*t*he *a*ctor's *h*

the actor's handbook

Editor: Barry Turner

BLOOMSBURY

First published 1989
by Bloomsbury Publishing Limited
2 Soho Square, London W1V 5DE

Publisher's note

The information in this book was correct to the best of the Editor's and Publisher's belief at the time of going to press. While no responsibility can be accepted for errors or omissions, the Editor and Publishers would welcome corrections and suggestions for items to include in future editions of the book.

British Library Cataloguing in Publication Data

Turner, Barry
  The actor's handbook.
  1. Acting — Manuals
    I. Title
    792'.028

  ISBN 0—7475—0249—8

Designed by Anita Plank, Panic Station
Typeset by Columns of Reading
Printed in Great Britain by
Richard Clay Ltd, Bungay, Suffolk

contents

Introduction

For a supposedly undemonstrative race, the British have a great love of acting. No part on stage or screen, however grotesque, is left unfilled for want of a volunteer. If the role is half decent, the queue of hopefuls will stretch all the way from the audition to the social security counter — and back again.

Why do they do it?

The flip response is that it's better than working. There is a snippet of truth here. Acting is as unlike conventional work as it is possible to imagine. The hours are variable, the pay is irregular, the location fluctuates erratically and the security is non-existent. These may not sound like virtues, but set against the humdrum nature of the typical career, they have an appeal that is not entirely masochistic.

Take the thorny question of pay. For an actor possessed of more than average ability, the prospects of a reasonable living are as good as in any occupation. The unexceptional minimum rates imposed by agreement between Equity and the various management bodies must be seen in context. Large parts of the business — television, film, commercials, West End theatre — are thriving and can pay very well indeed. A flick through a week's casting for mainstream productions reveals an impressive number of actors who are not short of a bob or two. Some of them may not last very long, it is true — from rags to riches to rags is a familiar saga — but the achievement of modest distinction is usually a fair indicator that the parts will continue to be offered. The pattern of work will fluctuate, but that is part of the excitement and pleasure of the game. Anyone who wants predictability should try chartered accountancy.

Even the Equity job statistics — a much publicized disincentive to would-be actors — should not be taken at face value. It may be true that, at any one time, two-thirds of Equity members are out of work, but a high proportion of them disqualify themselves from full-time employment by virtue of age (retirement is not in the actor's vocabulary), special aptitudes (there is not much call for transvestite fire eaters) and inclination (there are those who welcome only the occasional engagement).

What, then, does it take to make a career as an actor? Heed the voices of experience:

> Imagination! Imagination! I put it first years ago when I asked what qualities I thought necessary for success upon the stage.
>
> Ellen Terry

> Speak clearly! Speak clearly and be human.
>
> Sir Henry Irving

For an actress to be a success, she must have the face of Venus, the brains of Minerva, the grace of Terpsichore, the memory of Macaulay, the figure of Juno and the hide of a rhinoceros.

Ethel Barrymore

To act, you must make the thing written your own; you must steal the words, steal the thoughts and convey the stolen treasure to others with great art.

Ellen Terry

Acting is standing up naked and turning around very slowly.

Rosalind Russell

It is necessary for the young and ambitious actor to have a sense of the size of his life's task, to feel what Yeats called 'the fascination of what's difficult'. He must say to himself quite early on, 'What kind of actor do I wish to be?' He must think in terms of the size of his ambition, strengthen and enlarge every part of his equipment, his physical and vocal powers, his knowledge of dramatic literature and, indeed, his knowledge of all the arts.

Michael Redgrave

But the last word must go to Bill Fraser:

Anybody can walk on to a stage but it takes real talent to get off.

part **1**

getting started

1. So you want to be an actor . . .

Training physically tunes you. Performing is primarily a physical activity. You'll be made fit and taught how to keep that way.

Training will help you develop the actor's most important tool – the voice. A good actor has a voice of range, power and flexibility. This will not all happen at drama school. The prime of life is a vocal prime, too.

Drama students begin to think like actors. They look at the world like actors. Acting cannot be taught academically; it isn't something that can be mastered through knowledge. Degrees, honours, decorations are of no avail because, every time you act, you have to prove you can do it. Acting is doing. Straight acting is performing in a disciplined and rehearsed way and being able to do so in a variety of styles.

Drama school lets you practise before loosing you upon an unsuspecting public.

Clive Swift, *The Job of Acting*

At their best, the drama schools offer a higher education to rival any of the universities. Where else is a great cultural tradition brought to play on the whole personality, on the way one thinks, talks – and acts? Drama training, like training in the visual arts, but unlike any other form of arts education, combines the theoretical and the practical. Knowing *what* to do is only half the equation; the other half is knowing *how* to do it.

The wider educational benefits of drama training are emphasized because critics assume there aren't any. They see the typical drama course as cramped and confined, leading tunnel-like to a ludicrously overcrowded occupation. But it doesn't have to be like this. If, for one reason or another, acting ceases to appeal as a life-long career, there are plenty of other options. Teaching is the obvious example, but why stop there? The whole world of commerce is open to those who have learned the art of vocal communication. Employers are queuing up for sales people who can express themselves intelligently.

If, on the face of it, this seems a curious way to use a drama qualification, it is only because the connection is, as yet, rarely appreciated. But the evidence is clear. Last year, for example, the Institute of Directors ran a 'business challenge' competition that attracted teams from big companies such as IBM, Price Waterhouse, Cadbury and Proctor & Gamble, and one loner, Lynne Stabler, a graduate of Nene College in Northampton where she had majored in drama. Out of 900 entrants, Lynne came fifth, beating all the heavies not to mention the team entered by the London Business School.

Now a trainee accountant, Lynne argues that studying drama is an excellent preparation for business: 'It gave me a lot of confidence and a lot of social skills. It teaches you how to achieve what you want with other people, how to work with them. You also learn when you should back down.'

The only sense in which the value of drama school as a general education can be overstated is in encouraging yet more pressure on an already oversubscribed sector of learning. The leading drama schools are snowed under with applications. Last year, the Central School of Speech & Drama had over 1500 requests for places to set against just 28 vacancies. RADA's figures were much the same. Over at the Drama Centre in Camden Town, the administration (Gillian Diamond and an indefatigable assistant) copes with a demand for prospectuses that now exceeds 4000 a year.

Working down the scale, competition is less intense for places at schools still struggling for a reputation while, lower yet, there are establishments — often country house conversions in remote locations — where any student is sure of a welcome as long as he or she can pay the not inconsiderable fees.

A prestigious name is a fair indication of quality, but the more usual test of worthiness is accreditation by the National Council for Drama Training, an independent board of assessors who look into the philosophy and standards of teaching, the experience and qualifications of staff, the availability of reasonable premises and decent training facilities and the success rate of students. Absence of accreditation is not in itself a clear signal of inferiority (some schools refuse to submit to what they regard as high-handed interference in their affairs), but on the whole, approval by the NCDT is eagerly sought and highly valued by drama schools.

Students whose interests go beyond acting to writing, directing and design and who want to study drama in its widest sense are best advised to aim for one of the university courses or the Rose Bruford College of Speech & Drama where they offer degree-level courses in theatre arts. As with the acting schools, entry requirements vary from place to place and from year to year (see listings); the big difference is that, for admission to university courses a sound academic background weighs more heavily than evidence of natural talent.

So far, the typical student is seen as someone in their late teens on the first steps to a full-time career. However, drama training embraces all ages. More teeny than teenagers are the youngsters who attend afternoon drama classes at Anna Scher's Children's Theatre in north London. Miss Scher set up her classes 20 years ago, and since then, she has helped 5000 children express themselves through drama and more than a few to advance to successful acting careers. Last year, Jodhi May, a 12-year-old veteran of an Anna Scher course, shared the Best Actress award at the Cannes Film Festival.

Older students, some of whom have already spent half their working lives outside acting, are generally attracted to part-time courses such as those provided by the City Lit in Covent Garden. While unemployment seems to be endemic to acting, those embarking on a second career can take comfort from the fact that modern drama is beginning to reflect the increasingly middle-aged profile of society.

Younger part-timers also have a fair choice of training opportunities. A recent addition to the list is the appropriately named Poor School on London's Pentonville Road. Set up by former actor Paul Caister, the Poor School caters specifically for those who want to act but who also have to earn a living while they train, and are prepared to combine the two by spending four hours a night, four nights a week and one day at weekends pursuing their ambition. The fees at the Poor School are about £500 a term, which may sound a lot to someone who is used to heavily subsidized rates for other areas of adult education, but is chicken feed compared to the drama school fees for full-time students. In one of these establishments, a three-year course can cost up to £12,000 and more without taking into account those optional extras much loved by drama students such as late-night pub sessions on the meaning of life.

Grants for drama training are hard to come by. With characteristic myopia, local education authorities are disinclined to think of acting as real work, even though film and theatre are among the livelier growth industries and certainly generate more income and jobs than many more solid and respectable professions. Even the Inner London Education Authority, which used to lend a sympathetic ear to pleas for support, is down to 11 awards, just one each for the accredited schools within its boundaries.

Much depends on where a student comes from. Surrey and Essex are relatively good counties for a would-be actor to spend his formative years, but there are some local education authorities who reject all applications for drama school grants – and one LEA required a student to be accepted at four schools before taking his grant application seriously.

In the relative absence of grants from LEAs, a possible alternative to support from parents or indulgent relatives (assuming there is spare cash in the bank) is for students to throw themselves on the mercy of a charitable trust. The best prospects are usually with local institutions – those charities originally set up in the days before free state education to help the gifted offspring of poor but worthy families. Nowadays, with fewer regular clients, they can be more than happy to plug the gaps left by the bureaucratic benefactors.

If all else fails, there is always the chance of a Career Development Loan, a government-sponsored scheme administered by the leading banks. A sympathetic bank manager can help smooth the way, but since the government will be paying the interest on the loan for the duration of the course, the risk to the bank and to the manager's career prospects is correspondingly reduced. It has to be a very mean-minded banker to reject out of hand an actor's request for help. Career Development Loans are available for up to 80 per cent of course fees and living expenses for full-time students. However, the limit is £5000, not enough for students to avail themselves of a top drama school without the promise of further income.

Failure to gain first-time acceptance for a drama course is not the equivalent of a death penalty. Many youngsters benefit from a period of work experience outside their chosen career. If an interviewing panel takes the view that candidates need to gain maturity to benefit from drama school, they should respond constructively – with ideas, say, for travelling the world for a year or two. If, on their return, they are still of the same mind about acting, their perseverance is almost sure to be rewarded.

Drama school is the beginning but not the end of training. In earlier times, fledgling actors continued their practical education on the rep circuit, switching roles two or three times a week. However, provincial audiences are no longer willing to pay out to see a cast of unknowns go through the agonies of inexperience (they get enough of that for free on television). Anyway, the modern economics of popular theatre lead inexorably away from big casts with a wide choice of minor roles towards the two- or three-hander led by a star of the small or big screen. Today the fringe and the festivals offer the best chance to newcomers for extending their range.

The few who are taken on by the Royal Shakespeare Company and the National Theatre receive regular coaching as part of their contracts. Standards of instruction vary according to the availability of funds, but while the RSC bemoans over-large classes and the absence of voice training (once the company's strongest suit), the National Theatre Studio, next to the Old Vic, offers an impressively wide range of workshops. Where teachers agree is in urging young actors against an early career as a spear carrier — even with a prestigious company. The days when actors of the quality of Roger Rees and Ian Holm could work their way up the ranks are long past. Gillian Diamond, formerly casting director at the National and now running the Drama Centre, speaks for her colleagues: 'If you're the best spear carrier in the world, you do not end up playing Hamlet. I beg people not to take the job after drama school; they'd do better at Butlins.'

Although basking in an enviable reputation for quality, the leading drama schools are not beyond criticism. A popular insiders' view is that too much attention is given to the theatre at the expense of film and television. Susie Figgis, the casting director who introduced Emily Lloyd, Gabriel Byrne and Greta Scacchi to the screen, attacks 'the snobbishness in the drama schools which support the belief that real acting is only in the theatre and that film is a rather crass thing imported from America.'

The irony is, of course, that a high proportion of young actors are making their reputations in film — after three years of learning all about live theatre. The retort from the drama schools is to proclaim the all-embracing virtues of a theatre-based training. The easy interchange between film, television and theatre is one of the glories of British acting, much admired in the States where most students are trained for film and never venture before a live audience.

Perhaps the distinction should not be made between the different media but between the different attitudes towards acting. The drama schools pay such homage to the classics — Shakespeare particularly — that all other forms of entertainment are seen to be distinctly inferior. This tends to downgrade the 'boulevard actor' who, rejecting the great roles, is none the less central to the British acting tradition.

Although not arguing this specific point, Sheridan Morley made a relevant observation some time ago in an article about his father. 'Robert comes from a generation of actors who saw themselves as public servants,' he wrote. 'They were there not to educate or inform or convert the customers but purely and simply to entertain them; and to achieve that most difficult of all theatrical tasks, he has always had to be amused by what he was doing. Shakespeare he never found very amusing.'

There is, and always will be, only one Robert Morley. But it is a great pity that there are not more actors like him.

Drama school acting/stage management courses accredited by the National Council for Drama Training

Academy of Live & Recorded Arts	3-year acting course
Arts Educational Schools	3-year acting course
Birmingham School of Speech Training & Dramatic Art	3-year acting course
Bristol Old Vic Theatre School	2- and 3-year acting courses 2-year stage management course
Rose Bruford College	3-year degree courses in theatre arts & community arts 3-year stage management course
Central School of Speech & Drama	3-year acting course 2-year stage management course
Drama Centre London	3-year acting course
Drama Studio	1-year post-graduate course
Guildford School of Acting	3-year acting/musical theatre course 1-year post-graduate course 2-year stage management course
Guildhall School of Music & Drama	3-year acting course 2-year stage management course
London Academy of Music & Dramatic Art (LAMDA)	3-year acting course 2-year stage management course
Manchester Polytechnic	3-year acting course
Mountview Theatre School	3-year acting course 1-year post-graduate course 2-year stage management course
Royal Academy of Dramatic Art (RADA)	3-year acting course 2-year stage management course
Royal Scottish Academy of Music & Drama	3-year acting course 2-year stage management course
Webber Douglas Academy	2- and 3-year acting courses 1-year post-graduate course
Welsh College of Music & Drama	2 3-year acting courses 1-year Advanced Certificate course 3-year stage management course

2. Drama schools

Academy of Live & Recorded Arts (ALRA)

Royal Victoria Building, Trinity Road, London SW18 3SX
Tel (01) **870 6475**
Principal Sorrel Carson
Contact Gillian Davison (administrator)

Founded 1979 in a church hall in East Finchley with only six students. Grew rapidly in size and reputation, moving to its present historic premises in 1983. *Courses on offer*:
● Actors' course: 3-year full time, NCDT accredited. Min. age 20. Designed for students who wish to pursue a career in classical and modern theatre and the recorded media.
● Actors' course: 2-year full time. Min. age 18. Emphasis on modern theatre and recorded media.
● Performing arts dance course: 2- or 3-year full time. Min. age 16.
● Stage management course: 4 terms, full time.
● Post-graduate course: four terms, full time, designed for graduates and other advanced or mature students with experience.
● Summer courses.
Places available: no fixed numbers policy. Intake flexible according to demand and development of courses. Currently 150 students in the whole Academy on different courses. Eligible for student grants. Prospectus available.
Audition requirements: First audition: classes in voice, dance, improvisation; no pieces. Second audition: screen test and rehearsal of scenes from plays. Audition fee: £28.75 inc. VAT.
'. . . We believe that no art form can survive unless it relates to its own age and fully embraces its challenges. The Royal Victoria Building symbolizes our philosophy — for it has been transformed from a Victorian asylum into a centre of creative endeavour with its feet firmly planted in the 21st century.'

Ackerley Studios of Speech and Drama

Crane Building (5th floor), Hanover Street, Liverpool 1
Tel (051) **709 5995**
Principal Margaret Parsons

Founded 1919 by Mrs Harold Ackerley. *Courses available*: private tuition for ALAM Dip and LLAM Dip, LGSM and LRAM examinations. Telephone to make an appointment for interview. Auditions not given. Prospectus available.

Actors' Residential Theatre & Television School International (ARTTS)

Highfield Grange, Bubwith, Selby, N. Yorks. YO8 7DP
Tel (0757) **8088**
Principal John P. Sichel (artistic director)
Contact Norman Y. Smith (administrator)

Opening October 1989. Planned as a rural, residential school. Will offer one-year intensive course for post-graduate or other experienced students. Prior to opening, contact the Administrator, 15 Towers Road, Hatch End, Pinner, Middx HA5 4SQ, tel: (01) 428 1453.

Ads Agency & Stage School
Reform Road, Maidenhead, Berks. SL6 8BT
Tel (0628) **29346**
Contact Betty Curtis

A part-time school for children, with classes on Tuesday and Wednesday evenings and on Saturdays. Drama, some modern dance and tap. Ages 5–17, with one class available for adults. Classes are also held in Watford.

Arts Educational Schools Drama Department
Arts Educational School, 12 Errol Street, London EC1 8LX
Tel (01) **638 0946**
Contact Mr D. Robson (head of drama department)

Courses on offer: 3-year, NCDT-accredited, full-time acting course; and 1-year, full-time course for post-graduates, mature students and actors seeking a renewed focus in their work. Discretionary grants available. Ask for prospectus.
Audition requirements: 3-year course: full day's audition consisting of classes in movement, voice and improvization, followed by two short contrasting pieces of the candidate's own choice; there may also be an interview. 1-year course: two contrasting pieces, one classical and one modern, and an extensive interview; university degree and/or evidence of appropriate experience and talent is required. Audition fee: £15.00.
'The Drama Department offers a three-year acting course that is Stanislavsky based. The work is concentrated and demanding. Training places considerable emphasis on the education of the individual so that he/she may be sensitive to the requirements of any kind of text. Our aim is to produce actors who have a respect for the theatre, for acting and for themselves.'

Birmingham School of Speech Training & Dramatic Art
45 Church Road, Edgbaston, Birmingham B15 3SW
Tel (021) **454 3424**
Principal Patricia A. Yardley

Founded 1936. *Course on offer:* 3-year full-time acting course; 30–35 places available; NCDT accredited; students eligible for grants.
Audition requirements: speech from Shakespeare, speech from a modern play, a lyrical poem, a song – each of which must be no more than 2 minutes in duration. Sight reading, improvisation and movement will also be required. Audition fee: £19.00.
'Education is no longer limited to the mere absorption of knowledge; it is concerned with the development of the whole being – body, mind and spirit. Because of the special value of speech and drama in assisting in the development of the personality, the teaching at the Birmingham School of Speech and Drama is based on the realization that these arts have an ever-increasing part to play.'

Boden Studio
13 Essex Road, Enfield, Middx EN2 6TZ
Tel (01) **367 1836/2692**
Principal Maureen Boden/Tony Boden

Founded 1979. *Courses on offer:* part-time classes in speech, acting, singing and dance. Ages 3–20. All students work towards examination standard, and full-scale productions (23 in the last eight years) are frequently mounted. Summer courses are also held.

Braithwaite's Acrobatic School
8 Brookshill Avenue, Harrow Weald, Middx
Tel (01) **954 5638**
Principal Valerie Braithwaite

Founded 1968. *Courses on offer:* classes in acrobatics, singing, dance, drama for ages 6–20+. After normal school hours. Also operates as an agency.

Brighton Academy of Performing Arts
- *See* **Shandy Stage School.**

Brighton School of Music & Drama
12 Buxton Road, Brighton, E. Sussex BN1 5DE
Tel (0273) **552187**
Principal Carole Nina Best, LGSM, ANEA
Contact The Secretary

Founded 1883. For many years, a music school in central Brighton, then a full-time speech and drama school. For the last 20 years has been a part-time school for drama and singing. Private lessons are offered for all ages, and class lessons for those under 18. About 100 students per term; prospectus available. Class and general drama involve mime, improvisation, play production and festivals. Private drama lessons include Guildhall teaching work, performing for examinations and festivals and preparation of auditions for London colleges, drama schools and theatres.
Audition requirements: interview with the singing staff and trial lesson, one song, interview with the principal. No charge for audition.

Bristol Old Vic Theatre School
2 Downside Road, Clifton, Bristol BS8 2XF
Tel (0272) **733535**
Principal Christopher Denys
Contact Erika Neumann (secretary)

Founded 1946 by Laurence Olivier; moved to its present premises in 1956. *Courses on offer:*
- 3-year full-time acting course.
- 2-year full-time acting course: more suited to mature students, post-graduates and/or those with some theatre experience.
- 1-year post-graduate course: should only be undertaken by those with exceptional application, determination and stamina.
- 2-year stage management and technical course.
- 2-year design course.
- 1-year wardrobe course.
- Trainee directors' attachment (not a structured course).

The acting and technical courses are NCDT accredited; grants available. Ask for a prospectus.
Audition requirements: Preliminary audition: excerpts from one classical verse play (preferably Shakespeare) and one modern prose play, the two pieces together not exceeding 4 minutes. A short unaccompanied song is also required. Following the preliminary audition, candidates may be invited to attend a weekend school where they work with members of staff, who will then shortlist or offer them a place. Audition fee: £15.00.
The school aims to train and prepare actors for a career in theatre, radio, TV and

films, with a particular emphasis on preparation for work in the classical repertoire. All courses are essentially practical. No one 'philosophy' of teaching, acting, design or production is adhered to. The aim is to offer students the best possible training and preparation for a successful career in a profession that makes increasingly varied demands upon the individuals it employs.

The school has close links with the Bristol Old Vic Company, University of Bristol Drama Department, Bristol City Council and Avon Education Authority. As a result, there are opportunities to perform in a wide variety of venues: theatres, art centres and schools throughout the city and region. Links are also maintained with the BBC and HTV. Every effort is made to enable students to obtain as much professional work experience as possible.

British Ballet Organization

Woolborough House, 39 Lonsdale Road, London SW13 9JP
Tel (01) **748 1241**
Principal John Field, CBE (director)
Contact Tim Yeates (assistant to the director)

Founded 1930. An examining body conducting ballet and tap examinations in its own syllabus at venues throughout the country. Courses are open to all British Ballet Organization members and teachers.
Audition requirements: students must have passed Elementary Ballet and Higher Preliminary Tap.

Rose Bruford College of Speech & Drama

Lamorbey Park, Sidcup, Kent DA15 9DF
Tel (01) **300 3024**
Principal Phil Robins
Contact Chief administrative officer

Founded 1950, by Rose E. Bruford. Established a fine reputation for its training of actors and teachers. Developed and began the existing courses in 1976, becoming the first and only institution of its kind to offer professional training to degree and honours degree level. *Courses on offer*:
- BA (Hons) in theatre arts: 3-year full time; 30 places (600 applicants).
- BA in community theatre arts: 3-year full time; 30 places (200 applicants).
- Diploma in technical theatre arts: 3-year full time; 18 places (150 applicants).
All courses are accredited by the National Council for Drama Training. Grants for degree courses are mandatory, and discretionary for the diploma course. A prospectus is available. Application to the college should be made in September, and interviews/auditions are held from November to July.
Audition requirements: Vary according to course applied for. Candidates are informed of requirements when they are told of the date and time of the interview. Audition fee: £12.50.
'Our courses are all advanced courses of higher education, but at the same time are courses of vocational, professional training. The teaching on the courses is of the highest standard in both respects, and makes considerable academic, intellectual, physical and artistic demands upon the student. The staff expect, equally, that demands will be made on them.'

Advice to aspiring actors: 'Apart from a trained body and voice, you will require a trained mind in order to make critical choices and to fully engage in the process of making theatre. What you think is very important. Try to ensure that those involved in your training will allow you to be yourself before embarking on the making of a theatre event.'

Bush Davies Schools Ltd

Closing down in 1989.

Central School of Speech and Drama

Embassy Theatre, Eton Avenue, London NW3 3HY
Tel (01) **722 8183/4/5/6**
Principal Robert S. Fowler, MA (Oxon) LGSM, Dip ED
Contact Linda Cookson

Founded 1906 at the Albert Hall by Elsie Fogerty, moving to its present premises in 1956. *Courses on offer*:
● Diploma in acting: 3-year full time, NCDT accredited.
● Higher National Diploma in stage management (BTEC): 2-year full time, NCDT accredited.
● BEd (Hons) in drama and spoken language: 4-year full time.
● BA (Hons) in drama and a language: 3-year full time.
● BSc (Hons) speech and language pathology: 4-year full time.
● Central School Sesame Joint Certificate in the use of drama and movement in therapy: 1-year full time.
● Advanced Certificate in speech and drama.
● Part-time Diploma in drama in education.
● Advanced Diploma in voice studies.
The last three are post-experience/in-service courses. Applicants for acting course should normally be aged between 17 and 25 on starting the course. Grants available for degree courses, and discretionary grants for NCDT-accredited courses. Limited number of bursaries available for shorter courses. Ask for prospectus.
Auditions: Held throughout the year for entrance in the autumn. Audition fee: £15.00.
'The Central School of Speech and Drama is much older than many universities and polytechnics; and its traditions, confirmed by experience, constitute the basis of its reputation. At the same time, the school is alive to contemporary developments and offers its students the best possible preparation for a successful career in their chosen field.'
As is clear from the variety of its courses, the school's training has evolved into three main areas: acting and stage management; speech therapy; and teaching. It has contact with other institutions such as the Polytechnics of North and Central London, Thames Polytechnic and Westfield College (University of London). It has a student population of around 400, but it is still possible for staff to know all the students, and the school cherishes its family approach and friendly working environment, which is conducive to effective learning.

Constructive Teaching Centre

18 Lansdowne Road, London W11 3LL
Tel (01) **727 7222**
Contact The Secretary

Founded 1962. Four or five courses each year, taken by individual Alexander teachers. No regular system of courses. Actors interested in one-to-one Alexander technique lessons should contact: The Society of Teachers of the Alexander Technique, 10 London House, 266 Fulham Road, London SW10 9EL, tel: (01) 351 0828 (afternoons only).

Cygnet Training Theatre

Friars Gate, Exeter EX2 4AZ
Tel (0392) **77189**
Principal Monica D. Shallis, LRAM, LGSM
Contact Mary G. Evans (administrator)

Founded 1980, the company grew out of an association between Monica Shallis, Mary Evans and the Northcott Theatre Company. It is now a full-time training company, with Peter Brook as patron. Formal training in voice, movement, music, dance etc. are all part of the daily work of the company, but rehearsal and performance remain the strongest features of the experience-based training. Takes open-minded young actors who are expected to work with a fully professional attitude from their first day. High standards of technique and flexibility are aimed for, and among others, the disciplines of Stanislavsky and Michel Saint-Denis are in constant use. Has a good professional standing as a touring company, and aims to provide maximum contacts and opportunities of further work for actors.

Sixteen new members taken on each September. No set length of stay as members' needs and development vary. Receive about 200 applicants each year. Grant eligibility*. Prospective students should write with a large SAE for prospectus and application form. No academic qualifications are required. Professional actors may join company for three or six months, to refresh skills or to study and tour specific role.

Audition requirements: 2 contrasting pieces of own choice, plus interview and workshop session with other prospective candidates and company members. Audition fee: £16.00. A further fee of £7.50 is payable if an assessment of the audition is required.

*Because Cygnet is unique, it is not listed among conventional drama schools, and some local education authorities use this as a reason for refusing grants. However, the DES has stated that Cygnet is eligible for discretionary grants on the same footing as any drama school. Cygnet's fees are considerably lower than those of most schools, and Cygnet actors have an exceptionally high success rate in obtaining professional work as a result of appearances and contacts made during touring. This should encourage local education authorities to give financial help to applicants who obtain places.

Drama Centre London

176 Prince of Wales Road, Chalk Farm, London NW5 3PT
Tel (01) **267 1177**
Principal Christopher Fettes
Contact Gillian Diamond (registrar)

Founded 1963 when a group of directors and teachers — John Blatchley, Yat Malmgren and Christopher Fettes — broke away from the Central School of Speech and Drama and founded the Drama Centre London based on the teachings of Stanislavsky and the American Method. *Courses on offer*:
● Diploma acting course: 3-year full time; 30 places.
● Diploma professional instructors course: 2-year full time; 10 places.
Receive approximately 500 applications for the acting course each year. Accredited by the National Council for Drama Training; students eligible for grants. Prospectus available. Prospective entrants should complete an application form, giving reasons why acting is their chosen profession and why they are applying to the Drama Centre London in particular.

Audition requirements: one classical piece, chosen from five nominated by the Principal, and one modern piece of the applicant's own choice, plus a lengthy interview. Audition fee: £12.00.

'Before you start your training, you need to have seen something of what exists beyond the confines of school and home. You need to have thought about it and to have formed opinions. Don't go to school too soon, and don't go to a school like the Drama Centre London if you don't feel it a duty to make people ask questions and think about answers. . .

'The training of the actor consists essentially in learning how to bring feeling under control and how to confer form upon it – and, in particular, those especially powerful and especially fruitful feelings that have their origin below the threshold of consciousness. If you have been led to assume that training centres upon the mechanics of expression, speech and movement, you will have to think again. The aim of the Drama Centre London is to provide the student actor with a systematic approach to the problems of acting, which will lead to the eventual acquisition of this control; to teach him to make a proper use of himself as an organic being on the stage and to equip him with the freedom that derives not from the licence to "do his own thing" but from the mastery of his creative resources.'

Drama Studio London

Grange Court, 1 Grange Road, London W5 5QN
Tel (01) **579 3897**
Principal Peter Layton (executive director)
Contact Sheila Ward (secretary)

Founded 1966 by Peter Layton. *Courses on offer*: one-year three-term acting course; one-year three-term directing course. Both full-time. 55 places available on the acting course, with 500 applicants each year; 8 places available on the directing course, with 100 applicants per year. Applicants to both courses must be over the age of 21. The acting course is NCDT accredited, and discretionary grants are available from some authorities. Prospectus available.
Audition requirements: Acting course: all-day interview, consisting of group and individual acting and improvisation exercises, sight-reading tests and possibly some prepared work (which will be asked for when the appointment is made). Directing course: interview and practical exercises. Audition fee: £20.00.
'The primary objective of the school is the preparation of the student for a career in the theatre. The student learns to face positively the realities of the profession as it exists ... The work is serious but not solemn; it requires considerable self-discipline, hard work and a positive commitment from each student. The student must be prepared for searching self-analysis and have an unselfish concern for his fellow students. Drama Studio expects its graduates to make a significant contribution to their art, to exercise their best efforts in their professional lives and to establish and abide by their own standards of excellence and integrity.'

The Drama Studio London also operates in Berkeley, California, and is the only major drama school in North America to offer one-year full-time courses in acting and directing. Details are available from the London address or: The Drama Studio London/USA, 2325 Fourth Street, Berkeley, California 94710, USA, tel: (415) 549 1118.

Gina Dyke Stage School

240 Tolworth Rise South, Surbiton, Surrey KT9 5NB
Tel (01) **399 9429**
Contact Gina Dyke, Mary McLeish

Founded 1962. *Courses on offer*: evening and Saturday dance classes for all ages: ballet, tap, modern, jazz.

East 15 Acting School

Hatfields, Rectory Lane, Loughton, Essex IG10 3RU and
Sheriff Hutton Park, Sheriff Hutton, N. Yorks. YO6 1RH
Tel (01) **508 5983** and (03477) **442**
Principal Margaret Bury
Contact Mrs F. C. Stark (administrator, north)

Founded 1961 by Margaret Bury to create a school where actors could continue to explore and develop the creative way of working begun by Joan Littlewood at Theatre Workshop. *Courses on offer:*
● 3-year full-time acting course.
● 2-year full-time acting course: more pressurized and requiring a good educational background and some acting experience.
● 1-year post-graduate acting course: for mature students and also professionals wishing to extend their range.
● 3-year directors' course.
● 1-year stage management course.
● 1-year tutors' course: open to East 15 graduates and professional actors who wish to train as tutors using the school's acting methods.
Discretionary grants are available from some local education authorities. Minimum age for application is 18; there is no upper age limit.
Audition requirements: group workshop auditions are held every week. Audition fee: £15.00.
Students work at both Hatfields, where there is a TV studio and the fully equipped Corbett Theatre, and at Sheriff Hutton Hall, where performances are given in the historic rooms and in the arena theatre in the grounds.

The school's policy is 'to accept talented and ambitious students of differing ages, backgrounds and nationalities, who, under our demand and tuition, will strive for higher standards of theatre technique and craftsmanship, and aspire to acting as a creative art. Individual coaching is given in preference to class instruction. Training emphasis is on the study of human behaviour and emotions, and on each actor's use of imagery, body and voice. The training challenges the student to recall childhood experiences, to assess the codes of honour and behaviour he has assumed and the effect of his society upon him.

'It is only through an understanding of oneself that objective assessment of others becomes possible. An actor will only act himself until he can separate his private person from his public self, and when his body, mind and voice are flexible enough as instruments to create the observed truth and reality of others. Only through awareness of reality can theatricality be understood and created. Actors must first create their characters from observation of life.'

There is a professional company — East 15 Theatre Company — which employs mostly ex-students who have had experience in commercial theatre. The Galtres Theatre Company also consists of East 15 graduates, and works in the historic setting of Sheriff Hutton Park.

East Herts College

Dept of Adult Education, Turnford, Broxbourne, Herts. EN10 6AF
Tel (0992) **466451**
Course Tutor Organiser Miss Thelma Tillaney AGSM, LRAM

Course on offer:
● Theatre and Performing Arts Course: two-year full-time preparatory course combining dance, drama and general education.
The aim of the course is to prepare students for entry to an academy of drama/dance or a college of higher education where they can be prepared for careers in theatre, teaching or leisure management.
Entry requirements: preferably five 'O' levels including English (special considera-

tion is given to students without these qualifications should they show exceptional ability at audition). Leaflet containing application form is available from the college. Interviews and auditions are held between March and June.

The course is recognised as a Foundation Course for the London Studio Centre, and those students who successfully complete the course are offered a place at the Centre.

Evening Academy of Dramatic Art

189 Whitechapel Road, London E1
Tel (01) **624 5400**
Principal Tim Reynolds

Founded 1985. *Courses on offer*:
● 2-year acting course, Monday–Friday 6.30–10.30 pm and Saturday 10.00 am–3.00 pm;
● weekend course, Saturday 4.00–6.30 pm: flexible foundation training, ideal as a pre-drama school preparation.
● medallion course, weekday mornings: ages 16–18, intended as a bridge between school and drama school.
● international course: 2-year full time, specifically designed for overseas students.
● summer course.

There are 30 places on the full-time evening course, which attracts approximately 200 applications each year. Not eligible for grants, although the international course may attract grants from foreign governments. Write for prospectus and application form, and apply between January and July for entry in September.
Audition requirements: usually two speeches and a workshop, although this varies. Audition fee: £9–£10.00.

The Academy was set up in response to the large numbers of students who are unable to get grants or to support themselves while at drama school. However, the evening course is not an easy option, as it is very intensive and daytime work must take second place. It is vital that students see themselves as *actors* who earn money in their spare time. All tutors are working professionals, both actors and directors. No one method or theory is taught; students are offered a wide range of techniques and encouraged to develop their own style.

Stella Greenfield School

41 Bush Grove, Stanmore, Middx.
Tel (01) **952 1805**

Affiliated to the Stella Greenfield Agency. Run evening classes in speech and drama for children up to the age of 15. Mostly attended by local children.

Guildford School of Acting and Dance

20 Buryfields, Guildford, Surrey GU4 5DA
Tel (0483) **60701**
Principal Michael Gaunt
Contact Admissions officer

Founded 1964. *Courses on offer*:
● acting course: 3-year full time; 24 places (400 applicants);
● musical theatre course: 3-year full time; 24 places (150 applicants);
● post-graduate acting course: 3-year full time; 15 places (120 applicants);
● stage management course: 2-year full time; 18 places (110 applicants).

All courses are NCDT accredited. Grants available. Ask for prospectus.
Audition requirements: full day, to include two pieces, improvisation, learned song, taught dance routine and interview. Stage management admission is by

interview. Audition fee: £20.00. Auditions are held in Guildford, New York and Santa Barbara, California: 'Prepare all aspects for the audition as fully as possible: we want to see you at your best.'

The school believes that its training will provide the theatre with disciplined, balanced actors, stage managers and musical theatre specialists with a sense of responsibility to the theatre and community.

Guildhall School of Music and Drama

Barbican, London EC2Y 8DT
Tel (01) **628 2571**
Principal John Hosier
Contact Drama Department

Founded 1880. *Courses on offer:*
- Associate in Music Diploma (AGSM), 4-year full time.
- Diploma in Music (DipGSM), 3-year full time.
- Graduate in Music (GGSM), 3-year full time.
- Professional Acting (AGSM), 3-year full time; NCDT accredited; 24–26 places (700 applicants).
- Certificate in Stage Management (CSMGSM), 2-year full time; NCDT accredited; 24 places (180 applicants).

The following higher diplomas may be obtained on the satisfactory completion of not less than one year's full-time tuition on the appropriate courses: Concert Recital Diploma; Certificate of Advanced Study; Diploma in Music Therapy. Discretionary grants available. Ask for prospectus.

Audition requirements: Acting course: three contrasting pieces (including one Shakespeare or Jacobean verse piece, one comic piece) and an unaccompanied song. Stage management course: interview. Audition fee: £20.00.

The school follows a policy of classical theatre training.

Ernest Hopner Studios of Voice, Speech and Drama

34/35 Bluecoat Chambers, School Lane, Liverpool L1 3BX
Tel (051) **709 1966**
Principal Ernest Hopner, LLAM

Founded 1952. *Courses on offer:* voice production (singing and speech); dialects; microphone technique; audition technique; movement and mime; characterization; verse speaking; public speaking and self presentation; stage make-up.

All students are taught individually and privately by the Principal. 56 places are available, but the demand far exceeds this. Grants not available; no prospectus.

Audition requirements: students must show intelligence, imagination and capacity for hard work. Actors should memorize two pieces, one comedy and one dramatic. A short impromptu mime and a sight-reading are also given at the audition. There is no audition fee. 'Make sure you know your pieces *thoroughly* — that includes the play from which the extract has been taken. Be prepared to be asked searching questions on *why* you want to act. Don't let your nerves run away with you!'

The school has adopted the following policy: 'To develop to the full the student's abilities through a thorough mastery of technique so as to enable them to produce work of first-class professional standard.'

Italia Conti Academy of Theatre Arts

Italia Conti House, 23 Goswell Road, London EC1M 7BB
Tel (01) **608 0044**
Principal Mrs E. M. Sheward
Contact Mrs Beverley Thomas

Founded 1911 by Italia Conti, an actress. She was succeeded by her niece, Ruth Conti, in 1946 and by the present principal in 1967. *Courses on offer*:
● junior course: 9–16 years of age; general education to GCSE and vocational training in dance, drama and singing;
● performing arts course: 3-year vocational course from 16 years of age, majoring in dance with drama and singing, designed to teach the student to accept direction and to extend his/her individual potential in all aspects of drama, dance and singing. ISTD Associate examinations and LAMDA ALAM and LLAM examinations may be taken within the course by suitable applicants if required.
● drama course: 1-year foundation course for students aged 16+ who wish to specialize in drama.
Grants available. There are 70 places available on both the performing arts and the drama courses, and 700 applicants each year. Applicants should write for prospectus and application form. Entry is by written application with photograph, and audition.
Audition requirements: two pieces (one classical) and three dances (ballet, tap, modern, etc.). One song is required (bring taped music), and also improvization and sight reading. Audition fee: £20.00.

Desmond Jones School of Mime & Physical Theatre

St Luke's Church Hall, 450a Uxbridge Road, London W12
Tel (01) **747 3537**
Principal Desmond Jones
Contact Registrar (20 Thornton Avenue, London W4 1QG)

The longest-established school of mime in Britain. Course on offer: 3-month intensive study of mime technique and the arts of physical acting (9.30 am– 12.30 pm, Monday to Friday). Grants not available. Applicants are asked to attend an interview, which is not an audition, but is to help select those who would benefit most from the course. Those accepted range between the ages of 18 and 35, sometimes older. They will be largely beginners, mostly actors and actresses but also painters, sculptors, puppeteers and people with some mime experience who want to extend their technique.

'The technique is based on that of Etienne Decroux, the originator of modern mime. Through it, students will learn a sense of style and precision indispensable to the modern mime. They will be made aware of the body and how to use it, and of the infinite subtlety that the body is capable of.

The acting techniques draw on a variety of sources that have influenced modern theatre, from Jacques Lecoq to Keith Johnstone. It is not the intention of the school to produce carbon-copy performers, but to give the students a language of the body that they can use as they wish, whether it be for pure mime, clowning, the speaking theatre, or for daily life.'

The bulk of the teaching is undertaken by Desmond Jones himself. He has performed regularly throughout England and Europe, has choreographed for television and the English National Opera, and was Head of Movement on the films *Quest for Fire* and *Greystoke*. He lectures widely and is an adviser on mime not only to the Arts Council but to all the central organizations promoting mime and mime training.

Glyn Knowles Stage School

8 Hunters Way, Gillingham, Kent ME7 3BA
Tel (0634) **50745**
Principal Glyn Davies
Contact Linda Krause-Davies

Founded 1972. *Courses on offer:* children's drama classes, three days a week in Croydon, once a week in Bromley and on Saturday afternoons in Teddington. A class in the Medway area is due to open shortly, and the school holds summer drama courses during the holidays. Age range 5—16 years. Children join classes on a four-week trial basis; no audition is involved. Around 40 children attend the school. Prospectus available.

'Working principally through improvisation, the aim is to develop the child's own awareness of him/herself. This confidence building is taken at the child's pace. Video and microphones are used in classes.'

An agency — Glyn Knowles Direction — is attached to the school.

Laine Theatre Arts Ltd

The Studios, 25 High Street, Epsom, Surrey KT19 8DD
Tel (03727) **24648**
Principal Betty Lane
Contact Nicola Mumford

Courses on offer: 3-year full-time course comprising dance, drama and singing. Individual timetables are prepared for each student. All students are required to enter for the Associate teaching examinations of the Imperial Society of Teachers of Dancing in the third year. There is also a musical theatre course designed for the student who wishes to specialize in drama and singing, with dance as a subsidiary.

The school is accredited by the Council for Dance Education and Training. Discretionary grants available from some local authorities. Ask for prospectus.
Audition requirements: Girls: one-hour ballet class; modern dance solo; optional two-minute singing and drama pieces. Boys: one-hour jazz class; modern/jazz solo; optional two-minute singing and drama pieces. College policy is to audition a small number of students weekly throughout the year.

London Academy of Music and Dramatic Art

Tower House, 226 Cromwell Road, London SW5 0SR
Tel (01) **373 9883**
Principal Roger Croucher

Founded 1861. *Courses on offer:*
● acting course: 3-year full time; NCDT accredited;
● overseas course, with emphasis on Shakespeare and the classics for overseas students: 1-year full time;
● stage management/technical theatre course: 2-year full time; NCDT accredited.
Discretionary grants available. Ask for prospectus. Age of entry: 18—26.
Audition requirements: two pieces: one Shakespeare and one modern, lasting not more than three minutes. Audition fee: £15.00.

The school's policy is 'to train actors and stage managers to meet the demands and opportunities of the contemporary professional theatre, and to equip them with a strong technical basis for their craft. Directors and specialist technicians from the professional theatre contribute to the training and life of the school throughout the year.'

London Academy of Performing Arts
861–863 Fulham Road, London SW6 5HT
Tel (01) **736 0121**
Principal Celia Hocking
Contact Faith Sutherland

Founded 1985. *Courses on offer*:
- 2-year full-time acting course.
- 1-year post-graduate acting course.
- summer Shakespearean acting course; 4 weeks.

24 places are available on the one- and two-year courses, but there are several hundred applicants each year. Minimum age for entrance is 18, except for post-graduate course, which is 20. Discretionary grants available. Ask for prospectus.
Audition requirements: two contrasting speeches of candidate's own choice: one classical and one modern of 2–3 minutes each. Candidates may also be asked to sight-read a passage or to perform a short improvization. Audition fee: £18.00.

The school's policy is 'to concentrate on the basic studies of voice and movement, to develop the individual resources of each student, to stimulate the imagination and to free the creative instincts. The aim is to lay the foundations for a secure and firm technique for the actor's future role in the theatre.'

London and International School of Acting
LISA House, 138 Westbourne Grove, London W11 2RR
Tel (01) **727 2342**
Principal Brian Lidstone, DGGB
Contact Administration (please write; do not telephone)

Founded 1983. *Courses on offer*: 2-year diploma course; 1-year post-graduate course; 3-year career launching course; short-term courses from time to time. There are 20 places available. Students with grants do attend.
Audition requirements: prepared presentations. Audition fee £10.00.

Aimed strictly at training professionally orientated aspirants for classical and modern theatre.

London Studio Centre
42–50 York Way, London N1 9AB
Tel (01) **837 7741**
Principal Bridget Espinosa
Contact Sandra Johnston (registrar)

Founded 1978. *Course on offer*: 3-year full time, including dance and drama and individually structured from a curriculum of over 350 classes a week. The course accredited by Council for Dance Education and Training; grants available from most authorities. Entry is by audition, or by successful completion of the performing course at East Herts College. Audition fee: £15.00. Minimum age 16. In some cases, where students have already attended a dance or drama school, the course may be shortened.

'The London Studio Centre trains students who are dedicated to the pursuit of excellence in all aspects of theatre, with special emphasis on dance, drama, singing, film and TV techniques. The Studio Centre provides a bridge between school leaving and entry into the professional theatre. The majority of teaching staff are actively engaged in the theatre, thus enabling students to be aware of new techniques and trends.'

A classical graduate course has been designed to meet the needs of advanced ballet students who wish to make their careers in classical ballet companies. The London Studio Centre has close links with the London City Ballet, who train selected students to understudy roles for them.

London Theatre School

120 Putney Bridge Road, London SW15
Tel (01) **874 5852**
Principal Barbara Buckmaster, CSTD, LUD
Contact Administrator

Founded 1984 by Barbara Buckmaster and Belinda Quirey with colleagues from major drama schools and the professional theatre, who share the belief that a strong basis in classical theatre best equips an actor for all forms of drama. Currently undergoing accreditation by the NCDT. *Courses on offer:*
● 2-year acting course: full time; minimum age 18.
● 1-year post-graduate and mature student acting course: full time; minimum age 21.
● 6-month course: for the more academically mature student, or the professional actor seeking a refresher course.
● foundation course: 1 year, for 16–18-year-olds.
24 places per course are available each year; however, 1563 applied for the two-year course last year. Students eligible for grants. Applicants should write for prospectus and application form.
Audition requirements: two pieces (one Shakespeare, one 20th-century), not more than three minutes each; sight-reading, unaccompanied singing and possibly an acting exercise. Good health is considered essential.

The Mary Lynch Studio

322 Endsleigh Court, Upper Woburn Place, London WC1
Tel (01) **387 8023**
Principal Mary Lynch RAM, LRAM

Courses on offer: individual and group sessions for anyone who has to perform or speak in public. Stage, spotlight and camera work are used to allow people to experience being on show. Improvement of English speaking, pronunciation, conversation, speech-making, voice production and business presentation. Personal tuition can be arranged at offices and hotels. All sessions under the direction of Mary Lynch.

Manchester Polytechnic, School of Theatre

Dept of Communication, Arts & Design, Capitol Building, School Lane, Didsbury, Manchester M20 0HT
Tel (061) **434 3331**
Principal Mr A. Taylor, Head of School of Theatre

Course on offer: Diploma in Theatre Course, 3-year full time; NCDT accredited. Annual intake of 24 students. Minimum age for entry: 18. Discretionary grants available; ask for prospectus.
Audition requirements: maximum of three set-pieces, an improvisation and, when relevant, a hearing test. Selected applicants are asked to return.
'The course is focused sharply on the process of acting as the essence of theatrical experience. It is therefore principally concerned with (1) the development of the basic skills required of a flexible actor; (2) the experience of creating truthfully and imaginatively a wide range of characters; (3) the acquisition of supportive experiences to give breadth and depth to the acting; (4) the ability to communicate to a wide range of audiences in a variety of production forms and literary styles; and (5) the preparation of the student for the demands of a highly disciplined profession.

Morley Theatre School

Morley College, 61 Westminster Bridge Road, London SE1 7HT
Tel (01) **928 8501**
Principal Susan Fey, BA (Principal of College)
Contact Roy Kendall (Director of Theatre School) or General Office for enquiries

Founded 1939. *Course on offer*: a part-time theatre course, ideal for those with little background who need a foundation before applying for full-time courses. All students involved in productions, some of which take place at the George Inn, Southwark, as well as at the college. There are approximately 50 places available, with 100–150 applicants. No grants available. The course is subsidized by ILEA, so fees are low. The college prospectus is available in the summer. Enrolment is by interview/audition just before the start of the course in September.
Audition requirements: no pieces; workshop improvisation.

Mountview Theatre School

104 Crouch Hill, London N8 9EA and Ralph Richardson Memorial Studios, Clarendon Road, Wood Green, London N22
Tel (01) **341 5885/881 2201**
Principal Peter Coxhead
Contact Hilda Goddard (PA to Principal, 104 Crouch Hill), Laurie Bates (Registrar, Ralph Richardson Memorial Studios)

Founded 1940s. Has been a full-time school for about 15 years, and is growing all the time. It is due to move to a large new complex in Alexandra Palace in the near future. *Courses on offer*:
● Acting course: 3-year full time; 9 terms of about 10–11 weeks each. (The year is divided into four terms: autumn, spring, summer and late summer.) 1-year full time.
● Postgraduate acting course: 1-year full time; 4 terms,
● Stage management & technical theatre course: 2-year full time.
Number of places varies. Accredited by the National Council for Drama Training and eligible for student grants. A prospectus is available.
Audition requirements: unaccompanied song, one Shakespeare and one modern piece. Movement and voice sessions. Audition cost: £16.50.
A limited scholarship fund is available, as well as the Sir Ralph Richardson Memorial Scholarship for second- and third-year acting students, and the Mountview Acting Scholarship for a resident of the London Borough of Haringey, not currently a member of the school.

New Era Academy of Drama And Music

137b Streatham High Road, London SW16
Tel (01) **769 0384**
Principal Michael Bentine, President
Contact Bernard Price, Secretary

Not a drama school as such, but an examining body with a wide ranging syllabus including Speech and Drama, Spoken English, Interview Technique, Public Speaking, Solo Verse Speaking, Reading, Choral Speaking, Bible Reading, English as a Second Language, Mime, Stage Technique. Exams in these subjects can be taken at centres all over the UK in the presence of one or two of the Academy's Board of Directors. Adults and children are catered for and the Senior exams in Stage Technique are helpful for those wishing to take up theatre work as a career. No full time courses are available, but tutors attend the Academy on Wednesday evenings. Write for a syllabus which gives details of exams in all subjects.

The Oxford School of Drama
Samsomes Farm Studios, Woodstock, Oxford OX7 1ER
Tel (0993) **812882**
Patron Denholm Elliott, CBE
Principal George Peck
Contact The Administrator

Founded 1982. Developed from summer courses run by professional actors and directors. *Courses on offer*:
- Diploma acting course: 2-year full time; minimum age 17.
- Diploma acting course: 1-year full time; minimum age 20.
- Summer courses: introduction to acting, advanced acting, Edinburgh Festival performance course.

28 places on full time courses; approximately 70 applicants each year. The school is not yet accredited by the National Council for Drama Training, but discretionary grants are available from some authorities. A prospectus is available.
Audition requirements: One Shakespeare piece and one modern piece (2 minutes). Improvisation is required at recall auditions. Audition fee: £12.00.
Teaching policy: to develop existing potential by encouraging the imagination and liberating the individual physically.

Jackie Palmer Stage School
28 Easton Street, High Wycombe, Bucks. HP11 1NT
Tel (0494) **20978**
Principals Jackie Palmer, Marylyn Phillips
Contact Marylyn Phillips

Founded 1981. *Courses on offer*: classes for boys and girls in all subjects, from the age of 3 upwards; 300 places available. No prospectus available; write or telephone the principals for details and to apply.
Audition requirements: to show some potential in the work that has been learned, suitable for the child's age.

The school attempts to provide an all-round training for those interested in working in the theatre or TV, or who wish to go on to full-time further education in drama.

Rosina Pulley School of Stage Dancing
5 Lancaster Road, London E11
Tel (01) **539 7740**
Contact Rosina Pulley

Courses on offer: evening and weekend classes for children aged 4–16; ballet, tap and modern. No straight drama classes, though some dance classes include mime. Children are entered for examinations.

Redroofs Theatre School
Littlewick Green, Maidenhead, Berks.
Tel (062882) **2982**
Principal June Rose

Courses on offer:
- 3-year full-time student course; performance-orientated professional training in acting, singing and dance. Minimum age of entry: 16.
- children's co-educational day school with education to GCSE level and drama and dance training; from 9 years.
- part-time classes in all branches for adults and children.

Prospectus available.

Richmond Drama School

Richmond Adult & Community College, Parkshot, Richmond TW9 2RE
Tel (01) **940 0171**
Director David Whitworth, BA

Founded 1956, as De Leon Drama School. A previous course director, Sam Walters, is now artistic director of the Orange Tree Theatre.
Course on offer: 1-year full-time acting course; 24 places (70 applicants each year). Some authorities will give grants. The fees are low compared to other drama schools. A prospectus is available.
Audition requirements: One Shakespeare and one modern piece. Audition fee: £10.00.
This is a small school with excellent facilities. Students have the advantage of belonging to one of the largest adult education colleges in Europe. High professional standards are demanded, and a lot is packed into one year. For some students, a further course of study is advisable. Applicants are welcomed from a wide variety of backgrounds, the only criterion being whether they show potential for development to a professional standard of acting. Students have many opportunities to work with professional actors and directors, and strong links are maintained with the Orange Tree Theatre.

Royal Academy of Dramatic Art

62–64 Gower Street, London WC1E 6ED
Tel (01) **636 7076**
Principal Dr O. Neville
Contact The Secretary

Founded 1904 by Sir Herbert Beerbohm Tree, and has functioned in Gower Street since the following year. Has two fully equipped theatres — the Vanbrugh and the GBS — and a small studio theatre. *Courses on offer*:
● Diploma in acting: 9 terms, full time; 28 places per annum; minimum age 18; NCDT accredited.
● Diploma in stage management: six terms, full time; 6 places; minimum age 17; NCDT accredited.
● specialist diploma courses: usually four terms, may be taken in stage carpentry, scene painting and design and property-making; one person per course; minimum age 19.
Audition requirements: two pieces, one contemporary and one Shakespeare. Audition fee: £20.00.
'The training is vocational. A very favourable student/staff ratio enables the acquired skills of the actor, both vocal and physical, to be taught at an intensive level. Great emphasis is given to this part of the course. However, the acquiring of these skills is clearly directed towards our central purpose, which is to develop in the actor an ability to understand and communicate a playwright's intentions. Throughout the course, these interpretative and imaginative skills are also developed by working with professional directors whose teaching is integrated with an active career outside the Academy. Performances take place in three kinds of acting space. These circumstances combine to enable the student to explore his/her work from as many angles as possible, and to keep in touch with contemporary theatre.'

Royal Scottish Academy of Music & Drama

School of Drama, 100 Renfrew Street, Glasgow G2 3DB
Tel (041) **332 4101**
Principal Edward Argent (Director, School of Drama)
Contact Valerie Parker (Administrative assistant)

Founded 1950, as College of Dramatic Art. Took present title in 1968, and moved to purpose-built accommodation in 1987.
Courses on offer:
● Diploma in dramatic art: 3-year full time; 20 places (300 applicants).
● Diploma in stage management studies: 2-year full time; 12 places (90 applicants).
● BA in dramatic studies: 3-year full time; 20 places (200 applicants).
Both diploma courses are NCDT accredited, and eligible for grants; there is mandatory granting for the degree course, which is validated by the University of Glasgow. A prospectus is available. Applicants should write for an application form, and for details of the auditioning process.
Audition requirements: Diploma in dramatic art: two pieces — one Shakespeare and one contrasting; candidates who are successful at this stage will be recalled for an interview, and then for group improvisation. BA in dramatic studies: two contrasting pieces, sight reading of texts, interview and improvisation session. Audition fee: £10.00.

St Catherine's Drama Studio

26a Portsmouth Road, Guildford, Surrey GU2 5DH
Tel (0483) **68788**
Principal June Cooper, LGSM (Hons)
Contact Adrian Cooper (Director)

Founded 1978.
Courses on offer:
● Acting diploma course: 2-year full time.
● Acting diploma course: 1-year full time.
● Stage management & technical course: 1-year full time.
Some part time courses for adults and children. All full-time courses include TV work. There are 12 places on each acting course, and six for stage management. Discretionary grants available from some education authorities. Prospectuses are available for each course.
Audition requirements: Usually a workshop. Separate audition pieces. Audition fee: £10.00.
Only tutors with recent professional experience are employed to teach. A professional company, The Strolling Players, has recently been set up to employ students, who then become members of Equity.

Sandown College

Greenbank Annexe, Mossley Avenue, Liverpool L18
Tel (051) **733 5511**
Principal R. A. Humphries
Contact A. J. Cunningham

Founded 1986, from the reorganization of the City of Liverpool's further education colleges.
Courses on offer:
● Preparatory course in drama: 1-year full time.
● Diploma in theatre studies: 2-year full time.
● Preparatory course in dance: 1-year full time.
● Diploma in dance: 2-year full time.

- General course in performing arts (GCSE A-levels in dance, drama, music).
- Diploma in performance technology: 2-year full time.
- Community/evening programmes in performing arts: widely varied series of courses.
- Graduate diploma in music: 3-year full time.
- Diploma in light music: 2-year full time.
- Preparatory course in music: 1-year full time.
- Preparatory course in rock: 1-year full time; intended for the 16–18-year-old performer who cannot read music or who needs to widen his or her skill to progress.

Grants are available for Liverpool residents attending full-time courses, and discretionary grants may be available from other local authorities.

Audition requirements: applicants for all performing courses are auditioned, but requirements vary.

Policy: 'If it's to do with the arts – WE DO IT!'

Anna Scher Theatre

70–72 Barnsbury Road, London N1 0ES
Tel (01) **278 2101**
Principal Anna Scher
Contact Shireen Nelson-Williams (administrator)

Founded 1968, as a schools' drama club. Now attended by 900 children and young people. Classes are divided into Junior (6–11), Secondary (11–16) and Youth (16–21+). There are also two professional groups. Fees are paid per session or per term, with reductions for families. There is a long waiting list, and it takes about three years to get in. As well as classes, productions are put on for parents and for friends of the theatre. There are opportunities for members to work in films, on TV and on the stage under Anna Scher Theatre Management Ltd; see Agents section. (Children under 16 do not do modelling or advertising for commercial products.) 'Our motto is "Talent thrives on training together."' Emphasis is placed on professionalism, learning to share and being a good audience.

School of Dramatic Corporal Mime

F28 Royal Victoria Patriotic Building, Trinity Road, London SW18 3SX
Tel (01) **870 7895**
Principals Ms A. Pronk, Mr W. Dashwood

Founded 1984. The Principals founded Animate Theatre in 1981 after studying with Etienne Decroux in Paris. They then moved to Holland, where they taught at the National Theatre School, and toured the Continent. In 1984, they moved to London and founded the school.

Courses available:
- Mime training: 6 terms, involving balancing, mime technique, and improvisation/acting.
- Summer course: 10 days, intensive.
- Private classes and specialized tuition for stage, film and TV are also available.

Audition requirements: motivation and 3-minute movement piece. No audition fee.

Policy: 'A technique of movement is easier and best received from many short sessions over a long period. This sustained regularity helps to develop concentration and allows the body to adapt to the subtle changes necessary.'

Advice to aspiring actors: 'Have lots of initiative. Movement is the basis of action and the basis of acting.'

Shandy Stage School (affiliated to Brighton Academy of Performing Arts)

1 Chesham Place, Kemptown, Brighton, E. Sussex BN2 1FB
Tel (0273) **607316**
Principal Andrew Cameron

Founded 1984. The school operates under the same roof as the Brighton Music Centre, and together they are known as the Brighton Academy of Performing Arts.
Courses on offer: Full-time academic and performing arts education for young people aged 6–16. There are 9 places available each year, with 68 applicants. No grants are available.
Audition requirements: to attend the school for a day for assessment. No audition fee.
The school aims to produce well-accomplished and confident young adults with the best possible knowledge of the performing arts and high academic qualifications.

Barbara Speake Stage School

East Acton Lane, London W3 7EG
Tel (01) **743 1306/6096** (day); (01) **998 6596** (night)

Founded in 1945 as a dancing school and became a full time educational establishment for 5–16 year olds in 1963. Academic curriculum with one daily non-academic class in drama, singing, tap or modern dancing. Telephone or write for details. Also hold classes (approximately four hours daily) for over-16s. Also see Barbara Speake Agency and C.S.M. (Artistes) Ltd in Agents section.

Stardust Children's Theatre Workshop

57b Meads Lane, Seven Kings, Ilford, Essex
Tel (01) **590 5555**
Principals Phyllis Borden, Annette Fisher

Founded 1983. *Courses on offer*: ballet, tap, modern dance, theatre workshops. Classes for all ages of children and adults. Phone or write in to apply. No audition requirements.
Policy: 'Learning through an educative yet fun approach.'

Dacia Stevens Stage School

Glenavon Lodge, Lansdowne Road, South Woodford, London E18 2BE
Tel (01) **989 0166**
Principal Dacia Stevens RAD, RADA

Founded 1970. *Courses on offer*: all types of drama and stage training for children, 4–9 pm each day. Pupils entered for examinations and prepared for full-time stage school. 'Children need to be taught to speak correctly. They love to act. I teach them both.' Classes for older pupils by arrangement.

Webber Douglas Academy

30 Clareville Street, London SW7 5AP
Tel (01) **370 4151**
Principal Raphael B. Jago
Contact Judy Carter (administrator)

Founded 1906, in Paris. In 1926, moved to London where it became an opera school; became a fully fledged drama school in 1945.
Courses on offer:
● Diploma course: 3-year full time; 30 places (900 applicants).

- Diploma course: 2-year full time; 12/14 places (300 applicants).
- Post-graduate course: 1-year full time; 12/14 places (300 applicants).

All courses are NCDT accredited and eligible for student grants. A prospectus is available. Prospective students should complete an application form, attaching a small photograph.

Audition requirements: One Shakespeare piece, one modern piece. It is recommended that one piece should be comedy, one should include some movement, and that only one should be a direct address to the panel. Applicants may also be asked to sing unaccompanied and to improvise. Audition fee: £15.00.

Teaching policy: 'To create a professional well-equipped actor with a good working method.'

'The demands made on actors with the development of the range of the media since the middle 1950s, and the requirement that the modern actor should be able to sing, dance and stage fight as well as act, make great demands on the modern drama school. Nevertheless, the core of the course remains the development of skills primarily to enable the student actor to cope with the demands of the classical stage. Once this is achieved, the needs of the modern theatre, films, TV and radio can be satisfied by building on these foundations.'

Welsh College of Music & Drama

Castle Grounds, Cathays Park, Cardiff CF1 3ER
Tel (0222) **42854/5/6**
Principal Peter Fletcher
Contact Avril Harding

Founded 1949. *Courses on offer*:
Acting
- Performer's course: 3-year full time.
- Graduate diploma course: 3-year.
- Advanced certificate course: 1-year; for graduates or those with appropriate experience.

All the above acting courses are fully accredited by the NCDT.
Design & stage management
- Graduate diploma course: 3-year full time.
- Advanced certificate course: 1-year.

Education
- B Ed (Hons) course: 4-year full time, designed primarily for those who wish to qualify as teachers of drama, but also useful for radio and TV work with young people, and Theatre-in-Education.

Minimum age for all 3-year courses is 18; for 1-year courses, 21. Grants are mandatory for the degree course, and discretionary for the acting courses and the 1-year courses. A prospectus is available.

Audition requirements: candidates will be selected by audition and interview. A reference is required, which must be sent with the application form.

Policy: 'The acting courses are practical in philosophy and emphasis. They aim to:
- equip the student with control of both inner and external resources for acting.
- encourage the development of the actor as a thinking, feeling, passionate and self-confident individual.
- help the actor become aware of the opportunities for employment and expression which exist in the theatre and its related industries.
- build a foundation of commitment and care about the work and the arts, which will assist the individual to make the most of the profession and, in particular, the opportunities it presents for further development, learning and growth.

White Rose Studio

Castle Hill House, 21 Otley Road, Leeds LS6 3AA
Tel (0532) **757514**
Principals Mr S. J. Armstrong, Mrs J. M. Armstrong
Contact Miss J. A. Turner (secretary)

Founded 1968, as York Academy of Speech & Dramatic Art. *Courses on offer:* tuition in speech, drama, public speaking and dancing. Different classes to suit the needs of each individual, including private and small group lessons and group workshops. All ages catered for. A prospectus is available. No auditions, just a brief interview. There are lots of opportunities for public performance, for taking examinations and for taking part in festivals. Help is given with drama school entrance. The White Rose Studio Children's Theatre, made up of students and actors attending classes at the Studio, tours to schools in West and North Yorkshire, usually at Christmas.

Universities and further education courses

Central London Adult Education Institute ('The City Lit')

Stukeley Street, Drury Lane, London WC2B 5LJ
Tel (01) **430 0455**
Principal William Tyler
Contact John James (joint head of department)

Founded 1919. The City Lit Drama Department (under the auspices of the Inner London Education Authority) has a high reputation for all aspects of acting, different dance forms, mime, clowning and circus skills, as well as speech skills taught by professional actors and teachers at low cost to students. Prospectus available (two are usually issued each year). An average of 180 courses per year, with between 25 and 20 applicants for each course.

Audition requirements: Entry is by personal interview. Open auditions are held for specified dance classes where evidence of training is required, and prepared speeches may be asked for entry into some performance classes. There are no audition fees.

'The two-year part-time drama course aims to give a good introduction to acting skills for students who may hope to become professional actors. Other, more advanced courses are designed to extend performance skills and refresh working performers and teachers. Numerous professional actors/performers have entered the City Lit as beginners seeking to test a vocation/skill for work in the theatre and in other branches of entertainment. It is possible to begin in an introductory class and then proceed by carefully monitored stages to advanced classes, which may lead to drama school entry. The low fees are made possible by the educational policies of the ILEA, which seeks to make educational opportunities available to all in accordance with its equal opportunities statements.'

The City University

Dept of Arts Policy & Management, Level 12, Frobisher Crescent, Barbican, Silk Street, London EC2Y 8HB
Tel (01) **628 5641/2**
Head of Department Professor John Pick BA, PGCE, MA PhD, FRSA

Courses on offer:
● Diploma in Arts Administration: one-year full-time course in professional skills associated with administration in the arts. Candidates should hold a degree and

have professional experience in arts administration.
- MA in Arts Administration: one-year full-time or two-year part-time course. For practising arts administrators.
- MA in Arts Criticism: one-year full-time or two-year part-time course. For those with experience of criticism and evaluation in the arts.

Various other MA courses also available. All courses require applicants to have a good first degree and several years' professional experience.

Loughborough University of Technology

Loughborough, Leics. LE11 3TU
Tel (0509) **231983**
Head of English & Drama Department J. Lucas, BA PhD FRSA
Director of Drama M. G. Robinson, BA PhD

Courses on offer:
- BA Single Honours in Drama: three-year full-time course, designed to offer the opportunity of studying the subject both in practice on stage and in theory through the detailed examination of a wide range of dramatic texts.
- BA Joint Honours in English & Drama: three-year full-time course. During the third year, students may concentrate on either the practical or the theoretical elements of the drama side of the course.

Students intending to become teachers may take an alternative four-year course that leads to the award of a degree and a Certificate in Education.

Facilities for practical drama work include a 300-seat theatre and a multi-purpose drama workshop with 150 seats. Professional theatre companies often visit these, and the university is well situated for visits to theatres at Leicester, Nottingham, Derby, Coventry, Stratford, Birmingham and Sheffield.

Middlesex Polytechnic

Ivy House, North End Road, London NW11 7HU and Trent Park, Cockfosters Road, Barnet EN4 0PT
Tel (01) **458 4646** (Ivy House) or (01) **368 1299** (all other sites)
Director Dr R. M. W. Rickett (Trent Park)
Contact Dr Lesley Ferris (Acting Head of School of Drama). Messages can be left with Jane Dare at Ivy House.

Trent Park College and the New College of Speech and Drama joined Middlesex Polytechnic in 1975. *Courses on offer:*
- BA (Hons) Performance Arts: 3-year full time, with core of performance studies and choice of first study in dance, drama or music.
- BEd (Hons): 4-year full time, with study areas in dance and music.
- MA Performance Arts: 2-year part time.
- Post-graduate Certificate in Education: music or drama, 1-year full time.
- under the 'modular scheme', which offers 400 modules in 28 different subject areas: BA (Hons) in History of Art, Design and Film; BA (Hons) Contemporary Cultural Studies; DipHE in dance, drama and music. All three courses can be full or part time.

(The Diploma in Dramatic Art, the Certificate in Stage Management and Technical Theatre and the Certificate in Drama Skills have been suspended due to lack of funding, and at present, their future is unclear.)

Grants available. Normal entry requirements for degree courses are five GCSE passes including two at A-level, or four GCSE passes with three at A-level, or an equivalent standard of education. Applications from mature students with appropriate experience but no formal qualifications will be considered.

Audition requirements: vary for the different courses. No audition fees.

'Middlesex Polytechnic has a reputation for excellence in all the performing arts. This is based on the strengths of two of the Polytechnic's constituent colleges:

Trent Park College of Education and the New College of Speech and Drama. Both became part of the Polytechnic in 1975, offering staff expertise and specialist facilities for what is now a major centre for the teaching of dance, drama and music at degree, diploma and certificate levels.

Students at Middlesex have ample opportunity for involvement with performance in both academic work and extra-curricular activities. Concerts, plays, dance programmes and multi-media productions are staged throughout the year. In one academic session alone, student productions included dance workshops and dance programmes in the community, lunchtime recitals, major opera productions, Greek and Roman drama, Japanese Noh plays, performances of electronic music, major modern plays, musicals, revues and productions of the classics.'

Nene College

Moulton Park, Northampton NN2 7AL
Tel (0604) **715000**

BA and BSc (Hons) degrees in combined studies include drama, which can be taken for one, two or three years. Offers 'a unique blend of academic study and practical experience'. Those who take drama as a minor three-year subject study a selected element of the course in Modern British and European Drama and the practical course in its entirety. Prospectus available.

Newark Technical College

Chauntry Park, Newark on Trent, Notts. NG24 1PB
Tel (0636) **705921**
Principal Mr J. E. Ashton
Contact Mr L. Orton LRAM, LLAM (section head)

Course on offer:
● Foundation course in theatre arts: 2-year, full time; 15–20 places (20–30 applicants).
Free to students living in Nottinghamshire. Other local education authorities may give grants. Application should be made to the Principal of the college. A prospectus is available.
Audition requirements: Interview and workshop audition. No audition fee.
The course is based on modules – e.g. acting technique, voice production, dance, text study, etc. These provide a wide and varied training for qualification or further training in the areas of work outlined. Emphasis is placed on developing the career prospects of each student. English language and literature and drama can be taken at GCSE level, and English and drama at A-level.

Queen Margaret College

Clerwood Terrace, Edinburgh EH12 8TS
Tel (031) **339 8111**
Principal Donald Leach
Contact Alan S. Dunbar (Head of drama)

Founded 1971. The School of Drama, which is part of a multi-discipline college, was formed after the closure of a private school called the Edinburgh College of Speech & Drama.
Courses on offer:
● Diploma in drama (acting): 3-year full time.
● Diploma in drama (stage management): 3-year full time.
There are 20 places available, with 250–300 applicants per course. Grants are mandatory for Scottish students. A prospectus is available.
Audition requirements: the school provides a set classical piece, and the student

chooses a modern piece. Short-listed candidates are also given singing, movement and improvisation tests. There is no audition fee.

Policy: 'To train students, both acting and stage management, for work in the professional theatre and related media. We are looking for people who have talent and who are *totally committed* to the job.'

Stockton–Billingham Technical College

The Causeway, Billingham, Cleveland TS23 2DB
Tel (0642) **552101**
Principal A. Oyston, MA LRAM LTCL Cert Ed
Contact Mrs M. Smith (secretary to Principal)

Courses on offer:
- Foundation course in dance and human movement.
- Foundation course in drama and theatre arts: 2-year course.
- Foundation course in arts administration.
- Foundation course in theatre and TV crafts.

Students interested in gaining further qualifications will be guided to use non-foundation-course hours in pursuit of appropriate courses in other subjects, including the range of GCSE A-level courses.

3. Universities, polytechnics and further education courses

University of Birmingham
Dept of Drama & Theatre Arts, University of Birmingham, Birmingham B15 2TT
Tel (021) **414 5994**
Admissions Tutor for Faculty of Arts B. Standring, BA PhD

Courses on offer:
- BA Special Honours: 3-year full-time course in drama and theatre arts.
- BA Combined Honours: 3-year full-time course in drama and theatre arts, with one other subject: English, French, German, Greek (ancient or modern), history, Italian, Latin, music, physical education, Russian, sociology or Hispanic studies.

The Drama & Theatre Arts Department at Birmingham is a leader in the field of practical drama, having pioneered a course which puts at its centre the actor in performance. At the core are the complementary dramatic medium and theatre practice courses which all students follow, and from this stem the optional courses which aim to develop more specialized skills.

The Department also runs a special honours degree course in music, drama and dance in conjunction with the Music Department.

University of Bristol
Drama Dept, Senate House, Bristol BS8 1TH
Tel (0272) **303030**
Professor of Drama Professor E. Braun, MA, PhD (Cantab)

Courses on offer:
- BA Single Honours: 3-year full-time course in drama, designed to provide students with a training in the theory, criticism and history of dramatic literature and performance (including radio, film and TV drama), together with an introduction to practical aspects of the dramatic arts.
- MA in Drama Studies: 1-year full-time or 2-year part-time course for those seeking an advanced qualification in drama.
- Certificate in Radio, Film and Television: post-graduate 1-year course that is an introduction to the skills in practical work in the three media.

Facilities for research work leading to the degrees of M.Litt. and PhD are also offered by the Department.

University of Durham
Old Shire Hall, Durham DH1 3HP
Tel (091) **374 2000**
Head of School of Education Professor F. J. Coffield

No drama courses *per se*, but drama in education is offered as a curriculum option on two courses: Advanced Diploma in Education (remedial and special education; one-year, full-time) and Advanced Diploma in Education (primary education; one-year, full-time). Applicants for the primary course must have had five years of teaching experience, and applicants for the remedial course must have had three years' experience.

University of Essex

Dept of Literature, Wivenhoe Park, Colchester, Essex CO4 3SQ
Tel (0206) **872624**
Course director Roger Howard

> *Course on offer:*
> ● MA in Drama: 1-year full-time (or possibly 2-year part-time at the course director's discretion). Chiefly concerned with modern dramatic literature worldwide, with options available in English plays of the late medieval, Elizabethan and Jacobean stages. There are currently two main components to the course: 'The Theatre and Social Change' and 'Naturalism and Beyond'. Instead of a final written dissertation, students may offer: an original stage play of at least one hour's duration; the production and direction of a play of at least one hour's duration; or a prompt book for the production of a full-length play.
> The Dept of Literature has initiated a theatre writer's residency to provide students with an opportunity to work with a professional theatre writer during the writing of a play, usually leading to a production. Recent writers have included Edward Bond, Nick Dear, Steve Gooch and Michele Roberts.

University of Exeter

School of English, Drama Dept, Thornlea, New North Road, Exeter EX4 4JZ
Tel (0392) **77911 ext 241**
Head of Department Professor Peter Thomson

> *Courses on offer:*
> ● BA Single Honours: 3-year full-time course in drama, which has a national reputation for innovation and experiment. The studio-based project system of teaching and learning obliterates any final distinction between practical and academic work. Continuous assessment, a dissertation, a practical 'essay' (devised and performed, not written) and portfolios take their place alongside examination papers in the degree scheme.
> ● BA Combined Honours: 3-year full-time course in drama and English or drama and German.
> ● BA (Ed) Honours: 3-year full-time teaching course in English and drama. Offers opportunities to those who have equal interest in both subjects, or to those who prefer to concentrate on one or the other. The work seeks to involve students in the kinds of approaches they can readily adapt to teaching in schools.

University of Glasgow

Dept of Theatre, Film & Television Studies, Glasgow G12 8QQ
Tel (041) **339 8855**
Head of Department Professor Janet B. I. McDonald, MA

> *Courses on offer:*
> ● Theatre Studies: *1st year:* an introduction to the nature of the theatrical art. *2nd year:* a study of the major theatrical genres, current trends in non-text-based theatre, practical classes in direction and design. *Honours courses (3rd & 4th years):* students may choose from a wide range of options. Entry to the 1st-year class is limited to 100, preference being given to those who want to pursue the subject to honours level.
> ● Film & Television Studies: *1st year:* introductory course on film and TV. *2nd year:* two subjects — 'Genre in Film and Television' and 'Film, Television and British National Culture'. *Honours courses (3rd & 4th years):* a variety of topics are studied, and there is a substantial practical course in the 3rd year.

University of Hull
Dept of Drama, Cottingham Road, Hull HU6 7RX
Tel (0482) **46311 ext 6210**
Director of Drama Donald H. Roy, MA, Dip Ed, FRSA

Courses on offer:
● BA Special Honours: 3-year full-time course, designed for the student who wishes to concentrate on the study of drama in all its aspects. In addition, Special students are required to follow a supporting course outside the department for one year.
● Joint Honours: 3-year full-time course, designed for the student who wishes to read drama and one other subject.
● MA in Theatre & Media Production: 1-year full-time vocational course.

University of Kent
Drama & Theatre Studies, Rutherford College, The University, Canterbury, Kent CT2 7NX
Tel (0227) **764000**
Chairman of Drama & Theatre Studies Alan Pearlman

Courses on offer:
● BA Single Honours: 4-year full-time course in drama and theatre studies. The fourth year of this course is devoted to one specialist subject: directing; devising; or the funding and organization of the British theatre.
● BA Combined Honours: 3-year full-time course, with half the degree work in drama and half in another subject in the Faculty of Humanities.
● Visual & Performed Arts: 3-year full-time course. A package of courses may be chosen, related to film, drama and the history and theory of art.
'At this university, we start from the rejection of the notion (which dies hard in the English theatre) that skills of an intellectual and analytical kind are incompatible with skills of a creative and imaginative kind. We believe that the best theatre has always been created by people with developed minds as well as natural theatrical talent.
'At a drama school, you will be trained as an actor. If you are absolutely certain that you want to study acting exclusively, then perhaps a drama school is the better choice – university drama departments do not give specialist acting training. But if your interest in the theatre is more broad-based, if you want to study its literature and its history, if you are interested in writing and directing and design – if, in short, you want to study theatre in its widest sense, then a university drama course is the wiser choice ... The kind of training a degree in drama offers is relevant to all worlds of work: learning to meet work deadlines; learning to find and use information; learning to present coherent arguments; learning to work cooperatively in group projects ... Also bear in mind that people do much better at things that interest and stimulate them, than at things that they "ought" to be doing.'

University of Lancaster
Drama Dept, University House, Bailrigg, Lancaster LA1 4YW
Tel (0524) **65201**
Head of Department K. M. Sturgess, MA, B.Litt (Oxon)

Courses on offer:
● BA (Hons) Single Major in Theatre Studies: 3-year full-time. Based entirely around the Theatre Studies Department and involving the study of subjects and options which include: theatrecrafts; Stanislavski and Brecht; arts administration; mediaeval English theatre; one theatre, its Company and repertoire; TV drama; ritual theatre; feminist theatre.
● BA (Hons) Combined Major: 3-year full-time, in theatre studies and one

other subject: education; religious studies; English; French; German; sociology.
- MA in Theatre Studies: 1-year full-time. 'This course aims to provide laboratory facilities for and guidance into a variety of aspects of theatre.'

University of Leeds
Leeds LS2 9JT
Tel (0532) **431751**
Director Professor Martin Banham (at The Workshop Theatre, ext 7416)

Courses on offer:
- MA Theatre Studies: normally 1-year full-time. Students will be required to attend three courses: theory and practice of performance; history of theatre and methods of theatrical analysis; theatre practice. Applicants will be expected to have made some significant study of drama or theatre during the course of their studies at first-degree level.
- BA Drama Studies with English Literature: to be run from October 1989; details not currently available.

'The Workshop Theatre is the laboratory for the academic programme in theatre studies in the School of English. Much of the work that is to be seen in the Workshop Theatre is directly related to teaching programmes within the university, specifically the MA programme in theatre studies, but the Workshop Theatre also has a responsibility to the university as a whole, and originates a range of general theatrical activities that are designed to complement academic programmes and provide a richer cultural life for the university community.'

University of London: Goldsmiths' College
New Cross, London SE14 6NW
Tel (01) **692 7171** (enquiries to The Registry)
Admissions Tutor for Drama Miss N. Jones

Courses on offer:
- BA Drama & English: 3-year full-time.
- BA Drama & French: 4-year full-time (third year spent in France).
- BA Drama & German: 4-year full-time (third year spent in Germany).
- B Ed in Primary Education, with subject study in drama: 4-year full-time.
- Facilities are available for study for the post-graduate degrees of M.Phil and PhD in the following fields: Gogol, Ostrovsky, Chekov and Gorki; the Soviet Russian theatre – directors and designers; political theatre, Brecht to Fugard – all supervised by Dr V. Gottleib. Full- or part-time study may be undertaken.
- Postgraduate Teaching Certificate in drama as a subject for secondary school teaching: 1-year full-time.

'Goldsmiths' is a unique institution, in which the creative and performing arts co-exist at a high level of achievement with more traditional studies in the humanities, education, science and the social sciences.'

University of London: Royal Holloway & Bedford New College
Dept of Drama & Theatre Studies, Egham Hill, Egham, Surrey TW20 0EX
Tel (0784) **34455**
Professor & Head of Department D. Bradby

Courses on offer:
- BA Single Honours in Drama & Theatre Studies: 3-year full-time course, established 1980. Designed to extend knowledge and deepen critical appreciation of drama from the classical period to the present day. Practical work is undertaken with this end in view.
- BA Combined Honours: 3-year full-time course in drama and theatre studies combined with English, French or music.
- MA in Drama & Theatre Studies: 1-year full-time or 2-year part-time study.

All of the above courses include training in and use of theatre skills, production work, critical analysis, and study of the history of film and theatre, with many optional subjects. There is a Departmental Studio Theatre, and radio and TV facilities are available at the London University Audio-Visual Centre in central London. The Department also houses the Centre for the Study of Japanese Noh Theatre, which is building up a specialist library of videotapes and books.

University of London: Westfield College

Kidderpore Avenue, London NW3 7ST
Tel (01) **435 7141**
Director of Drama J. Redmond, MA Ed B (Glasgow), BA (Cantab), B.Litt (Oxon)

Courses on offer:
- BA Combined Honours Degrees as follows:

Classical Studies & Drama (3 years, full-time)
English & Drama (3 years, full-time)
French & Drama (3 and 4 years, full-time)
German & Drama (3 and 4 years, full-time)
Greek & Drama (3 years, full-time)
Latin & Drama (3 years, full-time)
Spanish & Drama (3 and 4 years, full-time)
- Graduate students are accepted for the degrees of M.Phil and PhD in Drama, and receive personal supervision.

Drama classwork for the combined degrees involves a wide variety of lectures, seminars, tutorials and practical studio and production work. Students are registered as undergraduates at Westfield, and attend most of their lectures and seminars there, but they also have membership of the Central School of Speech & Drama (*see* Drama schools), and take practical classes and mount productions there.

University of Manchester

Dept of Drama, The University, Manchester M13 9PL
Tel (061) **275 2000**
Head of Department Professor Kenneth Richards

Courses on offer:
- BA Single Honours: 3-year full-time course in drama. Largely an academic course, with a practical element.
- BA Double Honours: 4-year full-time course in English and drama.
- BA Joint Honours: 3-year full-time course in Italian and drama. Other combinations of subjects are also available on some occasions.
- Diploma in Drama: 3 terms. Occasionally the Department is able to offer supervised study for the Diploma in select areas of practical theatre work (e.g. design, playwriting).
- Facilities are also available for study for PhD and M.Phil degrees.

The Drama Department at Manchester is one of the largest in Britain, with approximately 90 undergraduates. There are a number of professional theatre companies in the city, and opera, ballet and contemporary dance flourish in the region.

University of Ulster at Coleraine

Faculty of Humanities, University of Ulster, Coleraine, Co. Londonderry BT52 1SA
Tel (0265) **4141**
Head of Department of English, Media & Theatre Studies Professor R. Welch, MA, PhD

Course on offer:
- BA (Hons) Humanities Combined Degree: 3-year full-time course. Theatre

studies may form a major, joint or minor option in combination with other approved subjects.

The course focuses on the relation of theory to practice and is modern in its overall emphasis. It has been found to be particularly popular with students who respond to the challenge of group work and collective practical activity as a process through which they can extend their creative, intellectual and academic skills.

Students taking theatre studies as a major option take part in a placement during their second year, which consists of a six-week period of intensive work, usually with a leading producing theatre company in Britain or Ireland.

University of Warwick

Coventry CV4 7AL

Tel (0232) **523523**

Professor of Theatre Studies & Dramatic Arts D. B. Thomas MA, PhD (Cantab)

Courses on offer:
- BA Single Honours: 3-year full-time course in theatre studies and dramatic arts. Allows students to emphasize, in their second and third years, either a practical or an historical and analytical approach to theatre.
- BA Joint Honours (English & Theatre Studies): 3-year full-time course. Approaches drama from two directions: through the literary analysis of texts, and via the understanding of playing places and performance. The degree provides no training for actors or directors, but does have a special concern with the role of the writer in the theatre: as critic and dramatist, in theory and practice.
- BA Combined Honours: 3-year full-time course in theatre studies with either French or Italian.
- BA Joint Honours (Film & Literature): 3-year full-time course. The only course of its kind at a British university.

University College of Wales Aberystwyth

The Old College, King Street, Aberystwyth, Dyfed SY23 2AX

Tel (0970) **623177**

Head of Department Mrs E. Closs Stephens

Courses on offer:
- BA Single Honours: 3-year full-time course in drama.
- BA Joint Honours: 3-year full-time. Drama with American studies; drama with art history; drama with classics.

Students can decide whether to take single or joint honours at the end of their first year.

'Drama at Aberystwyth is characterized academically by its emphasis on the indivisibility of theory and practice. Practical work is seen as illuminating and deepening the student's understanding of the written text; similarly, theoretical approaches are tested in the workshop of creative work.'

University College of North Wales, Bangor

Adran Ddrama (Dept of Drama), Bangor, Gwynedd LL57 2DG

Tel (0248) **351151**

As a result of a reorganization of drama departments within British universities, drama at Bangor is being phased out and all courses will be withdrawn by 1990. The Welsh Department will be retaining a course in 'Welsh Literature and Drama'.

4. Film and video courses

Bournemouth & Poole College of Art & Design
Wallisdown, Poole, Dorset BH12 5HH
Tel (0202) **533011**
Head of School of Film, Television & Audio Visual Studies Nick Wright

Courses on offer:
- BTEC Higher National Diploma in film and television: 2 years, full time.
- BTEC Diploma in audio visual design: 2 years, full time.
- Advanced Diploma in media production: 1 year, full time; specifically devised to offer an opportunity to 'especially gifted students' to extend and develop a chosen specialization within certain categories such as writing/direction, production management, editing, etc.
Prospectus available.

Croydon College
School of Art and Design, Barclay Road, Croydon, Surrey CR9 1DX
Tel (01) **688 9271**
Contact Eileen Baldwin/Kevin Gough-Yates

Courses on offer:
Postgraduate Certificate in film or animation: 1 year, full time. Students specialize in live-action film-making or animation, although in certain circumstances both areas can be studied (there is currently no video offered).

Gwent College of Higher Education
Faculty of Art and Design, Clarence Place, Newport, Gwent NP9 OUW
Tel (0633) **59984**
Contact Lez Mills

Course on offer:
BTEC Higher National Diploma in film and television: 2 years, full time; devised to provide vocational training in the practical skills of handling film and video equipment and materials and to encourage a creative yet professional attitude towards the film and television media.

Harrow College of Higher Education
Northwick Park, Harrow, Middx HA1 3TP
Tel (01) **864 5422**

Offer a BA (Hons) CNAA (Council for National Academic Awards) degree course in photography, film and video (3 years full time). Prospectus available.

Kent Institute of Art and Design

Maidstone College of Art and Design, Oakwood Park, Oakwood Road, Maidstone, Kent ME16 8AG
Tel (0622) **57286/9**
Head of Time—based Media David Hall

> *Course on offer:*
> BA (Hons) communication media—time based studies: 3 years, full time. Time based studies is for students with a particular interest in the exploration of new developments in the field. The practical and theoretical thrust aims to inform, encourage and develop a broad approach to video/TV production with special attention to creative authorship and visual innovation.

King Alfred's College of Higher Education

Sparkford Road, Winchester SO22 4NR
Tel (0962) **62281**
Contact Peter Sykes

> *Course on offer:*
> BA (Hons) (CNAA) in drama, theatre and television: 3 years. The focus is on the practice of communication through live performance and television with approximately equal integrated practical and theoretical units.

London College of Printing

Elephant & Castle, London SE1 6SB
Tel (01) **735 8484/9100**

> 3—year full-time course leading to a Council for National Academic Awards BA (Hons) degree in film and video. A production course with a strong theoretical input, concentrating on independent, new and innovative production. Students study all stages of film and video production within the context of past and current media structures and institutions. The course has a special interest in popular culture, women's cinema and Third World cinema, and prepares students for the possibilities of cross-ethnic, cross-cultural co-productions in the European and international context.

London International Film School

24 Shelton Street, London WC2H 9HP
Tel (01) **836 9642/240 0168**
Administrator Phil Mottram

> Diploma course, 2 years full time. The syllabus includes: basic principles for film-makers; scripting and planning; organization and production; directing and acting; photography; lenses; camera; lighting and special effects; animation and titling; projection and presentation; editing; sound; music; art department and design; make-up and wardrobe; film analysis and appreciation; written work, tests, etc.; dissertation. Prospectus available.

Manchester Polytechnic

Faculty of Art and Design, Dept of Communication Arts & Design, Capitol Building, School Lane, Didsbury, Manchester M20 OHT
Tel (061) **434 3331**
Head of School of Film & Television Graeme McCaig

> *Course on offer:*
> BA (Hons) Design for communication media/film and television: 3 years, full time with options in television film production or television production design (set design). General audio—visual design and animation 2D and 3D is also available.

The course is 60% practical and the main study is on television production and design with strong emphasis towards broadcasting.

Middlesex Polytechnic
Cat Hill, Barnet, Herts. EN4 8HT
Tel (01) **368 1299**

CNAA (Council for National Academic Awards) postgraduate diploma in video: 1 year, full time. 10 places on offer; local authority awards not available, but a small number of bursaries from the Department of Education and Science are awarded to UK students on the recommendation of course staff after interviews. Candidates should have a first-class or upper-second honours degree, a year or more away from formal *taught* course work, substantial experience in video production and evidence of formal critical/theoretical study of film, TV or media studies.

National Film & Television School
Beaconsfield Studios, Station Road, Beaconsfield, Bucks. HP9 1LG
Tel (0494) **671234** Fax (0494) **674042**
Contact Applications secretary

Offer two training programmes: full-time three-year course, and a short course. (Those wishing to be considered for admission to a short course should address their enquiries to the Administrator of the National Short Course Training Programme at the school.) The school's departments cover: animation, art direction, camera, direction, documentary, editing, music composition, producing, script, sound. Applicants are first interviewed in the areas of their proposed specialization. The selection process takes approximately five months, and the deadline for applications is in January. Prospectus available.

Newcastle upon Tyne Polytechnic
Faculty of Art and Design, Squires Building, Sandyford Road, Newcastle upon Tyne NE1 8ST
Tel (091) **232 6002**
Contact Peter Leake

Course on offer:
BA (Hons) Media Production: 3 years, full time. The course aims to produce graduates who will become professional practitioners whose basic technical proficiency is informed by firmly established critical perspectives. The film and video area offers an opportunity to engage in the processes of film and video production and criticism and seeks to develop individual and group skills, perceptions and roles to a level satisfying professional standards.

Polytechnic of Central London
18 Riding House Street, London W1P 7PD
Tel (01) **486 5811**
Contact The Registry

Undergraduate courses
Offer the following 3-year full-time courses: BA (Hons) degree in media studies; BA (Hons) degree in film, video and photographic arts; BSc and BSc (Hons) degrees in photographic and electronic imaging sciences.
Postgraduate courses
Linked MA and postgraduate diploma in film and TV studies (nine terms or six terms part-time evening). These courses lead to the postgraduate diploma of the CNAA (Council for National Academic Awards) in film and TV studies after six terms of study, and to the MA in film and TV studies of the CNAA after a further

three terms of study. Students with previous film and/or TV study experience may be directly admitted to year two.

'The Faculty of Communication is concerned with the study and practice of the modern media of communication – principally broadcasting, film, journalism and photography. It embraces a wide variety of academic disciplines. Our courses deal with the technology of the media, creative professional practice and the aesthetic and social implications of media products . . .'

Royal College of Art

Kensington Gore, London SW7 2EU
Tel (01) **584 5020**

Postgraduate 2-year full-time course in film and TV. Also facilities for mid-career course for artists and designers with at least five years' professional experience. Candidates should be over 21 and under 40 years old and have obtained the BA in art and design or a first degree of a British university or an equivalent overseas qualification. The upper age limit does not apply to mid-career students.

St Martin's School of Art

Film and Video Unit, 27–29 Long Acre, London WC2E 9LA
Tel (01) **437 0611**
Advanced Course Tutor Bill Foulk

Course on offer:
MA in independent film and video: 2 years, part time. An intensive programme of lectures and seminars which are designed to meet the needs of film and video–makers.

Suffolk College of Higher and Further Eduction

Dept of Art & Design, Rope Walk, Ipswich, Suffolk IPA 1LT
Tel (0473) **55885**
Head of Dept J R Lowe

Course on offer:
BTEC Higher National Diploma in visual communication: 2 years, full time. Includes options in film/TV graphics, animation and film/video production.

West Surrey College of Art & Design

Falkner Road, Farnham, Surrey GU9 7DS
Tel (0252) **722441**
Contact Art & Design Admissions Registry

Offer 3-year full-time CNAA (Council for National Academic Awards) degree courses in photography, film and video, and animation. Applicants are required to specify their chosen course in advance, and normally carry out their practical study almost entirely within that school. Prospectus available.

5. Directors' courses

Courses on directing are to be found at:

Bournemouth & Poole College of Art & Design
Wallisdown, Poole, Dorset BH12 5HH
Tel (0202) **533011**

> *See* Film & Video Courses *above*.

British Theatre Association
Regent's College, Inner Circle, Regent's Park, London NW1 4NW
Tel (01) **935 2571**

> *See* Associations & Societies.

Bristol Old Vic Theatre School
2 Downside Road, Clifton, Bristol BS8 2XF
Tel (0272) **733535**

> Trainee directors' attachment (not a structured course). *See* Drama Schools *above*.

East 15 Acting School
Hatfields, Rectory Lane, Loughton, Essex IG10 3RU
Tel (01) **508 5983**

> *See* Drama Schools *above*.

National Film & Television School
Beaconsfield Studios, Station Road, Beaconsfield, Bucks. HP9 1LG
Tel (0494) **671234**

> *See* Film & Video Courses *above*.

Regional Theatre Young Director Scheme
Independent Television Association, 56 Mortimer Street, London W1N 8AN
Tel (01) **636 6866**
Administrator Jack Andrews

> Founded 1960. A training scheme for those between the ages of 20 and 26 who have had some experience in theatre (professional or amateur) or the allied arts and who wish to make a career as directors in the professional theatre. Funded by the ITV companies, the training is for two years and may take place in one or more regional theatres. Usually four vacancies each year; applications should be made by early February (the closing date can be obtained from the Television Fund Secretary and is advertised in *The Stage*). The list of former trainees is long and distinguished, including Pip Broughton, Bill Bryden, Giles Havergal, Gregory Hersov, Barry Kyle, Kenneth Loach, Adrian Noble, Trevor Nunn, Michael Rudman, Sue Wilson.

part **2**

the opportunities of acting

6. Agents

The ideal agent is an entrepreneur, lawyer, counsellor and friend.

The bad news is, of course, that these paragons appear rarely. Easier to find is the agent with one or at best two of the prime qualities. Given the choice, the canny negotiator and the sharp legal brain are preferable to the agent who simply wants to be your chum.

To say that the entertainment business is open warfare is a laughable euphemism. It takes a tough operator to hold out for a fair deal against the massed ranks of the producers and their accountants. Actors are generally inhibited when it comes to arguing money. You have to be very brave to say, 'This is the figure I want because this is what I believe I am worth.' But agents who know the market rates can more easily assert the incomparable talents of their clients and press for decent rewards. Moreover, when money is due, agents are best equipped to put the squeeze on recalcitrant book-keepers.

The legal skill comes in charting a way through the mass of small print that turns every contract into a tome. The doubtless commendable tendency of Equity to make agreements with producers and management which cover all eventualities adds to the complexity of the game.

For the untutored, the greatest risks of misinterpretation are in calculating film and TV repeats and residuals. Failure to get the sums right can be expensive. Actors who appear in a popular TV series are quite accustomed to finding that they earn much more from repeats than from the original showing. Take ITV, for example: while a first repeat in Britain brings 100 per cent of the programme fee, a second repeat attracts 150 per cent. Residuals vary from a top rate of 550 per cent for the first showing on some American TV stations to just 1 per cent in Albania, but even these 1 per cents can add up to a few hot dinners.

Then there are the commercials. Nobody truly understands the pay structure for commercials; it is too early in the evolutionary process for the human brain to grasp such complexities. But a good agent with years of experience and computer back-up will make the best of a deal.

Actors who find it difficult to believe that calculating fees for commercials can be *that* difficult should give themselves a test run, starting with the Equity minimum of £95.00 for days on screen work and £57.50 per hour for voice-overs. These apparently measly figures can transform into a living wage when multiplied by a percentage of the studio fee paid every time the advertisement is shown. The percentages vary from one region to another (16 per cent in London; 2 per cent in the furthest north), from one company to another (TV-AM pays 42 per cent of ITV fees) and from one channel to another (Channel 4 gets away with 60 per cent of ITV fees). Anyone still paying attention at this stage should think about giving up acting in favour of chartered accountancy.

Agents should know where to go to find business. If they are respected by producers and casting directors, business will come to them, but they are not employment exchanges. Actors are their own best representatives. They need to work hard at finding and cultivating their own contacts. Those who sit back waiting for the telephone to ring are in for a lifetime of disappointment.

A vital part of the selling operation is a photograph in *Spotlight*, the multi-volume directory of performers which is part of the office furniture for every producer and casting director. A potential rival to *Spotlight* is the BBC's new electronic casting directory known as *Lasercast*. The aim is to put 100,000 full colour pictures and over half a million pages of text on to a single laser disc. More informative than *Spotlight* and far easier to use, it does mean more expense for the actor — a £35.00 registration fee in addition to £73.50 for a half-page in *Spotlight* with a new photograph.

Young actors in seach of agents have to work at it. *The Actors Handbook* offers a starting point, with a list of those agents prepared to consider taking on new clients. A close reading will reveal those who are likely to offer a fruitful partnership, but since there is no guarantee that any one of them will rise to the bait, it is wisest to draw up a shortlist of possibles. Ask the opinions of other actors whose experience may suggest additions to the list.

At least one may be a cooperative agency, staffed by actors who are themselves clients of the agency but who give a proportion of their time to managing the office and dealing with contracts. Though gaining ground in recent years, the cooperative ventures rarely meet with the approval of traditional agents, who argue that they lack the cutting edge of true professionalism. But cooperatives can be very helpful to young actors who quickly learn the ropes and find sympathetic support from fellow members during the inevitable spells of unemployment.

Now for the approach. A letter and CV, with an SAE, is best calculated to draw a response. A photograph is rarely needed at this stage, while videos tend to pile up until someone has the time to look at them (which can be never). It is different when established actors are considering changing their agents. In these circumstances, a picture can help to jog the memory ('I remember him, he was very good in . . .'), and a video is likely to be taken more seriously when it accompanies a healthy list of credits.

A CV should be edited down to fit one side of A4. At the same time, newcomers should try to give information beyond the parts they have played on stage or screen. Hobbies, interests and work outside the profession may not be strictly relevant to acting ability, but this extra information does give a more complete image of the writer. Agents are more likely to react favourably if they have something positive to go on. It is difficult to get enthusiastic over a list of minor roles, however well received by friends and relatives. Parts that do get a mention should be clearly related to production companies and directors. Familiar names always make a good starting point for discussion.

A neatly typed or printed CV will attract more attention than a hand-written one. There is a good practical reason for this: actors' handwriting is invariably illegible — the penalty, perhaps, of signing too many autographs. But in any case, typewritten correspondence looks more professional. This may be a sad reflection on the persuasive influence of office technology, but there it is.

At best, agents will respond cautiously to actors' supplications, probably suggesting a meeting as an opportunity for a mutual sizing-up. Agents will have stock questions to test the strength of purpose of their potential clients (there is no virtue in taking on someone who is liable to give up at the first disappointment) and will doubtless set out their terms of business. Now is the time to check out rates of commission. The usual base is 10 per cent, but it is not uncommon for 15 or even 20 per cent to be quoted as the mean, with rates above or below for particular types of work. Be warned: no self-respecting agent charges a registration fee or takes commission on rehearsal pay.

Top actors are liable to argue for a lower-than-average commission to take account of their higher-than-average fees, but hard bargaining, even from a position of strength, is not always productive. There is the story of Richard Burton and Elizabeth Taylor, when they were as one, negotiating with top New York agent Robert Lantz. With their vast earning power, they figured that half the usual commission was fair.

'Five per cent is our top,' declared Burton.

'I quite understand,' said Lantz, smiling sweetly as he got up from the table. 'Why don't you come back when you can afford me.'

There are agents (Robert Lantz is one) who would be more inclined to be lenient with young, talented but untried actors. Putting the harshest possible interpretation on their motives, it might be said that they recognize the advantage of investing in the future. But young actors should not look to many concessions. Agents need to cover their overheads (office, rent, secretarial salaries, postage, telephone, printing, stationery, photocopying, entertaining contacts) and make a living. The sad fact is that 10 per cent of the average actor's income does not go very far.

First meetings between agents and prospective clients will clear up a lot of outstanding questions but may not lead directly to a deal. Agents will want to see what the actors can do. A forthcoming stage performance is an ideal opportunity, but a demonstration tape or video may serve the purpose. At this stage of the negotiations, agents will make the time to assess all the material to hand.

If, after all this, the only result is a polite letter of rejection, do not become despondent. Think of it as Fate's reminder that you are in the business of hard knocks — and start again.

AAA Agency
Addlestone Moor, Weybridge, Surrey KT15 2QE
Tel (0932) **854184**
Contact Glyn Picton

> Represent mostly speciality acts — trapeze artists, lion tamers and so forth. Interested in anything unusual. Will consider telephoned or written approaches.

A & B Personal Management Ltd
5th floor, 114 Jermyn Street, London SW1Y 6HJ
Tel (01) **839 4433**

> Represent actors, writers, directors and a choreographer. Welcome queries from actors seeking representation. Send CV and photograph initially. Will consider video tapes of work done, not set-up demos.

ABA Associates
97 High Street, London SE20 7HW
Tel (01) **659 6639**
Contact Pat Armitage

> Founded 1975. Represent actors only, and welcome queries from those seeking

representation. Approach in writing in the first instance. Will consider demo tapes and video show reels.

AC Management
38 Mount Pleasant, London WC1X 0AH
Tel (01) **837 2413**
Contact Kate Day

> Founded 1976. Cooperative management. Represent actors only, and welcome queries from those seeking representation. Approach in writing in the first instance (with SAE). No unsolicited demo tapes or video show reels.

ACT Artistes Management
8 Elms Avenue, Muswell Hill, London N10 2JP
Tel (01) **444 6150**
Contact Alan Thomas

> Founded 1978. Represent actors, presenters, personalities, media persons, public-life figures. Welcome queries from actors seeking representation. Approach in writing in the first instance with follow up telephone call. Will consider demo tapes and video show reels if accompanied by SAE.

AIM (Associated International Management)
5 Denmark Street, London WC2H 8LP
Tel (01) **836 2001** Fax (01) **379 0848**
Contact Derek Webster, Marina Darling

> Founded 1984. Represent actors and film and TV directors. Welcome queries from actors seeking representation. Approach in writing in the first instance. No unsolicited demo tapes or video show reels.

A & J Management
551 Green Lanes, London N13 4DR
Tel (01) **886 3159**
Contact Jackie Michael

> Founded 1984. Represent actors and children (small number of adult clients). Do not welcome queries from actors seeking representation.

ANA (Actors Network Agency)
11 Mowll Street, London SW9 6BG
Tel (01) **735 0999**

> Founded 1985. Cooperative management. Represent actors only, and welcome casting queries from those seeking representation.

ART Casting
2 Mount Pleasant, Liverpool L3 5RY
Tel (051) **708 7669**
Contact Ron Tomlinson

> Founded 1980. Represent actors only, and welcome queries from those seeking representation. Send letter in the first instance, with CV and photograph. Welcome demo tapes and video show reels.

Abacus Agency
31 Chesfield Road, Kingston upon Thames, Surrey KT2 5TH
Tel (01) **546 3463**
Contact Jean Darnell

> Founded 1985. Represent child actors, and welcome queries from under 16s, or 16–18 with Equity if able to play down. Approach by telephone in the first instance. No unsolicited demo tapes or video show reels.

Marjorie Abel Ltd
50 Maddox Street, London W1R 9PA
Tel (01) **499 1343**
Contact Marjorie Abel

> Founded 1972. Represent actors, musical directors and orchestrators. Welcome queries from actors seeking representation. Approach in writing in the first instance. No unsolicited demo tapes or video show reels.

Acting Associates
Unit F10, 28 Tooting High Street, London SW17 0RE
Tel (01) **672 7801**

> Founded 1987. Cooperative management. Represent actors only, and welcome queries from prospective clients. Write in the first instance, stating interest in a cooperative agency.

Actor Factor (Barbara Pemberton Associates)
Imex House, 40 Princess Street, Manchester M1 6DE
Tel (061) **236 7768**
Contact Barbara Pemberton

> Founded 1987. Represent actors only, and welcome queries from those seeking representation. Approach in writing in the first instance, enclosing CV and photograph. Do not welcome unsolicited demo tapes or video show reels.

The Actors Agency
Clyde Chambers, 164 Howard Street, Glasgow G1 4HA
Tel (041) **221 7744** Fax (041) **221 3808**
Contact Douglas Stiven

> Founded 1984. Represent actors, directors, writers, producers, and also involved in co-productions, investment, etc. Welcome queries from actors seeking representation. Approach in writing in the first instance. Will consider demo tapes and video show reels.

Actors Alliance
Bon Marché Building, 444 Brixton Road, London SW9 8EJ
Tel (01) **326 0070**

> Founded 1976. Cooperative management. Represent actors only. Currently not considering requests for representation. No unsolicited demo tapes or video show reels.

The Actors' Exchange Ltd
Unit 503, 69/71 Bondway, London SW8 1SQ
Tel (01) **793 0028**

> Founded 1983. Cooperative management. Represent actors only. Usually advertise in *The Stage* when seeking new members, but will consider queries from

actors wanting representation. Approach by telephone in the first instance. Photographs and CVs should always be accompanied by an SAE. No unsolicited demo tapes or video show reels.

Actors Management Wales Ltd (Rheolaeth Actorion Cymru CYF)

House One, The Maltings, East Tyndall Street, Cardiff CF5 5EA
Tel (0222) **489032**
Contact Tracy Spottiswoode, Christopher Morgan, Sera Moore-Williams

Founded 1987. Cooperative management. Represent actors only, and welcome queries from those seeking representation. Approach in writing in the first instance, although 'if someone rings, we are happy to send information.' Will consider demo tapes and video show reels. 'It is vital to send a good photograph and informative CV as well as a letter stating interest. As we are a cooperative agency, it is essential that applicants are willing and able to man the office on a rota basis when not working. We would advise any actor who wants more control over his/her career to join a cooperative.'

Actors Network Agency

- *See* ANA.

ADS Agency

Reform Road, Maidenhead, Berks. SL6 8BT
Tel (0628) **39758/29346**
Contact Betty Curtis

Founded 1983. Represent children and some adults. Welcomes queries from actors seeking representation. Write in the first instance, sending photograph and CV. Demo tapes and video show reels welcome.

Afro-Caribs Ltd

11 Ingestre Court, Ingestre Place, London W1R 3LU
Tel (01) **439 1734**
Contact Graham Byers

Founded 1968. Represent actors only. Welcome queries from actors seeking representation. Contact by telephone or in writing in the first instance. Will consider demo tapes and video show reels.

Alpha Management

London House, 68 Upper Richmond Road, London SW15 2RP
Tel (01) **870 7066**

Founded 1983. Cooperative management. Represent actors only, and welcome queries from those seeking representation. Approach in writing in the first instance, enclosing photograph and CV. No unsolicited demo tapes or video show reels.

Amber Personal Management Ltd

Asia House, 82 Princess Street, Manchester M1 6NQ
Tel (061) **228 0236**

Founded 1987. Cooperative management. Represent actors only, and very much welcome queries from those seeking representation. Approach in writing in the first instance – 'your letter will be discussed at our monthly meeting.' Will consider demo tapes and video show reels. 'As Amber is a cooperative agency, we are interested in the reasons why a particular actor is searching for this kind of management as opposed to a commercial management, what they can bring to the agency and if they feel they can represent the existing members. This means that they must be free to work days in the office when they are not in employment.'

Susal Angel Associates

1st floor, 12 D'Arblay Street, London W1V 3FP
Tel (01) **439 3086**
Contact Susan Angel

Founded 1978. Represent actors; one designer on the books. Welcome queries from actors seeking representation. Approach in writing in the first instance. Do not welcome telephone calls, unsolicited demo tapes or video show reels.

Angel Star Theatrical Employment Agency

5 Lancaster Road, London E11
Tel (01) **539 7740**

Represent children and adults. Do not welcome queries from actors seeking representation as they are handling only their established clients at the moment.

Anglian Casting

Burgh Castle, Great Yarmouth, Norfolk NR31 9QH
Tel (0493) **780793/780465**
Contact Carl Adams

Founded 1980. Represent actors and supporting and crowd artists for TV, films and commercials. Specialize in location work in East Anglia, so handle mostly clients who live there. Welcome queries from actors seeking representation. Write in the first instance with CV and photograph. Demo tapes and video show reels welcome. All letters acknowledged.

Arena Personal Management Ltd

Bon Marché Building, 444 Brixton Road, London SW9 8EJ
Tel (01) **274 4000 ext 268**
Contact Catherine Chase, Simon Williamson

Founded 1985. Cooperative management. Represent actors only, and welcome queries from those seeking representation, 'especially from those over 40 years, those under 23 years and ethnic actors of all ages – all must be Equity members or from recognized drama schools'. Send letter with CV, photograph and SAE. No unsolicited demo tapes or video show reels.

Arlington Enterprises Ltd

1/3 Charlotte Street, London W1
Tel (01) **580 0702**

Represent presenters. No actors.

Mary Arnold Management

12 Cambridge Park, East Twickenham, Middx TW1 2PS
Tel (01) **892 4860**
Contact Mary Arnold

Founded 1965 as a variety agency; now deal only with actors. Some voice-over work. Welcome queries from actors seeking representation. Approach in writing with CV and photograph. Telephone calls and unsolicited demo tapes and video show reels not welcome.

Arts Management
Redroofs, Littlewick Green, Maidenhead, Berks.
Tel (0628 82) **2982**

> Represent actors and children. Do not welcome queries from actors seeking representation.

Avenue Artistes Ltd
47 The Polygon, Southampton, Hants SO1 2BP
Tel (0703) **227077**
Contact Terry Rolph

> Founded 1963. Represent actors and 'offer a full entertainment service covering every aspect of the entertainment industry'. Welcome queries from those seeking representation. Initial approach by either telephone call or letter. Will consider demo tapes and video show reels.

AZA Artistes Ltd
652 Finchley Road, London NW11 7NT
Tel (01) **458 7288**
Contact Morris Aza, Sheila Aza

> Founded 1958. Represent actors, comedians, writers and musicians. Welcome queries from actors seeking representation, but 'we are a small personal representation agency seldom taking on new clients.' Approach in writing in the first instance. Will consider demo tapes and video show reels. 'Artistes should choose their agents very carefully. The association often lasts longer than marriages.'

Paul Bailey Agency
22 Wolsey Road, East Molesey, Surrey KT8 9EL
Tel (01) **941 2034**

> Represent variety artists. No actors.

Yvonne Baker Associates
8 Temple Fortune Lane, London NW11 7UD
Tel (01) **455 8687**

> Do not represent actors.

George Bartram Enterprises Ltd
5 Commercial Street, Birmingham B1 1RS
Tel (021) **643 9346**

> Represent variety artists. No actors.

Julian Belfrage Associates
60 St James's Street, London SW1
Tel (01) **491 4400**
Contact Julian Belfrage

> Founded 1985 (previously Leading Artists). Represent actors only, and welcome queries from those seeking representation. Approach in writing in the first instance, with CV and photograph. Demo tapes and video show reels will be considered.

Billboard Personal Management

The Old Laundry Studios, 20/22 York Way, London N1 9AA
Tel (01) **837 8608**

> Founded 1987. Cooperative management. Represent actors and directors. Welcome queries from actors seeking representation. Approach in writing in the first instance. Will consider demo tapes and video show reels.

Nina Blatt Ltd

The Coach House, 1a Larpent Avenue, London SW15 6UP
Tel (01) **788 5602**

> Producers and directors only. Does not represent actors.

Boden Agency

13 Essex Road, Enfield, Middx EN2 6TZ
Tel (01) **367 1836/2692**
Contact Tony Boden

> Founded 1979. Represent actors only, and welcome queries from those seeking representation. Approach in writing in the first instance. Will consider demo tapes and video show reels. To newcomers: 'Try to get qualifications for something apart from acting before going to drama school.'

Bourne & Corner Associates

2.2.3. Greenwich Business Centre, 49 Greenwich High Road, London SE10 8JL
Tel (01) **469 2726**
Contact Clive Corner, Sheila Bourne

> Founded 1987. Represent actors and directors. Welcome queries from actors seeking representation. Send letter with CV, photograph and SAE (large enough for the return of the photograph). No unsolicited demo tapes or video show reels.

Michelle Braidman Associates

Third floor suite, 10/11 Lower John Street, London W1R 3PE
Tel (01) **437 0817** Fax (01) **439 3600**
Contact Michelle Braidman, Alan Turner

> Founded 1984. Represent actors, directors and designers. Welcome queries from actors seeking representation. Approach in writing in the first instance, enclosing CV, 10×8 photograph and SAE. Video show reels must always be accompanied by large enough SAE.

Braithwaite's Theatrical Agency

8 Brookshill Avenue, Harrow Weald, Middx HA3 6RZ
Tel (01) **954 5638**

> Linked with Braithwaite's Acrobatic School.

Claude Brooks

5 High Street, Slough, Berks.
Tel (0753) **20717**

> Represent variety artists. No actors.

Barry Brown Management

47 West Square, Southwark, London SE11 4SP
Tel (01) **582 6622**
Contact Barry Brown, Carrie Simcocks

> Founded 1972. Represent mostly actors, one or two 'personalities'. Welcome queries from actors seeking representation. Write with CV and photograph initially. Will not consider unsolicited demo tapes or video show reels. 'Let us know what you are doing, and when and where you're doing it; don't write at the end of a run. Be different — agents get around 25 queries every week.'

Darryl Brown

1 Dorset Road, Merton Park, London SW19
Tel (01) **540 3968**
Contact Darryl Brown

> Founded 1981. Represent actors only, and welcome queries from those seeking representation. Write in the first instance. Will not consider unsolicited demo tapes or video show reels.

Joan Brown

3 Earl Road, London SW14 7JH
Tel (01) **876 9448**

> (*See* Brunskill Management Ltd.)

Pete Brown Artist Management

33 Percy Street, London W1P 9FG
Tel (01) **637 5302** Fax (01) **631 4273**
Contact Pete Brown, Loretta Sacco, Anna Wilks

> Represent actors, musicians, bands, writers, producers and directors. Welcome queries from actors seeking representation. Approach in writing in the first instance. Will consider demo tapes and video show reels.

Brunskill Management Ltd

Suite 8a, 169 Queens Gate, London SW7 5EH and The Courtyard, Edenhall, Penrith, Cumbria CA11 8ST
Tel (01) **580 3388**/(076881) **430** Fax (01) **589 9460**/(076881) **850**
Contact Ms Aude Powell

> Represent actors, directors, producers, writers and musicians. Welcome queries from actors seeking representation. Approach in writing in the first instance. Will consider demo tapes and video show reels.

Barry Burnett Organisation Ltd

Suite 42, Grafton House, 2 Golden Square, London W1
Tel (01) **437 7048** Fax (01) **437 1098**

> Founded 1968. Represent actors only, but do not welcome queries from those seeking representation.

CCA Personal Management

4 Court Lodge, 48 Sloane Square, London SW1W 8AT
Tel (01) **730 8857** Fax (01) **730 6971**
Contact Howard Pays

> Founded 1965. Represent actors, directors, technicians. Welcome queries from

actors seeking representation. Write in the first instance. Will not consider unsolicited demo tapes or video show reels.

C & S Personal Management

Picardy House, 4 Picardy Place, Edinburgh EH1 3JT
Tel (031) **557 0790**
Contact Linda Crooks, Liz Smith

> Founded 1986. Represent actors, directors and choreographers. Welcome queries from actors seeking representation. Approach in writing in the first instance.

CSM (Artistes) Ltd

Suite 1, 52 Perryn Road, London W3 7NA
Tel (01) **749 5154**
Contact Carole Deamer

> Founded 1984. Represent actors, but do not welcome queries from those seeking representation.

Calypso

25–26 Poland Street, London W1V 3DB
Tel (01) **734 6415** Fax (01) **437 0410**
Contact Nigel Lewis

> Founded 1983. Represent actors only, and welcome queries from those seeking representation. Write in the first instance. Will not consider unsolicited demo tapes or video show reels.

Cameron, Hayward & Co. Ltd

3 Lord Napier Place, London W6 9UB
Tel (01) **748 9974** Fax (01) **741 1428**
Contact Clodagh Wallace

> Founded 1973. Represent actors and recording artists. Welcome queries from actors seeking representation. Write in the first instance, preferably giving details of work you are currently doing. Will consider unsolicited demo tapes and video show reels.

Sarah Cape

2 Hinde Street, London W1M 5RH
Tel (01) **486 3312**
Contact Sarah Cape

> Founded 1968. Primarily a model agency, although they do handle actors for commercials. Welcome queries from actors interested in representation for commercials. Write in the first instance. Will not consider unsolicited demo tapes or video show reels.

Cardiff Casting

Unit 15, Royal Stuart Workshops, Adelaide Place, Cardiff CF1 6BR
Tel (0222) **494465**

> Founded 1984. Cooperative management. Represent actors only, and welcome queries from those seeking representation – 'from time to time, we do increase our membership.' Send letter with CV and photograph. No unsolicited demo tapes or video show reels. 'Cardiff Casting is by no means a purely Welsh agency. However, due to the nature of our organization, it would be impractical to consider anyone for membership who is not resident in South Wales.'

Cast
1 Stronsa Road, London W12 9LB
Tel (01) **749 9491**
Contact Lorna Cotton

> Founded 1985. Represent mainly actors, and welcome queries from those seeking representation, especially if they can be seen working. As a rule, do not take anyone unless they have seen them. Write in the first instance. Will not consider unsolicited demo tapes or video tapes. Advice to aspiring actors: 'Get good photographs done!'

The Central Agency
112 Gunnersbury Avenue, London W5 4HB
Tel (01) **993 7441** Fax (01) **992 9993**
Contact Hazel Hemmings

> Founded 1980. Represent actors and light entertainment artists. Welcome queries from actors seeking representation. Write or telephone in the first instance. Will consider demo tapes and video show reels.

The Central Line
11 East Circus Street, Nottingham NG1 5AF
Tel (0603) **412937**

> Founded 1984. Cooperative management. Represent actors only, and welcome queries from those seeking representation. Send letter enclosing CV and photograph. No unsolicited demo tapes or video show reels.

Characters Agency
106 Wilsden Avenue, Luton LU1 5HR
Tel (0582) **456213**
Contact Ron O'Brien, Sussette O'Brien (supporting artists & walk-on)

> Founded 1983. Represent actors only, and welcome queries from those seeking representation. Send letter with photograph and CV in the first instance. Will consider demo tapes and video show reels. 'Ron O'Brien is also a casting adviser/director for many video production companies specializing in corporate and training videos.'

Peter Charlesworth Ltd
2nd floor, 68 Old Brompton Road, London SW7 2LQ
Tel (01) **581 2478** Fax (01) **589 2458**
Contact Peter Charlesworth, Priscilla Bergus

> Represent actors, directors, writers, designers, etc. Welcome queries from actors seeking representation – strictly by letter with SAE. No unsolicited demo tapes or video show reels.

Chatto & Linnit Ltd
Prince of Wales Theatre, Coventry Street, London W1V 7FE
Tel (01) **930 6677**
Contact Rosalind Chatto

> Founded 1970. Represent actors, designers and directors. Take for granted queries from actors seeking representation. Write in the first instance. Will not consider unsolicited demo tapes or video show reels.

City Actors' Management Ltd
5 Leonard Street, London EC2A 4AQ
Tel (01) **251 0917**

> Founded 1981. Cooperative management. Represent actors only, and always welcome queries from those seeking representation. Send brief letter, photograph, CV and *photo-size* SAE. No unsolicited demo tapes or video show reels — 'there just isn't time.'

Elspeth Cochrane Agency
11–13 Orlando Road, London SW4 0LE
Tel (01) **622 0314**

> Founded 1959. Actors, designers, writers and directors represented.

Shane Collins Associates
24 Wardour Street, London W1V 3HD
Tel (01) **439 1976**
Contact Shane Collins

> Founded 1986. Represent actors only, and welcome queries from those seeking representation. Send letter with full CV and photograph. No unsolicited demo tapes or video show reels.

Company Call
27 Romford Road, London E15 4LJ
Tel (01) **519 5909**

> Founded 1986. Cooperative management. Welcome queries from actors seeking representation. It is better to write in the first instance with photo, CV and SAE, as this is easier for the members to deal with. Will not consider unsolicited demo tapes or video show reels.

Jeremy Conway Ltd
109 Jermyn Street, London SW1Y 6HB
Tel (01) **839 2121** Fax (01) **930 3272**
Contact Jeremy Conway, Nicola van Gelder, Valerie Hoskins

> Represent actors, directors and writers. Will consider queries from actors seeking representation. Approach in writing in the first instance. No unsolicited demo tapes or video show reels.

Vernon Conway Ltd
19 London Street, London W2 1HL
Tel (01) **262 5506**
Contact Vernon Conway

> Founded 1977. Represent actors and writers. Welcome queries from actors seeking representation. Write in the first instance with photo and CV. Send SAE for reply and return of photo. Will not consider unsolicited demo tapes or video show reels.

Lou Coulson
37 Berwick Street, London W1
Tel (01) **734 9633**
Contact Lou Coulson

> Founded 1978. Represent actors only. Not actively seeking new clients — do not welcome unsolicited queries. Usually work on personal recommendation.

Crawfords

2 Conduit Street, London W1R 9TG
Tel (01) **629 6464**
Contact Nicholas Young, Veronica Pieters

> Founded 1981. Represent actors only, and welcome queries from those seeking representation. Approach in writing in the first instance. Will consider demo tapes and video show reels. 'Crawfords is the only agency specializing in representing actors and actresses for TV commercials.'

Crouch Associates

59 Frith Street, London W1V 5TA
Tel (01) **734 2167**
Contact Peter Crouch

> Founded 1959. Represent actors only, and welcome queries from those seeking representation. Write in the first instance with photo and CV. Will not consider unsolicited demo tapes or video show reels.

Culbertson Reeves Ltd

The Studio, 7a North Cross Road, London SE22 9ET
Tel (01) **693 9318**
Contact Carrie Culbertson, Fenella Reeves

> Founded 1985. Represent actors only, and welcome queries from those seeking representation — 'but it is difficult to get on to our deliberately small list.' Approach in writing in the first instance. No unsolicited demo tapes or video show reels. 'When sending a CV, always say what part played, which production and *where* (e.g. not just "*Romeo and Juliet*"). Not only is it important, but we may have seen it on our numerous theatre visits. Also, the director's name is helpful.'

DAC Directory

First floor, 548 Chiswick High Road, London W4 5RG
Tel (01) **995 1995**
Contact Rashna Homji, Jeanetta Laurence

> Founded 1983. Represent actors with dancing and singing abilities, and welcome queries from such actors seeking representation. Approach in writing in the first instance. Will consider demo tapes and video show reels.

Jimmy Daisley Associates Ltd

> Company in liquidation.

Liam Dale Associates Ltd

3 Culvers Avenue, Carshalton, Surrey SM5 2BN
Tel (01) **647 6627** Fax (01) **647 6628**
Contact Liam Dale, Vanessa Anstey

> Founded 1984. Represent actors, light entertainment, presenters and writers. Welcome queries from actors seeking representation — however, 'we are a personal management company dealing with artists accustomed to high-profile exposure; the company limits its responsibilities to 14 artists.' Approach in writing in the first instance. Will consider demo tapes and video show reels.

David Daly Personal Management
68 Old Brompton Road, London SW7 3LQ
Tel (01) **581 0121**
Contact David Daly

> Founded 1978. Represent actors, but do not welcome queries from them — 'our list is full.'

Larry Dalzell Associates Ltd
Suite 12, 17 Broad Court, Covent Garden, London WC2B 5QN
Tel (01) **379 0875** Telex **DALMAR LONDON**
Contact Larry Dalzell, Jean Clarke, Sarah Osborne

> Founded 1970. Represent actors, directors and designers. Welcome queries from actors seeking representation. Approach in writing in the first instance, enclosing SAE. Will consider demo tapes and video show reels if accompanied by SAE.

Dabber Davis Productions
24a Park Road, Hayes, Middx UB4 8JN
Tel (01) **848 9048**
Contact Dabber Davis, Mrs Paddy Davis

> Founded 1948/9. Represent comedians, singers and magicians — not actors.

Caroline Dawson Associates
Apt 20, 47 Courtfield Road, London SW7 4DB
Tel (01) **370 0708**

> Founded 1978. Represent actors only.

Denman Casting Agency
Commerce Chambers, Elite Buildings, Parliament Street, Nottingham NG1 2BP
Tel (0602) **418421/473257**
Contact Jack Denman, Alison Hope

> Founded 1958. Represent actors, walk-ons, supporting artists. Very large agency, operating countrywide with the largest casting directory in the country. Welcome queries from actors seeking representation. Write in the first instance with photo and CV. Will not consider unsolicited demo tapes or video show reels.

Denmark Street Management
Room 122, Canalot Production Studios, 222 Kensal Road, London W10 5BN
Tel (01) **960 8204/5**

> Founded 1985. Cooperative management. Represent actors only, and welcome queries from those (particularly older actors) who are seeking representation. Approach in writing in the first instance. No unsolicited demo tapes or video show reels. 'We are 15 members and, to date, are looking to expand to 18. Our main casting gap is men 40+.' Advice to newcomers: 'When dealing with an agent or casting director, an actor should never generalize — be specific: what roles you want to do, who you want to work with, which companies you want to try for, what work you do not want to do. Know your material; try and know what work directors have done. Ask direct questions and give direct answers. Be adroit and persevere. When dealing with agents, do not be frightened of chasing up your letter by phone — when agents get busy, it is very helpful to be reminded about people and what's going on; in a busy week, a new application will simply get left lying around.'

Felix de Wolfe
Manfield House, 376/378 The Strand, London WC2R 0LR
Tel (01) **379 5767** Fax (01) **222 7471** Telex **931770 A/B W1BU G**
Contact Felix de Wolfe

> Founded 1938. Represent actors, writers, designers, directors, composers, musical directors and producers. Welcome queries from *established* actors seeking representation. Approach in writing in the first instance. Will consider demo tapes and video show reels.

Direct Line Personal Management
Room 28, Vassalli House, 20 Central Road, Leeds LS1 6DE
Tel (0532) **444991**

> Founded 1985. Cooperative management. Represent actors only, and welcome queries from those seeking representation. Approach in writing in the first instance. Will consider demo tapes and video show reels.

Donna Maria Management
16 Bell Meadows, Dulwich Wood Avenue, London SE19 1HP
Tel (01) **671 7814**

> Linked to Donna Maria Children's Theatre Company of London. Represent children and adults.

Bryan Drew Limited
Mezzanine, Quadrant House, 80–82 Regent Street, London W1R 6AU
Tel (01) **437 2293** Fax (01) **437 0561**
Contact Bryan Drew & Dulcie Huston (theatre, film, TV); Bryan Drew (writers, directors); Kate Evans & Pauline O'Brien (voice-overs)

> Founded 1963. Represent actors, writers and directors. Welcome queries from actors seeking representation. Approach in writing in the first instance. Will consider demo tapes and video show reels.

Evan Dunstan Associates/EDA (TV) Ltd
1b Montagu Mews North, London W1
Tel (01) **486 3479/0**
Contact Evan Dunstan, Richard Talbot

> Founded 1973. Represent actors, singers and dancers. Welcome queries from actors seeking representation. Approach in writing in the first instance. Will consider demo tapes and video show reels. 'Where possible, it is always handy if artists have a play (even one in fringe) where we can see their performance before accepting them on to the books.'

Eastern Agency
114 Rainborough Close, London NW10 0TS
Tel (01) **451 1183**

> Founded 1983. Represent actors, walk-ons, supporting artists, models — mostly Afro-Caribbean, Asian and Oriental artists in the past, but now also representing Europeans. Welcome queries from actors seeking representation, if Equity members. Write in the first instance with CV and photograph. Will not consider unsolicited demo tapes or video show reels. The agency offers a 7-days-a-week, 24-hour service to casting directors.

Elliman's Agency

Flat 1, 10 Westbourne Villas, Hove, East Sussex BN3 4GQ
Tel (0273) **728307**
Contact Sonia Elliman

> Founded 1983. Represent actors, directors, designers, lighting designers, sound designers and other technical staff. Welcome queries from actors seeking representation. Approach either by telephone or in writing. No unsolicited demo tapes or video show reels.

Ellison Combe Associates, Personal Management

17 Richmond Hill, Richmond, Surrey TW10 6RE
Tel (01) **940 7863**
Contact Timothy Combe (managing director), Sarah Lermit & John Wilson (associate directors)

> Founded 1981. Represent actors, directors, producers and presenters. Welcome queries from actors seeking representation – 'many of our enquiries are by personal recommendation.' Approach in writing in the first instance. Will consider demo tapes and video show reels – 'we use these as a back-up to the interview.' 'Our policy is always to reply to applications, but a quicker response will be given to those with an SAE.'

Emanco Ltd

8 Great Russell Street, London WC1B 3NH
Tel (01) **323 0821**

> No longer represent actors. Technical people only.

June Epstein Associates

110 Golden House, 29 Great Pulteney Street, London W1R 3DD
Tel (01) **734 1154/5019**
Contact June Epstein, Esme McKinnon

> Founded 1973. Represent actors only, and welcome queries from prospective clients. Write in the first instance with SAE for reply. Will consider demo tapes or video show reels, but only if requested.

Jacqué Evans Management Ltd

54 Lisson Street, London NW1 6ST
Tel (01) **402 3248**

> Do not represent actors.

Face Over

6 Poland Street, London W1V 3DG
Tel (01) **734 6910**
Contact Jill Green, Joan Morley

> Founded 1985. Represent actors for voice-over work only – i.e. TV, radio commercials, videos, dubbing, etc. Welcome queries from actors seeking voice-over representation. 'A phone call is a good preliminary approach to us – followed up by a letter, CV and, in our case, a professional-quality voice tape. Video show reels also welcome.'

Kate Feast Management

43a Princess Road, London NW1 8JS
Tel (01) **586 5502**

Represent actors and the occasional director. Do not generally welcome queries from actors seeking representation — 'It depends who they are.' Will not consider unsolicited demo tapes or video show reels.

Film Rights Ltd

4 New Burlington Place, Regent Street, London W1X 2AS
Tel (01) **437 7151**
Contact Maurice Lambert, Judith Quinn

Founded 1932. Represent actors, film and stage technicians. Welcome queries from actors seeking representation. Approach in writing in the first instance, enclosing CV, photographs and SAE. No unsolicited demo tapes or video show reels.

Sheridan Fitzgerald Management

69b Credon Road, Upton Park, London E13 9BS
Tel (01) **471 9814**
Contact Sheridan Fitzgerald

Founded 1987. Represent actors, and will act on their behalf for any writing or directing they may do in addition to acting. Welcome queries from actors seeking representation. Send letter with SAE and follow up with a telephone call. No unsolicited demo tapes or video show reels. 'Always consult *Spotlight* for advice, and always have a *Spotlight* entry. Photos that are not honest to the subject are a total waste of time and money.'

Fletcher & Boyce

1 Kingsway House, Albion Road, London N16 0TA
Tel (01) **923 0606** Fax (01) **241 2313**
Contact Wendy Fletcher, Sandra Boyce

Represent mostly actors, a couple of directors. Welcome queries from actors seeking representation. Write in the first instance, with CV, photo and SAE. Will consider unsolicited demo tapes and video show reels.

Focus Management Ltd

Unit 312, Bon Marché Building, 444 Brixton Road, London SW9 8EJ
Tel (01) **737 7713**

Founded 1982. Cooperative management. Represent actors only, and welcome queries from those seeking representation. Send letter with CV, photograph and SAE. Will consider demo tapes and video show reels.

Aida Foster Ltd

33 Abbey Lodge, Park Road, London NW8 7RJ
Tel (01) **262 2181**
Contact Anita Foster

Founded 1945. Represent actors only, and welcome queries from those seeking representation. Approach in writing in the first instance. Will consider video show reels. 'Always send a truly representative photo, an up-to-date CV, including age and playing age, and an SAE.'

Fraser & Dunlop Ltd

5th floor, The Chambers, Chelsea Harbour, Lots Road, London SW10
Tel (01) **376 7676**
Contact Ginette Chalmers, Maureen Vincent

Founded 1951. Represent actors, writers, directors and producers. Welcome queries from actors seeking representation, although they tend to take on only people whose work they know and are interested in, or those who will fill a gap on their client list. Write in the first instance. Will not consider unsolicited demo tapes or video show reels.

Frazer Skemp Management Ltd

34 Bramerton Street, Chelsea, London SW3 5LA
Tel (01) **352 2922/3771/1969**
Contact Norma Skemp (director), Susan Shaper (assistant)

Founded 1972. Represent actors working in theatre, films and TV, and welcome queries from those seeking representation. Approach in writing in the first instance. Will consider demo tapes and video show reels. 'It is important that artists appreciate that, however talented they may be, we cannot represent them if we already have a similar actor or actress on our books, or if our books at the time are already full.'

Patrick Freeman Management

4 Cromwell Grove, London W6 7RG
Tel (01) **602 4035**
Contact Patrick Freeman

Founded 1973. Represent actors only. Write in the first instance with SAE; *no* telephone calls. Will consider unsolicited demo tapes and video show reels.

French's

26 Binney Street, London W1
Tel (01) **629 4159**
Contact Janet Welch

Founded 1974. Represent actors, directors, writers and technicians. Welcome queries from actors seeking representation. Write in the first instance. Will consider unsolicited demo tapes and video show reels.

Frontline Management

245a Coldharbour Lane, London SW9 8RR
Tel (01) **326 1382**

Founded 1985. Cooperative management. Represent actors only, and welcome queries from those seeking representation. Approach in writing in the first instance. No unsolicited demo tapes or video show reels.

Joy Galloway Management

15 Lexham Mews, London W8
Tel (01) **376 2288**
Contact Joy Galloway, Jill Moore

Represent actors only, and welcome queries from those seeking representation. Write in the first instance with CV and photograph.

Galloways Ltd
14 Rocks Lane, London SW13 0DB
Tel (01) **392 1313/1818** Fax (01) **878 2213**
Contact Hugh Galloway

> Founded 1971. Represent actors only, and welcome queries from those seeking representation. Send letter with current photo, *Spotlight* number and CV in the first instance. Video show reels/demo tapes only required at an interview. Advice to newcomers: 'Take as many classes/workshops as possible to gain experience and confidence.'

Kerry Gardner Management
15 Kensington High Street, London W8 5NP
Tel (01) **937 4478/3142** Fax (01) **376 2587**
Contact Kerry Gardner, Pauline Asper, Angela Collins, Julie Ann Gregory

> Founded 1975. Represent actors, directors, producers and a voice coach. Welcome queries from actors seeking representation. Approach in writing in the first instance – 'always send an SAE if you expect a reply.' No unsolicited demo tapes or video show reels.

Garricks
7 Garrick Street, London WC2 9AR
Tel (01) **240 0660/379 7476**
Contact Megan Willis, Ligeia Marsh

> Do not welcome queries from actors seeking representation.

Jimmy Garrod Management
St Martins, Sandhills Meadow, Shepperton, Middx TW17 9HX
Tel (0932) **246333/4**
Contact Jimmy Garrod

> Founded 1963. Represent actors only, and welcome queries from those seeking representation. Send letter with CV. No unsolicited demo tapes or video show reels. 'Aspiring actors should seek representation by an agent of repute and long established in the business. Avoid agents who represent too many actors.'

Noel Gay Artists
24 Denmark Street, London WC2H 8NJ
Tel (01) **836 3941** Fax (01) **379 7027** Telex **21760**
Contact Alex Armitage, Lorraine Hamilton

> Represent actors, presenters, composers, directors, writers and producers. Welcome queries from actors seeking representation. Approach in writing in the first instance. Will consider demo tapes and video show reels.

Giantpatch Ltd
8 The Path, London SW19 3BL
Tel (01) **540 9648**

> Do not represent actors.

Keith Gilbey Personal Management
11/15 Betterton Street, Covent Garden, London WC2H 9BP
Tel (01) **379 0344** Fax (01) **379 0801** Telex **265639** BETTS G
Contact Keith Gilbey

> Founded 1987. Represent actors, scripwriters, directors, and act as freelance

casting director to film/TV/corporate sectors. Welcome queries from actors seeking representation. Send letter with CV and 10×8 photograph. No unsolicited demo tapes or video show reels. Advice to newcomers: 'Pay attention to photographs; they are the window to the profession. Learn about your profession, and understand that it is a business and treat it as such.'

Bernard Gillman Ltd
28 Elmdene, Tolworth, Surbiton, Surrey.

Agency closed due to retirement.

Eric Glass Ltd
28 Berkeley Square, London W1X 6HD
Tel (01) **629 7162** Telex **296759** KALLIN G
Contact Eric Glass, Janet Crowley

Founded 1934. Represent actors, directors, authors and playwrights. Welcome queries from actors seeking representation. Favour initial approach in writing. Will consider demo tapes and video show reels.

Glyn Knowles Direction
8 Hunters Way, Gillingham, Kent ME7 3BA
Tel (0634) **50745**
Contact Glyn Davies

Founded 1972. Represent children who are attending the Glyn Knowles Stage School (*see* Drama Schools).

Jimmy Grafton Management
9 Orme Court, London W2 4RL
Tel (01) **221 9364** Fax (01) **221 3907** Telex **268312** WESCOM G

Founded 1950. Represent actors and light entertainment artists. Welcome queries from actors seeking representation. Write or telephone. Will consider unsolicited demo tapes and video show reels.

Peter Graham Associates
59 Frith Street, London W1V 5TA
Tel (01) **734 2203/4**
Contact Peter Graham, Sarah Hight, Andrew Lennox

Founded 1980/1. Represent actors only, and welcome queries from those seeking representation. Approach in writing in the first instance – prefer to see actors working. No unsolicited demo tapes or video show reels.

Joan Gray Personal Management
29 Sunbury Court Island, Sunbury on Thames, Middx TW16 5PP
Tel (01) **979 1789**
Contact Joan Gray

Founded 1960. Represent actors only. 'I have a complete list and am not taking on anyone else.'

Grays Management Ltd
38 Mount Pleasant, London WC1X 0AP
Tel (01) **278 1054**

Founded 1986. Cooperative management. Represent actors only, and welcome queries from those seeking representation. 'A phone call can be a quick check to see if your category is already covered by someone in the agency.' No unsolicited demo tapes or video show reels.

Green & Underwood (in association with Essanay)

2 Conduit Street, London W1R 9TG
Tel (01) **493 0308**
Contact Nicholas Young, Louise Hillman

> Founded 1937 (Essanay), 1962 (Green & Underwood). Represent actors, costume designers and theatre directors. Sometimes welcome queries from actors seeking representation: 'It is basically a matter of luck. If a letter arrives when we are looking for someone and they fill a gap, we will probably see them. Always approach by letter, unless an established actor.' No unsolicited demo tapes or video show reels. 'Always send an SAE; good photographs are a real asset.'

Stella Greenfield Agency

41 Bush Grove, Stanmore, Middx HA7 2DY
Tel (01) **952 1805** Fax (01) **952 1032**
Contact Stella Greenfield

> Founded 1970. Represent actors, children and teenagers. Welcome queries from actors seeking representation (teenagers should have Equity membership). Write in the first instance, with CV and photograph. Will consider demo tapes and video show reels, but please enclose an appropriate SAE for their return.

Carl Gresham Presentations

Salem House, 28a Manor Row, Bradford, West Yorks. BD1 4QU
Tel (0274) **735880** Fax (0274) **305149**
Contact Carl Gresham

> Founded 1970. Represent actors and general entertainers. Do not welcome queries from actors seeking representation. No unsolicited demo tapes or video show reels.

Jeanne Griffiths Agency

185 Oxford Street, London W1R 1TA
Tel (01) **437 2491**
Contact Jeanne Griffiths, Gary Trolan

> Founded mid-Sixties. Represent actors, presenters and voice artists. Welcome queries from actors seeking representation. Write in the first instance with CV and photograph, and enclose SAE. Will not consider unsolicited demo tapes or video show reels.

J. Gurnett Personal Management Ltd

2 New Kings Road, London SW6 4SA
Tel (01) **736 7828**

> Do not represent actors.

Hamilton & Sydney Ltd

21 Goodge Street, London W1P 1FD
Tel (01) **323 1162**
Contact Margaret Hamilton

> Founded 1960. Represent mostly actors, and will consider queries from those seeking representation. Write in the first instance with CV and photograph. Will not consider unsolicited demo tapes or video show reels.

Sue Hammer Management

Otterbourne House, Chobham Road, Ottershaw, Chertsey, Surrey KT16 0QF
Tel (093287) **4111/2**
Contact Sue Hammer, Nina Hendry, Alexes Weaver

> Founded 1980. Represent actors only, and welcome queries from those seeking representation. Send a letter with CV and photograph. No unsolicited demo tapes or video show reels.

Louis Hammond Management Ltd

Golden House, 29 Great Pulteney Street, London W1R 3DD
Tel (01) **734 1931** Fax (01) **437 0887**
Contact Louis Hammond, Saskia Nowell

> Founded 1982. Represent actors only, and welcome queries from those seeking representation ('It is something agents must expect'). Approach in writing in the first instance. Will consider demo tapes and video show reels.

Hamper–Neafsey Associates

4 Great Queen Street, London WC2
Tel (01) **404 5255** Fax (01) **831 1524**
Contact Sharon Hamper (managing director)

> Founded 1976. Represent actors, directors and designers. Welcome queries from actors seeking representation, but only 'when they are in a showcase where we can see their work before any interview is granted. Send photograph that looks like the actor and mention what parts played in what productions.'

Harbour & Coffey

9 Bleinhem Street, New Bond Street, London W1Y 9LE
Tel (01) **499 5548** Fax (01) **629 6923**
Contact Gillian Coffey, Harry Harbour

> Founded 1969. Represent actors only, and will consider queries from those seeking representation, especially if they have been recommended. Write in the first instance, with CV, photograph and SAE. Will not consider unsolicited demo tapes and video show reels, although 'it is worth mentioning that you have these available.'

Val Hastings Management

8 Wynfield Gardens, Birmingham B14 6EY
Tel (021) **443 3166**
Contact Val Hastings (manager)

> Founded 1981 as Val Hastings Casting Ltd; changed name 1988. Represent Midlands-based actors only. Welcome queries from actors (Equity only) seeking representation. 'I only recruit once a year in October for 12-month contracts starting the following January.' Send letter with good CV and photograph. Will consider demo tapes and video show reels. 'Actors must have good CVs, well printed and readable; good photos in black and white, head shots only. In our case, we do not represent actors who undertake walk-on work, so we are selective in whom we see. Actors must be able to talk well at interviews, and sight reading is of paramount importance for television auditions.'

Hatton & Baker Ltd

18 Jermyn Street, London SW1Y 6HN
Tel (01) **439 2971** Fax (01) **439 7633** Telex **263026**

> Represent actors and writers. Welcome queries from actors seeking representa-

tion. Write in the first instance with CV and photograph. will not consider unsolicited demo tapes or video show reels.

Duncan Heath Associates Ltd
162 Wardour Street, London W1V 3AT
Tel (01) **439 1471** Fax (01) **439 7274** Telex **263361**

> Founded early 1970s. Represent actors, directors, writers, producers, technicians, composers. Welcome queries from actors seeking representation. Write in the first instance. Will not consider unsolicited demo tapes or video show reels.

Hill–Urwin Associates (incorporating The Singers Agency)
22 Inverness Street, London NW1 7HJ
Tel (01) **267 6845/482 1831**
Contact David Urwin, Stephen Hill

> Founded 1980. Represent actors, musical directors and singers. Welcome queries from actors seeking representation. Send letter with photograph and CV. Will consider demo tapes from singers. 'We are principally a musical theatre-orientated agency, representing Equity members only.'

Hills Personal Management
1st floor, 7 Childwall Valley Road, Childwall Fiveways, Liverpool L16 4PB
Tel (051) **737 1939**
Contact Jonathan Swain, Sally Moss

> Founded 1986. Represent actors only; cooperative management. Welcome queries from actors seeking representation. Send a letter enclosing CV, photograph and details of any forthcoming performances where your work can be seen. Will consider demo tapes and video show reels.

Philip Hindin Ltd
33 Albert Street, London NW1 7LU
Tel (01) **380 0375**

> Do not represent actors.

Hope & Lyne
108 Leonard Street, London EC2A 4RH
Tel (01) **739 6200**
Contact Sally Hope, Dennis Lyne, Ann Hope, John Wood

> Founded 1975. Represent actors, directors and designers. Welcome queries from actors seeking representation, 'but it is only possible to take on a very few each year as our client list is small.' Approach in writing in the first instance. No unsolicited demo tapes or video show reels – 'we prefer to see actors working in theatre.'

The Bill Horne Partnership
15 Exmoor Street, London W10 6BA
Tel (01) **960 8281**
Contact Bill Horne, Peter Walmsley

> Founded 1970. Represent actors, directors, musical directors and choreographers. Welcome queries from actors seeking representation. Approach in writing in the first instance – 'no telephone calls please.' Will consider demo tapes and video show reels.

Howes & Prior Ltd
66 Berkeley House, Hay Hill, London W1X 7LH
Tel (01) **493 7570/7655**
Contact Rupert Prior

Founded 1969. Welcome casting queries from actors seeking representation. Approach in writing in the first instance. No unsolicited demo tapes or video show reels.

Jane Hughes Management
Suite 21, Rex Buildings, Alderley Road, Wilmslow, Cheshire SK9 1HY
Tel (0625) **530787** Fax (0625) **528064**
Contact Jane Hughes, Amanda Brown

Founded 1968. Represent actors, presenters and voice-over artists. Welcome queries from actors seeking representation. Write in the first instance, with CV and photograph. Will not consider unsolicited demo tapes or video show reels.

Hutton Management Ltd
200 Fulham Road, London SW10 9PN
Tel (01) **352 4825**
Contact Ann Hutton, Cristina Shepheard

Represent actors only, and welcome queries from those seeking representation. Write in the first instance. Will consider unsolicited demo tapes and video show reels.

ICM Ltd
388/396 Oxford Street, London W1N 9HE
Tel (01) **629 8080** Fax (01) **493 6279** Telex **885974** ICMLON G
Contact Laurence Evans, Dennis Selinger, Michael Anderson, Ronnie Waters

Represent actors, producers, directors and writers. Welcome queries from actors seeking representation. Approach in writing in the first instance. No unsolicited demo tapes or video show reels.

Inspiration Management
Room 2, Southbank House, Black Prince Road, London SE1 7SJ
Tel (01) **587 0947/735 8171 ext 127**

Founded 1986. Cooperative management. Represent actors only, and welcome queries from those seeking representation. Send letter with CV and photograph. Will consider demo tapes and video show reels. 'Inspiration is a cooperative agency which means helping with office duties and being the other members' agent. Being involved makes you feel you have a much stronger hold on your own career even when you are out of work.'

Inter-City Casting Ltd
515 Corn Exchange Building, Hanging Ditch, Manchester M20 8QL
Tel (061) **832 8848**

Founded 1984. Cooperative management. Represent actors only, and welcome queries from those seeking representation. Approach in writing in the first instance. Will consider demo tapes and video show reels. 'As a coop agency, we need applicants who have good administrative skills – though abilities as an actor are the prime consideration. We recently took on a personal manager who ran the office three days a week, and we believe this is the future for coop agencies. We would warn new actors that London agents are not always the "be all and end all" of good management since often a new actor finds he is a small fish in a very big sea.'

International Artistes Ltd
235 Regent Street, London W1R 8AX
Tel (01) **439 8401** Fax (01) **409 2070** Telex **295061** INTAM G
Contact Hugh J. Alexander, Jean Mirylees (actors), Laurie Mansfield, Bob Voice, Stuart Littlewood (variety)

Founded 1946. Represent actors and variety performers. Welcome queries from actors seeking representation. Approach in writing in the first instance (addressed to Jean Mirylees). Will consider demo tapes and video show reels.

Italia Conti Agency Ltd
Italia Conti House, 23 Goswell Road, London EC1M 7BB
Tel (01) **608 0044/5**
Contact Gaynor Sheward

Founded 1911. Specialize in young people (10 years to early 20s) in all branches of the media, mainly those training at the Italia Conti Academy of Theatre Arts. But 'opens its books from time to time to outsiders.' Approach in writing in the first instance. Will consider demo tapes and video show reels.

Richard Jackson Personal Management Ltd
59 Knightsbridge, London SW1X 7RA
Tel (01) **235 3671/2**
Contact Richard Jackson, John Huntley, John Cannon

Founded 1959. Represent actors, and also a play director from France, a fight director and two after-dinner speakers. Also involved in play production, mainly on London's Fringe (*see separate entry*). Welcome queries from actors seeking representation; 'all applicants are given serious consideration and some are granted interviews.' Approach in writing in the first instance. Will consider demo tapes and video show reels.

Jaclyn Agency
Thackeray House, Hempnall, Norwich NR15 2LP
Tel (050842) **241**
Contact Marilyn Sandiford (proprietor), Julie Parker, Claire Fox

Founded 1952. Represent actors who are mainly TV supporting artists, extras and walk-ons, background artists for TV commercials, audiovisuals and training films. Do not handle theatre work. Welcome queries from those seeking representation 'only if they are within the East Anglian/East Midlands region'. Approach in writing in the first instance. No unsolicited demo tapes or video show reels. 'The nature of the work we handle excludes those who do not have Equity membership.'

Carole James Management
14 Hill Street, Richmond, Surrey TW9 1TN
Tel (01) **940 8154**
Contact Carole James

Represent actors only, and welcome queries from those seeking representation. Send letter with CV and photograph. Will consider demo tapes for actors who also sing, but these are not essential.

Maureen James Management

38 Meadow Lane, Dove Holes, Buxton, Derbys. SK17 8DG
Tel (0298 81) **4001**
Contact Maureen James, Maureen Davie, James Davie

Founded 1987. Represent actors, including child actors, and welcome queries from those seeking representation. Send letter with CV and photograph. Will consider demo tapes and video show reels. Advice to newcomers: 'Be honest — I really want to know what your talents are, *not* that your drama school says that, if you sang, you would be a baritone! Give complete information — even if you feel that underwater swimming is not important, there just may be a casting director wanting that. Only give accents/dialects that you can do very well, *without* weeks of practice — "they" may want to see you tomorrow.'

Joseph & Wagg

2nd floor, 78 New Bond Street, London W1Y 9DA
Tel (01) **629 1048**
Contact Tod Joseph

Founded 1964. Represent actors only, and welcome queries from those seeking representation. Write in the first instance. Will not consider unsolicited demo tapes or video show reels.

Chuck Julian Agency

3rd floor, Cecil House, 41 Charing Cross Road, London WC2H 0AR
Tel (01) **437 4248** Telex **21120 Ref 2745**
Contact Chuck Julian, Helen Brindle, Sue Yager, Ann Molloy

Represent actors and a couple of directors. Do not welcome queries from actors seeking representation.

KD Management

64 Sussex Road, Harrow, Middx HA1 4LX
Tel (01) **861 0240**

Represent Afro-Asian artists.

Roberta Kanal Agency

82 Constance Road, Twickenham, Middx TW2 7JA
Tel (01) **892 2277**
Contact Roberta Kanal

Founded 1968. Represent actors only, and welcome queries from those seeking representation. Write in the first instance. Will not consider unsolicited demo tapes or video show reels.

Kean & Garrick

6–8 Paved Court, The Green, Richmond, Surrey TW9 1LZ
Tel (01) **940 5559**
Contact Jane Ball, Ralph P. Ball

Founded 1982. Represent actors only — comedy, straight and musical — and welcome queries from those seeking representation. Write in the first instance, with photograph and CV. Will not consider unsolicited demo tapes or video show reels.

Ivor Kimmel Casting

7 Andover Place, London NW6
Tel (01) **328 3125**
Contact Ivor Kimmel

>Founded 1973. Represent actors, stunt men and supporting artists. Do not welcome queries from actors seeking representation.

Rolf Kruger Management Ltd

Morley House, 314–322 Regent Street, London W1
Tel (01) **580 9432** Fax (01) **734 2165**
Contact Rolf Kruger, Suzi Earnshaw

>Founded 1969. Represent actors, directors (theatre, film, TV), theatre designers, action coordinators. Welcome queries from actors seeking representation. Approach in writing in the first instance. 'We are only interested in well-trained theatre actors with good theatre background, and only take on artists after we have seen a considerable amount of their work. Training is essential.'

LA Entertainments

13 Fenswood Mead, Long Ashton, Bristol BS18 9BL
Tel (0272) **393876**
Contact Dave Royal

>Founded 1983. Represent actors and walk-ons. Welcome queries from actors seeking representation. Initial approach by telephone. No demo tapes or video show reels.

LM Agency

213 Edgware Road, London W2 1ES
Tel (01) **262 9787**
Contact Mary Medea

>Founded 1950s. Represent actors only, and welcome queries from those seeking representation. Write or telephone in the first instance, although a letter is more explicit. Will not consider unsolicited demo tapes or video show reels.

LWA

61–63 Beak Street, London W1R 3LF
Tel (01) **434 3944**
Contact Eileen Williams, Jill Williams

>Founded 1968. Represent actors and freelance TV directors. Do not particularly welcome queries from actors seeking representation, but any initial contact must be made in writing. No unsolicited demo tapes or video show reels.

Mary Lambeth Associates

22 Acol Road, London NW6 3AG
Tel (01) **624 4858**
Contact Mary Lambeth

>Founded 1968. Represent actors and voice-over artists. Welcome queries from actors seeking representation. Approach in writing in the first instance. No unsolicited demo tapes or video show reels.

Tessa Le Bars Management
18 Queen Anne Street, London W1M 9LB
Tel (01) **636 3191** Fax (01) **436 0229**
Contact Tessa Le Bars

> Founded 1983. 'Not an actors agency as such but personal/business manage-
> ment and production for small group of performers/writers in the light
> entertainment field.' Do not welcome queries from actors seeking representation
> — 'new clients come through personal contact only.'

Bernard Lee Management
Moorcroft Lodge, Farleigh Common, Warlingham, Surrey CR3 9PE
Tel (08832) **5667**
Contact Bernard Lee

> Founded 1968. Represent actors and light entertainment artists. Welcome
> queries from actors seeking representation. Approach in writing in the first
> instance. Will consider demo tapes and video show reels.

L'Epine Smith & Carney Associates
10 Wyndham Place, London W1H 1AS
Tel (01) **724 0739**
Contact Terry Carney, Eric L'Epine Smith

> Founded early 1960s. Represent actors, directors, writers, technicians. Welcome
> queries from actors seeking representation. Write in the first instance. Will not
> consider unsolicited demo tapes or video show reels.

Brian Lidstone Representation
138 Westbourne Grove, London W11 2RR
Tel (01) **727 2342**
Contact Brian Lidstone

> Founded 1962. Represent actors, directors, writers, composers and teachers.
> Welcome queries from actors seeking representation. Approach in writing in the
> first instance. No unsolicited demo tapes or video show reels.

Links Management
22 Colombo Street, London SE1 8DP
Tel (01) **928 0806/3134**

> Founded 1984. Cooperative management. Represent actors only, and welcome
> queries from those seeking representation. Send letter with CV and photograph.
> Will consider demo tapes and video show reels.

Sarah Llewellyn
6 Sandstone Place, London N19 5TU
Tel (01) **263 0248**
Contact Sarah Llewellyn

> Founded 1974. Represent actors only, and welcome queries from those seeking
> representation. Write in the first instance. Will not consider unsolicited demo tapes
> or video show reels.

London Actors
10 Barley Mow Passage, Chiswick, London W4 4PH
Tel (01) **994 6477**

> Founded 1979. Cooperative management. Represent actors only, and welcome

queries from those interested in being in a cooperative agency. Approach in writing in the first instance. Will consider demo tapes and video show reels.

London Management

235/241 Regent Street, London W1A 2JT
Tel (01) **493 1610** Fax (01) **408 0065** Telex **27498**
Contact Address letter to the company

Founded 1959. Represent actors, composers, directors, designers, film technicians, illustrators, producers and writers. Welcome queries from actors seeking representation. Approach in writing in the first instance: 'Always put name and address on the back of photographs; do not send a $3\frac{1}{2}\times6$ or 9×4 SAE with a 10×8 photograph.' No unsolicited demo tapes or video show reels.

Look Alikes

46 Clapham Common Northside, London SW4 0AA
Tel (01) **720 0525** Telex **888941** LCCI Fax (01) **622 6366**
Contact Tracey Amos

Founded 1980. Represent actors, models, amateurs — anyone who looks like a personality. Welcome queries from actors seeking representation. Send a letter with photograph in the first instance. Will consider demo tapes and video show reels.

Pat Lovett Agency

14 Broughton Place, Edinburgh EH1 3RX
Tel (031) **557 5565**
Contact Pat Lovett, Morag Arbuthnot, Mo Hargreaves

Founded 1981. Represent actors only, and welcome queries from those seeking representation. Approach in writing in the first instance. No unsolicited demo tapes or video show reels.

Robert Luff Ltd

294 Earls Court Road, London SW5 9BB
Tel (01) **373 7003**

Do not represent actors.

MPC Artists and Management

113 Wardour Street, London W1V 3TD
Tel (01) **434 1861**

Do not represent actors.

McKenna & Grantham

39 York Road, Teddington, Middx TW11 8SL
Tel (01) **943 1256/7**
Contact John Grantham, Jenny McKenna

Founded 1987. Represent actors only, and welcome queries from those seeking representation. Send letter enclosing photograph and CV. No unsolicited demo tapes or video show reels.

Errol McKinnon

10 Barley Mow Passage, London W4 4PH
Tel (01) **994 6477** Fax (01) **994 2874**
Contact Errol McKinnon

> Founded 1966. Represent actors only, and welcome queries from those seeking representation. Write in the first instance. Will not consider unsolicited demo tapes or video show reels.

Bill McLean Personal Management

23b Deodar Road, Putney, London SW15 2NP
Tel (01) **789 8191**
Contact Bill McLean

> Founded 1972. Represent actors, directors, authors, musical directors and composers. Welcome queries from actors seeking representation. Approach in writing in the first instance. No unsolicited demo tapes or video show reels.

MacNaughton Lowe Representation Ltd (MLR)

200 Fulham Road, London SW10 9PN
Tel (01) **351 5442** Fax (01) **351 4560** Telex **91993T** MLRHTN
Contact Robin Lowe, Patricia MacNaughton, Caroline Renton

> Founded 1968. Represent actors, writers, directors, producers, designers and composers. Will consider queries ('very selectively') from actors seeking representation. Approach in writing in the first instance. No unsolicited demo tapes or video show reels.

Magnet Personal Management

Lancaster House, 67 Newhall Street, Birmingham B3 1NU
Tel (021) **236 0446**
Contact Vikki Chambers, Kim Durham, Mark Audley

> Founded 1986. Cooperative management. Represent actors only, and welcome queries from those seeking representation. Approach in writing in the first instance. Will consider demo tapes and video show reels.

Magnus Management

155 Park Road, Teddington, Middx TW11 0BP
Tel (01) **977 5471/2** Fax (01) **943 3898** Telex **9222958** SCHUF G

> Founded early 1960s. Represent children and teenagers for acting and modelling. Welcome queries from prospective clients. Write in the first instance, with SAE. Will consider demo tapes and video show reels.

John Mahoney Management

Lower ground floor, 94 Gloucester Place, London W1H 3DA
Tel (01) **486 2947**
Contact John Mahoney, David Gretton

> Founded 1960s. Represent actors, a fight director, a designer and several TV directors. Welcome queries from actors seeking representation; write in the first instance. Will consider unsolicited demo tapes and video show reels.

Hazel Malone Management Ltd

Suite 14, London House, 271 King Street, London W6
Tel (01) **741 0707**

> Founded late 1950s. Represent actors, singers and dancers. Welcome queries

from actors seeking representation. Write in the first instance. Will not consider unsolicited demo tapes or video show reels, as they like to meet prospective clients first.

Marmont Management Ltd

Langham House, 308 Regent Street, London W1R 5AL
Tel (01) **637 3183**
Contact Patricia Marmont, Rose Streatfeild

Founded 1983. Represent actors and directors. Client list is full, but welcome queries from actors seeking representation. Approach in writing in the first instance, enclosing an SAE. No unsolicited demo tapes or video show reels.

Derrick Marr Ltd

5 Bank Chambers, 13 Dorset Street, London W1H 3FP
Tel (01) **486 1603/7760**
Contact Derrick Marr, Paul Keylock

Founded 1950. Represent actors only, and welcome queries from those seeking representation. Approach in writing in the first instance. No unsolicited demo tapes or video show reels.

Ronnie Marshall Agency

66 Ollerton Road, London N11 2LA
Tel (01) **368 4958**
Contact Ronnie Marshall, Shelana Marshall

Founded 1970. Represent actors 'with song and dance skills of a very high standard, and with full Equity status'. Welcome queries from prospective clients. Approach in writing in the first instance. Will consider demo tapes and video show reels, 'providing the recording is of good quality and, in the case of video, VHS system'. 'New actors should furnish themselves with good photographs and, if possible, advertise in *Spotlight*.'

Scott Marshall Personal Management

44 Perryn Road, London W3 7NA
Tel (01) **749 7692** Fax (01) **749 3790**
Contact Scott Marshall, Denise Marshall, Lorna Dolan

Founded 1968. Represent actors and directors (TV & theatre). Welcome queries from actors seeking representation. Approach in writing or by telephone in the first instance. Will consider demo tapes and video show reels.

Marina Martin Associates Ltd

97 Axminster Road, London N7 6BS
Tel (01) **263 9391** Fax (01) **734 2165**
Contact Marina Martin, Daphne Schofield

Founded 1972. Represent actors only, but do not welcome queries from those seeking representation. 'Ours is a personal management, and I am attempting to keep the list at around 35 actors only.'

Nigel Martin-Smith Personal Management

Suite 544, The Royal Exchange, St Ann's Square, Manchester M2
Tel (061) **834 3403**
Contact Tracy Edge

Founded 1980. Represent actors, writers, directors, musicians, singers and photographic models. Welcome queries from actors seeking representation.

Send letter enclosing CV and photograph. Will consider demo tapes and video show reels.

Masque Management

38 Mount Pleasant, London WC1X 0AP
Tel (01) **278 7449**

Founded 1986. Cooperative management. Represent actors only, and welcome queries from those seeking representation. Write in the first instance with CV and photograph, and an SAE if you would like them returned. Will consider unsolicited demo tapes and video show reels.

Mayer Management Ltd (in association with James Sharkey Associates Ltd)

Grafton House, 2–3 Golden Square, London W1R 3AD
Tel (01) **434 1242** Fax (01) **494 1547** Telex **295251** JSA
Contact Cassie Mayer, Clare Eden

Founded 1985. Represent actors and directors. Welcome queries from actors seeking representation. Approach in writing in the first instance. No unsolicited demo tapes or video show reels.

Media Legal Management Services

75 Clarendon Road, Sevenoaks, Kent
Tel (0732) **460592**

Not an agency. Do research and provide information for films/TV using scenes involving legal procedure.

Janet Mills Associates

1 Thetis Terrace, Westerly Ware, Kew Green, Richmond, Surrey TW9 3AU
Tel (01) **948 4549**
Contact Janet Mills

Founded 1987. Represent actors, and also have a composer/lyricist, voice and dialogue coach and a choreographer on their books. Will consider queries from actors seeking representation. However, 'I prefer to keep a small list, so I am not anxious to add to it by more than two or three for the foreseeable future.' Approach in writing in the first instance. Will consider demo tapes and video show reels. 'I would not consider taking on any person whose work I had not seen, preferably in theatre.'

Montagu Associates

3 Bretton House, Fairbridge Road, London N19 3HP
Tel (01) **281 4658**
Contact Beverley Montagu, Ruth Berryman

Founded 1987. Represent actors only, and welcome queries from those seeking representation. Approach in writing in the first instance. Will consider video show reels.

Morgan & Goodman

1 Old Compton Street, London W1
Tel (01) **437 1383**

Mainly represent actors, but also have directors and musical directors on their books.

William Morris Agency (UK) Ltd
31/32 Soho Square, London W1V 5DG
Tel (01) **434 2191** Fax (01) **437 0238** Telex **27928**
Contact 'Too complex to list — address letter to the agency'

> Founded 1965. Also literary agents. Represent actors, directors, choreographers, designers (theatre & costume), dramatists and producers. Although innundated with queries from actors seeking representation, will consider letters. No unsolicited demo tapes or video show reels.

Murphy & Heathcote
2 Bow Street, London WC2
Tel (01) **379 0705**
Contact Elaine Murphy, George Heathcote

> Founded 1985. Represent actors only, and welcome queries from those seeking representation. Write in the first instance. Will not consider unsolicited demo tapes or video show reels.

The Narrow Road Company
22 Poland Street, London W1V 3DD
Tel (01) **434 0406**
Contact Tim Brown, Richard Ireson

> Founded 1986. Represent actors, directors, writers, designers and lighting designers. Welcome queries from actors seeking representation. Approach in writing in the first instance.

1984 Personal Management Ltd
5 Leonard Street, London EC2A 4AQ
Tel (01) **251 8046**
Contact Robin Brown, Susan McGoun

> Founded 1984. Cooperative management. Represent actors only, and welcome queries from those seeking representation. Approach in writing in the first instance. Will consider demo tapes and video show reels if accompanied by covering letter and CV.

North One Management
Unit C20, Metropolitan Workshops, Enfield Road, London N1 5AZ
Tel (01) **254 9093**

> Founded 1987. Cooperative management. Welcome queries from actors seeking representation. Send letter with CV and photo in the first instance. Will consider video show reel.

'North of Watford' Actors Agency Ltd
Bridge Mill, Hebden Bridge, West Yorks. HX7 8EX
Tel (0422) **845361**

> Founded 1984. Cooperative management. Represent actors only, and welcome queries from those seeking representation. Approach in writing in the first instance. Will consider demo tapes and video show reels.

Oriental Casting Agency Ltd
34 Grafton Terrace, London NW5 4HY
Tel (01) **485 9338**
Contact Niall Toland

> Founded 1963. Represent Afro/Asian actors, walk-ons and supporting artists only. Do not welcome queries from actors seeking representation.

Otto Personal Management Ltd
Regency House, 75–77 St Mary's Road, Sheffield S2 4AN
Tel (0742) **752592**
Contact Chris Wilkinson, John Graham Davies, Robin Polley

> Founded 1985. Cooperative management representing actors only. Welcome queries from actors seeking representation (Equity members only). Initial approach by letter preferred, with CV, photograph and SAE. If work is not known to members of the agency, give details of current/forthcoming performances, broadcasts, etc.; 'For economic and practical reasons, we favour actors living locally.' 'Otto expects actors to provide their own 10×8 photos; new members pay £100 joining fee. Current pay commissions: 15% — TV, film and commercial; 12% — voice-over, training and video; 10% — radio and theatre. Members to attend six-weekly business meetings. The agency has an annual brochure launch of 250; circulates members' availability monthly; issues weekly newsletter to members; has a current restriction to 20 members.'

PBR Management
138 Putney Bridge Road, London SW15 2NQ
Tel (01) **871 4139**
Contact Simon Cutting

> Founded 1986. Represent actors and a couple of choreographers. Write in the first instance. Will not consider unsolicited demo tapes or video show reels.

PTA
Bugle House, 21a Noel Street, London W1V 3PD
Tel (01) **434 9513** Fax (01) **439 3814** Telex **8955398**
Contact Virginia Sharp, Roxane Vacca, Louisa Stevenson

> Founded 1986. Represent actors and technicians. Welcome queries from actors seeking representation. Approach in writing in the first instance. Will consider demo tapes and video show reels.

Pan Artists Agency
112 Washway Road, Sale, Cheshire M33 1RF
Tel (061) **969 7419**

> Founded 1973. Represent actors, supporting artists and walk-ons. Welcome queries from actors seeking representation; experience preferred. Write in the first instance. Will not consider unsolicited demo tapes or video show reels.

Park Personal Management Ltd
508 Butler's Wharf Business Centre, 45 Curlew Street, London SE1 2ND
Tel (01) **407 2561**

> Founded 1986. Cooperative management. Represent actors only, and welcome queries from those seeking representation. Send letter with CV and photograph. No unsolicited demo tape or video show reels.

Phyl Payne
7 Chesney Court, Shirland Road, London W9 2EG
Tel (01) **286 1270**

No longer working as an agent.

Performance Actors Agency
137 Goswell Road, London EC1V 7ET
Tel (01) **251 5716/3974**

Founded 1984. Cooperative management. Represent actors only, and welcome queries from those seeking representation. Write in the first instance. Will not consider unsolicited demo tapes or video show reels.

Performer and Choreographic Enterprises
Flames Studio, Galena Road, Hammersmith, London W6 0LT
Tel (01) **741 5133/9488** Telex **934386** BMS G
Contact Catriona Keenan, Lynne Rendell

Founded 1986. Represent actors, dancers, singers, and stage production shows and cabaret. Welcome queries from prospective clients. Approach in writing in the first instance: 'Always send a well-prepared CV and letter.' Will consider demo tapes and video show reels.

Performing Arts
6 Windmill Street, London W1P 1HF
Tel (01) **255 1362** Fax (01) **631 4631** Telex **266708** AJHLDN **(Ref: Perfar)**
Contact Richard Haigh

Founded 1983. Represent directors, designers, lighting designers, choreographers and conductors — do not represent actors.

Frances Phillips
Laynes House, 526/528 Watford Way, London NW7 4RS
Tel (01) **906 1200/0911**
Contact Frances Phillips

Founded 1986. Represent actors, choreographers and directors. Welcome queries from actors seeking representation. Approach in writing in the first instance. Will consider demo tapes and video show reels 'if a meeting is agreed'. Member of the Personal Managers' Association (PMA). Each year, 'try to take on one drama student without a card.'

Hilda Physick
78 Temple Sheen Road, London SW14 7RR
Tel (01) **876 0073**
Contact Hilda Physick

Represent actors only, but do not welcome queries from those seeking representation.

Piccadilly Management Actors' Cooperative
Colwyn Chambers, 24 Mosley Street, Manchester M2 3AG
Tel (061) **228 7734**

Founded 1986. Cooperative management. Represent actors only, and welcome queries from those seeking representation. Send letter with CV, photograph and any show dates. No unsolicited demo tapes or video show reels. 'We welcome applications from actors of all ages and backgrounds who are Equity members based in or around Manchester. We expect a high degree of commitment from our members, as well as a willingness to work in a cooperative environment.'

Pineapple Agency
6 Langley Street, London WC2H 9JA
Tel (01) **836 9477**

> Represent dancers. No actors.

Peter Pitts Management
6 South Parade, Headingley, Leeds LS6 3LF
Tel (0532) **789789**
Contact Peter Pitts

> Founded 1964 (in Scarborough). Represent actors and organize outdoor events such as the first commercial *It's a Knockout*, beer competitions, etc. (Member of National Outdoor Events Association and Institute of Entertainment and Arts Management.) Also represent bands and groups. Welcome queries from actors seeking representation, 'preferably from the northern provinces'. Approach in writing in the first instance. No unsolicited demo tapes or video show reels.

Plant & Froggatt Ltd
4 Windmill Street, London W1P 1HF
Tel (01) **636 4412** Fax (01) **637 5233**
Contact Peter Froggatt, Pippa Markham

> Founded 1965. Represent actors only, and welcome queries from those seeking representation. Write in the first instance. Will not consider unsolicited demo tapes or video show reels.

Plunket Greene Ltd
4 Ovington Gardens, London SW3 1LS
Tel (01) **584 0688**
Contact Mr. Plunket Greene

> Founded 1952. Represent actors only, and welcome queries from those seeking representation. Write in the first instance, with SAE. Will consider video tapes and demo show reels, if they are of work done and not set-up 'audition pieces'.

Gordon Poole Ltd
Kingston House, Pierrepont Street, Bath BA1 1LA
Tel (0225) **63061** Fax (0225) **69845** Telex **449212** LANTEL G
Contact Gordon Poole, Jill Poole

> Founded 1965. Represent actors, and also are general booking agents for all types of entertainers. Welcome queries from actors seeking representation. Approach in writing in the first instance. Will consider demo tapes and video show reels.

Portfolio Management
58 Alexandra Road, London NW4 2RY
Tel (01) **203 1747**

> Founded 1984. Represent actors, singers, dancers, musical ensembles, one-man shows. Welcome queries from actors seeking representation. Write in the first instance. Will consider unsolicited demo tapes and video show reels.

David Preston Associates Ltd
9 Blenheim Street, London W1
Tel (01) **495 1812**
Contact David Preston

> Founded 1965. Represent actors and opera singers. 'Occasionally' welcome queries from actors seeking representation. Approach in writing in the first instance. No unsolicited demo tapes or video show reels.

Peter Prichard Ltd
118 Beaufort Street, London SW3 6BU
Tel (01) **352 6417**

> Represent light entertainment artists only. No actors.

Professional Artists Management
18–19 Warwick Street, London W1R 5RB
Tel (01) **439 8195** Fax (01) **434 4478** Telex **263899** GENMAN G
Contact Sally-Ann Lipson, Victoria Tinker

> Founded 1985. Represent actors, directors, choreographers and musical directors. 'Within reason', welcome queries from actors seeking representation. Approach in writing in the first instance, enclosing CV and photograph. No unsolicited demo tapes or video show reels.

Profile Management Associates
7 Henrietta Street, London W1M 9AG
Tel (01) **636 1480/6728** Fax (01) **408 1286**
Contact Bill Merrow, Suzy Hansford, Jane Bullen (Los Angeles)

> Founded 1980. Represent actors, directors, musical directors, composers, dancers/singers. Welcome queries from prospective clients. Either telephone or send a letter. Will consider demo tapes and video show reels.

RAP Management
98 Bromley Common, Bromley, Kent BR2 9PF
Tel (01) **464 2630** Fax (01) **305 2320** Telex **8951182** GCOMS G
Contact Paul Edwards

> Founded 1984. Represent actors only, and welcome queries from those seeking representation. Write in the first instance. Will consider demo tapes and video show reels. 'No callers without appointment, please!'

RB Management
10a The Avenue, Hatch End, Middx HA5 4EP
Tel (01) **421 2470**
Contact Ron Barnes

> Founded 1985. Represent actors only, and welcome queries from those seeking representation. Send letter with CV and photograph. No unsolicited demo tapes or video show reels. Restricted number of clients: 'In this way, I can maintain a good working relationship with them all and can suggest them with confidence as I see everything they do.'

Reactors Management Ltd
London House, 68 Upper Richmond Road, Putney, London SW15 2RP
Tel (01) **870 7357/871 1505**

> Founded 1985. Cooperative management. Represent actors only, and welcome

queries from those seeking representation. Approach in writing in the first instance. Videos welcomed.

Joan Reddin Ltd

Hazel Cottage, Wheeler End Common, Lane End, Bucks. HP14 3NL
Tel (0494) **882729**
Contact Joan Reddin

Founded 1954. Represent actors only, but do not welcome queries from those seeking representation.

Red Letter Personal Management

85/86 Darlington Street, Wolverhampton WV1 4EX
Tel (0902) **311889**

Founded 1986. Cooperative management. Represent actors only, and welcome queries from those seeking representation. Approach in writing or by telephone in the first instance. Will consider demo tapes and video show reels. 'We are a Midlands-based cooperative agency scratching a living off the scraps thrown to us from the "rat- race"-oriented metropolis, at the same time proving that there is life north of Watford.'

Redroofs Agency

Littlewick Green, Maidenhead, Berks.
Tel (062882) **2982**

Attached to Redroofs Theatre School. Represent actors, singers, dancers and children, but do not welcome queries from actors seeking representation.

John Redway and Associates Ltd

16 Berners Street, London W1P 3DD
Tel (01) **637 1612** Fax (01) **493 0511** Telex **22914** ccc
Contact John Redway, David Booth

Represent actors, directors and writers, and welcome queries from actors seeking representation. Approach in writing in the first instance. Will consider demo tapes and video show reels.

Stella Richards Management

42 Hazlebury Road, London SW6 2ND
Tel (01) **736 7786** Fax (01) **731 5082**
Contact Paul McGurk, Stella Richards

Founded 1978. Represent actors, directors, designers, musical directors, film editors, choreographers, etc. Do not welcome queries from actors seeking representation. Will 'possibly' consider demo tapes and video show reels. 'Failure to enclose an SAE tends to lead to no reply!'

Rigal Management

109 Albert Bridge Road, London SW11 4PF
Tel (01) **228 8689**
Contact Muriel Rigal, Hans Baernhoft

Founded 1985. Represent actors only, and very much welcome queries from those seeking representation. Approach in writing in the first instance. Will consider demo tapes and video show reels. 'We do not actively seek for work in the areas of stills photography or voice-overs. We never deal with extra or walk-on work.'

Rogues & Vagabonds Management
Garden Studios, 11–15 Betterton Street, Covent Garden, London WC2H 9PB
Tel (01) **379 0344** Fax (01) **379 0801** Telex **265639** BETTS G

> Founded 1987. Cooperative management. Represent actors only, and welcome queries from those seeking representation. Approach in writing in the first instance. No unsolicited demo tapes or video show reels. 'Anyone accepted by us should be prepared to take a share of the work in manning the office and also to make a financial contribution.'

Jon Roseman Associates Ltd
103 Charing Cross Road, London WC2 0DT
Tel (01) **439 8245**

> Represent presenters. No actors.

Rossmore Associates
1 Rossmore Road, London NW1
Tel (01) **258 1953**
Contact Sylvia Young

> Founded 1988. Represent actors only, and welcome queries from those seeking representation. Write in the first instance with CV and photograph. Will not consider unsolicited demo tapes or video show reels.

Royce Management
44 Nasmyth Street, London W6 0HB
Tel (01) **741 4341**

> Founded 1980. Represent actors only, and welcome queries from those seeking representation. Approach in writing in the first instance. No unsolicited demo tapes or video show reels. 'We carefully consider all applications for representation, but only see people for interview if we feel there is a reasonable possibility that we could move on to offer a proposition. If applicants want photos and CVs returned, they must include an SAE and should never, in any case, send original or indispensable photos.'

SCA Management Ltd
23 Goswell Road, London EC1M 7BB
Tel (01) **608 0047/8**
Contact Anne Sheward

> Primarily represent actors, but also have singers/dancers and particularly specialize in musicals. Welcome casting queries from actors seeking representation. 'We represent a small select number of artists whose playing ages range between 18 and 35 years.' Approach in writing in the first instance. Will consider demo tapes and video show reels.

Saraband Associates
265 Liverpool Road, Islington, London N1 1LX
Tel (01) **609 5313/4**
Contact Sara Randall, Bryn Newton

> Founded 1973. Mainly represent actors, but also directors and choreographers. 'Sometimes' welcome queries from actors seeking representation. Always approach in writing in the first instance. Will consider demo tapes and video show reels.

Anna Scher Theatre Management Ltd
70–72 Barnsbury Road, London N1 0ES
Tel (01) **278 2101**
Contact Anna Scher

> Founded 1975. Represent actors only, and welcome queries from those seeking
> representation. Approach in writing in the first instance. Will consider demo tapes
> and video show reels. 'New clients must participate in classes at the Anna Scher
> Theatre. We only represent actors who train or have trained with us.' Anna Scher
> represents actors of all ages.

Screenlite
Lee International Studios, Studios Road, Shepperton, Middx TW17 0QD
Tel (0932) **562611 ext 2271/2** Fax (0932) **68989** Telex **929146 MOVIES G**
Contact Carlie Tovey, Kerry Tovey

> Founded 1982. Represent actors and children, and welcome queries from those
> seeking representation. Approach in writing in the first instance. No unsolicited
> demo tapes or video show reels.

Seven Muses
5 Milton Avenue, Highgate, London N6 5QF
Tel (01) **348 7256** Telex **918774 SEVMUS G**
Contact Nicholas Curry

> Founded 1983. Represent actors, classical musicians (soloists and ensembles), as
> well as well-known actors in words-and-music programmes. Do not welcome
> queries from actors seeking representation.

James Sharkey Associates Ltd
Third floor suite, 15 Golden Square, London W1R 3AG
Tel (01) **434 3801/6** Fax (01) **494 1547** Telex **295251 JSALON G**
Contact James Sharkey, Sophie James, Jon Bagley, Jane Augustus

> Founded 1983. Represent actors; also have a literary department (chief
> executive, Sebastian Born). Welcome queries from actors seeking representation.
> Approach in writing in the first instance. Will consider demo tapes and video
> show reels.

Vincent Shaw Associates
20 Jay Mews, London SW7 2EP
Tel (01) **581 8215**
Contact Vincent Shaw, Cherry Palfrey

> Founded 1958. Represent actors, stage managers, company managers and
> directors. Welcome queries from actors, but only if they can be seen working. Will
> consider demo tapes and video show reels if they are of work done.

Elizabeth Shepherd
29 Eversley Crescent, London N21 1EL
Tel (01) **364 0598**
Contact Elizabeth Shepherd

> Founded 1986. Represent actors, musical directors and composers. Welcome
> queries from actors only, and in moderation. Write in the first instance. Will not
> consider unsolicited demo tapes or video show reels.

Siân-Lucy Management
9 Mount Stuart Square, Cardiff CF1 6EE
Tel (0222) **488120** Fax (0222) **553399**
Contact Siân-Lucy, Yvette Wall

Founded 1985. Personal management for actors, walk-on artists and models. Welcome queries from actors seeking representation. Approach in writing in the first instance. No unsolicited demo tapes or video show reels.

Pamela Simons
9/15 Neal Street, London WC2H 9PU
Tel (01) **240 0228**
Contact Pamela Simons

Founded 1961. Represent actors only, and welcome queries from those seeking representation. Approach in writing in the first instance. No unsolicited demo tapes or video show reels: 'As I have only a limited number of artists, I must see their work before representing.'

Robert Smith Agency
20 Royal York Crescent, Clifton, Bristol BS8 4JY
Tel (0272) **738265**
Contact Robert Smith

Founded 1986 (in present form). Represent actors, musicians, variety performers, etc. Welcome queries from actors seeking representation. Send letter with CV, Equity number, etc. Will consider demo tapes and video show reels.

Snowshaft Theatrical Agency
Room 217, Wickham House, 10 Cleveland Way, London E1 4TR
Tel (01) **791 3373** and (0277) **227271** Telex **932011** GENFING
Contact Aleene Hatchard

Founded 1984. Represent actors, models, promotions people, dancers, singers. Welcome queries from actors seeking representation. Send a letter enclosing CV, recent photograph or Index Card. Will consider demo tapes for voice and vocal ability.

South East Theatrical & Promotion Agency
25 Samos Road, London SE20 7UQ
Tel (01) **778 4101**

Represent children. No adult actors.

Barbara Speake Agency
East Acton Lane, London W3 7EG
Tel (01) **743 1306/6096**
Contact Mrs June Collins

Mainly represent pupils, aged five to sixteen, of the Barbara Speake Stage School. Graduates of the school are represented by C.S.M. (Artistes) Ltd (see entry).

Barrie Stacey Promotions
9 Denmark Street, London WC2
Tel (01) **836 6220**
Contact Barrie Stacey

Founded 1966. Represent actors only. Specialize in musical comedy, panto and commercials. Welcome queries from actors seeking representation. Write in the first instance with photo and CV. Will not consider unsolicited demo tapes or video show reels.

Stage Centre
41 North Road, London N7 9DP
Tel (01) **607 0872**
Contact Patricia Henson

Founded 1982. Represent actors only — cooperative management. Welcome queries from those seeking representation. Send letter enclosing photograph and CV. Will consider demo tapes and video show reels: 'Please send SAE large enough for return of photos, show reels and video tapes.'

Stellaris Management
47 Greencoat Place, Westminster, London SW1
Tel (01) **828 1678** Telex **265871 MONREF G quoting 72: MAG 95881**
Contact Heidi Cook, Sophia Mallett

Founded 1970. Represent actors, singers and dancers. Welcome queries from actors seeking representation. Approach in writing in the first instance. Will consider demo tapes and video show reels.

Renée Stepham Ltd
2 Arthur Court, Queensway, London W2 5HW
Tel (01) **221 5550**

Do not represent actors.

Annette Stone Associates
9 Newburgh Street, London W1V 1LH
Tel (01) **734 0626** Fax (01) **434 2014**
Contact Annette Stone, Camilla Valentine Warrack

Founded 1983. Represent actors and directors. Do not welcome unsolicited queries from actors seeking representation; rely on personal recommendation. No unsolicited demo tapes or video show reels.

Roger Storey Ltd
71 Westbury Road, London N12 7PB
Tel (01) **346 9411**
Contact Roger Storey

Founded 1965. Represent actors only. Welcome queries from those seeking representation, but only if there is a strong possibility of work being seen. Write in the first instance. Will not consider unsolicited demo tapes or video show reels.

Swap Enterprises International Ltd
10 Barley Mow Passage, Chiswick, London W4 4PH
Tel (01) **994 6477** Fax (01) **994 1533** Telex **8811418**
Contact Mr W. Pestano, Miss J. De Lane

Alongside representation of actors, Swap Enterprises run a promotions company, and stage exhibitions, conferences and trade shows. Welcome enquiries from prospective clients. Approach by telephone or letter. Will consider demo tapes and video show reels.

T & S Management Ltd

The Old Clubhouse, Cambridge Park, St Margaret's, Twickenham, Middx TW1 2JE
Tel (01) **892 2261**
Contact Les Hines

> Founded 1988. Represent actors only, and welcome queries from those seeking representation. Write in the first instance, with CV and photograph. Will consider demo tapes and video show reels, but please send SAE for their return.

Talkies

10 St Martin's Court, London WC2
Tel (01) **836 2392**
Contact Beth Owen

> Founded 1979. Represent actors only, just for voice work. Sometimes welcome queries from actors as prospective clients. Write in the first instance. Demo tapes will only be considered if an interest has been expressed by the agency.

Target Casting Ltd

St Leonard's House, St Leonard's Gate, Lancaster LA1 1NN
Tel (0542) **67354**
Contact Cooperative management

> Founded 1983. Represent actors only, and welcome queries from those seeking representation. Approach in writing in the first instance; will consider video show reels. 'We are a successful actors' cooperative, and acceptance is limited by our geographical position (members should live in the north-west) and by our wish to hold the number of members to a manageable level.'

Ruth Tarko Agency

50/52 Cecil Street, Glasgow G12 8RJ
Tel (041) **334 0555** and **339 8037**
Contact Ruth Tarko, Arlene Carroll

> Founded 1970. Represent actors only, and welcome queries from those seeking representation. Send letter with CV and photograph. Will consider demo tapes and video show reels.

Theatre World Ltd

Cotton's Farmhouse, Whiston Road, Cogenhoe, Northants NN7 1NL
Tel (0604) **891487**
Contact Lena Davis

> Founded 1982. Represent actors, writers, directors, singers, etc. 'Sometimes' welcome queries from actors seeking representation. Approach in writing in the first instance. Will consider demo tapes and video show reels.

Thomas & Benda Associates Ltd

361 Edgware Road, London W2 1BS
Tel (01) **723 5509** Fax (01) **724 7287**
Contact Mr Thomas, Mr Benda

> Founded 1980. Represent actors and a couple of musical directors. Welcome queries from actors seeking representation; write in the first instance. Will not consider unsolicited demo tapes or video show reels.

Jim Thompson

134 Tooley Street, London SE1 2TU
Tel (01) **403 6033**
Contact Jim Thompson

> Founded 1980. Represent actors, writers, directors and personalities. Welcome queries from actors seeking representation. Approach in writing in the first instance. Will consider demo tapes and video show reels.

Thornton Agency

72 Purley Downs Road, Croydon, Surrey CR2 0RB
Tel (01) **660 5588**
Contact Leslie Collins, Jaqui Lillywhite

> Founded 1963. Represent actors and some TV variety artists. Welcome queries from actors seeking representation. Write in the first instance with CV and photograph. Will consider unsolicited demo tapes and video show reels.

Tobias Management

766 Wilmslow Road, Manchester M20 0DR
Tel (061) **434 0434**
Contact Sharon Tobias, Julia Donat

> Formerly Zena Sharpe Personal Management (founded 1971). Represent actors, and also have a musical director on their books. Welcome queries — 'in moderation' — from actors seeking representation. Approach in writing in the first instance. Will consider demo tapes and video show reels.

Tops Casting

The Royal Institution, Office 61, Coquitt Street, Liverpool L1
Tel (051) **708 7752**
Contact Mark Roscoe

> Founded 1985. Represent actors and children. Welcome queries from actors seeking representation. Either telephone or send letter with CV and photograph. Will consider video show reels.

Sheila Tozer Management & Agency

143 Nevill Avenue, Hove, East Sussex BN3 7NE
Tel (0273) **774388**
Contact Sheila Tozer

> Represent actors. New clients acquired mainly through personal recommendation.

Trapeze

123 Tottenham Court Road, London W1P 9HN
Tel (01) **388 8781**
Contact Charlotte Kelly

> Founded 1987. Represent actors and directors. Welcome queries from actors seeking representation. Approach in writing in the first instance, 'although if someone wants to know more about the agency first, I am happy to speak to them.' Will consider demo tapes and video show reels: 'I would not consider taking anyone on until I had seen their work first — either live or on a fairly thorough tape — preferably both. Circular letters (particularly ones addressed "Dear Sir"!) go in the bin.'

Trends Management
54 Lisson Street, London NW1 6ST
Tel (01) **723 8001** Fax (01) **258 3591** Telex **912881**
Contact Francesca Lucy, Robert Briggs

> Founded 1950. Represent actors, dancers and singers. Welcome queries from actors seeking representation. Approach in writing in the first instance. Will consider demo tapes and video show reels.

Joan Underwood
5 Sudbrook Gardens, Ham Common, Richmond, Surrey
Tel (01) **940 8888**
Contact Joan Underwood

> Formerly Encore Agency Ltd, founded in the 1950s. Represent photogenic teenagers and young, classically trained singers. Welcome queries from actors seeking representation ('if within the range of my interests'). Approach in writing in the first instance, enclosing a photograph. Will not consider unsolicited demo tapes or video show reels. Also offer a consultation service to help with all aspects of presentation for auditions and interviews, choice of pieces, songs and so forth.

Universal Productions
1 Haggard Road, Twickenham, Middx TW1 3AL
Tel (01) **892 5530**
Contact Elizabeth A. Roberts

> Founded 1948. Represent actors and children for television and all types of dancers. Do not welcome queries from actors seeking representation 'at present', but will consider demo tapes and video show reels.

Paul Vaughan Associates
Gayfere House, 22–23 Gayfere Street, London SW1P 3HP
Tel (01) **222 8161** Fax (01) **799 1457**
and Alpha Tower, Paradise Circus, Birmingham B1 1TT
Tel (021) **642 4011**
Contact Anthony Blackburn (London), Stephen Pink (Birmingham)

> Founded 1978. Represent actors and presenters. Welcome queries from actors seeking representation. Write in the first instance. Will not consider unsolicited demo tapes or video show reels.

Adza Vincent
11a Ivor Place, London NW1 6HS
Tel (01) **262 9356**

> Founded 1957. Represent actors only, but do not welcome queries from those seeking representation.

Voice Box
126 Stamford Park Road, Hale, Altrincham, Cheshire WA15 9ER
Tel (061 928) **3222**

> Represent actors for voice work, and actors and presenters for vision work on corporate videos. Do not welcome queries from actors seeking representation.

Voicecall
Apt 2, 12 Cambridge Park, East Twickenham, Middx TW1 2PF
Tel (01) **891 1264**

> Represent actors for voice-over work. Have a long list of established clients, and do not welcome queries from actors seeking representation at the moment.

Voiceover
59 Frith Street, London W1V 5TA
Tel (01) **437 3060/2713**
Contact Heather Fooks

> Founded 1974. Represent actors for voice-over work only. Very rarely take on new clients; do not really welcome queries from actors seeking representation.

Voice Shop Ltd
Bakerloo Chambers, 304 Edgware Road, London W2 1DY
Tel (01) **402 3966** Fax (01) **706 1002**
Contact Maxine Wiltshire

> Founded 1979. Represent actors for voice-over work only, and welcome queries from those seeking representation. Approach in writing in the first instance, enclosing demo tape.

Voices Ltd
Suite 116, Golden House, 29 Great Pulteney Street, London W1R 3DD
Tel (01) **734 3934**
Contact Jenni Waters

> Founded 1984. Represent actors for voice work only, and welcome queries from those seeking representation. Write in the first instance. Will consider unsolicited demo tapes.

Thelma Wade
54 Harley Street, London W1N 1AD
Tel (01) **580 9860** Fax (01) **637 8022**
Contact Thelma Wade

> Founded 1985. Represent actors, singers and dancers. Welcome queries from actors seeking representation, despite being 'inundated'. Approach in writing in the first instance. Will consider demo tapes and video show reels. 'Good clear presentation of CV is essential, to include colouring, height, training, skills, languages, hobbies — so many miss valuable selling details.'

Penny Wesson
26 King Henry's Road, London NW3 3RP
Tel (01) **722 6607**

> Consultancy and advisory service.

West Central Management (WCM)
Suite 121, Panther House, 38 Mount Pleasant, London WC1
Tel (01) **833 8134**

> Founded 1986. Cooperative management. Represent actors only, and very much welcome queries from those seeking representation. Send letter with CV and photograph. Will consider demo tapes and video show reels. 'WCM is an actors' cooperative agency. A willingness to participate fully in the life of WCM is essential. This involves office duty (one day a week minimum), attendance at

regular meetings and a creative input generally. The constitution of WCM is available on request to all prospective members. All decisions and matters of policy are decided collectively and cooperatively.'

David White Associates

2 Ormond Road, Richmond, Surrey TW10 6TH
Tel (01) **940 8300**
Contact David White

Founded 1965. Represent actors and directors. Welcome queries from actors as prospective clients, but only if the first approach is by letter with a photograph and a brief CV so that neither side need waste time. 'The agent might already represent someone of the actor's type, and at least then a gentle rebuff can be sent as opposed to a flat "NOT INTERESTED" if one really is busy.'

Michael Whitehall Ltd

125 Gloucester Road, London SW7 4TE
Tel (01) **244 8466** Fax (01) **244 9060**

Founded 1985. Represent actors, directors and writers. Welcome queries from prospective clients. Write in the first instance. Will consider unsolicited demo tapes and video show reels. Have a large voice-over department.

Newton Wills Management

Utopia Studios, 7 Chalcot Road, London NW1
and
17 Church Street, Belton-in-Rutland, Leics. LE15 9JV
Tel (01) **586 3434**
Contact Newton Wills

Founded 1980. Represent actors, TV presenters, singers/actors. Welcome queries from actors seeking representation. Contact by telephone or letter in the first instance. Will consider demo tapes and video show reels. 'Send as much information as possible — full CV, good photographs, etc. Never ask an agent to return your call when making enquiries for representation!'

The Wendy Wisbey Agency

2 Rupert Road, London W4 1LX
Tel (01) **994 1210/5378**
Contact Dinah Bland, Wendy Wisbey

Founded 1956. Represent actors only: 'We are always prepared to consider enquiries.' Send a letter with an SAE in the first instance. No unsolicited demo tapes or video show reels.

April Young Ltd

2 Lowndes Street, London SW1X 9ET
Tel (01) **259 6488**
Contact April Young

Founded 1974. Represent actors and writers. Do not welcome queries from actors seeking representation, as no longer in a position to take on any new clients.

Young Casting Agency
7 Beaumont Gate, Glasgow G12 9EE
Tel (041) **334 2646**
Contact Freddie Young

> Founded 1967. Represent actors, walk-ons and supporting artists. Welcome queries from actors seeking representation if they are based in Scotland and can be seen working. Write or telephone with details of work. Will consider unsolicited demo tapes and video show reels.

Sonny Zahl Associates
57 Great Cumberland Place, London W1
Tel (01) **724 3684** Telex **94014150** ANNZ
Contact Ann Zahl

> Founded 1975. Represent actors, choreographers, light entertainment artists, designers and directors. Welcome queries from actors seeking representation, although a small agency with not many actors on its books. Write in the first instance. Will consider unsolicited demo tapes and video show reels.

Peter Zander Artist & Concert Management
22 Romilly Street, London W1V 5TG
Tel (01) **437 4767**
Contact Peter Zander

> Founded 1983. Represent actors, musical directors, musicians and singers. Also a promoter of opera, plays, concerts and concert seasons, music competitions, arts festivals. Counsel actors on the handling of their careers and self-promotion. Commercial sponsorship of the arts. Welcome queries from actors seeking representation — 'but telephone first; do not send bumph uninvited.' No unsolicited demo tapes or video show reels.

7. Freelance casting directors

The casting director is the go-between for actors and directors. It is his job to interpret how the director visualizes his production, and then to find the actors who can realize that vision.

The ITV companies, the big theatre companies such as the National and the RSC and some regional theatres such as Manchester Royal Exchange and Sheffield Crucible have in-house casting directors (*see* relevant sections) whose responsibilities can extend beyond setting up interviews and auditions to the negotiation of contracts and the financial planning of a production. However, most casting directors are freelancers who limit themselves to finding faces that fit.

Because he takes pressure off the director — and spares him the embarrassment of telling an actor precisely why he is not wanted — the casting director holds a position of strength in the production team which should not be underestimated simply because he is not constantly in attendance. It helps to know a casting director; it helps even more to be able to impress him.

The opportunity for a young actor to make a mark is in performance (though casting directors are notoriously averse to seeing anything on spec) or at audition or screen testing. These will be set up by the casting director on behalf of the director, who will make a final decision.

The audition, at its worst, gives new meaning to the word sadism. The dreaded signal of rejection — 'Thank you. Next.' — has entered common currency as the dismissal of minor talent. But short of an unimpeachable CV, the audition is the only known technique for matching horses to courses, and it does not have to be a painful or humiliating experience. Any agent worth his salt gives his actor a full briefing on the role and how best to present himself at the audition. Even if it does not lead directly to a contract, a rigorously prepared and properly conducted audition will leave a lasting impression. If one role is not within your range, there are plenty of others that are. Expect the casting director to call again.

Michael Barnes Ltd
Suite 201, Golden House, 29 Great Pulteney Street, London W1R 3DD
Tel (01) **439 9716** Fax (01) **437 0824**
Contact Michael Barnes, Karin Stretford-Grainger

> TV, films, commercials and training videos. Do not welcome casting queries from actors, but will consider demo tapes and video show reels.

Laura Cairns
Flat 2, 7 Streathbourne Road, Tooting Bec, London SW17 8QZ
Tel (01) **767 8607**

> Films, TV, video and theatre. Welcomes casting queries from actors; approach in

writing in the first instance. 'I try and see as many shows as I can if the contact is made in writing, but of course, I cannot see everyone. The main reason for contacting a casting director is in the hope that he/she may be able to see you working. If I had sufficient secretarial assistance, I should certainly want to set aside more time to interview actors personally. I do not think actors need to include an SAE with a CV and photograph. However, it is necessary in the case of returning a video.'

Di Carling
36 Wardour Street, London W1V 3HJ
Tel (01) **437 0841**

TV films, commercials and training films. Very occasionally holds general interviews, but does not particularly welcome casting queries from actors. No unsolicited demo tapes or video show reels. Credits include: *The Birmingham Six Appeal.*

Maggie Cartier
Pinewood Studios, Iver Heath, Bucks.
Tel (0753) **651 700**

Feature films and films for TV. Credits include: *Empire of the Sun, Valmont, Amadeus, Ragtime* and *Jack the Ripper* (Euston Films). CVs, photographs and performance notices welcomed. No unsolicited demo tapes or video show reels.

The Casting Company
9 Newburgh Street, London W1V 1LH
Tel (01) **734 4955**
Contact Michelle Guishe, Debbie McWilliams

Feature films, TV and some commercials. Do not welcome general letters, but will try to see actors' work if performance notices sent. Credits include: *Queen of Hearts* (feature film) and *Des Res* (Michelle Guishe); *Danny, the Champion of the World* and the feature film of Kenneth Branagh's *Henry V* (Debbie McWilliams).

Beth Charkham
122 Wardour Street, London W1V 3LA
Tel (01) **734 0202** Fax (01) **439 8568**
Contact Beth Charkham, Emma Goldman

TV films and commercials. Do not welcome casting queries from actors. Will consider demo tapes and video show reels. Hold general interviews. Credits include: *Robin of Sherwood* and *Pulaski.*

Jackie Coote
27 Britannia Road, London SW6 2HJ
Tel (01) **731 1061**

Stills advertisements and commercials. Will consider CVs and photographs. No unsolicited demo tapes or video show reels.

Kathy Curshen
26 Ulundi Road, Blackheath, London SE3 7UG
Tel (01) **858 9291**

Approach by letter in the first instance. No unsolicited demo tapes or video show reels.

Davis & Zimmerman Casting

31 King's Road, London SW3 4RP
Tel (01) **730 9421**
Contact Noel Davis, Jeremy Zimmerman

Feature films, TV films and commercials, training films. Approach by letter in the first instance. No unsolicited demo tapes or video show reels. 'Forty-five per cent of photographs have no name on the back. Needless to say, they go into the bin. Letters, photographs and CVs should be stapled or clipped together. Actors should learn that casting directors are not agents. We do not answer letters from actors, but we file the information and refer to it when casting. Every actor must advertise in *Spotlight*; otherwise, they are dead.' Credits include: *The Dresser* and *Madame Sousatzka*.

Liz England Casting

34 Connaught Street, London W2 2AF
Tel (01) **723 1332**
Contact Simone Ireland

Commercials, films and TV. Prefer to be approached in writing in the first instance. Will consider demo tapes and video show reels, but 'We like to be told in advance that they're going to be sent. Videos that arrive unasked for can sometimes be put to one side until we have time to view them.' 'It is very important to have an agent for numerous reasons — e.g. money negotiations, availability checks. It is very time-consuming chasing actors without agents.'

Ann Fielden Casting

36 Wardour Street, London W1V 3HJ
Tel (01) **434 1331**

TV, film, corporate video, commercials. Approach by letter in the first instance. No unsolicited demo tapes or video show reels. Credits include: *The Fear, The Monocled Mutineer* and *Shanghai Surprise*.

Susie Figgis

12 Flitcroft Street, London WC2
Tel (01) **379 7808**

Feature films. Welcomes letters and performance notices from actors. Credits include: *Ghandi, The Killing Fields, The Mission, Mona Lisa, Local Hero, Wish You Were Here*.

Bernice Fildes

56 Wigmore Street, London W1
Tel (01) **935 1254**

General casting — films, TV, etc. Will consider CVs, photographs and performance notices; also demo tapes and video show reels. Very occasionally holds general interviews.

Allan Foenander

59 North Eyot Gardens, St Peters Square, London W6 9NL
Tel (01) **748 9641**

Films, TV, commercials and documentaries. Credits include: *Deadline* and *The Most Dangerous Man in the World* (both BBC); *Friendships in Vienna* (Disney TV); *Shirley Valentine* (Paramount); *Great Expectations* (Walt Disney Primetime). Will consider CVs, photographs and performance notices. No unsolicited demo tapes or video show reels.

Celestia Fox

5 Clapham Common Northside, London SW4
Tel (01) **720 6143**

>Feature films. Credits include: *A Room with a View, Maurice, A Handful of Dust, Mountains of the Moon.* Does not welcome unsolicited photographs and CVs, but will consider performance notices. No unsolicited demo tapes or video show reels.

Paul de Freitas

3rd floor, 2 Conduit Street, London W1R 9TG
Tel (01) **434 4233/4**

>TV commercials and training films. Will consider letters from actors, but no unsolicited demo tapes or video show reels. Does not usually hold general interviews.

Jane Frisby Casting

51 Ridge Road, London N8 9LJ
Tel (01) **341 4747**

>Commercials, training films, TV drama, theatre. Approach by letter in the first instance. No unsolicited demo tapes or video show reels.

Joyce Gallie

37 Westcroft Square, London W6 0TA
Tel (01) **741 4009**

>Feature films, commercials and some TV. Does not particularly welcome unsolicited letters from actors – 'we are inundated' – nor demo tapes and video show reels.

Lesley Grayburn

74 Leigh Gardens, London NW10 5HP
Tel (01) **969 6112**

>TV commercials and corporate videos. Approach in writing in the first instance, enclosing CV and photograph. No unsolicited demo tapes or video show reels.

Anne Henderson Casting Ltd

93 Kelvin Road, Highbury, London N5 2PL
Tel (01) **354 3786**

>Films, TV, commercials. Does not welcome casting queries from actors, or unsolicited demo tapes or video show reels. 'Only contact casting directors by letter when you have something to be seen in, either TV or theatre.' Credits include: *A Very British Coup, Porterhouse Blue* and *Taggart.*

Rebecca Howard

37 Wharton Street, London WC1X 9PG
Tel (01) **837 2978**
Contact Rebecca Howard, Cathy Bell

>Film and TV. Approach by letter in the first instance. No unsolicited demo tapes or video show reels. Credits include: *A Very Peculiar Practice* and *Salome.*

Sharon Howard Field

27 Neal Street, London WC2H 9PR
Tel (01) **240 0388**

>Feature and TV films. Does not particularly welcome letters from actors; prefers to

receive performance notices. No unsolicited demo tapes or video show reels. Credits include: *The Attic* (YTV) and *Drowning by Numbers*.

Hubbard Casting

6 Noel Street, London W1
Tel (01) **494 3191** Fax (01) **437 0559**
Contact John Hubbard, Ros Hubbard, Sue Needleman

Feature and TV films, plays and commercials, theatre. Approach by letter in the first instance. Hold general interviews. Will consider demo tapes and video show reels. Credits include: *Out of Order* and *Twins*. 'Get known by all casting directors. Keep them posted about progress. Persevere.'

Priscilla John

22 Cardross Street, London W6 0DR
Tel (01) **741 9615**

Feature films and TV. Credits include: *A Fish Called Wanda* and *Who Framed Roger Rabbit?* Happy to receive CVs, photographs and performance notices. No unsolicited demo tapes or video show reels.

Marilyn Johnson

The Basement, 115 Chesterton Road, London W10 6ET
Tel (01) **969 7128/9**

TV and films. 'Rarely see people for general interviews.' Does not welcome letters from actors; prefers to receive performance notices. No unsolicited demo tapes or video show reels. Credits include: *Piece of Cake, Inspector Morse* and *Slipstream*.

Doreen Jones

107 Warwick Road, London SW5 9EZ
Tel (01) **373 0171**
Contact Doreen Jones, Amanda Fisher

TV and film (was Head of Casting for Granada TV until 1987). Approach by letter in the first instance. No unsolicited demo tapes or video show reels. Credits include: *Game, Set and Match* and *Shake Hands Forever*.

Just Casting

128 Talbot Road, London W11 1JA
Tel (01) **229 3471**
Contact Leo Davis

Feature films and TV. Performance notices, but no unsolicited demo tapes or video show reels. Credits include: *Absolute Beginners, For Queen and Country*.

Suzy Korel

20 Blenheim Road, London NW8 0LX
Tel (01) **624 6435**

Approach by letter in the first instance. No unsolicited demo tapes or video show reels. 'I like letters to be sent, and then I try to meet the actor.' Sometimes considers demo tapes and video show reels, but 'only after I have met the actor'.

Irene Lamb
Flat 4, Avenue House, 97 Walton Street, London SW3 2JY
Tel (01) **589 6452**

> Feature films and TV. Approach in writing in the first instance, enclosing CV and *Spotlight* number. No unsolicited demo tapes or video show reels. Credits include: *Brazil*, *The Lonely Passion of Judith Hearne* and *Eric the Viking.*

Jane L'Epine Smith
2 Chertsey Road, St Margaret's, Twickenham, Middx
Tel (01) **891 1685**

> Corporate videos. Tries to see as many actors as possible. Welcomes letters and performance notices (sees at least three shows per week). No unsolicited demo tapes or video show reels.

Sharon Levinson
48 Yale Court, Honeybourne Road, London NW6 1JG
Tel (01) **435 3329**

> Commercials, corporate video, TV. Occasionally holds general interviews. No unsolicited demo tapes or video show reels.

Julia Lisney
c/o 'The Bill' office, Thames Television, 85 Barlby Road, London W10
Tel (01) **969 6699**

> TV, films, commercials, training films. Credits include: *The Bill*, *The Gemini Factor*, *Gems.*

Jill Pearce
Suite 16, 6 Langley Street, London WC2
Tel (01) **240 0316**

> TV and cinema commercials. Performance notification – preferably by phone. No unsolicited demo tapes or video show reels.

Lesley de Pettitt
2 Parkview, The Ride, Hatfield, Herts. AL9 5HG
Tel (07072) **64301**
Contact Lesley de Pettitt

> Film, TV and commercials. Approach in writing in the first instance, enclosing CV and photograph.

Poole and Crowley Casting
2nd floor, 82 Wardour Street, London W1V 3LS
Tel (01) **437 4444**
Contact Gilly Poole, Suzanne Crowley

> Founded 1988 (formerly with The Casting Company). Feature films, commercials, TV, theatre, etc. No demo tapes or video show reels.

Simone Reynolds
60 Hebden Road, London SW17 7NN
Tel (01) **672 5443**

> Film, TV, theatre and some commercials (for directors such as John Mackenzie). Credits include: *Chariots of Fire*, *The Long Good Friday*, *We Think the World of*

You and *The Firm* (BBC *Screen on 2*). Does not welcome letters; performance notice cards preferred. No unsolicited demo tapes or video show reels.

Maggie Sangwin
61 Flanders Mansions, Flanders Road, London W4 1NF
Tel (01) **995 7523**

Feature films, TV, commercials and photographic work. Welcomes letters and performance notices from actors. Enclose CV and photograph. Will consider demo tapes and video show reels. Credits include: *The Bill* (Thames TV) and *Tank Malling* (film).

Mary Selway
Twickenham Film Studios, The Barons, St Margaret's, Twickenham, Middx TW1 2AW
Tel (01) **892 4477**

Feature films. Credits include: *Out of Africa, White Mischief, Dry White Season, Gorillas in the Mist, Strapless, Paris by Night*. Is happy to receive CV, photograph and performance notices.

Hazel Singer
1 Newcastle House, Luxborough Street, London W1

Mainly corporate videos and training films.

Maude Spector
16 Upper Brook Street, London W1Y 1PD
Tel (01) **493 3478**

Feature films and TV. Does not welcome unsolicited letters or demo tapes and video show reels. Prefers to deal only through agents.

Gail Stevens & Janey Fothergill
37 Berwick Street, London W1
Tel (01) **437 1562**

Films, TV, commercials, etc. Do not hold general interviews. No demo tapes or video show reels; send letter with CV and photograph. Credits: *The Lair of the White Worm, Resurrection, The Rachel Papers* and two projects for Jim Henson.

Sylvia Taylor
40 Brookville Road, London SW6 7BJ
Tel (01) **385 9716**

Commercials and stills. Will consider CVs and photographs. Demo tapes and video show reels *only on request*.

Rose Tobias Shaw
219 Liverpool Road, London N1 1LX
Tel (01) **607 0762**
Contact Rose Tobias Shaw

Film, TV and commercials. Approach in writing in the first instance, enclosing CV and photograph. Will try to cover a show if performance notice sent. Does not hold general interviews. No unsolicited demo tapes or video show reels. Credits include: *Voice of the Heart* and *Around the World in 80 Days*.

Valerie Van Ost
57 Oakwood Court, Kensington, London W14 8JY
Tel (01) **602 0088**

> Commercials and some TV films. Welcomes letters, including *Spotlight* number and CV. Does not hold general interviews. No unsolicited demo tapes or video show reels.

The Vocal Casting Company
25–26 Poland Street, London W1V 3DB
Tel (01) **437 4492**
Contact Alan Fitter

> Voice-over casting service and consultancy. Welcome demo tapes for consideration.

Sue Whatmough
34 Cadogan Road, Surbiton, Surrey KT6 4DJ
Tel (01) **390 6225**

> TV and feature films. Credits include: *Gentlemen and Players*. Photographs, CVs and performance notices will be considered. No phone calls and no unsolicited demo tapes or video show reels.

8. Repertory and regional theatres

The theatre has never been so prosperous, yet everywhere there is talk of doom and disaster.

The paradox is explained by changes in the politics of arts subsidy, changes in production economics and changes in the power structure of live entertainment. For all those who have gained by the revolution, about the same number feel angry and aggrieved. As ever, the voices of unhappiness speak loudest.

The clampdown on Arts Council expenditure has caused anguish at the National Theatre and the Royal Shakespeare Company, and throughout the provincial network of rep companies, though not for the same reasons. The big subsidized companies resent the Arts Council policy of diverting resources away from the centre (while paying lip service to the need for a thriving regional theatre); the reps, though grateful for any extra that comes their way, are under pressure to make money with popular and undemanding plays.

Last October, Bill Pryde, artistic director of the Cambridge Theatre Company, one of the touring companies much touted by the Arts Council in its devolutionary campaign, delivered his protest at 'artistic restrictions' in the form of his resignation. He claimed that financial stringency had made theatre managers timid: as they could no longer afford for every show not to be a box-office success, there was no room for artistic risk-taking. The small war in Cambridge caused rumblings of discontent throughout the country. There was even talk of such prestigious theatres as the Manchester Royal Exchange having to close for six months in the year in order to survive.

And yet, and yet ... Examples of exciting and original work are not hard to find. Residents of Watford, say, or of Derby, Lancaster or Chester, who share a rich and varied diet of live drama, might wonder what all the fuss is about. The Leicester Haymarket is not alone in making up a local shortfall in income with successful West End transfers. What shame is there in that?

On tour, the Renaissance Company has scored a huge success without a penny of public subsidy. The promoters hastily disclaim any wish to stand as champions of Thatcherite enterprise, but they can hardly deny the spoils of their own spectacular victory or deter others from following in their wake.

In London, meanwhile, where the griping from the subsidized sector is unremitting, the signs of imminent collapse are hard to detect. As Bernard Levin, one-time theatre critic and now political sage, advises his *Times* readers, the premonitions of catastrophe never come true: 'For the past 17 years, Mr Nicholas de Jongh has been saying three times a day after meals that the Royal Shakespeare Company is going to close down permanently next Wednesday, and the RSC has recently opened its sixth playhouse.' Last year, the RSC employed some 240 performers, the highest number since it set up shop.

On the commercial side, publicity has focused on a succession of monster flops, climaxing with the departure of the musical spectacular *Ziegfield* from the Palladium, leaving behind a £3 million shortfall. However, in most of London's first-rank theatres, business is booming. In 1987, some 11 million people paid £130 million into the collective box office, achieving the best year since the Society of West End Theatres started collecting statistics at the beginning of the decade.

One might argue about the standard of the productions, but the supply side of second-rate musical revivals is thinning out. The punter who comes fresh to the West End now has a wide choice of quality drama — wider by far than in any Continental or American city. For this achievement alone, British theatre is entitled to a vote of thanks.

Yvonne Arnaud Theatre
Millbrook, Guildford, Surrey GU1 3UX
Tel (0483) **64571**
Artistic director Val May

Founded 1965. Seating capacity: just under 600. Mostly co-produce with managements such as Triumph and Bill Kenwright for pre- and post-West End productions and nationwide tours. 20–25 shows per year. Recent productions: *The Admirable Crichton* (directed by Michael Rudman), *Holmes and the Ripper* (John David), *Hand over Fist* (Mark Piper; co-production with the Theatre Royal Windsor), *The Secret of Sherlock Holmes* (Patrick Garland), *The Royal Baccarat Scandal* (Val May; Chichester Festival production). Do not welcome casting queries from actors. Recommend that the actors contact the co-producing company as unlikely to hold auditions at the Yvonne Arnaud.

Touring company: Millstream (*see* Touring companies).

Belgrade Theatre
Belgrade Square, Coventry CV1 1GS
Tel (0203) **56431**
Artistic director Robert Hamlin

Founded 1958. Seating capacity: 866. Two seasons: September to July. Nine productions: musicals, classics, revivals, premières and pantomime. Cast sizes range from four to 25. Recent productions: *Guys and Dolls, Guardian Angels* and *Lock Up Your Daughters* (directed by Robert Hamlin); *The Prime of Miss Jean Brodie* and *The Crucible* (Simon Dunmore); *Jack and the Beanstalk* (Ian Watt Smith); *Amadeus* (Simon Dunmore & Miriam Segal); *The Elephant Man* (Miriam Segal); *Bare Necessities* (Rob Bettinson). Do not advertise for actors, but welcome casting queries. Approach by letter in the first instance. Hold general auditions and also see people for individual productions.

Studio theatre with a seating capacity of 60. Seven plays annually with a maximum cast size of five. Recent productions: *Sad Arthur's Trip* (Rob Bettinson); *Never the Sinner* and *The Act* (Miriam Segal); *The Way to Go Home* (Pip Broughton); *The Hole in the Top of the World* (Simon Dunmore). TIE company (*see* Theatre-in-Education companies).

Comment
The West Midlands is extremely well served with high-quality theatre, and the Belgrade is no exception. This lively rep theatre offers an adventurous and varied programme. Named after the Yugoslav capital, which presented the timber used in its interior, The Belgrade, built in 1958, was Britain's first civic theatre.

Birmingham Repertory Theatre
Broad Street, Birmingham B1 2EP
Tel (021) **236 6771**
Artistic director John Adams
Associate director Derek Nicholls

Founded 1913 by Barry Jackson; moved to present modern home 1970. Seating capacity: 834–99 (flexible stage). Autumn and spring seasons of approximately four to five plays per season. Recent productions: *A Midsummer Night's Dream* (directed by Robin Midgley); *The Contractor* and *Alice in Wonderland* (Derek Nicholls); *An Inspector Calls* and *Who's Afraid of Virginia Woolf?* (John Adams). Generally hold auditions twice a year. Very occasionally advertise in Equity *Job Grapevine*. Welcome casting queries, either by telephone or letter: 'But please do not follow up a letter with a telephone call. We carefully file all photographs and CVs for future reference.'

Studio theatre: seating capacity 109–140. Touring productions as well as home-produced contemporary and classical works. Recent production: *Blood Brothers* (Maggie Ford).

Comment
The launching pad for many leading actors — Olivier, Richardson, Scofield — the Birmingham Rep has a long-established reputation for unusual and avant-garde drama going back to its beginnings in 1913. The Rep was the first British theatre to introduce a subscription ticket scheme and, in 1976, was the first regional rep to present productions at the National Theatre (*Measure for Measure* and *The Devil is an Ass*). One of the foremost rep theatres in the country.

Brunton Theatre Company
Ladywell Way, Musselburgh, East Lothian EH21 6AA
Tel (031) **665 9900** Fax (031) **665 7495**
Artistic director Charles Nowosielski

Founded 1979. Seating capacity: 312. One season (August–March) of eight plays, one pantomime and late-night shows. Wide range of productions: musicals, Scots plays, new work. Average cast size of ten (including musicians). Recent productions: *Cabaret*; *The Prime of Miss Jean Brodie*; *Jungle Book*; *The Taming of the Shrew*; *The Cauldron*; *Holy Isle* (all directed by Charles Nowosielski). Hold auditions in May/June. Advertise in *SBS*, *The Stage* and Scottish national daily papers. Welcome casting queries; approach by letter only. 'Persevere with applications and know about the theatre to which you are applying to join.'

Byre Theatre Company
Byre Theatre, Abbey Street, St Andrews, Fife KY16 9LA
Tel (0334) **76288**
Artistic director Adrian Reynolds

Founded 1933. Seating capacity: 145. Produce six to seven plays annually with an average cast size of five. 'The season is structured around the variety of patrons visiting the historic town of St Andrews: May–June — small cast, middle-range work; July–August — popular entertainment; September — handsome, bigger-cast work; October — adventurous fare.' Recent productions (all directed by Adrian Reynolds): *The Miracle Worker*; *I Ought to be in Pictures*; *The Decorator*; *Absent Friends*; *Agnes of God*; *Abigail's Party*. Hold general auditions as well as casting for each production — 'some cross casting is essential, but standards have risen through more specialized casting on shorter contracts.' Occasionally advertise in *SBS*. Welcome casting queries from actors. 'A vast amount of mail lands on the artistic director's desk every day. The Byre Theatre does respond, but only if an SAE is enclosed. The Byre faces a nationwide problem: funding does not keep pace with salary increases. It is advisable to apply for auditions only when you think you are suitable for particular casting as small casts are dominant at the Byre each year and may get smaller!' Occasionally do theatre-in-education work based on project funding.

Comment
This tiny theatre started life as a cow byre and was converted into an amateur theatre in 1933. During the war, it was taken over by a small professional company, and in 1969, the old Byre was demolished and the present purpose-built theatre was established.

Churchill Theatre Trust Ltd
Churchill Theatre, High Street, Bromley, Kent BR1 1HA
Tel (01) **464 7131**
Director Nick Salmon

Founded 1977. Seating capacity: 760. Three seasons of approximately three months each. Annually produce eight to ten plays plus a pantomime with occasional tours. Cast size ranges between four to 12 (more for musicals). Recent productions: *King's Rhapsody* (directed by Kim Grant); *Oklahoma!* (Eoin McManus); *Dangerous Obsession* (Roger Smith); *Dangerous Corner* (Leon Rubin); *Time and Time Again* (Christopher Renshaw); *See How They Run* (Leslie Lawton); *Blithe Spirit* and *Something to Hide* (John David); *Time and the Conways* (Keith Baxter). Sometimes advertise in *The Stage* when producing musicals. Hold general auditions and also see people for individual productions.

Citizens Company
Citizens Theatre, Gorbals, Glasgow G5 9DS
Tel (041) **429 5561**
Artistic directors Giles Havergal, Philip Prowse, Robert David MacDonald

Founded 1945. Seating capacity: 641. Three seasons — spring, summer, autumn/winter — of approximately three months each. Ten plays (British and European classics) produced annually with an average cast size of ten. Recent productions: *No Man's Land* (directed by Giles Havergal); *Lady Windermere's Fan* (directed & designed by Philip Prowse); *Joan of Arc* (Robert David MacDonald). Cast for each production. Do not advertise for actors, but welcome casting queries in the form of a letter and photograph.

Theatre About Glasgow company (*see* Young people's theatre companies).

Comment
An internationally renowned theatre with low seat prices and a good, hard-hitting repertoire of unusual, high-quality plays. Contemporary drama, little-known classics and European works make up the rich and varied programme.

Civic Theatre
Fairfield Road, Chelmsford, Essex CM1 1JH
Tel (Newpalm Productions) (01) **349 0802**
Artistic director John Newman

Fortnightly rep performed by Newpalm Productions since 1970. Season of ten plays (including pantomime and children's show) from October to May, with an average cast size of nine. Seating capacity: 512. Recent productions: *Jesus Christ Superstar* (directed by John Dryden); *A Day in the Death of Joe Egg*; *And Then There Were None*; *One for the Road*. Do not hold general auditions and do not advertise for actors as most of the company taken from Newpalm touring productions (*see* Independent managements). Will file details and photographs, but do not reply to query letters due to pressure of work.

Contact Theatre Company

Oxford Road, Manchester M15 6JA
Tel (061) **274 3434**
Artistic director Anthony Clark

Founded 1972. Seating capacity: 300. Between seven to nine plays produced between September and July, rehearsing for three weeks and playing for 3–4 weeks. Average cast size of ten. Classics, plays with music and a lot of new works. Recent productions: *The Caucasian Chalk Circle* and *Translations* (directed by John Ginman); *Homeland* (Anthony Clark); *Stigg of the Dump* (Richard Williams). General auditions held in November and May. Try to cross cast as much as possible. Do not advertise for actors, but welcome casting queries. Write, enclosing CV, photograph and SAE. 'We always reply to those people who send an SAE. We keep the information on file, up-dating each year, and refer to our files on a regular basis.'

Studio theatre: seating capacity 60. Used by the company's youth theatre, but it is hoped that in-house productions may be staged there in the future.

Comment
Although Contact's brief is to be a young people's theatre, its reputation extends far beyond that as a result of such productions of award-winning plays as Charlotte Keatley's *My Mother Said I Never Should* (George Devine award) and premières of plays by locally based writers. Also noted for its regular inclusion of Brecht plays in its repertoire – Anthony Clark describes the University Theatre, Contact's home, as 'made for Brecht'.

Crucible Theatre Trust Ltd

55 Norfolk Street, Sheffield S1 1DA
Tel (0742) **760621**
Artistic director Clare Venables
Associate director Mike Kay

Founded 1971. Seating capacity: 1000. Two seasons: September to March and May to July; eight productions annually. Recent productions: *The Importance of Being Earnest* (directed by Clare Venables); *Of Mice and Men* and *Cinderella* (Mike Kay); *The Winter's Tale* (Steven Pimlott); *The Park* (Steven Pimlott with Clare Venables); *The Cherry Orchard* (Clare Venables with Steven Pimlott); *Wuthering Heights* (Jane Collins); *Gregory's Girl* (Mike Kay & Phil Clark). Cast for each production. Do not advertise for actors, but welcome letter with full CV and photograph. Write to Nicholas Horsey (casting director).

Studio theatre with seating capacity of 150–200, producing wide range of productions, favouring new plays and modern work. Four to six plays annually ('depending on grants'). Recent productions: *Out with a Bang* (Bob Eaton); *The True Story of the Titanic* (Stephen Daldry); *The Event* (Martin Duncan); *American Buffalo* (Mike Kay).

TIE company (*see* entry for 'Sheffield Crucible Theatre-in-Education Company' in Theatre-in-Education companies).

Comment
Possibly for economic reasons, the Crucible's programming has become increasingly conservative. However, the studio theatre continues to produce new and challenging work. With its two restaurants, wine bar, exhibitions and televized snooker, the theatre is an essential part of Sheffield life.

Derby Playhouse Company

Derby Playhouse, Theatre Walk, Eagle Centre, Derby DE1 2NF
Tel (0332) **363271**
Artistic director Annie Castledine
Associate director Susan Todd

Seating capacity: 500. A season of nine plays, produced between September and June, with a strong emphasis on European design. Recent productions: *Gaslight* (directed by Susan Todd); *The Children's Hour* and *Sunday's Children* (Annie Castledine). Cast from a 'known pool' of actors; do not advertise. Do not welcome casting queries.

Studio theatre with a seating capacity of 75+. Three new plays annually.

TIE company (*see* Theatre-in-Education companies).

Duke's Playhouse

Moor Lane, Lancaster LA1 1QE
Tel (0524) **67461**
Artistic director Ian Forrest

Founded 1971. Seating capacity: 300. One season from October to April, with a season of open-air theatre ('Summer Park') from June to August. Four plays (including pantomime) in the main season, with an average cast size of seven. Recent productions: *Dracula, Aladdin, Othello* and *When I Was a Girl, I Used to Scream and Shout* (all directed by Ian Forrest); *Woman in Mind* (open-air production). Hold general auditions each summer — through casting as much as possible. Do not advertise, but welcome casting queries from actors. Approach in writing in the first instance, enclosing CV, photograph and SAE.

Studio theatre: Theatre-in-the-round. Seating capacity: 176. Production policy currently under review. Productions have included: *Alice through the Looking Glass* (Ian Forrest) and *As You Like It* (Jonathan Petherbridge).

TIE company (*see* Theatre-in-Education companies).

Dundee Repertory Theatre

Tay Square, Dundee DD1 1PB
Tel (0382) **27684**
Artistic director Robert Robertson
Associate directors Cliff Burnett & Neil Murray

Founded 1939 (new theatre opened 1982). Seating capacity: 450. Autumn and spring seasons (August to April) with four productions each season plus a pantomime. Broad spectrum of productions, including new plays. Recent productions: *The Hound of the Baskervilles* (directed by Cliff Burnett); *Sweeny Todd* and *Beauty and the Beast* (Neil Murray); *Blithe Spirit* (Cliff Burnett); *Still Life* (Robert Robertson). Hold general auditions in May/June (one week in London and one week in Scotland). Do not advertise, but welcome casting queries from actors. Approach in writing in the first instance, enclosing, CV, photograph and SAE. 'We keep details on file, and the director looks through them in May when compiling the audition list. We also feel an entry in *Spotlight* is essential to an actor.'

Everyman Theatre

Regent Street, Cheltenham, Glos. GL50 1HQ
Tel (0242) **512515**
Artistic director John Doyle (until Spring 1989)

Re-opened in 1986 after a £2.5 million refit. Seating capacity: 680. Autumn and spring seasons, with approximately five productions each season. Average cast size of eight to ten. Wide range of productions including musicals and new drama. Recent productions: *The Crucible* and *Sweeny Todd* (directed by John Doyle); *The Rivals* (John Durnin); *Acts of Kindness* (Graham Berowne); *Harvey* (Terry Wale). Very occasionally hold general auditions, but usually specific casting. The autumn 1988 season consisted of a permanent company of actors. Sometimes advertise in *SBS* and Equity *Job Grapevine*. Welcome casting queries from actors. Write in the first instance, enclosing CV, photograph and SAE.

Studio theatre: The Richardson Studio. Seating capacity of 50/60. Emphasis on alternative drama. Recent productions: *Crimes of the Heart* (John Doyle), *The Duchess of Malfi* (John Durnin) and Ted Hughes' adaptation of Seneca's *Oedipus*.

Everyman Theatre
Hope Street, Liverpool L1 9BH
Tel (051) **708 0338**
Artistic director John Doyle

Founded 1964. Seating capacity: 402. Three seasons from October to June/July; five or six plays with an average cast size of 13. A wide range of productions. Recent productions: *Hamlet* and *The Winter's Tale* (directed by Glen Walford); *The Three Sisters* and *Entertaining Mr Sloane* (Kevin Robinson); *The Hunchback of Notre Dame* (Graham Callan); *Cinderella and Her Rocking Feller* (Peter Rowe). Mostly cast for each individual production. Rarely advertise for actors, but welcome casting queries. Write in the first instance, enclosing CV and photograph, and SAE if reply required.

Comment
The Everyman has established itself as an important community theatre presenting new and challenging work. Local writers and actors have always been encouraged, and it was the starting point for the famous four — Alan Bleasdale, Chris Bond, Bill Morrison and Willy Russell — who then moved down the road to liven up the Liverpool Playhouse. John Doyle's production policy for the Everyman was not known at the time of writing.

Farnham Repertory Co. Ltd
Redgrave Theatre, Brightwells, Farnham, Surrey GU9 7SB
Tel (0252) **727000**
Artistic director Graham Watkins

Seating capacity: 362. Produce 13/14 plays throughout the year, with an average cast size of eight to nine. Recent productions: *Corpse* (directed by Gerald Moon); *The Glass Menagerie*, *A Taste of Honey*, *Woman in Mind* and *The Snow Queen* (Graham Watkins). Cast for each production, and also hold general auditions. Do not advertise for actors, but will consider letters ('preferably specific queries relating to productions we are planning — i.e. suggest yourself for a specific part ... Enclose an SAE or we cannot reply').

Studio theatre with a seating capacity of 45. 'Rarely used due to financial restrictions.'

TIE company: 'specifically formed once or twice a year for schools tours.'

Gateway Theatre
Hamilton Place, Chester CH1 2BH
Tel (0244) **44238**
Artistic director Phil Partridge
Associate director Laurence Honeyford

Founded 1968. Seating capacity: 440. Autumn season of three plays plus a tour; spring season of four plays plus a tour; Christmas show and summer show.

Produce classics, new writing and populist contemporary work. Average cast size of seven. Recent productions: *Made in Bangkok*, *The Tempest* and *Teddy Bear's Picnic* (directed by Phil Partridge); *Revelations* and *Educating Rita* (Laurence Honeyford); *Dick Whittington* (Peter Fieldson). Advertise occasionally in *SBS*. Welcome casting queries from actors. 'We prefer always to be contacted by letter, and like many theatres, only reply to an SAE, though it is usually a printed note. We *do* consider *every* letter, and see actors if it's possible and useful. We advise brief letters, small photos and *clear* CVs.'

Studio theatre with a seating capacity of 50, which takes incoming tours plus productions by the main-house company. Ten plays annually with an average cast size of four. Recent productions: *Stains upon the Silence* (Tranter Theatre; directed by Padraig Tolan); *Christie in Love* (Vox Company; Dave Bond); *All Quiet on the Western Front* (Pentabus; Peter McCann).

No TIE company, but do co-productions with Action Transport Theatre Company.

Graham Players

Civic Theatre, Craigie Road, Ayr, Ayrshire KA8 0EZ
Tel (0292) **263755**
Artistic director Victor Graham
Associate director Suzanne Jeffries

Founded 1956. Seating capacity: 350. Summer seasons of two-weekly rep (weekly until last year); 14-week season of comedies and drama. Company of six to nine actors. Recent productions: *On Golden Pond*, *Duet for One*, *How's the World Treating You?*, *Educating Rita* and *Season's Greetings* (all directed by Suzanne Jeffries). Do not advertise, but welcome casting queries from actors. Applications for the general auditions, held in London in May every year, should be made by letter in March.

Grand Theatre

Singleton Street, Swansea SA1 3QJ
Tel (0792) **475242**
Artistic director (temporary) Brian Sullivan

Seating capacity: 1021. Repertory (two weekly) of four productions annually, plus eight-week pantomime season. Average cast size of eight. Recent productions: *Deadly Nightcap* and *Arsenic and Old Lace* (directed by Simon Whitfield); *The Man* and *Boeing Boeing* (Mark Woolgar). Hold general auditions as well as casting for each production. Do not advertise for actors, but welcome written casting queries.

Greenwich Theatre

Crooms Hill, Greenwich, London SE10 8ES
Tel (01) **858 4447**
Artistic director Sue Dunderdale

Founded 1969. Seating capacity: 426. One season: October to July. 1988/89 productions: *The Millionairess* (directed by Penny Cherns); *The Woman in White*, *Othello* and *Apocalyptic Butterflies* (Sue Dunderdale); *Himself* (Bill Bryden). Also community play in July, written and presented by the local community. Do not hold general auditions as they cast play by play. Do not advertise but will keep letters and actors' details on file. Enclose CV and photograph.

Hampstead Theatre ● *See* Fringe and Alternative Theatre

Harrogate Theatre Company

Harrogate Theatre, Oxford Street, Harrogate, N. Yorks. HG1 1QF
Tel (0423) **502710**
Artistic director Andrew Manley

Founded 1900. Seating capacity: 476. Season of nine to ten plays from September to the end of April; from classical to modern plays, plus musicals. Average cast size of nine. Recent productions: *The Secret Diary of Adrian Mole* (directed by Peter Fieldson); *An Ideal Husband*, *The Rivals*, *Nora*, *Woman in Mind*, *The Normal Heart*, *Piaf* and *The Midsummer Gathering* (Andrew Manley). 'Usually hold general auditions in June or July, and perhaps again in December. Best to write before these times. There is a high degree of permanency in the company, though there is some casting for each production.'

Studio theatre with a seating capacity of 50, which is used by visiting companies, local colleges and amateurs.

TIE company (*see* Theatre-in-Education companies).

Haymarket Theatre

Belgrave Gate, Leicester LE1 3YQ
Tel (0533) **530021**
Artistic director Peter Lichtenfels
Associate director Chris Ellis

Founded 1972. Seating capacity: 752. Productions throughout the year. Recent productions: *Julius Caesar* and *Creon* (directed by John Dexter); *Oh What a Lovely War* (Tim Supple); *French without Tears* (Simon Usher); *Easter* (David Leveaux). No general auditions; specific casting only. Sometimes advertise in *SBS*. Prefer to deal with agents, but will consider letters from actors (an SAE does *not* guarantee a reply).

Studio theatre: seating capacity 150. In-house and touring productions throughout the year. Recent productions: *The Broken Heart* and *Timon of Athens* (Simon Usher); *The Last Supper* (co-production with The Wrestling School; Kenny Ireland); *Crimes of Passion* (Youth theatre production: Keith Boak).

Youth theatre: Tim Supple (director). Workshops and productions with local young people aged 8–18.

Horseshoe Theatre Company

The Shrubbery, Cliddesden Road, Basingstoke RG21 3ER
Tel (0256) **55844**
Artistic director Ian Mullins
Associate director Kit Thacker

Founded 1974. Seating capacity: 420. Autumn and spring seasons (September to May) with seven plays. A balanced and contrasting programme with cast size ranging from two to 13 actors. Recent productions: *Busman's Honeymoon* and *Pluck'd in a Far-off Land* (directed by Ian Mullins); *The Real Thing* (Kit Thacker). Do not advertise for actors – 'no need to, we get more applications than we can cope with.' Approach in writing (enclosing SAE) in the first instance.

Studio theatre: Queen Mary's 6th Form College run the Central Studio, with Gareth Thomas as artistic director. Seating capacity: 100+. Two productions annually with an average cast size of five. Recent productions: *Master Harold ... and the Boys* and *Who Killed Hilda Murrell?* (Kit Thacker).

No TIE company – 'but we have done a few sessions with schools as a special request.'

Stephen Joseph Theatre-in-the-Round (Scarborough Theatre Trust Ltd)

Valley Bridge, Scarborough, N. Yorks. YO11 2PL
Tel (0723) **370540**
Artistic director Alan Ayckbourn

Founded in 1955 by Stephen Joseph as the Studio Theatre Co. Seating capacity: 307. One season from June to January, sometimes followed by a tour. Approximately eight main house productions, plus two studio lunchtime shows and one studio late-night show. Average case size of eight. Comedy, drama, farce; considerable output of new work; classics plus some European drama. Recent productions: *All My Sons, Serjeant Musgrave's Dance* and *Can't Pay? Won't Pay!* (directed by Robin Herford); *Bröntes of Haworth* and *The Parasol* (Alan Ayckbourn); plus world premières of Alan Ayckbourn's plays directed by the author. Hold general auditions — 'like to cast through three months at a time'. Do not advertise for actors: 'We don't object to casting queries from actors, but we are inundated with applications and it is impossible to see everyone who contacts us.' Contact Michele Tidy (casting director) by letter with CV, photograph and SAE. 'We cannot afford to reply to people who do not enclose an SAE.'

Studio theatre situated in restaurant area, with a seating capacity of 100. Produce 3–4 in-house plays annually, with an average cast size of 2–5. Musical revues, full-length plays, one-act plays, one-man shows, Punch & Judy, concerts (pop and classical). Recent productions: *Bar & Ger* (directed by Stephen Mallatratt); *The Woman in Black* (Robin Herford); *The Haunt of Mr Fossett* (Alan Ayckbourn).

Comment
Stephen Joseph first pioneered the American idea of 'theatre-in-the-round' in 1955 at the public library in Scarborough. The aim was to create a writers' theatre — a concept that was greeted with much suspicion by the diehards, who firmly believed that writers should be kept at a good distance. It was as a result of this policy of encouraging bright young writers that Alan Ayckbourn, an erstwhile stage manager and actor, wrote and had his first play produced in 1959. Full seasons were not possible at the library in the early years, so Joseph took his company on tour, travelling the country with his theatre-in-the-round. It was not until 1976, nine years after his death, that the company found a permanent home in the Municipal School, Scarborough.

Leeds Playhouse

Calverley Street, Leeds, W. Yorks. LS2 3AJ
Tel (0532) **442141**
Artistic director John Harrison

Founded 1971. Seating capacity: 721. Autumn and spring seasons, five plays per season, with an average cast size of 10–12. Varied range of productions — classics, comedies and new plays. Recent productions: *Intimate Exchanges* (directed by Angie Langfield); *Coloured* (John Harrison); *London Assurance* (Tim Luscombe); *The Gingerbread Man* (Rex Doyle); *The Little Foxes* (Helena Kaut-Howson). Hold general auditions twice yearly (February & August) in London, plus locally once a year. Do not advertise for actors, but welcome casting queries. Approach in writing in the first instance, enclosing CV, photograph and SAE.

TIE company (*see* Theatre-in-Education companies).

Comment
Work is underway on the West Yorkshire Playhouse, which will house the Leeds Playhouse company from 1990. The new artistic director Jude Kelly, will take over from John Harrison at that time.

Library Theatre Company

Library Theatre, St Peter's Square, Manchester M2 5PD
Tel (061) **236 9422**
and Forum Theatre, Leningrad Square, Wythenshawe M22 5RT
Artistic director Christopher Honer
Associate director Roger Haines

Seating capacity: 308 (Library), 483 (Forum). Season at the Library: September
to April (7 plays); Forum: October to June (5 plays). Wide range of productions
including new plays, musicals, contemporary drama, some classics, plus pantomime and children's shows at Christmas. Recent productions: (*Library Theatre*)
Greek (directed by Paul Kerryson); *Tom and Viv* (Christopher Honer); (*Forum
Theatre*) *Ain't Misbehavin'* (Roger Haines); *Soapbox* (Kay Patrick). Only advertise
if looking for actors with specialist skills. Welcome written casting queries. 'The
directors try to see a number of actors every year for a general audition, but most
of the casting is done play by play.'

Comment

Housed in the basement of the Central Library, this was the first theatre in Britain to be
funded from the public purse and opened in 1934. The Forum Theatre opened in the
mid-1970s as a sister theatre to the Library Theatre. Both theatres offer a distinctive
rep programme with an emphasis on new and unusual plays.

Liverpool Playhouse

Williamson Square, Liverpool L1 1EL
Tel (051) **709 8478**
Artistic director Ian Kellgren
Associate director Kate Rowland

Founded 1911. Seating capacity: 758. One season (September to May/June)
with six productions. A wide-ranging season including comedies, classics, musicals
and new plays. Recent productions: *Arsenic and Old Lace, Macbeth* and *Camelot*
(directed by Ian Kellgren); *Of Mice and Men* (Julian Webber); *Crimes of the
Heart* and *Journeyman Jack* (Kate Rowland). Audition for each show in London,
plus general auditions in Liverpool in the summer. Occasionally advertise in *SBS*.
Welcome casting queries from actors. Write in the first instance, enclosing CV,
photograph and SAE.

Studio theatre: seating capacity 100. production plans under review.

Comment

This is the oldest surviving repertory theatre in the country. Having started life in 1866
as the Star Music Hall, it became a rep theatre in 1911. The original stucco exterior still
survives, but in 1968, a drum-like extension — housing restaurant, bars and workshops
— was added, offering a stark contrast to the Victorian elegance of the old music hall
architecture. In March 1988, the Arts Council cut the Playhouse grant (as well as that
of the Everyman) by 5 per cent because the local council refused to meet its funding
responsibilities.

Lyceum Company

Lyceum Theatre, 10 Heath Street, Crewe CW1 2BZ
Tel (0270) **215523**
Director Stephen Wischhusen (theatre proprietor)
Associate director Colin McIntyre

Founded 1911. Seating capacity: 750. One season (September to March) with
20 productions in weekly repertory. Popular drama and comedy plus some
classics. Average cast size of ten. Recent productions: *Macbeth, The Secret Diary
of Adrian Mole, One of Us* and *Cards on the Table* (directed by Colin McIntyre).

Advertise in *Rep Report* and hold general auditions. Do not welcome casting queries from actors.

Lyric Players' Theatre

55 Ridgeway Street, Stranmillis, Belfast BT9 5FB
Tel (0232) **669660**
Artistic director Roland Jaquarello

Founded 1969. Seating capacity: 305. One season (August to June/July) with usually 11 plays. Classics, comedies, new works, Belfast plays. Recent productions: *Mrs Warren's Profession* and *Culture Vultures* (directed by Roland Jaquarello); *Juno and the Paycock* and *Romanoff and Juliet* (Tom Jordan). Sometimes hold general auditions, but also cast for individual productions. Do not advertise, but welcome casting queries from actors. Approach in writing in the first instance, enclosing CV and photograph.

Lyric Theatre Hammersmith & Lyric Studio

King Street, London W6 0QL
Tel (01) **741 0824**
Artistic director Peter James

The Lyric have an original and exciting programme of new work and international plays. Produce seven to eight plays in the main house annually, and there are usually two in-house productions annually in the Studio, plus in-coming shows. Recent productions: *The House of Bernarda Alba, Faust, The Infernal Machine* and *Medea*. Subsidized rep contracts. Do not advertise for actors, but keep CVs and photographs on file for reference.

Comment
One of the best restored theatres in London (re-opened in 1979), having been originally built in 1895.

Mercury Theatre

Balkerne Gate, Colchester, Essex CO1 1PT
Tel (0206) **577006**
Artistic director Michael Winter

Founded 1972. Seating capacity: 497. Spring and autumn seasons; five productions per season plus a pantomime. Recent productions: *One for the Road, The Taming of the Shrew, Look Back in Anger* and *Dick Whittington and his Cat* (directed by Michael Winter). Hold general auditions as well as casting for individual productions. Do not usually advertise, but welcome casting queries from actors. Write enclosing CV, photograph and SAE.

Studio theatre: seating capacity approximately 65. Occasionally take in touring productions but rarely used in-house.

The Mill at Sonning (Theatre) Ltd

Sonning Eye, Reading, Berks. RG4 0TW
Tel (0734) **696039**
Artistic director Sally Hughes

Founded 1982. Seating capacity: 197. Produce nine plays (both commercial theatre and new) throughout the year, with an average cast size of six. Recent productions: *Hotel Arusha* (directed by Geoff Bullen); *Dial M for Murder* (Chris Johnston); *Romantic Comedy* (Sebastian Graham-Jones); *Sound of Murder* and *Table Manners* (Anna Barry); *Old Time Music Hall*. Cast for each production; advertise for actors in *Report* and *SBS*. Will consider casting queries from actors. Approach in writing in the first instance.

Kenneth More Theatre

Oakfield Road, Ilford, Essex IG1 1BT
Tel (01) **553 4464**
Artistic director Vivyan Ellacott

Founded 1974. Plays, musicals, opera, pantomime and studio work. Productions include: *Amadeus, Bent, Sweeny Todd, The Rocky Horror Picture Show, Don Giovanni* (all directed by Vivyan Ellacott). Do not advertise for actors, but welcome casting queries — 'by letter only. As a repertory theatre, the director is almost always in rehearsal and phone calls cannot be dealt with.' Do not hold general auditions. 'Since this theatre specializes in providing opportunities for young actors, singers and dancers very early on in their careers, there is no shortage of available artistes. The standard required is a high one, but formal drama school training is not an absolute necessity. A recommendation from someone known to us can be helpful.'

National Theatre

Upper Ground, South Bank, London SE1 9PX
Tel (01) **928 2033** Telex **297306**
Artistic director Richard Eyre
Executive director David Aukin
Casting directors Serena Hill (head of casting), Adriana Quaradeghini, Edel Musselle

Founded 1963. In 1976, the company moved from the Old Vic to its new home on the South Bank. The National houses three separate theatres: the Olivier (seating 1160), the Lyttelton (890) and the Cottesloe (400). The NT also has a Studio, based at the Old Vic Annexe, which is used as an experimental workshop for the company and to encourage new writing. Sir Peter Hall was succeeded by Richard Eyre as artistic director in September 1988.

Present a diverse repertoire embracing classics and new and neglected plays. Productions are cast from play to play with some cross casting. The casting directors occasionally hold interview sessions, but general auditions are not held. Performance notices are welcomed; the casting directors independently cover shows every night of the week. Letters and CVs from actors referring to a specific production are kept in the relevant production file for reference when casting. General letters enclosing CV and photographs are also kept on file for future reference. Actors must be full Equity members (although, on a few occasions, Equity has waived this ruling).

New Victoria Theatre

Etruria Road, Newcastle-under-Lyme, Staffs. ST5 0JG
Tel (0782) **717954**
Artistic director Peter Cheeseman
Associate director Chris Martin

The New Vic moved from Stoke-on-Trent to its new theatre-in-the-round in Newcastle-under-Lyme in 1986. Seating capacity: 665. Season from July to January, with a programme of six plays (three in repertoire). Average cast size of eight. Recent productions: *Of Mice and Men* and *Hay Fever* (directed by Bob Eaton); *Aladdin* (Chris Martin); *Blood Knot* (Peter Cheeseman). Do not hold general auditions. Actors are usually contracted for three or four productions. Do not advertise —'a lot of our actors are people who have written in with their details.' Unlikely to be able to reply even if an SAE is enclosed due to pressure of work.

Stephen Joseph Studio Theatre: seating capacity 150. Not used on a regular basis for productions.

Comment
The company was previously based at the Victoria Theatre in Stoke-on-Trent, which

was opened in 1962 under the eagle eye of Stephen Joseph, the pioneer of British theatre-in-the-round. The Vic quickly established itself as a dynamic centre with its roots firmly planted in the community. Under the direction of Peter Cheeseman, it is one of the few regional theatres that steers clear of recycled West End successes.

Northampton Repertory Players Ltd

Royal Theatre, Guildhall Road, Northampton NN1 1EA
Tel (0604) **38343**
Artistic director Michael Napier Brown

Founded 1927 (theatre built 1884). Seating capacity 426 (plus 150 in the Gallery). An average season of 11 plays, plus pantomime, from September to July. Average cast size of eight. Recent productions: *An Inspector Calls* (directed by Peter Dews); *Relatively Speaking* (Malcolm Farquhar); *Special Occasions* (Graham Callan); *To Kill a Mockingbird* (Chris Hayes); *Happy Event* and *The Subject was Roses* (Michael Napier Brown). Hold general auditions; occasionally advertise in *The Stage*. Welcome casting queries: 'write legibly and to the point, enclosing an SAE if you would like a reply.'

Studio theatre at the Derngate, situated next door to the theatre, with a seating capacity of 120. Produce 3–4 plays annually with average cast size of 2–3. Recent productions: *Kiss of the Spiderwoman* and *Statements after an Arrest under the Immorality Act* (Michael Napier Brown); *Happy Jack* (Mark Clements).

TIE company (*see* entry for 'Royal Theatre-in-Education Company' in Theatre-in-Education companies).

Comment

The Royal Theatre opened in 1884 and is a fine example of late Victorian theatre architecture. Resplendent with red plush seats, ornate boxes and an elaborate ceiling, it has been splendidly preserved.

Northcott Theatre Company

Stocker Road, Exeter EX4 4QB
Tel (0392) **56182**
Artistic director George Roman
Associate director Martin Harvey

Founded 1967. Seating capacity: 433. Between nine and ten plays produced annually, from mid-April to end of January. Wide range of productions, from musicals and serious contemporary work to classics. Recent productions: *On the Razzle*, *Monsignor Quixote* (world première) and *The Winter's Tale* (directed by George Roman); *The Wizard of Oz* and *Close of Play* (Martin Harvey). Usually hold general auditions once a year. Do not advertise for actors but welcome casting queries — 'although there is a very limited number we can see.' Approach in writing in the first instance.

Studio theatre seating up to 100, producing mainly contemporary plays (two per year with a cast size of 2–6). Recent productions: *Two-way Mirror* (George Roman); *Orphans* (Warren Hooper).

Nottingham Playhouse

Wellington Circus, Nottingham NG1 5AF
Tel (0602) **474361**
Artistic director Kenneth Alan Taylor
Associate directors Martin Jamieson

Founded 1948. Seating capacity: 685–766. Ten plays produced annually, playing for three weeks each. A wide range of productions, from Shakespeare to pantomime, with an average cast size of ten. Recent productions: *September in the Rain, To Kill a Mockingbird* and *Cinderella* (directed by Kenneth Alan Taylor); *Prisoners* and *The Act* (Martin Jamieson); *Death of a Salesman* (Richard Frost); *Larkrise to Candleford* (Richard Frost). Rarely advertise for actors. Cast for each production, holding specific and general auditions in London and Nottingham. Will consider letters from actors: 'Always enclose photo, CV and SAE with first application.'

Do not have a studio theatre, but 'do studio productions in small venue directed by the three directors of the main company.'·

TIE company (*see* entry for 'Roundabout Theatre Company' in Theatre-in-Education companies).

Nuffield Theatre
University Road, Southampton SO9 5NH
Tel (0703) **671871**
Artistic director Patrick Sandford

Founded 1964. Seating capacity: 506. Autumn/spring season, with occasional late spring and early summer productions. Approximately seven plays, plus a Christmas show each year. Recent productions: *Rhinoceros, Swallows and Amazons* (adapted by Denise Deegan) and *The Beaux Stratagem* (directed by Patrick Sandford). Do not, as a rule, hold general auditions; occasionally advertise for actors. Welcome casting queries; write enclosing CV and photograph, and SAE if a reply is required.

TIE: hoping to start a company in the not-too-distant future.

Comment
This lively rep company has a reputation for producing new plays, modern American classics and European plays not previously seen in the UK. A number of shows transfer to London's West End. *Daisy Pulls It Off* was the most successful recent transfer.

Octagon Theatre
Howell Croft South, Bolton, Lancs. BL1 1SB
Tel (0204) **29407**
Artistic director Andrew Hay
Associate director Romy Baskerville

Founded 1967. Seating capacity: 350–420 (flexible). Two seasons – spring and autumn; four plays per season. Average cast size of 10/11. New plays, musicals. Recent productions include: *In the Midnight Hour* and *Road* (directed by Andrew Hay); *Cricket at Camp David* and *No Worries* (Romy Baskerville). Do not usually hold general auditions; try to through cast. Occasionally advertise in *The Stage*. Welcome casting queries: approach in writing in the first instance. 'Although we get swamped with letters, we do try to reply to them all if an SAE is enclosed.'

Studio theatre: seating capacity 100. Takes in touring productions.

Youth theatre: Simon Stallworthy (director). For local children. Two groups: 11–13 and 14–18 years old. Two or three performances each year in the studio theatre.

Oldham Coliseum
Fairbottom Street, Oldham, Lancs. OL1 3SW
Tel (061) **624 1731**
Artistic director Paul Kerryson

Founded 1887 (theatre), 1978 (company). Seating capacity: 564. Season from September to June, comprising eight plays and one pantomime. Wide range of productions — new plays, northern classics, musicals. Average cast size of ten. Recent productions: *Twelfth Night* and *Educating Rita* (directed by John Retallack); *Stage Fright* and *The Threepenny Opera* (Paul Elkins); *The Steamie* (Renata Allen). Cast for each production, but also hold general auditions. Do not advertise for actors but welcome casting queries. Approach in writing in the first instance. 'We receive thousands and answer all, but no theatre favours an initial approach by phone. Try to explain your particular interest in a specific company or play rather than "Dear Sir ..."'

Palace Theatre
Clarendon Road, Watford WD1 1JZ
Tel (0923) **35455**
Artistic director Lou Stein

Founded 1908. Seating capacity: 663. Autumn season: September to December. Spring season: January to May. Nine plays annually with average cast size of seven to eight. Produce new adaptations of classics, musicals, comedy and specially commissioned works. Recent productions: *Madame Bovary*, *The Price* and *Winter in the Morning* (directed by Lou Stein); *Mary Rose* (Matthew Francis). Cast for each production; occasionally advertise in *The Stage*. Welcome casting queries from actors, either by telephone or in writing.

TIE company (*see* entry for 'Watford Palace Theatre in Education' in Theatre-in-Education companies).

Comment
This superb Edwardian theatre often takes on the West End at its own game and wins.

Palace Theatre
London Road, Westcliff-on-Sea, Essex SS0 9LA
Tel (0702) **347816**
Artistic director Christopher Dunham

Seating capacity: 500. Autumn/winter and spring seasons, and occasionally one in the summer. Recent productions: *It Runs in the Family*, *The Lion, the Witch and the Wardrobe* and *The Unexpected Guest*. Do not hold general auditions. Do not welcome query letters: 'we are inundated with them.'

Studio theatre and TIE company (*see* Theatre-in-Education companies).

Perth Repertory Theatre
185 High Street, Perth PH1 5UW
Tel (0738) **38123**
Artistic director Joan Knight OBE

Founded 1935. Seating capacity: 470. Produce ten plays, plus a traditional pantomime, each year between August and May. Average cast size of ten. Recent productions: *Stepping Out*, *Hobson's Choice* and *Passage to India* (directed by Joan Knight); *Benefactors* (Liz Carruthers); *Pravda* (Patrick Sandford); *Pirates of Penzance* (Clive Perry). General auditions usually held in June. Do not advertise, but welcome casting queries from actors. Approach in writing in the first instance. 'Perth Theatre has a policy of employing mainly Scottish, or Scottish-based, actors.'

Studio theatre with a seating capacity of 100. Produce two plays annually with an average cast size of four. Recent productions: *The Caretaker* (John Buick); *Precarious Living* (Colette O'Neill).

Pitlochry Festival Theatre

Port-na-Craig, Pitlochry, Perthshire PH16 5DR
Tel (0796) **3054**
Artistic director Clive Perry

Founded 1951. Seating capacity: 544. Season (repertoire) of six plays, May–October. Average company of 22/25 actors. 1988 season: *Pygmalion*, *See How They Run* and *Woman in Mind* (directed by Clive Perry); *When We Are Married* (Joan Knight); *Pride and Prejudice* (Michael Meacham); *Daphne Laureola* (Bill Pryde). Auditions held each January in London, plus additional auditions in Edinburgh in mid-February. A lot of cross casting, and actors must be prepared to accept a seven-month contract (rehearsals begin mid-March). Do not advertise, but welcome letters with CVs and photographs at the end of the year.

Queen's Theatre

Billet Lane, Hornchurch, Essex RM11 1QT
Tel (04024) **56118**
Artistic director Bob Tomson

Founded 1954. Seating capacity: 506. Four/five weekly rep from September to June plus national tours, West End transfers and ten-week pantomime. Eight plays annually with an average cast size of ten. Recent productions: *Blood Brothers* – national tour/West End transfer; *A Midsummer Night's Dream*; *One Careful Owner* – world première musical; *Stags and Hens* and *Tom Thumb* – world première (directed by Bob Tomson); *It's A Madhouse* – national tour (Kenneth Alan Taylor); *Are You Lonesome Tonight?* – national tour (Bill Kenwright). Do not hold general auditions. Cross cast, but 'not longer than two productions because of tax code laws'. Try to employ from within a 25-mile radius. Do not advertise but welcome casting queries from actors. Write in the first instance enclosing CV, photograph and SAE. Bob Tomson particularly looks for actors with varied skills, e.g. circus skills. 'Since the Arts Council withdrew funding four years ago, the company has to earn seventy per cent of its costs (thirty per cent coming from local government and Greater London Arts). Productions tend to be populist therefore and usually contemporary.'

Royal Exchange Theatre Company

Royal Exchange, St Ann's Square, Manchester M2 7DH
Tel (061) **833 9333**
Artistic directors Gregory Hersov, James Maxwell, Braham Murray, Casper Wrede
Associate directors Nicholas Hytner, Ian McDiarmid, Sophie Marshall

Founded 1973 (formerly 69 Theatre Co., founded 1968). Seating capacity: 730. Produce eight to ten plays annually between September and August, with runs of 2½–6½ weeks. Plays range from Shakespeare, Shaw and Chekhov to modern playwrights such as Iain Heggie and Jonathan Moore. Recent productions: *Twelfth Night* (directed by Braham Murray); *Loot* (Paul Unwin); *Don Carlos* (Nicholas Hytner); *All My Sons* (Gregory Hersov); *Don Juan* (Ian McDiarmid). Do not advertise for actors, but season details are mailed to agents, *PCR* and *Job Grapevine*. Each production is cast separately. Will consider letters from actors, but 'please leave time for us to read them before ringing to check they have arrived! We only keep CVs and photos on file if they are likely to be relevant to our casting over subsequent months – otherwise, we would have thousands of out-of-date CVs and drawers too full to cope with. If actors send an SAE, we will reply eventually.' Letters should be addressed to the casting director: Sophie Marshall.

Comment
This is one of the country's foremost producing theatres, featuring a mixture of classics, revivals and new work. With top names and quality productions, a number of plays end up in London's West End.

Royal Lyceum Theatre Company
Royal Lyceum Theatre, Grindlay Street, Edinburgh EH3 9AX
Tel (031) **229 7404** Fax (031) **228 3955**
Artistic director Ian Wooldridge
Associate director Hugh Hodgart

Founded 1965. Seating capacity: 773. Three seasons — autumn, spring and summer. Four plays in each, plus Christmas show. Classics, new Scottish plays, translations and adaptations. Average cast size of 11. Recent productions: *Hobson's Choice* (Ian Wooldridge); *Shadow of a Gunman* (Hugh Hodgart); *As You Like It* (Hamish Glen). Do not advertise, but welcome casting queries from actors. Approach in writing in the first instance. 'We cast for each production, but also hold auditions for Scottish-based actors when time allows.'

Royal National Theatre ●*See* National Theatre in Repertory/Regional Theatre section

Royal Shakespeare Company
Barbican Theatre, Barbican Centre, London EC2Y 8DS and Royal Shakespeare Theatre, Stratford-upon-Avon, Warwicks. CV37 6BB
Tel (01) **628 3351** (Barbican Theatre) Fax (01) **628 6247**
Artistic director Terry Hands

The Royal Shakespeare Company has two centres. At Stratford is the Royal Shakespeare Theatre (seating 1500) and the Swan Theatre (400); the Other Place is currently closed for rebuilding until 1990. In London, there is the Barbican Theatre (seating 1162) and The Pit (200).

Apart from its Shakespeare productions, the RSC has a commitment to new plays and new writers. Only Shakespeare's plays are presented at the Royal Shakespeare Theatre, but at the Swan Theatre, recent productions have ranged from plays by contemporaries of Shakespeare to the work of Edward Bond. In London, recent productions have ranged from works of Marlow to that of Howard Brenton. An actor's life within the company usually starts in Stratford and then transfers to London. A number of new plays are added to the London season which means that some additional actors join the company according to production requirements. Until now, contracts have been for two years (one year in Stratford and one year in London), but this may change in the near future.

Do not hold general auditions. Actors are invited to audition after a casting director or director has seen their work. Welcome CVs, photographs and performance notices. Advise making contact around Christmas time when casting for the new season at Stratford commences. Correspondence should be addressed to Siobhan Bracke (casting director) at the Barbican Theatre.

Salisbury Playhouse
Malthouse Lane, Salisbury, Wilts. SP2 7RA
Tel (0722) **20117**
Artistic director David Horlock

Founded 1976. Seating capacity: 516. One season from September to July with 10–11 productions. Recent productions: *Wuthering Heights, Habeus Corpus* and *Aladdin* (directed by David Horlock); *The Day After the Fair* (Lynn Wyse); *Not Now Darling* (Michael Stroud). Do not hold general auditions. Try to cross cast as much as possible. Do not advertise for actors, but happy to receive enquiry letters enclosing CV, photograph and SAE. Details are kept on file for a certain period of time.

Salberg Studio Theatre: seating capacity 100. In-house and touring companies. Approximately 12 productions from September to July. Tend to use visiting directors. Recent productions: *Entertaining Mr Sloan* (Hugh Walters); *Stevie* (Millstream Touring Co.); *One of Us* (Sue Wilson).

TIE company (*see* Theatre-in-Education companies).

Sherman Theatre
Senghennydd Road, Cardiff CF2 4YE
Tel (0222) **396844**
Artistic director Mike James

Founded 1974. Seating capacity: 472. Autumn and spring seasons; approximately seven to eight plays annually. Take in touring productions as well as touring their own shows. Recent productions: *Intimate Exchanges* (directed by Kit Thacker); *A Streetcar Named Desire* (Mike James); *Gigi* (co-production with Torch Theatre, Milford Haven; Ian Granville Bell). Do not hold general auditions; cast per show. Sometimes advertise in *SBS* and Equity *Job Grapevine*. Welcome casting queries; write with CV and photograph. 'We keep details on file and always refer to them when casting.' Send SAE if acknowledgement required.

Arena Theatre – studio space seating 150/160. Touring and a number of in-house productions. Recent productions: *True West* (Mike James).

Hold workshops and summer schools for local youngsters. Education officer: Jane Oliver.

Swan Theatre
The Moors, Worcester WR1 3EF
Tel (0905) **726969**
Artistic director Pat Trueman
Assistant director Paul Newham

Founded 1963. Seating capacity: 350. One season: August to March. Six productions plus a Christmas show. Average cast size of ten. Broad range of productions. Recent productions: *Entertaining Strangers* and *The School for Wives* (Pat Trueman); *Woman in Mind* (Peter Fieldson). Sometimes hold general auditions. Do not advertise for actors. Welcome casting queries; write enclosing CV, photograph and SAE.

Studio theatre: not currently in use.

Theatr Clwyd
County Civic Centre, Mold, Clwyd CH7 1YA
Tel (0352) **56331**
Artistic director Toby Robertson

Founded 1978. Seating capacity: 530–570 (flexible staging). Spring, autumn and winter seasons plus a summer festival. Approximately 10–12 productions (including studio theatre). Wide range of productions, including a lot of new work. Recent productions: *The Revenger's Tragedy* (directed by Toby Robertson); *Treasure Island* (Roger Haines); *Paris Match* (Roger Smith). Do not hold general auditions but hoping to do so in the future. Cast from show to show, with some cross casting. Do not advertise for actors. Approach in writing, enclosing CV, photograph and SAE ('although sometimes it is impossible to respond to query letters due to pressure of work').

Emlyn Williams Theatre: flexible studio space with a seating capacity of 160–250. Recent productions: *Night Must Fall* (Sue Wilson); *Captain Carvallo* (Toby Robertson).

TIE company: have close ties with Cwmni Theatr Outreach Theatre Company (*see* Theatre-in-Education companies).

Comment

Dynamic company producing a broad spectrum of shows from the classics to challenging world premières (1989 sees an adaptation of Kingsley Amis' novel, *The Old Devils*), which frequently transfer to London's West End.

Theatre Royal

King Street, Bristol BS1 4ED
Tel (0272) **277466**
Artistic director Paul Unwin

One of the country's oldest theatres, built in 1766. Seating capacity: 645. Autumn and spring seasons, with four plays per season. Production policy has been revised since Paul Unwin took over as artistic director in 1988. The autumn season last year was launched with a community production of *A Town in the West Country*, in which 150 local people took part. Other recent productions: *Look Back in Anger* (directed by Steve Unwin); *The School for Scandal* (Les Waters); *The Three Musketeers* (adapted by David Pownall; Paul Unwin). Do not hold general auditions and do not advertise for actors: 'We cast from *Spotlight*.' Welcome casting queries; write in the first instance, enclosing CV, photograph and SAE.

New Vic Studio: seating capacity is flexible, with a maximum of 200. Emphasis on new plays. Recent productions: *Bag Lady* (Jude Kelly); *Inventing a New Colour* (Phyllida Lloyd); *Rag Doll* (Terry Johnston); *The Little Prince* (Steve Woodward).

Theatre Royal & The Drum

Royal Parade, Plymouth, Devon PL1 2TR
Tel (0752) **668282**
Artistic director Roger Redfarn

'We do not run a permanent company. The majority of main-house productions are done in conjunction with commercial managements (*see* Non-producing theatres). Drum Theatre Productions — the studio company — occasionally tour. We rarely hold general auditions because of the very nature of our work, and for large-scale musical productions, we always hold open auditions, which are advertised in *The Stage*. We are always anxious to hear of actors who live in the West Country or have a West Country background.'

Thorndike Theatre

Church Street, Leatherhead, Surrey KT22 8DF
Tel (0372) **376211**
Artistic director Roger Clissold

Founded 1969. Seating capacity: 526. Each year is divided into two seasons of five or six months — i.e. January to June and August to December. Thirteen productions plus studio work, YPT, TIE and occasional Sunday shows. A wide range of productions including West End transfers ('Regrettably, we are not able to build on our studio work record'). Average cast size of eight. Productions include: *Stepping Out* (première; directed by Julia McKenzie); *The Country Girl* (Robin Lefevre); *The Maintenance Man* (Roger Clissold). No general auditions. Normally cast show by show, with some cross casting. Do not advertise for actors, but welcome written casting queries with SAE.

The Casson Room studio theatre: seating capacity 60–100. Very little home-based work; mostly incoming tours, plus YPT activity.

TIE company (*see* Theatre-in-Education companies).

Torch Theatre Company Ltd
Torch Theatre, St Peter's Road, Milford Haven, Dyfed SA73 2BU
Tel (06462) **4192**
Artistic director Ian Granville Bell

Founded 1977. Seating capacity: 297. One season of eight plays from July to March. Produce drama, comedy, classics, musicals and a Christmas show. Average cast size of nine. Recent productions: *Animal Farm* (directed by Graham Watkins); *Sleuth* (Denise Newton); *Relatively Speaking, Snow Queen, Dr Faustus* and *Blood Brothers* (Ian Granville Bell). Through casting with some one-offs. Advertise in *SBS*, and welcome letters of enquiry from actors.

Comment
This is very much a theatre for the community, with a good mixture of plays and musicals from the resident company.

Traverse Theatre
112 West Bow, Grassmarket, Edinburgh EH1 2HH
Tel (031) **226 2633**
Artistic director Ian Brown

Founded 1963. Seating capacity: 100. Usually have a season between March and August (11 plays in 1988) with an average cast size of four. Renowned for its policy of producing new plays by British and international writers previously unperformed in Britain. Recent productions: *The Straw Chair* (directed by Jeremy Raison); *Man to Man* and *Kathie and the Hippopotamus* (Stephen Unwin); *Losing Venice* (Jenny Killick). Do not advertise for actors, but welcome casting queries. 'Replies and acknowledgements only sent if SAE has been enclosed. Do not bother to send more than one CV per year. Do not follow up a CV with a phone call asking for an audition. If you are Scottish, do mention it when writing to Scottish theatres – Scots are filed separately here. Put name and address on back of photo.'

Studio theatre: seating capacity 75.

Comment
One of the mainstays of the annual Edinburgh Festival, the Traverse presents a programme of progressive new work with the emphasis on Scottish playwrights. It has long been hailed as one of the most original theatre companies in Britain. Once a warehouse, what the theatre lacks in luxury it makes up for in creativity.

The Tyne Theatre Company
Tyne Theatre & Opera House, Westgate Road, Newcastle upon Tyne NE1 4AG
Tel (091) **232 3366**
Artistic director Andrew McKinnon

Founded 1988. Seating capacity 900–1100. This is a newly formed company that is planning a wide range of broadly popular work, with a season of seven plays from September to April (first season 1988/89). Will generally audition for each production. Rarely advertise but will consider letters from actors, 'provided that the volume of applications is understood. It is not possible for us to acknowledge or reply to actors' letters without an SAE. We expect to receive a considerable number of letters each year, and it is unfortunately impossible for us to meet more than a small percentage of those who write.'

TIE company (*see* entry for 'Tynewear Theatre in Education' in Theatre-in-Education companies).

Comment
Reincarnation of the former Tyne Wear Company, which used to be based at the Playhouse on the University of Newcastle campus.

Watermill Theatre
Bagnor, nr Newbury, Berks. RG16 8AE
Tel (0635) **45834**
Artistic director Jill Fraser

Founded 1967. Seating capacity: 185. Five plays in the main season (April–January) plus a Christmas show. Average cast size of six. Recent productions: *Sweeny Todd* (directed by Tim Prager); *Private Lives* (Graham Callan); *The Winter's Tale* (Ceris Sherlock); *My Wife Whatsername* (Christopher G. Sandford). Do not advertise for actors, but welcome letters of enquiry. Hold auditions for each production; no general auditions.

Windsor Theatre Company
Theatre Royal, Thames Street, Windsor, Berks. SL4 1PS
Tel (0253) **863444**
Artistic director Mark Piper

Founded 1938. Seating capacity: 633. Produce 14 plays throughout the year, with an average cast size of nine. A programme of comedy, thrillers, classics and pantomime. Recent productions: *Black Coffee* (directed by Joan Riley); *Present Laughter* (Tom Conti); *Noises Off* (Stephen Barry); *Dear Octopus* (Mark Piper); *Lyric for a Tango* (Sue Wilson). Cast for each production. Do not advertise for actors, and do not welcome casting queries.

Comment
Splendid in its Regency elegance, the Theatre Royal is ideally suited to the weary commuter. The beautiful cream, gold and red decor offers the perfect setting, and the play always entertains but never taxes the imagination.

Wolsey Theatre Company
Civic Drive, Ipswich, Suffolk IP1 2AS
Tel (0473) **328922**
Artistic director Antony Tuckey
Associate director Gerry Tebbutt

Founded 1979. Seating capacity: 410. Produce 12–14 plays over a 46-week period. Average cast size of 13. Recent productions: *Half a Sixpence*, *Little Shop of Horrors* and *Private Lives* (directed by Gerry Tebbutt); *Glen Garry Glen Ross* (Phyllida Lloyd); *Pravda* (Antony Tuckey). Cast for each production, but also hold general auditions. Do not generally advertise for actors, but welcome casting queries. Send a letter with an SAE if a reply is required.

TIE company (*see* Theatre-in-Education companies).

York Theatre Royal
St Leonard's Place, York YO1 2HD
Tel (0904) **658162** Fax (0904) **611534**
Artistic director To be appointed

Founded 1934. Seating capacity: 899. Produce ten shows annually, with five incoming tours. Average cast size of ten. Classics, new writing and pantomime. Recent productions: *Epsom Downs* (directed by Jonathan Petherbridge); *Noises*

Off and *Lucky Chance* (Martin Houghton); *Trumpets and Drums* (Richard Williams). Hold general auditions as well as casting for each production. Do not advertise for actors, but welcome casting queries.

TIE company (*see* Theatre-in-Education companies).

Comment
There has been a theatre on the present site since 1765 although the building has often been reconstructed over the years. The auditorium and stage of the current theatre date from 1902. In 1967 an entrance foyer, restaurant and bars were added in the new, glass-walled pavilion at the side of the theatre.

Geographical index
England

Oldham, Lancs.
Oldham Coliseum

Plymouth
Theatre Royal & The Drum

Reading, Berks.
The Mill at Sonning (Theatre) Ltd

Salisbury, Wilts.
Salisbury Playhouse

Scarborough, N. Yorks.
Stephen Joseph Theatre-in-the-Round
(Scarborough Theatre Trust Ltd)

Sheffield
Crucible Theatre Trust Ltd

Southampton
Nuffield Theatre

Watford, Herts.
Palace Theatre

Westcliff-on-Sea, Essex
Palace Theatre

Windsor, Berks.
Windsor Theatre Company

Worcester
Swan Theatre

York
York Theatre Royal

Northern Ireland

Belfast
Lyric Theatre

Scotland

Ayr
Graham Players

Dundee
Dundee Repertory Theatre

Edinburgh
Royal Lyceum Theatre Company
Traverse Theatre

Glasgow
Citizens Company

Musselburgh, East Lothian
Brunton Theatre Company

Perth
Perth Repertory Theatre

Pitlochry, Perthshire
Pitlochry Festival Theatre

St Andrews, Fife
Byre Theatre Company

Wales

Cardiff
Sherman Theatre

Milford Haven, Dyfed
Torch Theatre Company Ltd

Mold, Clwyd
Theatr Clwyd

Swansea
Grand Theatre

9. Producing theatres and independent managements

Akela Ltd
14 Talbot House, 98 St Martin's Lane, London WC2N 4AX
Tel (01) **379 0123**
Contact Colin Brough

> A new company that aim to carry on the operation of the Lupton Theatre Company, Colin Brough's previous outfit, which produced *Rose* by Andrew Davies, *When the Wind Blows* by Raymond Briggs, *Big in Brazil* by Bamber Gascoigne, Racine's *Phaedra* and other West End and touring shows. Will advertise if producing. Do not welcome casting queries from actors, especially as there is 'nothing cooking at the moment'.

Albemarle of London
74 Mortimer Street, London W1N 7DF
Tel (01) **631 0135**
Contact Sulie Branscombe

> Pantomimes and an occasional tour. Productions include: *Snow White* and *The Pied Piper*, both directed by Basil Chritchley. Occasionally advertise in *The Stage*. 'Don't mind casting queries, but usually deal through agents and our casting director, so do not keep actors' details on file. Telephone — followed, if requested, with photo and CV.' Hold general auditions.

Aldersgate Productions Ltd
12 Palace Street, London SW1E 5JF
Tel (01) **828 6591**
Contact Ronald Mann (artistic director)

> Produce plays of a broadly Christian nature, for children and family and church groups. Productions have included: *Ride Ride*, a musical about John Wesley; *Sentenced to Life*, a play about euthanasia; *Song of the Lion*, a one-man show about C. S. Lewis; and *The Lion, the Witch and the Wardrobe*. Advertise very seldom and do not welcome queries from actors. Often individual directors of shows will do casting. Occasionally hold auditions.

Artattack (Stage) Ltd
Unicorn House, White Lyon Court, Barbican, London EC2Y 8UH
Tel (01) **588 5858** Telex **914685** ROYALB G Fax (01) **382 9320**
Contact Adrian Gilpin (managing director)

> Plays and musicals; also film and TV productions. Occasionally advertise in *PCR*, but do not welcome casting queries from actors. Do not hold general auditions. 'Remember, the production companies and casting directors get literally thousands of photographs and *curriculum vitaes* sent to them through the post. Your photograph and your *curriculum vitae* are vital business documents. They are your advertising. The general standard of presentation seems to be getting lower and lower — please remember that first impressions are absolutely vital!'

Jean Charles Productions

4a Jointon Road, Folkestone, Kent CT20 2RF
Tel (0303) **52413**
Contact Jean Charles

> Founded 1962. Variety shows. Do not advertise for actors, but welcome query
> letters. Do not hold general auditions. 'I do use actors with singing and dancing
> skills in pantomimes and sometimes in summer shows.'

Chichester Festival Theatre Productions Ltd

Oaklands Park, Chichester, W. Sussex PO19 4AP
Tel (0243) **784437** Fax (0243) **787288**
Artistic director John Gale

> Founded 1962. Festival season from April to September. 1988 productions: *Hay
> Fever* (directed by Tony Britton); *Major Barbara* (Christopher Morahan); *The
> Royal Baccarat Scandal* (Val May); *Ring Round the Moon* (Elijah Moshinsky). Do
> not advertise for actors, but welcome casting queries. Write, early in the new
> year, to Clare Rankin, the production secretary. Sometimes hold general
> auditions. 'We have a policy of trying to help whenever possible.'

City Theatre Productions

11a Friern Mount Drive, London N20 9DP
Tel (01) **445 7961**
Contact Jon Rumney

> Have enjoyed great success at the Edinburgh Festival, with international plays
> and new work. Currently dormant. Do not advertise, and do not welcome queries
> from actors, either by letter or telephone. Occasionally hold general auditions.

Alan Clements Productions

Mill House, St Ives Cross, Sutton St James, Spalding, Lincs.
Tel (094) **585466**
Contact Alan Clements

> Small-scale operation, producing pantomimes and one or two plays a year. Do
> not advertise in *The Stage*, and do not welcome query letters or phone calls from
> actors. Do not hold general auditions. Except in exceptional circumstances, use
> people on recommendation, or who they have worked with before.

Ron Coburn International Productions

Vaudevilla, Elliot Road, Dundee DD2 1SY
Tel (0382) **69025**
Contact Ron Coburn, Mary Scanion

> Founded 1963. Scottish musical entertainments, pantomimes, world tours,
> Canadian/American tours, theatre revues, TV shows. Credits include: *A Breath of
> Scotland, The Waggle o' the Kilt, Shamrocks and Heather, The Royal Clansmen*.
> Do not advertise, but welcome letters from actors, which 'will be entered on file
> and used if the occasion arises'. Do not hold general auditions. 'Only interested in
> actors in my own area. In this way, local actors, artistes and Equity members are
> not passed over by TV companies by bussing people in from the larger cities due
> to the lack of information on the availability of people in the east of Scotland,
> north of the Forth.'

Michael Codron Ltd
Aldwych Theatre Offices, Aldwych, London WC2B 4DF
Tel (01) **240 8291**
Contact Joe Scott Parkinson

Manage the Aldwych and Adelphi Theatres and own the Vaudeville Theatre in
the West End. Usually big-time fare like *Woman in Mind* with Julia McKenzie. Do
not advertise for actors, although query letters from actors are welcome and will
be acknowledged if an SAE is enclosed. Casting is usually up to individual directors
of each play, in association with Mr Codron.

Compass Theatre Limited
13 Shorts Gardens, London WC2H 9AT
Tel (01) **379 7501**
Contact Edward Kemp (assistant director), Julian Forrester (general manager)

Founded 1984. Plays (mainly classical) on No. 1 tours and West End. Credits
include: *The Clandestine Marriage* (directed by Anthony Quayle); *St Joan*
(Clifford Williams); *King Lear* and *The Government Inspector* (Don Taylor). Do not
advertise, but welcome casting queries from actors. Approach in writing in the first
instance. Do not usually hold general auditions.

Condor Productions Ltd
3/5 St John Street, London EC1M 4AE
Tel (01) **608 2131**
Contact Robert Cogo-Fawcett

Founded 1986. West End plays. Credits include: *Journey's End*, directed by Justin
Greene. Do not advertise, but welcome casting queries from actors. Approach in
writing in the first instance. Do not hold general auditions.

Mervyn Conn Organization
MC House, 14 Orange Street, London WC2H 7ED
Tel (01) **930 7502**

The *Annie* tour is the first piece of theatre the organization have produced. Next
production scheduled for 1989 or 1990. Will advertise start of casting in *The
Stage* and other theatrical publications. Do hold general auditions, but do not
welcome queries from actors, as there can be such long lapses between
productions.

Ray Cooney Presentations Ltd
1/3 Spring Gardens, London SW1A 2BD
Tel (01) **839 5098**
Contact Mr H. S. Udwin

Founded 1965. Mainly comedies in the West End, Australia, United States and
Canada. Credits include: *Rookery Nook, Run for Your Wife, Two into One* and
Pygmalion, all directed by Ray Cooney. Do not advertise for actors, and do not
welcome casting queries. Hold general auditions.

Co-Producers
161a Kennington Park Road, London SE11 4JJ
Tel (01) **735 0769** Fax (01) **735 6273**
Contact Joanna Hole, Eric Standidge (joint artistic directors)

Founded 1986. Provincial touring on large and middle scale, straight plays, new
plays and classical revivals. Productions include: *Not about Heroes* and *Knuckle*
by David Hare, and *Macbeth* (all directed by Eric Standidge); *Simplicity* by Lady

Mary Wortley Montagu (Sonia Fraser). Advertise for actors in *SBS* and Equity *Job Grapevine*. Welcome casting queries from actors, either by telephone or letter. Do not hold general auditions. 'We usually co-produce with subsidized repertory theatres and then tour.'

Cotes Logan Productions Ltd

Reg. office: Chancery House, Chancery Lane, London WC2
Production office: 7 Hill Lawn Court, Chipping Norton, Oxon
Tel (0608) **41208**
Contact Peter Cotes, Joan Miller, John Stannard

Founded 1947. West End and touring productions. Credits include: *The Children's Hour, A Pin to See the Peepshow, Home of the Brave, Candida, Land of the Living, The Long Mirror, For Services Rendered, Back to Methuselah, Miss Julie, Anna Christie, Rocket to the Moon* (all directed by Peter Cotes). Do not advertise, but welcome casting queries from actors. Approach in writing in the first instance. Hold general auditions 'when the occasion arises'.

Cwmni Theatr Gwynedd

Theatr Gwynedd, Fford Deiniol, Bangor, Gwynedd LL57 2TL
Tel (0248) **351707**
Contact Graham Laker, J. O. Roberts, John Ogwen, William R. Lewis.

Founded 1983. English musicals for summer seasons and, since 1986, a wide range of Welsh-language productions. Productions include: *Happy as a Sandbag, Relatively Speaking, Sleuth, Oliver* and *O Law I Law* (all directed by Graham Laker); *Cymerwch Chi Sigaret?* (William R. Lewis); *Lle Mynno'r Gwynt* (Greg Evans); *Plas Dafydd* (John Ogwen). Do not advertise for actors, but welcome casting queries; write in the first instance with photograph and CV. Do not hold general auditions, but cast for each production with auditions as required. 'The company concentrates mainly on Welsh-language productions, touring within Wales, and always welcome information from Welsh-speaking actors.'

Charles Dickens Theatre Company

Meadowsweet, Wash Lane, Witnesham, Ipswich, Suffolk IP6 9EW
Tel (047385) **672**
Contact Charles Peter Mugleston

A new company that hope to produce plays of all kinds, about 25 per cent of output being Dickens related. The Dickens International Theatre is projected for the future. Do not advertise for actors. Welcome query letters or telephone calls, and keep a file of details. General auditions are held. Opportunities for actors are limited at the moment, but expansion is planned.

Dramatis Personae Ltd

122 Kennington Road, London SE11 6RE
Tel (01) **735 0831**
Contact Maria Aitken, Nathan Silver

Founded 1983. Plays (West End and tours) and TV co-productions. Productions include: *Happy Families* by Giles Cooper and *Are You Sitting Comfortably?* by Sue Townsend (directed by Maria Aitken); *Sister Mary Ignatius Explains It All for You* by Christopher Durang (Richard Digby Day). Do not advertise for actors. Do not especially welcome queries from actors as 'we prefer to make enquiries ourselves.' Write in the first instance – replies are not guaranteed due to staff limitations. To date, have not held general auditions. 'Our production work is sporadic and currently mainly in television.'

E & B Productions Ltd

Suite 1, Waldorf Chambers, 11 Aldwych, London WC2B 4DA
Tel (01) **836 2795**
Contact Paul Elliott, Brian Hewitt-Jones

Previous productions include: *Run for Your Wife, Double Double, Crown Matrimonial, Gaslight, Crystal Clear, The Secret Life of Cartoons* (new play by Clive Barker), as well as up to 14 pantomimes each winter. Advertise in *The Stage* for dancers, and welcome query letters from actors for the Christmas shows. Hold general auditions.

Each World Productions

1 King's House, 396 King's Road, London SW10 0LL
Tel (01) **352 1852** Telex **27918**
Contact David Adams, Mandie Joel

Founded 1984. Specialize in plays, pre-London tours, musicals, TV drama. Productions include: *Tales from a Long Room* (world première) and *Uncle Mort's North Country* at Lyric Hammersmith (directed by Peter James); *Cowboys No. 2* (British première) by Sam Shepard (David Adams); two West End productions of *Wren*, musical written and directed by David Adams. Advertise for actors in *PCR*, *SBS* and Equity *Job Grapevine*. Welcome casting queries from actors; write in the first instance, unless it has been specified in casting publications that it is all right to telephone. Do not hold general auditions. 'It is always a bonus if an actor knows about the part he is going up for — reading the book or play is always a good idea, also dressing up for the part.'

English Shakespeare Company Ltd

60 Paddington Street, London W1M 3RR
Tel (01) **434 2046**
Contact Kirsten Oploh (general manager), Sue Evans (administrative assistant)

Founded 1986. Recent productions: *The Wars of the Roses* (Shakespeare's history cycle consisting of *Richard II, Henry IV* [parts 1 & 2], *Henry V, Henry VI* [*House of Lancaster* and *House of York*] and *Richard III*), directed by Michael Bogdanov. Do not advertise, but welcome casting queries from actors; approach in writing in the first instance. Do not hold general auditions.

Vanessa Ford Productions Ltd

62 Uverdale Road, Chelsea, London SW10 0SS
Tel (01) **352 1948**
Contact Vanessa Ford, Jo Toy

Founded 1979. Tours of plays — family entertainment and classics. Productions include: *A Man for All Seasons, Rosencrantz and Guildenstern Are Dead, The Importance of Being Earnest*, 15 productions of Shakespeare plays, *The Lion, the Witch and the Wardrobe, Winnie the Pooh*. Do not usually advertise, but welcome casting queries; send letter with CV and photograph. Sometimes hold general auditions.

Clare Fox & Brian Kirk Ltd

Suite 17, 26 Charing Cross Road, London WC2H 0DG
Tel (01) **379 4985/4676** Fax (01) **379 5898**
Contact Clare Fox, Brian Kirk

West End plays and tours. Credits include: *The Amen Corner* (directed by Anton Phillips). Do not advertise for actors, but welcome query letters. Do not hold general auditions.

Robert Fox Ltd
6 Beauchamp Place, London SW3 1HG
Tel (01) **584 6855** Telex **936221** Fax (01) **225 1638**
Contact Ken Grant, Clare Howard

Founded 1980. Plays and musicals in the West End. Credits include: *Lettice and Lovage* (directed by Michael Blakemore); *Chess* (Trevor Nunn); *Another Country* (Stuart Burge). Occasionally advertise in *The Stage*. Prefer correspondence from actors when they are casting. Do not hold general auditions.

Freeshooter Productions Ltd
10 Clorane Gardens, London NW3 7PR
Tel (01) **794 0414**

Founded 1979. Plays and musicals, West End and touring. Credits include: *The Petition* (directed by Sir Peter Hall); *Kipling* (Patrick Garland); *Godspell* (Paul Kerryson); *March of the Falsettos*; *Siegfried Sassoon*. Sometimes advertise in *SBS*, but do not welcome casting queries from actors. Do not hold general auditions.

Jill Freud & Company
22 Wimpole Street, London W1M 7AD
Tel (01) **580 2222**
Contact Jill Freud

Founded 1980. Annual summer season at Southwold, plus an autumn tour of a classic such as *Under Milk Wood* and *Arms and the Man*. Credits also include: *You're a Good Man, Charlie Brown* (directed by Michael Richmond); *The Glass Menagerie* (Cathy Ingram); *Ten Times Table* (Kit Thacker); *Pack of Lies* (Nat Brenner). Casting takes place from February to April each year.

Mark Furness Ltd
10 Garrick Street, London WC2E 9BH
Tel (01) **836 7373**

Recent productions have included two West End productions: *Peter Pan* (the musical) and *Dangerous Obsession*. Tours have included: *Run for Your Wife*, *The Mating Game* and *Mixed Feelings*, a new play by Donald Churchill. Do advertise in *The Stage* and *PCR*, and welcome query letters from actors, which are put on file and referred to. Hold general auditions for dancers and singers for musicals.

Gallery Productions Ltd
Old Fire Station, Station Road, Merstham, Surrey RH1 3EE
Tel (07374) **4833/4/5**
Contact Robert Kennedy, Lee Dean

Founded 1985. Plays: touring productions and Christmas shows. Credits include: *Romantic Comedy* (directed by Charles Savage); *The Owl and the Pussycat* (Lou Stein); *The Rivals* (Stephen Barry); *On Approval* (Harvey Ashby); *A Sting in the Tale* (Jack Douglas); *Rough Crossing* (Roger Smith); *Whodunnit?*, *Widow's Weeds* and *The Haunting of Hill House* (Philip Grout); *Alphabetical Order* (John David). Do not advertise, and do not really welcome casting queries from actors. Occasionally hold general auditions.

Trevor George Entertainments (UK) Ltd (Trevor George Entertainment Agency/Stairway Productions)

42 Marldon Road, Shiphay, Torquay, Devon TQ2 7EJ
Tel (0803) **63752/64887**
Contact Trevor George (chairman), Billie George (managing director), Trevor Ashford (director)

> Founded 1959. Pantomime and summer shows in the provinces. Productions include various pantomimes directed by Billie George. Occasionally advertise for actors in *The Stage*. Welcome casting queries from actors; write in the first instance. Do hold general auditions.

Derek Glynne (London) PTY

> No longer based in London, now operate from Melbourne. Took Royal Shakespeare Company's *Richard III* to Australia. No opportunities for individual UK based actors. (*See* International Plays Ltd).

Francis Golightly Productions

7 Riverside Walk, Colchester, Essex CO1 1RD
Tel (0206) **65057**
Contact Francis Golightly, Roy Cloughton

> Founded 1973. Revue, pantomime and variety shows in provincial theatres. Occasionally advertise in *The Stage*, and welcome casting queries from actors. Telephone in the first instance. Do not hold general auditions.

Hetherington Seelig

28 Museum Street, London WC1R 1LH
Tel (01) **637 5661** Fax (01) **323 1151** Telex **268553** HSARTS G
Contact Anthony Smee

> Founded 1977. Drama, musicals, opera, dance, ballet, mime, concerts, touring and festivals. Do not advertise for actors and do not welcome casting queries. Do not hold general auditions. In 1988 Hetherington Seelig bought out Charles Vance Ltd. giving them control of the Beck Theatre in Hayes, previously managed by Charles Vance.

Philip Hindin Ltd

33 Albert Street, London NW1 7LU
Tel (01) **380 0375** Telex SHOWBIZ LONDON
Contact Philip Hindin

> Founded 1937. Plays, musicals, imported overseas dance companies, variety and revue. Credits include: *The Merry Widow* and *The World of Suzie Wong* (directed by Stanley Willis Croft); *The Sunshine Boys* (Danny Simons). Do not advertise for actors, and do not welcome casting queries. Hold general auditions. 'I always approach agents when casting.'

Hiss & Boo Productions Ltd

Strand Theatre, Aldwych, London WC2B 5LD
Tel (01) **379 0453** Fax (01) **240 2056**
Contact Ian Liston

> Founded 1976. West End and touring musicals, plays and children's shows. Credits include: *Novello: A Chance to Dream; Dear Ivor* and *Nunsense* (directed by Richard Digby Day); *Benefactors* (Stephen Barry); *Cluedo* (Hugh Goldie); *Corpse!* (Gerald Moon); *See How They Run* (Leslie Lawton); *Groucho: A Life in Revue* (with Triumph Theatre Productions; directed by Arthur Marx). Occasionally

advertise in *The Stage*; do not hold general auditions. Will consider letters from actors: 'We will always reply to applicants who enclose an SAE. Actor's details are kept on file and frequently referred to during the course of the year.'

Bruce Hyman & Harvey Kass Ltd

5 Brewer Street, London W1R 3FN
Tel (01) **439 1984** Fax (01) **494 2570**
Contact Bruce Hyman, Harvey Kass

Founded 1986. Plays and musicals – West End and tours. Credits include: *The Life of Napoleon* (directed by Kenneth Branagh); *The Foreigner* (Nick Broadhurst); *The Mystery of Edwin Drood* (Wilford Leach). 'Rarely' advertise for actors. Welcome casting queries; approach in writing in the first instance. Do not hold general auditions.

Richard Jackson Personal Management Ltd

59 Knightsbridge, London SW1X 7RA
Tel (01) **235 3671**
Contact Richard Jackson, John Huntley, John Cannon

Founded 1959. Plays and musicals on London's fringe, with the occasional West End transfer: 'Our policy is to produce new plays, mainly from France and Germany, but not to discount any English or American script of quality which come our way. They need to have small casts and be suitable for producing in fringe venues such as the Offstage, New End and Latchmere.' Credits include: *A Day in Hollywood, a Night in the Ukraine* (directed by Ian Davison); *The Singular Life of Albert Nobbs, Appearances, Portrait of Dora, The Revolt* and *The Human Voice* (directed by Simone Benmussa); *Flashpoint* (Anton Rodgers); *I Ought to Be in Pictures* and *Swimming Pools at War* (Robert Gillespie); *Tribute to Lili Lamont* (Jack Gold); *Better Days, Better Knights* (Max Stafford-Clark); *Pier Paolo Pasolini* (Tim Luscombe); *An Evening with Quentin Crisp*. Do not advertise for actors. Do not really welcome casting queries: 'Nearly all the casting is done by invitation on consultation with the play's director. Although all casting enquiries by letter are considered, actors whose work is unknown to us are rarely used.'

Bill Kenwright Ltd

55–59 Shaftesbury Avenue, London W1V 7AA
Tel (01) **439 4466**

Revivals and new shows for West End and touring theatres. Productions include: *The Business of Murder* (by Richard Harris); *A Fighting Chance* (by Norman Crisp); *Up on the Roof* (written and directed by Jane Prowse & Simon Moore); *James and the Giant Peach* for children. Occasionally advertise in *The Stage* for actors for touring shows. Welcome query letters from actors, which will be kept for one year. Auditions are sometimes held for understudies, ASMs and smaller parts; for major parts in big West End shows, individual directors usually do their own casting.

David Kirk Productions

12 Panmuir Road, London SW20 0PZ
Tel (01) **947 0130**

Commercial management touring post-London revivals and some new plays to provincial and suburban theatres. Productions have included the post-London tours of *Middle-Age Spread, Taking Steps, Master Class, Strippers, A Month of Sundays* and *Diary of a Somebody*. New plays have included: *Murder Sails at Midnight* by Ngaio Marsh; *The Gold Umbrella* by William Douglas Home; *Local Murder* by Peter Whalley; *Mr Fothergill's Murder* by Peter O'Donnell; *Agenda for Murder* by Denis Cleary & Joseph Boyer. Do not advertise, and do not welcome queries from actors. Do not hold auditions. Most plays have small casts, and are cast from TV names and a pool of people already known to the management; other supporting roles are cast through agents.

Knightsbridge Theatrical Productions
15 Fetter Lane, London EC4A 1JJ
Tel (01) **583 2266**

Straight plays suitable for production in the West End. Very occasional tours. Do not advertise for actors, and do not welcome query letters. Have not held auditions for several years.

Logan Theatres Ltd
112 Hamilton Avenue, Pollokshields, Glasgow G41 4EX
Tel (041) **427 6743**
Contact Jimmy Logan

Comedy and family shows, mostly starring Jimmy Logan. Past productions include: *Run for Your Wife*, *A Bedful of Foreigners*, *Not Now Darling* and *Lauder*. Do not advertise. Welcome casting queries from actors, especially Scottish-based actors or those with authentic Scottish accents. Although interested in new faces, there are limited casting opportunities, as sometimes the same company of actors will be employed for a year or more. Do hold auditions, usually in a theatre; also use agents and have contacts with Scottish drama schools.

Lyric Theatre Hammersmith ● *See* **Repertory/Regional Theatres section.**

Cameron Mackintosh Ltd
1 Bedford Square, London WC1B 3RA
Tel (01) **637 8866**
Contact The Casting Department

Founded 1980. Musicals. Credits include: *Cats*, *Les Miserables*, *Follies* and *The Phantom of the Opera* (co-production with The Really Useful Theatre Company). Advertise for actors in *The Stage*. Welcome casting queries from actors, which should be addressed to the Casting Department. Hold general auditions, which are always advertised in *The Stage*.

Lee Menzies Ltd
20 Rupert Street, London W1V 7FN
Tel (01) **437 0127** Fax (01) **439 0297**
Contact Lee Menzies

New commercial plays. Recent productions: Jeffrey Archer's *Beyond Reasonable Doubt*; *Dry Rot* with Sir Brian Rix. Do not advertise for actors. Do not welcome query letters except from actors they know and have already worked with; correspondence from others will be thrown away or returned if there is time and an SAE has been enclosed. Do not hold general auditions. Casting is usually the responsibility of the director working on each show.

National Theatre ● *See* NATIONAL THEATRE in Repertory/Regional Theatres section.

Newgate Company & Air Play

P.O. Box 175, Bath BA1 2FX
Tel (0225) **318335/743782**
Contact Glenys Gill, Jo Anderson, Alec Reid

Founded 1976 (Newgate), 1988 (Air Play). *Newgate Company* is principally involved in theatre production but often tied in with broadcasting media; ensemble-based, it re-assembles with specific projects. *Air Play*, an affiliated company, is based on audio-stereo drama tape recordings of new plays, screenplays and teleplays; has its own studio facilities. Projects initiated and developed by Newgate Company: *Ludwig* (directed at the Roundhouse in 1977 by Tony Craven; film version in association with Ken Russell is ongoing project based on film repertory company); *Oldest Profession* (Globe Bankside Shakespeare Festival, 1987; BBC Radio 4 version directed by Ed Thomason; at various theatres during the summer of 1988); *Hitler's Whistle* (in association with Orchard Theatre, 1989); *Solstice* (in association with Bristol Express Theatre Company; directed by Andy Jordan; Lyric Hammersmith showcase, 1987). Sometimes advertise in *PCR, Spotlight* or *SBS*. 'We welcome introductions from *new*, graduating drama students, but *prefer* updates from working actors – i.e. we like to see actors in action. Always send a letter. With regard to Air Play, we like to keep a file on actors who have *extensive* radio drama experience, can lift off the page and who have a good vocal range – do send a CV.' Do not hold general auditions. 'We prefer to cover actors we do not know when they are doing a showcase, have a "spot" on TV or radio, etc. Or invite them in for a "workout" session. Auditions prove little. Both Newgate Company and Air Play always have very specific requirements, and we are always very specific in itemizing those specifications in detail, so it is not all that worthwhile responding to our advertisements unless you really fit the bill.'

Newpalm Productions

26 Cavendish Avenue, Finchley, London N3 3QN
Tel (01) **349 0802**
Contact Phil Compton, Daphne Newpalm

Usually produce national tours of such plays as *Noises Off, Seven Brides for Seven Brothers* and *Rebecca* at regional repertory theatres. Advertise for big productions in *The Stage* and *PCR*. Will accept casting queries from actors by letter. Details are kept on file and are consulted when audition lists for specific parts are being drawn up. Unless a suitable part is being cast, the chances of a reply are slim. Auditions for specific parts are sometimes held. There are no general auditions; use agents for casting.

The Niccol Centre

Brewery Court, Cirencester, Glos. GL7 1SP
Tel (0285) **67181**
Contact Alison Rochfort (director), Danielle Charleson—Gallacher (arts director)

Founded 1984. A small theatre-in-the-round with a seating capacity of 120. Plays, recitals, poetry readings, one-man shows. Productions include: *Born in the Gardens* (directed by Jaqui Crago); *The Old Ladies* (David Buxton); *Relatively Speaking* (Andrew Charleson); *The Glass Menagerie* (Danny Charleson-Gallacher). Do not advertise for actors (except through personal contacts and word of mouth), and welcome casting queries from actors. Write in the first instance to the arts director. Auditions are held for specific productions.

North Bank Productions

103b Victoria Road, London NW6 6TD
Tel (01) **328 8163**
Contact Chris Hayes

> Founded 1985. Plays and musicals, mainly touring; future plans for the West End
> and touring abroad. Credits include: *The Anastasia File, Hancock's Finest Hour,
> Romeo and Juliet, Super Gran* and *To Kill a Mockingbird* (directed by Chris
> Hayes); *Funny Peculiar* (Stewart Trotter); *Educating Rita* (John Davis); *Happy
> Event* (Michael Napier Brown). Sometimes advertise in *SBS* and *PCR*, and
> welcome casting queries from actors; approach in writing only. Rarely hold
> general auditions. 'Although we are always interested to hear from young actors,
> weight of numbers prevents us replying individually to "unsolicited enquiries"
> unless SAE is enclosed. All letters/CVs/photos are filed for future casting
> opportunities. Interviews/auditions are always arranged by telephone. Sending
> an SAE merely ensures acknowledgement of receipt.'

Old Vic

Waterloo Road, London SE1
Tel (01) **928 2651**
Artistic director Jonathan Miller
Contact Pippa Ailion, Emma Harris

> Classical revivals: *Andromache, One-Way Pendulum, The Tempest, Candide*
> (directed by Jonathan Miller); *Too Clever by Half* (Richard Jones). Do not
> advertise, but welcome casting queries from actors. Send a letter enclosing CV
> and photograph. Do not hold general auditions.

The Opera House

Gloucester Street, St Helier, Jersey, Channel Isles
Tel (0534) **35348**
Contact Dick Ray

> Founded 1902. Wide range of productions. Advertise in *The Stage*, and welcome
> casting queries from actors; approach in writing in the first instance. Hold general
> auditions.

Permutt-Hadley Productions Ltd

6 Exchange Court, London WC2
Tel (01) **379 5612** Fax (01) **497 2038** Telex **826085** ELAINR G
Contact Val Perry

> Founded 1983. Plays and musicals, West End and tours; variety tours. Credits
> include: *The Girlfriend, The Little Shop of Horrors, The Cat and the Canary, A
> Chorus Line, Godspell, Two and Two Make Sex, Don't Misunderstand Me, Cards
> on the Table, Everything in the Garden, La Cage aux Folles, Sweeny Todd.*
> Advertise for actors in *SBS,* Equity *Job Grapevine* and *The Stage.* Welcome
> casting queries from actors — 'by letter only'. Do not hold general auditions.

Pola Jones Associates Ltd

5 Dean Street, London W1
Tel (01) **439 1165**
Contact Caroline Signell

> Founded 1981. Mostly comedy. Credits include: *When Did You Last See Your
> Trousers?* (directed by Roger Smith); *Arturo Ui* (David Gilmore); *The Nerd* (Mike
> Ockrent); *The Gambler* - musical. Do not advertise for actors. Will accept casting
> queries from actors and keep a file of details, although casting opportunities are

limited and whoever is directing a show will usually make casting requests and decisions. Write in the first instance. Do not hold general auditions.

Quill Theatre Productions

247 Norwood Road, London SE24 9AG
Tel (01) **674 1050**
Contact Ann Parnell McGarry (artistic director)

Quill exist to produce new work, which may be serious plays, fast, witty comedies, musicals and childrens' plays. When decent new work cannot be found, as is often the case, there are huge gaps in the production schedule. Casting is therefore spasmodic, and opportunities for actors are limited. Casting queries from actors are not really welcomed, though details will be kept on file. Casting policy varies with the needs of each production. Occasionally advertise and audition for specialist parts. The artistic director is more interested in an actor with 'the ability to do it as much as having done it before'. Use casting directors and agents for West End productions.

Dick Ray Productions ● *See* THE OPERA HOUSE.

Really Useful Theatre Company

Palace Theatre, Shaftesbury Avenue, London W1V 8AY
Tel (01) **734 0762** Fax (01) **734 6157** Telex **266756** PALMUS G

Andrew Lloyd Webber's company, which produces West End musicals, plays and comedies. Credits include: *Cats* and *Starlight Express* (directed by Trevor Nunn); *Daisy Pulls It Off* and *Lend Me a Tenor* (David Gilmore); *Phantom of the Opera* (Hal Prince). Advertise in *The Stage*, and welcome casting queries from actors; approach in writing in the first instance. Hold general auditions. 'Do not attend auditions for jobs if your Equity status prevents you from taking the job simply in order to "be seen". Be honest and accurate about musical and dancing ability and vocal range.'

Michael Redington

10 Maunsel Street, London SW1P 2QL
Tel (01) **834 5119**

Plays, including *84 Charing Cross Road* (adapted and directed by James Roose-Evans) and *The Best of Friends* by Hugh Whitemore (directed by James Roose-Evans); *Pack of Lies* and *Breaking the Code* by Hugh Whitemore (Clifford Williams); *Mr and Mrs Nobody* by Keith Waterhouse (Ned Sherrin). Do not advertise for actors. Do not welcome casting queries, and do not hold general auditions.

The Renaissance Theatre Company

Formed in April 1987 by Kenneth Branagh and David Parfitt. 'It was a natural development of the work that David Parfitt and I had been doing periodically on the London fringe, producing and appearing in lunchtime shows, new plays and finally a full scale production of *Romeo and Juliet*.' Their first season included *Public Enemy*, *Life of Napoleon*, and *Twelfth Night*. In 1988 their productions of *Much Ado About Nothing* (directed by Judi Dench), *As You Like It* (Geraldine McEwan) and *Hamlet* (Derek Jacobi) attracted full houses on tour and in the West End.
Further information withheld by Renaissance to stem the flow of enquiries from actors.

Rigoletto Ltd/Stanley Sher Enterprises Ltd

28 Oakhampton Court, Park Avenue, Leeds LS8 2JF
Tel (0532) 731348
Contact Stanley Sher, June Sher

> Founded 1963. Pantomimes, plays, children's shows and concerts. Do not advertise for actors, but welcome query letters. Hold general auditions.

Royal Court Theatre (English Stage Company Ltd)

Sloane Square, London SW1W 8AS
Tel (01) 730 5174
Artistic director Max Stafford-Clark
Associate director Simon Curtis
Casting director Lisa Makin

> The English Stage Company was founded by George Devine in 1956 to put on new plays. John Osborne, John Arden, Arnold Wesker, Edward Bond, Caryl Churchill, Howard Barker and Michael Hastings are among the writers this theatre has discovered. Recent productions: *A Lie in the Mind* (directed by Simon Curtis); *Bloody Poetry*, *The Recruiting Officer* and *Our Country's Good* (Max Stafford-Clark). Cast from play to play; West End contracts. Do not hold general auditions, but Lisa Makin, the casting director, tries to cover actors' work and therefore likes information about what is going on. Actors' details are kept on file and referred to: 'It is not necessary to keep on sending in new photographs, etc.'

> *Theatre Upstairs*: Seating capacity: 60. Cast from play to play. Rep contract. 'Equity cards can be issued with Theatre Upstairs contracts.'

> **Comment**
> With its Young Writers' Festival and its ambitious Theatre Upstairs, the Royal Court is one of the few British theatres to hold out any hope to contemporary playwrights, actors and directors.

Royal National Theatre ● *See* National Theatre in Rep/Regional Theatres section.

Royal Shakespeare Company ● *See* Repertory and Regional Theatres section.

RTC

Novello Theatre, High Street, Sunninghill, nr Ascot, Berks.
Tel (0990) 20881
Contact June Rose (artistic director), Samantha Keston (administrator)

> Children's plays and musicals. Recent productions: *Worzel Gummidge*, *Alice in Wonderland*, *Snoopy*, *A Midsummer Night's Dream*. Advertise in *The Stage* and *SBS*. Do not welcome casting queries from actors.

Sadler's Wells Theatre Company

Lilian Baylis Theatre, Sadler's Wells, Rosebery Avenue, London EC1R 4TN
Tel (01) 278 6563
Artistic director Nick Hamm

> A new company formed in 1988 as a 'middle ground between the pub circuit and Shaftesbury Avenue'. Opening season of three productions: *The House of Blue Leaves* by John Guare and *The Madwoman of Chaillot* by Jean Giraudoux (directed by Nick Hamm); *School for Clowns* by Waechter, translated by Ken Campbell (Martin Duncan).

St George's Theatre

49 Tufnell Park Road, London N7 0PS
Tel (01) **607 7978**
Artistic director George Murcell

Founded 1976, by George Murcell who was determined that Shakespeare should be presented without any frills or modern interpretations. The St George's Theatre (seating capacity: 600), presents Shakespeare only, always aiming to recreate the original Elizabethan stagings. Three ten-week seasons that follow school terms. Casting takes place each September, January and April. Company of 12 actors on Equity contracts for the season, with cross casting in at least two plays. Do not advertise, but welcome letters enclosing CV and photograph: 'We do not have the time to reply, unless interested in seeing an actor, so an SAE is not needed.' Require actors who have at least rep experience of performing Shakespeare (drama school Shakespeare is not sufficient).

Barrie Stacey Promotions (Barrie Stacey Productions/Sante Fe Productions Ltd)

3rd floor, 9 Denmark Street, London WC2H 0LA
Tel (01) **836 6220/4128**
Contact Barrie Stacey

Founded 1966. Children's musicals, pantomimes, the occasional straight play and many variety concerts. Productions include: *Snow White and the Seven Dwarfs* (directed by Barrie Stacey); *Adventures of Pinocchio* (Henry Metcalfe/Vernon Morris); *David Copperfield* (Keith Hopkins). Advertise in *PCR*, *SBS* and Equity *Job Grapevine*. Welcome casting queries from actors, by letter with photograph and resumé. Hold general auditions bi-monthly. 'Make sure you know your type and what parts you think you are right for and would like to play.'

Stagestruck Productions Ltd

57 Duke Street, Grosvenor Square, London W1M 5DH
Tel (01) **629 2334** Fax (01) **493 3808** Telex **22713**
Contact Simon Caplan (managing director), Theo Gobat (director)

Founded 1978. Plays and musicals; West End and tours. Credits include: *The Club* (directed by Tony Tanner); *Flashpoint* (Anton Rodgers); *Killing Jessica* (Bryan Forbes); *Separation* (Michael Attenborough). Advertise in *PCR*, and welcome casting queries from actors; send a letter enclosing biography/resumé only. Hold general auditions. 'Will consider new Equity members as well as experienced actors.'

Stoll Productions Ltd

Cranbourn Mansions, Cranbourn Street, London WC2H 7AG
Tel (01) **437 2274** Fax (01) **434 1217**

One of the most influential theatre empires, with 12 theatres (including the Globe, Lyric, Apollo and Queen's in Shaftesbury Avenue) that tend to host straight plays; Her Majesty's and the Palladium are more often musical venues. Recent productions have included *Up on the Roof*, *The House of Bernarda Alba*, *Barnum* and *La Cage aux Folles*. Do not advertise, do not welcome query letters from actors and do not hold general auditions. All casting is handled by individual directors of shows.

Talbot Hay Productions Ltd

2a Roebuck Road, Rochester, Kent ME1 1UD
Tel (0634) **812584**
Contact Philip Talbot, Pamela Hay

Founded 1987. New production company whose first show was a tour and West End run of Catherine Cookson's *The Fifteen Streets*, directed by Rob Bettinson. Advertise in *The Stage*, and welcome casting queries from actors: 'Prefer letter with CV and photograph.' Hold general auditions 'if necessary'. 'Don't audition for something in which you are not interested "just for experience" or for which you are unsuited. For example, if a particular accent has been specified, it will be wanted at the audition; the director will be unlikely to be satisfied that it can be mastered. If the show is a musical, take the music of the chosen song or songs to the audition; do not expect the accompanist to "busk it". Do not ask to accompany yourself on a guitar if the show will have an orchestra. Do not expect sound amplification at the audition. Do not go at all if you really cannot sing (unless the management have specifically asked to see you — they may have a good reason).'

Stephen Tate & June Epstein Ltd

111 Golden House, 29 Great Pulteney Street, London W1R 3DD
Tel (01) **734 2574** Fax (01) **494 1946**
Contact Simon Spencer, Cathy McMahon

Founded 1987. West End musicals. Credits include: *Rage, Wuthering Heights* and *The Dancing Years*. Advertise in *The Stage*, but do not welcome casting queries from actors. Hold general auditions.

H. M. Tennant Ltd

Globe Theatre, Shaftesbury Avenue, London W1V 7HD
Tel (01) **437 3647**
Contact Sheila Formoy

London's oldest established theatre production company. Recent productions have included: *A Month of Sundays, Number One* and *Ducking Out*. Do not advertise for actors, but welcome query letters. Actors' details are kept on file for 18 months; individual directors of shows will consult the file if they need to. Do not hold general auditions.

Theatre of Comedy Company Ltd

Shaftesbury Theatre, 210 Shaftesbury Avenue, London WC2H 8DP
Tel (01) **379 3345** Fax (01) **240 0961**
Contact Mary Price (assistant to the producer)

Founded 1983. Comedies; West End and tours. Credits include: *Run for Your Wife* (directed by Ray Cooney); *When We Are Married* (Ronald Eyre). Do not advertise, and do not welcome casting queries from actors. Hold general auditions 'when appropriate'.

Theatre Projects Consultants Ltd

3 Apollo Studios, Charlton Kings Road, London NW5 2SU
Tel (01) **482 4224**

West End and touring shows. Productions include: *Edward II, Richard III, She Stoops to Conquer, I'm Not Rappaport, Cabaret, Fiddler on the Roof, A Little Night Music*. Not currently in production and do not know when they will be. Do not welcome queries from actors. Do not keep a file of details, as productions are infrequent and each one is cast 'from scratch'.

Theatre Royal, Margate Ltd

Addington Street, Margate, Thanet, Kent CT9 1PV
Tel (0843) **221913**
Contact Managing director

Theatre founded in 1786, and the company in 1988. The theatre is currently undergoing restoration and is due to re-open in late 1988, when it is hoped to stage in-house productions. Michael Ward Theatre Productions will be using the theatre as a base when it re-opens.

Thomas & Benda Associates Ltd

361 Edgware Road, London W2 1BS
Tel (01) **723 5509** Fax (01) **724 4523/7287**
Contact Peter Benda

Founded 1978. Plays, musicals and trade shows. Productions include national tours of *A Chorus Line* and *The Little Shop of Horrors*. Advertise for actors in *SBS*, and welcome query letters from actors, although 'we do not have time to reply and deal with casting letters unless we are looking for specific people for parts in a specific production.' Do not hold general auditions.

Trafford & Parnell Productions

8 Jesmond Avenue, Blackpool, Lancs. FY4 1EJ
Tel (0253) **48069/66928**

Founded 1974. Plays, summer seasons, pantomimes. Productions include: summer seasons at the Spa Theatres, Bridlington and Whitby (directed by Ronnie Parnell); summer season at the Spa Theatre, Scarborough and at New Leisure World, Bridlington (Keith Hopkins); summer season at Talk of the Coast, Blackpool (Ronnie Parnell & Chris Nicholl). Do not advertise for actors, but welcome casting queries. Telephone in the first instance, when photograph and CV may be requested. Do hold general auditions.

Triumph Theatre Productions

Suite 4, Waldorf Chambers, 11 Aldwych, London WC2B 4DA
Tel (01) **836 0187**
Chairman and Managing Director Duncan C. Weldon
Deputy Managing Director Peter Wilkins

A major producer of West End and touring shows, mostly revivals but with a regular output of new work. Productions have included co-producing *Kiss Me Kate* at the Old Vic; *You Never Can Tell*; *The Deep Blue Sea*; *A Touch of the Poet*; *Melon*; *A Piece of My Mind*. Under the auspices of Triumph, 1988 saw the first production by **The Peter Hall Company** of *Orpheus Descending*, starring Vanessa Redgrave. Do not hold general auditions; sometimes use freelance casting directors. Do not advertise for actors.

Charles Vance Ltd/Prestige Plays Ltd

83 George Street, London W1H 5PL
Tel (01) **486 1732**
Contact Jill Streatfeild (personal assistant to Charles Vance)

Founded 1960. Tours, repertory, musicals and pantomimes. Productions 'too numerous to mention!' Advertise for actors through *PCR*. Rarely hold general auditions. Welcome casting queries from actors, by letter only: 'Keep applications succinct, with clear CV, good photograph and SAE.' Merged with Hetherington Seelig in 1988 giving them control of the Beck theatre in Hayes, the council-owned venue previously managed by Charles Vance.

Viva Theatre Productions Ltd

42–46 St Lukes Mews, London W11
Tel (01) **221 5101** Fax (01) **221 3374** Telex **297314** ANSA HITTZ
Contact Christopher Malcolm (managing director)

> Founded 1985. Productions include: *Steaming* and *Viva* (directed by Roger
> Smith); *Pal Joey* and *Yakety Yak* (Robert Walker); *Façades* by William Humble
> (Simon Callow); *Metamorphosis*; *Sink the Belgrano*; *Decadence*; *Greek* (written &
> directed by Stephen Berkoff); *When I Was a Girl*; *Tuesday's Child*. Do not
> advertise for actors, but sometimes welcome query letters from them: 'Direct
> approaches only work if actors feel they are absolutely right for a project the
> producers are involved in. General sending out of information is usually a waste
> of time.' Do not hold general auditions; casting is usually done through casting
> directors: 'Actors should know and inform casting directors whenever they feel a
> change or improvement in their careers merits a communication.'

Michael Ward Theatre Productions

39 Thames Street, Windsor, Berks. SL4 1PR
Tel (0753) **863982**
Contact Michael Ward

> Founded 1980. Tours and pre-West End try outs. When the Theatre Royal,
> Margate, re-opens, they intend to transfer all activities there as a base theatre. Do
> not hold general auditions, do not advertise for actors, and do not really
> welcome casting queries from actors as 'we do like to go out and about a fair bit
> ourselves.' Write in the first instance, if you do contact them.

Westminster Productions Ltd

12 Palace Street, London SW1E 5JB
Tel (01) **834 7882** Fax (01) **821 5819**
Contact Howard Bird

> Founded 1984. West End shows and provincial tours. Productions include: *An
> Inspector Calls* (directed by Peter Dews); *The Miracle Worker* (Adrian Reynolds);
> *The Lion, the Witch and the Wardrobe* and *The Voyage of the Dawn Treader*
> (Richard Williams). Do not hold general auditions. Occasionally advertise for
> actors in *The Stage*, and welcome casting queries from actors; write in the first
> instance.

Michael White

13 Duke Street, St James's, London SW1Y 6DB
Tel (01) **839 3971** Fax (01) **839 3836**
Contact Michael White

> High-output company. Recent productions have included *On Your Toes* and *A
> Chorus Line*. Casting is done through casting directors, who will advertise
> auditions in *The Stage*. Do not welcome query letters, which are simply passed on
> to casting directors.
> See Michael White Productions in Film and Video section.

Maurice Winnick (Associates) Ltd ● *See* PHILIP HINDIN LTD.

10. Fringe and alternative theatre

Poverty and the Fringe are inseparable. Paying actors less than the going rate, holding out on bills for essential services, hoping that the public health inspector will not interpret the rules too precisely and praying for a stage-struck bank manager — these are the standard features of the Fringe theatres. If suddenly they were blessed with respectable budgets, they would rise from the Fringe to join the ranks of 'alternative' theatre — Hampstead, the Young Vic, Stratford East — where actors may not get rich but can at least expect to earn the Equity minimum.

Fringe theatre managers dream of a life without the debt collector — the purist who believes that a balanced account will compromise his artistic integrity is now a rarity. However, minority theatre tends to bring in minority receipts, and commercial sponsorship is not attracted to small-scale ventures.

The last resort — adequate funding by the Arts Council or local authorities — is about as likely as a win on the pools. Or, rather, that's how it was until recently. Changes in the rules by which the drama panel of the Arts Council distribute grants mean that henceforth an application from a Fringe company attempting original or unusual work may not be a total waste of time. Under the new system, those Fringe companies who have traditionally enjoyed a lifeline to the Arts Council are required to show why they are more deserving than other claimants. Last year, two leading drama groups — Foco Novo and Joint Stock — were set adrift. Foco Novo promptly sank; Joint Stock is still floundering. There was a loud outcry from the arts lobby at such wanton cruelty, but the arts panel argued that a reallocation of scarce resources was long overdue.

Among those benefiting from the discomfiture of the old guard (in Fringe terms, anything predating 1980 is positively ancient) are the mime company Théâtre de Complicité and Trestle, a company distinguished by its imaginative use of masks. Others new to the list of Arts Council beneficiaries include the Asian group Tara; the black group Talawa; Quicksilver, which plays to young people; and Forkbeard Fantasy, an experimental group based, improbably, in Somerset. These last four attract grants totalling £239,200 — not a great fortune by West End standards but enough to release a few pent-up ideas.

Many other groups committed to new writing and innovative theatre are trying to catch the eye of the Arts Council. But given the tightness of funds, if they win support it can only be at the expense of some of the old stagers for whom the yearly handout has become a prop to conformity.

For the actor, the Fringe is an opportunity to be noticed, often in highly original productions. If the pay is rotten, it can be better (marginally) than not working at all, and there is always the outside chance of a transfer to a theatre where Equity rates apply. This is why Dan Crawford, doyen of the pub theatre managers, can attract such fine talent to the King's Head. His recent revival of Noel Coward's *Easy Virtue* went on to do good business in the West End. But this exception relied heavily on the known appeal of a famous dramatist. New and experimental writing has much less chance of attracting support from mainstream theatre, with notable exceptions such as Tricycle's *Crystal Clear*, which started life at the Old Red Lion.

The deal to watch out for — and to reject if money is any consideration — is the profit-share. True, a London Fringe production is an excellent showcase for an actor with a decent role, but since the project for which the profit-share is the only option seldom realizes any profits, the actor who covers his own expenses can end up working at a loss. There are easier ways of starving.

Albany Empire
Douglas Way, London SE8 4AG
Tel (01) **691 8016**
Artistic director Teddy Kiendl

> The Albany moved to its new, purpose-built home in 1981. The base for the Combination Theatre Company, it is a lively community centre, and stages three or four in-house productions per year plus in-coming tours of theatre, dance, music and cabaret. Shows are targeted at the local community, which is predominantly Afro-Caribbean and white working-class. Recent productions: *Mass Carib*, *Romeo and Juliet* (set in Trinidad), *The Gut Girls* — all directed by Teddy Kiendl. Do not advertise for actors (tend to work through agents), but welcome casting queries, particularly from local actors. ITC/Equity small-scale contract of 8–9 weeks; cast from show to show.
>
> The Albany is also the company base for IRIE, an Afro-Carib dance company (artistic director: Beverly Glean).

Almeida Theatre ● *See* **Non-producing theatres.**

Artaud Theatre Company ● *See* CAFÉ THEATRE UPSTAIRS.

Battersea Arts Centre ● *See* **Non-producing theatres.**

Bush Theatre
Shepherds Bush Green, London W12 8QD
Tel (01) **602 3703**
Joint artistic directors Nicky Pallot and Brian Stirner

> An exciting studio theatre, seating 105, producing new plays by British and foreign writers. Recent productions: *The Brave* by Sharman Macdonald (directed by Simon Stokes); *Raping the Gold* by Lucy Gannon (Debbie Shewell); *Handful of Stars* by Bill Roche (Robin Lefevre). Equity contracts. Do not advertise, and do not welcome casting queries from actors. 'Casting breakdowns are not given out, but a list of actors suitable for any part is drawn up. Their availabilities are checked so that casting proceeds from the theatre outwards rather than the reverse. The policy is to cast actors whose work we know. It is helpful, therefore, if actors keep us up to date with where their work can be seen.'

Café Theatre Upstairs
Bear & Staff, 37 Charing Cross Road, London WC2
Tel (01) **240 0794**
Artistic director Michael Almaz

> The London base for the Artaud Theatre Company, founded as a touring company in 1973; have been in London since 1981. Produce at least 25 plays per year with the emphasis on adaptations. Productions include: *Intimacy* by

Jean-Paul Sartre (directed by Michael Almaz); *Underground Man* by Feodor Dostoevsky (Israel Zohar). All productions are profit-share. Occasionally advertise in *PCR* or *The Stage*. Hold general auditions, and welcome letters enclosing CV and photograph. Address them to: D41 Odhams Walk, Long Acre, London WC2H 9SB.

Common Stock Theatre Company
182 Hammersmith Road, London W6 7DJ

After losing its grant in the early 1980s, Common Stock is now only involved in local community youth theatre projects that do not involve professional actors.

The Corner Theatre
Hen & Chickens Pub, 109 St Paul's Road, Highbury Corner, London N1 2NA
Tel (01) **226 3724**
Artistic director Tony Heywood

Small pub theatre seating 64 (beautiful tip-up seats rescued from the theatre on Brighton pier). Try to produce two in-house shows annually, but generally play host to incoming companies. Interested in new writing, and aim to promote women's theatre (2–3 women's companies annually). Try to have one foreign theatre company a year. Recent productions: *Philadelphia Here I Come* (directed by John Quinn); *Now and at the Hour of Our Death* (devised by Trouble & Strife Company); *The Glass Hill* (Phelim Mcdermott). All in-house productions are on a profit-share basis. In-house casting advertised in *The Stage*, *Time Out* 'Theatreboard', *Casting Report*. Welcome queries from actors; telephone call in the first instance.

Cut-Cloth Theatre
41 Beresford Road, London N5 2HR
Tel (01) **359 4150**
Artistic director Robert Duirs

Workshops and profit-share productions. Recent production: *The Long and the Short and the Tall*. Advertise in *The Stage*. Do not welcome casting queries from actors.

Donmar Warehouse Theatre ● *See* **Non-producing theatres.**

The Drill Hall ● *See* **Non-producing theatres.**

Foco Novo Theatre Company ● *See* **Touring companies.**

Forkbeard Fantasy ● *See* **Touring companies.**

Gate Theatre
11 Pembridge Road, London W11
Tel (01) **229 5387**
Artistic director Giles Croft

Small venue, seating 60, which opened in 1979 above the Prince Albert Pub in Notting Hill and specializes in translated plays. Recent productions: *Naomi* (directed by Giles Croft); *Pains of Youth* (Patti Love); *The Audition* (Astrid Hilne); *Turcaret* (Janet Amsden); *Struggle of the Black Man and the Dogs* (M. Batz). Usually operate on a non-Equity basis. Advertise in *SBS*, and welcome casting queries from actors – 'a phone call is sometimes more successful as letters are easier to ignore.'

Half Moon Theatre
213 Mile End Road, London E1 4AA
Tel (01) **791 1141**
Artistic director Chris Bond's successor unknown at the time of writing

> Founded 1977. Flexible seating: maximum 320. This creative centre in the heart of the East End produces five in-house productions each year, with an emphasis on new writing. Recent productions: *Macbeth, As Is* and *Poppy* (all directed by Chris Bond); *Every Black Day* (Phyllida Lloyd). Cast from play to play; Equity contract. Do not advertise, but welcome letters enclosing CV and photograph; hold general auditions. 'Particularly interested in considering local actors.'

Hampstead Theatre
Swiss Cottage Centre, London NW3 3EX
Tel (01) **722 9224**
Artistic director Jenny Topper
Associate directors John Dove, Robin Lefevre

> Founded 1959. Seating capacity: 176. Leading London company that produces six plays a year and concentrates on promoting new work by new and established writers, with the occasional revival of a classic. Recent productions: *Aristocrats* by Brian Friel (directed by Robin Lefevre); *Danger: Memory!* by Arthur Miller (Jack Gold); *Smelling a Rat* (devised and directed by Mike Leigh). Do not hold general auditions; cast separately for each production. Do not advertise for actors, but welcome letters with CV, photograph and SAE.

ICA Theatre ● *See* Non-producing theatres.

Joint Stock Theatre Group ● *See* Touring companies.

King's Head Theatre Club
115 Upper Street, Islington, London N1 1QN
Tel (01) **226 1916**
Artistic director Dan Crawford

> Founded 1970. Seating capacity: 110. Leading fringe venue producing five in-house productions each year for six-week runs, plus in-coming companies. In 1988, two plays transferred to the West End. Productions include: *Easy Virtue, Artist Descending a Staircase* and *When She Danced* (all directed by Tim Luscombe). Non-Equity contracts (1988 rate of £100 per week). Advertise in *The Stage*, and welcome letters with CVs and photographs in response to these ads; do not, however, have the facilities to keep information on file.
>
> There is also a lunch-time theatre (artistic director: Sid Golder); in-coming productions only.

Latchmere Theatre
503 Battersea Park Road, London SW11 3BW
Tel (01) **223 3108**
Artistic director Chris Fisher

> Purpose-built studio theatre (seating 95) above the Latchmere Public House and base for the London Actors Theatre Company. Productions range from theatre for young people to new plays and revivals for the general public. Recent productions: *Rosencrantz and Guildenstern Are Dead, Hamlet, Sleeping Beauty* and *The Screamer* (all directed by Chris Fisher); *Romeo and Juliet* (Chris Fisher & Mark Freeland). Some productions are profit-share, some Equity contracts. Advertise for actors in *The Stage, SBS* and *PCR*. Do not welcome casting queries: 'Plays are cast on a production-to-production basis, and actors are advised to

apply for auditions for specific productions, not general casting/unsolicited auditions, etc.'

London Actors Theatre Company ● See LATCHMERE THEATRE.

Man in the Moon Theatre Club
392 King's Road, Chelsea, London SW3 5UZ
Tel (01) **351 2876**
Artistic director Leigh Shine

> Small theatre (44 seats) above a pub, presenting new plays including adaptations of contemporary significance, with the accent on encouraging new writers at an early stage of their careers. In addition, they present revivals of rarely performed plays. Only 2–3 in-house productions per year; play host to in-coming plays. Recent in-house productions: *Our Own Red Blood* by Cecil Jenkin (directed by Paul Moore); *Significant Others* by Charles Dennis (Angela Langfield); *The Best Years of Your Life* by Clive Jermain (Rod Bolt). Usually profit-share or an agreed fee. Sometimes advertise in *The Stage*, but do not welcome casting queries from actors.

Millfield Theatre
Silver Street, Edmonton, London N18 1PJ
Tel (01) **807 6186**
Artistic director Graham Bennett

> New, purpose-built theatre, seating 356–400, which opened in December 1988 with *Humpty Dumpty*. Productions (both amateur and professional), tours, concerts, recitals, etc. Equity contracts. Advertise in *The Stage*, and do not welcome unsolicited casting queries from actors.

New End Theatre ● See Non-producing theatres.

Old Red Lion Theatre
St John Street, Islington, London EC1V 4NJ
Tel (01) **833 3053**
Director Richard Hansom

> Founded 1979. Seating capacity: 60–80. Mainly a venue for visiting fringe companies such as Inner City and Empty Space, producing new plays. In 1983, the theatre had its first transfer to the West End with *Crystal Clear*. Recent productions: *Up Against It* (stage version of Joe Orton's screenplay written for The Beatles); *American Eagle*. Most productions that visit the Old Red Lion are profit-share.

Orange Tree Theatre
45 Kew Road, Richmond, Surrey TW1 2NQ
Tel (01) **940 0141/3633**
Artistic director Sam Walters

> Theatre-in-the-round seating 80. New plays, classics, musicals and revivals of neglected or overlooked work. Recent productions: *Absolute Hell* by Rodney Ackland, *The Secret Life* by Harley Granville Barker, *No More A-Roving* by John Whiting; *Mother Courage* by Bertolt Brecht and *Largo Desolato* by Vaclav Havel (all directed by Sam Walters); *Definitely the Bahamas* by Martin Crimp (Alec McCowen); *The Hole in the Top of the World* by Fay Weldon (Stephanie Turner). Equity contracts. Do not advertise, but welcome casting queries from actors; send letter with CV and photograph.

Comment
Currently fund-raising for a new 200-seat theatre in Richmond. Sam Walters — who also founded the Oval House Theatre (*see* Non-producing theatres) — won a *Time Out/01 for London* award in 1988 in recognition of an exceptional season of revivals of little-known works at the Orange Tree.

Oval House Theatre ● *See* Non-producing theatres.

Pentameters Theatre
Three Horseshoes, 28 Heath Street, London NW3
Tel (01) **435 6757**
Contact Leonie Scott-Matthews

Founded 1968 to promote poetry and new writing. Seating capacity: 100. Recent production: *Don't Blame It on the Moonlight*. Generally profit-share productions. Rarely advertise for actors, but welcome casting queries by telephone. Particularly interested in people who take an active interest in the theatre, which is run as a club. Leonie Scott-Matthews is always present on performance nights.

Pioneer Theatres Ltd ● *See* THEATRE ROYAL STRATFORD EAST.

Riverside Studios
Crisp Road, Hammersmith, London W6 9RL
Tel (01) **741 2251**
Artistic director Di Robson

Founded in 1976 by Peter Gill who established its reputation as an international theatre. Mainly hosts visiting companies — approximately 10–15 each year — with only one or two in-house productions. Autumn 1988 saw: *A Doll's House* (in-house) and Bristol Old Vic's production of *Bag Lady* by Frank McGuinness. Do not advertise for actors, and due to so few in-house productions, do not welcome casting queries.

Soho Poly Theatre
16 Riding House Street, London W1P 7PD
Tel (01) **580 6982**
Artistic director Tony Craze

A studio basement theatre seating approximately 55. A front-runner in encouraging new writing. Recent productions include: *Going West* by Tony Craze (directed by Sue Dunderdale); *Holy Days* by Sally Wemeth (Brian Stirner); *Children of the Dust* by Anne Aylor (Terry Johnson). Equity contracts. Do not advertise for actors, but welcome casting queries; approach in writing in the first instance.

Tabard Theatre
2 Bath Road, Turnham Green, Chiswick, London W4 1LW
Tel (01) **995 6035**

Theatre, with a seating capacity of 75, has a policy of producing new work that is well written and stimulating and has potential. Recent productions: *Allegiance* (directed by 'collective effort under new management'); *For You, My Sons* (Rowena Rolton-McGann). All productions are on a profit-share basis. Advertise in *The Stage*, *PCR* and Equity *Jobgrapevine*. Welcome casting queries from actors; send letter with CV, photograph and SAE: 'Please make sure CVs are neatly typed. Find something memorable about you but don't go overboard. Always enclose a SAE. At an audition, be friendly but please do not invade the director's space.'

Talawa Theatre Company Ltd
38 King Street, Covent Garden, London WC2E 8JT
Tel (01) **379 6509**
Artistic director Yvonne Brewster

Founded 1985 by Yvonne Brewster, Inigo Espejel, Mona Hammond and Carmen Munroe. With the aim of using ancient African rituals and black political experience, they set out to expand modern black British theatre and make it more accessible to British people. Usually perform in London venues but have co-produced *The Importance of Being Earnest* with the Tyne Theatre Company for a Number 1 tour. Other productions include: *The Black Jacobins, An Echo in the Bone* and *O Babylon!* (directed by Yvonne Brewster). Equity contracts. Cast for each production. Do not advertise but welcome casting queries from actors. Send photograph, CV and SAE; details are kept on file for future reference.

Théâtre de Complicité ● *See* Touring companies.

Theatre Royal Stratford East (Pioneer Theatres Ltd)
Gerry Raffles Square, Newham, London E15 1BN
Tel (01) **534 7374**
Artistic director Philip Hedley

A leading theatre, well known throughout the country, producing Afro-Asian and Afro-Caribbean drama, family shows, melodramas, pantomimes, populist plays, variety and youth shows. A Victorian theatre built in 1884 with a seating capacity of 476. Recent productions: *Fatty* and *King of England* by Barrie Keefe (directed by Philip Hedley); *Twelfth Night* (Jeff Teare); *The Ragged Trousered Philanthropists* (Stephen Daldry). Equity contracts. Sometimes advertise in *PCR*, but usually cast from their own files. Welcome letters with CV and photograph.

Comment
Joan Littlewood's Theatre Workshop moved to the Theatre Royal in 1953, but the high ideal of 'A British People's Theatre', which she had hitherto pursued with commendable single-mindedness, soon gave way to the many attractions — not least financial — of staging West End transfers. Popular and critical success followed with such productions as *The Hostage, A Taste of Honey, Fings Ain't Wot They Used to Be* and *Oh What a Lovely War!*.

Three Horseshoes ● *See* PENTAMETERS THEATRE.

Trestle Theatre Company ● *See* Touring companies.

Tricycle Theatre
269 Kilburn High Road, London NW6 7JR
Tel (01) **372 6611**
Artistic director Nicolas Kent

Founded in 1972 as a touring company and moved to its London base in 1980. The theatre was destroyed by fire in 1987, but will be re-opening in 1989 with a seating capacity of 225. Produce new plays; particularly interested in writing from ethnic minorities. Credits include: *The Great White Hope, Playboy of the West Indies, The Hostage*. Also host visiting theatre companies. Equity contracts, normally six weeks long. Do not advertise for actors, but welcome casting queries. Approach in writing in the first instance; details are kept on file. No general auditions.

Tron Theatre Company

38 Parnie Street, Glasgow G1 5HB
Tel (041) **552 3748/5940**
Artistic director Michael Boyd

Formerly a church, the theatre opened in 1982 with a seating capacity of 215, having established a lively reputation with performances in its café/bar which opened in 1980. Produce major new plays from experienced Scottish writers, as well as new American and European writing. Also host Scottish touring companies such as Communicado, as well as such international companies as Pocket Opera, Moscow Studio Theatre of the South-west, Shaliko and La Mamma from New York. Recent in-house productions include: *Dr Faustus, Philadelphia Here I Come* and *Sleeping Beauty* (all directed by Michael Boyd); *Gamblers; Babes in the Wood* (Hamish Glen); *The White Bird Passes* (Andi Ross). Equity contracts. Do not advertise, but will consider letters of enquiry from actors.

Warehouse Theatre Croydon

62 Dingwall Road, Croydon, Surrey CR0 2NF
Tel (01) **681 1257**
Artistic director Ted Craig

Major fringe theatre with a policy of producing new writing. A flexible performance space with seating of 100/120. According to the *Financial Times*, 'The auditorium has a genuine atmosphere under its splendid roof of beams and rafters.' The main aim of the theatre is to produce its own productions — usually six per year — running for 5—6 weeks each. Also promote touring companies who have a commitment to new work. Recent productions: *In the Image of the Beast* (written & directed by Jonathan Holloway; co-production with Red Shift Theatre Company); *Children of the Dust* by Anne Aylor (Terry Johnson); *Sinners and Saints* by James Mundy (Celia Bannerman); *Savannah Bay* by Margurite Duras (Sue Todd; co-production with Foco Novo); *Pommies* by David Allen (Ted Craig). Equity contracts. Occasionally advertise in *SBS, PCR* and Equity *Job Grapevine* when special skills are required. Welcome casting queries from actors; send letter with SAE: 'General letters can only be filed for further reference when casting. By far the most useful letter is one informing us of an appearance in a play or production which we are able to cover.'

The Young Vic

66 The Cut, Waterloo, London SE1 8LZ
Tel (01) **633 0133**
Artistic director David Thacker

Leading fringe venue with a main house theatre-in-the-round (seating 500) which can be adapted to thrust (seating 430), and a studio theatre seating 114. Produce classics, new plays, plays by contemporary writers, and plays for family audiences. Recent productions: *Solomon and the Big Cat* by David Holman, *A Touch of the Poet* by Eugene O'Neill, *Romeo and Juliet* and *Comedians* by Trevor Griffiths (directed by David Thacker); *Doctor Faustus* (Anthony Clark); *The Small Poppies* by David Holman (Matthew Marsh). Equity contracts. Do not advertise for actors, but welcome casting queries; approach in writing in the first instance.

Comment

The Young Vic was opened in 1970, under the direction of Frank Dunlop, as an offshoot of the National Theatre (at the time, based almost next door at the Old Vic). It broke away from the National in 1974 and reaffirmed its reputation under Michael Bogdanov and, latterly, David Thacker.

11. Touring companies

Aba Daba Company (Pindar Productions – Water Rats Theatre)
Water Rats Dinner Theatre, 328 Gray's Inn Road, London WC1
Tel (01) **722 5395**
Contact Aline Waites, 30 Upper Park Road, London NW3 2UT

Founded 1970 at the Pindar of Wakefield pub, now known as the Water Rats Dinner Theatre. Musical comedy, revue, cabaret and music hall. Most productions are specially commissioned and use original music and comedy. Apart from performing at their base theatre, they tour to theatres, hotels, schools – 'anywhere there is space, a piano and a dressing room.' Company of 6–7 actors on contracts of varying length (profit share and guarantee). Very occasionally advertise in Equity *Jobgrapevine*. Welcome casting queries, although 'we have too many to cope with individually.' Approach in writing in the first instance, then telephone. 'Most actors we use have been in the business over five years. There are opportunities for younger people in pantos. We do not take anyone without a card except in *very* exceptional circumstances.'

Actors Touring Company
Alford House, Aveline Street, London SE11 5DQ
Tel (01) **735 8311**
Artistic director To be announced in 1989
General manager Joanne Reid

Founded 1978. Leading small-scale touring company which, under the direction of its past directors, John Retallack and Mark Brickman, has established an excellent reputation for producing innovative and inventive theatre ranging from 'classic epic texts with a collaborating ensemble to "big theatre on a small scale" '. Recent productions: *Faustus* (adapted by Mark Brickman); *Princess Ivona* by Witold Gombrowicz; *The Illusion* by Corneille. Perform in arts centres, studio theatres, educational and outdoor venues with a company of 5/6 actors plus stage management of two. ITC/Equity contract of approximately four months. Perform single nights, two nights, split weeks, whole weeks, plus three weeks in London. Advertise in *SBS*, *PCR* and Equity *Jobgrapevine*, and welcome casting queries from actors; approach in writing in the first instance.

Age Exchange Theatre Trust
The Reminiscence Centre, 11 Blackheath Village, London SE3 9LA
Tel (01) **318 9105**
Artistic director Pam Schweitzer

Founded 1983. Tour 'reminiscence' shows based on the memories of pensioners on a range of topics such as work and leisure in the 1920s and 1930s and life in general 50 years ago. Perform in old people's homes, sheltered housing units, community centres. Usually four tours annually. ITC/Equity small-scale touring contract of 7–13 weeks. Advertise in *The Stage*. Welcome casting queries; approach in writing in the first instance, enclosing CV, photograph and SAE. Most shows have a musical content, and it is important that actors can sing and, preferably, play a musical instrument. Also a youth theatre that holds workshops, etc. for local children aged 10–15 years.

Animus

22 Boydell Court, St John's Wood Park, London NW8 6NJ
Tel (01) **722 0323**
Artistic directors Sean Aita, Adam Henderson

Founded 1984; formerly The Commercial Theatre. Productions range from 'Shakespeare to improvised spectacle performed for unsuspecting audience'. Recent production: *Strange as an Angel* at the Almeida and Edinburgh Festivals. 'We tend to open on the London fringe and then search for arts festival bookings.' Company of 2–8 performers; non-Equity, 'but there is genuine profit to share'. Sometimes advertise in *SBS*, *PCR* and *The Stage*, but welcome casting queries from actors; approach in writing in the first instance.

Avon Touring Theatre Company

Albany Centre, Shaftesbury Avenue, Montpelier, Bristol BS6 5LL
Tel (0272) **555436**

Founded 1974. A Bristol-based cooperative that produces challenging and thought-provoking shows for non-theatre-going audiences. Productions include: *The Ballad of Mary Burton* (directed by Clair Grove), *Trapped in Time* (Philip Tyler), *Half Hearts and Quarter Measures* (Paulette Randall). Tour to non-theatre venues such as village halls, schools and drop-in centres, as well as small-scale theatres. Three tours annually: a devised show for 13- to 17-year-olds, which tours in tandem with an autumn tour of an adaptation of a classic, and a spring tour of a community show based on research in the South-west. Company of four actors on ITC/Equity small-scale touring contracts. Initial probationary period of three months, then open-ended contract. Advertise in *The Stage* and *The Voice*. Do not welcome general casting queries – prefer letters to be written in response to advertisements. 'We look for actors with a wide range of skills, not only acting and musical but also management skills. The company is run as a cooperative, and part of the actor's job is to be a company manager.'

Bagatelle

Flat 3, 411 Wilmslow Road, Withington, Manchester M20 9NB
Tel (061) **225 2413**
Artistic director Boo Bennett

Founded 1984. Science-fiction clown shows for 4–11-year-olds (*The Robot from Gorf* and *Koggs Ace Space Adventure*) and alternative cabaret/plays for teenagers. 'Company-devised touring productions that are vividly theatrical, using original writing, design, music and songs. These are backed up by an adaptable workshop service. Also produce versions for special-needs and deaf children.' Perform in schools, community venues and festivals. Company of three performers (more for special projects) on one-year contracts. Advertise in local listings and regional arts association magazines. Welcome casting queries from actors: 'Letter and CV first, then phone. Applications in November for workshop auditions in December to join the company at the end of January.'

Black Theatre Cooperative

61 Collier Street, London N1 9BE
Tel (01) **833 3785**
Artistic director Malcolm Frederick

Founded 1980. Small-scale touring company performing plays that touch on the black experience universally. Venues range from main houses to community centres, including a main London fringe venue. Recent productions: *Slipping into Darkness*, *The Cocoa Party*, *11 Josephine House*. Company of five actors on Equity minimum contracts of up to five months in length. Do not advertise, but welcome casting queries from actors; send letter with CV and photograph.

Bootleg Theatre Company

Sherborne House, 20 Greyfriars Close, Salisbury, Wilts. SP1 2LR
Tel (0722) **21250**
Artistic director Colin Burden

Founded 1981. Tour new or rarely performed plays with socially relevant subjects such as unemployment, drug abuse, rape, etc. to art centres, studio venues, schools, colleges and youth clubs. Company of two actors. 'We negotiate performance contracts on number of performances.' Advertise in *The Stage* and welcome casting queries from actors; approach in writing in the first instance, enclosing CV. 'We formed the company through disillusionment with the type of plays on show. We wanted to stage good, new or obscure material that we believed was necessary, and although we have had several major setbacks (and this probably sounds very clichéd), we feel that sheer determination and belief in yourself is the only way to achieve any success at all.'

Borderline Theatre Company

Darlington New Church, North Harbour Street, Ayr KA8 8AA
Tel (0292) **281010**
Artistic director Morag Fullerton

Founded 1974. Tour to main house theatres in city centres and small venues in outlying districts, plus the Edinburgh Festival, Mayfest and, occasionally, London. Mainly new and contemporary work, plus revivals. Productions include: *Trumpets and Raspberries*, *Threepenny Opera*, *Writer's Cramp*, *A Night in the Ukraine*. Company of 6/8 actors on subsidized rep contracts of 8–15 weeks. Only advertise (in *SBS*) if seeking a specific type: 'We have a body of regular actors we use.' Welcome casting queries; details are kept on file and looked at when casting.

BP Springboard Theatre Company

20 Lansdowne Road, London N10 2AU
Tel (01) **883 4586**
Artistic director Clive Wolfe

Founded in 1987 to take accessible work into small scale venues, Springboard is the professional counterpart of the National Student Theatre Company using actors who have progressed from student drama to the professional stage. Productions have included: *Journeys Among the Dead* by Eugene Ionesco and *Handle with Care* by Jane Thornton. 'Anyone now at school or college who would like to work with Springboard later on can do no better than to start by attending the National Student Drama Festival.' Funded by British Petroleum.

Bristol Express Theatre Company

20 Mocatta House, Brady Street, Whitechapel, London E1 5DL
Tel (01) **247 4156**
Artistic director Andy Jordan

Founded 1978. Mainly produce new work by new writers, but the overall range is 'from the commercial to the difficult and challenging'. Usually seven productions annually. Recent credits: *Elsie and Norm's Macbeth* by John Christopher; *Winter Darkness* by Allan Cubitt; *Child's Play* by Jon Wolfman. Tour to a wide range of venues, from small-scale to No. 1 theatres. ITC/Equity contract of 20 weeks.

Advertise in *The Stage*, and welcome casting queries from actors: approach in writing in the first instance – details are kept on file.

Bruvvers

Ouseburn Warehouse Workshops, 36 Lime Street, Stepney, Newcastle upon Tyne NE1 2FQ
Tel (091) **261 9230**
Artistic director Michael Mould

Founded 1969. Community tours for all age ranges. Productions have included: *The Adventures of Little Red Riding Hood* (instructional show against child sexual abuse); *You've Got Me Singing the Blues* (on poverty and mental illness). Tour to schools, hospitals, community centres, youth clubs, tenants huts, etc. Company of six actors on long-term contracts (musical ability necessary). Rarely advertise, but welcome casting queries from actors.

Buster Theatre

2 Trinity Church Square, London SE1 4HV
Tel (01) **407 5192**
Artistic directors Sarah Harper, Sarah Cahn

Small-scale tours of devised work for an audience age range of 14 years upwards. Company of nine on 10–week contracts; pay Equity rates. Advertise in *The Stage*, and welcome casting queries from actors; approach in writing in the first instance. Auditions held twice a year.

Cambridge Theatre Company

8 Market Passage, Cambridge CB2 3PE
Tel (0223) **357134**

Founded 1969. Classics, modern plays and new works. Tour nationwide (from Inverness to Poole) and also abroad, performing in middle-scale theatres. Recent productions: *A Tale of Two Cities, A Woman of No Importance, The Alchemist.* Company of 6–10 actors on Esher contracts: four weeks rehearsal plus 6–9 weeks touring. Do not advertise for actors.

At the time of writing, the artistic director for the past six years, Bill Pryde, announced his resignation. He was reported as saying that the Arts Council's current funding policies had created too many artistic restrictions for him to continue, and that there was 'no room for artistic risk-taking'.

Carib Theatre Productions

Linburn House, 342 Kilburn High Road, London NW6 2QJ
Tel (01) **624 5860**
Artistic director Anton Phillips

Founded 1981. Tours to middle-scale venues for approximately eight weeks in the spring, plus Theatre-in-Education (TIE) tour centred on London for the summer and autumn terms (8–15 weeks). Recent productions: *The Prophet* (devised by Renu Setna); *The Amen Corner* by James Baldwin; *Smokey* by Judith Hepburn (TIE for under 5s); *All I Can't Do Is See* (TIE for 7–12-year-olds); *Crown Versus Cramer* by Alan Cooke (TIE for 13–17-year-olds). Equity contracts. Sometimes advertise in *SBS*, and welcome casting queries from actors; approach in writing in the first instance. 'Carib Theatre was formed to give black actors, writers, designers, directors, technical staff and stage managers more opportunities to practise and develop their skills. Carib's work reflects the multi-cultural nature of British society and aims at the highest possible professional standards. Carib commissions new scripts for TIE work.'

Century Theatre

Lakeside, Keswick, Cumbria CA12 5DJ
Tel (07687) **72282**
Artistic director Han Duijvendak

Founded 1949. Commenced touring in 1950 in the purpose-built mobile theatre known as the 'Blue Box' – a collection of trailers which, when assembled, comprise a 225–seat theatre. The Blue Box is still the base for the company and is used for their summer season in Keswick; however, since 1981, Century Theatre have toured without it. Originally only toured in Yorkshire, but now perform in middle-scale venues nationwide and are the third largest Arts Council-funded middle-scale touring company (after the Cambridge Theatre Company and the Oxford Stage Company). Tour 4–5 shows annually for a total of 35 weeks, plus a summer season of 15 weeks with a repertoire of three or four shows. Aim to produce mainstream theatre in exciting new ways by scaling down large-scale productions to meet the needs and restrictions of middle-scale venues. Recent productions include: *Cabaret* (using an ensemble company of 11 actor/musicians); *Hobson's Choice* and *The Glass Menagerie* (both incorporating music); *Accidental Death of an Anarchist*. Tours last from 6 to 15 weeks. Company of 4–15 actors on subsidized rep contracts. Advertise in *SBS*, Equity *Jobgrapevine* and *PCR*. Happy to receive letters with CVs and photographs. Do not hold general auditions. In working towards building an ensemble company for each project, Han Duijvendak does not require audition pieces; instead the actor reads from the play and takes part in a workshop: 'This enables both sides to see how well they can work together.'

Channel Theatre Company

Granville Theatre, Victoria Parade, Ramsgate, Kent CT11 8DG
Tel (0843) **588260**
Artistic director Philip Dart

Founded 1980. Tour a wide range of productions to small- and middle-scale venues. Recent credits: *The Normal Heart, What the Butler Saw, Intimate Exchanges* and *Made in Bangkok* (all directed by Philip Dart). Usually three tours annually of 6–10 weeks. Equity subsidized rep contract. Have a core of actors which are used regularly. Advertise in *The Stage* and Equity *Jobgrapevine*. Prefer letters to be in response to advertisements; always enclose SAE.

Charabanc Theatre Company

The Ulster Hall, Linenhall Street, Belfast BT2 8BG
Tel (0232) **234242**
Joint directors Marie Jone, Carol Scanlan, Eleanor Mathven

Founded 1983. Tour throughout Ireland, UK, USA and Europe to small/middle scale venues. Perform new writing. Company of four to seven actors on 2-month contracts (currently applying to ITC for Equity contracts). Do not advertise for actors. Due to having only one administrator, they are unable to reply to queries from actors. 'We have never recruited from unsolicited applications from actors as we usually cast from people whose work we know.'

Cheek by Jowl

Alford House, Aveline Street, London SE11 5DQ
Tel (01) **793 0153/4**
Artistic directors Declan Donnellan, Nick Ormerod

Founded 1981. Award-winning touring company much lauded for its innovative productions of world classics. Middle- and small-scale tours annually, both national and worldwide. Recent productions: *Twelfth Night, The Cid* by Pierre

Corneille; *Macbeth*; *A Family Affair* by Alexander Ostrovsky. Company of 8–13 actors plus stage management of 2/3. Use both ITC/Equity and TMA subsidized rep contracts, depending on type of tour (pay 30–40% above minimum rate); 5–10 months in length. Never advertise for actors, and do not welcome casting queries. 'We always use a casting director who produces an audition list for us. We regularly use people straight out of drama school who have been suggested in this way. We believe that a drama school training is essential for our style of work. We actively pursue an integrated casting policy.'

The Cherub Company

Flat 4, 14 Canfield Gardens, London NW6 3JU
Tel (01) **624 7802**
Artistic director Andrew Visnevski

Founded 1978. Middle-scale tours of popular and neglected classics, new adaptations of world drama (e.g. Kafka, Calderon) and new plays that fit the company's policy. Average company size of 10–12 on Equity minimum contracts. Tour a minimum of three nights, plus 'tours abroad for the British Council, commercial managements and impressarios'. Recent productions: *Twelfth Night* and *The Castle*. Do not advertise, but welcome casting queries from actors; send letter with CV and SAE. 'It is important, when agents send clients for auditions, they understand exactly what they are auditioning for! Too often, agents send clients who are undoubtedly talented but totally unsuited to the job, which wastes everyone's time. It should also be understood if the applicant is going to be asked to "do a piece" or "read". Applicants turn up with nothing prepared or do not wish to read for a part, thinking it is merely an interview and not an audition. It is always wise for young artists to have something up their sleeves in case they are asked to do something. Choice of audition piece should be something that suits their talents and personality and, preferably, *not* the inevitable Hamlet or Juliet. Originality is a plus mark.'

Clean Break Theatre Company

Basement, 34a Stratford Villas, London NW1 9SG
Tel (01) **485 0008**

Founded 1979. Small-scale touring company that mainly employs female ex-prisoners. Have produced 18 shows since the company was formed, including: *Voices from Prison* (devised by the company); *Te Awa I Tahutu* (*The River that Ran Away*) by Rena Owen. Perform in a wide range of venues, from the Barbican main stage to the Oval House, Albany Empire, Theatro Technis, prisons, youth custody centres, drug–alcohol rehabilitation centres and mental-health day centres. Company of three actors on ten-week Equity small-scale touring contracts. Advertise for actors in *The Stage*. Welcome casting queries ('women only'); approach in writing in the first instance. 'We try to centralize the experiences of women, the law and imprisonment by creating dramas, plays and workshops for touring to different communities. The afterplay discussion is always invaluable in breaking down the myths surrounding women and crime. It is helpful if the actors have experience of prison, interest in the penal system, etc.'

The Commercial Theatre ● *See* ANIMUS.

Communicado

Royal Lyceum Theatre, Grindlay Street, Edinburgh EH3 9AX
Tel (031) **229 7404**
Artistic director Gerard Mulgrew

Founded 1983. Small-scale touring company performing in anything from village halls to small- or medium-scale theatres. A wide range of productions, including new writing. Recent productions: *Mary Queen of Scots Got Her Head Chopped Off*; *Tales of the Arabian Nights*. Over the past few years, have opened a show at the Edinburgh Fringe, followed by a 6–8 week tour (1988 saw the première of a new translation of *Blood Wedding*, much acclaimed and seen at the Donmar Warehouse in London soon after the Festival). Company of 8–10 on ITC contracts of a minimum of six weeks (maximum 16 weeks). Occasionally advertise in *The Stage*. Welcome casting queries from actors; approach in writing in the first instance. 'We are an association of theatre artists working (mainly) in Scotland, interested in evolving an eclectic style of theatre which is at once popular and innovative, in which respect we mix text, live music, visual imagery and the physical resources of the performer as well as an awareness of our indigenous culture. The nature of our work is Scottish and international, specific but universal.'

Compass Theatre Company (Actors Cabal Ltd)
The Leadmill, 6–7 Leadmill Road, Sheffield S1 4SF
Tel (0742) **755328**
Artistic director Neil Sissons

Founded 1981. Mainly tour classical works, with an occasional new play normally written by Neil Sissons and Nicholas Chadwin. Past productions have included: *Volpone*, *The Winter's Tale*, *Romeo and Juliet*, *The Tempest*, *A Higher Passion*, *Macbeth*, *Spartacus*, *The Odyssey*. Perform in a wide variety of venues — No. 1 theatres, small- and middle-scale venues, arts and community centres and schools. Currently tour 30 weeks a year, including six weeks in Germany. Company of six actors plus one stage manager on nine-month contracts (September to July) with Equity rates of pay. Advertise in *The Stage*, and welcome query letters from actors. 'Compass specialize particularly in the narrative language of the piece, combined with the physical style of performance suited to an ensemble company. To join Compass, actors need to have initiative, versatility and, above all, endurance for what is a very heavy and tiring schedule.'

Crummles Theatre Company
86 Queen Alexandra Mansions, Judd Street, London WC1
Tel (01) **837 0587** Telex **265871 MONREF G (quote 72:MAG36007)**
Contact Ellie Dickens (artistic director), Roger Bilder (administrator)

Founded 1983. Productions include: *Absurd Person Singular* and *Absent Friends* (both directed by Doug Fisher); *Othello* (Joseph Marceu); *My Dearest Kate* (John Dryden). Tours (3–4 weeks) to small- and middle-scale venues, including annual visit to the Edinburgh Fringe. Occasionally profit-share. Advertise in *The Stage*, and welcome casting queries from actors; approach in writing in the first instance.

Cumbernauld Theatre Company
Cumbernauld Theatre, Kildrum, Cumbernauld G67 2BN
Tel (0236) **737235**
Director Robert Robson

Founded 1979. Produce popular theatre, new plays by Scottish writers, children's shows, educational drama and established plays. Tour to community centres, halls, schools and art centres, as well as performing at the Cumbernauld Theatre. Recent productions: *Checking Out* by Marcella Evaristi; *A Christmas Carol*; *Shakers* by John Godber and Jane Thornton. Company of 4–6 on Equity subsidized rep contracts of eight weeks. Occasionally advertise in *The Stage*, and welcome casting queries from actors; write in the first instance.

DAC

School House, Church Lane, Barnburgh, Doncaster DN5 7EU
Tel (0709) **892462**
Artistic director Ron Rose

Founded 1979. Community tours, theatre-in-education (TIE) and mainstream theatre — all new or very recent work. 'We aim in the main to play to non-theatre audiences plays drawn from their history and experience; to represent South Yorkshire; to conduct occasional main-house incursions in London.' Recent productions: *Perdition* by Jim Allen; *Cinderella* by Martin Riley; *What Was It Like?* by Ron Rose; *Esther's Tomcat* by Ian McMillan; *Tilly Mint and the Dodo* by Berlie Doherty; *Fun City* by Barry Hines. Perform in clubs, pubs, schools and theatres (twice daily for TIE; once-nightly, local touring). Average company of 6–9 on 9–15-week ITC contracts. Pay above Equity minimum. Do not advertise for actors: 'We file letters, but only very occasionally use them.' 'We work with people who want to do the work we do, play to the audiences we play, wish to be associated with DAC. No non-Equity, no careless approaches. We have a core group of performers.'

dereck dereck productions

24 Idlecombe Road, Tooting, London SW17 9TB
Tel (01) **767 3042**
Joint artistic directors Julia Bardsley and Phelim McDermott

Founded 1984. Tour to festivals and middle-scale venues. Movement-based productions including an adaptation of Ted Hughes' poem *Gaudete* (directed by Julia Bardsley and Phelim McDermott); *The Cupboard Man* by Ian McEwen (Julia Bardsley). In January, took part in the International Mime Festival at the Almeida Theatre. Company of 1 to 8 actors. In 1989, hope to be able to issue Equity contracts (funding by the Arts Council is pending). Advertise through ITC. Welcome casting queries from actors; details kept on file.

Dr Foster's Travelling Theatre Company

The Old Convent, Beeches Green, Stroud, Glos. GL5 4AD
Tel (04536) **71903**

Founded 1980. Community and outdoor shows plus educational projects, all of which are suitable for mainly non-theatre going audiences in rural areas. Recent productions: *The Secret Agent* (adapted by Chris Stagg from the novel by Conrad); *Lives Worth Living*; *Wall to Wall*; *Windfall*. Perform in village halls, community centres, schools, small arts centres and non-theatre venues. Generally one-night stands in the South-west plus occasional weeks outside the region. Company of four actors on ITC/Equity contracts of 16 weeks. Advertise for actors in *The Stage* and SBS. Prefer enquiries to specific job adverts, but will reply to query letters.

Dual Control Theatre Company Ltd

4 The Close, Rochester, Kent ME1 1SP
Tel (0634) **402598**
Artistic director Michael Bath

Founded 1985. 'We are a new writing company — promoting writers from the South-east — work which is both innovative and of a high standard.' Tour to arts centres, schools and theatres — from small-scale to No. 1 venues. Two tours each year performing one-night stands, split and full weeks, and residencies. Recent productions: *Ouch*; *Black Nightingale*. Company size can be from 5 to 32, depending on the production; Equity contracts. Advertise in *PCR*, Equity

Jobgrapevine and through agents. Welcome casting queries from actors; write in the first instance.

Durham Theatre Company

The Arts Centre, Vane Terrace, Darlington, Co. Durham DL3 7AX
Tel (0325) **469861**
Artistic director Laurence Sach

Founded 1977. Autumn tour (usually a production with musical content) and annual pantomime. Productions include: *Every Night Something Awful* by Denise Deegan; *Mother Goose*; *Trafford Tanzi* by Claire Luckham; *Sinbad*; *Godspell*; *The Beggar's Opera*; *Robinson Crusoe*. Perform in community centres, village halls, schools and small arts centres. One-night stands (returning to base each night), mainly in Co. Durham but also Cleveland and Tyne & Wear. Company of five actors and stage management of two on ITC/Equity contracts. Usually through cast from autumn tour to panto, which means a 23-week contract. Sometimes advertise in *Report* and Equity *Jobgrapevine*. Welcome letters from actors ('do not phone'); CVs and photographs kept on file for three years.

Eastern Angles Theatre Company

The Drama Centre, Gateacre Road, Ipswich, Suffolk IP1 2LQ
Tel (0473) **218202**
Artistic director Ivan Cutting

Founded 1982. 'All productions use music and are original to the company. They often reflect some flavour of the region.' Tour a wide range of venues, from 'the smallest village hall to the largest theatre', mostly in the region, returning to base most nights. Performances are from Tuesday to Saturday. Recent productions: *John Barleycorn* (new play with music for village halls); *Moll Flanders* (new adaptation for larger-scale venues in towns); *Mr Pickwick's Victorian Christmas*. Company of 4–6 on ITC/Equity contracts ('Pay above minimum, but rarely pay overtime') of not less than ten weeks. Sometimes advertise in *The Stage*. Welcome casting queries, provided the actor is familiar with the company's work or has special skills such as ability to play an instrument.

Empty Space Theatre Company

15 Alleyn Road, London SE21 8AB
Tel (01) **670 5529**
Artistic director Andrew Holmes

Founded 1985. Small scale touring with limited runs at a London fringe venue. Ensemble-based work with a strong emphasis on adaptations of literary originals. Productions include: *The Comfort of Strangers* by Ian McEwan, *The Rainbow* by D. H. Lawrence and *The Aspern Papers* by Henry James. Company of 4/6 actors; non-Equity. Advertise in *PCR*, Equity *Jobgrapevine* and *The Stage*. Actors need to have experience of improvisational work.

Entertainment Machine

22a Birchington Road, London NW6 4LJ
Tel (01) **624 5361**
Artistic director David McGillivray

Founded 1975. Tour to every type of venue, from church hall to main house theatres; normally two national tours each year. Comedy shows: *The Farndale Avenue Housing Estate Townswomen's Guild Dramatic Society's Production of 'A Christmas Carol'* (1987/88); *The Farndale Avenue Housing Estate Townswomen's Guild Dramatic Society Murder Mystery* (1988). Average company of 6–7 actors on three-month contracts. Advertise in *The Stage*, and welcome casting queries from actors; approach in writing in the first instance, enclosing CV and photograph. 'Acting ability alone is not enough. We also require resilience, compatibility, sense of humour and happy-go-lucky attitude regarding our risible wages.'

Field Day Theatre Company

Northern Counties Building, 22 Waterloo Place, Derry BT48 6BU
Tel (0504) **360196**

Founded 1980. Touring company committed to new Irish writing that is relevant to Ireland today. Tour in northern and southern Ireland to theatres, town halls, schools and community halls. Recent productions: *Translations*, *The Communication Cord* and *Making History*, all by Brian Friel; *Boesman and Lena* by Athol Fugard; *Double Cross* by Thomas Kilroy; *Pentecost* by Stewart Parker. Average company of 5/6 actors plus stage management of three on Equity contracts of 3–4 months. Do not advertise, but welcome casting queries from actors; telephone in the first instance.

Foco Novo Theatre Company

1/2 Alfred Place, London WC1E 7EB
Tel (01) **580 4722**
Artistic director Roland Rees

Founded 1972. Leading middle- and small-scale touring company founded by Roland Rees, Bernard Pomerance (author of *The Elephant Man*, subsequently produced by the company) and producer David Aukin. Present new writing and modern classics in an innovative form, performing middle- and small-scale theatres; also neighbourhood shows. Productions include: *Savannah Bay* by Marguerite Duras; *The Cape Orchard* by Michael Picardie; *Bloody Poetry* by Howard Brenton (commissioned by Foco Novo).

At the time of writing, it was announced that the company's Arts Council grant had been cut, resulting in the cancellation of their prestigious new show, *Consequences* by Howard Brenton, Tunde Ikoli, Nigel Williams, Tom Stoppard, Trevor Griffiths, Nell Dunn, Olwen Wymark, Joshua Sobol and Snoo Wilson. The company's future is now in doubt.

Forest Forge Theatre Company

Ringwood Comprehensive School, Manor Road, Ringwood, Hants BH24 1RA
Tel (0425) **470188**
Artistic director Karl Hibbert

Founded 1981. Small-scale touring company that performs TIE projects, specific projects for day centres and old people's homes, and a Christmas family show. Also committed to organizing community projects involving local people. Shows generally devised by the company, music being an integral part of the productions. Annually tour three projects from September to March. A core of four actors, which is added to as required, on ITC/Equity small-scale touring contracts of six months. Advertise in *The Stage*, the ethnic minority press and through ITC's mailing. Prefer to receive letters only in response to specific advertisements. The company pursues an equal opportunities policy. 'Actors in the company must be very versatile — musical skills an advantage.'

Forkbeard Fantasy

Moor Cottage, Huntsham, Tiverton, Devon EX16 7NF
Tel (03986) **329**

Founded 1974. (Recent beneficiary of new Arts Council policy on funding). Cooperative touring company performing devised comedy shows throughout the

UK and Europe. Also tour to small cinemas and film clubs as the 'Britonioni Brothers' with their 16mm films. Two tours annually plus educational residencies, working with schools and handicapped people (usually four sessions per year). Productions include: *Work Ethic, Who Shot the Cameraman?* (performance film) and *Red Strimmers* (outdoor theatre). Do not advertise for actors or welcome casting queries as all performances are by the cooperative directors, Tim Britton and Chris Britton.

GW Theatre Company Ltd
Abraham Moss Centre Theatre, Crescent Road, Crumpsall, Manchester M8 6UF
Tel (061) **740 1491 ext 336**

Founded 1986. A workers' cooperative company committed to touring original drama with a clear contemporary impact. Perform in theatres, youth clubs, community centres, studio spaces, schools, colleges, probation centres, drop-in centres locally and nationally. At least one show per venue, split and full weeks. Company of 2–5 actors on Equity rates or Equity contracts of 6–8 weeks. Occasionally advertise in *The Stage* and the local press, and welcome casting queries from actors; approach in writing in the first instance.

Gay Sweatshop
PO Box 820, London NW1 8LW
Tel (01) **722 1491**
Artistic directors Kate Owen, Philip Osment, Tierl Thompson, Richard Sandells

Founded 1975. Tour new work written by and for lesbians and gay men, ranging from text-based plays and company-devised pieces to the presentation of new plays as rehearsed readings during festivals. Usually present two productions annually, opening in London followed by small-scale touring of 3–5 weeks in the North-west, Midlands, Southern region and Scotland. Perform in arts centres, studio theatres, civic theatres, university and college theatres. Productions have included: *Poppies* by Noel Greig; *Telling Tales* by Philip Osment; *Raising the Wreck* by Sue Frumin; *Compromised Immunity* by Andy Kirby; *This Island's Mine* by Philip Osment. Company of seven on Equity contracts (minimum rate) of 10–11 weeks. Advertise in *The Stage*, lesbian and gay press (*Capital Gay, The Pink Paper*), black press (*The Voice*) and feminist press (*Spare Rib*). Welcome casting queries; send letter with CV and photograph. 'Gay Sweatshop is an equal opportunities employer, operating integrated casting, and it welcomes applications irrespective of gender, race, age or abilities. We actively encourage applications from lesbians and gay men, so if you do identify yourself as homosexual, please say so in your letter. Applicants should have a commitment to challenging heterosexism and supporting the rights of lesbians and gay men, and should draw attention to any relevant work experience or areas of study. All casting information on file is consulted by directors for every production prior to advertising.'

Gemini Productions
22 Cumberland Court, Carlisle Avenue, St Albans, Herts. AL3 5LS
Tel (0727) **41661**
Artistic director Nigel Austin

Tour with a range of productions including new writing and adaptations, comedy and drama, to venues seating 100–400. Tour once a year with an average company of 4–6 on basic Equity contracts of 4–10 weeks. Recent productions: *The Fox* (adaptation of D. H. Lawrence story); *True West* by Sam Shepard; *The Farndale Avenue Housing Estate Townswomen's Guild Dramatic Society's Production of Macbeth* by McGillivray; *No Why* by John Whiting. Advertise for actors in *SBS*. Welcome casting queries 'only to specific work planned'; approach in writing in the first instance.

Gog Theatre Company Ltd

The Assembly Rooms, High Street, Glastonbury, Somerset BA6 9DU
Artistic directors Tom Clark, Caryne Clark

Annual Theatre-in-Education (TIE) production for Somerset primary schools. Recent residency and performance tour with *North–South – Across the Divide*. Creative video-making and teaching theatre workshops and communication skills sessions. Perform in schools, colleges, community venues and arts centres. Company of eight on three-month contracts; non-Equity. Occasionally advertise in *The Stage, ITC Newsletter* and local press. Always welcome casting queries, preferably by letter. 'We interview people by workshopping over a period of time – we don't audition as a company. Gog is a small-scale theatre company which is involved in innovative projects which differ in skills required usually in the "rep" theatre. For this reason, and for financial reasons, the company does not employ many new actors. However, we are always very interested in hearing from anyone especially interested in theatre as a tool for change.'

Good Company

46 Quebec Street, Brighton, E. Sussex BN2 2UZ
Tel (0273) **606652**
Artistic director Sue Pomeroy

Founded 1986. Tour from small- to large-scale theatres; particularly concerned with new writing. Approximately one tour each year. Credits include: *Ear, Nose and Throat* by Sue Townsend (No. 1 tour); *Crowned with Fame* by Michael Ellis; *I, Bertolt Brecht* (in collaboration with Bristol Old Vic). Occasionally advertise in *SBS*. Welcome casting queries from actors; approach in writing in the first instance, enclosing CV, photograph and SAE. Musical skills an advantage.

Graeae

The Diorama, 18 Park Square East, London NW1 4LH
Tel (01) **935 5588**

Founded 1981. Touring company using disabled actors; productions are therefore primarily concerned with some aspect of disability experience. Writers are commissioned to produce new work on a particular theme (e.g. the 1987 tour was performed and produced by an all-women company). Perform in arts centres, studio theatres, colleges, day and community centres. Also tour Theatre-in-Education (TIE) programmes for junior schools. Recent productions: *Opportunity Blocks* (TIE); *A Private View* by Tasha Fairbanks. Company of four actors on Equity/ITC contracts of approximately 14 weeks (28 weeks for TIE). Advertise in *The Stage, The Voice, Disability Now, Asian Times, City Limits* and the newsletters of organizations for disabled people. Welcome casting queries from eligible actors; approach by telephone in the first instance.

Great Eastern Stage

Steinkirk Buildings, Dunkirk Road, Lincoln LN1 3UJ
Tel (0522) **34924**
Artistic director Michael Fry

Founded 1977. Some new plays but mainly established work: *Tess of the D'Urbevilles* (directed by Michael Fry); *Waiting for Godot, Taking Steps* and *When the Wind Blows* (Ian McKeand, the previous artistic director). Tour to small-scale venues in Lincolnshire and Humberside, plus some national dates. ITC/Equity contracts, usually six weeks in length. Cast from tour to tour. Advertise in *SBS* and welcome casting queries from actors; approach in writing in the first instance. Details are kept on file.

HAC Theatre Ltd
65a Kingsley Road, Hounslow, Middx. TW3 1QB
Tel (01) **570 9681**
Contact Cavelle Priestley (administrator)

Founded 1985. Small-scale tours of original work that specifically addresses contemporary social issues facing young British Asians, coupled with the wider issues facing the youth of today. Perform in arts centres and community venues. Two major productions a year (April/October); workshops (June–August); cabaret (June). Recent productions: *The Curse of the Dead Dog* by R. Gill and Parv Bancil; *How's Your Skull ... Does It Fit?* by Parv Bancil. Equity contracts of approximately 12 weeks. Advertise in *The Stage*, and welcome casting queries from actors; send letter with CV. 'Although we are interested in all young talent, we particularly welcome CVs from young Asian actors. An essential part of HAC's policy is to promote and develop all young artistic talent; we are therefore always interested in potential playwrights, designers, etc.'

Hull Truck Theatre Company
Spring Street Theatre, Spring Street, Hull HU2 8RW
Tel (0482) **224800**
Artistic director John Godber
Associate director Neil Sissons, Richard Lewis, Robert Sian

Founded 1975 by Mike Bradwell. With the close collaboration of John Godber and Barry Nettleton (Hull Truck's administrator for the past 14 years), the company has grown into one of the leading small- to middle-scale touring companies, with shows transferring to London and regularly winning awards at the Edinburgh Festival. Until recently concentrated on new writing, but now including classics in their programming. Recent productions include: *A Hard Day's Night* by Frederick Harrison; *Up 'n' Under*, *Salt of the Earth* and *Teechers* (West End transfer), all by John Godber; *A Midsummer Night's Dream*; *Viva España* by John Burrows. Tour to small- and middle-scale venues nationwide, and currently planning to include large-scale touring. One major tour annually plus 2–4 smaller tours. Company of four actors on contracts varying between five weeks and nine months; Equity/ITC small-scale touring contract. Recruit from a pool of regular actors, but occasionally advertise in *SBS*. Keep details of actors on file. Recommend making contact a couple of months before their new season commences (at the Edinburgh Festival in August).

Impossible Theatre
160 Huddersfield Road, Holmfirth, W. Yorks. HD7 1JD
Tel (0484) **681262**
Artistic directors Charlott Diefenthal, Chris Squire

Founded 1983. Small-scale touring theatre to large outdoor spectaculars. Productions are 'intriguing visual and physical theatre with live music'. Number of company members varies from 2–5 up to 20 for some events; contracts vary according to project. Do not advertise for actors, and do not welcome casting queries unless acquainted with their work. 'Our group approach to working means we must be able to depend on good working relationships. We must see people at work or in workshops.'

Inner City Theatre Company

Unit A43, Metropolitan Workshops, Enfield Road, London N1
Tel (01) **249 1711**
Artistic director Adrian Bean

Founded 1982. Small-scale touring company committed to new writing (usually on social issues), plus farces and musicals. Recent productions: *Hot Stuff*; *I'm Dreaming the Hardest*. Perform in arts centres and colleges, with a touring pattern of two- to three-nighters, split weeks, one-night stands and three-week runs. Company of four actors and stage management of two on 12–14 week Equity small-scale touring contracts. Advertise in *SBS*, and do not welcome casting queries from actors.

Interim Theatre Productions Ltd ● *See* Theatre-in-Education companies.

Interplay Community Theatre

Armley Ridge Road, Leeds LS12 3LE
Tel (0532) **638556**

Founded 1970. Community tours, residencies at the Interplay Community Theatre for groups and organizations, schools tours and summer outdoor touring shows. 'Our work is self-devised and specially designed for its particular audience and performing situations.' Recent productions: *Peacock's Peculiar Pavilion, Scrooge's Yuletide Makemerry*. Perform in small-scale community venues — village halls, social clubs, leisure and community centres — plus festivals, galas and special schools. Half of the touring is in Yorkshire, with 2–4 weeks per project in the regions. Six weeks touring the community show or special schools project, and 12 weeks touring the summer outdoor show. Company of four actors on ITC contracts of 3–5 months in length; gross weekly wage: £157.00. Advertise for actors in the *Guardian, The Stage* and the ITC noticeboard. Welcome casting queries; send letter enclosing CV. 'We are confirmed eclectics, ever open to a variety of forms, developing a style that includes music, humour, poetry, movement, visual imagery and audience participation, with a content that is non-racist and anti-sexist.'

Joint Stock Theatre Group

123 Tottenham Court Road, London W1P 9HN
Tel (01) 388 9719

Founded 1974. Leading touring company renowned for its unique method of production, involving close collaboration between director, writer, actors and designers on a wide range of subject matters. 'Projects are chosen on the strength of idea and the creative team and the potential for it to be developed via the "Joint Stock Method".' Productions include: *A Child in the Heart* by Karim Alrawi (directed by Nick Broadhurst); *Sanctuary* by Ralph Brown (Paulette Randall); *A Mouthful of Birds* by Caryl Churchill & David Lan (Ian Spink & Les Waters). Previous Joint Stock/Caryl Churchill collaborations have produced *Light Shining in Buckinghamshire, Cloud Nine* and *Fen*. Perform in repertory theatres, arts centres, university and civic theatres nationwide. Recently toured two productions a year, both full and split weeks (6–12 weeks) plus a London run of 3–4 weeks. Company of six actors on £170 per week (1988). Split contract: initial three-week workshop; ten-week gap; six-week rehearsal period; then tour and London run. Do not advertise, but welcome letters from actors. 'All companies are multi-racial. A commitment to multi-racial, integrated casting is central to our artistic policy.'

At the time of writing, it had been announced that Joint Stock's 1989 Arts

Council grant is to be cut. If sponsorship is not forthcoming, the company's future could be in doubt.

Live Theatre Company

'The Live Theatre', Broad Chare, Quayside, Newcastle upon Tyne NE1 3DF
Tel (091) **261 2694**
Artistic director Max Roberts

Founded 1973. Extensive touring, both regional and national, of in-house productions, collaborations with other theatre, film and TV companies, workshops and community projects. 'Our policy is to perform new work with a commitment to those writers, performers and technicians from the North-east whose work is innovative and challenging. These plays reflect experiences of working-class life, past and present, in a way that is neither exclusive nor parochial.' Recent productions: *In Blackberry Time* by Alan Plater & Mike Chaplin; *Jack Commons — Kiddars Luck* by Phil Woods; *Yesterday's Children* and *The Long Line* by Tom Hadaway. Perform in a wide range of community venues and arts centres, small- and middle-scale theatres, as well as in their own 200-seat theatre. Spring tour — early February to April; autumn tour — September to November; small-scale Christmas tour; and other projects throughout the year, including building-based productions. Company of 5–6 actors plus stage management of two on ITC/Equity minimum contracts of 11 weeks in length. Advertise for actors in *The Stage* and the local press. Welcome casting queries; approach in writing in the first instance.

London Bubble Theatre Company

3 & 5 Elephant Court, London SE16 4JD
Tel (01) **237 4434**
Artistic director Peter Rowe

Founded 1972. Popular community theatre company performing in their tent in parks and open spaces around London, plus community touring to community centres, arts centres, tenants' halls, etc. Classics, rock musicals, kids' shows and late-night cabaret. Recent productions: *I Fought Yuppie Zombies from Hell* by Alan Gilbey; *A Midsummer Night's Dream*; *Sir Gawain and the Green Knight* by David Holman; *Groping for Words* by Sue Townsend; *Blood Brothers* by Willy Russell. Community touring company of four from February to March (five weeks); tent touring company of nine from June to August (10/12 weeks). ITC/Equity standard contract. Advertise in *The Stage, The Voice, Asian Times*, etc.; do not welcome casting queries from actors. 'We work in a particular style and in a particular environment, quite often playing to a non theatre-going audience. Come and see the work.'

Lumiere & Son Theatre Company

70 Silverthorne Road, London SW8 3HE
Tel (01) **622 4865**
Artistic director Hilary Westlake

Founded 1973. Perform new work only, either written by co-founder David Gale or devised and directed by Hilary Westlake. Tours plus large-scale site-specific shows using music, choreography, projection and text. Recent productions: *Panic*; *Deadwood* (Kew Gardens); *Brightside*; *Circus Lumiere*; *Culture Vulture*. Perform in arts centres and studio theatres. Site-specific — e.g. Kew Gardens, Thames Barrier, Singapore Zoo. Tour in autumn, spring and summer; outdoor work in summer. Touring company of 9–10; site-specific company of 50–150+. ITC/Equity contracts of 3–6 months. Advertise in *The Stage*, and welcome casting queries from actors; approach in writing in the first instance. 'Find out about the company *before* writing.'

M6 Theatre Company
The Theatre Workshop, Heybrook School, Park Road, Rochdale OL12 9BJ
Tel (0706) **355898**
Resident director Eileen Murphy

Founded 1977 from Bolton TIE Company. Tour one show per year to community venues throughout Rochdale, Greater Manchester and north-west England; three TIE productions to Rochdale schools; and a community show at Christmas at two large-scale Rochdale venues. Cooperative company of 12 (on average); open-ended Equity contracts. Advertise in *The Stage*, *The Voice*, Equity *Jobgrapevine*; also mail other theatre companies. Welcome casting queries from actors: 'we reply to all letters, but we usually refer actors to *The Stage*.'

The Made-in-Wales Stage Company
Mount Stuart House, Mount Stuart Square, Cardiff CF1 6DQ
Tel (0222) **484017**
Artistic director Gilly Adams

Founded 1982. Touring company that is committed to producing new work by Welsh or Wales-based writers, writing in English. Recent productions: *A Blow to Bute Street* by Laurence Allan; *On the Black Hill* by Charles Way; *The Tuscan* by Alan Osborne; *The Poor Girl* by Michael Bosworth. Perform in theatres in Wales — principally the Sherman Theatre in Cardiff and Theatre Clwyd in Mold — but also the Waterman Arts Centre in Brentford (London): 'Our touring work is beginning to expand.' Open in Cardiff or Mold, then tour for at least a week to each venue. Average company of ten on six-week Equity contracts (MRSL II). Advertise ('if necessary') in *The Stage*, *SBS* and Equity *Jobgrapevine*. Welcome casting queries from actors; write in the first instance. 'Actor training is part of the production process. Actors who are interested in the particular challenges of new work and who are prepared to take risks are welcomed.'

The Magic Roundabout Theatre Company
Wyvern Theatre, Theatre Square, Swindon, Wilts. SN1 1QJ
Tel (0793) **614864**
Artistic director Derek Hewitson

Community theatre, Theatre-in-Education (TIE) and small-scale touring productions in Wiltshire and surrounding area. Perform in village halls, community centres, schools, arts centres and mainstream theatres. Recent productions: *Stronger than Superman* by Roy Kift (middle-school TIE); *A One-Man Protest* by Alan Ayckbourn (tour); *A Peace of Aggro* by Carol Anne Duffy (secondary-school TIE); *Simon Says* by David Campton (tour); *Macbeth* (secondary-school TIE). Company of 3–8 actors, depending on production, with tours of 3–6 weeks. Some through casting; standard Esher contract. Advertise in *The Stage*, Equity *Jobgrapevine*, *SBS* and *PCR*. Welcome casting queries from actors — 'strictly by letter'.

Major Road Theatre Company
29 Queens Road, Bradford, W. Yorks. BD8 7BS
Tel (0274) **480251**
Artistic director Graham Devlin

Founded 1973. Major Road's policy is to create and commission new work by new writers and to develop a highly visual style of theatre. Their special concerns are theatre for youth and aural history-based projects. The work involves a fusion of forms such as dance and music. Also run theatre residences in various settings, educational programmes and community work. Specialize in large-scale 'civic spectacular'. Tour to small-scale venues (particularly to youth clubs). Company of 4–8 actors on ITC/Equity contracts of 10–15 weeks. Advertise in *The Stage*, *Asian Times* and *Caribbean Times*. Welcome casting queries from actors; approach in writing in the first instance, enclosing CV, photograph and SAE (big enough for return of photograph). Details are kept on file. Major Road actively pursue an equal opportunities policy.

Manchester Actors Company

c/o Administration, 14 Lynton Street, Rusholme, Manchester M14 7PS *or* c/o North-West Arts, 12 Harter Street, Manchester M1 6HY
Tel (061) **225 2616**
Artistic director Stephen Boyes

> Founded 1980. Community theatre – small-scale touring to all branches of the community throughout Greater Manchester, plus some national touring. Recent productions: *Robocat* (children's show); *A Short History of the Female Detective* (adult show; pub tour); *Dracula* (promenade version); *Tales Never Told* (children's show; tour of libraries). 'We devise, or commission writers to produce, work tailor-made for specific areas in the community – i.e. youth clubs, elderly people, infant schools.' Perform in shopping precincts, schools, village halls, community centres, sports centres, studio theatres – 'we have played the Royal Exchange Theatre, Manchester.' Average of three shows per year. Company of four actors on six-week contracts. Sometimes profit-share – 'we try to use Equity as a guideline.' Advertise for actors in *The Stage*, and welcome casting queries; send a letter enclosing CV and photograph. 'Our type of work provides a good, practical training ground for young actors with lots of stamina who are interested in taking theatre to non-theatre venues.'

Mikron Theatre Company Ltd

31 Warehouse Hill, Marsden, Huddersfield, W. Yorks. HD7 6AB
Tel (0484) **845264**
Artistic director Mike Lucas

> Founded 1972. Waterborne theatre company touring musical shows on a variety of topics, but all with a 'quality of life' theme – i.e. conservation of our heritage in tandem with technological progress. Productions include: *Flight of Fancy* (one day in the life of a canalside community; an evocation of rural life in the 1930s); *Rise and Fall* (the story of the first boatlifts in the world and their relevance today). Perform in canal and riverside pubs, museums, rallies and festivals. Generally a summer tour by narrowboat throughout the waterways of England, and in the autumn, a South Pennine tour and a Belgo-French tour by barge. Company of four on 8–9-month contracts. Advertise in *The Stage*, and welcome casting queries from actors; approach in writing in the first instance.

Millstream Theatre Company

Yvonne Arnaud Theatre, Millbrook, Guildford, Surrey GU1 3UX
Tel (0483) **64571**
Artistic director Christopher Masters

> Founded 1982. Revivals and seldom-seen classics. Tour to theatres seating from 70 to 500. Recent productions: *Stevie*, *Sufficient Carbohydrate*, *Fool for Love* and *Berlin and Beyond* (all directed by Christopher Masters). Two 9–10-week Millstream tours annually, plus a month-long Surrey Theatre Link tour (joint productions of new works with the Thorndike Theatre, Leatherhead, the Redgrave Theatre, Farnham, and Millstream). Company of five actors on

subsidized rep contracts. Advertise in *SBS*, and do not particularly welcome casting queries from actors. *See also* entry for Yvonne Arnaud Theatre in Rep/Regional Theatres section.

Monstrous Regiment
123 Tottenham Court Road, London W1P 9HW
Tel (01) **387 4790**

Founded 1975 by a group of professional actors who wanted to make 'exciting, political theatre based on women's experience; tired of seeing that experience marginalized or trivialized, we wanted to take it out of the wings and place it at the centre of the stage.' One of Britain's leading feminist theatre groups, managed by a collective of six women. Produce commissioned new plays (usually by women writers) and tour split and full weeks to studio theatres and arts centres. Recent productions: *My Song is Free* by Jorge Diaz; *Alarms* by Susan Yankowitz; *My Sister in This House* by Wendy Kesselman; *Waving* by Carol Bunyan; *Island Life* by Jenny McCleod. Maximum cast size of four on Equity/ITC contracts of 12–16 weeks. Do not advertise, but welcome casting queries; approach in writing in the first instance. As a women's company, we normally encourage enquiries by women, but as we only do two productions a year with casts of no more than four, we cannot be too encouraging.'

Moving Being Ltd
St Stephen's Theatre Space, West Bute Street, Cardiff CF1 6EP
Tel (0222) **480961**
Artistic director Geoff Moore

Founded 1968 in London; moved to Cardiff 1972. Used to tour extensively, but in 1982, bought St Stephen's Theatre Space and now perform there, although it is thought that touring may recommence in the future. Wide range of productions – classics plus new or devised work. Usually 2–3 productions annually. TMA subsidized rep contract, usually of 4–7 weeks. Very rarely advertise, but welcome casting queries from actors. Approach in writing in the first instance – details are kept on file.

Mummerandada
East Ford, Tedburn St Mary, Exeter, Devon EX6 6ET
Tel (064 724) **376**
Artistic director Bim Mason

Founded 1984. Perform original 'circus' theatre – incorporating mumming, mime, mask, acrobatics, music, comedy, slapstick and illusion – at outdoor venues such as parks, fairs, festivals and tents and in indoor venues such as arts centres, bars and theatres. Tour from May to October each year. Company of six performers on six-month contracts. Advertise in *The Stage*. Do not welcome casting queries from actors 'unless skilled in specific areas. Mummerandada require a high level of skill in circus techniques such as mime, clowning and/or music.' Approach in writing in the first instance.

National Student Theatre Company
20 Lansdowne Road, London N10 2AU
Tel (01) **883 4586**
Artistic director Clive Wolfe

Since their first appearance at the Edinburgh Festival in 1977, the NSTC have presented nearly 80 productions, mostly of new work, and helped 130 or more students to a career start in the world of entertainment. Together with the National Student Drama Festival, the NSTC has also given birth to a professional offshoot, the BP Springboard Theatre Company. Productions have included: *Going Clear* by Brian B. Thompson, *Tommy's Girl* by Katy Dean, *Wildsea-Wildsea* by Eric Prince and *Blind Man's Buff* by Beverley Newns. Advertise in *The Stage* and circularize colleges. Applications should be sent to the artistic director by the third week of April for auditions in May.

Natural Theatre Company
Kingsmead North, Bath BA1 1XB
Tel (0225) **69131**
Artistic director Ralph Oswick

Founded 1969. Medium-scale touring indoor shows, and also peripatetic street theatre using visual and verbal comedy and virtuoso musicians. Perform in medium-to-large theatres, arts centres, school halls with facilities and studio theatres; outdoor performances in busy streets or squares, fun parks, conferences, etc. Indoor show tours November to April; outdoor work tours in Britain in the summer months and any other time in 'sunny countries'. Recent productions: *Scarlatti's Birthday Party* (European tour); *Spy Society* (British & European tour); street theatre performances at Quebec Festival d'Été; Great British Bike Ride; Glasgow Garden Festival (6-month residency). Average company of 4–5 on Equity/ITC contracts, indoor show for six-month contract; outdoor show ranges from one day to six-month contract. Advertise in *The Stage*, ITC news-sheets, local press. Do not welcome casting queries 'unless we are currently advertising, as we get overwhelmed with requests for work. (Letters are better, or phone for a brochure.) We had 850 applications for our last vacancy. Half of them didn't know what they were applying for. I think aspiring actors should find out something about the companies they apply to and think hard about whether they really would be suitable. We keep all our applications for future reference, but I am sure many companies have very big wastebins. Don't apply for everything just for the sake of it.'

Northern Lights Theatre Company
1 Nether Green, Clipston, Market Harborough, Leics. LE16 9SA
Tel (085 886) **416**
Artistic directors Debbie Stroud, Bill Downing

Founded 1982. Produce Shakespeare with small casts, feminist comedies, classic tales and psychological drama, plus workshops for sixth-formers. Recent productions: *Pilgrim's Progress*, *Outcry*, *Female Parts*. Perform in arts centres, small theatres, festivals, schools and colleges, on yachts, in bird sanctuaries and churches. Company of two. Have done Equity tours in the past but currently not advertising for actors; it would be 'a waste of their time' if they write in.

Northumberland Theatre Company
The Playhouse, Bondgate Without, Alnwick, Northumberland NE66 1PQ
Tel (0665) **602586**
Artistic director Ronan Paterson

Founded 1977. Perform new writing, major classics, children's and Christmas shows and shows of local relevance, in theatres, arts centres, schools, village halls and community centres. Audience age range from 5 upwards. Recent productions: *The Tempest*; *All-Hallow Eve* by James Hogg; *O'er the Hills* by Rigby, Taylor, Flush & Armstrong; *The Frog Prince*. Main tours in early autumn and early spring, with schools shows, a Christmas show and smaller-scale community tours in between. Company of five actors on show-to-show contracts of 9–10 weeks. ITC/Equity small-scale touring contract. Sometimes advertise in *The Stage* and the ethnic press; will consider letters from actors. 'As we tend to do a lot of productions with local relevance, we try to cast firstly from performers who are, broadly speaking, local (really between Leeds and Edinburgh). We tend to look for actors who have some understanding of rural audiences, but neither of these criteria is exclusive.'

Orange Box Theatre Company

20 Kingstone Road, Ipswich, Suffolk IP1 4BQ
Tel (0473) 463134
Artistic director Rob Horton

Founded 1985. Community and schools tours of technically simple shows with an emphasis on the actor — few props and in-the-round. Productions have included: *The Merchant of Venice* (modern adaptation by Steve Mara) and *Bear Tale* (modern adaptation by Steve Mara of *A Winter's Tale*). Perform in schools, village halls and small local theatres. Three tours per year, each lasting approximately 12 weeks. Company of four actors on three-month contracts. Advertise in *The Stage* and Equity *Jobgrapevine*, and welcome casting queries from actors; approach in writing in the first instance.

Orchard Theatre

108 Newport Road, Barnstaple, Devon EX32 9BA
Tel (0271) **71475**
Artistic director To be appointed

Founded 1971. Britain's first rural touring company performs a mix of new work (commissioned or otherwise), classics and a number of plays relevant to the West Country, in towns and villages throughout Devon, Cornwall, Dorset, Somerset, Avon and Gloucestershire. Productions (all directed by Nigel Bryant the previous artistic director) include: *Macbeth*; *The Life of the Land* by Jane Beeson; *The Death of Arthur* by John Fletcher; *The Pied Piper*. Perform mainly one-night stands in small-to-middle-scale venues (village halls, schools, Northcott Theatre, Exeter and the Brewhouse Theatre, Taunton). Company of 6/7 actors on ten-week Equity contracts. Occasionally advertise in *The Stage*. Welcome casting queries from actors; letters are kept on file and referred to when casting. 'Our touring schedule is demanding, and actors who apply to us must take into account that a lot of energy and commitment is required for performing, plus helping with get-outs.'

Oxford Stage Company

12 Beaumont Street, Oxford OX1 2LW
Tel (0865) **723238**
Artistic director Richard Williams

Founded 1974. Tour English and foreign classics, new plays and adaptations to middle-scale (300–1000-seat) theatres in towns without repertory theatres. Recent productions: *Dr Faustus, Woman in Mind, The Miracle Plays, Robeson — Song of Freedom*. Company of 4–6 on Esher contracts of 11–15 weeks (September to May). Do not advertise for actors.

Oxfordshire Touring Theatre Company

Cricket Road Centre, Cricket Road, Oxford OX4 1SP
Tel (0865) **778119**
Artistic director Mollie Guilfoyle

Founded 1982. Tour adaptations of classics, new writing, issue-based projects to village halls, community centres, art centres, theatres and schools in Oxfordshire, Berkshire, Buckinghamshire and Hampshire; occasionally go outside these counties. Recent productions: *Devil Take the Future (or Who'll Fix It When Jimmy*

Savile's Dead?) by Steven K. Wilson and *Shahrazad* (both directed by Peter Cooper). Company of 2–5 actors on ITC Equity contracts (minimum rate) of 12–15 weeks. Advertise in *The Stage*, ITC and through agents, and welcome casting queries from actors; write in the first instance.

Paines Plough – the writers' company
121–122 Tottenham Court Road, London W1P 9HN
Tel (01) **380 1188**
Artistic director Pip Broughton

Founded 1974. Produce new works only, and support the development of writers at all stages. Recent productions (all directed by Pip Broughton) include: *Such as Women* by Kay Adshead; *Berlin Days, Hollywood Nights* by Nigel Gearing; *The Way to Go Home* by Rona Munro; *Germinal* by William Gaminara. Tour to middle- and small-scale venues nationwide, both whole and split weeks. Company of eight actors on 12-week Equity contracts. Advertise for actors in *SBS* and Equity *Jobgrapevine*.

Pascal Theatre Company
149 Cavendish Mansions, Clerkenwell Road, London EC1R 5EQ
Tel (01) **837 5390**
Artistic director Julia Pascal

Founded 1983. Tour new plays on contemporary issues – e.g. Ireland, South Africa, Israel – and European writing to London venues such as Riverside Studios, Lyric Studio, Young Vic Studio, Drill Hall. Recent productions: *Salt River* by Yana Stajno; *Traitors* by Melanie Phillips; *The Murphy Girls*; *The German Connection*; *Soldiers* by Seamus Finnegan. Company of six on Equity minimum rates. Sometimes advertise in *The Stage*; do not welcome casting queries from actors as they have no full-time administrator.

Pit Prop Theatre
Railway Road, Leigh, Lancs. WN7 4AF
Tel (0942) **605258**

Founded 1979. Community theatre and Theatre-in-Education (TIE) tours of new plays written or devised from within the company, although writers are sometimes commissioned. Productions include: *Lilford Mill* and *On the Rock 'n' Roll* by Neil Duffield; *Out of Mind* (company-devised piece). Tour in the Wigan borough of Greater Manchester, and sometimes to other North-west boroughs. Collective of 11 people, mostly on open-ended contracts. ITC/Equity small-scale touring contract. Advertise in *The Stage*, the *Guardian*, *The Voice* and *Caribbean Times*. Welcome casting queries; telephone in the first instance. 'Applicants are advised to write showing some understanding and interest in the particular forms of theatre we are involved in.'

Rainbow Theatre Company
1 Ashurst Drive, Goring-by-Sea, Worthing, W. Sussex BN12 4SN
Tel (0903) **502741**
Artistic director Nicolas Young

Produce children's classics, Shakespeare workshops, 'Living History' total participation shows, dramas, cabaret, 'problem solving' for audiences of 5–20-year-olds and old people in schools, colleges, old people's homes and studio theatres. Company of four actors on contracts of term length. 'Periodically' pay Equity rates. Advertise in *The Stage*, and welcome casting queries from actors 'with an ability to work happily and creatively in a small group, and an enjoyment in playing to and with children'. Approach in writing in the first instance. Teaching qualifications are not required, but music and dance skills an advantage. Auditions held each term. 'Hard work and cheerfulness early in the morning are essential requisites for Rainbow company members.'

Raskolnikoff Theatre

Pearce Institute, 840 Govan Road, Govan, Glasgow
Tel (041) **334 4203**
Artistic director Laura Raskolnikoff

Founded 1984. Children's theatre, variety, Theatre-in-Education (TIE), community involvement – drama projects, pageants, panto, street theatre. Perform in community halls, schools, studio theatres – six weeks at Christmas and ten weeks in the summer. Company of 4–6 actors on Equity minimum contracts of 8–10 weeks. Welcome casting queries from local actors; approach in writing in the first instance. 'We usually cannot afford to pay subsistence, so do not send CV unless you live in Glasgow or want to stay in Glasgow. Look for actors who can sing, dance, possibly juggle or do acrobatics or anything visually unusual.'

Ratskins Theatre Company

121 Hammersmith Grove, London W6 0NJ
Tel (01) **748 2498**
Contact Richard Crowe

Founded 1985. 'Ratskins is essentially a two-man acting/writing partnership. All scripts are new, developed by the company through improvisation with an emphasis on human relationships and, to a lesser degree, social issues.' Perform in studio theatres (e.g. Lyric Studio, Hammersmith and Croydon Warehouse Theatre), arts centres and fringe venues. Company of five on three-month Equity contracts. Do not advertise for actors, and do not welcome casting queries, 'although we are more than willing to give any advice we can'. 'Ratskins hopes to be able to increase the size of its productions but, in the present financial climate, finds it difficult to do so. When it does, we will advertise for actors, stage management and so on. We receive many casting queries, often quite expensive packages, all unsolicited, which we try our best to answer and return photos. However, this is not always possible, and it is surprising how many enquiries arrive without an SAE. These we simply cannot afford to answer, which means someone has wasted valuable time and money. Always phone first to see if the company is casting or is able to consider doing so in the near future. Don't accept defeat. If you want to stay in the business but can't get a job, make your own work. Get together a group of like-minded people (there are plenty around), advertise if necessary and do a profit-share or do it for nothing. It's worth it to get people to see you work.'

Red Shift Theatre Company

11 Many Gates, Cornford Grove, Balham, London SW12 9JE
Tel (01) **673 5539**
Artistic director Jonathan Holloway

Founded 1982. Adaptations of classic plays and novels and new plays performed in a highly visual/physical ensemble style. Two tours each year – January to June and August to January – to small-scale venues. Productions include: *In the Image of the Beast*, written and directed by Jonathan Holloway (Edinburgh Fringe First winner); *Cowboys* by Anne Caulfield; *The Mill on the Floss* (adapted by Robin Brown); *Le Misanthrope* (Edinburgh Fringe First winner); adaptation of *Timon of Athens*. Company of 5–7 actors, contracted project to project; ITC/Equity small-scale touring contracts. Advertise in *The Stage* and

Equity *Jobgrapevine*; welcome letters enclosing CV, photograph and SAE. Details are kept on file.

Riding Lights Theatre Company

39 Micklegate, York YO1 1JH
Tel (0904) **655317**
Artistic director Paul Burbridge

Founded 1977. Tour new full-length plays, classics, musicals, revues, adaptations of literature, children's shows and workshops, both locally and nationwide. Perform in major theatres, arts centres, schools and arts festival venues. Major tours in autumn/Christmas/spring; schools tour at Christmas; small-scale tours at other times of the year; international tour during January–March. Recent productions: *On Christmas Night* by Nigel Forde; *St John's Gospel*; *Daniel* (musical) by Watts/Norton. Company of 6–8 on Equity small-scale touring contracts of about 8–12 weeks. Advertise in *The Stage*, and welcome casting queries from actors; write in the first instance. 'We often work with actors, devising the production in rehearsal, aiming for a strong actor-based style of ensemble playing. Singing abilities are often relevant, as well as other kinds of musical abilities.'

7:84 Theatre Company, Scotland

3rd floor, 302 Buchanan Street, Glasgow G2 3LB
Tel (041) **331 2219**
Artistic director David Hayman
Associate director Gerard Kelly

Founded 1973. Perform mainly new writing but also adaptations and classics. Productions include: *The Cheviot, the Stag and the Black, Black Oil*; *Blood Red Roses*; *There Is a Happy Land*; *In Time of Strife*; *The Gorbals Story*. Tour to a wide variety of venues throughout Scotland, from village halls to No. 1 theatres. Subsidized rep contracts of 12 weeks in length. Do not advertise for actors. Will consider letters from actors only if SAE enclosed.

This leading, left-wing company (its name comes from the premise that 7 per cent of the population owns 84 per cent of the country's wealth) lost its Arts Council grant in 1988, leading to the resignation of its founder/director, playwright John McGrath.

Shadow Syndicate Ltd

36 Ritherdon Road, London SW17 8QF
Tel (01) **672 0606**

Founded 1984. Small-scale touring company presenting new works and adaptations in a highly visual style with a strong element of surprise. Music is integral to all their productions. Credits include: *The Turn of the Screw, The Last Days of Nosferatu, Blood of Angels, Between the Devil and the Deep Blue Sea, Scream Blue Murder*. Tour to small-scale venues, including an annual visit to the Edinburgh Fringe. Company of 5–6 actors on ITC/Equity small-scale touring contracts of varying length. Do not advertise, but welcome casting queries from actors; approach in writing in the first instance. 'All information is kept on file and referred to when casting.'

Shared Experience Ltd

The Soho Laundry, 9 Doufour's Place, London W1V 1FE
Tel (01) **434 9248**
Artistic director Nancy Meckler

Founded in 1976 by Mike Alfreds. Recent productions: *The Bacchae, True West.*

Tour to small- and middle-scale venues; 6–8-week tours with 4–5 weeks in London. Equity contracts. Do not advertise, but welcome casting queries from actors; approach in writing in the first instance.

In 1988, an appeal for funds reached their target of £95,000, enabling the company to retain their premises in the Soho Laundry where rehearsals and workshops for actors are held.

Solent People's Theatre
The Heathfield Centre, Valentine Avenue, Sholing, Southampton, Hants SO2 8EQ
Tel (0703) **443943**
Artistic director Sue Charman

Founded 1976. Community theatre company that tours the Hampshire, Southampton and Southern Arts region. Eight projects per year; mainly new writing, but also classics and some company-devised pieces. Most productions include workshops of some nature. Recent shows: *Penny for Your Thoughts* (1940s reminiscence piece); *Room for Improvement* (ecological cabaret); *The Forgotten Forest* (schools tour), *Bright Lights and Promises* (community show on homelessness) and *Eat Your Heart Out* (street theatre), all by Chris Stagg. Tour to old people's homes, special schools, community centres, middle schools, arts centres, village halls, hospitals and colleges; return to base each night. Six of the eight annual projects will be tours of approximately 3–4 weeks: 1–2 shows per day for 5–6 days per week. Company of five actors on ITC/Equity small-scale open-ended contracts ('but everyone has made an informal commitment to stay for 1–2 years or more'). Advertise in *The Stage*. 'We are currently working towards a full equal opportunities policy, so although we keep people on file, they need to apply for each job as advertised. We only see performers when we have a job to offer. Performers need to be extremely versatile – a large playing range, good musical skills, ability with accents, physical skills, plus experience and enjoyment of devised work. In addition to devising, performing, workshop-leading and liaison skills, performers need a cooperative attitude towards the work that the company shares, including decision-making, planning, assessment, tea/coffee-making, keeping the building clean and organizing the work in general. A clean driving licence would also be useful.'

Splash Theatre Company Ltd
Danish Buildings, 44–46 High Street, Hull, N. Yorks. HU1 1PS
Tel (0482) **24256**

Founded 1983. Tour to schools, youth centres, residential homes and day centres for the elderly, as well as playschemes and outdoor venues in the local area. 1988 productions: *Weaving Webs and Spinning Tales* (performance and workshops for 8–15-year-olds); *Chewing the Fat* (youth clubs show). Company of four on eight-week Equity contracts. Occasionally advertise in *The Stage*, and welcome casting queries from actors; write in the first instance. 'Our policy is to take theatre to those areas of the community which would not normally have access to it. As such, we work with children, young people, the elderly, and mentally and physically handicapped children and adults.

Strathcona Theatre Company
c/o Strathcona Social Education Centre, Strathcona Road, Wembley, Middx.
Tel (01) **451 7419**
Artistic directors Joan Greening, Janet Bliss

Founded 1982. Dance and drama all written and created by the company. Perform in fringe theatres, community centres, schools and colleges. Constant company of 10 actors and two directors.

TAG (Theatre About Glasgow) Theatre Company ● *See* Young People's Theatre.

Tara Arts Group

356 Garratt Lane, London SW18 4ES
Tel (01) **871 1458**
Artistic director Jatinder Verma

'Tara Arts began in 1976/7 as a community theatre group in South London. Today, it is a professional, subsidized Asian theatre company, newly arrived on the Arts Council grants list, touring nationally and internationally with its own building base in London. Born of a need to express the Asian experience in Britain, Tara Arts' policy is to present each year plays ranging from the classic to the contemporary; all offering entertaining, informative and provocative insights into the Asian experience. Drawing upon Indian traditions of theatre-craft, Tara Arts aims to offer challenging alternatives to conventional theatre in Britain. The group's extensive touring, workshop and building-based programmes throughout the year seek actively to promote Asian creative work as widely as possible.' The *Tara Arts Theatre Company* has taken theatre shows and workshops to various venues both in London and throughout the UK. A total of 30 productions have been staged since the company was formed, each touring an average of nine weeks. Average company of six actors. Advertise in drama schools and *The Stage* and welcome casting queries from actors; approach in writing in the first instance, enclosing CV and photograph.

Temba Theatre Company Ltd

Dominion House, 101 Southwark Street, London SE1 0JH
Tel (01) **261 0991**
Artistic director Alby James

Founded 1972. Middle- and small-scale touring; seasons of small- and middle-scale work in London. community outreach and education workshops. Recent productions: *Black Sheep* by Derrick Cameron; *Romeo and Juliet* and *A Visitor to the Veldt* by Mfundi Vundla (directed by Alby James); *Black Love Song No. 1* by Kalamu ya Salaam (Heather Goodman). Small-scale tour of 16 weeks (one-nighters); middle-scale tour of eight weeks — one venue per week. Average company size: three actors for small scale; ten for middle scale. Sixteen-week contract, both ITC and IMA. Rarely advertise, but welcome casting queries from actors; send letter with CV and current photograph. Temba's policy is to: enable people to share in the artistic expression of black cultures and experience; to enable people in Britain to see black people in the wider context of the heritage and experience of black people around the world; to assist the development and representation of black writing in British theatre.

Theatr Bara Caws

Y Coleg Normal, Bangor, Gwynedd LL57 2DE
Tel (0248) **355579/355436**
Co-operative company no directors

Founded 1977. From pub shows to chapel shows — all original productions. 'The show must be of interest and relevance to the community.' Three new productions toured annually and 'New Authors Festival' held. Some productions tour nationally, others in Clwyd and Gwynedd only. Equity contracts of 3 months in length. 'Everyone on equal pay.' Advertise for actors in *The Stage*, *Y Cymro* and *Y Papurau Bro*. 'Greatly' welcome casting queries from actors. Send a letter enclosing CV and photograph. 'We should like all new faces to get in touch with us. We are always looking for new talent — actors, technicians and writers. We hold annual auditions. The company's policy is to promote original, Welsh artistic work.'

Sylfaenwyd 1977. O sioeau tafarn i berfformiadau capel — pob cynhyrchiad yn wreiddiol. 'Rhaid i'r sioe fod o ddiddordeb ac yn berthnasol i'r gymuned'. Teithio tair sioe newydd y flwyddyn a chynnal 'Gwyl Awduron Newydd'. Y mae rhai cynyrchiadau yn teithio'n genedlaethol ac eraill yng Nghlwyd a Gwynedd yn unig. Cytundeb Equity o dri mis, pawb ar gyflog cyfartal. Hysbysebu am actorion — *The Stage, Y Cymro, Y papurau bro.*

'Hoffem petai pob actor newydd yn cysylltu â ni, rydym wastad yn chwilio am dalent newydd — actorion, technegwyr a dramodwyr. Yr ydym yn cynnal cyfweliadau blynyddol. Polisi'r cwmni yw hybu gwaith artistig, gwreiddiol Cymraeg.'

Théâtre de Complicité

108 Upper Street, London N1 1QN
Tel (01) **226 7025**

Founded 1983. Successful versatile company which specializes in physical theatre (most company members have trained at the Jacques Lecoq School in Paris). Tour to small and middle scale venues throughout the UK, including the Highlands and Islands; also Eire, Hong Kong, South America, USA, Italy, Belgium, Spain, Germany, Netherlands. In 1988 had a three and a half month residency at the Almeida Theatre in North London; touring four shows in 1989. Productions include: *Anything For a Quiet Life* and *The Phantom Violin* (directed by Simon McBurney); *The Visit* (Annabel Arden). Cast size ranges from 1 to 8; Equity contracts. Audition by workshop sessions. Actors who wish to be considered for these sessions should apply for inclusion on the workshop mailing list.

Theatre Foundry

The Drama Centre, Old School, Slater Street, Darlaston, W. Midlands WS10 8EE
Tel (021) **526 6947**
Artistic director Jeremy Bell

Founded 1982. Community plays, schools productions and a Christmas show toured to arts centres, colleges, schools and clubs in the West Midlands (mainly in the boroughs of Walsall, Dudley and Sandwell). Recent productions: *One in a Million* by David Holman; *Red Devils* by Debbie Horsfield; *Trafford Tanzi* by Claire Luckham; *The Island* by Athol Fugard; *Mother Courage* by Bertolt Brecht. Company of 4—6 actors on Equity MRSL Scale 2 contracts of 10—12 weeks. Do not normally advertise for actors — usually send script breakdown to agents. Welcome casting query letters.

Theatre Nova

69 Highbury Road, Kings Heath, Birmingham B13 7QW or Padworth House, Padworth, Reading, Berks. RG7 4NP
Tel (021) **443 4763** or (073529) **2645/3963**
Joint artistic directors Nigel Stewart, Don McGovern

Founded 1984. Touring company whose special concerns are writing and devising new poetic texts, adapting and translating existing ones — 'to create a theatre in which visual image, movement, word and sound are given a new organic relation.' Perform in studio theatres, arts centres and educational venues — split weeks, whole weeks and sometimes longer. Productions include: *Cross Purposes* by Don McGovern; *Let Me Speak.* Company of 10—15; profit-share and occasional Equity minimum (depending on funding). Advertise in *The Stage*, and welcome casting queries; approach by letter in the first instance.

Theatre Rotto

Bosulval Farmhouse, Newmill, Penzance, Cornwall TR20 8XA
Tel (0736) **65158**
Artistic director Julia Mclean

Founded 1981. Children's shows for schools and theatre venues, adult mainstream productions, cabaret, theatre training workshops. 'The emphasis is on comedy and music and a sense of the weird and wonderful. While the group is mixed, women's ideas are important.' Annual tour of schools in the South-west with children's show; one mainstream show every two years. Nucleus of four actors with others joining depending on the show. Advertise in local publications, and welcome casting queries from actors; approach in writing or by telephone.

Theatre Venture

Three Mills School, Abbey Lane, Stratford, London E15 2RP
Tel (01) **519 6678/8769**
Artistic director Heather Peace

Founded 1981. In the past few years, the company has toured plays to community centres and for deaf children, two short shows for OAPs and a large-scale community play. Venues include community centres, schools, hospitals and fringe venues. Productions must be accessible to 'an audience of people who do not usually go to theatre, have positive images of women and minorities and have a strong musical content'. Recent productions: *Castles in the Air* and *SOS* by Trevor Lloyd; *Ringroad* by Dave Fox; *The Dancing Years* (company devised). Mainly one-night stands. Company of four performers on ITC/Equity contracts of varying lengths. Advertise in *The Stage*, *Asian Times*, *The Voice* and *SBS*; do not welcome casting queries from actors. 'When responding to an advertisement, send a clear photocopy-able CV that is not cluttered with irrelevant details (e.g. O-level grades), an honest photograph and a covering letter explaining why you are interested in the job. A distressing number of applications manage to reveal that the applicant knows nothing about the company or the kind of work that it does. Many applicants do not read what the advertisement asks them to do. We don't expect any detailed knowledge, but we do expect applicants to have some understanding of community theatre and the practicalities of touring one-nighters from a van!'

Theatre Workshop Edinburgh

34 Hamilton Place, Edinburgh EH3 5AX
Tel (031) **225 7942**
Artistic director Adrian Harris

Founded 1965. Small-scale tours, Theatre-in-Education (TIE), children's shows and community plays. 'We tend towards commissioning new work but not exclusively. Plays have to be accessible to both rural-based and city-based Scottish audiences.' Recent productions: *State of Confusion* by David Kane; *Ye Cannae Put a Pink Blanket on His Bed* and *Has Anybody Here Seen Jo?* by Janet Fenton; *The Swan with the Golden Wings* by Paula Malgee. Perform in schools, community centres, village halls, theatres, studio theatres and arts centres throughout Scotland. Company of six actors plus stage management of two on nine-week Equity/ITC contracts. Do not advertise for actors, but welcome casting queries; approach in writing in the first instance. 'Our casting policy tends to favour actors based in Scotland.'

Theatr Powys

The Drama Centre, Tremont Road, Llandrindod Wells, Powys LD1 5EB
Tel (0597) **4444**
TIE director Louise Osborn
Community arts director Guy Roderick

> Founded 1972. Theatre-in-Education (TIE) to Powys schools and small- to middle-scale theatre to community centres, primarily in Powys, but also to theatres throughout Wales. Usually two TIE and two community tours each year, with the second community tour mainly scheduled for autumn or early spring. Recent productions: *Mary Morgan, Beauty and the Beast, Grandmother's Footsteps, Careless Talk, Robin Hood, Inside Stories.* 'Productions must have relevance to our community as a part of the world today, to empower, educate, stimulate communication, reflection and action in society. To demystify the arts and encourage participation in them.' Company of five permanent actor/teachers. Company house agreements on Equity subsidized rep long-term contracts, on teachers' pay scale. Advertise in *The Stage* and *Y Cymro.* Welcome casting queries from actors; approach in writing in the first instance.

Trestle Theatre Company

47 Wood Street, Barnet, Herts. EN5 4BS
Tel (01) **441 0349**
Administrator Penny Mayes

> Founded 1981. Cooperative theatre company that performs in small- and middle-scale venues. The work is company-devised mask theatre – highly original and visual. The masks are made by the company members. Tour for three weeks, with one week rest; company of three performers/devisers/mask makers on one-year ITC/Equity contracts. Advertise in *The Stage*, ITC, the *Guardian, The Voice* and *City Limits.* Welcome casting queries from actors; approach in writing in the first instance – letters are kept on file. 'We specialize in mask and mime, so it helps to mention skills in any field on your CV.'

Umbrella Theatre

The Basement, 46 Compton Avenue, Brighton, E. Sussex BN1 3PS
Tel (0273) **775354**
Joint artistic directors David Lavender, Colin Granger

> Founded 1979 to produce in English unusual and exciting works from abroad. Small-scale touring to venues seating up to 500. Recent productions: *The World of the Café Waiters* (original French cabaret); *Joseph and Mary* by Peter Turrini. Usually profit-share. Advertise in *The Stage*, and welcome casting queries from actors; approach in writing in the first instance.

Umoja Theatre

The Base, Thompson's Avenue, Camberwell, London SE5
Tel (01) **701 6396**
Artistic director Gloria Hamilton

> Founded 1983. Tour both adult and children's productions on topics of relevance today, to community centres, arts centres and schools – London only in the case of the children's show and nationwide for the adult show. Recent productions: *Nine Nights* by Edgar White; *Success or Failure* by Gloria Hamilton. Company of 15 on four-month Equity contracts. Sometimes advertise in *The Stage, The Voice, City Limits* and *Time Out.* Welcome casting queries from actors; telephone in the first instance. Also run theatre training courses, workshops and an employment agency.

Wildcat Stage Productions

Sir Henry Wood Building, Jordanhill College, Southbrae Drive, Glasgow G13 1PP
Tel (041) **954 0000**
Artistic director David Maclennan

Founded 1978. Tour new works of music theatre by writers working in Scotland to large- and medium-scale theatres, town and village halls and community centres. Six productions each year touring for 7–8 weeks each. Recent productions: *The Steamie, The Magic Snowball, The Importance of Being Honest, The Celtic Story, Waiting on One.* Company of 8–10 actors on 12-week Esher standard contracts for subsidized repertory. Do not advertise, but welcome casting queries from actors; write in the first instance, enclosing CV. 'We prefer to work with actors who are musicians and vice versa, and they should be good singers.'

Winged Horse Touring Productions

6 The Old Schoolhouse, 1 Dean Path, Edinburgh EH4 3BG
Tel (031) **226 3520**
Artistic director John Carnegie

Founded 1979. Produce either specially commissioned work by Scottish-based authors or plays reworked by contemporary authors from existing texts. Tour to theatres, community centres, studio theatres, village halls and art centres in the spring and autumn. A mixture of one- and two-night stands and full weeks. Recent productions: *Tales of an Island People* and *The Cry of Spain* by Robin Munro; *Blood and Ice* by Liz Lochhead. Company of 1–7 on Equity/ITC contracts of approximately nine weeks. Do not advertise, but welcome casting queries from Scottish-based actors. Send letter with an SAE, 'otherwise we will not reply.'

The Women's Theatre Group

5 Leonard Street, London EC2A 4AQ
Tel (01) 251 0202

Founded 1972. National small-scale touring. The WTG commissions plays by women playwrights specifically for the company. Perform in arts centres, studio theatres, colleges and community centres from the autumn to spring/early summer. Recent productions: *Picture Palace* by Winsome Pinnock; *Lear's Daughters* by WTG & Elaine Feinstein; *Holding the Reins* (company devised); *Our Lady* by Deborah Levy. Average company of 4–5 on iTC/Equity contracts of varying lengths. Advertise in *The Stage, The Voice, Caribbean Times* and *Outwrite*. Welcome casting queries; approach in writing in the first instance. 'We present new work which is intended to record and expand the real experiences of women and, ultimately, change the way women are perceived in society. It is the aim of the company to make the work innovative, accessible, meaningful and entertaining.'

Word & Action (Dorset) Ltd

43 Avenue Road, Wimborne, Dorset BH21 1BS
Tel (0202) **883197**

Founded 1972. Specialize in audience participatory 'instant theatre', and also work with poetry and limited scripted pieces. Perform in schools, youth clubs, hospitals, day centres, community centres, village halls, universities, colleges, prisons and old age pensioner homes. Three, and sometimes four, teams of three actors work concurrently all over Britain, Ireland and Europe for 7–8 months. Non-Equity (cooperative company); length of stay indeterminate. Advertise in the *Guardian, Peace News, Venue, Due South* and *City Limits*, and welcome casting queries either by telephone or in writing. 'Membership is open to anyone, providing space is available, but the group requires a strong interest and commitment to seeking out a new form of relationship between actor and audience. Long hours and low pay but highly rewarding.'

Yorkshire Theatre Company

LCVS, 229 Woodhouse Lane, Leeds LS2 9LE
Tel (0532) **444053**

Founded 1982. 'YTC is committed to encouraging new plays dealing with crucial cultural and social issues.' Tour to arts centres, studio theatres, universities, colleges, schools, prisons and community centres nationwide. Split weeks and 1–2 nights performance pattern. Company of 5–6 on Equity contracts of approximately 20 weeks. Advertise in *The Stage* and local press. Welcome casting queries from actors; send letter with CV and photograph. 'The company is committed to producing easily accessible theatre which broadens its audience beyond the accustomed theatre-goer by virtue of its subject matter and/or form. Recent production, *State of Play* by Ian Hartley and Toby Swift, was a highly stylized, physical and, above all, comic examination of the male ego.'

12. Non-producing theatres

The non-producing theatre is a peculiarly British institution. In most countries, the producer and his theatre are as one, but here, it is more common for a producer to rent theatre space only when occasion demands. Whatever the administrative advantages of this arrangement, it does mean that certain well-known theatres lack a consistent character. From high drama to low comedy, the stage is held by whatever or whomever can pull in the audiences.

Note All telephone numbers listed are management *not* box office.

London

Adelphi Theatre
Strand, London WC2E 7NA
Tel (01) **836 1166**

> *Seating capacity*: 1554. Dates back to 1806; it was the home of melodrama in the last half of the 19th century, and had its own real-life drama in 1897, when the leading actor, William Terriss, was stabbed to death outside the Royal Entrance in Maiden Lane. Legend has it that his ghost still haunts the theatre. The present theatre, the fourth on the site, opened in 1930. Today it is the musicals that bring in audiences, including most recently *Me and My Girl*. Part of the James Nederlander Theatres group. *Funding*: self-financing.

Albery Theatre
St Martin's Lane, London WC2
Tel (01) **867 1125**

> *Seating capacity*: 900. Plays, musicals. Renowned for the Olivier/Richardson seasons of the 1940s. Other successes include *Oliver!* (which ran for five years from 1960, returning to sweep the board again in 1977), and a number of transfers from the subsidized section — including *Children of a Lesser God* from the Mermaid. Part of the Maybox Theatres group (Chesterfield Properties). *Funding*: self-financing.

Aldwych Theatre
Aldwych, London WC2B 4DF
Tel (01) **379 6736**

> *Seating capacity*: 1057. Designed to pair the Strand Theatre, it opened seven months after its twin in December 1905. Between the wars, the theatre was renowned for the famous 'Aldwych' farces, many by Ben Travers. The Aldwych also housed the World Theatre seasons that Peter Daubeny presented from 1964 to 1975. The theatre was bought by James Nederlander, the Broadway producer, in 1982, when he outbid Andrew Lloyd Webber. Tom Stoppard's *Hapgood* is among its recent productions. *Funding*: self-financing.

Almeida Theatre

Almeida Street, London N1 1TA
Tel (01) **226 7432**

> *Seating capacity*: 300. Full range of performance arts, with an excellent balance of contemporary British and international works, and an emphasis on contemporary music. Theatre presentations include a three-month residency by Théâtre de Complicité at the end of 1988, and several seasons in conjunction with the Royal Shakespeare Company, who offered a nine-week season of three plays in August/September 1988: Lucy Gannon's *Keeping Tom Nice*, Athol Fugard's *Hello and Goodbye* and Seneca's *Oedipus*, translated by Ted Hughes. Mainly funded by Greater London Arts; additional funding from London Borough Grants Scheme (LBGS), the London Borough of Islington and the Arts Council. 'Invaluable work in mounting new plays' – *Sunday Telegraph*.

Ambassadors Theatre

West Street, London WC2H 9ND
Tel (01) **836 4797**

> *Seating capacity*: 450. Opened in 1913, the theatre initially made its name with the London debuts of Vivien Leigh and Ivor Novello. But it is chiefly remembered as the home of London's longest-running play, *The Mousetrap*, which was here for 22 years before transferring to St Martin's Theatre next door. Currently showing the Royal Shakespeare Company's *Les Liaisons Dangereuses*. *Funding*: self-financing.

Apollo Theatre

Shaftesbury Avenue, London W1V 7HD
Tel (01) **437 3435**

> *Seating capacity*: 756. A turn-of-the-century theatre, the Apollo specialized in musicals in its early days. However, its most famous production was the comedy, *Boeing Boeing*, which ran for 3½ years from 1962. Alfred Uhry's *Driving Miss Daisy* was among its recent productions. *Funding*: self-financing.

Apollo Victoria

17 Wilton Road, London SW1
Tel (01) **834 6318**

> *Seating capacity*: 2170. Hosts major musicals and international artists. Currently showing Andrew Lloyd Webber's *Starlight Express*. *Funding*: self-financing.

Battersea Arts Centre

Old Town Hall, Lavender Hill, London SW11 5TF
Tel (01) **223 2223**

> *Seating capacity*: 100–120. The Arts Centre was originally opened by the local authority, but closed in 1980 because of local government cuts. An independent trust reopened the Centre in January 1981. It hosts small-scale touring companies, fringe companies, cabaret and jazz. *Funding*: Greater London Arts and Wandsworth Council.

Bloomsbury Theatre

15 Gordon Street, London WC1H 0AH
Tel (01) **388 5976**

> *Seating capacity*: 560. Opened in 1968 and operated by University College, London as a student theatre until 1974 when, to help finances, visiting professional companies were encouraged to present shows. Now runs an all-

year programme of visiting theatre, opera, dance and concerts, plus in-house and student productions. *Funding*: University College, London.

Cambridge Theatre

Earlham Street, London WC2H 9HU
Tel (01) **240 7664**

Seating capacity: approximately 1000. Reopened in 1987 with American musical version of *Peter Pan* and in 1988 staged the musical *Budgie* starring Adam Faith and Anita Dobson. Contact Stoll Moss Theatres, Cranbourn Mansions, Cranbourn Street, London WC2H 7AG. Tel (01) 437 2274.

Comedy Theatre

Panton Street, London SW1Y 4DN
Tel (01) **839 5522**

Seating capacity: 820. Opened in 1881, the Comedy had – until its refurbishment in 1954 – the oldest surviving auditorium in London. In the mid-1950s, the theatre was an important centre for strong contemporary drama and became the base for the New Watergate Club which presented American works banned by the Lord Chamberlain. With plays by Arthur Miller and Tennessee Williams on offer, the Club's membership rocketed to 68,000, making it an important force in weakening the power of the censor. The Comedy went traditional with the long-running *There's a Girl in My Soup*, then was again associated with new and innovative work when Nell Dunn's *Steaming* transferred from the Theatre Royal, Stratford East. Now owned by Roger Wingate's Chesterfield Properties. *Funding*: self-financing.

Criterion Theatre

Piccadilly Circus, London W1V 9LB
Tel (01) **867 1127**

Seating capacity: 647. One of the most important surviving mid-Victorian theatres. Everything, except the entrance and foyer, is below street level, a great novelty when the theatre was built in 1874. Probably the most spectacular run here was the 1039 performances of Rattigan's *French Without Tears*. Over the years, the theatre has proved that there is an audience for the off-beat and original with *Loot, Bent* and *Can't Pay? Won't Pay!* Part of the Maybox Theatres group (Chesterfield Properties). *Funding*: self-financing.

Donmar Warehouse Theatre

41 Earlham Street, London WC2H 9LD
Tel (01) **240 2766**
Artistic director Nica Burns

Seating capacity: 250. Founded 1982. Leading venue for touring companies such as Cheek by Jowl. 'Pick of the Fringe' season each autumn features award-winning shows from the Edinburgh Festival. 1988 season included: *Blood Wedding* (Communicado Theatre Company) and *Salt of the Earth* (Hull Truck). Rarely produce in-house. Owned by Maybox Theatres group (Chesterfield Properties). *Funding*: self- financing.

The Drill Hall

16 Chenies Street, London WC1E 7ET
Tel (01) **637 8270 (box office)**

Seating capacity: 280. Opened in 1976 as the base for Action Space, the Drill Hall is now used by touring companies with a committed political programme.

Sexual politics are high on the list, with regular visits from Monstrous Regiment and Gay Sweatshop. *Funding*: Camden Council, London Boroughs Arts Scheme and Greater London Arts.

Duchess Theatre
Catherine Street, London WC2B 5LA
Tel (01) **839 1134**

Seating capacity: 484. One of the smallest West End theatres, the Duchess was built to an original design by the architect Ewen Barr in 1929. The theatre is on two different levels; the circle is narrower than the stalls and is supported by steel girders from the roof, giving it some of the best sight lines of any London theatre. J. B. Priestley began a long association with the theatre in 1933, and a number of his plays were seen here. Coward's *Blithe Spirit* had a triumphant opening in 1942 and ran for 1997 performances. *Oh Calcutta!* occasioned some raised eyebrows in 1974, even though it had already run for four years at the Royalty. *Funding*: self-financing.

Duke of York's Theatre
St Martin's Lane, London WC2H 0HD
Tel (01) **836 6260**

Seating capacity: 640. An unassuming but attractive theatre, owned by Capital Radio. The first theatre to open in St Martin's Lane, it was unusual in that the auditorium was heated by three roaring fires. Legend has it that the building is haunted by Violette Melnotte, one half of the acting team that founded the theatre in 1892. *Funding*: self-financing.

Fortune Theatre
Russell Street, London WC2B 5HH
Tel (01) **240 1514**

Seating capacity: 435. This tiny theatre, opened in 1924, was the first to be built after World War I. Standing in the shadow of the famous colonnade of the Theatre Royal, Drury Lane, its history has been chequered. In the 1950s and 1960s, revues proved popular, *Beyond the Fringe* being the best-remembered. *The Promise* and David Storey's *The Contractor* brought a return to drama, though thrillers proved the success of the 1970s. N. J. Crisp's *Dangerous Obsession* is among recent productions. *Funding*: self-financing.

Garrick Theatre
Charing Cross Road, London WC2H 0HH
Tel (01) **836 8271**

Seating capacity: 710. The Garrick opened in 1889 with Pinero's play *The Profligate*. Among its greatest successes were *Love on the Dole* in 1935, which introduced Wendy Hiller to the West End, Theatre Workshop's *Fing's Ain't Wot They Used to Be* and that old stalwart *No Sex Please, We're British*. More recently, Coward's *Easy Virtue* transferred from the King's Head. *Funding*: self-financing.

Globe Theatre
Shaftesbury Avenue, London W1V 8AR
Tel (01) **437 6003**

Seating capacity: 897. Designed in Louis XVI style and built in 1906 as a pair to the Queen's Theatre, the Globe has seen successful productions by Maugham,

Coward, Novello, Rattigan, Fry, Bolt and, more recently, Ayckbourn and Frayn. *Funding*: self-financing.

Hackney Empire
291 Mare Street, Hackney, London E8 1EJ
Tel (01) **986 0171**

> *Seating capacity*: 1000. Built 1901, with a large but friendly auditorium and splendid Edwardian decor. All facilities are constantly being improved, as the theatre was used as a bingo hall until its conversion and reopening in 1986. Management intend to create a national theatre of entertainment, comedy and music, with some in-house events and outside promoters and companies suitable for the wide appeal of the theatre. Will not accept racist or sexist material. *Funding*: self-financing.

Her Majesty's Theatre
Haymarket, London SW1Y 4QR
Tel (01) **930 5337**

> *Seating capacity*: 1210. The history of Her Majesty's is long and illustrious. The original theatre – designed by the architect and playwright, Sir John Vanbrugh – opened in 1705. Two further theatres, both with established reputations for fashionable opera, occupied the site until the present theatre opened in 1897. One of the larger London theatres, this final version was built by the famous actor/manager, Max Beerbohm Tree. In his day, there were spectacular revivals of Shakespeare, the first production of Shaw's *Pygmalion* and the musical *Chu Chin Chow*. Musicals have proved popular fare in recent years: *West Side Story*, *Fiddler on the Roof*, *Ain't Misbehavin'* and currently *Phantom of the Opera*. Owned by Stoll Moss group.

ICA Theatre
Nash House, Carlton Terrace, The Mall, London SW1
Tel (01) **930 0493**

> *Seating capacity*: 220. The theatre opened in 1973. It has a large acting space that lends itself well to free-ranging experimental drama. No in-house productions; this is a centre for British and foreign touring companies offering highly visual new works. *Funding*: Westminster Council, the British Council and Greater London Arts.

London Coliseum
St Martin's Lane, London WC2N 4ES
Tel (01) **836 0111**

> *Seating capacity*: 2358. The Coliseum is London's largest theatre. It was built on a grand scale in 1904 by Oswald Stoll, and had a special escalator to take royal parties to their boxes, lifts to conduct patrons to the upper levels and foyer facilities for typing and sending telegrams. Moreover, the theatre was equipped with the first revolving stage in Britain. The exterior was equally impressive with columns, arches, chariots, lions and a globe designed to revolve. When this was declared illegal, Stoll resorted to simulating movement with flashing lights. In the early days, spectaculars of all kinds were staged here. Musicals took over in the 1930s, and the English National Opera moved here from Sadler's Wells in 1968. *Funding*: Arts Council of Great Britain, City of Westminster.

London Palladium
Argyll Street, London W1A 3AB
Tel (01) **437 6166**

> *Seating capacity*: 2317. Although now heavily dependent on TV to provide it
> with star turns, this last refuge of variety is probably the best-known London
> venue for those in search of a good night out. The Palladium started life in the
> 1880s as the home of Hengler's Circus, so it is entirely fitting that *Barnum*, the
> story of the 19th-century circus impresario, should have had a run of several
> years here. After Hengler's death in 1887, a skating rink replaced the circus, until
> the new music hall opened in 1900. One of its unique features was a box-to-box
> telephone system that enabled patrons to talk to their friends! The Palladium can
> still be relied upon to provide spectacular entertainment, albeit of a transatlantic
> flavour. Owned by Stoll Moss group. *Funding*: self-financing.

Lyric Theatre
Shaftesbury Avenue, London W1V 8ES
Tel (01) **437 1231**

> *Seating capacity*: 967. Opened in 1888 with a long-forgotten, but then highly
> popular, operetta. It was the second theatre in the Victorian grand design for
> Shaftesbury Avenue. Completely redecorated in 1933, it still retains its 1930s
> style. *Funding*: self-financing.

May Fair Theatre
Stratton Street, London W1A 2AN
Tel (01) **629 7777**

> *Seating capacity*: 310. An integral part of the May Fair Hotel, the theatre started
> life as the Candlelight Ballroom where Ambrose and Harry Roy made their
> famous big-band broadcasts in the 1930s. It was opened as a theatre in 1963.
> Small-scale productions, often from the fringe, have proved successful. *Funding*:
> self-financing.

Mermaid Theatre
Puddledock, Blackfriars, London EC4 4DB
Tel (01) **236 9521**

> Opened in 1959. At the time of writing, the theatre was dark and likely to remain
> so for the foreseeable future.

New End Theatre
27 New End, Hampstead, London NW3 1JD
Tel (01) **794 0022**

> *Seating capacity*: 80. Housed in a building that was once a mortuary, the theatre
> first opened in 1974. No in-house productions — visited by fringe theatre
> companies.

New London Theatre
Drury Lane/Parker Street, London WC2B 5PW
Tel (01) **242 9802**

> *Seating capacity*: 900. Opened in 1973. A highly versatile theatre: stage, seats
> and even walls move at the flick of a switch. *Cats* has been a sensational hit here.

The Old Vic
Waterloo Road, London SE1 8NB
Tel (01) **928 2651**

> *Seating capacity*: 1000. Opened as the Royal Coburg in 1818 and renamed as the Royal Victoria Theatre in 1833. In 1912 Lilian Baylis became theatre manager and founded The Old Vic Shakespeare Company in 1914. The legendary productions starring actors such as Sybil Thorndike, Edith Evans, Peggy Ashcroft, John Gielgud, Laurence Olivier, and Ralph Richardson carried on until 1941 (Tyrone Guthrie took over from Lilian Baylis in 1937), when the war forced the theatre to close. It reopened in 1950 and The Old Vic Company played 49 seasons until the advent of the National Theatre in 1963. The Prospect Theatre Company made the Old Vic its London base until 1981 and in 1982 the theatre was bought by Canadian businessman Ed Mirvish. A nine-month £2 million facelift followed and the theatre reopened in 1983 with a new Tim Rice musical, *Blondel*.
> See also Producing Theatres and Independent Managements.

Oval House Theatre
52–54 Kennington Oval, London SE11
Tel (01) **735 2786**

> *Seating capacity*: 100 (downstairs studio) and 50 (upstairs studio). Visited by 50 fringe companies each year such as Intimate Strangers, Random Pact and Red Rag Theatre Company. Experimental new work workshops plus Youth Theatre.

Palace Theatre
Shaftesbury Avenue, London W1V 8AY
Tel (01) **434 0088**

> *Seating capacity*: 1394. This extraordinary red brick and terracotta theatre took two years to build, and was opened by Richard D'Oyly Carte in 1891 as the Royal English Opera House. His hopes for English grand opera were short-lived, however, for a year later, it became a variety theatre, changing its name to the Palace. Its greatest successes have been musicals: *The Sound of Music* played here for six years and *Jesus Christ Superstar* played for eight. *Les Miserables*, the Royal Shakespeare Company production (and British première) of the musical by Alain Boblil and Claude-Michel Shonberg, is currently playing. *Funding*: self-financing.

Phoenix Theatre
110 Charing Cross Road, London WC2H 0JP
Tel (01) **836 7431**

> *Seating capacity*: 1012. The Phoenix opened in 1930 with Noel Coward's *Private Lives*. Post-war, *The Canterbury Tales* opened in 1968 and ran for over 2000 performances. Recently hosted a season by Kenneth Branagh's Renaissance Theatre Company. Now owned by Roger Wingate's Chesterfield Properties. *Funding*: self-financing.

Piccadilly Theatre
Denman Street, London W1V 8DY
Tel (01) **437 2397**

> *Seating capacity*: 1232. Built in 1928 and then taken over by Warner Bros to become a screening venue for the country's first talkies. Live entertainment returned in the 1930s when Noel Coward scored a hit with *Blithe Spirit*. Gielgud's *Macbeth* and the musical *Panama Hattie* played to wartime audiences until the

theatre was damaged by flying bombs in 1944. Donald Albery took over in 1960, and under his management, links were formed between commercial and subsidized theatre. A number of transfers, mainly from the Royal Shakespeare Company, have been housed here: *Wild Oats*, *Privates on Parade*, *Piaf*, *Once in a Lifetime* and *Educating Rita*. Part of the Maybox Theatres group (Chesterfield Properties). *Funding*: self-financing.

Playhouse Theatre

Northumberland Avenue, London WC2N 5DE
Tel (01) **839 4292**

Seating capacity: 786. First opened as the Royal Avenue Theatre in 1882 and extensively rebuilt in 1907 after part of Charing Cross Station collapsed on top of it in 1905. Used by the BBC as a radio studio for *The Goons*, *Tony Hancock* and other productions from 1951. Reopened in 1988 with the musical *Girlfriends* by Howard Goodall (directed by John Retallack). Jeffrey Archer now a 60 per cent owner.

Prince Edward Theatre

Old Compton Street, London W1V 6HS
Tel (01) **437 2024**

Seating capacity: 1647. The theatre has had a chequered career since it was opened in 1930. Designed as a musical and revue venue, it was converted into a cabaret restaurant in 1936 and renamed the London Casino. In 1954, it housed the spectacular Cinerama, and in 1974, it became a dual-purpose theatre offering both films and shows. In 1977, live entertainment had its revenge when the musical *Evita* moved in. Currently houses *Chess*, the musical by Benny Anderson, Tim Rice and Bjorn Ulvaeus. *Funding*: self-financing.

Prince of Wales Theatre

31 Coventry Street, London W1V 8AS
Tel (01) **930 1867**

Seating capacity: 1133. Actor/manager Edward Bruce opened the first theatre on this site in 1884. Gracie Fields laid the foundation stone of the present theatre which was redesigned and rebuilt in 1937. An ideal venue for musicals, it recently housed *South Pacific*. *Funding*: self-financing.

Queen's Theatre

Shaftesbury Avenue, London W1V 8BA
Tel (01) **734 1348**

Seating capacity: 979. The Queen's was originally built in 1907 as the twin to the Globe. After bomb damage, it was almost completely restored in 1958, when Hugh Casson and Bryan Westwood designed the present glass frontage (preserving the Edwardian interior). In recent years, the theatre has been associated with a string of prestigious productions – *Otherwise Engaged*; *Saturday, Sunday, Monday*; *Another Country*; and recently *Beyond Reasonable Doubt* by Jeffrey Archer. *Funding*: self-financing.

Royalty Theatre

Portugal Street, off Kingsway, London WC2A 2HT
Tel (01) **242 9136**

Seating capacity: 1000. Musicals, pop concerts, drama. Opened with *The Visit*, directed by Peter Brook, and has since seen service as a cinema, and as the home for Paul Raymond's risqué revue *Birds of a Feather* as well as the American musical *Bubbling Brown Sugar*. *Funding*: self-financing.

Sadler's Wells Theatre
Rosebery Avenue, London EC1R 4TN
Tel (01) **278 6563**

> *Seating capacity*: 1499. Home of New Sadler's Wells Opera and Sadler's Wells Royal Ballet. Also attracts top British and international opera, ballet, dance and mime companies. *Funding*: London Boroughs Grants Scheme, London Borough of Islington.

St Martin's Theatre
West Street, London WC2H 9NH
Tel (01) **836 1086**

> *Seating capacity*: 554. Since 1974, home of Agatha Christie's *The Mousetrap*, which has now been running in London for 35 years. *Funding*: self-financing.

Savoy Theatre
Savoy Court, Strand, London WC2R OET
Tel (01) **836 8117**

> *Seating capacity*: 1122. Opened in 1881 by Richard D'Oyly Carte as the home for Gilbert & Sullivan operettas, the Savoy was the first theatre to have electric light. In 1902, it became a general West End venue, and the entrance was switched from the Embankment to its present position in the front courtyard of the Savoy Hotel. Complete rebuilding took place in 1929 when the interior was swept away to be replaced by the present striking art deco design. *Funding*: self-financing.

Shaftesbury Theatre
Shaftesbury Avenue, London WC2H 8DP
Tel (01) **379 3345**

> *Seating capacity*: 1327. This theatre has always been slightly disadvantaged by its position — at least a quarter of a mile from its nearest rival. It opened in 1911, and was forced to close in 1973 when the roof collapsed during the run of the musical *Hair*. A campaign by Paul Scofield and Alec Guinness saved the theatre from threatened redevelopment, and it now hosts large-scale musicals, such as *Follies*, and major comedy productions by the Theatre of Comedy Company. *Funding*: self-financing.

Strand Theatre
Aldwych, London WC2B 5LD
Tel (01) **836 4144**

> *Seating capacity*: 923. Opened May 1905, the theatre was designed, like its twin the Aldwych, by W. G. R. Sprague. It has had a history of long-running comedies: *Arsenic and Old Lace* played 1337 performances to wartime audiences, while *No Sex Please, We're British* played here for over a decade before moving to the Garrick. Recently Agatha Christie's *And Then There Were None* has been revived here.

Theatre Royal, Drury Lane
Catherine Street, London WC2B 5JF
Tel (01) **836 3687**

> *Seating capacity*: 2237. This theatre — now a Grade I listed building — has the

longest continuous theatrical tradition in the UK. The first theatre on the site was built in 1663, and was rebuilt in 1774 and 1812. Garrick acquired the patent to the theatre in 1747, and was replaced on his retirement by Sheridan, who presented *School for Scandal* in 1777. The 1880s were famous for Augustus Harris's great spectaculars – sea battles and chariot races were re-enacted with no expense spared. Then followed a move towards romantic musicals, which reached their peak in the 1930s with a series of Ivor Novello successes. ENSA made the theatre their wartime headquarters; the post-war period has been devoted almost entirely to musicals. Owned by Stoll Moss group. *Funding*: self-financing.

Theatre Royal Haymarket

Haymarket, London SW1Y 4HT
Tel (01) **930 8890**

Seating capacity: 905. Although this theatre dates back to 1720, it was not granted the essential 'Royal' patent until 1766. Even then, it was only allowed to open in the summer months when the two grand houses – Drury Lane and Covent Garden – were closed. The present Grade I-listed theatre, with its splendid portico, was designed by John Nash and opened in 1821. It has a long and distinguished history as an upmarket venue, and this tradition is continued today with its starry programme of classics. *Funding*: self-financing.

Vaudeville Theatre

Strand, London WC2R ONH
Tel (01) **836 3191**

Seating capacity: 690. This small theatre was built in 1870 and remodelled in 1891. The next change occurred only in 1969, when its new owner, Sir Peter Saunders, gave it a complete decorative overhaul; now owned by Michael Codron. Its most memorable productions include: *Salad Days*, which ran for over 2000 performances from 1954; *The Man Most Likely To*; *Move Over, Mrs Markham*; and *Present Laughter*. *Funding*: self-financing.

Victoria Palace

Victoria Street, London SW1 5EA
Tel (01) **834 2781**

Seating capacity: 1564. Designed as a music hall, the Victoria Palace has been associated with variety and musical productions throughout its history. The Crazy Gang installed themselves here in 1949 and remained until 1962, when *The Black & White Minstrel Show* began its eight-year run. *Annie* and *The Sound of Music* have proved lucrative in recent years. Owned by Stoll Moss group. *Funding*: self-financing.

Westminster Theatre

Palace Street, Buckingham Palace Road, London SW1E 5JB
Tel (01) **834 7882**

Seating capacity: 585. The theatre stands on the site of a chapel built in 1776 by an off-beat clergyman who used his wife's lottery winnings to finance the building! In 1931, Anmer Hall transformed this former chapel-of-ease into a theatre (naming it after his former school), and a bold policy of presenting Pirandello, Shaw, Ibsen and O'Neill put the theatre in the forefront of its contemporaries. In 1946, Moral Rearmament took over, and the theatre opened for 'worthy' shows and the profitable Christmas season. *Funding*: self-financing.

Whitehall Theatre
14 Whitehall, London SW1A 2DY
Tel (01) **867 1129**

> *Seating capacity*: 680. The Whitehall was one of a rash of theatres to open in 1930 and is best known as the post-war home of British farce. Paul Raymond took it over in the 1970s for his sex revues, but there was a return to the good old days in 1981 when the political farce *Anyone for Denis?* swept in. Now part of the Maybox Theatres group (Chesterfield Properties). *Funding*: self-financing.

Wimbledon Theatre
The Broadway, Wimbledon, London SW19 1QG
Tel (01) **543 4549**

> *Seating capacity*: 1600. The theatre offers a wide range of entertainment. It is on the circuit for big touring opera and ballet companies, and stages the occasional pre-West End run. There is an annual pantomime. *Funding*: self-financing.

Wyndham's Theatre
Charing Cross Road, London WC2H 0DA
Tel (01) **867 1125**

> *Seating capacity*: 800. One of London's most romantic theatres, Wyndham's was built in 1899 by the actor/manager Charles Wyndham. The auditorium is decorated in cream, gold and blue, and the bust above the proscenium is said to be of Mary Moore, Wyndham's leading lady and later his wife. The theatre has had a long and close association with the fringe, and its successful transfers include *A Taste of Honey*, *Oh What a Lovely War!*, *No Man's Land* (with John Gielgud and Ralph Richardson), *Once a Catholic*, *Piaf*, *Accidental Death of an Anarchist*, *Crystal Clear* and more recently *Serious Money* and *The Secret of Sherlock Holmes*. Now part of the Maybox Theatres group (Chesterfield Properties). *Funding*: self-financing.

England (excluding London)

Alexandra Theatre
Station Street, Birmingham B5 4DS
Tel (021) **643 5536**

> *Seating capacity*: 1367. This top touring venue attracts star TV names in musicals, light comedies and pantomime, and hosts many pre- and post-West End shows. *Funding*: City of Birmingham.

Alhambra Theatre
Morley Street, Bradford, W. Yorks. BD7 1AJ
Tel (0274) **753623**

> *Seating capacity*: 1482. The theatre is the venue of touring opera, ballet, plays, musicals, variety and concerts. In 1986, it underwent a £6 million refurbishment by well-known theatre architects RHWL. The exterior, with towers and cupolas, was completely restored, with the addition of some ultra-modern design features, including a glass-fronted staircase inside the main rotunda which unites all the interior levels. The National Theatre is planning to make the studio at the rear of the theatre into its northern home. *Funding*: Bradford Metropolitan District Council.

Apollo Theatre
Ardwick Green, Manchester M12 6AP
Tel (061) **273 6921**

> *Seating capacity*: 2641. Although opera, ballet and drama are seen here, the theatre is mostly used for rock concerts. *Funding*: self-financing.

Ashcroft Theatre
Park Lane, Croydon, Surrey CR9 1DG
Tel (01) **681 0821**

> *Seating capacity*: 763. The theatre houses touring companies, producing mostly comedies and thrillers. There is an annual pantomime. *Funding*: London Borough of Croydon.

Babbacombe Theatre
Babbacombe Downs, Torquay TQ1 3LU
Tel (0803) **528693**

> *Seating capacity*: 600. Summer season only; amateurs. *Funding*: self-financing.

The Beck Theatre
Grange Road, Hayes, Middlesex
Tel (01) **561 8371**

> *Seating capacity*: 598 (flexible). The Beck Theatre, named after a local worthy, was opened in 1977. Offers a mixed programme of touring drama, mostly light comedies and thrillers.

Birmingham Hippodrome
Hurst Street, Birmingham B5 4TB
Tel (021) **622 7437**

> *Seating capacity*: 1367. Blockbuster tours of plays, musicals, operas, ballet; an annual panto; and some variety. Many pre- and post-West End plays. *Funding*: City of Birmingham.

Bournemouth Pier Theatre
Bournemouth, Dorset BH1 5AD
Tel (0202) **290250**

> *Seating capacity*: 850. Open May to October only. Summer seasons, concerts. *Funding*: self-financing.

Buxton Opera House
Water Street, Buxton, Derbys. SK17 6XN
Tel (0298) **71573**

> *Seating capacity*: 946. Varied programme of professional and amateur productions, one-night stands and a festival in July and August (*see* Festivals). *Funding*: North Western Arts, High Peak Borough Council, Derbyshire County Council.

Cambridge Arts Theatre
PO Box 17, Cambridge CB2 3PW
Tel (0223) **355246**

> *Seating capacity*: 650. A traditional theatre built in 1936, that offers standard comedies and thrillers as well as new work from such touring companies as the

Cambridge Theatre Company and the Oxford Playhouse Company. Also ballet, films and panto. *Funding*: University of Cambridge.

Chatham Central Hall Theatre
170 High Street, Chatham, Kent ME4 4AS
Tel (0634) **48584**

> *Seating capacity*: 945. One-night stands and weekly productions: music, plays. *Funding*: self-financing.

City Varieties Music Hall
The Headrow, Leeds LS1 6LW
Tel (0532) **450366**

> *Seating capacity*: 586. A traditional music hall over 200 years old. Variety, revue, pantomime, drama and music. *Funding*: self-financing.

Connaught Theatre
Union Place, Worthing, W. Sussex BN11 1LG
Tel (0903) **31799**

> *Seating capacity*: 514. Mixed programme of amateur and professional shows; some films. *Funding*: Worthing Borough Council.

Corby Civic Theatre
George Street, Corby, Northants. N17 1QB
Tel (0536) **402551**

> *Seating capacity*: 530. Part of Corby civic centre, built in 1966. Ballet, opera, rock and classical concerts. *Funding*: Corby District Council.

Gordon Craig Theatre
Stevenage Leisure Centre, Lytton Way, Stevenage SG11 1LZ
Tel (0438) **317956**

> *Seating capacity*: 507. This venue provides a wide programme of light touring drama, music, films, children's shows and an annual panto, aiming to suit all tastes and ages. *Funding*: Stevenage Borough Council, Eastern Arts.

Daneside Theatre
Park Road, Congleton, Cheshire
Tel (0260) **278481**

> *Seating capacity*: 300. Mostly amateur productions, but available for professional bookings. *Funding*: self-financing.

Darlington Civic Theatre
Parkgate, Darlington DL1 1RR
Tel (0325) **468006**

> *Seating capacity*: 599. An Edwardian theatre, built in 1907, it houses major tours of plays, ballet, opera, recitals, concerts and a pantomime season. Director Brian Goddard claims the highest average attendance of any provincial theatre, by booking popular shows and then marketing them so that people know what is on. *Funding*: Darlington Borough Council.

Devonshire Park Theatre
8 Compton Street, Eastbourne, E. Sussex
Tel (0323) **412424**

> *Seating capacity*: 936. Major touring productions, pre- and post-West End; some classical plays. *Funding*: self-financing.

Doncaster Civic Theatre
Waterdale, Doncaster, S. Yorks. DN1 3ET
Tel (0302) **22817**

> *Seating capacity*: 511. Used mostly by amateur companies; available for bookings at other times. *Funding*: Doncaster Metropolitan Borough Council.

Empire Theatre
Lime Street, Liverpool 1
Tel (051) **709 3514**

> *Seating capacity*: 2348. One of the major touring houses in the North-west, attracting top drama, opera and ballet companies. *Funding*: self-financing.

Forum Theatre
Town Centre, Billingham, Cleveland TS23 2LJ
Tel (0642) **551389**

> *Seating capacity*: 631. Part of a large, multi-purpose centre comprising a swimming pool and other leisure facilities, the theatre offers a mixed programme of good-quality touring drama, children's shows, one-night stands, music and an annual panto. *Funding*: Stockton Borough Council.

Georgian Theatre Royal
Victoria Road, Richmond, N. Yorks. DL10 4DW
Tel (0748) **3021**

> *Seating capacity*: 231. This remarkable theatre, originally built in 1788, re-opened in 1963 after being used as a wine store and an auction house: everything from the paybox to the proscenium arch doors is authentic. It offers an interesting programme of touring drama, music and one-night stands, as well as hosting the local amateur dramatic society. *Funding*: self-financing.

Grand Theatre
Church Street, Blackpool FY1 1HT
Tel (0253) **28309**

> *Seating capacity*: 1238. Originally built in 1894, designed by the great theatre architect Frank Matcham, the Grand reopened as a touring venue in 1981: top drama; musicals; concerts; ballet; the usual comedy acts and one-night stands on offer during the summer; annual panto. *Funding*: local authority.

Grand Theatre
Lichfield Street, Wolverhampton, W. Midlands WV1 1DE
Tel (0902) **28165**

> *Seating capacity*: 1200. Drama, opera, pantomime, light entertainment, children's shows, amateur musicals, concerts. *Funding*: Wolverhampton City Council.

Grand Theatre & Opera House
New Briggate, Leeds LS1 6NZ
Tel (0532) **456014**

> *Seating capacity*: 1550. One of Britain's finest examples of a Victorian theatre and opera house, and the home of Opera North. It offers a varied programme of opera, one-night stands, touring ballet and major touring drama productions. *Funding*: Leeds City Council.

Harlequin
Warwick Quadrant, Redhill, Surrey RH1 1NN
Tel (0737) **765547**

> *Seating capacity*: 494. Middle-scale touring productions; pantomime season. *Funding*: Reigate & Banstead Borough Council.

Harrogate Theatre
Oxford Street, Harrogate, N. Yorks. HG1 1QF
Tel (0423) **502710**

> *Seating capacity*: 476. Victorian theatre with many outstanding features. There is a repertory company resident from late August to the end of April (*see* Rep/Regional Theatres), but from May to August, there is a touring season with a full range of performing arts: drama, dance, music, mime, children's shows. Bookings range from whole weeks to one-night stands. *Funding*: Yorkshire Arts, Harrogate Borough Council, N. Yorks. County Council.

Hull New Theatre
Kingston Square, Hull, N. Humberside HU1 3HF
Tel (0482) **20244**

> *Seating capacity*: 1200. Large touring productions, opera, ballet and concerts. Produces a large annual panto. *Funding*: Hull County Council, Beverley Borough Council, Hull Leisure Services.

Key Theatre
Embankment Road, Peterborough, Cambs. PE1 1EF
Tel (0733) **52437**

> *Seating capacity*: 399. Plays, musicals, jazz, amateur shows – entertainment of all kinds. *Funding*: Peterborough County Council.

King's Theatre
Albert Road, Southsea, Hants PO5 2QT
Tel (0705) **811394**

> *Seating capacity*: 1750. Drama, opera, musical, ballet – covering a wide range of tastes. *Funding*: self-financing, Southern Arts grid/circuit funding.

Limelight Theatre
Queens Park Centre, Queens Park, Aylesbury HP21 7RT
Tel (0296) **431272**

> *Seating capacity*: 150. Visiting small-scale theatre and dance companies. *Funding*: Buckinghamshire Arts Association.

Malthouse Theatre

Malthouse Lane, nr Hurstpierpoint College, Hassocks, W. Sussex
Tel (04446) **41047**
Artistic director Sandra Scriven

>*Seating capacity*: 100. Medieval barn with adjoining restaurant and bar. Visiting companies ranging from opera and music hall to drama and one-man shows. *Funding*: self-financing.

Marlowe Theatre

The Friars, Canterbury, Kent CT1 2AS
Tel (0227) **767246**

>*Seating capacity*: 986. Touring, concerts, pantomime, one-night stands. *Funding*: Canterbury City Council.

Marina Theatre

Marina, Lowestoft, Suffolk NR32 1HH
Tel (0502) **569646**

>*Seating capacity*: 751. Variety, dance, music, opera, star names - one-night stands and weekly bookings. Cinema. *Funding*: Waveney District Council.

Mayflower Theatre

Commercial Road, Southampton SO1 0GE
Tel (0703) **330083**

>*Seating capacity*: 2299. The largest regional theatre in the South, it presents opera, ballet, pantomime, rock and pop concerts, drama and musicals (pre- and post-West End). *Funding*: self-financing.

Mountbatten Theatre

East Park Terrace, Southampton SO9 4WW
Tel (0703) **221991**

>*Seating capacity*: 515. Amateur and professional musicals, comedies, occasional drama, concerts and films. *Funding*: Hampshire County Council.

The Music Hall

The Square, Shrewsbury, Salop SY1 1LH
Tel (0743) **50761**

>*Seating capacity*: 410. Drama, musicals, dance, pop and classical concerts; one-night stands and weekly shows. *Funding*: Shrewsbury & Atcham Borough Council.

Neptune Theatre

Hanover Street, Liverpool 1
Tel (051) **709 7844**

>*Seating capacity*: 445. Available for hire by professional and amateur companies. *Funding*: Liverpool City Council.

New Theatre Royal

Guildhall Walk, Portsmouth PO1 2DD
Tel (0705) **864611**

>*Seating capacity*: currently 250. The theatre is undergoing restoration and rebuilding, and facilities are very limited. At present, performances and events can take place only in the auditorium. *Funding*: Hampshire County Council, Portsmouth City Council.

North Pier Theatre

Westover Road, Bournemouth, Dorset BH2 5BH
Tel (0202) **20980**

> *Seating capacity*: 1518. Opera, ballet, musicals, summer shows, one-night stands, pantomime. *Funding*: self-financing.

Opera House

Quay Street, Manchester M3 3HP
Tel (061) **834 1787**

> *Seating capacity*: 2000. Presents extended runs of major musicals. *Funding*: self-financing.

The Orchard

Home Gardens, Dartford, Kent DA1 1ED
Tel (0322) **343222**

> *Seating capacity*: 900. Can be used in the round or with proscenium arch. A top touring venue with mixed programme of drama, music, dance, opera and films. *Funding*: Dartford Borough Council.

Palace Theatre

Oxford Street, Manchester M1 6FT
Tel (061) **228 6255**

> *Seating capacity*: 2000. A leading touring venue, it houses drama, ballet, music and visits from the Royal Opera. *Funding*: self-financing.

Palace Theatre

Alcester Street, Redditch, Worcs. B98 8EA
Tel (0527) **61544**

> *Seating capacity*: 399. Professional and amateur productions; bought-in one/two-night stand music, theatre, dance. Also exhibitions, films, youth theatre, holiday activities for young people. Policy of community involvement and access to the arts. *Funding*: Redditch Borough Council.

Pavilion Theatre

North Pier, The Promenade, Blackpool FY1 1NE
Tel (0253) **21452**

> *Seating capacity*: 1564. Summer season only. *Funding*: self-financing.

Pavilion Theatre

The Esplanade, Weymouth, Dorset DT4 8ED
Tel (0305) **786732**

> *Seating capacity*: 1000. Summer season, pantomime, one-night stands, concerts; some amateur use. *Funding*: Weymouth & Portland Borough Council.

Pavilion Theatre

Marine Parade, Worthing, W. Sussex BN12 4ET
Tel (0903) **39999** ext. **129**

> *Seating capacity*: 850. Wide range of shows — concerts, children's entertainment, dance. *Funding*: Worthing Borough Council.

Phoenix Theatre
6 Newarke Street, Leicester LE1 5TA
Tel (0533) **554854 (box office)**

Reopened in 1988, after extensive refurbishment, as an arts centre run in conjunction with Leicester Polytechnic. Visiting companies plus films.

The Playhouse
The High, Harlow, Essex CM20 1LS
Tel (0279) **24391**

Seating capacity: auditorium 435, studio 110. Wide programme of touring drama, dance and music. Amateur work mainly in the studio. *Funding*: Harlow District Council, Eastern Arts.

Pomegranate Theatre
Corporation Street, Chesterfield, Derbys. S41 7TX
Tel (0246) **234633**

Seating capacity: 549. Touring, plays, pantomimes, musicals, variety, Sunday concerts; some one-night stands and amateur shows. *Funding*: Chesterfield Borough Council, Derbyshire County Council.

Princess Theatre
Torbay Road, Torquay TQ2 5EZ
Tel (0803) **528693**

Seating capacity: 1514. Summer shows, pantomime, touring plays, ballet, opera; weekly or one-night stands. *Funding*: self-financing.

Richmond Theatre
The Green, Richmond-upon-Thames, Surrey TW9 1QJ
Tel (01) **940 0220**

Seating capacity: 920. Mostly light drama, much of it pre-West End. *Funding*: self-financing.

Ritz Theatre
High Street, Lincoln LN5 7PJ
Tel (0522) **537127**

Seating capacity: 1400. Drama, films, one-night stands, concerts. *Funding*: self-financing.

Royal Hippodrome Theatre
Seaside Road, Eastbourne, E. Sussex
Tel (0323) **411818**

Seating capacity: 643. Summer season, variety, musicals, concerts. *Funding*: self-financing.

Spa Terrace
South Marine Drive, Bridlington, Yorks.
Tel (0262) **678255**

Seating capacity: 1031. Summer shows, professional tours and amateur shows. *Funding*: East Yorks. Borough Council.

Sunderland Empire Theatre
High Street West, Sunderland SR1 3EX
Tel (091) **514 2517**

> *Seating capacity*: main auditorium 1550, studio 150. Pantomime, variety, opera, plays and concerts. *Funding*: Sunderland Borough Council, Grid/circuit funding (No. 1 circuit).

Tameside Theatre
Oldham Road, Ashton-under-Lyne, Greater Manchester OL6 7SE
Tel (061) **330 2095**

> *Seating capacity*: 1262. Tours, plays, music, pantomime, one-night stands, children's shows, TV transmissions. *Funding*: Tameside Municipal Borough Council.

Theatre Royal
Sawclose, Bath, Avon BA1 1ET
Tel (0225) **65074**

> *Seating capacity*: 950. One of the oldest theatres in the country, superbly restored. Often premières shows, and has close links with the National Theatre, who preview a number of their productions here in advance of the South Bank. Caters for all tastes, with opera, drama and comedy. *Funding*: self-financing.

Theatre Royal
New Road, Brighton BN1 1SD
Tel (0273) **27480**

> *Seating capacity*: 951. A venue for top touring companies, with a traditional programme of comedies and thrillers, many of them pre-West End. *Funding*: self-financing.

Theatre Royal
Westgate Street, Bury St Edmunds, Suffolk IP33 1QR
Tel (0284) **755127**

> *Seating capacity*: 350. A charming period theatre that for many years served as a brewer's warehouse; now owned by the National Trust. Plays, dance, opera, music, films and pantomime; one-night stands, weekly and half-weekly bookings. *Funding*: Suffolk County Council, St Edmundsbury Borough Council.

Theatre Royal
Grey Street, Newcastle upon Tyne NE1 6BR
Tel (091) **232 0997**

> *Seating capacity*: 1350. Recently refurbished at a cost of £8 million, the bars and foyers have been expanded and backstage facilities completely modernized, while the superb Matcham interior has been faithfully restored. It houses top touring productions, usually thrillers and comedies, and also opera and ballet. *Funding*: Newcastle City Council.

Theatre Royal
Theatre Street, Norwich NR2 1RL
Tel (0603) **623562**

> *Seating capacity*: 1275. This claims to be the most profitable civic theatre in Europe. Revues, variety acts and musicals share the stage with opera, ballet and top drama; there is an annual pantomime. *Funding*: self-financing.

Theatre Royal

Theatre Square, Nottingham NG1 5ND
Tel (0602) **483505**

> *Seating capacity*: 1188. Large-scale touring opera, ballet, variety, concerts, pantomime and light drama. *Funding*: Nottingham City Council.

Theatre Royal

Corporation Street, St Helens, Lancs. WA10 1LQ
Tel (0744) **28467**

> *Seating capacity*: 703. Touring venue for dance, music and limited drama. Also has films, lectures, children's shows, amateur events and pantomime. *Funding*: Theatre Royal (St Helens) Trust.

Theatre Royal

7 Pall Mall, Hanley, Stoke-on-Trent ST1 1EE
Tel (0782) **266343**

> *Seating capacity*: 1424. All types of productions; week, split week and one-night stands. *Funding*: self-financing.

Theatre Royal

Jewry Street, Winchester SO23 8SB
Tel (0962) **842122**

> *Seating capacity*: 409. Touring drama, music and one-night stands — a varied but light programme. *Funding*: Winchester City Council, Hampshire County Council.

Theatre Royal & The Drum

Royal Parade, Plymouth PL1 2TR
Tel (0752) **668282**

> *Seating capacity*: Theatre Royal 1296, Drum 205. In-house productions; also touring opera and ballet, children's shows and concerts. Visiting fringe groups and experimental drama in The Drum. *Funding*: Arts Council and Local Authorities. (*See also* Rep/Regional Theatres.)

Theatre Royal & Opera House

Drury Lane, Wakefield, W. Yorks. WF1 2TE
Tel (0924) **373757**

> *Seating capacity*: 530. All forms of music, dance and drama. *Funding*: Wakefield Municipal District Council, Yorkshire Arts.

Towngate Theatre

Towngate, Basildon, Essex
Tel (0268) **531343**

> *Seating capacity*: main house 550, studio 200. Built by architects RHWL and opened in April 1988, the theatre has a traditional Georgian horseshoe format, but can be transformed into a flat floor space using the latest air castor technology. It houses touring dance, music and drama, the latter ranging from new and alternative work to popular comedies; also films. *Funding*: local authority.

Watermans Arts Centre
40 High Street, Brentford, Middx. TW8 0DS
Tel (01) **847 5651**

> *Seating capacity*: 240. Opened 1983. Touring theatre companies, dance and music. Also co-produce large-scale open air shows such as *Deadwood* which was performed in Kew Gardens. *Funding*: Greater London Arts, the London Borough Grants Scheme and Hounslow Council.

West Cliff Theatre
Tower Road, Clacton-on-Sea, Essex
Tel (0255) **426526**

> *Seating capacity*: 598. Summer season; also bookings by professional and amateur companies. Closed four months of the year. *Funding*: District Council grant.

Isle of Man
Gaiety Theatre
Harris Promenade, Douglas, Isle of Man
Tel (0624) **25001**

> *Seating capacity*: 1168. Opened in 1900, this has a splendid opulent auditorium, recently restored to the original specification. Musicals, plays, opera, ballet and rock, jazz and classical concerts. *Funding*: Isle of Man Government.

Northern Ireland
Ardhowen: The Theatre by the Lakes
Dublin Road, Enniskillen, Co. Fermanagh
Tel (0365) **23233**

> *Seating capacity*: 300. Mainly touring professional theatre and music, but some community theatre, folk, traditional and jazz music, dance, opera and light entertainment. *Funding*: local authority, Arts Council of Northern Ireland.

Belfast Civic Arts Theatre
41 Botanic Avenue, Belfast BT7 1JG
Tel (0232) **242819**
Administrator Mr W. E. Brown

> *Seating capacity*: 500. Having been closed for some years, the theatre reopened in 1977 with the Ulster Actors Company in residence. Variety and children's shows, drama, dance, plus the occasional in-house production with guest directors. *Funding*: Arts Council of Northern Ireland and Belfast City Council.

Grand Opera House
Great Victoria Street, Belfast BT2 7HR
Tel (0232) **667687**

> *Seating capacity*: 1001. A splendid Victorian theatre, and Northern Ireland's only large venue for touring opera, drama and ballet. Light comedies and shows with TV names are most popular. *Funding*: Arts Council of Northern Ireland.

Scotland

Ayr Civic Theatre
Craigie Road, Ayr, Ayrshire KA8 OE7
Tel (0292) **263755**

> *Seating capacity*: 350. A small theatre linked to the Gaiety Theatre (*see below*), it is housed in an old converted church. It offers a summer repertory season and a modest programme of plays and concerts. *Funding*: Kyle & Carrick District Council.

Eden Court Theatre
Bishop's Road, Inverness IV3 5SA
Tel (0463) **239841**

> *Seating capacity*: 791. Mixed programme: music, films, some drama. *Funding*: Scottish Arts Council, Inverness District Council.

Gaiety Theatre
Carrick Street, Ayr
Tel (0292) **264630**

> *Seating capacity*: 570. Broad policy — touring plays, musicals, ballet. Resident season. *Funding*: Kyle & Carrick District Council. (*See also* AYR CIVIC THEATRE.)

His Majesty's Theatre
Rosemount Viaduct, Aberdeen
Tel (0224) **637788**

> *Seating capacity*: 1456. Opened in 1906, and designed to give a sense of luxury and (despite the large capacity of the auditorium) a feeling of intimacy, this is a premier theatre for large touring companies presenting opera, ballet, concerts and quality mainstream drama. *Funding*: local authority and self-financing.

King's Theatre
2 Leven Street, Edinburgh EH3 9LQ
Tel (031) **229 4840**

> *Seating capacity*: 1336. All types of large-scale touring productions: ballet, opera, mainstream drama, comedy. *Funding*: Edinburgh District Council, Scottish Arts Council grid/circuit funding.

King's Theatre
Bath Street, Glasgow G2 4JN
Tel (041) **248 5332**

> *Seating capacity*: 1785. Top touring venue offering drama, comedy, musicals, pantomimes, opera, ballet and one-night stands. Occasional Sunday concerts. *Funding*: Glasgow City Council, Scottish Arts Council grid/circuit funding.

Mitchell Theatre
Granville Street, Glasgow G3 7DR
Tel (041) **227 5033**

> *Seating capacity*: 418. Opened in 1981, this acts as an overspill venue for top touring drama, ballet and music companies. *Funding*: Glasgow City Council.

Orkney Arts Theatre

Mill Street, Kirkwall, Orkney KW5
Tel (0856) **2131 (day)** and (0856) **4803 (evenings)**

> *Seating capacity*: 324. Modern facilities for local and touring companies. *Funding*: Orkney Islands Council.

Palace Theatre

9 Green Street, Kilmarnock KA1 3BN
Tel (0563) **37710**

> *Seating capacity*: 503. Dance, opera, local dramatics — broad variety. *Funding*: Kilmarnock District Council, Scottish Arts Council grid/circuit funding.

Pavilion Theatre

121 Renfrew Street, Glasgow G2 3AX
Tel (041) **332 7579**

> *Seating capacity*: 1449. Plays, variety, pantomime; rock and pop concerts. *Funding*: self-financing.

Adam Smith Theatre

Bennochy Road, Kirkcaldy, Fife KY1 1ET
Tel (0592) **202855**

> *Seating capacity*: 475. Touring plays, variety, children's theatre; occasional one-night stands. Some in-house productions including pantomime. *Funding*: Kirkcaldy District Council.

Theatre Royal

Hope Street, Glasgow G2 3QA
Tel (041) **332 3321**

> *Seating capacity*: 1547. Home of Scottish Opera from October to June, and of Scottish Ballet for seven weeks. It takes in top touring companies for the remainder of the year. *Funding*: Scottish Arts Council, Glasgow District Council, Strathclyde Regional Council.

Whitehall Theatre

Bellfield Street, Dundee DD1 5JA
Tel (0382) **22684**

> *Seating capacity*: 750. Open 20–25 weeks of the year. Touring shows, one-night stands, local opera and music societies. *Funding*: self-financing.

Wales

New Theatre

Park Place, Cardiff CF1 3LN
Tel (0222) **394232**

> *Seating capacity*: 1168. An Empire-style Edwardian theatre, completely refurbished by theatre architects RHWL, who have expanded the inadequate bar and foyer space. The home base of Welsh National Opera who perform here for 15–20 weeks a year. Top-quality touring theatre, housing the Royal Shakespeare Company, National Theatre and other major companies. Dance (classical and modern), musicals, children's shows, six-week pantomime. *Funding*: Cardiff City Council.

Theatre Hafren

Llanidloes Road, Newtown, Powys SY16 2EN
Tel (0686) **25447**

> *Seating capacity*: 448. Dance, opera, classical music and celebrities. *Funding*: Powys County Council, grid/circuit funding – North Wales Arts touring scheme and Mid Wales Entertainment.

13. Festivals

There are two types of actors who go to festivals: those who are invited for a fee, and those who pay their own way. The first group make a little money; the second group invariably lose their savings.

For example, at the Edinburgh Festival, the biggest and the best, there is more money thrown away than on a fair day at the races. Last year, the Edinburgh Fringe attracted no fewer than 473 companies; their average size of audience was just 14. Against this pathetic return must be set expenditure of several thousand pounds. Even with the actors on profit-share, living on starvation diets and sleeping in garrets, a company of six with a half-decent set and booking with an established venue should count on spending £6000 to £7000. No wonder that Edinburgh is playing host (if that is quite the word) to an increasing number of two-handers and one-man shows. New writing and experimental work have all but disappeared from the programme.

Throughout the country, there are some 120 festivals. Tending towards the conservative, most support goes to music and art of the order least likely to upset the punters. Where drama does get a look in, it is the established companies with their tried and tested routines which do best. But even for them, the rewards can be disappointing, with actors attracting less than the going rate.

Bath International Festival
Festival office: Linley House, 1 Pierrepont Place, Bath BA1 1JY
Tel (0225) **62231/66411**

> Annual festival; 1989 dates: 26 May–11 June. Concentration on music and visual arts.

Belfast Festival at Queen's
Festival House, 25 College Gardens, Belfast BT9 6BS
Tel (0232) **667687**

> Founded 1963. Annual festival held at and near Queen's University. 1989 dates: 8–25 November. Opera, theatre, music, dance, cinema, exhibitions, jazz as well as literary, children's and fringe events. 1988 theatre included: Royal Shakespeare Company in *The Beaux Stratagem* and *A Midsummer Night's Dream*; Leicester Haymarket's productions of *Julius Caesar* and *Creon*; and Alec McCowen in his one-man show, *Shakespeare, Cole & Co.*

BP Young Directors Festival
Festival office: Battersea Arts Centre, Old Town Hall, Lavender Hill, London SW11 5TF
Tel (01) **223 2223**
Administrator Jane Dawson

> Annual festival, financed by British Petroleum for young directors under the age

of 35 who are not in full-time education. Entry is by written application to the above address by September; advertisements appear in the national press. A list of 12 directors is drawn up which is subsequently narrowed down to three through a series of workshops held in December. The final three directors go on to direct a professional production in May/June and it is hoped that each will receive a bursary to enable them to work in the professional theatre for a year. (BP provide one bursary.)

Brighton Festival

Festival office: Marlborough House, 54 Old Steine, Brighton, E. Sussex BN1 1EQ
Tel (0273) **29801**

Founded 1967. Annual international festival held in May. Theatre, music, dance, opera, visual arts and literature. 1989 festival – 5–28 May – will have a theme of liberty and independence with an emphasis on France with American influences. 1988 drama highlights included: Abbey Theatre Company productions of *The Mother of All the Behans* and *Playboy of the Western World*; the Wrestling School's production of *The Last Supper*; and Theatre on a String Company from Czechoslovakia in *Ballet Macabre*.

Bristol Community Festival

Festival office: First floor, 26 Broad Street, Bristol BS1 2HF
Tel (0272) **294100**

Founded 1974. Month-long festival in association with the Bristol Old Vic theatre. Held in March, and funded in 1988 by Bristol Old Vic and the Bristol *Evening Post*. Due to a withdrawal of local council funding, the future of the festival is uncertain. The programme consists of theatre, cabaret, jazz, exhibitions and workshop projects involving local schools and people with special needs. 1988 drama included: Avon Touring Theatre Company in *On the Plastic*; Ian McKellen in *Acting Shakespeare*; and Barebones Theatre in *Faustus*.

Buxton Festival

Festival office: 1 Crescent View, Hall Bank, Buxton, Derbys. SK17 6EN
Tel (0298) **70395**

Founded 1979. Three-week summer festival of opera, drama, music and films. 1988 drama included: *The Daughter-in-Law* performed by the 'Not The National Theatre' Company. 1989 dates: 22 July to 13 August.

The Calderdale Festival Theatre Company (formerly Hebden Bridge Festival Theatre)

Festival office: Linden Mill, Linden Road, Hebden Bridge, W. Yorks. HX7 7DP
Tel (0422) **844917**

Founded 1987. Summer festival of drama, June to August. Currently looking for a permanent home which may be Hebden Bridge but if not, will be located in the Calderdale area. Do not advertise but welcome casting queries from actors. Approach in writing. Auditions usually held between January and April.

Cambridge Festival

Festival office: Mandela House, 4 Regent Street, Cambridge CB2 1BY
Tel (0223) **358977**

Founded 1962. Annual two-week summer festival with a theme – in 1989, this will be French. Music, theatre, jazz, film, community arts, visual arts and dance. 1988 (American theme) drama included: Cambridge Arts Theatre production of

Intimate Exchanges; Clap Trap Theatre Company in *Death of a Salesman* and the Spare Tyre Theatre Company in *A Look at Love*.

Canterbury Festival
Festival office: 59 Ivy Lane, Canterbury, Kent CT1 1TU
Tel (0227) **452853**

Founded 1984. Annual festival of music, drama, dance, film, master classes and talks. 1989 festival dates: 15 October to 4 November. 1988 drama included: Oxford Stage Company's production of *A Doll's House* and Shared Experience's *The Bacchae*.

Chichester Festival Theatre ● *See* Independent Managements

Dumfries & Galloway Festival
Festival office: Gracefield Arts Centre, 28 Edinburgh Road, Dumfries DG1 1JQ
Tel (0387) **61234**

Annual ten-day festival held in May/June. Theatre and music. 1988 drama included: Theatre About Glasgow's production of *Great Expectations*.

Edinburgh Festival
Festival office: 21 Market Street, Edinburgh EH1 1BW
Tel (031) **226 4001**

Founded 1947. Leading annual international festival of music, theatre, film, jazz, dance and tattoo, as well as a fringe consisting of some 500 events. 1989 dates: 13 August to 2 September. 1988 drama included: Manchester Royal Exchange's production of *A Midsummer Night's Dream* and the Japanese Ninagawa Theatre Company's production of *The Tempest*.

Exeter Festival
Festival office: Room 2–1, Civic Centre, Exeter, Devon EX1 1JN
Tel (0392) **265200**

Founded 1974 as a community festival and expanded into its current professional status in 1980. Annual event with theatre, music, dance, visual arts and community-based activities. 1989 dates: 24 May to 10 June – 'The Gothic' will be its theme. 1988 productions included: National Youth Music Theatre in *The Ragged Child* and Northcott Theatre's *Monsigneur Quixote*.

Greenwich Festival
Festival office: 25 Woolwich New Road, London SE18 6EU
Tel (01) **317 8687**

Founded 1970. Annual two-week festival held in June. 1989 dates: 2–18 June – with a theme of revolution and chance. Theatre, dance, music and visual arts. 1988 drama included: Roger Rees and Virginia McKenna in *Sons and Mothers*.

Harrogate International Festival
Festival office: Royal Baths, Harrogate, N. Yorks. HG1 2RR
Tel (0423) **62303**

Founded 1966. Annual two-week summer festival. Mainly music with some drama and exhibitions.

Henley Festival

Festival office: 103–109 Wardour Street, London W1V 4HE
Tel (01) **734 2505**

> Founded 1983. Five-day festival in early July. Orchestral concerts performed on a stage floating on the Thames, riverside exhibitions and cabaret and recitals performed in restaurants in the Festival enclosure. 'Gentlemen are requested to wear black tie or formal rowing blazers.'

London International Festival of Theatre (LIFT)

Festival office: 28 Neal Street, London WC2
Tel (01) **836 7186**

> Biennial festival bringing the best of contemporary performance to London for a three-week season every other summer. Performances take place in large and small venues and outdoor locations all over London. Next festival – the third – begins on 23 July 1989. In the past, festivals have included companies from the USSR, US, China, Latin America, Europe, Africa and India. The directors, Lucy Neal and Rose de Wend Fenton, won the International Theatre Institute's 'Award for Excellence in International Theatre' in 1988.

Ludlow Festival

Festival office: Castle Square, Ludlow, Salop NY8 1AY
Tel (0584) **2150**

> Annual summer festival – 1989 will be its 30th year. Drama, music, films, exhibitions. During the two weeks of the festival, a Shakespeare play is performed in the grounds of Ludlow Castle: in 1988, Michael Napier Brown directed *Twelfth Night*.

Mayfest (Glasgow's International Festival)

Festival office: 46 Royal Exchange Square, Glasgow G1 3AR
Tel (041) **221 4911**

> Founded 1983. Three-week festival each May – the second largest in the UK. 1989 dates: 1–21 May. International and Scottish theatre, dance, music, cabaret, opera, visual arts and community events. 1988 drama included: Peter Brook's production of *The Mahabharata*, Glasgow Citizens Company in *Lady Windermere's Fan*, the Maly Drama Theatre of Leningrad in *Stars in the Morning Sky*, Wildcat Stage Productions in *The Celtic Story* and Joint Stock's production of *A Child in the Heart*.

National Student Drama Festival

Festival office: 20 Lansdowne Road, Muswell Hill, London N10 2AU
Tel (01) **883 4586**

> March/April 1989 saw the 34th festival, sponsored by The Sunday Times and ITV. The only regular focus for British student drama, it includes workshops and discussions, performances and social events. Leaders and speakers who have taken part in the past include Terry Hands and Bill Alexander of the RCS, Max Stafford-Clark of the Royal Court and actors John Hurt, Warren Mitchell, Joan Plowright and Prunella Scales. Productions can be entered for adjudication – details from the above address.

Newbury Spring Festival

Festival office: Suite 3, Town Hall, Newbury, Berks. RG14 5AA
Tel (0635) **49919**

> Founded 1979. Annual festival of music held in May.

Nottingham Festival

Festival office: Victoria Centre, Nottingham NG1 3QB
Tel (0602) **483504**

Founded over 20 years ago but only recently developed into the large-scale annual event it now is. 1989 dates: 30 May to 15 June, with a theme of British art, 1880–1915. Theatre, music, opera and jazz. In 1988 (with a theme of Lord Byron), drama included: English Chamber Theatre's *Mad, Bad and Dangerous to Know*, Industrial & Domestic Theatre Company's *Newstead: An Eccentric History* and Royal Exchange Theatre Company's *Don Juan*.

Perth Festival of the Arts

Festival office: Concorde Box Office, 17 Scott Street, Perth
Tel (0738) **38353**

Founded 1975. Annual 11-day festival; 1989 dates: 17–28 May. Music, theatre and opera. 1988 drama included Theatre About Glasgow's production of *Great Expectations*.

Pitlochry Festival Theatre ● *See* Rep/Regional Theatres.

Polesden Lacey Open Air Theatre

Festival office: National Trust, Polesden Lacey, Dorking, Surrey RH5 6BD
Tel (0372) **57223**

Annual three-week festival of open-air amateur drama and music. 1989 dates: 21 June to 9 July. 1988 drama production was *Othello*.

Reading Festival

Festival office: P.O. Box 17, Civic Centre, Reading RG1 7TD

Three-week festival (May/June) with an emphasis on music and dance.

Salisbury Festival

Festival office: The King's House, 65 The Close, Salisbury, Wilts. SP1 2EN
Tel (0722) **23883**

Four-year cycle of festivals celebrating the four elements of earth, fire, water and air. 1988 festival devoted to fire and held for two weeks in September. Music, drama, film, dance, exhibitions, literary events and festival fringe. 1988 drama included: Barebones Theatre Company in *The Fire Raisers* and Salisbury Playhouse Company in *The Day after the Fair*.

Wallington Festival

Adminstrator, Wallington, Cambo, Morpeth, Northumb. NE61 4AR
Tel (067 074) **283**

Founded 1986. Annual festival held in and around this National Trust House. Festival varies in length depending on how many events are booked. 1988 festival was held from 24 June to 3 July and featured performances of *A Winter's Tale* by Theatre Set Up company on the lawns of the house.

Warwick Arts Festival

Festival office: Northgate, Warwick CV34 4JL
Tel (0926) **492468**

Founded 1979. Annual summer festival. 1989 dates: 5–16 August. Music, theatre, dance and visual arts. 1988 drama included a performance of *Romeo and Juliet* in Warwick Castle.

York Festival & Mystery Plays
Festival office: 1 Newgate, York YO1 2LA
Tel (0904) **610266**

Quadrennial summer festival — the next one is in 1992. Four weeks of drama, dance, music, film, opera, lectures and many fringe events. 1988 drama productions included: *The Wars of the Roses* (English Shakespeare Company); *Trumpets and Drums* (York Theatre Company); *A Hard Day's Night* (Hull Truck). The York Mystery Plays are performed by local amateurs, with the role of Christ being taken by a professional actor.

14. Children's and young people's theatre

Young people's theatre

Age Exchange Theatre Trust ● *See* Touring companies.

Bagatelle ● *See* Touring companies.

Bolton Octagon Youth Theatre ● *See* Repertory and regional theatres.

Cannon Hill Puppet Theatre
Midlands Arts Centre, Cannon Hill Park, Birmingham B12 9QH
Tel (021) **440 4221**
Artistic director John Blundall

> Founded 1968. Britain's largest residential professional puppet theatre company, it has played to over half a million children at its home base at the Midlands Arts Centre and many more on tour in the UK and Europe in over 54 productions. These feature all kinds of puppet figures, from small hand-held ones to large elaborate rod puppets and masks, all of which are designed and constructed in the theatre's own workshops. Material includes original scripts written specially for the company as well as adaptations based on music, folk literature and classical children's literature. Do not hold general auditions. Advertise for actors in *The Stage*, and welcome casting queries from actors/puppeteers who can sing. Write with CV and photograph in the first instance.

Carib Theatre Productions ● *See* Touring companies.

Contact Theatre Company ● *See* Repertory and regional theatres.

DAC ● *See* Touring companies.

Forest Forge Theatre Company ● *See* Touring companies.

Globe Players Theatre Company
36 St James Avenue, Hampton Hill, Middx TW12 1HN
Tel (01) **979 5497**

> Shakespeare and fairy stories only, for touring to schools throughout the London area. Welcome queries from actors in October, when they are casting for the busy Christmas season which runs from November through December, with seven companies of 5–6 actors on the road. Write or phone in the first instance. Queries at any other time of year will be referred to October.

Gog Theatre Company Ltd ● *See* Touring companies.

Graeae ● *See* Touring companies.

Greenwich Young People's Theatre Ltd

Burrage Road, Plumstead, London SE18 7JZ
Tel (01) **854 1316 and 855 4911**
Artistic director Chris Vine

Theatre-in-Education (TIE) programmes for primary, secondary and further education audiences; youth theatre and arts workshops for an age range of 7–25 years. Perform in the Greenwich Young People's Theatre Centre (studio), schools, colleges, community venues. Company of eight actors on full-time, permanent lecturer contracts (NATFHE) by arrangement with Equity. Advertise for actors in *The Stage*, the *Guardian* media page, *Asian Times* and *The Voice*. Do not welcome casting queries as all auditions are advertised as vacancies occur (on average, twice yearly). Do not require teaching qualifications, but 'a commitment to work with young people is essential and knowledge of education/teaching strategies an advantage. All actors are full company members with a role in developing the artistic and educational policy of the company. They are required to run workshops as well as perform. A minimum commitment of two years to the company is preferred; previous knowledge and experience of TIE/YPT is an advantage. GYPT is a multi-racial company and equal opportunities employer. Policy development is towards diversity of cultural forms, and content that is educationally and socially relevant to inner-city young people.'

Half Moon Young People's Theatre

213 Mile End Road, London E1 4AA
Tel (01) **791 1141 ext 6**
Artistic director Deborah Bestwick

Theatre-in-Education (TIE), young people's and touring community productions for an audience age range of 5 to 25. Perform in schools and community centres. Open-ended Equity contracts with an average company of four actors. Do not require teaching qualifications, but look for workshop and devising experience and a genuine interest in education. An ability to speak Bengali is very helpful. Advertise for actors in *The Stage*, *The Voice*, *Asian Herald* and *Surma*. As they have a small turnover of actors, do not welcome casting queries unless they have advertised; unable to maintain casting files. Hold auditions 'when necessary – about twice a year'.

Leicester Haymarket Youth Theatre ● *See* Repertory and regional theatres.

M6 Theatre Company ● *See* Touring companies.

Magic Carpet Theatre

18 Church Street, Sutton-on-Hull, N. Humberside HU7 4TS
Tel (0482) **709939**
Artistic director Jon Marshall

Children's theatre productions and shows for family audiences performed in schools, theatres, arts centres, civic halls, village halls and out-of-doors. Company of four on one-year contracts; pay Equity rates. Occasionally advertise in *The Stage*, but welcome casting queries from actors. Approach in writing in the first instance. Do not require teaching qualifications – 'much of our work is based on circus and magical skills.'

Magic Roundabout Theatre Company ● *See* Touring companies.

Merseyside Young People's Theatre Company
5 Hope Street, Liverpool L1 9BH
Tel (051) **708 0877**
Artistic director Paul Harman

Founded 1978. Tour schools in the Merseyside region, playing to audiences from 3 to 18 years old. In 1981, Willy Russell was commissioned to write *Blood Brothers* for the company. Company of four or five actors on year-long Equity contracts. Advertise once a year in *The Stage*, usually in February and welcome casting queries from actors. Letters and details are kept on file. Teaching qualifications not essential but require actors who have experience of working with children.

Molecule Theatre of Science for Children
Bloomsbury Theatre, 15 Gordon Street, London WC1H 0AH
Tel (01) **388 5739**
Artistic director Josephine Wilson

Founded 1967. Tour scientific adventure plays for 7- to 11-year-olds to middle-scale theatres (one tour annually). Also a Theatre-in-Education company playing to 11- to 13-year olds in schools (one tour annually). Company of ten actors for the middle-scale tour, and four actors for the TIE tour; all on Equity contracts. Advertise in Equity *Jobgrapevine*. Letters enclosing details should be sent only in May/June.

National Youth Theatre of Great Britain
443/445 Holloway Road, London N7 6LW
Tel (01) **281 3863**
Artistic director Edward Wilson

Founded 1956 by Michael Croft who was the company's director until his death in 1986. Starting in the East End of London, the NYT proved so successful that soon young people from all over the country were applying to join. It reached the West End in 1959 and, in 1960, was given national status and financial support by the Department of Education and Science, which has grant-aided it ever since.

The NYT's record has been one of continual development and expansion, despite limited resources. It now presents an annual season of both contemporary and classical plays in London every summer, and has toured abroad many times with the British Council. The NYT also mounts national and regional tours. From its earliest days, it has also played a key role in developing youth theatre in the provinces, and has helped to set up many of the over 400 regional youth theatres in Great Britain.

The NYT's aims are to give young people practical experience of the theatre, to set them high standards and, in doing so, offer them a valuable form of teamwork. Membership is open to young people aged between 14 and 21. Selection is by interview and audition, but the latter is often of secondary importance. Members are often selected because they have lively personalities or show qualities that seem to be suited to the teamwork essential in the NYT. It is hoped that technical members will show more evidence of ability, but this is not essential. Applications should be made in October of each year.

Comment
The 1988 NYT production of *The Caucasian Chalk Circle* attracted praise from reviewers, including John Coldstream of the *Daily Telegraph*: '... There is much to relish in the revitalization of this admirable troupe, now 32 years old and buffeted by the fates – above all, by the death in 1986 of its irrepressible founder, Michael Croft. A new permanent home has opened in the Holloway Road; there is miraculous talk of

Arts Council support; Sainsbury's provide trolleyloads of fivers; and, to judge by the contingent at present mustered under Mr Wilson's firm hand in WC1, morale is high.'

Oily Cart Company

Workshop 17, Royal Victoria Patriotic Building, Fitzhugh Grove, Trinity Road, London SW18 3SX
Tel (01) **877 0743**

Comedy, puppet shows, participation plus day-long interactive drama projects at special schools. Shows for under 5s, 7- to 11-year-olds and mentally handicapped children aged 5–16. Perform in nursery schools, playgroups, one o'clock clubs, community centres, schools, arts centres, theatres, language units, libraries, festivals, etc. Company of three actors on contracts of varying lengths; pay Equity rates. Advertise in *The Stage*, and do not welcome casting queries from actors – 'not necessary as company is too small'. Only hold auditions when 'our actress leaves – other two actors are partners/directors.' Do not require teaching qualifications.

Pandemonium Theatre

13 Royal Stuart Workshops, Adelaide Street, Cardiff CF1 6BR
Tel (0222) **482821**
Artistic director Paul Bassett

Perform to primary school children – infant and junior. 'We aim to produce entertaining pieces of live theatre to the primary age range (3–12). All of our plays have an educational content, but we are not TIE [Theatre-in-Education].' Recent productions: *Out of the Valley*; *A Flying Visit*; *The Mary Celeste*; *The Owl and the Pussycat*. Three companies of ten actors tour nationally during school terms; 12-week contracts, renewable if required (non-Equity). Advertise in *The Stage*, and welcome casting queries from actors. Approach in writing in the first instance.

Pilot Theatre

St Peters School, Schoolyard, Queen Street, Horbury, Wakefield, W. Yorks. WF4 6LP
Tel (0924) **262200**

Four projects per year – two school shows, one street show and one youth/community workshop project. Perform in schools, colleges, community centres and street. Company of five on ten-week contracts; Equity rates. Advertise for actors in *The Stage*, *Leeds Other Paper* and *The Voice*; do not welcome casting queries. Auditions held when they need to replace company members. Teaching qualifications not required.

Pit Prop Theatre ● *See* Touring companies.

Polka Children's Theatre

240 The Broadway, Wimbledon, London SW19 1SB
Tel (01) **542 4258**
Artistic director Vicky Ireland

Full stage productions for children and young people, including puppet shows, musicals and straight drama. Audience age range of 3 years to early teens, performing in main theatres. Company of six, contracted per production (approximately two months); pay Equity rates. Advertise in *SBS* and *PCR*, and do not welcome casting queries from actors. General auditions are held once a year, with restricted auditions per production. Teaching qualifications are not required; they look for skills in mime and movement, mask work and puppetry.

Premier Theatre Company Ltd
1 Chester Road, Tuebrook, Liverpool L6 4DY
Tel (051) **260 8999**
Contact Richard Gardiner

Mainly small-scale touring shows of set texts — e.g. Shakespeare — in schools in the north-west. Also company-devised productions on subjects such as drug abuse, careers and bullying. Audience age range of 11 to 16. Company of three actors on contracts of 4–7 weeks; pay ITC/Equity minimum. Have not as yet advertised for actors, but planning to do so in *The Stage*, local press and through ITC. Welcome casting queries — approach in writing in the first instance. Auditions held once or twice per year. Do not require teaching qualifications.

Quicksilver Theatre for Children
4 Enfield Road, London N1 5AZ
Tel (01) **241 2932**
Artistic director Guy Holland

Founded 1978. Tour 2–3 productions per year for the 3–7 and 7–11 age ranges. Tours of 11–16 weeks, one or two shows daily; perform in schools, community and arts centres, small- and middle-scale theatres in London and the regions. Company of five actors on contracts of 15–20 weeks' duration; pay ITC/Equity small-scale touring rates. Advertise in *The Stage* and Equity *Job Grapevine*, and welcome casting queries from actors — send letter and CV. 'As a member of ITC, Quicksilver Theatre is committed to a policy of integrated casting, and actively seeks applicants from ethnic minorities.'

Rainbow Theatre Company ● *See* Touring companies.

Raskolnikoff Theatre ● *See* Touring companies.

Royal Court Young People's Theatre
309 Portobello Road, London W10 5TD
Tel (01) **960 4641**
Artistic director To be appointed

Youth theatre productions for an audience ranging up to the age of 30. Perform in community venues. *The Royal Court Young People's Theatre never requires actors*: 'Actors — especially drama school leavers — think it appropriate to write to the company [but it] is a non-professional organization for young people.'

Salamander Theatre
2 Cresswell Road, Twickenham, Middx TW1 2DZ
Tel (01) **891 0425**
Artistic director Glynn Caren

Infant show for 4–8-year-olds; junior show for 7–12-year-olds; also lower secondary school pupils. Perform in schools, colleges, special schools, community centres, libraries, parks, small theatres and arts centres. Company of five on six-month contracts; pay Equity rates. Advertise in *The Stage*, and welcome casting queries from actors — 'all applications are given equal consideration.' Approach in writing in the first instance. Auditions held twice yearly. Require actors to have teaching qualifications — 'but not every company member has to be a teacher. Languages are a help, also musical skills. We like actors with all-round skills: acting/musical and physical. We work mainly in Hounslow and Ealing where there is a large Asian/black community, and a lot of our work is involved with language skills. We, therefore, feel it is desirable to have black or Asian company

members, but very few apply! We do, however, cast the person we feel will make
the best all-round company member for a particular production.'

Scottish Youth Theatre

48 Albany Street, Edinburgh EH1 3QR
Tel (031) **557 2224/0962**
Artistic director Robin Peoples

Small-scale touring, Theatre-in-Education (TIE) in community, open-air and main-
house theatre venues. Company of six (on average) with contracts of seven
weeks; pay Equity rates. Rarely advertise or hold auditions, but welcome casting
queries despite 'limited opportunities'. Approach in writing in the first instance.
Occasionally require actors with teaching qualifications.

Snap Theatre Company

Millars One House, Southmill Road, Bishop's Stortford, Herts. CM23 3DH
Tel (0279) **504095/503066**
Artistic director A. M. Graham

Schools-based project residencies, youth club show/workshops, infant, primary
and junior school programmes, small-scale tours and national children's theatre
tour. Perform in schools, arts centres, village halls, youth clubs, small- and middle-
scale theatres. Company of 3–7 on contracts which range in length from 6 to 20
weeks; pay Equity rates. Advertise for actors in *The Stage, SBS* and *Rep Report.*
Welcome casting queries from actors; approach in writing in the first instance.
Hold auditions four times a year. Teaching qualifications 'useful but not essential'.
'Prepare audition pieces most suited to you. Avoid Shakespeare unless asked
specifically. Gain as much experience as you can in working with young people –
i.e. youth clubs, schools, etc. Skills: mime (drama school alone won't do), musical
instruments an advantage, ability to sing, devising and improvisation skills
essential, drivers preferred. State on application why the interest apart from the
job prospects. Send SAE and *up-to-date* photo. Arrive on time; phone if any
problems. Files on actors are only kept if actors up-date Snap's administration –
i.e. a postcard on what they've been doing.'

Soapbox Theatre Company

Durning Hall, Earlham Grove, Forest Gate, London E7 9AB
Tel (01) **519 4394**
Artistic director Russell Daymond

Educational theatre for young people aged 3 to 17 years old. Perform in schools
and community venues. Company of four actors on 12-week contracts; pay
Equity rates. Advertise in *The Stage,* and welcome ('within reason') casting queries
from actors; approach in writing in the first instance. Auditions held twice a year.
Teaching qualifications not required but 'an advantage'. 'We have a policy of
mixed race and gender casting.'

TAG (Theatre About Glasgow)

Citizens Theatre, Gorbals, Glasgow G5 9DS
Tel (041) **429 2877**
Artistic director Alan Lydiard

Founded 1967. Perform new plays, small-scale adaptations of Shakespeare,
plays for primary and secondary schools as well as plays for adults. 'The plays
must have a strong storyline and reflect aspects of modern life, and are produced
in a strong visual way.' Venues range from school halls to 2000-seat theatres.
School tours are usually in the Strathclyde region, and adult tours all over
Scotland, Northern Ireland and the north of England. Recent productions: *Great*

Expectations, Othello, Stramash (open-air primary school play), *Visible Differences* (secondary school tour). Average company of eight actors on 12-week Equity contracts. Do not advertise for actors, and do not particularly welcome casting queries, as 'we usually cast inside Scotland.' Will consider letter with CV, photo and SAE.

Taking Steps Community Theatre Co. Ltd
c/o Midlands Arts Centre, Cannon Hill Park, Birmingham B12 9QH
Tel (021) **440 4108**
Artistic director Karen Benjamin

Perform Theatre-in-Education (TIE), street theatre and circus in schools, youth clubs, community centres and out-of-doors. Audience age range of 5–90, with school ages of 6–11 and 12–16 years. Company of two or three on 10/12-week contracts; pay Equity rates 'when on contract'. Sometimes advertise in *The Stage*, and welcome casting queries from actors; send letter giving full details. Auditions held annually. Do not require actors to have teaching qualifications, but sometimes need teaching experience or circus skills – depending on tour.

Theatre Centre
Hanover School, Noel Road, London N1 8BD
Tel (01) **354 0110**
Artistic director Libby Mason

Commission five new plays each year for young people, all within a particular theme. 1987/88 theme was 'In Transit'. Audience age range: 4–8, 9–14, 15–18. Tour to schools and small-scale venues. Company of ten on contracts of four months minimum; pay 'slightly above' Equity rates. Advertise in *The Stage, Asian Times* and *The Voice*. 'We are always happy to meet and talk with actors; unsolicited CVs and photographs are, however, RETURNED.' Audition/workshop held once a year over two days, plus periodic special auditions to replace performers mid-way through the year. Do not require actors with teaching qualifications. 'Theatre Centre is not a TIE company. Generally we audition for the year in June/July. We endeavour to get to as many productions as possible and, in that way, acquaint ourselves with new performers. We specialize in the production of new plays for young audiences and have two performing units: an all-women's company (four performers + stage manager) and a mixed company (four performers + stage manager). The shows tour schools and venues throughout Britain and internationally, and we positively welcome applications from Asian/African and Afro-Caribbean people. We do not discriminate on the grounds of gender, sexual orientation or physical disability.'

Theatre West Glamorgan/Gorllewin Morgannwg
Sandfields Comprehensive, Southdown View, Port Talbot SA12 7AH
Tel (0639) **898077**
Artistic director Tim Baker

Theatre-in-Education (TIE) programmes for junior schools in English and Welsh language; community theatre productions to local audiences in English and Welsh language. Company of five on one-year or single-tour (16 weeks) contracts; Equity rates – 'well above minimum'. Advertise for actors in *The Stage*, the *Guardian, Western Mail* and *Y Cymro*. Welcome casting queries – send letter explaining interest in this field of work. Auditions held annually, although the present company has been maintained for two years. Teaching qualifications not required, but look for 'talent and musical ability'. The company's policy is very locally based – 'members need an interest and commitment to Wales and the area. The company tends to write its own material, therefore an interest in writing/devising a distinct advantage. Singing skills (not necessarily trained) are almost essential, musical skills an advantage. Operate an equal-wage policy for all members. Any interested actors welcome to write for "package" including details of nature of work and company policy.'

Theatr Powys ● See Touring companies.

Theatre Workshop Edinburgh ● See Touring companies.

Unicorn Theatre
6/7 Great Newport Street, London WC2H 7JB
Tel (01) **379 3280**
Artistic director Chris Wallis

Leading London young people's theatre company which produces plays 'that help children understand their world and gain power within it'. Audience age ranges from 4 to 12 years old. Perform in their own theatre in Great Newport Street. Average number of actors in the company is six. Try to cross cast as much as possible. Equity contracts. Do not usually advertise for actors, but welcome letters enclosing CV and photograph, which are kept on file. Sometimes hold general auditions. Teaching qualifications not required.

Upstream Children's Theatre
St Andrew's, Short Street, London SE1 8LJ
Tel (01) **928 5394**
Artistic director Roy Poole

Founded 1978 as part-time project; became full-time company in 1980. Performances and drama workshops, usually devised by the company, with emphasis on themes of anti-racism, anti-sexism and non-violence for children aged 4 to 11 years old. Perform in infant and junior schools, youth clubs, community play schemes plus the Upstream Theatre. Summer tour to community venues and a Christmas tour to schools plus a week in the Upstream Theatre. Permanent company of three actors – the company is extended according to production requirements. Equity/ITC contracts of varying lengths. Advertise in *The Stage*, *The Voice* and through other companies. Prefer responses to advertisements rather than general enquiries, although the director will meet actors who have a genuine interest in the work of the Upstream Children's Theatre. The company is committed to working as a mixed sex/racial company.

Whirligig Theatre
14 Belvedere Drive, Wimbledon, London SW19 7BY
Tel (01) **947 1732**
Artistic directors David Wood & John Gould

Full-length musical plays for children of primary school age. Perform in middle-scale and large theatres at low seat prices. Company of 8 to 12 actors on 12-week contracts; pay Equity rates. Advertise for actors in *SBS* and *PCR*, and welcome casting queries – by letter only. Hold auditions for every production, usually once a year. Do not necessarily require actors with teaching qualifications, but look for 'good acting, singing and moving plus a genuine interest in the work. Please do not approach us if you see children's theatre work as simply a rung on the ladder, a stepping stone to "greater things". The work demands great commitment as well as skills and the ability to be on top form for morning and afternoon performances, working in front of audiences of up to 1500 children. When coming to an audition, it is essential that you have a couple of songs under your belt and do not arrive with no music, or ask to look over the pianist's shoulder. Although we sometimes like people to play musical instruments, an audition is best sung with piano accompaniment provided.'

Zuriya Theatre Company

38 Brixton Road, London SW9 6BT
Tel (01) **582 9479**
Artistic director John Adewole

Perform traditional African storytelling, musical and full dramatic productions plus workshops for schools, for audiences from primary school age to further education. Venues include schools, community centres and fringe theatres. Company of six actors on contracts of 3–6 months; non-Equity. Advertise for actors in educational and local publications, and also at venues; welcome written casting queries. Teaching qualifications not essential but favour experience of working with children. Musical and dance skills required. Auditions held according to demand.

Theatre-in-Education (TIE) Companies

Big Brum Theatre-in-Education Company Ltd

Midlands Arts Centre, Cannon Hill Park, Birmingham B12 9QH
Tel (021) **440 2087**
Artistic director Peter Wynne-Willson

TIE programmes for secondary school children (11–18 years), mostly devised but a few commissioned; always aimed specifically at Birmingham schools and colleges. Occasionally perform in studio and community venues. Company of (on average) 3–4 actors on contracts of one term to one year in length; pay Equity rates. Advertise for actors – usually in the *Birmingham Post & Mail*, local radio and careers services, and sometimes nationally in *The Stage* and *TES*; also in Afro-Caribbean and Asian papers. Particularly welcome casting queries from local Birmingham actors. Approach in writing or by telephone. Only hold workshops and interviews (no auditions) for specific vacancies – on average, twice yearly. Do not specifically require actors with teaching qualifications, but look for teaching *ability*. 'We tend to look much more closely at abilities and instincts than at qualifications. We have always taken on a number of untrained local people alongside more experienced actor/teachers. Acting ability and experience probably come lower down in our priorities than many applicants realize – instinctive grasp of the point of our work, commitment, ability to communicate with young people, suitability for the balance of the company at the time, all these can turn out to be more important. The best actors in the world might be disastrous company members. Genuine feeling for young people in Birmingham is the most sought-after attribute for Big Brum.'

Big Wheel Theatre Company

8 Boults Lane, Old Marston, Oxford OX3 0PW
Tel (0865) **241527**
Artistic director Roland Allen

Workshops for schools on the Continent, for those starting English, for those beginning English literature and for advanced students of English literature. Perform in schools to an age range of 11–19 years. Company of three on one-year contracts; non-Equity. Advertise for actors in student journals, *The Stage*, *Time Out, City Limits*, national newspapers. Welcome casting queries – approach in writing in the first instance. Do not require teaching qualifications. Auditions held twice yearly. 'Actors must be genuinely interested in working with young people whose English may be poor. TIE work is extremely demanding and exhausting: teachers *make* pupils see our shows, so if they like them, they are a wild success, but if they get bored, they make this very clear.'

Cambridge Syllabus Players Ltd

12 Guildford Street, London WC1N 1DT
Tel (01) **242 8672**
Artistic director Timothy Seward

Perform plays, adaptations of novels, poetry in connection with GCSE examination texts for audiences of 12–18-year-olds in school halls and occasionally in theatres or arts centres. Company of seven on contracts for one term, although the actors 'often stay for two or even three terms'; non-Equity. Advertise in *The Stage*, and welcome letters from actors: 'We do not have time to reply to them as they come in, but examine them all at our next casting session and reply to them all then.' Hold auditions on average once or twice a year, with major auditions usually in August or September. Do not require teaching qualifications. 'We tend to take people who have previous TIE experience and usually some form of drama training, but this is not a hard and fast rule. As members of ITC, we abide by all their rulings with regard to equal opportunities, etc., though we are not as yet an Equity company. We look not only for acting talent but also for a personality that we feel will work well under the exacting conditions of eight- or nine-week tours and will respond in a friendly way to secondary school children. Our workshops always involve close work with students as well as performance.'

Channel Theatre TIE Company

Granville Theatre, Victoria Parade, Ramsgate, Kent CT11 8DG
Tel (0843) **588260**
Artistic director Philip Dart

Productions and occasional workshops for infant-to-secondary pupils in Kent schools. Company of seven actors on one year's Equity contract. No teaching qualifications required. Advertise once a year in *The Stage*, and hold general auditions following that.

Cockpit Theatre-in-Education Team

Gateforth Street, Marylebone, London NW8 8EH
Tel (01) **262 7907**
Contact Stuart Bennett (director, Cockpit Theatre and Arts Workshop)

TIE programmes of theatre performance, role-play and drama workshops for secondary school pupils; occasional work with primary school children. Performances take place at the Cockpit Theatre, occasionally followed up with workshops in the schools. Company of four actors on contracts of one term in length. Pay Lecturer Grade I rates – funded by ILEA. Advertise for actors in *The Stage*, the *Guardian* and the ethnic press. Welcome casting queries from actors: 'we always respond to letters and keep details on file.' Enclose SAE. Auditions held when a vacancy occurs. Teaching qualifications not required, but an understanding of education and educational theory is an advantage.

Cwmni'r Frân Wen

Coleg Harlech, Harlech, Gwynedd LL46 2PU
Tel (0766) **780179**
Artistic director Carys Huw

TIE company that works in Welsh, performing to a wide age range: 5- to 16-year-olds in schools. Recent projects have dealt with substance abuse (12–13 years); Bardsey Island (top junior); and a project in multi-coloured inflatables based on the Mabinow folk tale of 'Blodenwedd'. Future projects will include conservation, acid rain and the life and poetry of Wales' premier poet of the Middle Ages, Dafydd Ap Gwilym. Company of three actors (on average) on four-month contracts; pay Equity rates (MRSL 1). Advertise for actors in *Y Cymro*, *Liverpool Daily Post*, *Western Mail* and *The Stage*. Welcome casting queries from actors; approach in writing in the first instance. 'Teaching qualifications an advantage.' Hold auditions once a year.

Cwmni Theatr Outreach Theatre Company
Outreach Theatre Centre, Glanrafon Road, Mold, Clwyd CH7 1PA
Tel (0352) **56331 ext 298**
Artistic director Kevin Lewis

Perform to a wide age range in schools and community venues. 1987/8 productions included: *High Time* (secondary school programme on drugs education); *Edrych Ymlaen* (Welsh language junior programme); *Silas Marner* (community show); *Follow My Leader* (infant programme); *The Dark Cloud* (secondary schools); *Leonardo* (junior). Company of four actor/teachers; length of contract varies. Pay Equity rates. Teaching qualifications are useful but not necessary. Advertise in *The Stage*, and welcome written casting queries from actors. Usually hold auditions once a year. 'The company devise a lot of their work, so experience of devising, research and improvisation is important. The company performs work in English and Welsh, and is interested in hearing from Welsh-speaking performers as well as English-speaking ones. Commitment to TIE and community theatre is essential.'

Electric Theatre Company
21 Slagrove Place, London SE13 7HT
Tel (01) **690 6164** and **314 5676**
Artistic directors (partnership) David Zoob, David Annen

TIE for fourth-year GCSE students and above. Programmes mix economical, energetic performance with active participatory drama work, usually lasting two hours. Programmes complement aims and content of exam syllabi. Perform in secondary schools throughout ILEA and surrounding boroughs; occasional performances in youth centres, clubs, etc. Company of three on contracts of 13 weeks' duration (i.e. one term); usually pay Equity rates – 'all company members on equal salaries that vary according to funding.' Do not advertise, but use actors on other TIE companies' recommendation, via word of mouth and those who contact the company – 'these channels have satisfied requirements in the past.' Approach in writing or by telephone call. Auditions are held 'as required'. Ideally prefer actors with teaching qualifications, devising and administrative ability and a genuine concern and interest in education. 'Work for ETC demands a heavy touring schedule, unflagging commitment, inspired audience interaction and a lot of time sitting in traffic jams in the middle of London. Enthusiasm, adaptability and good humour essential.'

Gazebo Theatre-in-Education Company Ltd
The Old School, Slater Street, Darlaston, W. Midlands WS10 8EE
Tel (021) **526 6877**
Artistic director Annie Lambert (acting)

TIE programmes for all ages and abilities, serving schools within the Wolverhampton & Walsall LEA. Company of six, generally on permanent contract but with some of three months; pay Equity rates. Advertise for actors in *The Stage*. Hold auditions only when, on the rare occasion, a vacancy arises; do not therefore welcome casting queries. Teaching qualifications not a necessity.

Gwent Theatre in Education Company

The Drama Centre, Pen-y-Pound, Abergavenny, Gwent
Tel (0873) **3167**
Artistic director Gary Meredith

Theatre-in-Education projects for infant, junior and secondary schools (6–7; 10–12; 16–18 years); community touring. Perform in schools, village halls, leisure centres, theatres ('we occasionally present "on site" productions – venues to date have included a large country house, a castle and a colliery'). Company of nine. Contracts renewable every six months, but 'we prefer people to stay with us for at least a year – most stay for two or more years.' Pay Equity rates (MRSL 1). Advertise in *The Stage*, Equity *Jobgrapevine* and a circular to all theatre companies in Wales; welcome casting queries from actors. 'It is important that the letter is detailed and demonstrates clearly the reasons why the writer wants to work in TIE and the qualities they feel they have that make them suitable for this kind of work. Casual enquiries and duplicated letters receive a polite acknowledgement only. As the average length of stay for team members is a couple of years, auditions are infrequent – perhaps once a year or every 18 months. Teaching qualifications are desirable but not essential – a genuine interest in education and working with young people is far more important. We prefer actors to have had some formal professional training. Most of the company's work is devised and written by the team under the direction of the artistic director. Strong performing skills are essential, as well as devising skills or the desire to develop them. Music plays an important part in our work, and although it is not a requirement for anyone seeking work with the company to be able to play a musical instrument, it is important that they are able to sing reasonably well. We welcome visitors; anyone wishing to see our work should contact our administrator, Julia Davies, to arrange a visit.'

Humberside Theatre in Education

Hessle High School, Lower School, Boothferry Road, Hessle, nr Hull HU13 9AR
Tel (0482) **640876**
Director Dave Broster

Perform existing work, new work and company-devised shows for 5–18-year-olds in schools. Company of four actor/teachers on contracts that vary from short to long term; pay Equity/ITC rates. Advertise for actors in *The Stage*, *Minority Arts Advisory Service Job Bulletin* and ITC *Job Bulletin*. Do not necessarily require actors with teaching qualifications, although 'educational background/experience may be useful.' Welcome casting queries and will keep CVs on file; hold auditions when necessary. 'The company works as a cooperative. Members have to: take responsibility; be honest and open; work under pressure and as a team; be fair; challenge in a creative way.'

Interim Theatre Productions Ltd

254 Portland Road, South Norwood, London SE25 4SL
Tel (01) **654 9282**
Artistic director Terry Ruane

Founded 1978. Originally a small-scale touring company but since 1984 have been concentrating on Theatre-in-Education for deaf and handicapped children. Perform in arts centres, middle-range theatres, schools and colleges, with a touring pattern of some split weeks and one-night stands. Company of seven actors on 12+ -week subsidized rep contracts. Advertise in *The Stage*, and welcome letters from actors.

Learning Through Action

Learning Through Action Centre, Cumberland Road, Reading, Berks. RG1 3JY
Tel (0734) **665556**
Artistic director Annette Cotterill

Separate programmes devised for infant, junior and secondary schools, mostly in Berkshire. At least three programmes are presented each year, and the scope of subject matter is very wide – emphasis is always placed on multi-cultural, cross-curricula teaching and on conservation-related issues. Company of ten on one-year contracts. Teaching qualifications required. Do not pay Equity rates – teachers must have LEA secondments. Do not advertise, and do not welcome casting queries from actors; auditions held annually. 'Learning Through Action's teachers use role-play and artefacts to create simulated environments that facilitate learning. While working for the company, the teachers also study for a Learning Through Action Diploma, awarded by Berkshire's Local Education Authority.'

Playtime Productions

'No Worries', 9 Thorsby Close, Lincoln LN5 9DF
Tel (0522) **721947**
Artistic director Hayley Joy

Puppet shows, children's plays, TIE, youth club productions and a variety of workshops. Perform in schools, village halls, youth clubs and community arts centres. 'All productions are specially written for Playtime Productions or are devised by the company through improvisation sessions for either 4–12-year-olds or 13–20-year-olds, and have a non-violent/non-sexist/strong moral or educational element.' Company of four actors on contracts of 5–10 weeks; non-Equity. Do not advertise for actors, but welcome casting queries. Send letter with full CV, photograph and SAE. 'We require actors who are hard working, extremely versatile and capable of devising productions through improvisation. We look for actors with skills in mime, circus skills, creative movement, mask work, puppetry and some musical skills – who are also capable of leading workshops in these skills. It would be advantageous if actors had experience of work with the handicapped and any technical experience. Most important of all, though, is a sense of humour. Playtime Productions is an equal opportunities employer.'

Skin and Bones Theatre Company

Skin and Bones Theatre Collective, Ouseburn Warehouse Workshops, Lime Street,
Newcastle upon Tyne NE1 2PN
Tel (091) **232 3276**
Contact Maysie Sharp, Gwyneth Lamb

Productions for young people including TIE, participatory work and pantomime in schools, colleges and community centres. Audience age range of 3–18 years. Company of six on an initial contract of 3–6 months, often extended, with the possibility of a permanent contract; pay Equity rates. Do not usually advertise for actors. Do not object to receiving casting queries from actors, but 'cannot often respond'. Approach in writing in the first instance. Usually hold auditions once a year. Teaching qualifications would be an advantage. 'Find out something about us before applying. CVs which just list the parts you have played are of no use to us. We value other experience – other jobs, voluntary work, etc. – as well as acting experience. Tell us about it.'

The Theatre Company Blah Blah Blah
48 Harold Mount, Leeds LS6 1PW
Tel (0532) **754091**
Artistic director None – 'artistic decisions are taken by the company'

Junior and senior programmes for schools and youth clubs (ages: 5–7, 7–11, 14 upwards). 'We devise our own shows, and would expect any person joining the company to enter into the devising process. The content of the show reflects questions that company members confront in their work and which are then tested against the age range for which we devise the show.' Average company of four actors on three-month contracts; non-Equity. Rarely advertise, and do not welcome casting queries from actors. Hold auditions annually. Teaching qualifications required or 'at least a good knowledge of theories of learning'.

Theatre of Fact
Stantonbury Campus, Stantonbury, Milton Keynes, Bucks. MK14 6BN
Tel (0908) **322568**
Artistic director Roy Nevitt

Issue-based TIE plays and participatory programmes for 9–16-year-olds. Perform in schools, small-scale theatres and community centres. Company of four actors on 14-week contracts; Equity rates. Advertise for actors in *The Stage*. Welcome casting queries from actors; approach by telephone call in the first instance. Auditions held as necessary – once or twice a year. Teaching qualifications not required.

TIE Break Theatre in Education
St William's Primary School, St William's Way, Norwich NR7 0AJ
Tel (0603) **39965**
Artistic director David Farmer

Production themes include disability, conservation, racism, prejudice, sexism and local history for an audience age range of 5 to 25 years. Perform in schools, youth clubs and arts centres. Company of 3–6 on contracts that vary from two months to a year; pay Equity rates. Advertise in *The Stage*, and prefer to hear from actors only in response to these adverts. Auditions held, on average, twice a year. Teaching qualifications not always required, but welcome drama or teacher training and preferably some experience in TIE/YPT. 'We look for company members who have good experience in TIE/YPT or who wish to make this their chosen area of work.'

TIE companies attached to Rep/Regional Theatres ● *see also* Rep/Regional Theatres

Belgrade Theatre in Education Company
Belgrade Theatre, Belgrade Square, Coventry CV1 1GS
Tel (0203) **56431**
Head of Department Brian Bishop

Half-day, whole-day and multi-visit TIE programmes: 'A combination of performance pieces, workshops and participation in role work.' Audience age ranges from 4 to 18. Perform in school halls and classrooms, with occasional performances in the Belgrade Studio Theatre. Average size of the company is 13, with a core of 11 on open-ended contracts. Freelance workers are employed on an average 12-week contract; pay above MRSL 2. Advertise in *The Stage*; hold auditions only when a company member leaves (sometimes three or four times per year). 'Applications are helped if they are accompanied by a letter clearly stating the applicant's ideas on and commitment to TIE and education, and why they have applied to this company in particular.' Do not require teaching qualifications – however, 'such applicants might be viewed with more interest.'

Derby Playhouse TIE Company
Derby Playhouse, Theatre Walk, Eagle Centre, Derby DE1 2NF
Tel (0332) **363271**
Artistic director Annie Castledine

Wide audience age range; perform in varied venues. Average length of contract is 12 weeks, with a company of six actors. Do not advertise for actors, and only need one letter of enquiry each year. Do not require teaching qualifications.

Duke's Theatre in Education Company
Duke's Playhouse, Moor Lane, Lancaster LA1 1QE
Tel (0524) **67461**
Artistic director Warwick Dobson

A range of productions for primary and secondary school children (7–18 years), including *Peterloo, Breaking the Magic Spell, Black and Blue, The Big Lie*. Perform in schools. Company of five actor/teachers on open-ended permanent contracts; pay Equity rates. Advertise in *The Stage*; do not generally welcome casting queries from actors as they only hold auditions as and when a vacancy occurs, which is not often. Teaching qualifications are a 'decided advantage' as is a degree. 'If young actors are *genuinely* interested in TIE, they should take every opportunity to see companies at work. (From our point of view this is the best kind of preliminary approach.)'

Harrogate Theatre-in-Education
Harrogate Theatre, Oxford Street, Harrogate, N. Yorks. HG1 1QF
Tel (0423) **502710**
Artistic director Nobby Dimon

Biased towards role-play and interactive drama, but do occasionally mount 'plays' for young people. Audience age ranges from 5 to 18. Perform in schools in North Yorkshire. Average size of company is three, with an average contract length of ten weeks; pay Equity rates. Advertise in *The Stage*, and welcome casting queries from actors; approach in writing in the first instance. 'Pro-forma letters such as the drama schools seem to encourage, with a string of productions listed and parts played, are, as far as we are concerned, useless without a letter which gives us some idea about the person behind the boring statistics, his or her attitudes to TIE, children, hopes, fears, etc.' Do not exclusively require actors with teaching qualifications but do prefer them: 'Improvisational skills essential.'

Palace-go-Round
Palace Theatre, London Road, Westcliff-on-Sea, Essex SS0 9LA
Tel (0702) **347816**
Artistic director Christopher Dunham

Leeds Playhouse Theatre-in-Education
Quarrymount School, Pennington Street, Leeds, W. Yorks. LS6 2JP
Tel (0532) **442145**
Artistic director Gillian Hambleton

Present company-devised programmes plus some scripted work, performing in schools plus one annual production in Leeds Playhouse. Audience age ranges from 5 to 18. Average size of company is nine; offer an open-ended contract – 'company members tend to stay for a long time' – and pay above Equity rates (teachers' salary levels). Advertise in *The Stage* and *Leeds Other Paper*; do not welcome casting queries from actors – 'we only advertise when we need to replace a company member.' Teaching qualifications are not essential. 'Applications to become a company member should indicate the actor's views on theatre-in-education. We are looking for acting excellence and integrity and a knowledge of and a willingness to explore educational theory in relation to theatre as a learning medium. Company members are required to take on responsibility for all company activities including policy-making (artistic and educational); devising; acting; discussing the work with teachers, theatre workers and other educationalists.'

Roundabout Theatre Company

Nottingham Playhouse, Wellington Circus, Nottingham NG1 5AF
Tel (0602) **474361**
Artistic director Rick Hall

Founded in 1973, this is the TIE and community touring company of Nottingham Playhouse whose aim is 'to use theatre as a medium for learning'. Play to schoolchildren from 5 to 18 years, including those with special needs; there is also a community tour through Nottinghamshire and the East Midlands to non-theatre-going audiences. Six TIE programmes per year plus one tour. Productions include: *Women Beware Women* and *No Longer Kids*. Company of eight actors on open-ended contracts (having completed probationary period); 56 days' notice, TMA/Equity Esher TIE contract – MRSL II. Advertise in *The Stage*, actors' centres, the black press and through other TIE companies. Prefer letters from actors only in response to advertisements; general auditions usually held once a year. Do not require teaching qualifications.

Royal Theatre-in-Education Company

Royal Theatre, Guildhall Road, Northampton NN1 1EA
Tel (0604) **27566**
Artistic director Jonathan Landsberg

Tour schools in the county, playing to four age ranges between years 4 to 18. Also do a community show each year, touring community centres. Average company of four actors on Equity contracts, usually of ten weeks. Advertise for actors in *The Stage*, and welcome casting queries, 'although we do not keep extensive files'. 'We want actors who write to us to explain why they have a particular interest in theatre-in-education work.' Usually hold auditions twice a year. Do not require teaching qualifications.

Salisbury Playhouse Theatre-in-Education Company

Malthouse Lane, Salisbury, Wilts. SP2 7RA
Tel (0722) **20117**
Artistic director Lynn Wyfe

Tour schools in Wiltshire, Dorset and part of Hampshire, playing to children from 5 to 18 years old. Company of four actors on Equity contracts of 6–9 months. Sometimes advertise in *The Stage*. Hold auditions once a year. Welcome casting queries from actors; approach in writing in the first instance, enclosing CV, photograph and SAE. Teaching qualifications not 'entirely' essential.

Sheffield Crucible Theatre-in-Education Company

Crucible Theatre, 55 Norfolk Street, Sheffield S1 1DA
Tel (0742) **760621**
Artistic director Phil Clark

Theatre-in-education and community shows; perform in old people's homes, youth clubs, working-men's clubs, community centres, schools and the Crucible

Studio Theatre. Cuts in funding have reduced the company to a core of four full-time actors on Equity contracts, which are renewed yearly. The company tends to be of mixed race, and actors with disabilities are encouraged to apply. Do not advertise for actors and do not hold general auditions. Welcome letters enclosing CV and photograph, which will be kept on file.

Thorndike Young People's Theatre Company

Thorndike Theatre, Church Street, Leatherhead, Surrey KT22 8DF
Tel (0372) **376211**
Artistic director Seona McKinnon

Tour primary and secondary schools twice a year (autumn and spring terms) – workshops as well as performances. Average company of 4/5 actors on Equity contracts of 8–10 weeks. Hold general auditions once a year – usually in September. Welcome casting queries from actors; approach in writing, enclosing CV and photograph. Do not require teaching qualifications.

Tynewear Theatre in Education

Tyne Theatre & Opera House, Westgate Road, Newcastle upon Tyne NE1 4AG
Tel (091) **232 3366**
Artistic director Christopher Bostock

Infant, junior and secondary projects plus pre-school shows and projects for young people with severe learning difficulties. Audience age ranges from 3 to 18+. Perform in school and community venues plus small studio theatres. Average company of 4–8 performers; Equity contract of three months' to one year's duration. Advertise in *The Stage*, and hold auditions once or twice a year. Welcome casting queries from actors either by telephone or letter. Do not necessarily require actors with teaching qualifications, but musical skills are 'useful'.

Watford Palace Theatre in Education

Theatreyard, Grosvenor Road, Watford WD1 2QT
Tel (0923) **33439/35455 ext 48**
Artistic director Alan Orme

Plays, participatory drama and teachers' workshops. Perform mainly in schools and youth clubs (community show planned). Audience age ranges from 5 to 25. Company of four actors with contracts of 9–46 weeks; pay Equity rates. Advertise in *The Stage* and various ethnic-minority papers; do not particularly welcome casting queries from actors. Hold auditions 'once a year whenever possible; try to do all casting in July.' Teaching qualifications not essential. 'When applying to the company, a full letter of application is preferred, detailing why the actor wishes to work in TIE.'

Wolsey Theatre-in-Education

Wolsey Theatre, Civic Drive, Ipswich, Suffolk IP1 2AS
Tel (0473) **220092**
Artistic director Andrew Breakwell

Perform in schools and youth/community venues to audiences aged 5–18 in two-year age bands. Past productions have included such topics as Northern Ireland, drug education, evacuees and 'how kids play'. Average company of four with contracts of 10–12 weeks; pay above Equity rates, depending on age and experience. Sometimes advertise in *The Stage*. Welcome casting queries – 'particularly from older and experienced actors'. Approach in writing in the first instance. Auditions held twice yearly. Teaching qualifications not required –

'professional theatre training desirable and an interest in working with children/teachers'.

York Theatre Royal Young People's Theatre

York Theatre Royal, St Leonard's Place, York YO1 2HD
Tel (0904) **658162** Fax (0904) **611534**
Artistic director Anthony Ravenhall

TIE for age range of 4 to 18 years; theatre for young people for all age groups (including family shows); participation events; young writers' festival; youth theatre work. Perform in schools, colleges, community venues, youth clubs and in the Theatre Royal. Company of 4–6 actors on six-month contracts; pay MSLR 2 Equity rate. Advertise in *The Stage* and the *Guardian*, and welcome casting queries from actors; approach in writing in the first instance. Hold auditions approximately three times per year depending on the demands of each programme. Wherever possible, use actors with teaching qualifications and experience of working with young people, plus as wide a range of qualifications and experience as is possible. 'An understanding of TIE practice is essential – very few "new" actors have seen many TIE shows, and very few drama schools prepare them for this field. A schools tour of a set text is not the same as TIE. However, when making the initial approach, please do not send a 15-page thesis on what TIE is.'

15. Film, video and independent production companies

The British film business is going through one of its periodic bouts of optimism. Cinema admissions may be half of what they were ten years ago, but the seemingly inexorable decline has been reversed, and with 75 million tickets sold last year, a visit to the movies is once again the single most popular excuse for getting out of an evening.

Of course, admission figures alone are no guarantee of a thriving home industry. All those multiplexes springing up round the country can still do very nicely by projecting just American movies on to their numerous screens. And even if they do show an occasional British film, it is a near certainty that, even for a blockbuster, the returns in this country alone will not be high enough to cover the production costs. In those far off days when Colin Welland was waving an Oscar above his head to herald a resurgence of British film-making, he forgot to mention that the success of *Chariots of Fire* was entirely due to American enthusiasm. Even *Gandhi* only grossed a quarter of its production costs on the home circuit.

So what's new? Without losing all sense of proportion, there are signs that the British might at last be finding a way into the American market that is not a dead end. The success of *A Fish Called Wanda*, recently breaking box-office records across the States, owes more than a little to John Cleese's realization that there is a form of humour, not entirely British and not entirely American, which can appeal on both sides of the Atlantic. Parochial themes such as those milked by Cleese in his previous film, *Clockwise* and by *Wanda*'s vintage director Charles Crichton in his Ealing comedies *The Titfield Thunderbolt* and *The Lavender Hill Mob* go down in America like the proverbial lead balloon.

The lesson applies just as strongly with lower-budget movies. The films of Merchant Ivory (*Room with a View*, *Maurice*), though unmistakably British in tone, deal with subjects which have transatlantic appeal. It may not extend beyond the art houses, but that is more than enough to make sense of the budgets. Perhaps the secret is to have a gifted director like James Ivory who is American-born yet enjoys working in a European setting.

As if to endorse the British film-makers' claim to a share of the American market, there is at last emerging a group of young actors who are equally bankable in Hollywood and wherever it is around London they make films nowadays. Gary Oldman and Daniel Day-Lewis lead the pack, but there are others hovering — Miranda Richardson, Kenneth Branagh, Emma Thompson. Two years ago, Timothy Dalton was the only youngish British actor with any recognition in the States and that was only because he played James Bond.

If American sales are the difference between a thumping loss and a decent profit, increasing opportunities for fireside viewing can help to raise income another few notches above the safety margin. The overlap between cinema, television and video may be confusing to the purists, but it has a financial logic that the producers understand only too well. An increasing proportion of films are sold to television even before they go into production as a way of guaranteeing at least part of the budget. In the near future, the same sort of deal will be made with the video distributors.

The link between television and the creative side of film-making was forged by Channel 4 as part of its overall policy of farming out all production to independents. (There is a warning here for would-be television actors: there is no point in plying for work in Charlotte Street; those with the power to cast are at other addresses.) Inspired backing has associated Channel 4 with an enviable run of credits, including *My Beautiful Laundrette*, *The Draughtsman's Contract*, *A Room with a View*, *Dance with a Stranger*, *Mona Lisa*, *Sammy and Rosie Get Laid* and *Prick Up Your Ears*. And all this on an investment budget of just £10 million a year.

Under government edict to open more of its programme-making to competitive tender, the BBC has now decided to back at least six films a year. For an investment of about £800,000 of the £4–5 million total cost of a film, the BBC will secure UK television rights and a share of the equity. Several of the independent companies are following suit, though their preference is for associated production companies. Anglia Films, the production arm of Anglia Television, is sufficiently ambitious to invite David Puttnam on to its board. The end result may be no more than a succession of made-for-TV movies, an area of modest achievement so far dominated by Hollywood, but given the available talent – acting, writing and directing – it is reasonable to pitch expectations higher.

Let us hope that plans do not fall foul of the administrative cock-ups that used to be second nature to the BBC. Who was it, for example, who allowed the superb Falklands film, *Tumbledown*, to be made without an actors' agreement on a big screen showing? This unforgivable omission cost the BBC a £1 million deal with the Cannon cinema chain when three of the cast of 55 exercised their right to object. The problem originates with the huge discrepancies in actors' pay for film and television. No one suggests that a settlement will be easy to achieve, but an agreement with Equity is a must if there is to be free interchange between cinema, television and video, and if the financially hard-pressed BBC is to exploit fully its vast archive of rarely seen classics.

Still, the unknown factor in the development of film and television is the impact of satellite broadcasting, which is soon to increase the viewing choice for the typical household by up to 15 channels. British Satellite Broadcasting (BSB) – supported by, among others, Granada, Anglia TV, Pearson, Virgin and Reed International – has given a commitment to feature film production, but it is not immediately clear how much money is on offer for origination as opposed to buying in programmes. Such massive sums are needed for technology and marketing that whatever is left is bound to be modest in the short run, although resources have been found for a stockpile of 100 movies from Warner Bros. Over at Astra, a Luxemburg-based satellite with a 16-channel potential, Rupert Murdoch is making the running without pausing to declare how he intends to fill the viewing time at his disposal.

The general mood of uncertainty is intensified by the imminent deregulation of the existing independent television sector. With franchises going to the highest bidder, who can say what will happen to production standards?

The cynics claimed that we are in for a deluge of tatty quiz shows and American soaps. This must be taken as the accountant's option: buying in programmes is at least two-thirds cheaper than origination. However, viewers may not be ready to cooperate. Audience research suggests that produced programmes of high quality are far more popular than the drop-offs from the Hollywood conveyor belt. A surfeit of inferior product will have an adverse effect on advertising revenue, which in turn will force the programme-makers to mend their ways. This is what happened when the BBC and ITV began to share the screen in the mid-1950s: viewers were thrown a lot of rubbish early on, but over a period, standards did improve. Does anyone argue that television today on four channels is not infinitely better than the television of 30 years ago when it was dominated by a single public service channel?

Actors have every reason to look on the bright side.

ACT Films Ltd

111 Wardour Street, London W1V 4AY
Tel (01) **437 8506**
Contact Richard Gates (executive director)

> Low-budget feature films and documentaries (primarily political). Use casting directors but also welcome casting queries from actors. Send letter in the first instance.

A & M Sound Pictures

136 New Kings Road, London SW6 4LZ
Tel (01) **736 3311** Telex **916342**
Contact Steven Lavers

> Not currently acting as producers: commission other production companies when required.

Air Play

> Affiliated to Newgate Company, Air Play makes audio-stereo drama tape recordings of new plays, screenplays and teleplays. See *Newgate Company & Air Play* in Producing Theatres and Independent Managements section.

ANV Productions

47a Kendal Street, London W2 2BV
Tel (01) **262 3074**
Contact Antony Norris

> Film and video business TV; corporate and training programmes. Always use casting directors. Do not welcome casting queries from actors, but will consider demo tapes for voice-overs.

AVC Group

Walters Farm Road, Tonbridge, Kent TN9 1QT
Tel (0732) **365107** Fax (0732) **362600** Telex **95586** PROBES G
Contact Claudia Fraser

> Video — corporate and training. Welcome casting queries from actors. Send letter in the first instance. Foreign-language voice-over opportunities; welcome demo tapes.

AVP

School Hill Centre, Chepstow, Gwent NP6 6PH
Tel (02912) **5439** Fax (02912) **79200**
Contact Laurence Nauen

> Film and video — documentary, training, educational. Always use casting directors. Do not welcome casting queries from actors. Occasional voice-over opportunities, but do not welcome unsolicited demo tapes.

Abacus Film Productions Ltd

31 Shelton Street, London WC2H 9HT
Tel (01) **240 1277** Fax (01) **836 7014**
Contact Ron Trainer

> TV commercials, documentaries, corporate videos. Usually use casting directors. Do not welcome casting queries from actors, but will consider demo tapes or video show reels. Advice to newcomers: 'Keep in touch with casting directors; get a good agent. Demo tapes are important.'

Abbey Video Ltd

Five Lamps Studio, West Avenue, Derby DE1 3HR
Tel (0332) **40693**
Contact Richard Faulkner

> Makers of corporate videos for a variety of industrial clients.

Acme Arts Ltd

12 Vauxhall Grove, London SW8 1SY
Tel (01) **735 9099**
Contact Jim Field

> Horticultural and educational films for TV and video.

Action Time

23 Woodstock Street, London W1R 1HF
Tel (01) **409 3421** Telex **262187**
Contact Jeremy Fox

> Makers of TV programmes: 'format shows' such as *Game for a Laugh*, *Odd One Out* and *The Krypton Factor*, both for the UK and America.

Advent Video Production

Ely House, 37 Dover Street, London W1X 4AH
Tel (01) **409 1343**
Contact Dominic Roncoroni

> Documentary, educational and corporate videos; also commercials.

After Image Ltd

32 Acre Lane, London SW2 5SG
Tel (01) **737 7300**
Contact Jane Thorburn

> Makers of TV programmes, with a particular interest in the arts and unusual people and events. *Output*: *Alter Image*, the alternative arts magazine, with no presenter; *Pookiesnackenburger*, musical series; *Map of Dreams*, arts video, dance and effects.

Agender Films

25 Denmark Street, London WC2H 8NJ
Tel (01) **379 5304/5346**
Contact Sarah Boston, Rachel Trezise

Documentaries. *Output:* most recent, *Just Sex* and *Merely Mortal* for Channel 4.

Aisling Films

17–21 Bruce Street, Belfast BT2 7JD
Tel (0232) **327434** Fax (0232) **327820**
Contact Bill Hiskelly, Marie Jackson

Documentary and drama film. *Output: End of the World Man* (BBC children's drama serial); *In the Name of God* (Channel 4 documentary). Use casting directors, but also welcome casting queries from actors. Will consider demo tapes and video show reels.

Britt Allcroft Group Ltd

61 Devonshire Road, Southampton SO1 2GR
Tel (0703) **331661** Fax (0703) **332206** Telex **47408 BALAHA G**
Contact Britt Allcroft, Angus Wright

TV programmes – notably specializing in family and children's, led by *Thomas the Tank Engine and Friends.*

Allied Stars

17 Waterloo Place, London SW1 4SR
Tel (01) **839 5285**
Contact Luke Randolph

Feature films. *Output: Chariots of Fire; Breaking Glass; F/X Murder by Illusion; Government Issue; Rocket.*

Alligator Productions Ltd

68–70 Wardour Street, London W1V 4JA
Tel (01) **734 0101** Telex **25554 PECLDN**
Contact Catherine Skinner

A group of freelance directors and other professionals who make commercials and promo films for video and TV.

Amber Films

5 Side (rear), Newcastle upon Tyne NE1 3JE
Tel (091) **232 2000**
Contact Peter Roberts, Murray Martin, Ellin Hare

Broadcast and non-broadcast video; broadcast film drama and documentary. *Output: Byker* (Channel 4 documentary); *Seacoal* and *T. Dan Smith* (Channel 4 docu-drama features). Welcome casting queries from actors. Approach by letter in the first instance. Occasional voice-over opportunities; will consider demo tapes. 'Our work is almost exclusively based in the north-east of England, concentrating on subjects rooted in contemporary working-class life. Actors with this kind of background are therefore obviously of main interest to us.'

The Animation Partnership Ltd and Carl Gover Associates
8 Percy Street, London W1P 9FB
Tel (01) **636 3300** Fax (01) **580 9153** Telex **297002**
Contact Carl Gover

Film, video and TV — documentary and commercials, with a possibility of forthcoming drama production. Use casting directors, but also welcome casting queries from actors. Prefer to be approached in writing, 'because the information contained in a letter can be filed for future use'. Welcome demo tapes and video show reels. 'Many voice-over opportunities on the animation side of our business because every character needs a voice. Demo tapes are always useful for reference, but video show reels demonstrate the use of the right voice for the appropriate occasion.'

Antelope Films Ltd
3 Fitzroy Square, London W1P 5AH
Tel (01) **387 4454** Fax (01) **388 9935** Telex **266205** AFL G
Contact Clive Syddall

Makers of drama and TV documentaries. *Output: The Triple Crown: The Paradox of the Papacy*; *The Spirit of the Alcazar: 50 Years in a Spanish City*; *Vidal in Venice*; *Heart of the Dragon*, 12-part series on China for Channel 4; *Portrait of Russia*, 7-part series for Turner Broadcasting; *Testament*, 7-part series for Channel 4.

Antonine Productions/Black Cat Studios
830 Springfield Road, Glasgow G31
Tel (041) **554 4667**
Contact Paddy Higson

Films for TV, feature films (particularly thrillers and road movies). *Output: The Girl in the Picture*, 1985; *Brond*, Channel 4, 1987.

Apple Television
A2 Connaught Business Centre, Hendon, London NW9 6JL
Tel (01) **205 6687/7514**
Contact Ronnie Cairnduff

Videos — corporate, business, commercials, documentary, training films. Use casting directors, but also welcome casting queries from actors. Contact by telephone in the first instance. Welcome demo tapes and video show reels. 'A straight-to-camera photo — updated each year. If an accent is asked for, say no if you can't do it rather than bodge it.'

Arbor Productions Ltd
10 Museum Street, London WC1A 1LE
Tel (01) **379 5847**
Contact Mary Jane Walsh

Makers of TV programmes, cinema, corporate and educational video. Specialize in music, arts, documentary and drama. *Output: Body Styles* for Channel 4.

Aspect Film & Television Production Ltd
36 Percy Street, London W1P 9FG
Tel (01) **636 5303** Fax (01) **436 0666**
Contact Marian Lacey

Corporate films and videos. Do not mind receiving casting queries from actors, but do not have many opportunities for them. Send a letter in the first instance. 'Prefer to contact agents.'

Aspen Spafax Television
1 Gayford Road, London W12 9BY
Tel (01) **743 8618** Fax (01) **740 9333** Telex **25221**
Contact Mike Raggett, Amanda Thompson

Corporate film and video for promotion, training and communications using presenters, actors and voice-overs. *Output:* promotional dramas for Leeds Building Society; training programmes for British Gas, British Telecom, Marks & Spencer, Woolworth; communications for *Financial Times*, Pearson, TieRack, RHM, Glaxo and Wellcome; commercials for Post Office's QTV. Occasionally use casting directors, but welcome casting queries from actors. Approach by letter in the first instance. Frequent voice-over opportunities; welcome demo tapes and video show reels.

Astramead Ltd
38 Gloucester Mews, London W2 3HE
Tel (01) **723 4678**
Contact Mark Shivas

TV programmes, cinema and drama on film and video. *Output: Telford's Change, Can You Hear Me at the Back?* and *The Price* for Channel 4; *Late Starter* for BBC.

Aurora Sound & Vision
05 Hellesdon Park Road, Drayton High Road, Norwich NR6 5DR
Tel (0603) **789509**
Contact Steve Bloomfield, Trevor Machin

Video sales and training filmes; radio commercials; conference presentations. Welcome casting queries from actors. Approach by letter in the first instance. Will consider demo tapes for voice-overs.

Robert Austen Communications Ltd
The Chequers, 2 Church Street, High Wycombe, Bucks. HP11 2DE
Tel (0494) **443777** Telex **265871** MON REF G TCC097
Contact Bob Austen, Charlene Hamlin

Film and video — commercials, corporate, documentary, dramatized documentary. Occasionally use casting directors, but most productions are cast internally. Do not welcome casting queries from actors. Welcome demo tapes for voice-overs — a wide range required in age, sex, region. Foreign voices especially welcome. 'We work mostly through theatrical or casting agencies. However, we do have some agencies who have given us bad treatment in the past. If we have trouble with an agent, we eliminate every artist represented by that agent. Advice to young actors: choose your agent carefully.'

BBC Enterprises Ltd
Woodlands, 80 Wood Lane, London W12 0TT
Tel (01) **576 0216** Fax (01) **743 0393** Telex **934678**
Contact Denise Evans (business affairs manager, home entertainment)

Responsible for the release of BBC Video and BBC Record titles, usually reflecting BBC-TV and BBC Radio output. No outlet for actors apart from occasional voice-overs. Do not welcome unsolicited demo tapes.

BFVW Ltd

2nd floor, Pitman Buildings, 161 Corporation Street, Birmingham B4 6PH
Tel (021) **233 3423**
Contact Rob Burkitt

TV documentary and features; corporate. Use casting directors, but welcome casting queries from actors. Prefer to be approached by letter with CV and photograph. 'We are particularly keen to develop regionally based talent. However, vacancies occur only irregularly.'

Behr Cinematography

22 Redington Road, London NW3 7RG
Tel (01) **794 2535**
Contact Arnold Behr, Betty Burghes

Documentary, educational and corporate film and video, on subjects ranging from care of the terminally ill through sport for the handicapped to custom building of motor cars.

Stuart Bell & Partners Ltd

40 Frith Street, London W1V 5TF
Tel (01) **439 2700**
Contact Stuart Bell

Video and film: commercials, corporate and training, broadcast documentaries.

Bentorm Ltd

26b Thorney Crescent, London SW11 3TR
Tel (01) **585 1592**
Contact David Deutsch

Films and TV drama. *Output*: *Shakespeare Lives* and *Reflections* (Channel 4); *Tales of the Unexpected* (Anglia TV); *The Chain* (Rank). Always use casting directors. Do not welcome casting queries from actors. Welcome demo tapes and video show reels.

Paul Berriff Productions Ltd

The Chesnuts, Woodfield Lane, Hessle, N. Humberside HU13 0EW
Tel (0482) **641158**
Contact Paul Berriff

TV documentary features. *Output*: *Lakeland Rock* for Channel 4; *Lifeboat* series and *Animal Squad* for BBC1; *Fire* for BBC *40 Minutes*; *Dianne's Children* for BBC2.

Stuart Black Productions

79 Charlbert Court, Eamont Street, London NW8 7DB
Tel (01) **722 7636**
Contact Stuart Black, Crystal Black

Not currently active as producers. Mainly providing a script service and production management for other producers.

Blackrod Ltd

Threeways House, 40–44 Clipstone Street, London W1P 7EA
Tel (01) **637 9376** Fax (01) **580 9143** Telex **269859**
Contacts Michael Rodd, Nick Crombie

Corporate TV – drama and documentary. Always use casting directors. Do not welcome casting queries from actors, but will consider demo tapes and video show reels.

Blackwell Videotec Ltd

7 John Street, London WC1N 2ES
Tel (01) **430 0044**
Contact Jo-Anne Winston

> Subsidiary of Blackwell Scientific Publications. Educational, medical, scientific, corporate and promotional programmes. *Output: Risk*, looking at the risks in medical practice, which won the gold award at the 1985 New York Film & TV Festival.

Matt Boney Associates

'Woodside', Holdfast Lane, Grayswood, Haslemere, Surrey GU27 2EU
Tel (0428) **56178**
Contact Matt Boney

> Video, TV – documentary, commercials, travel and sport.

British Film Institute

29 Rathbone Street, London W1P 1AG
Tel (01) **636 5587** Fax (01) **580 9456** Telex **27624** BFILDNG
Contact Davina Nicholson, Eliza Mellor

> Film, video, drama. *Output: Friendship's Death; On the Black Hill; Distant Voices/Still Lives; La Deuda Interna.* Use casting directors. Do not welcome casting queries from actors. Not really any voice-over opportunities for actors. Do not consider unsolicited demo tapes or video show reels.

British Lion

Pinewood Studios, Iver, Bucks. SL0 0NH
Tel (0753) **651700** Telex **847505**
Contact Peter Snell (chief executive), Lesley Keane

> Film and TV. *Output: Turtle Diary, Lady Jane, Prayer for the Dying* (all feature films); *Tears in the Rain* (Yorkshire TV); *A Man for All Seasons* (Turner Network TV, USA). Use casting directors, but will respond to casting queries from actors 'only when in production'.

Broadwick Productions

26 Charlotte Street, London W1P 1HJ
Tel (01) **580 1923**
Contact Sarah Wickham, Simon Lethbridge

> Wide range of corporate productions, including training, educational, financial, documentary, point-of-sale programme making and production of pop promos.

Brook Productions

103–109 Wardour Street, London W1V 3TD
Tel (01) **439 9871**
Contact Anne Lapping

> Makers of documentary, music, arts and current affairs TV. *Output: A Week in Politics* for Channel 4; *Shape of the World, Voices, The Writing on the Wall* and *David Low.*

Burrill Productions

51 Lansdowne Road, London W11 2LG
Tel (01) **208 0866** Fax (01) **450 1544**
Contact Timothy Burrill

> Feature film production company. *Output: Alpha Beta* (BBC); *Tess* (Roman Polanski); *Pirates of Penzance; Supergirl; The Fourth Protocol.*

CHG Communications

108 Clarendon Road, London W11 2HR
Tel (01) **727 4388** Fax (01) **727 3918**
Contact Charlotte Cain, Anthony Smith

> Film, video, TV – drama/documentary, corporate. Occasionally use casting directors, but welcome casting queries from actors. Approach by letter and follow up with a telephone call. A lot of opportunities for experienced voice-over actors. Welcome demo tapes. 'Provide realistic photographs, accurate, well-presented CVs and a demo tape of your work (if available). We avoid rude agents who have chips on their shoulders about non-broadcast programmes.'

CTR Productions

31 Lismore Crescent, Broadfield, Crawley, W. Sussex RH11 9DA
Tel (0293) **548475**
Contact Ian Cunningham, Roseanne Coils

> Video and TV – documentary, music, children's, religious. Welcome casting queries from actors. Approach in writing in the first instance. Very occasionally have voice-over opportunities. Will consider demo tapes and video show reels.

The Callender Company

4th floor, 82 Wardour Street, London W1V 3LF
Tel (01) **240 8644** Fax (01) **240 8647**
Contact Andi Wright

> Major drama series and feature films. *Output: The Belly of an Architect* (Peter Greenaway); *The Bretts* (co-produced with Central TV for Mobil Masterpiece Theatre).

Candid Cameras (Rental) Ltd

Centerpoint 16/18 St Giles High Street, London WC2H 8LN
Tel (01) **379 0537** Fax (01) **379 3027**
Contact Peter Hartman, Hamid Rahman

> Video – social documentaries and promos. Do not welcome casting queries from actors, but will consider demo tapes and video show reels.

Carpenter Audio Visual

Skyport House, Bath Road, Heathrow, West Drayton, Middx UB7 0BX
Tel (01) **897 2736** Fax (01) **759 3565**
Contact John S. Carpenter

> Video – documentaries, drama, training, commercials. Use casting directors, and do not 'usually' welcome casting queries from actors, but will consider demo tapes and video show reels. 'An appropriate SAE for return of show reels or demo tapes always earns a plus point – but if possible, we like to retain material for future casting.'

Pearl Catlin Associates

16a Carlisle Mansions, Carlisle Place, London SW1P 1HX
Tel (01) **834 1660**
Contact Pearl Catlin, Paul Bernard, Philip Bond

> Film and video — corporate and educational; TV commercials, some programme material. Welcome casting queries from actors, but 'can't reply to them all.' Approach by letter or telephone. No unsolicited demo tapes or video show reels. 'Keep on at your agent — not at companies, please.'

Celador Productions Ltd

39 Long Acre, London WC2E 9JT
Tel (01) **240 8101** Fax (01) **836 1117** Telex **264593** COMCEL G
Contact Bob Louis (director of productions), Paul Smith (managing director)

> Broadcast light entertainment, light features. International movies and mini-series. *Output*: *Television Scrabble* (Channel 4 game show); *The Longest Running Show on Earth* (Channel 4 telethon); *Celebrating St Patrick* (1-hour specials for ITV); *Comedians Do It on Stage* (Channel 4); *Lucan* (TV film). Always use casting directors. Do not welcome casting queries from actors.

Centre Films Ltd

118 Cleveland Street, London W1P 5DN
Tel (01) **387 4045** Fax (01) **388 0408** Telex **23733** CENTRE G
Contact Kent Walwin, Jeffrey Taylor, Derek Granger, Mona Bauwens

> Film and TV drama. *Output*: *Happy Valley* (BBC co-production); *The Four-Minute Mile* (co-production BBC/ABC Australia/CB Films); *Death of a Son* (4-hour mini-series, BBC co-production). Use casting directors, and do not welcome casting queries from actors. 'If actors will insist on writing to us, we would ask that they make their letters clear, short and an enjoyable read, which give some insight into their personality and not just a dry, monotonous list of what they have done (or worse, what they would like to do).' Very limited opportunities for voice-over work. Will consider demo tapes and video show reels.

Charisma Films

Russell Chambers, Covent Garden, London WC2E 8AA
Tel (01) **379 4267**
Contact David Gideon Thomson

> Contrary to popular belief, do not make music promos (the company grew out of Charisma Records). Theatrical and drama TV producers. *Output*: *The Best of British* — a compilation of old Rank film clips for the BBC, and the feature film *Sir Henry at Rawlinson End*.

Cinexsa Film Productions Ltd

209 Manygate Lane, Shepperton, Middx TW17 9ER
Tel (0932) **225950** Telex **266389** KINLON G
Contact Mr J. E. F. Wright (director)

> Film, video, documentary, shorts. Clients include: British Telecom, Shell UK Ltd, Manpower Services Commission, St Dunstan's, British Red Cross Society and RYA Seamanship Foundation. Use casting directors, but also welcome casting queries from actors. Contact by telephone in the first instance.

The City Rises
33 Berwick Street, London W1
Tel (01) **494 2101**
Contact Tanya Cochrane, Peter Granger

> TV commercials and film. Usually use casting directors. Do not welcome casting queries from actors, but will consider demo tapes for voice-overs.

Clappers Video Productions
11 The Meade, Chorltonville, Manchester M21 2FA
Tel (061) **881 8185**
Contact Benny van den Burg

> Training films, commercials. Use casting directors, but also welcome casting queries from actors. Approach by telephone call in the first instance. Voice-over opportunities. Welcome demo tapes and video show reels. 'We are a very small company — do not expect too much.'

Peter Claridge Pictures Ltd
Post 59, Shepperton Studios, Studios Road, Shepperton, Middx TW17 0QD
Tel (0932) **562611** Fax (0932) **568989**
Contact Geraldine Morgan

> Film and video — commercials, promos, corporate. Clients include: Philips, Barclays Bank. Rarely use casting directors. Welcome casting query letters from actors. Will consider demo tapes and video show reels.

Cleveland Productions
5 Rainbow Court, Oxhey, Herts. WD1 4RP
Tel (0923) **54000**
Contact Michael Gosling

> Film and video — commercials, corporate, sales, promo programmes. Use casting directors, but welcome casting queries from actors. Approach by letter or telephone. Welcome demo tapes for voice-overs.

Colstar Communications Entertainment Ltd
1 Wardour Mews, D'Arblay Street, London W1V 3FF
Tel (01) **437 5725** Telex **8951859** BASIL G
Contact Robert Angell

> Make sponsored, corporate, training and promotional films, plus documentary films for an international market. *Output*: *The Poacher*, *The Hunter*, *The Gamekeeper* and *Roots of Tomorrow*.

Communications Concept Ltd (trading as **Concept**)
Five Lamps Studio, West Avenue, Derby DE1 3HR
Tel (0332) **383322** Fax (0332) **291268**
Contacts Mollie Kirkland, David Regan

> Industrial video, conferences and audio-visual.

Compass Film Productions Ltd
Third floor, 18–19 Warwick Street, London W1R 5RB
Tel (01) **439 6456**
Contact Simon Heaven

> Specialists since 1974 in documentary, educational and promotional programmes

for TV and corporate clients. *1987/8 output: Another Way of Life*, on mental handicap, for Channel 4; *Music of the Outsiders* for Channel 4.

Concept ● *see* COMMUNICATIONS CONCEPT LTD

Cosmos Productions

42–44 Hanway Street, London W1P 9DE
Tel (01) **631 3041**
Contact Ronis Varlaam

TV makers. *Output: Enthusiasts*, six half-hour documentaries for Channel 4; *Well, You Didn't Expect Us to Sit Around Doing Nothing, Did You?*, on unemployment, also for Channel 4.

Creative Film Makers Ltd

Pottery Lane House, Pottery Lane, London W11 4LZ
Tel (01) **229 5131** Fax (01) **229 4999**
Contact Gaby Seligman

TV commercials and programmes; videos for advertising and marketing. Sometimes use casting directors, but also have one in-house. Welcome casting queries from actors: 'send letter only.' Will consider demo tapes for voice-overs. 'Plenty of opportunities for keen young actors just now.'

The Crew Multi-Media

186 Monkmoor Road, Shrewsbury, Salop SY2 5BH
Tel (0743) **3684**
Contact Terry Herz, Simon Rea

Film, video, TV – documentary, commercials, sales, training, corporate and feature. Use casting directors, but also welcome casting queries from actors. Approach by letter in the first instance. Will consider demo tapes and video show reels.

Cromdale Films Ltd

17 St Paul's Road, London N1 2QN
Tel (01) **226 0178**
Contact Ian Lloyd

Film, video, TV, drama and documentary. *Output: The Face of Darkness* (feature film); *Drift to Dawn* (rock music drama); *The Overdue Treatment* (documentary).

Crystalvision Productions Ltd

Communications House, Blue Riband Estate, Roman Way, Croydon, Surrey CR9 3RA
Tel (01) **681 7171** Fax (01) **681 2340** Telex **8814079**
Contact Marcus Ascott (corporate), Frazer Ashford (broadcast television)

Corporate and industrial film and video; TV documentaries, commercials, sport and children's programmes. Do not welcome casting queries from actors, but will consider demo tapes for voice-overs.

Cygnet Ltd

Bilton Centre, Coronation Road, High Wycombe, Bucks. HP12 3TA
Tel (0494) **450541** Fax (0494) **462403** Telex **83659** BIGGS
Contact Philip Lee

Film and video: corporate, educational (medical) and TV commercials. Sometimes use casting directors, but welcome casting queries from actors. Send letter in the first instance. Will consider demo tapes and video show reels.

DBI Communication
21 Congreve Close, Warwick, Warwicks. CV34 5RQ
Tel (0926) **497695**
Contact David Impey

> Video — corporate, training, safety, promotional. Clients have included: Massey Ferguson, Courtaulds, ICI, Peugeot Talbot, Forte International. Welcome casting queries from actors. Send letter in the first instance. Welcome demo tapes and video show reels.

DMA Productions
41 Carnaby Street, London W1A 1PD
Tel (01) **437 9950**
Contact David Mead

> Film and video for business. Use casting directors, but also welcome casting queries from actors. Approach by letter in the first instance. Will consider demo tapes and video show reels.

Dareks Production House
58 Wickham Road, Beckenham, Kent BR3 2RQ
Tel (01) **658 2012** Telex **265871** MONREF G (Quote ref: **MAG10088**)
Contact David Crossman, Barry Wale, Tony Phillips

> Broadcast and sponsored film and video drama. *Output: Horace's Day Out; The Pocket Money Programme* (Channel 4). Use casting directors, but also welcome casting queries from actors. Send letter with CV and photograph — no phone calls. Will consider video show reels if on VHS format (SAE essential). 'Please provide details of where we can see your work — including theatre.'

Dateline Productions Ltd
79 Dean Street, London W1V 5HA
Tel (01) **437 4510/1834**
Contact Miranda Watts

> Film and video — broadcast documentary, corporate, drama, commercials. Occasionally use casting directors, but also welcome casting queries from actors. Approach by letter in the first instance. Will consider demo tapes and video show reels.

Dibgate Productions Ltd
Studio 4, Parkstead Lodge, 31 Upper Park Road, London NW3 2UL
Tel (01) **722 5634**
Contact Nicholas Parsons

> Make documentary and travel films for TV, and increasingly in recent years, shorts for cinema audiences. *Output: A Fair Way to Play, Mad Dogs and Cricketers, Relatively Greek, Viva Menorca* and *Terribly British.*

The Directors Video Company Ltd
89a Victoria Road, Aldershot, Hants GU11 1JE
Tel (0252) **316429** Fax (0252) **344362**
Contact A. J. Barton

> Video: documentary, corporate, training, promotional. Welcome casting queries from actors. Approach by letter in the first instance. Will consider demo tapes and video show reels.

Diverse Productions Ltd
6 Gorleston Street, London W1H 8XS
Tel (01) **688 6336** Fax (01) **603 2148** Telex **28363** DIVERS
Contact Frank Dynes

Corporate video; TV (current affairs, satellite business news, educational programmes). *Output: Friday Alternative, Diverse Reports, On Course* and *Dispatches* (all for Channel 4). No outlets for actors.

Drake A–V Video Ltd
89 St Fagans Road, Fairwater, Cardiff CF5 3AE
Tel (0222) **560333** Fax (0222) **554909** Telex **497618** TYPES G DRAKED
Contact Ian Lewis

Corporate A–V film and video — mostly documentary and promotional.

Duncan of Jordanstone College of Art (Postgraduate diploma in electronic imaging)
Perth Road, Dundee DD1 4HT
Tel (0382) **23261**
Contact Stephen Partridge (production) Colin Macleod (course leader)

Corporate video and TV drama. Welcome casting queries from actors. Send letter in the first instance. Will consider demo tapes and video show reels. 'We train young, aspiring writers, directors and producers who often need actors, and welcome the opportunity of testing themselves against fellow aspiring professionals. Budgets are extremely limited but enthusiasm is high!'

EPM Production
The Production Office, 8b St Vincent Street, Edinburgh EH3 6SH
Tel (031) **557 4609**
Contact Kenneth Andrew, Avis Moore

Corporate video — promotion, training, company information, documentary. Do not welcome casting queries from actors, but will consider demo tapes for voice-overs.

Ecce Productions
3/73 Station Road, Sidcup, Kent DA15 7DR
Tel (01) **302 1667**
Contact Stuart McKears

Film and video — documentary and drama. Do not use casting directors. Will consider demo tapes and video show reels. No telephone calls.

Emitel
65 Beak Street, London W1R 3LF
Tel (01) **439 9882**
Contact Malcolm Craddock

Shorts for the cinema, corporate video, training and educational films, sponsored films. Multi-award-winning company.

Eng Video Ltd
3 Nimrod Way, Elgar Road South, Reading, Berks. RG2 0EB
Tel (0734) **751555** Fax (0734) **861482**
Contact Sue Smith (producer)

Corporate television. Rarely use casting directors; welcome casting queries from actors. Approach by letter in the first instance. Will consider demo tapes and video show reels.

Enigma Productions Limited

The Old House, Lee International Studios, Studios Road, Shepperton, Middx. TW17 0QD
Tel (0932) **569144**

With the reestablishment of Enigma Productions, David Puttnam resumes his role as one of the film industry's most active producers, following his period as chairman and chief executive officer of Columbia Pictures. Enigma films include: *Chariots of Fire, The Killing Fields, Cal, The Frog Prince, The Mission*, and *Defence of the Realm*. Always use casting directors and do not welcome queries from actors.

Enlightenment AV & Video Productions

The Studio, Warrens Lane, Botesdale, Diss, Norfolk IP22 1BW
Tel (0379) **898434** Fax (0379) **898987**
Contact Adrian Taylor, Phil Whetter

Video — training, industrial sales, conferences. Welcome casting queries from actors with demo tapes and video show reels — 'more useful than picture and CV'.

Eurofilm Productions Ltd

47 Ossington Street, London W2 4LV
Tel (01) **243 1613**
Contact Andrzej Swoboda

Output: Modern Polish Composers for Channel 4 and *King Size*, a short science-fiction comedy feature.

Euston Films Ltd

365 Euston Road, London NW1 3AR
Tel (01) **387 0911** Fax (01) **388 2122**
Contact Andrew Brown, Bill Launder

Feature films; TV series and serials. *Output: The Fear; Consuming Passions; Bellman & True*. Always use casting directors. Do not welcome casting queries from actors.

Farnham Film Company Ltd

34 Burnt Hill Road, Lower Bourne, Farnham, Surrey GU10 3LZ
Tel (0252) **710313** Fax (0252) **725855** Telex **265871 ref: MMU279**
Contact Ian Lewis, Melloney Roffe

Film and TV drama, documentary, corporate. Use casting directors, but welcome casting queries from actors. Send letter in the first instance. No unsolicited demo tapes or show reels.

Fidelity Films Ltd

34–36 Oak End Way, Gerrards Cross, Bucks. SL9 8BR
Tel (0753) **884646** Fax (0753) **887163** Telex **864723 AUDVIS G**
Contact John Fewlass, Graham Harris

Corporate, training, sales, exhibition videos.

Filmworks

65 Brackenbury Road, Hammersmith, London W6
Tel (01) **741 5631** Fax (01) **748 3198** Telex **8954111** REPLAY
Contact Geraldine Easter

> Film, video, TV (drama and documentary); corporate programmes for business TV. Use casting directors. Approach by letter in the first instance. No unsolicited demo tapes or video show reels.

Fitting Images Ltd

Alfred House, 127a Oatlands Drive, Weybridge, Surrey
Tel (0932) **840056** Fax (0932) **858075**
Contact Sue Fleetwood, Venetia Rickerby

> Video – corporate, promotion and training films. Use casting directors, but welcome casting queries from actors. Prefer to be contacted by telephone in the first instance. Will consider demo tapes and video show reels, but 'we can't guarantee a speedy return.' 'We expect actors to have read and learned the script (unless otherwise directed). We expect a sympathy with the demands and expectations of our clients – mainly blue chip, Conservative organizations – i.e. attitude to content of scripts should be serious; clients' dress code and behaviour rules on smoking, drinking and swearing should be observed.'

Flickering Images Ltd

8 The Causeway, Teddington, Middx TW11 0HE
Tel (01) **943 3290**
Contact Michael Ferguson

> Script writing and project development only.

Flickering Picture Productions Ltd

Rosemount Studios, Pyrford Road, West Byfleet, Weybridge, Surrey KT14 6LD
Tel (09323) **53757** Fax (09323) **49008**
Contact Paul Gawith, David Haggas

> Film and video – medical, educational and corporate documentary.

Flickers Productions

Dumbarton House, 68 Oxford Street, London W1N 9LA
Tel (01) **580 0044** Telex **269578** FLICKS G
Contact Neil Zeiger, Baz Taylor

> Feature films and comedies. *Output*: *Lamb* by Bernard MacLaverty.

Forever Films

82d Warwick Avenue, London W9 2PU
Tel (01) **286 1948**
Contact Clare Downs

> Feature films. *Output*: *The Dress* and *High Season*. Always use casting directors. Do not welcome casting queries from actors.

Formula Enterprises Ltd
19a Marlowes, Hemel Hempstead, Herts. HP1 1LA
Tel (0442) **50427**
Contact Colleen Bending, Steve Arnold

> Video — commercial, corporate, training; AV multi-image production, conferences, presentations. Do not welcome casting queries from actors, but will consider demo tapes and video show reels.

Mark Forstater Productions Ltd
42a Devonshire Close, London W1N 1LL
Tel (01) **631 0611** Fax (01) **580 2248** Telex **8954665** VBSTLX G **ref.** MFP
Contact Nicola Land

> Active in the selection, development and production of material for film, TV and theatre. *Output*: *Monty Python and the Holy Grail*; *The Odd Job*; *The Grass Is Singing*; *Xtro*; *Forbidden*; *The Fantasist*.

Freeway Films
67 George Street, Edinburgh
Tel (031) **334 2993**
Contact John McGrath, Susie Brown

> Film outlet for John McGrath's work. *Output*: *Blood Red Roses* and *There Is a Happy Land* (Channel 4); *The Dressmaker*, from the novel by Beryl Bainbridge, scripted by John McGrath (Film on 4 International/British Screen). New projects: *Border Warfare*, a three-part series on Anglo-Scots relations; *The Long Roads*, a feature film.

Frontroom Productions Ltd
79 Wardour Street, London W1
Tel (01) **734 4603**
Contact Angela Topping

> TV and cinema, both short and full-length features. *Output*: *Acceptable Levels*, *Ursula Glenys*, *Intimate Strangers* and *The Love Child*.

Futuremedia Ltd
44a Aldwick Road, Bognor Regis, W. Sussex PO21 2PN
Tel (0243) **867811** Fax (0243) **868063** Telex **86402**
Contact Dr Peter Copeland

> Video — training programmes and company promotional films. Always use casting directors. Do not welcome casting queries from actors, but will consider demo tapes for voice-overs.

GPA Films
22 Romilly Street, London W1V 5TG
Tel (01) **734 6994** Fax (01) **734 1406**
Contact Celine Cawley (producer)

> TV commercials for UK, Ireland, Italy, Africa and the Far East. Some voice-over opportunities for actors. Always use casting directors. Do not welcome casting queries from actors. 'Get to know the casting directors!'

Gateway Audio Visual & Video
470–472 Green Lanes, London N13 5XF
Tel (01) **882 0177** Telex **896462**
Contact Graham L. Smart

> Corporate and training video and film. Some TV commercials. Always use casting directors. Do not welcome casting queries from actors, but will consider demo tapes for voice-overs.

Gibb Rose Organization Ltd
Pinewood Studios, Iver, Bucks. SL0 0NH
Tel (0753) **651700** Fax (0753) **656935** Telex **847505** PINEW G
Contact Sydney Rose (managing director), Keith Belcher (creative director)

> Film, video, TV. Corporate and sales videos through to independent productions for ITV (music, film, documentary) and full-length feature films.

Grandplay Ltd
Orchard House, Adam & Eve Mews, 169 Kensington High Street, London W8 6SH
Tel (01) **938 4766** Fax (01) **938 4992** Telex **917293**
Contact Yves Pasquier, Katri Skala

> TV and feature film drama. *Output: Hemingway*, Channel 4 series starring Stacey Keach.

Grasshopper Productions Ltd
50 Peel Street, London W8 7PD
Tel (01) **229 1181**
Contact Joy Whitby

> Children's programmes and adult drama.

Greenpark Productions Ltd
'St Wilfrids', 101 Honor Oak Park, London SE23 3LD
Tel (01) **699 7234** Fax (01) **291 6319** Telex **25247** GPK
Contact David Morphet

> Short film and video production. Always use casting directors. Do not welcome casting queries from actors, but will consider demo tapes for voice-overs.

Greenpoint Films
5a Noel Street, London W1V 3RB
Tel (01) **437 6492**
Contact Ann Scott, Patrick Cassavetti

> A small company whose members act as individual producers and directors.

Colin Gregg Films Ltd
Floor 2, 106 Falconberg Court, London W1V 5SG
Tel (01) **439 0257**
Contact Colin Gregg

> Feature films for Channel 4 and BBC2. *Output: Remembrance; To the Lighthouse; Lamb; Hard Travelling.*

Griffin Productions Ltd
3 Fitzroy Square, London W1P 5AH
Tel (01) **388 5811** Fax (01) **388 9830** Telex **8813271** GECOMS G
Contact Adam Clapham

Drama, documentary, arts and current-affairs TV. *Output: Painting with Light*, with Tom Keating (Channel 4); *The Bombay Hotel*, for *Forty Minutes* (BBC2); *Odyssey*, monthly magazine (Channel 4); *Maharajas* (BBC2).

Guild Sound & Vision Ltd
6 Royce Road, Peterborough, Cambs. PE1 5YB
Tel (0733) **315315** Fax (0733) **315395** Telex **32683** GSV G
Contact John Dent

Film and video (training and educational); sponsored corporate videos (usually drama with 3–5 actors). Always use casting directors. Do not welcome casting queries from actors. 'Get a good agent or get yourself known to casting directors.'

Nick Hague Productions
Film House, 142 Wardour Street, London W1V 3AV
Tel (01) **637 4904** Fax (01) **437 1854** Telex **24865** SVCLTD
Contact Nick Hague, Michael Algar, Rosalind Allen

Corporate video, training films, commercials, in-flight entertainment. Occasionally use casting directors. Welcome demo tapes and video show reels.

David Hall Productions
30–38 Dock Street, Leeds LS10 1JF
Tel (0532) **422584/465757**
Contact David Hall

Makers of TV drama and documentaries, film, corporate video. *Output: Maggie's Children* and *All of You Out There* (both documentaries for Channel 4); *Silver Shadows* (feature film in development).

Hamilton Film & Television Ltd
Lee International Studios, Shepperton, Middx TW17 0QD
Tel (0932) **562611** Fax (0932) **68989** Telex **929416** MOVIES G
Contact Christopher Hamilton

International co-productions, film, TV, drama, commercials.

Hamilton Perry
Carnaby House, 27–29 Beak Street, London W1R 3LB
Tel (01) **434 3041** Fax (01) **437 1586** Telex **894039**
Contact Kenneth Moon, Angie Laycock

Video production. Corporate videos for a wide range of clients in the UK and Europe.

Handmade Films
26 Cadogan Square, London SW1X 0JP
Tel (01) **581 1265** Fax (01) **584 7338** Telex **8951338** EURODO

Output: Mona Lisa; Shanghai Surprise; A Private Function; Privates on Parade; The Missionary; Time Bandits; Withnail and I; Five Corners; Bellman & True; Track 29; The Lonely Passion of Judith Hearne. Use casting directors. Do not welcome queries from actors; these are simply passed on to casting directors.

Charles Harris

17 Langland Gardens, London NW3 6QE
Tel (01) **435 1330**
Contact Charles Harris, Elaine Harris

> Feature films, TV drama, drama documentary. Always use casting directors. Do not welcome casting queries from actors. 'I am always looking for new talent, but when I am casting for a specific film and have specific needs, I advertise.'

John Hemson Associates

The Bakehouse Media Resource Centre, Bedford Road, Aspley Hill, Milton Keynes MK17 8DH
Tel (0908) **583062**
Contact John Hemson, Barbara Bilbow

> Film and video — corporate, documentary and drama. Welcome casting queries from actors. Approach by letter in the first instance. Will consider demo tapes and video show reels. 'Our output is mainly corporate video, using actors where possible plus voice-overs.'

Hidden City Films Ltd

23 Hamilton Gardens, London NW8 9PU
Tel (01) **586 8602**
Contact Irving Teitelbaum

> Film and TV. *Output: Hidden City* (feature film). Always use casting directors. Do not welcome casting queries from actors. No unsolicited demo tapes or video show reels.

Holmes Associates Ltd/Holmes Productions plc

10–16 Rathbone Street, London W1P 1AH
Tel (01) **637 8251** Fax (01) **637 9024**
Contact Stephen Taylor, Andrew Holmes

> Film and video for both broadcast and non-broadcast TV. *Output: Piece of Cake* (LWT drama); *Arts Weekly* and *Well Being* (Channel 4 documentaries); *Chish 'n' Fips* (Central TV); *Video & Chips* (HTV); *Four Up Two Down* (Channel 4 music programme). Always use casting directors; do not welcome casting queries from actors. 'Our needs, when they occur, are very specific, and it just isn't worth your while sending us material "on spec" — we won't have time to look at it.'

ICM International

ICM House, 53–55 Frith Street, London W1V 5TE
Tel (01) **434 0929**
Contact Linda Lewis

> Prominent makers of corporate videos for major commercial and industrial clients.

Ice International Video Films Ltd

31–33 King Street West, Manchester M3 2PN
Tel (061) **834 3992**
Contact David Kent-Watson (executive director)

> TV commercials and films; video presentations. Welcome casting queries from actors. Send CV with photograph. Also welcome demo tapes and video show reels. 'Films are budget — outside UK, usually exotic. Opportunities for actors and actresses to gain experience and suntan!'

Illuminations

16 Newman Passage, London W1P 3PE
Tel (01) **580 7877** Telex **23152** MONRET G
Contact Linda Zuck

Primarily a documentary production company, making cultural programmes for a Channel 4 audience. *Output: State of the Art*, six-part documentary series; *Ghosts in the Machine*, six-part video series; plus other documentaries about art and TV.

Imagicians

5 Newburgh Street, London W1V 1LH
Tel (01) **439 2244** Fax (01) **734 6813** Telex **299200** MOLI G
Contact Alan Scales

Diverse productions, from TV documentary features to in-flight videos. *Output: The Great Palace: The Story of Parliament.*

Independent Business Television Ltd

22–25 Portman Close, London W1A 4BE
Tel (01) **487 4474** Fax (01) **997 8738** Telex **24672** CFSLAB
Contact Sue Tramontini, Patrick Veale

Corporate film and video. Always use casting directors. Do not welcome casting queries from actors, but will consider demo tapes for voice-overs.

Independent Film Production Associates

87 Dean Street, London W1V 5AA
Tel (01) **734 3847** Fax (01) **734 0776** Telex **265871** Ref: MMU **441**
Contact Aileen McCracken

Makers of documentary and entertainment TV, plus corporate video.

Infovision Ltd

63 White Lion Street, London N1 9PP
Tel (01) **837 0012**
Contact John Mayhew (managing director)

Corporate video makers in the area of training, marketing and internal communications. Household-name clients.

In-House Corporate Video

Boundary House, Old Warwick Road, Lapworth, Warwicks. B94 6LU
Tel (05643) **3958**
Contact John Pluck

Corporate film and video programmes — training and marketing. Do not welcome casting queries from actors. 'Few opportunities for actors, and it is generally not worth getting in touch. Actors and presenters are hired through agents.'

Insight Productions Ltd

Gidleigh Studio, Gidleigh, Chagford, Newton Abbot, Devon TQ13 8HP
Contact Brian Skilton

Feature film, arts, documentary, entertainment, drama (TV). *Output: Playing Away* (Film 4 International); *Dartmoor, the Threatened Wilderness* (4 one-hour environmental documentaries); *Streets Ahead* (contemporary dance & music). Use casting directors, but welcome casting queries from actors. Write in the first instance. No voice-over opportunities currently; do not welcome unsolicited demo tapes or video show reels.

Integrated Video
5 Burton Close, Harpenden, Herts. AL5 4QT
Tel (05827) **64302/460921**
Contact Graham Reed, Dave Howell

> Video — promotional, pop and corporate. Use casting directors, but also welcome casting queries from actors. Will consider demo tapes and video show reels.

Interesting Television Ltd
Boundary House, Old Warwick Road, Lapworth, Warwicks. B94 6LU
Tel (05643) **3958**
Contact John Pluck

> Independent broadcast TV productions — documentaries and popular factual programmes. Although they do not in general welcome casting queries from actors, they will consider query letters. 'There are very few opportunities for actors apart from possible drama-documentaries and voice-overs. We would like to hear from actors with an interest in our main areas of production. We also use well-known actors to present programmes.'

International Broadcasting Trust
2 Ferdinand Place, London NW1 8EE
Tel (01) **482 2847** Telex **946240 Attn 19020600**
Contact Anthony Isaacs, Paddy Carlton

> Documentary company specializing in Third World issues. No opportunities for actors.

Iona Productions
22 Woodstock Street, London W1R 1HF
Tel (01) **493 8623** Fax (01) **493 1538** Telex **262187** ACTION G
Contact Alan Wright, Michelle Arnold

> Broadcast drama and documentary. *Output*: *Land* (BBC); *Route 66* (Central TV); *Beyond Belief* (Channel 4). Welcome letters with photographs for their files, 'but unless casting, there just isn't time to see actors.' Will consider demo tapes for voice-overs.

Peter Isaac Ltd
94 High Street, Bildeston, Suffolk IP1 7EB
Tel (0449 741) **248**
Contact Peter Isaac

> Film, video, TV, documentary, commercials. Special interest in medical subjects and animal husbandry.

Paul Joyce Productions
5 Townley Road, Dulwich, London SE22
Tel (01) **693 6006**
Contact Paul Joyce

> Development and production of drama, documentary, music, arts, adventure and current affairs TV and cinema. *Output*: *Nothing as It Seems*; *Summer Lightening* (Film on 4); *Tickets for the Titanic: Everyone a Winner* with Jonathan Pryce and Anna Carteret.

Kay Communications Ltd

Gauntley Court Studios, Gauntly Court, Nottingham NG7 5HD
Tel (0602) 781333 Fax (0602) 783734
Contacts John Alexander, Gary Hope

Makers of industrial video programmes and training programmes.

Kestrel II Ltd

23 Hamilton Gardens, London NW8 9PU
Tel (01) 586 8602
Contact Irving Teitelbaum

Film and TV – feature films and documentaries. *Output: Fatherland* (feature film); *About Now* (documentary). Always use casting directors; do not welcome casting queries from actors. No unsolicited demo tapes or video show reels.

King Rollo Films Ltd

Dolphin Court, High Street, Honiton, Devon EX14 8LS
Tel (0404) 45218/9 Fax (0404) 45328 Telex 24637 WIGMOR
Contact Clive Juster

Animated films for TV – mostly for children but some for adults. *Output: Mr Benn; King Rollo; The Adventures of Spot; Ric.* Do not welcome casting queries from actors as this is inappropriate to their work, but will consider demo tapes for voice-overs if relevant to their specialist output. 'For our type of work, it is useful to know if actors can also sing!'

Knaves Acre Productions

The Crest, Hoe Lane, Abinger Hammer, Dorking, Surrey RH5 6RL
Tel (0306) 731007
Contact Brian Izzard

Makers of broadcast television, principally for Channel 4 and ITV. Unusual biographies of unusual composers, comedy (particularly sit-com), popular drama (live soaps). *Output: The Middle of the Road* (HTV); *The Garden of Evelyn* (Channel 4); *Video Alice*, 90-minute special (Channel 4).

LTV Productions

147 Newline, Greengates, Bradford, W. Yorks. BD10 0BU
Tel (0274) 614809
Contact Simon Allison

Video drama, documentary, commercials.

Landseer Film & Television Productions

100 St Martin's Lane, London WC2N 4AZ
Tel (01) 240 3161

Drama, documentary, music, arts, children's, adventure and current affairs TV. *Output: Mr Pye* with Derek Jacobi; *A Penny for Your Dreams*, co-production with BBC Wales and S4C.

Lawson Productions Ltd

2 Clarendon Close, London W2 3NS and 8489 West Third Street, Los Angeles, California 90048, USA
Tel (01) 706 3111
Contact Sarah Lawson

Film and TV – drama and comedy. *Output: You Again?* (NBC comedy series for

USA); *The Dawning* (feature film); *That's Love* (TVS comedy series). Always use casting directors; do not welcome casting queries from actors.

Lewis Productions

Unit 3, River Gardens Business Centre, Feltham, Middx
Tel (01) **890 1111** Fax (01) **751 5797**
Contact Jonathan Lewis (managing director), Caroline Hardy (project manager)

Film and video — in-house promotional. Do not use casting directors. Welcome casting queries from actors. Send letter in the first instance. Will consider demo tapes and video show reels.

Limehouse Productions

Limehouse Studios, Canary Wharf, West India Docks, London E14 9SJ
Tel (01) **987 2090** Telex **296149** LIMHSE D
Contact Janet Walker, Terence Pritchard

Dramatic adaptations made for TV and video. *Output: But What if It's Raining?; Rocket to the Moon; To Have and to Hold.*

Linkward Productions Ltd

Shepperton Studios, Shepperton, Middx
Tel (0932) **562611** Fax (0932) **568989** Telex **929416** MOVIES G
Contact Phil Bowden, Pat Chapman

Video — medical and educational (children's); TV programmes. *Output: Bodytalk* (Channel 4). Occasionally use casting directors, but also welcome casting queries from actors. Write with photograph in the first instance. Will consider demo tapes and video show reels.

Little King Productions

13–14 Bateman Street, London W1V 6EB
Tel (01) **437 9611** Fax (01) **734 7143**
Contact Dr Simon Nicholas, Simon Manley Cooper

Film and video documentary (mainly medical). Do not generally welcome casting queries from actors, but will consider demo tapes and video show reels.

London Film Productions Ltd

44a Floral Street, London WC2E 9DA
Tel (01) **379 3366** Fax (01) **240 7065** Telex **896805**
Contact Rose Baring

Makers of a wide range of international TV and film. *Output: The Scarlet Pimpernel; Kim; Country Girls; Poldark; I Claudius.*

M2 VIDEO

7a Rushbrook Crescent, London E17 5BR
Tel (01) **527 5165**
Contact Peter Muir

Video, documentary, corporate, commercials. Do not welcome casting queries from actors, but will consider demo tapes for voice-overs.

MJW Productions

10 Museum Street, London WC1A 1LE
Tel (01) **379 5847**
Contact Mary Jane Walsh

> Film and TV – mainly arts documentaries, specializing in music. Will consider demo tapes and video show reels.

MNV

7 Althorp Road, Wandsworth Common, London SW17 7ED
Tel (01) **767 7501**
Contact Michael Norman

> Video – corporate communications, training, sales, promotions, exhibitions and conferences. Sometimes use casting directors, but also welcome casting queries from actors. Approach by telephone in the first instance. No unsolicited demo tapes or video show reels.

Magda Films Ltd

The Old Vicarage, Cragg Vale, Hebden Bridge, W. Yorks. HX7 5TB
Tel (0422) **882755**
Contact Lorne Magory

> Film, video, TV, corporate, documentary, children's drama.

Magic Hour Productions Ltd

143 Chatsworth Road, Willesden Green, London NW2 5QT
Tel (01) **459 3074**
Contact Ms D. J. Robinson

> Makers of TV and films for a serious adult audience. TV and feature films, drama series, serials, documentaries, shorts.

Magic Lantern Ltd

Metropolitan Wharf-GBL, Wapping Wall, London E1 9SS
Tel (01) **480 6811** Fax (01) **702 3509**
Contact Bill Johnson, Sylvia Johnson

> Mainly corporate video, training and promotional programmes on both film and video. Clients include: British Airways, RCA Records, Coates Viyella. Sometimes use casting directors, but also welcome casting queries from actors. Approach by telephone in the first instance. Mostly use voice-over actors; will consider demo tapes.

Malone Gill Productions Ltd

16 Newman Passage, London W1P 3PE
Tel (01) **580 6594** Fax (01) **637 1310** Telex **8951182** GECOMS G
Contact Georgina Denison, Mandy Field

> Principally documentary series on film for TV, but some drama and drama documentary. *Output: Vintage: The Story of Wine; Paul Gauguin; The Savage Dream; No Man Hath Seen God; Matisse in Nice; How to Handle a Wine* (all documentaries); *The Ghost Writer* (drama). Do not welcome casting queries from actors, but will consider demo tapes for voice-overs, giving range of accents and dialects. 'Our drama output is so limited that it is simply not worth applying to us speculatively.'

Mar-Com Production

1 Heathlands, Heath Gardens, Twickenham, Middx TW1 4BP
Tel (01) **891 5061**
Contact Shaun Gale, Tina Simmonite

Film and video — corporate drama/documentary. Welcome casting queries from actors. Approach by letter in the first instance, and follow up with a telephone call. Voice-over opportunities: welcome demo tapes and video show reels — 'This is the easiest and quickest way of assessing someone's potential.'

Marking Inc Productions

18 Sandringham Court, Dufours Place, London W1V 1FB
Tel (01) **494 1555**
Contact Stacy Marking

TV drama and drama documentary. *Output: Channel 4 Guide to Genius:* 'Freud' and 'Einstein'. Always use casting directors. Do not particularly welcome casting queries from actors, but 'the one useful piece of information is notification of an upcoming TV performance. But it must be *enough* of a part to be worth catching.'

Martak

Prospect Place, Mill Lane, Alton, Hants. GU34 2SX
Tel (0420) **88011** Fax (0420) **82497**
Contact Tim Cazalet, Bruce Vigar

Video — documentary, corporate. Use casting directors, but also welcome casting queries from actors. Write in the first instance. Will consider demo tapes and video show reels.

Medical & Scientific Productions

PO Box 493, Cookham, Maidenhead, Berks. SL6 9TD
Tel (06285) **31148** Fax (0628) **810029** Telex **849462**
Contact Peter Fogarty

Corporate — medical programmes for health-care professionals.

Meditel Productions Ltd

Bedford Chambers, The Piazza, Covent Garden, London WC2 8HA
Tel (01) **836 9216/9364** Fax (01) **831 9498** & (01) **405 1656** Telex **262284 Ref: 3348**
Contact Joan Shenton, Jad Adams

Intelligent documentaries; afternoon programmes, factually based but with an element of fun; evening programmes with hard story lines. *Output: Who Cares?*, series of four health-care documentaries; *Kill or Cure?*, two series on the international drugs industry; *10 Million*, two consumer series for the over-60s.

Merchant Ivory Productions

46 Lexington Street, London W1R 3LE
Tel (01) **437 1200** Fax (01) **734 1570** Telex **94013757** MIPLG
Contact Paul Bradley

Output: Maurice; The Deceivers; Room with a View; Slaves of New York; The Europeans; Heat and Dust; The Bostonians. Use casting directors, but also welcome casting queries from actors. Approach by letter in the first instance. Will consider demo tapes and video show reels.

Mersey Casting
35 Brookside, West Derby, Liverpool L12 0BA
Tel (051) **259 1602** Fax (051) **708 7750**
Contact Dorothy Andrew

> Film, TV, video — pop videos and commercials. *Output: Brookside* and all Mersey TV programmes; *First of the Summer Wine* and *Truckers* (BBC); *Business as Usual* (feature film).

Metropolis Pictures Ltd
147 Crouch Hill, London N8 9QH
Tel (01) **340 4649**
Contact Nick Dubrule, Elizabeth Taylor-Mead

> Film for TV: documentary and drama documentary. Feature films in development. *Output: Of Muppets and Men; John Cooper-Clarke — Ten Years in an Open-necked Shirt; Pottery Ladies; My Mama Done Told Me.* Always use casting directors. Do not welcome casting queries from actors.

Midnight Films Ltd
26 Soho Square, London W1V 5FT
Tel (01) **434 0011** Fax (01) **434 9625** Telex **268157**
Contact Iain Brown, Juliet Naylor

> Film — documentary and pop promos. *Output: White City* (film); *Pretenders: The Singles* (documentary). Do not welcome casting queries from actors.

John Mills Video Productions
11 Hope Street, Liverpool L1 9BJ
Tel (051) **709 9822**
Contact Andrew Mills

> Video documentary, sales and training films. Clients include: Nabisco, AC Delco, Alfred McAlpine. Welcome casting queries from actors. Approach by letter in the first instance. Will consider demo tapes and video show reels.

Mosaic Film & Video Productions
68 Clarence Road, Teddington, Middx TW11 0BW
Tel (01) **977 5554**
Contact Adrian Antrum

> Film, video and TV documentaries; training and public service films. Always use casting directors; do not welcome casting queries from actors. 'It always benefits actors to be punctual, reliable and consistent in all aspects of their work. To be truthful about their abilities is a must. Don't say you can ride a horse or drive a car just to get the job! You won't be thanked for the result.'

Moving Direction
Ground floor, 97 Strawberry Vale, Twickenham, Middx TW15 4SJ
Tel (01) **891 2604**
Contact Shaun Gale (director/producer)

> Makers of documentary and fictional productions on video and film. *Output: Truckers Delight; Dick Head* (gangster spoof for children's TV).

Moving Picture Company
25 Noel Street, London W1V 3RD
Tel (01) **434 3100** Fax (01) **437 3951**
Contact David Jeffers

> Drama and documentary for TV, corporate video and commercials. *Output: In the Shadow of Fujisan* (BBC); *Heinz Superchamps* (children's programme for Channel 4); *The Assam Garden* and *Stormy Monday* (features).

Multicord Video & Audio-Visual Studios
1–6 Ravensworth View, Dunston, Gateshead NE11 9DG
Tel (091) **460 9209**
Contact Ken McKenzie

> Video, mainly documentary and industrial; radio commercials. Do not use casting directors; welcome casting queries from actors. Write in the first instance. Voice-over opportunities for experienced actors. Will consider demo tapes and video show reels.

Multiple Image Productions
Milton Road Baths, Milton Road, Swindon SN1 5JA
Tel (0793) **611741**
Contact John Hay, Tim Langford

> Non-broadcast drama and documentary. *Output: We're Not Mad ... We're Angry!* (drama/documentary); *Looking Back* (drama). Do not use casting directors; welcome casting queries from actors. Approach either by letter or telephone in the first instance. Will consider demo tapes and video show reels.

Network 5
11 Ospringe Road, London NW5 2JA
Tel (01) **267 9492**
Contact Kathy O'Neil

> TV current affairs, documentary and drama. Welcome casting queries from actors. Approach by letter in the first instance. Will consider demo tapes and video show reels.

Normandy Film Productions
49 Observatory Road, East Sheen, London SW14 7QB
Tel (01) **878 2646**
Contact David Turnbull

> Broadcast TV: documentary and drama. *Output: The Song and the Story*, Prix Jeunesse winner (Munich 1982), BAFTA nominated.

North West Video Productions
9a New Street, Carnforth, Lancs. LA5 9BX
Tel (0524) **735774**
Contact Steve Le Cheminant (managing director)

> Corporate and training videos. Clients include: K Shoes, British Steel, Rexei.

Original Film & Video Productions Ltd
13 Bateman Street, London W1V 6EB
Tel (01) **734 9721** Fax (01) **734 7143**
Contact Boyd Catling, Julie Marler, Lisa Jenks

> Corporate video, sponsored film documentaries, commercials, video publishing,

broadcast. Always use casting directors. Do not welcome casting queries from actors, but will consider demo tapes and video show reels.

Original Image Ltd
3 Grosvenor Gardens, London SW1 0BD
Tel (01) **630 7552** Fax (01) **630 5893** Telex **8956658** TPSH
Contact Edward Riseman, Nick Scott

> Makers of drama and documentary programmes. *Output*: *Lichfield on Photography*; *Daley Thompson's Bodyshop* (Channel 4).

Pace Productions Ltd
12 The Green, Newport Pagnell, Bucks. MK16 0JW
Tel (0908) **618767** Fax (0908) **617641**
Contact Chris Pettit, Aileen Spankie

> Film and video – drama, commercials, documentaries, corporate. Clients include: Inland Revenue, Kodak, Crayola. Rarely use casting directors, preferring to deal with agents, but will consider letters and keep them on file. Welcome demo tapes for voice-overs. 'Prefer actors with some camera experience, but not averse to giving some their first break. At casting sessions, listen to the way the director wants the character played. Do not lose native accents.'

Pacesetter Productions Ltd
New Barn House, Leith Hill Lane, Ockley, Surrey RH5 5PH
Tel (0306) **70433** Fax (0306) **881021**
Contact Adele Spencer

> Feature and documentary films, TV, corporate and educational material.

Palace Productions
16–17 Wardour Mews, London W1V 3FF
Tel (01) **734 7060**
Contact Stephen Wooley, Nik Powell

> *Output*: *Company of Wolves*; *Letter to Brezhnev*; co-produced *Absolute Beginners*. Use casting directors, but also welcome casting queries from actors. Write in the first instance.

Peak Viewing Film & Video Productions Ltd
130 Canalot Production Studios, 222 Kensal Road, London W10 5BN
Tel (01) **969 7139**
Contact Wendy Smith

> Film, video – documentary and drama/documentary. Welcome letter with photograph and CV. Greater opportunities in voice-overs; will consider demo tapes.

Picture Palace Productions Ltd
65–69 Beak Street, London W1R 3LF
Tel (01) **439 9882** Fax (01) **734 8574**
Contact Malcolm Craddock, Tim O'Mara

> Film/video: commercials, drama, documentary TV programmes, corporate. *Output*: *Ping Pong* (feature film); *Tandoori Nights* (Channel 4 comedy drama series); *Eurocops – Hunting the Squirrel* (Channel 4 drama). Always use casting directors; do not welcome casting queries from actors.

Picture Partnership Productions

73 Newman Street, London W1
Tel (01) **637 8056**
Contact Brian Eastman

Feature films and popular entertainment TV, with the emphasis on comedy. *Output: Father's Day* (Channel 4); *Blott on the Landscape* (BBC); *Whoops Apocalypse; Porterhouse Blue.*

Poseidon Productions Ltd

113–117 Wardour Street, London W1V 3TD
Tel (01) **734 4441/5140**
Contact Frixos Constantine

TV and film makers/distributors, for an adult, educated art-loving audience. *Output: Pavlova* (drama); series for Channel 4 on the Greek philosophers.

Primetime Television Ltd

Seymour Mews House, Seymour Mews, Wigmore Street, London W1H 9PE
Tel (01) **935 9000** Fax (01) **487 3975** Telex **22872** TV FILM G
Contact Madeline Warburg & Deirdre Simms (directors), Helen Stroud (assistant to directors)

Specialize in international co-productions: adult and family drama series/serials and TV films. *Output: Nicholas Nickleby* and *Deliberate Death of a Polish Priest* (filmed theatre productions); *John Silver's Return to Treasure Island, Seal Morning, Lost Belongings* and *Fortunes of War* (drama series); *Durrell in Russia, Ourselves and Other Animals* and *Amateur Naturalist* (natural history documentaries). Always use casting directors. Do not welcome casting queries from actors, and they rarely have a chance to view video show reels sent on the off-chance. 'We tend to collect initial casting ideas by reference to *Spotlight* or other casting directories, and request biographical details from agents to follow up. Having approached a number of agents for availabilities, we are generally prepared at this stage to accept suggestions from the agents already approached.'

Priory Production Ltd

40 Priory Road, Kew, Richmond, Surrey TW9 3DH
Tel (01) **940 9062**
Contact Alexandra Collison

Film, video and TV documentaries. Do not welcome casting queries from actors. No unsolicited demo tapes or video show reels.

The Production Pool Ltd

52 Tottenham Street, London W1P 9PG
Tel (01) **323 0691**
Contact Ann Wingate

Film and TV drama. *Output: Making Waves*, short film for screen and Channel 4.

Professional Magnetics Ltd

Cassette House, 329 Hunslet Road, Leeds LS10 1NJ
Tel (0532) **706066** Fax (0532) **718106** Telex **55293** CHACOM G PROTAPE
Contact Hilary Rhodes, Barrie Rhodes

Video – corporate, sales and training. Do not use casting directors; welcome casting queries from actors. 'We frequently use voice-overs on our technical videos, and welcome demo tapes or show reels for casting purposes.'

Public Image Productions Ltd
22–25 Portman Close, London W1A 4BE
Tel (01) **487 4474** Fax (01) **997 8738** Telex **24672** CFSLAB
Contact Sue Tramontini, Patrick Veale

Drama and documentary. Always use casting directors. Do not welcome casting queries from actors, but will consider demo tapes for voice-overs.

Purves, Wickes Video Projects Ltd
11 West Street, London WC2H 9NE
Tel (01) **240 2756**
Contact Peter Purves, Alan Wickes

Video – corporate and training. Clients include: BT Mobile Communications, Dunlop Oil & Marine, British Gas, Midland Bank. Occasionally use casting directors, but will consider letters from actors 'though our output using actors has been limited'. Will consider demo tapes and video show reels. 'On our side of the business, we are invariably looking for someone very specific, and our advice would be not to get disillusioned when you miss out on parts which, on the face of it, would seem to fit you to perfection.'

Quad Production Company
Studio One, 2 Downshire Hill, London NW3 1NR
Tel (01) **435 6953**
Contact Andy Dean, Graham Grimshaw

Promotional and training programmes for commerce and industry. Radio commercials. Specialize in property, financial services and engineering.

Quanta Ltd
44 Newman Street, London W1P 3PA
Tel (01) **580 7222/7223**
Contact Nicholas Jones

Documentary makers, specializing in science. Also produce interactive corporate material.

Ragdoll Productions
34 Harbourne Road, Edgbaston, Birmingham B15 3AA
Tel (021) **454 5453/4344**
Contact Anne Wood

Makers of children's TV programmes. *Output*: *Pob's Programme* and *Pob's Playtime* (Channel 4); *Playbox* (Central TV).

Alvin Rakoff Productions Ltd
1 The Orchard, London W4 1JZ
Tel (01) **994 1269** Fax (01) **995 3191**
Contact Alvin Rakoff

Film, video and TV drama. *Output*: *Paradise Postponed* (TV series); *Mr Halpern & Mr Johnson* (TV drama); *A Voyage Round My Father* (TV film); *Dirty Tricks* (feature film). Always use casting directors; do not welcome casting queries from actors. 'Ours is a small personal company formed to supply the services of the director, Alvin Rakoff, and his actress wife. It does not have the personnel or time to answer actors' queries.'

Cyril Randell Pictures Ltd
47 Brewer Street, London W1R 3FD
Tel (01) **437 3331** Fax (01) **734 4166** Telex **261426** ADFONE G
Contact Jeremy Phipps

> Film, video and TV — documentary. Always use casting directors; do not welcome casting queries from actors. Occasional voice-over opportunities, but do not welcome unsolicited demo tapes.

Recorded Picture Company
8–12 Broadwick Street, London W1V 1FH
Tel (01) **439 0607** Fax (01) **434 1192** Telex **9419035**

> Feature films. Always use casting directors. Willing to give telephone information on current casting information — i.e. name of casting director involved. Credits include: *The Last Emperor* and *Merry Christmas Mr Lawrence*.

Rediffusion Films Ltd
Buchanan House, 3 St James's Square, London SW1Y 4LS
Tel (01) **925 0550** Fax (01) **839 2135** Telex **919673**
Contact Jette Bonnevie

> Video (training and educational); film and TV drama. *Output: The Irish RM* (Channel 4); *The Bostonians* (feature film). Use casting directors, but will consider demo tapes and video show reels.

Red Rooster Films
11–13 Macklin Street, London WC2B 5NH
Tel (01) **405 8147**
Contact Linda James, Christian Routh

> Independent film and TV production company, with productions ranging from drama series and feature films to documentaries, all destined for international distribution. A speciality in the past has been quality drama for children. *Output: Joni Jones* (five-part drama series about 1940s Welsh childhood); *Coming Up Roses* (feature film for SC4); *The Falcon's Malteser* (comedy feature film).

Regent Productions
235 Regent Street, London W1A 2JT
Tel (01) **493 1610**
Contact William G. Stewart, Christine Rye

> Drama, situation comedy, current affairs, quiz shows. *Output: The Lady Is a Tramp; Tickets for the Titanic* (Channel 4 series); *Fifteen-to-One; The Nineteenth Hole*. Use casting directors; do not welcome casting queries from actors. Occasionally consider demo tapes for voice-overs.

Renaissance Vision
Unit 16, Drayton Industrial Estate, Taverham Road, Drayton, Norwich NR8 6RL
Tel (0603) **260280**
Contact Brian Gardner

> Corporate video, 16mm films, documentaries and commercials. Welcome casting queries from actors: approach by letter in the first instance. Will consider demo tapes and video show reels. 'We already have several contacts, but we are always interested to hear from different people.'

Right Angle Productions Ltd
31 Ransomes Dock, 35 Parkgate Road, London SW11 4NP
Tel (01) **228 9968** Fax (01) **223 8116**
Contact Anise Driessen, Mike Goodman

> Corporate video. Occasionally use casting directors. Will consider demo tapes and video show reels.

Riverfront Pictures Ltd
Dock Cottages, Peartree Lane, Glamis Road, London E1 9SR
Tel (01) **481 2939**
Contact Jeff Perks, Tony Freeth (producer/directors)

> Arts, comedy, documentary, drama, music and young people's programmes. *Output: Our Lives, A Wee Bit Cheeky, Everyone a Special Kind of Artist, Breaking Through, The New Eastenders, Cola Cowboys, Raag Rung* and *Chorus Theatre of Manipur* (all for Channel 4); *Night Moves* (for BBC).

SBM Vision Ltd
1 Whitfield Place, London W1P 5SF
Tel (01) **387 9808** Fax (01) **387 9106**
Contact Mike Brown

> Corporate video programmes for training, information and marketing. Do not welcome casting queries from actors. 'We use actors occasionally in recreating business situations. We also use professional presenters on camera and as voice-overs. However, the person appointed to direct a drama is responsible for suggesting the cast who will then be auditioned.'

Sands Films Ltd
Grice's Wharf, 119 Rotherhithe Street, London SE16 4NF
Tel (01) **231 2209** Telex **886040** SANDS G Fax (01) **231 2119**
Contact Trevor Ingman

> Feature films. *Output: Little Dorrit.* Welcome casting queries from actors. Send letter with CV and photograph.

The Saville Group
Millfield Lane, Nether Poppleton, York YO2 6PQ
Tel (0904) **782782** Fax (0904) **782700**
Contact Sue Atkinson, Sue Rhodes

> Video — training, promotional, corporate. Sometimes use casting directors, but welcome 'intelligent' casting queries from actors. Approach in writing in the first instance. Welcome demo tapes and video show reels: 'We often require actors for voice-overs.'

Scan Film Productions
30 Heol Aradur, Danes Court, Llandaff, Cardiff CF5 2RE
Tel (0222) **552469** Telex **497492** CHACOM G ATT SCAFIL
Contact Frances Gallaher, Geoffrey Thomas, Robert Thomas

> Film, TV, video — drama documentary and commercials. *Output: The Welsh Connection* (drama/documentary series); *George Borrow* (drama series); *Pastor Dan* (drama). Do not welcome casting queries from actors.

Scimitar Films Ltd
6–8 Sackville Street, London W1X 1DD
Tel (01) **734 8385**
Contact Michael Winner (chairman)

> Feature films for the international market. *Output: The Sentinel; The Big Sleep; Death Wish I, II and III; The Wicked Lady; Appointment with Death; Chorus of Disapproval.*

Shand Pictures Ltd
Rosehill House, Rose Hill, Burnham, Bucks. SL1 8NN
Tel (06286) **5129**
Contact Ian Shand

> Documentaries, commercials, TV, feature films. *Output: Wombling Free* (feature film); *Homes of History* (TV series); training and corporate videos. Use casting directors, but welcome casting queries from actors. Write in the first instance. Voice-over opportunities. Will consider demo tapes and video show reels.

Skyline Productions Ltd
1st floor, 24 Scala Street, London W1P 1LU and 4 Picardy Place, Edinburgh EH1 3JT
Tel (01) **631 4649** Fax (01) **436 6209** and Tel (031) **557 4580** Fax (031) **558 1555**
Contact Steve Clark-Hall (London), Trevor Davis (Edinburgh)

> Major supplier of programmes to Channel 4, Skyline also make health, educational and corporate films. *Output: Years Ahead, Radicals, 98 Not Out, Roy and Bob* (all for Channel 4).

Smith Bundy Video & Film
10a The Pavement, Clapham Common, London SW4 0HY
Tel (01) **627 1109**
Contact Beryl Richards, Gill Brown

> Video (training, commercials); documentaries for broadcast TV. *Output: Dispatches* (Channel 4); *Moving Away from Home* (drama for Shelter). Use casting directors, but also welcome casting queries from actors. Write in the first instance with 'short' CV. 'Turn up on time for auditions. Let us know if you are substantially younger or older than the part you are up for. Send a note if you are appearing on television and have worked with us in the past – that way we may remember you!'

Spectacle Films Ltd
16 Chelmsford Road, London E11 1BS
Tel (01) **539 2306**
Contact Roger Ashton-Griffiths

> Film and video drama; business TV. Always use casting directors, and therefore do not welcome casting queries from actors. 'In common with most people, we look for what we want *when* we want it and not otherwise. This company is run by people with an acting background, so we are quite well placed to emphasize that the only route to the studio floor for an actor is through a casting director via an agent. The first qualification an actor needs is sufficient tenacity to get an agent – without this, therefore, there is no hope.'

Spectre Productions
41 & 45 Beak Street, London W1R 3LE
Tel (01) **439 1381** Telex **94013376** LARG G
Contact Simon Hartog

Film and TV drama. *Output: Further & Particular; The Return.* Do not welcome casting queries from actors. 'Don't bother a small company with intermittent production. We'll use a casting director.'

Strictly The Business Ltd
60 The Bond, Hanover Street, Newcastle upon Tyne NE1 3NF
Tel (091) **232 1818**
Contact Robert Smeaton, Andy Mathews

Pop videos, training films, drama and documentary. Use a local casting director when necessary. Do not welcome casting queries from actors.

Supervision Ltd
St Andrews House, 17 St Andrews Road, Croydon, Surrey CR0 1AB
Tel (01) **680 4612** Fax (01) **680 3127**
Contact Charles Marriott (director/producer)

Film and video — documentary, industrial and corporate.

Swanlind Ltd
The Production Centre, Stafford Road, Fordhouses, Wolverhampton WV10 7EL
Tel (0902) **784848/789212** Fax (0902) **788840** Telex **338490**
Contact Mike Davies, Tom Coyne

Video and TV — drama, documentary, commercials, corporate. *Output: Great Western Railway* (Channel 4); *Ar-y-Frordd* (S4C Welsh motoring series); *Hidden Attractions* and *It's No Big Deal* (award-winning dramas). Use casting directors, but welcome casting queries from actors. Approach by letter in the first instance. No unsolicited demo tapes or video show reels.

The Television Cooperative
7 Strath Terrace, London SW11 1RF
Tel (01) **223 4951**
Contact John Underwood

Production cooperative specializing in the media, arts, politics, making documentary TV. *Output: Ireland, the Silent Voices* (Channel 4), *A Beauty Awakes* (National Trust); *Between Object and Image* (British Council).

Teliesyn
3 Mount Stuart Square, The Docks, Cardiff CF1 6EE
Tel (0222) **480911** Fax (0222) **481552**
Contact Mary Simmonds, Richard Staniforth

Film and video — broadcast TV drama, documentary music and sport. Involved in the Celtic Film Festival and Cyfle (Welsh language film training course). *Output: Will Six* (1920s period drama); *Paris—Dakar Motor Rally; Dihirod Dyfed* (West Wales murder series); *In Two Minds* (feature film); *Cracking Up* (documentary series for Channel 4).

Topaz Productions Ltd
Manchester House, 46 Wormholt Road, London W12 0LS
Tel (01) **749 2619**
Contact Anne Taylor

> Corporate and broadcast TV. Clients include: Lloyds Bank, GKN, Alliance &
> Leicester Building Society. Usually use a casting director, but also welcome casting
> queries from actors. Send a letter with SAE in the first instance. 'We constantly use
> *Spotlight*, and suggest it is almost a prerequisite for actors to take space in this
> publication. It rarely happens that an actor writing in is suitable for imminent
> casting; they are better off concentrating mail shots to individual casting directors
> rather than small, independent companies.'

Torbay Video
58 Dolphin Crescent, Paignton, Devon TQ3 1JZ
Tel (0803) **558138**
Contact David C. Jackson

> Industrial videos. Do not welcome casting queries from actors, but will consider
> demo tapes for voice-overs.

Transport in Vision
20 Chancellors Street, London W6 9RL
Tel (01) **741 8691**
Contact Barry Coward

> Film and video documentary. Do not welcome casting queries from actors, but
> will consider demo tapes for voice-overs.

Transworld TV Productions Ltd
Whitecrook Centre, Whitecrook Street, Clydebank, Glasgow G81 1QS
Tel (041) **952 4816**
Contact Peter McNeill, Mr F. Taylor

> Video, non-broadcast TV (documentary). Clients include: Glasgow Airport, John
> Brown Engineering, Clydesdale Bank, Silverstream Films, Rolls Royce Hillington.
> Welcome casting queries from actors. Approach in writing in the first instance.
> Will consider demo tapes and video show reels.

Tridec Television Ltd
2 Dinsdale Road, Croft Industrial Estate, Bromborough, Wirral, Cheshire L62 3PY
Tel (051) **334 7939/9346**
Contact Belinda Talbot Smith

> Industrial and commercial video covering corporate, training, promotion, sales
> and public information. Use casting directors, but also welcome casting queries
> from actors. Approach by letter in the first instance. Will consider demo tapes and
> video show reels. 'A great proportion of our requirement is for new and
> interesting voice-overs. Please be quite clear what rate is going to be charged,
> and do not think that you can record a voice-over without some experience and
> practise.'

Tripod Films Ltd
111a Wardour Street, London W1V 3TD
Tel (01) **439 0729** Fax (01) **437 0304**
Contact Evan Morgans

> Film and video — TV documentary, corporate, commercials.

Triskel Communications Ltd
55 East Street, Epsom, Surrey KT17 1BP
Tel (03727) **42468**
Contact W. A. Eakins, J. Hutchens

> Video — training and education programmes in the field of finance; company promotional videos. Do not welcome casting queries from actors, but will consider demo tapes and video show reels.

Turners Film & Video Productions/Television Media Associates
Pink Lane House, 7–15 Pink Lane, Newcastle upon Tyne NE1 5HT
Tel (091) **232 1809** Fax (091) **232 9823**
Contact John Grant, Stephen Salam

> Film and video: TV documentary, commercials and dramatized documentary. Always use casting directors, but welcome demo tapes for voice-overs.

Turnham Productions Ltd
1st floor, 28 Poland Street, London W1V 3DB
Tel (01) **437 8281** Fax (01) **439 0152**
Contact Patrick Wallis, Georgina Cole

> Video —mainly corporate, plus training, promotional and instructional. Welcome casting queries from actors. Send letter with CV and photograph. Welcome demo tapes and video show reels, which are then kept in their library. Specialize in foreign voice-overs.

Tyburn Productions Ltd
Pinewood Studios, Iver Heath, Bucks. SL0 0NH
Tel (0753) **651700** Fax (0753) **656844** Telex **847505**
Contact Kevin Francis (managing director), Gillian Garrow (director of research & development)

> Film and video — drama/light entertainment. Producers of TV programme material, specializing in popular drama. *Output: The Masks of Death, Murder Elite* and *The Abbot's Cry* (TV films); *Courier* (TV series). Do not welcome casting queries from actors.

Ty Gwyn Films Ltd
Y Ty Gwyn, Llanllyfni, Caernarfon, Gwynedd LL54 6DG
Tel (0286) **881235**
Contact Gareth Wynn Jones

> Situation comedy, contemporary gritty Welsh subjects, spy thrillers. Bilingual productions. Their primary role is to provide output for the Welsh channel, S4C.

Umbrella Films Ltd
31 Percy Street, London W1P 9FG
Tel (01) **631 0625** Fax (01) **436 9442** Telex **296538** UMBRLA
Contact Simon Perry, Stacy Bell, Marc Samuelson

> Feature films and TV drama. *Output: White Mischief; Nineteen Eighty-Four; Nanou; Another Time, Another Place.* Always use casting directors; do not welcome casting queries from actors. 'Much better to contact casting directors than us as the casting process occupies such a small part of the year and we have no system to store CVs, etc.'

United British Artists

Russell Chambers, Covent Garden, London WC2E 8AA
Tel (01) **240 9891**
Contact Richard Johnson, Peter Shaw

> Feature films and TV drama. *Output: Turtle Diary; Castaway; The Lonely Passion of Judith Hearne; The Biko Inquest* (Channel 4). Sometimes use casting directors, but only welcome casting queries if the actor is known to them. Send letter with 'extensive CV' and photograph; these will then be put on their casting file.

Upstream

Ridings House, 66 Alma Road, Windsor, Berks. SL4 3EZ
Tel (0753) **858895** Fax (0753) **864123**
Contact Allan Bosley

> Corporate film, video and multi-image production. Use casting directors, but welcome casting queries from actors. Send letter in the first instance. Will consider demo tapes and video show reels.

Video Arts Ltd

Dumbarton House, 68 Oxford Street, London W1N 9LA
Tel (01) **637 7288**
Production executive Margaret Tree

> Training videos. Creative team includes John Cleese. Occasionally use casting directors but mainly cast from a core of actors known to the company.

VPS Ltd

22 Brighton Square, Brighton, E. Sussex BN1 1HD
Tel (0273) **728686/821567**
Contact Alan Holden (production director), Tracy Garrett (production manager)

> Film and video — corporate training, medical, interactive video production.

Video at Work

10 King Street Lane, Winnersh, Berks. RG11 5AS
Tel (0734) **790500** Telex **847423** COCRG
Contact Mr G. A. Clarke

> Video, corporate. Use casting directors; do not welcome casting queries from actors. Voice-over opportunities for actors, but will not consider unsolicited demo tapes or video show reels.

Video Express

7 Bedford House, The Avenue, London W4 1UD
Tel (01) **995 2250** Telex **937441**
Contact Beata Romandwski, David Lindsay

> Video — corporate, drama, documentary. Welcome casting queries from actors. Send letter in the first instance. Will consider demo tapes and video show reels.

Video One Professional

155 Baird Street, Glasgow G4 0PT
Tel (041) **552 7865**
Contact Harry Woolfries

> Video: documentary, commercials, training. Clients include: British Rail, Strathclyde Regional Council, Sony Centre. Welcome casting queries from actors. Approach by letter in the first instance. Will consider demo tapes and video show reels.

Videotel Productions/Living Tape Productions
Ramillies House, 1–2 Ramillies Street, London W1V 1DF
Tel (01) **439 6301**
Contact Nick Freethy

> Film, video, TV, mainly but not exclusively of a broadly educational nature. *Output: Catering with Care* (Open College/Channel 4); *Tourism: The Welcome Business* (Open College/Channel 4); *Dead Ahead – AIDS Advice for Seafarers* (Royal Navy).

Vidox Video Productions Ltd
Milton House, Roper Close, Canterbury, Kent CT2 7EP
Tel (0227) **763888** Fax (0227) **450744**
Contact Robin Ochs, Chantal Cleven

> Video – corporate, training, promotional, TV commercials. Use casting directors, but also welcome casting queries from actors. Will consider demo tapes and video show reels. 'We keep all letters on file and keep all show reels. In any production requiring actors, we will first look at the show reels, CVs, etc. that *we* have, before going to agents.'

Virgin Films & Video
328 Kensal Road, London NW10 5XJ
Tel (01) **968 8888**
Contact Mike Watts

> Cinema, educational and animated films. *Output: Gothic* (directed by Ken Russell, 1987); *Absolute Beginners*; *Captive*. No TV at present. Likely to bid for one of Britain's new national commercial radio stations.

The Visual Connection (TVC) Ltd
1 Rostrevor Mews, London SW6 5AZ
Tel (01) **731 6300** Fax (01) **736 9462** Telex **995801 Ref V1**
Contact Hugh Price

> Corporate film and video. Clients include: British Airways, NSPCC, Next. Use casting directors, but also welcome casting queries from actors. Send letter in the first instance. Will consider demo tapes for voice-overs.

Vulgar Productions
3–5 St John's Street, London EC1M 4AE
Tel (01) **608 2131**
Contact Sue Hayes

> Makers of TV programmes. *Output: Arthur & Phil* (Channel 4).

WSTV Productions Ltd
4th floor, Tennyson House, 159–163 Portland Street, London W1N 5FD
Tel (01) **580 5896**
Contact Bill Stewart, Rex Berry, Sian Coombes

> Corporate video, commercials, TV programmes.

The Walnut Production Partnership
Crown House, Armley Road, Leeds LS12 2EJ
Tel (0532) **456913** Telex **265871** MONREF G (**Quote: 72:**MAG**31593**)
Contact Alison Wright (production assistant)

> Corporate video. Sometimes use casting directors, but welcome casting queries

from actors. Approach by letter in the first instance. 'Telephone queries are of little use because of the small amount of drama work we do. However, information received through the post is retained in our files for reference.' Will consider demo tapes and video show reels.

Warner Sisters

21 Russell Street, London WC2B 5HP
Tel (01) **836 0134** Fax (01) **836 6559**
Contact Lavinia Warner, Jane Wellesley

TV and film drama, documentaries. *Output: Tenko; Lizzie – An American Adventure; GI Brides; Wish Me Luck.*

Watershed Television Ltd

53 Queen Square, Bristol BS1 4LH
Tel (0272) **276864**
Contact Ninon Jerome, Jenny Jillich

Corporate film and video; commercials; broadcast drama and documentary. Use casting directors, but also welcome casting queries from actors. Send a letter with photograph. Will consider demo tapes and video show reels, but 'always write first'.

Michael White Productions Ltd

13 Duke Street, St James's, London SW1Y 6DB
Tel (01) **839 3971** Fax (01) **839 3836** Telex **923753**
Contact Michael White

Feature films and theatre. *Output: White Mischief; Rocky Horror Picture Show; Monty Python and the Holy Grail; Ploughman's Lunch; My Dinner with André* and the *Comic Strip* series, including *The Strike.* 'Casting is not done through our office – always through a casting director. The most we can do is tell you if anything is in pre-production and who the casting director is.'

Wood Visual Communications

500 Leeds Road, Bradford, W. Yorks. BD3 9RU
Tel (0274) **732362** Fax (0274) **736164**
Contact David Wood

Film, video and TV – documentaries and commercials. Do not welcome casting queries from actors, but will consider demo tapes for voice-overs.

Working Title Ltd

10 Livonia Street, London W1V 3PH
Tel (01) **439 2424**
Contact Tim Bevan, Sarah Radclyffe

Feature films. Its subsidiary 'Working Title TV Ltd' handles television. *Output: My Beautiful Launderette; Caravaggio; Personal Services; Wish You Were Here; Sammy and Rosie Get Laid; A World Apart; For Queen and Country.* Use casting directors; do not welcome queries from actors.

Wyvern Television Ltd

18 Lansdown Road, Swindon, Wilts. SN1 3NE
Tel (0793) **615615**
Contact Leslie Jenkinson

Film, video, TV – drama, commercials, documentary. Sometimes use casting directors, but welcome casting queries from actors. Send letter with CV and photograph. Will consider demo tapes and video show reels.

Yorkshire Film Company Ltd

Tong Hall, Tong, Bradford, W. Yorks. BD4 0RR
Tel (0532) **853113** Fax (0532) **854811**
Contact Keith Hardy

> Film and video — corporate, training, information, TV commercials. 'Actors are quite frequently used — video compilations of any actor's range of work might be useful.'

Greg Younger Associates

Barons Croft, Hare Lane, Blindley Heath, Surrey RH7 6JA
Tel (0342) **832515** Fax (0342) **833768**
Contact Greg Younger, Christine Younger

> Film, video, TV, documentaries, commercials, corporate, training. *Output*: corporate, training and product video for Ford; corporate and sales video for Canary Wharf.

Yo-Yo Films

108 Grove Park, London SE5 8LE
Tel (01) **733 1806**
Contact Philip Bartlett, Laurens Postma

> Film, video, TV — drama, documentary and commercials. Always use casting directors. Do not welcome casting queries from actors, but will consider demo tapes for voice-overs.

Zenith Productions Ltd

8 Great Titchfield Street, London W1P 7AA
Tel (01) **637 7941**
Contact Scott Meek (head of development)

> Feature films and TV. Formerly the feature arm of Central TV; now owned by Carlton Communications, one of the leading independents. *Output*: *The Hit; The Dead; Insignificance; Wetherby; Personal Services; Prick Up Your Ears; Slam Dance; Wish You Were Here.* Television: *Heart of the Country; Finnegan Begin Again; Fields of Fire; Escape from Sobibor; Inspector Morse.* Always use casting directors — 'not always the same ones'. Do not welcome casting queries from actors. 'Make yourself known to all the main casting directors.'

16. National TV and radio

BBC Radio & Television

BBC Radio Drama

Room 6070, BBC Broadcasting House, London W1A 1AA
Tel (01) **927 4251**
Contact Karen Rose (auditions and publicity assistant)

Radios 3 and 4 transmit some 500 new plays every year – 50 times more than the National Theatre and the Royal Shakespeare Company put together. This output amounts to an annual 96 hours on Radio 3 (1.5 per cent of the total) and 852 hours on Radio 4 (11 per cent). No other country does so many radio plays.

The main slots are on Radio 4:

● **The Monday Play** (repeated on Saturday afternoons – 75 or 90 minutes, sometimes longer). Original plays often on complex themes, but also a showcase for classical stage plays and the occasional dramatization of novels.

● **Saturday Night Theatre** (repeated Monday afternoons – 75 or 90 minutes). Family entertainment with a strong narrative line.

● **The Afternoon Play** (Wednesday & Thursday – 45–55 minutes). A balanced diet of original, entertaining and demanding plays.

● **Thirty-minute Theatre** (Tuesday afternoons). Drama equivalent of the short story.

'To qualify for a radio drama audition, an actor must have had at least a year's professional acting experience with an emphasis on playing as many varied roles as possible, and be resident in the south-east region. Radio experience is not essential but an awareness is. Listen to as much radio drama as possible in order to recognize the range of work the department produces. Unfortunately, it is not enough to merely demonstrate a "pleasant" voice. Once you have done a radio drama audition, it is not possible to re-audition for another eight years. Auditions are not held specifically for the Radio Drama Company. Vacancies are discussed as they occur – some artists may be asked to attend a workshop at a later date; however, these cannot be applied for, although a general drama audition is the first step to this end.' Write to Karen Rose for further information.

BBC Natural History Unit

Broadcasting House, Whiteladies Road, Bristol BS8 2LR
Tel (0272) **73221**
Senior producer Michael Bright

'Actors for Natural History Unit TV programmes are usually obtained via agents, publicity material and *Spotlight*. Actors for Natural History Unit radio programmes (usually narrators for radio features) are obtained via personal contacts. It is useful for actors to send audition tapes (cassette is best), to include straight narrative readings.'

BBC Northern Ireland
Broadcasting House, 25–27 Ormeau Avenue, Belfast BT2 8HQ

Radio Drama
Tel (0232) **244400 ext 516**
Senior radio producer Jeremy Howe

Usually cast from a pool of actors based in Northern Ireland, with additions from the Radio Drama Company, but are interested to hear from actors either living in Northern Ireland or from actors who are going to be working there in the future (give at least two months' notice).

TV drama
Tel (0232) **244400 ext 240**
Head of TV drama Robert Cooper

Welcome casting queries from actors: 'Write, if enquiring about a specific production; telephone, if a general enquiry.' Do not hold general interviews.

BBC Radio Scotland (Drama Department)
27–35 Thistle Street, Edinburgh EH2 1DY
Tel (031) **225 3131**
Contact Stewart Conn (senior producer), Patrick Rayner

'We don't cast exclusively either Scottish actors or for Scottish parts. At the same time, we have an obvious obligation to our catchment area and to artists resident in Scotland. A worthwhile reminder to young actors and those newly out of college is that radio is not the easy option some seem to think, but a specialized field of acting, requiring timing, sensitivity and awareness of expression and considerable technique. For audition purposes, we prefer an indication of someone's emotional and vocal range and an understanding of the text – rather than an ability to double or play what in the theatre would be thought of as character roles.' Welcome letters giving advance notice if actors from the south are coming to work in Scotland. General auditions are held twice yearly.

BBC Scotland (Television Drama)
Queen Margaret Drive, Glasgow G12 8DG
Tel (041) **330 2345**
Head of drama Bill Bryden
Producers Norman McCandlish, Andy Park, Tom Kinninmont, Peter Broughan, Aileen Forsyth

Output has included: *Tutti Frutti*; *The Dunroamin' Rising*; *Down Where the Buffalo Go*; *The Dark Room*. Welcome casting queries from actors, either by telephone or letter. Do not hold general auditions.

BBC Television
Television Centre, Wood Lane, London W12 7RJ
Tel (01) **743 8000**

Casting of actors in BBC TV programmes is the responsibility of individual producers, directors and their production staff. There is no point of contact for general auditions. Producers or directors occasionally engage freelance Casting Advisers for special projects but they do not negotiate fees or contracts. That is the responsibility of the BBC's Artists Contracts department, and members of this department will give general casting advice. (Recently, two members of this department, Sarah Bird and Jonathan McLeish, have been casting and negotiating contracts for such productions as *The Franchise Affair*, *South of the Border*, and *Shadow of the Noose*.)

BBC Wales (TV & Radio)
Broadcasting House, Llantrisant Road, Llandaff, Cardiff CF5 2YQ
Tel (0222) **564888**
Head of drama John Hefin
Contact Dawn Walters (drama manager)

> Welcome casting queries from actors, either by telephone or letter. Will consider demo tapes. Occasionally hold general auditions — usually when planning a major series.

Commercial Television

Anglia Television
48 Leicester Square, London WC2H 7FB and Anglia House, Norwich, Norfolk NR1 3JG
Tel (01) **321 0101** Fax (01) **930 8499** Tel (0603) **615151** Fax (0603) **631032**
Head of drama John Rosenberg
Casting director Pat Jarvis (London office)

> Output includes: *Tales of the Unexpected* series; P. D. James murder mysteries such as *A Taste for Death*; *The Intercom Conspiracy* (directed by John Gorrie).

Border Television
18 Clerkenwell Close, London EC1R 0AA and The Television Centre, Carlisle CA1 3NT
Tel (01) **253 3737** Tel (0228) **25101**

> Very little drama output, apart from two productions in the children's drama series, *Dramarama*. No in-house casting directors.

Central Independent Television
35/38 Portman Square, London W1H 9AH and Central House, Broad Street, Birmingham B1 2JP and East Midland TV Centre, Nottingham NG7 2NA
Tel (01) **486 6688** Tel (021) **643 9898** Tel (0602) **863322**
Controller of drama Ted Childs
Head of casting Barry Ford
Casting directors Jane Arnell, Derek Barnes, Pam O'Connor, Sally Fincher (light entertainment) — all at 8 Great Titchfield Street, London W1

> Large drama output, including: the Birmingham-based series, *Boon*; *Inspector Morse*; *Hard Cases*; *Les Girls* and *The Bretts*.
>
> In 1988, Central Television set up a new film arm, Central Films, to replace Zenith. Managing director: Ted Childs. Recent output has included two mini-series, both filmed in Australia: *Tananmera* and *Edens Lost*; and a TV film, *The Grass Cutter* starring Frances Barber and Ian McElhinney. Central Films use freelance casting directors for each project.

Grampian Television
Queen's Cross, Aberdeen AB9 2XJ
Tel (0224) **646464**

> No drama output, apart from very occasional independent commissions.

Granada Television

Granada TV Centre, Manchester M60 9EA and 36 Golden Square, London W1R 4AH

Tel (061) **832 7211** Tel (01) **734 8080**

Casting directors Carolyn Bartlett (head of casting), Susie Bruffin and Margaret Crawford (London office), James Bain and Judi Hayfield (Manchester office)

> Britain's longest-established independent television company has a very large drama output including series, films and plays. Past successes include: *Brideshead Revisited*, *The Jewel in the Crown* and *The Adventures of Sherlock Holmes*, and *Coronation Street* continues to be as popular as ever. Recent productions include: *Game, Set and Match*; *The Return of Sherlock Holmes*; *The Hound of the Baskervilles*; *A Tale of Two Cities* and *After the War*.

HTV (Wales)

The Television Centre, Culverhouse Cross, Cardiff CF5 6XJ

Tel (0222) **590590**

HTV (West)

The Television Centre, Bath Road, Bristol BS4 3HG

Tel (0272) **778366**

> The Cardiff studios produce both Welsh- and English-language drama.
>
> Following the departure of their head of casting, Liz Jeffries, HTV intend to use freeland casting directors 'as and when required'. The first major drama production made by a British independent, Portman Productions, for HTV is *Voice of the Heart*, based on the Barbara Taylor Bradford novel.

London Weekend Television

South Bank Television Centre, Kent House, Upper Ground, London SE1 9LT

Tel (01) **261 3434**

Head of casting Diana Parry

Casting directors Anthony Arnell, Jane Davies, Nikki Finch, Corinne Rodriguez

> LWT provides a significant proportion of the network's drama, and is also one of the largest suppliers of programmes to Channel 4. Output includes: *Dempsey and Makepeace*; *London's Burning*; *The Charmer*; *Troubles*; *Wish Me Luck*; *Ticket to Ride*; *Bust*; *Piece of Cake*; *Poiret*; *Square Deal*; *The Two of Us*; *Hot Metal*.

Scottish Television

Cowcaddens, Glasgow G2 3PR

Tel (041) **332 9999**

Controller of drama Robert Love

> Scottish Television's networked drama continues to draw increased viewing figures, particularly the Glasgow detective series, *Taggart* starring Mark McManus (two or three 3-part series are screened annually). The networked soap, *Take the High Road*, which is mainly filmed on location at Loch Lomond, consists of 104 twice-weekly episodes each year. Apart from this regular output, they also produce occasional one-off dramas and series such as *Bookie* and *Winners and Losers* (starring Leslie Grantham).
>
> No in-house casting directors. Freelance casting directors have been increasingly employed.

Thames Television

Thames Television House, 306 Euston Road, London NW1 3BB
Tel (01) **387 9494**
Controller of drama Lloyd Shirley
Head of casting Liz Sadler
Casting directors Linda Butcher, Pat Hayley (light entertainment), Pat O'Connell, Julian Oldfield, Shirley Teece (light entertainment), Brian Wheeler (*The Bill*)

> Large drama output, including: *The Bill* (twice weekly); *Rumpole of the Bailey*; *Paradise Postponed*; *King and Castle*; *Gems*; *The London Embassy*; *Hannay*. Thames also has a subsidiary company — Euston Films — which produces filmed drama such as *Minder*, *The Fear* and *Jack the Ripper*.

TSW (Television South West)

Derry's Cross, Plymouth, Devon PL1 2SP
Tel (0752) **663322**

> Very limited drama output, including: *Where There's a Will* (starring Patrick McNee). Freelance casting directors used.

TVS (Television South)

Television Centre, Northam, Southampton SO9 5HZ
Tel (0703) **634211**
Controller of drama Graham Benson

> Output includes: *Gentlemen and Players*; *Act of Betrayal*; *Murder Is Among Us — Simon Wiesenthal*; *Heroes*; Ruth Rendell mysteries such as *A Guilty Thing Surprised* and *Shake Hands Forever*.
> Use freelance casting directors.

Tyne Tees Television

The Television Centre, City Road, Newcastle upon Tyne NE1 2AL
Tel (091) **261 0181**

> No drama department. Very little drama output at present, apart from an adaptation of the Cecil P. Taylor play, *And a Nightingale Sang* (a co-production with Portman Productions).

Ulster Television

Havelock House, Ormeau Road, Belfast BT7 1EB
Tel (0232) **328122**

> Not one of the major drama-producing companies, but output includes: *The Hidden Curriculum*; *The Last of a Dyin' Race* by Christina Reid; *Undertow of the Armada* (for *Dramarama*); *God's Frontiersmen* (a four-part drama documentary on the Scots-Irish emigration to America).
> Use freelance casting directors.

Yorkshire Television

Television House, 32 Bedford Row, London WC1R 4HE and The Television Centre, Leeds LS3 1JS
Tel (01) **242 1666** Tel (0532) **438283**
Head of casting Malcolm Drury (London office)
Casting directors Ruth Boyle and Paddy Stern (London), Linda Kremer (Leeds)

> Output includes: *The Beiderbecke Tapes*; *Emmerdale Farm*; *Cloud Waltzer*; *Dreams Lost, Dreams Found*; *The Refuge*.
> Welcome casting queries — in writing only.

part **3**

people in the business

17. Directors

Directors are having a hard time. For years, their authority was undisputed across stage and screen. Now, these proud monarchs (some might choose to call them despots) are under attack for every known professional vice starting and ending with overweening pride.

The assault is led by the younger theatre actors. Taking their cue from Simon Callow (whose views are vividly presented in his book *Being an Actor*), they accuse directors of ignoring modern drama because this would bring them up against living writers who might have their own ideas on how their plays should be staged, and of hijacking the classics for their own selfish purposes. In Callow's words: 'Instead of using their position to uncover the limitless spectrum of other worlds, other visions of human experience embedded in the range of world drama, they have plundered the past for works on which they can impose their personalities, or exemplify the playing styles of their companies.' Yet, as Simon Callow goes on to argue, 'the idea of a director's style or indeed a company's style seems inherently to threaten the individuality of the work itself.'

Television and film, it has been argued, offer the chance of a more democratic relationship between actors and directors. For Peter Barkworth, writing in his book *About Acting*, 'a television director is a performer too, supervising the cameras' moves and the cuts from one camera to another. He is not just an onlooker.' However, this does not necessarily stop him from wanting to dominate, to force through his own interpretation irrespective of the views of actors or writer.

All that can be said in favour of directors as final arbiters is that they must take the blame for failure — even, if Kingsley Amis is to be believed, the blame for the failure of the entire film industry. Although the director's views can tend towards the dotty, Mr Amis has undoubtedly started heads nodding with approval for his assertion 'that the much-acknowledged decline in cinema audiences may have been largely caused by the increase in the power and standing of the director, who wants to show he is an artist and be damned to the rest of us, and the decrease in those of the producer, who used to try to please the public.'

Given that dissatisfaction with the functions of the director is not just a passing phase (though one does have the feeling that, if the RSC and the National, the source of much ill feeling, pulled themselves together, criticism would be quickly muted), what is the remedy?

The British Actors' Touring Company, set up by Kate O'Mara and Peter Woodward, has, as its name implies, dispensed with directors altogether, while in his latest role as actor-manager, Kenneth Branagh has taken the brave step of inviting fellow actors of great repute to direct the Rennaisance Company's trilogy of Shakespearean productions. For both companies, the results have been entirely encouraging, but while others may follow, the overlapping of the functions of actor and director (or writer and director, for that matter) has limited scope. Those with a talent so wide are a rare breed.

The only alternative is to accept that directors as specialists are here to stay and to give them the training backup that will put them more in sympathy with their actor and writer colleagues.

The question then arises, what sort of training? At the British Theatre Association, one of the few institutions to give the matter the consideration it deserves, Victoria Thompson, Director of Studies, accepts that views on the content of a training programme for directors are many and varied. The briefest examination of the director's task will show why this is so.

> He needs a knowledge of all aspects of theatrical art. Theories of direction and directional exercises are notoriously fickle and cannot be carried over from one production to the next. The basis of the skill lies in confidence and that intangible intuitive sense which can only be effectively gained through experience. The problem is to find an environment in which the young director can make the first stumbling steps towards production without destroying himself or his actors.

That was Bruce Huett writing in *The Stage* nearly 20 years ago, and since then, no one has seriously taken issue with his diagnosis. However, Victoria Thompson believes she is at least close to finding the right training environment with her latest and most ambitious courses. The first is a restructuring of the traditional 13-week course, which now covers directional styles, design, stage management, sound, lighting and allied technical skills, costume, masks, acting craft (including mime, movement technique, stage fighting) and theatre history. All these facets reappear in extended form in a full one-year course, which also takes in a show placement with a working theatre or a major drama school.

No other organization is doing quite so much for directors' education — in fact, there are few organizations doing anything at all. Taking theatre and film schools together, there cannot be more than 200 places a year available for trainee directors.

It should be said that many directors are themselves not unhappy about this state of affairs. One of the foremost young theatre directors, Nicholas Hytner, who traces his development through student opera and regional theatre to the RSC and beyond, believes that, for all its faults, the UK practice of learning by experience is preferable to a system of formal training: '[In Germany] you train, you get your chance, everyone goes to see it; if it's good, you have a career, if it's bad, you don't. That's awful. The best training for a director is to direct.'

No doubt, his opinion will have been noted by the team of professionals set up by the Gulbenkian Foundation to examine directors' training. Due to report shortly, the enquiry has also heard some harsh comments from performers, including one devastating observation from a well-known (but, so far, anonymous) actress:

> 'I've worked with dozens of directors and not one of them was worthy of the name.'

*   *   *

Maria Aitken

Theatre director and actress. Credits include: *Happy Families* and *Private Lives* for the theatre. Devised and presented a chat show on television (*Private Lives*) and also devised a television drama series: *Poor Little Rich Girls*.

Bill Alexander

Theatre director. One of the six associate directors of the Royal Shakespeare Company, the others being John Barton, John Caird, Ron Daniels, Barry Kyle and Adrian Noble. His first production for the RSC was *Richard III* with Antony Sher in 1984. This subsequently transferred to the Barbican and then toured Australia. In 1985, he opened the Stratford season with *The Merry Wives of Windsor* and directed three new productions for the Pit at the Barbican: *Today* by Robert Holman, and *Downchild* and *Crimes in Hot Countries* by Howard Barker. In 1986, *The Merry Wives of Windsor* opened in London and won the Laurence Olivier Award for Best Production. At Stratford in 1986, Bill Alexander directed *A Midsummer Night's Dream* and *Country Dancing* by Nigel Williams, both of which transferred to the Barbican the next year. In 1987, he was artistic director of The Other Place in Stratford and directed *The Merchant of Venice*, *Twelfth Night* and *Cymbeline* there, all of which transferred to London in 1988.

Mike Alfreds

Theatre director and writer. Founded Shared Experience Theatre Company in 1975 (where his credits included *Too True to Be Good* and *The Three Sisters*), and though he has now left and is freelancing, he still works largely with classic texts. Has been voted 'Best Director' by the London critics for the production of *The Cherry Orchard* that he directed for Ian McKellen at the Cottesloe, and has directed and co-written (with Michelene Wandor) a five-hour production of *The Wandering Jew* at the Lyttelton.

In *Plays and Players* (August 1987), he said that he likes to adapt novels for the stage because: '19th-century novelists were frustrated playwrights, perhaps unable to work on the frivolous, artless, stage of that day ... There's a sense of purpose; of meeting; of struggling; something that's lacking in contemporary writing where you get a lot of wit and comment, but rarely any real, rich theatrical blood. There seems to be an inability to mesh together characters and concepts ... technology is crushing the actor. It is the suggestiveness of theatre that is so wonderful, but we're losing it. There's nothing except competence around. We are dull – no one's breaking new ground.' Recent direction includes *Countrymania* by Goldoni at the Olivier.

Jonathan Alwyn

TV producer and director. Credits (all BBC-TV) include: *The Trial of Lady Chatterley*; episodes of *Juliet Bravo*; *By the Sword Divided*; and episodes of *Bergerac*.

Sarah Pia Anderson

Theatre and TV director. Theatre credits: *The Caucasian Chalk Circle* (Crucible Theatre, Sheffield); *The Nest* by Frank Xavier Kroetz; *Rosmersholm* (National Theatre, 1987). TV credits: *A Woman Calling* by Ann Devlin (BBC N. Ireland); *This Is History, Gran* by Robert Holman and *Pity in History* by Howard Barker (both BBC-TV).

Michael Apted

TV and film director. Credits include: *Coal Miner's Daughter* (1980); *Continental*

Divide (1981); *Gorky Park* (1982); *P'tang Yang Kipperbang* (Channel 4, 1982); *First Born* (1984); *28-Up* (Granada TV, 1984); *Bring on the Night* (1985); *Critical Condition* (1986).

Moira Armstrong

TV and video director. Credits include: *Testament of Youth* (1979), *Minor Complications, How Many Miles to Babylon?* (1982), *Freud* (1984) and *Bluebell* (all BBC-TV); *Inside Story* (location video for Anglia).

Michael Attenborough

Theatre director. Son of Sir Richard Attenborough. Was artistic director at Hampstead Theatre for over four years and is now setting up a new production company, Turnstyle. Previous posts include: associate director of the Mercury Theatre, Colchester, Leeds Playhouse and Young Vic; artistic director of Watford Palace Theatre. Recent productions include *The Summer* by David Edgar.

While at Hampstead, he persuaded the Board of the need for a literary manager to cope with the volume of new scripts being sent in — around 600 per year. In an interview with Robert Gore-Langton in *Plays & Players* (May 1988), he said: 'If there's a good play out there, it will get done. Talent will out . . . Not enough new work is being re-done. Plays are coming and going far too fast. Very few new plays get an after-life, so the writer's income suddenly stops and they are immediately forced to accept another commission before they are ready.' He was sorry to leave Hampstead, but 'the sheer facts of subsidized theatre are stark at the moment.'

Sir Richard Attenborough, CBE

Film director. Began his career as an actor, undertaking an ambitious range of characterizations including Pinky in *Brighton Rock* (1947). Went on to produce and direct. Among his credits as a director are: *Oh! What a Lovely War* (1969); *Young Winston* (1972); *A Bridge Too Far* (1977), *Magic* (1978) and, most recently, *A Chorus Line, Gandhi* starring Ben Kingsley (for which director, actor and film all received Academy Awards), and *Cry Freedom* about the life and death of Steve Biko.

David Attwood

TV, video and pop promo director. Credits include: *Flowers in the Rain, All Together Now* and *Rockliffe's Babies* (all for BBC-TV); *Crossroads* (Central TV).

Alan Ayckbourn

Theatre director and writer. Began directing at the age of 19 for Stephen Joseph's Studio Company in Scarborough, and has directed approximately 150 plays to date. As a BBC radio drama producer in Leeds, he directed an average of two plays a month for six years, working mostly with new writers. He left the BBC in 1970 to become artistic director of Scarborough's Library Theatre, responsible for a summer repertoire of four or five plays, one of which traditionally was his own annual offering. He managed to establish the company on a permanent basis and, in 1976, masterminded the transfer of the company from the Library Theatre into a converted Victorian high school, where it became the Stephen Joseph Theatre-in-the-Round (*see* Rep/Regional Theatres).

Ayckbourn usually re-directs the London productions of his own plays when they transfer from Scarborough. These have included: *Ten Times Table; Joking Apart; Season's Greetings; Way Upstream; Intimate Exchanges; A Chorus of Disapproval* and *Woman in Mind*. In 1977, he was nominated for a Broadway

Tony award for his co-direction, with Peter Hall, of the National Theatre production of *Bedroom Farce*.

In 1986, Ayckbourn took a two-year sabbatical from Scarborough to work with his own group of actors at the National Theatre. He has directed the 1920s farce *Tons of Money*; his own play, *A Small Family Business*; Arthur Miller's *A View from the Bridge* (for which he was nominated for 'Director of the Year' in the Olivier Awards, and won the *Plays & Players* Award); and *'Tis Pity She's a Whore*. In 1988, he also directed *Henceforward*, his latest play, in the West End.

Roger Bamford

TV and video director. Credits include: *Auf Wiedersehen, Pet*; *Blott on the Landscape*; *Rumpole of the Bailey*; *Orbital*; and various pop promos.

Frith Banbury

Theatre director and manager. As an actor in the 1930s, he appeared in many West End plays including John Geilgud's *Hamlet*. Turned to direction in 1947, and has since produced and/or directed over 50 plays in London, including the original productions in the West End of *The Deep Blue Sea*, *Flowering Cherry*, *Waters of the Moon*, *The Holly and the Ivy* and *The Wings of the Dove*. Vanessa Redgrave made her first London appearance under his direction in N. C. Hunter's *A Touch of the Sun* in 1958. Banbury has worked on and off Broadway, and in many other cities all over the world. Recent London credits include: *Dear Liar* (with Robert Hardy & Sian Phillips); *The Aspern Papers* (with Vanessa Redgrave, Christopher Reeves & Dame Wendy Hiller); and *The Corn Is Green* (with Deborah Kerr) at the Old Vic.

Humphrey Barclay

TV director (light entertainment and video drama). Credits include: *Relative Strangers*, *Hot Metal*, *Whoops Apocalypse*, *Me and My Girl*, *A Fine Romance*, *Two's Company*, *No Honestly* and *Doctor in the House*.

Lezli-An Barrett

Film director. Credits include: *An Epic Poem* (short film about suffragettes, screened by Channel 4 in 1982); *Business as Usual* (1987). Financed the latter film (her first) with £900 she saved from her job as a cinema usherette. It defeated work by more experienced women directors to win an award in Paris.

John Barton

Theatre and TV director. Associate director of the Royal Shakespeare Company. Joined the RSC in 1960 and devised two anthology programmes: *The Hollow Crown* and *The Art of Seduction*. He co-directed the Stratford histories cycle with Peter Brook and edited *The Wars of the Roses*. Subsequent productions include: *Love's Labours Lost*; *Henry IV Parts I & II* and *Henry V* (co-direction); *All's Well that Ends Well*; *Julius Caesar*; *Troilus and Cressida*; *The Tempest*; *Othello*; *When Thou Art King*; *Richard II*; *King John*; *Cymbeline*; *Much Ado about Nothing*; *A Winter's Tale* (with Trevor Nunn); *King Lear* (with Trevor Nunn & Barry Kyle); *A Midsummer Night's Dream*; *The Merchant of Venice*; *Hamlet*. Non-Shakespearean work includes: *Dr Faustus*; *Perkin Warbeck*; *Pillars of the Community*; *The Way of the World*; and, recently, *The Three Sisters* at the Barbican. He has also directed *The School for Scandal* at the Haymarket Theatre, and *Waste* at the Lyric Theatre, Hammersmith. For TV, he has directed *Morte d'Arthur*, and has devised and presented the series *Playing Shakespeare*.

Roy Battersby

Film and TV director (documentaries and drama). Film credits include: *The Body* (1970); *Winter Flight* (1985); *Mr Love* (1986); *The Palestinian* (film documentary, 1978). TV credits: *No Excuses* (Central TV, 1983); *King of the Ghetto* (BBC-TV, 1986).

Stephen Bayley

Film director. Credits include: *Coming Up Roses/Rhosyn A Rhith* for S4C – the first film to be both financed in Wales and made in the Welsh language, and *The Falcon's Malteser*. Previously, he worked with Tony Scott and Ridley Scott before going to the National Film School.

Alan Bell

TV and video director: Credits include: *Chinese Puzzle*, *Gaskin* and *Death on the Mountain* (all for BBC-TV); *King and Castle*, *Gems* and *Couples* (all for Thames TV); *Fallen Hero* (Granada); *Cats' Eyes* (TVS).

Rodney Bennett

TV director. Credits include: *Dombey and Son* (BBC-TV); *Dearly Beloved* (Yorkshire TV); *Edwin* and *Love Song* (both for Anglia); *Monsignor Quixote* (Euston Films); *Rumpole of the Bailey* (Thames TV).

Bruce Beresford

Australian film, documentary and commercial director. Feature films include: *The Getting of Wisdom* (1977); *Breaker Morant* (1979); *The Club* (1980); *Puberty Blues* (1981); *Tender Mercies* (1982); *King David* (1984); *The Fringe Dwellers* (1985); *Crimes of the Heart* (1986).

Steven Berkoff

Theatre director, actor, writer and designer. Credits include: *Metamorphosis*; *The Trial*; *The House of Usher*; *East*; *Greek*; *West*; *Decadence*. Most of these have been produced several times, on the fringe and in the West End – for example, *Greek* was recently seen at Wyndham's. He has also directed *Coriolanus* at Joseph Popp's Public Theatre in New York.

Kevin Billington

TV, theatre and film director. Theatre credits include: *The Deliberate Death of a Polish Priest* (Almeida, 1986). Film credits include: *Interlude* (Columbia, 1968); *The Rise and Rise of Michael Rimmer* (Warner, 1969); *The Light at the Edge of the World* (1970). Television credits include: *Outside Edge* (LWT, 1982); *The Good Soldier* (Granada, 1981); *Henry VIII* (BBC-TV, 1979); *Reflections* (Court House Films/Channel 4, 1984).

Michael Blakemore

Theatre and film director, actor and writer. Born in Australia, and came to England in 1950. Studied at RADA and in 1966 joined the Glasgow Citizens Theatre as an actor and co-artistic director. Here he directed Peter Nichols' prize-winning play *A Day in the Death of Joe Egg*, which transferred to London and New York. Other prize winners he has directed include *Arturo Ui*; *Forget-Me-Not Lane*; and Michael Frayn's *Make and Break* and *Noises Off*. The latter two transferred from the Lyric, Hammersmith (where Blakemore was resident director) to the West End. The Broadway production of Frayn's *Benefactors* (also a prize winner) played on Broadway at the Brooks Atkinson, as did *Noises Off*. Blakemore was an associate director at the National Theatre for five years, where his successes included *The National Health*, *Plunder*, *Long Day's Journey into Night* and *The Front Page* (the latter two winning the *Plays & Players* 'Best Director' award). Other West End credits include: *Design for Living*, *Knuckle*, *Candida*, *Separate Tables*, *Privates on Parade*, *Deathtrap* and *All My Sons*.

He directed the film version of *Privates on Parade*, and wrote, directed and acted in the film *A Personal History of the Australian Surf*, for which he received the Peter Sellers Award for comedy in the (London) *Evening Standard* Film Awards. He has also written a novel about the theatre called *Next Season*. Recent West End productions include: *Made in Bangkok* by Anthony Minghella at the Aldwych Theatre; *Lettice and Lovage* by Peter Shaffer at the Globe Theatre; and *Uncle Vanya* with Michael Gambon at the Vaudeville Theatre.

Michael Bogdanov

Theatre, TV and opera director. Associate director, Tyneside Theatre Company (1971–3); director, Phoenix Theatre, Leicester (1974–7) and Young Vic (1978–80); associate director, National Theatre, since 1980; joint artistic director, English Shakespeare Company. Work for the National Theatre includes: *Sir Gawain and the Green Knight*; *The Hunchback of Notre Dame*; *The Romans in Britain*; *Hiawatha*; *One Woman Play*; *The Mayor of Zalamea*; *The Hypochondriac*; *Uncle Vanya*; *The Caucasian Chalk Circle*; *The Spanish Tragedy*; *Macbeth*; *Lorenzaccio*; *You Can't Take It with You*; *Strider – The Story of a Horse*; *Orwell's England*; *The Ancient Mariner*. For the Royal Shakespeare Company productions include: *Shadow of a Gunman*; *The Knight of the Burning Pestle* (1981); *Romeo and Juliet* (1987). In the West End, he directed the musical *Mutiny*, and won the 'Director of the Year' SWET award for his production of *The Taming of the Shrew*. For TV, he directed his own series *Broad and Narrow* and *Shakespeare Lives*; and at the Royal Opera House, *Donnerstag aus Licht*. For the English Shakespeare Company in 1987, he directed *The Henrys*, which made a national tour and appeared at the Old Vic.

John Boorman

Film director. Began as a TV director, switching to films in the 1960s. Has since moved to the US and has spent much time recently trying to keep the Irish film industry afloat. Credits include: *Leo the Last* (1970); *Deliverance* (1972); *Zardoz* (1973); *Exorcist II – The Heretic* (1977); *Excalibur* (1981); *The Emerald Forest* (1984); *Hope and Glory* (1987). 'Hope and Glory confirms Boorman as a worthy inheritor of Powell's role as the great risk-taking romantic of British cinema' (Charles Barr, *Monthly Film Bulletin*).

Liz Brailsford

Theatre director. Has worked extensively in children's theatre. Credits include: *Now You See It* by Shirley Barrie (Tricycle Theatre); *The Iron Man* by Ted Hughes (Nottingham Playhouse); *Fantastic Mr Fox* by Roald Dahl (Theatre-in-Education direction for Nottingham Playhouse); *Something Wicked This Way Comes* by Ray Bradbury (Nottingham Playhouse; Crucible Theatre, Sheffield; Theatre Royal, York); *The Lion, the Witch and the Wardrobe* by C. S. Lewis (Westminster Theatre).

Kenneth Branagh

Theatre director, actor and writer. (*See* Young Actors section for biography and acting credits.)

Much of the profits from his leading role in BBC-TV's *Fortunes of War* went into the founding of Renaissance Theatre Company with fellow actor David Parfitt. As an independent operation aiming to create opportunities for people to stretch themselves beyond their usual roles as actors, directors or writers, Renaissance has proved highly successful. Branagh has appeared in his own production of *Romeo and Juliet*, has directed *Twelfth Night* with Richard Briers at the Riverside Studios and, in 1988, inaugurated a series of Shakespearean productions directed by well-known actors. He has also written and appeared in his own play *Public Enemy*. To quote Kenneth Hurran in *Plays & Players* (February 1988): 'What a remarkable talent is amongst us in young Branagh. I begin to think there has not been such a boy wonder since Orson Welles. Not only is he one of the finest actors of his generation, he also writes plays (not, so far, with spectacular success, but that may well come), has formed his own Renaissance Theatre Company ... and he directs with, it may be said on the evidence of his *Twelfth Night*, considerable distinction.'

Yvonne Brewster

Theatre director. Credits include: *The New Hardware Store* (Arts Theatre); *Raisin in the Sun* (Black Theatre Cooperative); *Two Can Play* (Bristol Old Vic); *The Good Doctor* (Arts Theatre); *Black Jacobins* (Riverside Theatre); *School's Out* (Theatre Royal, Stratford East); *Flash Trash* (Half Moon Theatre). Also worked on the feature film *The Harder They Come* in Jamaica.

Alan Bridges

Film, TV, theatre and opera director. Credits include: *Film*: *The Hireling*, *Very Like a Whale*, *The Return of the Soldier*, *The Shooting Party*; *TV*: *The Lie* and *Oedipus* BBC-TV); *Saturday, Sunday, Monday* (Granada); *Film/TV*: *Pudden Head Wilson* (US).

Peter Brook, CBE

Theatre, film and opera director. Educated at Oxford. Directed his first theatre production, *Faustus*, at the Torch Theatre in 1943. Other theatre credits include: *Hamlet* (directed the Stratford Shakespeare Memorial Company at the Moscow Arts Theatre in 1955 and in London in 1956); *The Power and the Glory*, *A View from the Bridge* and *La Chatte sur un toit brulant* (*Cat on a Hot Tin Roof*) at the Theatre Antoine, Paris (1956); *Titus Andronicus* and *The Tempest* (1957; also composed music and designed sets); *Irma la Douce*, *The Visit* (opening play at the Lunt–Fontaine Theatre) and *Eugene Onegin* (Metropolitan Opera) (New York, 1958); *The Fighting Cock* (New York); *The Balcony* in Paris, *The Visit* in London and *Irma la Douce* in New York (1960); *King Lear* (1962; also designed); *The Physicists*, *The Perils of Scobie Prilt* and *Sergeant Musgrave's Dance* (1963); *Marat/Sade* (1964 & 1965; New York Drama Critics Award for Best Director); *US* (London, 1966); Seneca's *Oedipus* (London, 1968; also designed); *A Midsummer Night's Dream* (New York, London, Stratford, 1970–1).

In 1971, Brook founded the Centre International de Créations Théâtrales in Paris. Activities with the Centre have included: *Orghast* for the Shiraz Festival at Persepolis in Iran (1971); a tour of central Africa in 1972, presenting mime plays; *Timon of Athens* (Paris, 1974); *The Ik*, tour 1975–6, including the Round House, London; *Ubu* (1977); *Antony and Cleopatra* (Royal Shakespeare Company, 1978); *Conference of the Birds* (1979); and recently *The Mahabharata* in Paris, Glasgow and all over the world. Film credits include: *The Beggar's Opera* (1953); *Moderato Cantabile* (also co-wrote; 1960); *Lord of the Flies* (also screenplay; 1964); *Marat/Sade* (1967); *Tell Me Lies* (film version of *US*; 1967); *King Lear* (1969); *Meetings with Remarkable Men* (1979); *Carmen* (1983). Peter Brook also wrote two TV plays in the 1950s, and a book about directing: *The Empty Space*. His latest book, *The Shifting Point*, was published in 1988. He was made a Commander of the British Empire in 1965.

Bill Bryden

Theatre, TV and film director and writer. Directed his first professional production, *Misalliance*, at the Belgrade Theatre, Coventry, in 1965, and then worked as assistant to William Gaskill at the Royal Court (1966–8). Productions for the Royal Court include: *Journey of the Fifth Horse, Backbone, Passion, Corunna* and *The Baby Elephant*. In 1971, Bryden was appointed associate director of the Royal Lyceum Theatre, Edinburgh, where his productions included: *Benny Lynch* and *Willie Rough* (both written by Bryden); *The Iceman Cometh*; *The Flowers of Edinburgh*; *How Mad Tullock Was Taken Away*. At this time he also wrote the libretto for the opera *Hermiston*. In 1975, he was appointed an associate director of the National Theatre, where he directed: *Spring Awakening*; *Romeo and Juliet*; *The Playboy of the Western World*; *Watch It Come Down*; *Il Campiello*; *Counting the Ways*; *The Passion* (co-director); *Old Movies* (also author); *The Plough and the Stars*. In 1978, he was appointed director of the Cottesloe Theatre, where he has directed: *Lark Rise* (co-director); *American Buffalo*; *The World Turned Upside Down*; *Dispatches* (co-adapted); *Candleford* (co-director); *The Long Voyage Home*; *Hughie*; *The Iceman Cometh*; the York mystery plays; *Glengarry, Glenross*; *A Midsummer Night's Dream*; *The Mysteries* (National Theatre/Lyceum Theatre). TV work has included: *Ill Fares the Land* (Channel 4, 1982); *The Holy City* (BBC-TV, 1986).

Stuart Burge, CBE

Theatre, TV and film director. Began his career as an actor and stage manager at the Old Vic and started directing in 1948 with a travelling repertory company. First London production: *Let's Make an Opera*, at the Lyric Theatre, Hammersmith, 1949. Since then he has run the Queen's Theatre, Hornchurch; Nottingham Playhouse; and, more recently, the Royal Court. Notable theatre productions have included: the first performance of *The Ruling Class* by Peter Barnes at Nottingham, and Wedekind's *Lulu*, which was seen at Nottingham and later at the Royal Court and the Apollo Theatre in London. Co-directed *The Devil Is an Ass* and *Measure for Measure* at the Edinburgh Festival with Birmingham Repertory Theatre, which transferred to the National Theatre in 1977. Other productions at the Royal Court have included: *Fair Slaughter*; *The Eclipse*; *The London Cuckolds* (also at the Lyric, Hammersmith, 1985). In 1982, he directed *Another Country* at the Queen's Theatre, and, more recently, *Curtains* by Stephen Bill at Hampstead Theatre Club. Work for BBC-TV has included: *Sons and Lovers* (1981); *The Old Men at the Zoo* (1984); *Breaking Up* (1986); *Naming the Names* (1987). Films include: *There Was a Crooked Man* (1960); *Othello* (1966); *The Mikado* (1967); *Julius Caesar* (1970). Made a Commander of the British Empire in 1974.

John Caird

Theatre director. Born in Canada, he worked there for a time in touring, fringe, community and university theatre before coming to England to train as an actor. He soon decided that he preferred directing to acting, and joined the Royal Shakespeare Company in 1977. He directed several successes at the Warehouse including: *Dance of Death*; *Savage Amusement* by Peter Flannery; *Look Out, Here Comes Trouble* by Mary O'Malley. In 1977, he began a series of productions co-directed with Trevor Nunn, starting with *The Merry Wives of Windsor* and *As You Like It*, continuing in 1979 with *Nicholas Nickleby*, which went on to achieve enormous success, with three seasons at the Aldwych, a transfer to Broadway and a TV film. This production won 16 awards in the UK and US, including four for 'Best Director'. Other collaborations with Nunn include *Les Miserables* and *Peter Pan*. Other work for the RSC (where he is now an associate director) includes the first production in The Pit — *Our Friends in the North* by Peter Flannery — as well as *Twelfth Night*, *Red Star*, *Philistines* and *The New Inn* by Ben Jonson. Outside the RSC, he has directed *Song and Dance* (the Andrew Lloyd Webber musical) and *As You Like It* in Stockholm, which was filmed for Swedish TV.

Ken Campbell

Theatre director, actor and writer. Founded his own company, Ken Campbell's Roadshow, which toured from 1971 to 1974, visiting venues ranging from public bars to the Theatre Upstairs, in shows such as *Bar-room Tales*, *An Evening with Sylveste McCoy*, *The Human Bomb* and *Stonehenge Kit the Ancient Brit*. His musical, *Bendigo* (co-written with Dave Hill & Andy Andrews) was performed at Nottingham Playhouse in 1974, and he played the part of Stu Lyons in his own play *The Great Caper* at the Royal Court in the same year. In 1976, he co-founded the Science Fiction Theatre of Liverpool and was artistic director until 1980. Their marathon *Illuminatus* (which he adapted) was the opening production at the National Theatre's Cottesloe. Other productions for this company include the ten-play cycle *The Warp* and *The Hitch-Hiker's Guide to the Galaxy* (Rainbow, London). Was director of the Everyman Theatre, Liverpool in 1980, where productions included *The Disco Queen* and *War with the Newts*. As an actor, he has recently been seen on TV in the Sherlock Holmes series with Jeremy Brett and Edward Hardwicke.

Martin Campbell

TV and film director. TV credits include: *Muck & Brass* (Central TV, 1979); *Reilly: Ace of Spies* (Euston Films, 1981); *Charlie* (Central TV, 1983); *Edge of Darkness* (BBC-TV, 1985); *Frankie & Johnnie* (BBC-TV, 1985); also episodes of *Minder* and *The Professionals*. Currently breaking into films with *Criminal Law*.

Annie Castledine

Theatre director. Has worked as artistic director of the Northern Studio Theatre, and as associate director of Theatr Clwyd, Mold, where productions have included: *Hedda Gabler*, *Translations*, *The Three Sisters*, *Maria Marten*. Is currently artistic director of Derby Playhouse, where she is pursuing an adventurous policy with such recent productions as *The Children's Hour* and *Sunday's Children*.

Michael Caton-Jones

Film director. After appearing in films as 'hired brawn', went to night school and film school, and is now working on his first feature, *Scandal*, with Bridget Fonda and Joanne Whalley. His TV film, *Lucky Sunil*, was seen on BBC-TV in 1988.

James Cellan Jones

TV and film director. Head of BBC plays in the 1970s. Film credits include: *Bequest to the Nation* (1971); two films for Video Arts (1982). TV credits include: *The Day Christ Died* (1980); *A Fine Romance* (from 1981); *Comedy of Errors* (1983); *Oxbridge Blues* (1984); *Slip Up* (1985); *Fortunes of War* (1988).

Robert Chetwyn

Theatre and TV director. Early experience in repertory, then became an associate director at the Mermaid Theatre, London. West End productions include: *There's a Girl in My Soup* (also Broadway and Australia); *The Flip Side; The Importance of Being Earnest; The Real Inspector Hound* (at one time had four simultaneous West End productions); *What the Butler Saw; The Bandwagon; When We Are Married; Hamlet* (with Ian McKellen). Other London productions include: *Arms and the Man* (with Felicity Kendall); *Brimstone and Treacle* by Dennis Potter; *Bent* (with Ian McKellen & Tom Bell); *Moving* (with Penelope Keith). In 1983, he directed a new play by Peter Ustinov at the Vaudeville Theatre: *Beethoven's Tenth*. TV work includes *The Irish RM* (Channel 4); *Making Faces* (six plays by Michael Frayn); *Private Schultz* (six-hour mini-series; BBC-2).

Ted Childs

Film and TV director. Film credits include: *The Sweeney* and *Sweeney II* (EMI/Euston Films); *The Quatermass Conclusion* and *Charlie Muffin* (Euston Films); *Oliver Twist* (Claridge Films). TV credits include: *Special Branch, The Sweeney* and *Quatermass* (Euston Films).

Roger Christian

Film director. Worked as art director on *Star Wars* and *Alien*, and did second-unit work on *The Return of the Jedi*. Credits include: *Black Angel* (short film); *The Dollar Bottom* (Academy Award-winning short film); *The Sender; Lorca and the Outlaws* (1985, shot in Australia as *2084*).

Anthony Clark

Theatre director. Currently artistic director of Contact Theatre, Manchester. Previously ran the Orange Tree Theatre, Richmond and served as director to Tara Arts, as the only white member of the company. Now at Contact, he follows an integrated casting policy that is sometimes controversial: 'When you put black actors on stage, there is an assumption that it has to be about race. But it is about accessibility. Young audiences tend to be multiracial. An audience needs empathy with the characters on stage. They have to think, "I could be that character," and an all-white, middle-class cast adds extra barriers to a young black person's empathy' (*Plays & Players*, March 1988). Recent credits include: *The Snowman, Homeland, Mother Courage, To Kill a Mockingbird, Faustus*.

Alan Clarke

Film director. Credits include: *Road; Scum* (1979); *Rita, Sue and Bob Too* (Film Four International/Umbrella Entertainment). The latter has been compared to such 1960s slice-of-life films as *A Taste of Honey*.

Jack Clayton

Film director. Credits include: *The Bespoke Overcoat* (1956); *Room at the Top* (1958); *The Innocents* (1961); *The Pumpkin Eater* (1964); *Our Mother's House* (1968); *The Great Gatsby* (1974); *Something Wicked This Way Comes* (1983); *The Lonely Passion of Judith Hearne* (with Maggie Smith & Bob Hoskins, 1987).

Ray Cooney

Theatre and TV director, actor, writer and manager. Has worked extensively as a director of West End comedy and farce, founding the Theatre of Comedy Company in 1983. Credits as a director include: *Two into One, Pygmalion* and

See How They Run (Shaftesbury, 1984); *Run for Your Wife* (Criterion, 1983); *Wife Begins at Forty* (Ambassadors, 1985); TV production of *See How They Run* (TVS, 1984).

Ron Daniels

Theatre director. Associate director of the Royal Shakespeare Company. Born in Brazil, where he was a founder member of the Workshop Theatre of São Paolo. Came to England and worked as an actor at St Andrews Repertory Theatre, and at the Victoria Theatre, Stoke-on-Trent, where he became assistant director in 1969 and directed: *Who's Afraid of Virginia Woolf?*, *Sweeny Todd*, *Major Barbara*, *Drums in the Night*, *Ghosts*. He also directed for the Shaw Theatre, Bristol Old Vic, Yale Repertory Theatre in Connecticut, RADA and the National Youth Theatre. On the London fringe, he directed *Female Transport* (Half Moon Theatre) and *By Natural Causes* (Cockpit Theatre). In 1974, he directed his first show at The Other Place — *Afore Night Come* by David Rudkin — and, in 1976, *Destiny* by David Edgar, which transferred to the Aldwych.

In 1977, he became director of The Other Place and directed: *'Tis Pity She's a Whore* by John Ford; *The Lorenzaccio Story* by Paul Thompson; *The Sons of Light* and *Hippolytus*, both by David Rudkin; *Women Pirates* by Steve Gooch (at the Aldwych); *Pericles*; *The Suicide* by Nikolai Erdman (transferred to The Other Place and the Aldwych). In 1980 at Stratford, he directed *Romeo and Juliet*, *Timon of Athens* and *Hansel and Gretel* by David Rudkin, all of which transferred to London; and in 1981, he directed *A Midsummer Night's Dream* in Stratford and *The Beastly Beatitudes of Balthazar B* with Simon Callow and Patrick Ryecart at the Duke of York's Theatre in London. Subsequent productions in Stratford, which have transferred to London, include: *The Tempest* and *Peer Gynt* (both starring Derek Jacobi); *Hamlet*; *Camille* by Pam Gems (transferred first to the Comedy Theatre and then to the Long Wharf Theatre in Connecticut). Other recent work includes: *Maydays* by David Edgar; *Breaking the Silence* by Stephen Poliakoff; *Real Dreams*; *The Danton Affair*; *Much Ado about Nothing*; *The Plain Dealer*; *Hamlet*.

Howard Davies

Theatre director. Started work as associate director of Bristol Old Vic, where credits included: *Narrow Road to the Deep North*, *Candida*, *Long Day's Journey into Night*, *Early Morning*, *Fear and Miseries of the Third Reich*, *Woyzeck*, *Spring Awakening*. He then worked in fringe and repertory theatre for three years before joining the Royal Shakespeare Company to direct *Man Is Man*, *Schweyk in the Second World War* and *The Iceman Cometh*. A year later, he became an associate director of the RSC and established and ran the Warehouse Theatre in London for five years. Productions included: *Bandits*; *Bingo*; *The Fool*; *The Bundle*; *The Jail Diary of Albie Sachs*; *No Limits to Love*; *The Innocent*; *Outskirts*; *Good* and *Piaf* (which both transferred to the West End and Broadway). More recent RSC productions have been: *The Time of Your Life*; *Macbeth*; *Henry VIII*; *Softcops*; *The Party*; *Troilus and Cressida*; *Flight*; *Les Liaisons Dangereuses*, which is currently in the West End and was for a time on Broadway. He has also recently directed *Cat on a Hot Tin Roof* at the Lyttelton Theatre, with Ian Charleson, Lindsay Duncan and Eric Porter, and the *Shaughraun* at the Olivier Theatre.

John Davies

TV and film director. Credits include: *Nana*; *Germinal*; *The Woodlanders*; *War and Peace*; *Clayhanger*; *Cover Her Face* (adaptation of P. D. James novel); *Miss Marple*; *Kim* (three-hour film).

Tudor Davies

Theatre, dance, light entertainment and TV director. Theatre credits include: *Cowardy Custard, Call Me Madam, Dear Anyone, Aladdin.* TV credits include: *Pennies from Heaven* by Dennis Potter; *She Loves Me; Showstoppers.*

Barry Davis

Theatre, musicals, TV and radio director. Credits include: *Theatre: The Contractor* and *Romeo and Juliet* (both in New York); *Can You Hear Me at the Back?* (Piccadilly Theatre); *TV: Telford's Change, The Bell* (adaptation of Iris Murdoch novel), *Oppenheimer* and *Late Starter* (all for BBC-TV); *TV/Theatre: Wait until Dark* (US).

Ross Devenish

Film, TV and theatre director. Credits include: *Boesman and Lena* (Bluewater Films); *Marigolds in August* (Serpent Films); *Bleak House* (BBC-TV).

Clive Donner

Film and TV director. Credits include: *Stealing Heaven; Dead Man's Folly; Babes in Toyland; A Christmas Carol; Nothing but the Best; The Caretaker; Some People; The Scarlet Pimpernel; Rogue Male.*

Bill Douglas

Film director. Won a place at the London Film School with his drawings and went on to make an autobiographical trilogy of films: *My Childhood* (1971), *My Ain Folk* (1972) and *My Way Home* (1979). In 1986, made *Comrades*, about the Tolpuddle Martyrs.

Patrick Dromgoole

TV director and producer. Credits include: *as producer: Robin of Sherwood; Three Wishes for Jamie; The Canterville Ghost; Return to Treasure Island; as director: Chateau Arsenic; Succubus.*

Nancy Duguid

Theatre director. Born in Kentucky and came to England to study at the Central School of Speech and Drama. Has been associated with feminism and the gay movement (has directed numerous productions for Gay Sweatshop) but believes that 'content and breadth are as important as the issue' (*Time Out*, September 1986). Credits include: *Angels Descend on Paris* by Noel Greig (Albany Theatre); *Passion Play* by Peter Nichols (National Theatre of Israel); *The Daughter-in-Law* (Duke's Playhouse, Lancaster); work with the Suzuki Company of Toga in Japan; *Request Programme* by Franz Xavier Kroetz (Donmar, Bush, Traverse, Edinburgh); and, recently, *Sore Throats* by Howard Brenton and *Roosters* by Milcha Sanchez Scott. She has also directed a Greek-language version of *A Street Car Named Desire* in Athens.

Peter Duguid

TV and theatre director. Theatre credits include: *Just Between Ourselves* (Palace Theatre, Watford). TV credits include: *Funny Man; King and Castle; Jury; Ladies in Charge.*

Christine Edzard

Film director. Credits include: *Stories from a Flying Trunk*; *The Nightingale*; *Biddy*; *Little Dorrit* (in two parts).

Ian Emes

Film director. Credits include: *Tent* (short); *Goodie Two Shoes* (short); *Knights and Emeralds* (feature); *The Yob* (for the Comic Strip in association with Channel 4).

Richard Eyre

Theatre, film and TV director. Succeeded Peter Hall as artistic director of the National Theatre on 1 September 1988. Started as an actor, but moved into directing after a depressing stint in the chorus of *The Boyfriend* at Leicester. Directed his first production — *The Knack* — at Leicester Phoenix Theatre in 1965. Became associate director of the Royal Lyceum Theatre in Edinburgh in 1967, and director of productions from 1970 to 1972. Productions there included: *The Three Sisters*; *Uncle Vanya*; *Trumpets and Drums*; *The White Devil*; *The Crucible*; *Juno and the Paycock*; *Othello*; *Macbeth*; *The Changeling*; *Random Happenings in the Hebrides*; *Confessions of a Justified Sinner*. He won STV awards for 'Best Production' in 1969, 1970 and 1971. As artistic director of Nottingham Playhouse, his productions included: *The Taming of the Shrew*; *The Plough and the Stars*; *The Government Inspector*; *The Churchill Play*; *Bendigo*; *The Comedians* (later also for the National Theatre and BBC-TV); *Bartholomew Fair*; *The Alchemist*; *Deeds*; *Touched*; *The Cherry Orchard*. Work in London has included his own adaptation of *The Ha-Ha* (Hampstead Theatre); *The Great Exhibition*; *Hamlet*; *Edmund*; *Kafka's Dick*; *The Shawl* and *High Society* (Leicester Haymarket and Victoria Palace, London). For the Royal Shakespeare Company, he has directed *Jingo*, and for the National Theatre (as associate director) *The Beggar's Opera*; *Schweyk in the Second World War*; *Guys and Dolls* (highly successful production that won the SWET and [London] *Evening Standard* Awards for 'Best Director'); *The Government Inspector*; *Futurists*; *The Changeling*.

From 1978 to 1981, he was producer of the BBC *Play for Today* series, and also directed: *Waterloo Sunset*; *The Cherry Orchard*; *The Imitation Game*; *Pasmore* (his own adaptation); *Country*; *The Insurance Man* (Tokyo Prize winner); *'V'*; *Tumbledown*. Films include: *The Ploughman's Lunch* ([London] *Evening Standard* Award for 'Best Film'); *Loose Connections*; *Laughterhouse*.

In an interview with the *Sunday Times* on 26 June 1988, Eyre said, 'I have never created a public image, indeed I have been self-conscious about not doing so. Such publicity as I have attracted has come about through my work, and that's the way I like it. I have no desire to become a quasi-celebrity.' However, Trevor Griffiths warns: 'Just you watch, he will take hold of that place [the National Theatre] and start to make it what he thinks it should be. When people try to stop him, that's when things will happen.'

Ronald Eyre

Theatre, opera and TV director and writer. Theatre credits include: *London Assurance* (Royal Shakespeare Company, 1970); *Saint Joan*; *A Patriot for Me*; *When We Are Married*. TV credits include: *The Long Search* (BBC-TV, 1978); many plays, including some written by himself, such as *A Crack in the Ice* (BBC-TV, 1964), *Bruno* and *Are You There?*. Opera credits include: *Falstaff*; *Jason*; *Beatrice and Benedict*.

Christopher Fettes

Theatre and opera director. Productions include: *Dr Faustus* and *Faith Healer* (both starring the late Patrick Magee); Racine's *Britannicus* and *Berenice* (first professional London productions); *The Lonely Road* by Arthur Schnitzler (also co-author of English version with Ronald Adam); *Intermezzo* by Arthur Schnitzler; Handel's *Orlando* for Scottish Opera.

Bryan Forbes

Film, TV and theatre director, producer, screenwriter and actor. Started his career as an actor and appeared in many films, including *An Inspector Calls* (1954), *The League of Gentlemen* (also screenplay; 1960) and *The Guns of Navarone* (1961). Credits as a director (including many of his own screenplays) include: film: *Whistle Down the Wind* (1961); *The L-Shaped Room* (1962); *Seance on a Wet Afternoon* (1964); *King Rat* (1965); *The Raging Moon* (1971); *International Velvet* (1978); *The Naked Face* (1984); television: *Jessie* (BBC-TV); theatre: *Killing Jessica*.

Bill Forsyth

Film director and screenwriter. Formerly a maker of documentary films, whose first feature was made with boys from the Glasgow Youth Theatre. Credits include: *That Sinking Feeling* (1979); *Gregory's Girl* (1981); *Local Hero* (1983); *Comfort and Joy* (1984); *Housekeeping* (1987).

Giles Foster

Film and TV director. Credits include: *Northanger Abbey, Hotel Du Lac, Silas Marner, The Aerodrome, Last Summer's Child* and *The Obelisk* (all for BBC-TV); *Dutch Girls* (LWT). Feature film: *Consuming Passions* (1988). He has also directed three Alan Bennett films for LWT and the BBC.

Karl Francis

Film and TV director. A major Welsh talent, who has concentrated on the difficulties faced by the Welsh community. Credits include: *Above Us the Earth*; *Giro City*; *Ms Rhymney Valley*; *The Happy Alcoholic*; *Boy Soldier*.

Stephen Frears

Film and TV director. Worked as an assistant at the Royal Court Theatre on *Inadmissible Evidence* and *Waiting for Godot* in 1964, and then assisted Karel Reisz on *Morgan, a Suitable Case for Treatment*, Albert Finney on *Charlie Bubbles* and Lindsay Anderson on *If ...* He has also worked on commercials. Credits include: film: *The Burning* (1967); *Gumshoe* (1971); *The Hit* (1984); *My Beautiful Launderette* (1987); *Prick Up Your Ears* (1987); *Mr Jolly Lives Next Door* (Comic Strip/Channel 4); *Sammy and Rosie Get Laid* (1987); television: *Walter* and *Walter and June* (1982; Channel 4); *Saigon — Year of the Cat* (1983; Thames); *Song of Experience* (BBC-TV). Due to direct Glenn Close and John Malkovich in *Les Liaisons Dangereuses* in Hollywood.

Martyn Friend

TV director. Credits include: episodes of *Rumpole of the Bailey* (Thames TV); *All Passion Spent, The Daily Woman, The Daughter-in-Law, Anna of the Five Towns, Shackleton* (1983), *Fair Stood the Wind for France* (1981) and *The Voyage of Charles Darwin* (1978) (all for BBC-TV).

Patrick Garland

Theatre, opera and film director. Began career as actor with Bristol Old Vic. First directing credits include *Brief Lives* (which he also wrote, and which was produced in London, on Broadway, and for TV) and Alan Bennett's *Forty Years On* (1970). After directing *An Enemy of the People*, *The Apple Cart* and *look after Lulu* at Chichester, he was made artistic director there in 1980. During his four-year stint, eight productions transferred to London, including *Kipling*, a one-man show starring Alec McCowen. Opera credits include *Don Giovanni* for Pavilion Opera, and two Royal Gala Performances: *Fanfare for Europe* (1976) and *Fanfare for Elizabeth* (1971). He has also directed the musicals *Billy* (with Michael Crawford), *Hair* (in Israel) and *My Fair Lady* (in the US). Film credits include *The Doll's House*, nominated at the Cannes Film Festival in 1974. Most recently, he directed *The Secret of Sherlock Holmes*, with Jeremy Brett and Edward Hardwicke, at Wyndham's Theatre.

William Gaskill

Theatre director. One of the young directors brought on by George Devine in the early years of the English Stage Company at the Royal Court, where he directed plays by Osborne, Wesker, Arden and N. F. Simpson. Directed for the Royal Shakespeare Company for a short period — *Cymbeline*, *Richard III*, *The Caucasian Chalk Circle* — and then became one of Laurence Olivier's associates at the National Theatre (*The Recruiting Officer*, *Mother Courage*, *The Beaux Stratagem*). From 1965 to 1972, he was artistic director at the Royal Court, where he directed the first productions of Edward Bond's *Saved*, *Early Morning*, *Lear* and *The Sea*, and a controversial version of *Macbeth* with Alec Guinness and Simone Signoret. Since 1972, he has been a freelance. He was a founder–director of the Joint Stock Theatre Group, for whom he directed or co-directed *The Speakers*, *Fanshen*, *A Mad World My Masters*, *Yesterday's News*, *The Ragged Trousered Philanthropists*, *An Optimistic Thrust* and *The Crimes of Vautrin*. Recently, he directed *Infidelities* at the Lyric Theatre, Hammersmith, and *The Way of the World* at the Theatre Royal, Haymarket.

William Gaunt

Actor and director. Artistic director of Liverpool Playhouse 1979–81, he worked with several Liverpool writers, including Willy Russell, with whom he produced *One for the Road* and at the Lyric Theatre, London, and *Educating Rita*. *Here's a Funny Thing* and *Skirmishes* were two other of his Liverpool productions from that period that were subsequently seen in London. Gaunt's production of *Judgement* by Barry Collins won a Fringe First at the Edinburgh Festival. Acting roles include: Arthur Crabtree in the popular BBC-TV series *No Place Like Home* among numerous other TV roles, and a starring role in *When Did You Last See Your Trousers?* at the Garrick Theatre.

Peter Gill

Theatre and TV director and writer. Born in Cardiff. Associate director of the Royal Court (1970–2) and directed many productions there in the 1960s and '70s, including: *A Collier's Friday Night* by D. H. Lawrence; *The Ruffian on the Stair* by Joe Orton; Chekhov's *A Provincial Life* (also adapted); *Crete and Sergeant Pepper* by John Antrobus. From 1976 to 1980, he was director of the Riverside Studios, Hammersmith, where among his productions were: *Small Change* (which he also wrote); *The Changeling* by Myddleton & Rowley; *Julius Caesar*; *Scrape Off the Black* by Tunde Ikoli. Associate director at the National Theatre, 1980–4, where his productions included: Turgenev's *A Month in the Country*; Molière's *Don Juan*; Shaw's *Major Barbara*; *Fool for Love* by Sam Shepard; *Antigone* by Sophocles; and his own *Kick for Touch* and *Small Change*. In 1984, he became director of the National Theatre Studio, where he has directed the Festival of New Plays in 1985, his own *Mean Tears* in 1987 and *Mrs Klein* by Nicholas Wright in 1988. Television direction includes: *Grace* by James Joyce, *Girl* by James Robson, *A Matter of Taste* by Alex La Guma and *Fugitive* by Sean Walsh (all BBC-TV); *Hitting Town* by Stephen Poliakoff (1976; Thames). In addition to those already mentioned, he has written two plays — *Sleeper's Den* and *Over Gardens Out* — and also adapted *The Merry-go-round* and *Touch and Go* (from plays by D. H. Lawrence), *The Cherry Orchard* (a new version of the Chekhov play) and *As I Lay Dying* (from the novel by William Faulkner).

David Gilmore

Theatre director. Artistic director of the Nuffield Theatre, Southampton from 1979 to 1984, where he directed *Nuts* by Tom Topor, which transferred to the Whitehall Theatre; *Dead Men* by Mike Scott and *Working-class Hero*, a new play by Bob Mason, the latter two he had commissioned for the Nuffield Theatre. He directed the national tour of *An Ideal Husband*, several rock musicals and a production of Andrew Lloyd Webber's *Song and Dance* in Australia. Recent West End productions include: *Daisy Pulls It Off* (Globe Theatre); *The Resistable Rise of Arturo Ui* (with Griff Rhys Jones as Ui, Queen's Theatre) and Jeffrey Archer's *Beyond Reasonable Doubt* (Queen's Theatre).

John Glen

Film director. Credits include: *Octopussy* (1983); *A View to a Kill* (1985); *The Living Daylights* (1987).

Jim Goddard

Film director. Credits include: *Reasonable Force; A Tale of Two Cities; Kennedy* (1984); *Bones* (1984); *Shanghai Surprise.*

Jack Gold

TV, film and theatre director. Started his career as a TV cameraman. Credits include: television: *Praying Mantis* (1982; Channel 4); *Red Monarch* (1983; Goldcrest); *Macbeth* (BBC-TV); *Murrow* (1985; HBO/TVS); *Escape from Sobibor* (CBS/Central); *Sakharov* (HBO/BBC); films: *The Bofors Gun* (1968); *The Reckoning* (1969); *The Medusa Touch* (1978); *The Chain* (1986; Quintet/Rank).

David Green

TV and film director. Credits include: *The Chinese Detective, East Lynne* and *The Golden Land* (3 films) (all BBC-TV); *Whicker Aboard the Orient Express* and *1914 All Out* (Yorkshire TV). Films: *Car Trouble* (1985); *Buster* (1988).

Peter Greenaway

Film director. Described by Derek Malcolm in the *Guardian* as 'a true original with an eccentric and bizarre sense of humour', Greenaway is an experimental film-maker whose *Draughtsman's Contract* (1983; BFI/Channel 4) broke through to a wider audience while retaining his enigmatic style. Other credits include: *A Walk Through H* (1978); *Vertical Features Remake* (1978); *The Falls* (1981); and, recently, *A Zed and Two Noughts, The Belly of an Architect* and *Drowning by Numbers.*

Justin Greene

Theatre director and writer. Has directed productions at Nottingham Playhouse, Leicester Haymarket Theatre, Derby Playhouse, Young Vic and for the touring company Paines Plough. Directed with Michael Bogdanov at the National Theatre in 1982, collaborating on two workshop productions: *The Caucasian Chalk Circle* and *Macbeth*. In 1984, his production of David Pownall's *Master Class* with Timothy West as Stalin was seen at the Old Vic and at Wyndham's Theatre. As artistic director of the Nuffield Theatre in Southampton, his productions included: *Music to Murder By*; *Roll on Friday*; *Animal*; *The Assignment*. In the West End, he has directed *A Month of Sundays* with George Cole at the Duchess, *A Piece of My Mind* by Peter Nichols at the Apollo, and *Journey's End* by R. C. Sheriff at the Whitehall. He has written several stage and radio plays: *Ludwig and Bertie*, written with Steve Cook, was a very successful platform piece at the National Theatre, and *Totally Foxed*, also written with Cook, was performed at the Nuffield Theatre in 1986.

Andrew Grieve

Film and TV director; also commercials. Credits: *Storybook International* series (HTV); *Young Sherlock Holmes* (1985; EMI); *Suspicion* (1986; Hemisphere); *On the Black Hill* (1987; BFI/Channel 4).

Mike Grigsby

TV and film director. Worked as a cameraman for Granada. In 1957, formed an independent film-making group, Unit Five Seven. Has made documentaries and drama/documentaries, using the people concerned and sometimes professional actors. Short films include: *Engineman* (1957; BFI); *Tomorrow's Saturday* (1962; BFI). Television films include: *Unmarried Mothers* (1983), *Inside* (1965), *Deckie Learner* (1965), *The Pommies* (1966), *Death by Misadventure: SS Lusitania* (1967), *Deep South* (1969), *If the Village Dies* (1969), *I Was a Soldier* (1970), *Freshman* (1971), *Working the Land* (1972), *A Well-kept Secret* (1972), *A Life Apart* (1973), *A Life Underground* (1974), *The People's Land: The Eskimos of Pond Inlet* (1976), *Bag of Yeast* (1976; drama), *The Village that Would Not Die* (1978), *Living on the Edge* (1987) – all Granada TV; *Before the Monsoon* (1979; 3 episodes) and *For My Working Life* (1981) – both ATV; *Too Long a Sacrifice* (1985; Central). Subjects he has tackled include India, Northern Ireland, prisons, illiteracy, lives of deep-sea trawlermen, civil rights in the southern states of America. 'Mike Grigsby's remarkably consistent *oeuvre*, which has allowed the exploited, the forgotten, the taken-for-granted, the voiceless, to speak at some length and in their own words ... *Living on the Edge* paints a terrifyingly bleak picture of contemporary Britain without really offering any solutions ...' (Julian Petley). Of this last film, Grigsby said, 'The theme of so many of my films is betrayal of one kind or another, and this is a summation of that experience. It is about the betrayal of my own land' (*Monthly Film Bulletin*).

Val Guest

TV and film director and producer. In the 1930s, in the early days of his career, he worked as a writer on the screenplays of comedies for Will Hay, Arthur Askey and the Crazy Gang. Credits include: television: *Mark of the Devil*, *In Possession*, *Child's Play*, *Mistress of the Seas*; film: *Boys in Blue*.

Tom Gutteridge

TV director and producer. Credits include: *A Kick Up the Eighties*; *Footlights*; *Molly Keane*; *The Hot Shoe Show*; *Song and Dance*; *Blue Suede Shoes*; Wayne Sleep's *Dash*; *Fire and Ice*.

Piers Haggard

TV, theatre and film director. Credits include: television: *Pennies from Heaven* (1978), *Mrs Reinhardt* (1981), *Knockback, Return to Treasure Island, Visitors*; film: *A Summer Story, The Secret Plot of Dr Fu Manchu, Venom*; theatre: *The Ticket-of-Leave Man* (1981; National Theatre).

Sir Peter Hall

Director of the National Theatre for 15 years; left on 1 September 1988 to set up his own company in the West End.

Prior to founding the Royal Shakespeare Company in 1960, which he ran until 1968, he directed the première of Samuel Beckett's *Waiting for Godot*. With the RSC, he directed 18 Shakespeare plays including *The Wars of the Roses* and *Hamlet* with (David Warner in the title role). In addition, he also directed the premières of *A Delicate Balance* and *All Over* by Edward Albee, *The Homecoming, Landscape, Silence, Old Times, No Man's Land, Betrayal* and *Other Places*, all by Harold Pinter; as well as premières of plays by Anouilh, Peter Shaffer, John Mortimer and John Whiting.

In 1973, he became director of the National Theatre where he directed *John Gabriel Borkman, Happy Days, Hamlet, Judgement, Tamburlaine the Great, Bedroom Farce, Volpone, The Country Wife, The Cherry Orchard, Amadeus, Othello, The Oresteia, The Importance of Being Earnest, Animal Farm* (his own adaptation), *Coriolanus, Martine, Yonadab* and *Coming in to Land*. He has worked many times on Broadway, winning Tony awards for *The Homecoming* and *Amadeus*.

He is artistic director of Glyndebourne, where he has directed the operas *La Calisto, Il Ritorno D'Ulisse, The Marriage of Figaro, Don Giovanni, Cosi Fan Tutti, Fidelio, The Dream, Orfeo, L'Incoronazione di Poppaea, Carmen, Albert Herring*, and *Simon Boccanegra*. He has also directed opera at Covent Garden, New York, Bayreuth and Los Angeles.

He has directed *Carmen, The Oresteia, Albert Herring* and *L'Incoronazione di Poppaea* for TV and has made seven films, including *A Midsummer Night's Dream* (1968), *Three into Two Won't Go* (1969), *The Homecoming* (1973) and *Akenfield* (1974).

In his last two years at the National Theatre (1987–8), he directed *Antony and Cleopatra* with Judi Dench and Anthony Hopkins, *Entertaining Strangers* by David Edgar and the late Shakespeares: *The Winter's Tale, The Tempest* and *Cymbeline*.

In *Plays & Players* of June 1988, Michael Billington remarked how struck he was with 'how much Hall's own style as a director had changed over the years. When he started out he was a romantic. He confessed that his famous production of *Waiting for Godot* at the Arts in 1955 was probably far too cluttered and full of extraneous effects. His great years at the Royal Shakespeare Company from 1960 to 1968 marked a shift towards contemporary relevance: his production of *The Wars of the Roses* with John Barton coincided with a marked public cynicism about power, and his *Hamlet* with David Warner seemed all about youthful alienation in a morally bankrupt world. After the romantic and political Hall, we now have the classical Hall: a director obsessively concerned with divining the author's purpose. One actor who is in the current season of late plays said to me that it was almost like being directed by Shakespeare himself.'

Terry Hands

Theatre and opera director. Artistic director and chief executive of the Royal Shakespeare Company. Founded the Liverpool Everyman Theatre in 1964 and was artistic director there for two years. In the late 1960s and in the 1970s, his work for the RSC included: Triana's *The Criminals*, *The Merry Wives of Windsor*, *Pericles*, *Women Beware Women*, *Richard III*, Jean Genet's *The Balcony*, Etherege's *Man of Mode*, *The Merchant of Venice*, T. S. Eliot's *Murder in the Cathedral*, *Romeo and Juliet* and *The Bewitched*. In 1975, he directed all four productions in the centenary season at Straford and the Aldwych: *Henry V*, *Henry IV Parts I & II* and *The Merry Wives of Windsor*. (*Henry V* was seen in New York as the official British Theatre offering to the US to celebrate their bi-centenary.) For his direction of the three parts of *Henry VI* in 1977, he was joint winner of the *Plays & Players* award for 'Best Production' and was also the Society of West End Theatres 'Director of the Year' for 1978.

He was awarded the Meilleur Spectacle de l'Année by the Paris drama critics for his production of *Richard III* for the Comédie Française in 1973. The following year, he was appointed consultant director of the Comédie Française, and Chevalier of Arts and Letters by the French government. His Paris production of *Twelfth Night* in 1976 won another Meilleur Spectacle de l'Année, and he has also directed the plays *Le Cid* and *Murder in the Cathedral* and the opera *Otello* in Paris. (The latter production was the official French operatic offering for the US bi-centennial celebrations.)

In 1979, he directed *Parsifal* at the Royal Opera House, and with productions of *Richard II* and *Richard III* in Stratford, he completed the whole of the Shakespeare history cycle, which he began in 1975. Among his other productions have been: *As You Like It*; *Troilus and Cressida*; *Much Ado about Nothing* (with Derek Jacobi & Sinead Cusack); *Arden of Faversham* (with Jenny Agutter); the musical *Poppy* by Peter Nichols and Monty Norman at the Barbican (winner of SWET award for 'Musical of the Year'). He also directed Derek Jacobi in a new production of Rostand's *Cyrano de Bergerac* at the Barbican, which collected nine awards including the SWET award for 'Best Director' and the Drama Awards' 'Best Director of a Classical Revival'. Recent credits include *Julius Caesar* (a production in which the crowd was notably absent), *A Winter's Tale* at the Barbican and Jean Genet's *The Balcony* at Stratford.

David Hare

Playwright and theatre, film and TV director. Plays he has written include: *Slag*; *The Great Exhibition*; *Brassneck* (co-wrote with Howard Brenton); *Knuckle*; *Fanshen* (with Joint Stock Theatre Group); *Teeth 'n' Smiles* (at Royal Court & Wyndham's — also directed); *Plenty* (National Theatre and Broadway; also directed; won the New York Critics' award Best Director); *A Map of the World* (National Theatre and Adelaide Festival; also directed); *Pravda* (National Theatre; co-wrote with Howard Brenton; also directed). Has directed many plays by his contemporaries, including Trevor Griffiths, Christopher Hampton and Howard Brenton. He co-founded Portable Theatre and Joint Stock Theatre Group, and has been resident dramatist at the Royal Court and at Nottingham Playhouse. For TV, he has written: *Licking Hitler* (1978) and *Dreams of Leaving* (1980; also directed) — both BBC *Play for Today*; *Saigon — Year of the Cat* (1983; Thames TV); *Paris by Night* (Zenith/Channel 4, also directed). He has written three screenplays: *Wetherby* (also directed; Golden Bear for 'Best Film' at Berlin Film Festival); *Plenty* (adaptation of his own play); *The Butter Mountain*.

Frank Hauser, CBE

Theatre director. Started his career as a BBC Radio producer, working with Alec Guinness, Peter Ustinov, Pamela Brown, John Gielgud and others. In this capacity, he engaged the then unknown Richard Burton to play Henry V. A few years later, Burton returned the favour by funding the Oxford Playhouse Company, which Frank Hauser ran for 17 years, and where many new plays were pioneered, including the stage version of *A Passage to India*, Aruzov's *The Promise*, Sartre's

Kean and Molnar's *The Wolf* (the last two were translated by Hauser). He has also written the book, lyrics and music for three pantomimes, including *Cinderella*, which was mounted in London and gave Twiggy her stage debut as Cinders. In 1987, he became a Commander of the British Empire, and has since been freelancing. Work has included: *Captain Brassbound's Conversion* (with Penelope Keith); *A Village Wooing* (Judi Dench & Michael Williams); *The Assassin* (Edward Woodward); *Agnes of God* (Susannah York); *An Enemy of the People* (his own translation; with Roy Dotrice in New York). Recent credits include *Thursday's Ladies* at the Apollo, and *A Man for All Seasons* (with Charlton Heston) at the Savoy and on tour.

Jim Henson

American film and TV director of animation/puppets, light entertainment and children's productions. Credits include: film: *The Muppet Movie, Labyrinth, The Muppets Take Manhattan, The Dark Crystal, The Great Muppet Caper;* television: *The Muppet Show, Muppet Babies, Fraggle Rock, The Storyteller.*

Mike Hodges

Film and TV director. Film credits include: *Get Carter* (1971); *Pulp* (1972); *The Terminal Man* (1973); *Flash Gordon* (1980); *Squaring the Circle* (1984); *Morons from Outer Space* (1984); *Buried Alive* (1985); *A Prayer for the Dying* (1987).

Harry Hook

Film director. Credits include: *Art and Madness; Unknown Region; Sins of the Father; Snakes 'n' Ladders; Before I Die For Ever; The Kitchen Toto* (1987).

Hugh Hudson

Film director. Credits include: *Fangio; Chariots of Fire* (1981; Academy Award for 'Best Picture'); *Greystoke: The Legend of Tarzan, Lord of the Apes* (1984); *Revolution.*

Nicholas Hytner

Theatre and opera director. An associate director of the Royal Exchange Theatre in Manchester since 1985. Has directed at several repertory theatres, including Exeter and Leeds, and after impressing English National Opera director Colin Graham with one of his student productions at the Edinburgh Festival, he has worked as Jonathan Miller's assistant at the ENO and has directed several operas there including Wagner's *Rienzi and Xerxes*, which won the 1987 Laurence Olivier award for 'Best Opera Production'. Other operas he has directed include *King Priam, Turn of the Screw* and *Marriage of Figaro* for Kent Opera, and Handel's *Julius Caesar* in Paris. He has also directed the new opera, *The King Goes Forth to France* at Covent Garden. Theatre work has included: *Mumbo Jumbo; As You Like It; Jumpers* (with Julie Walters & Tom Courtenay); *Edward II* (Ian McDiarmid); *The Country Wife* (Cheryl Campbell); Schiller's *Don Carlos; The Scarlet Pimpernel* (Donald Sinden; at Chichester and in the West End). Recent credits include: *Measure for Measure* for the RSC in Stratford; *The Tempest* at Stratford; *The Magic Flute* for the ENO; *The Knot Garden* for the Royal Opera.

James Ivory

Film director. In partnership with producer Ismail Merchant and writer Ruth Prawer Jhabvala, he has made films touching on British colonial and expatriate experience, many of which are set in India. Credits include: *Savages* (1972); *Helen, Queen of the Nautch Girls* (1973); *Mahatma and the Mad Boy* (1974);

Autobiography of a Princess (1975); *The Wild Party* (1975); *Roseland* (1977); *Hullabaloo over George and Bonnie's Pictures* (1978); *The Europeans* (1979); *Jane Austen in Manhattan* (1980); *Quartet* (1981); *Heat and Dust* (1983); *The Bostonians* (1984); and, recently, *A Room with a View* and *Maurice*.

Paul Jackson

TV director and producer. Credits include: *The Two Ronnies; Three of a Kind* (1981); *Carrott's Lib* (1982); *The Young Ones* (1983); *Happy Families* (1985); *Saturday Live* (1985); *Girls on Top* (1985); *Red Dwarf; Spitting Image* (1984).

Derek Jarman

Film director. Worked as an art director for Ken Russell and has made promotional pop videos. Credits include: *Sebastiane* (1976); *Jubilee* (1978); *The Tempest* (1979); *Caravaggio* (1986); *The Last of England* (1987).

Roland Joffe

Film and TV director. In his early career, became the youngest director at the National Theatre, under Laurence Olivier, in 1973. Credits include: film: *The Killing Fields* (1984); *The Mission*; television: *The Spongers* (1978; BBC-TV *Play for Today*); *No, Mama, No; 'Tis Pity She's a Whore* (1980; BBC-TV); *United Kingdom* (1981; BBC-TV).

Richard Jones

Opera and theatre director. Initially worked as a jazz musician, before being awarded an Arts Council trainee director's bursary in 1982 to work with Scottish Opera. Recent opera productions include: *The Love for Three Oranges* (Opera North/English National Opera); *The Plummer's Gift* (David Blake's new opera for English National Opera); *The Rheingold and The Valkyrie* (Scottish Opera). Theatre credits include: *Too Clever by Half* by Ostrovsky, at the Old Vic for Jonathan Miller.

Terry Jones

Film director. Came to prominence as an actor with the TV series of *Monty Python's Flying Circus*. Film credits include: *Monty Python and the Holy Grail* (co-directed with Terry Gilliam); *Monty Python's Life of Brian*; *Monty Python's the Meaning of Life*; *Personal Services*.

Marek Kanievska

Film Director. Worked in television, where credits include: *Coronation Street* and *Muck and Brass* before directing the feature films: *Another Country* and *Horror Movie*.

Nicolas Kent

Theatre and TV director. Has been an associate director at the Traverse Theatre in Edinburgh and the Oxford Playhouse. Currently artistic director of the Tricycle Theatre. Credits include: theatre: *Class Enemy* (1979; Young Vic), *Love of a Good Man* and *No End of Blame* by Howard Barker (1980 & 1981; Royal Court), *The Great White Hope* (1985; Tricycle Theatre). TV: *Oceans Apart* by Olwen Wymark, *The Prodigal Grandfather* by Donald Churchill, *Playboy of the West Indies* — all for BBC-TV.

Irvin Kershner

Film and TV director. Credits include: TV: *Amazing Stories* (1985; NBC/Universal), *Raid on Entebbe* (1977); film: *Never Say Never Again* (1983), *The Empire Strikes Back* (1980), *The Eyes of Laura Mars* (1978), *The Return of a Man Called Horse* (1976).

Jenny Killick

Theatre director. In 1986, when she was 25, she took over as artistic director of the Traverse Theatre in Edinburgh where she succeeded in maintaining the theatre's reputation as a powerhouse for new writing. Financial constraints were met with an ambitious programme of visiting productions. New work included a 'Scottish Accents' season in 1988, comprising four plays by young Scottish writers. In an interview with Sarah Hemming in *Plays & Players* (February 1988), Killick said: 'I think if you don't want audience support you make a film or television. But you do theatre because you're a big show-off. You want the immediacy of response. But I think that's been forgotten. So I'm trying to stimulate that response again, to show that contemporary work can come from that very basic communicative root. A lot of new plays I've read have been terribly clever, but they have not moved me in the way that classical ones have. And I suppose the thing is to get contemporary work to aspire to those fundamental responses that are achieved by classical plays.' Jenny Killick left the Traverse Theatre in 1988, to be replaced by Ian Brown.

Christopher Lloyd King

TV director. Credits include: *Pulasky* (BBC-TV) and episodes of *Boon* (Central).

Alex Kirby

TV director. Credits include: *Maneaters of Kumaon* (BBC-TV) and episodes of *Boon* (Central).

Robert Knights

TV director. Credits include: *The Glittering Prizes* (1976; BBC-TV; co-directed with Waris Husain); *The History Man* (1981; BBC-TV); *The Ebony Tower* (1984; Granada); *Tender is the Night* and *The Dawning* (1985; BBC-TV).

Ian Knox

Film and TV director. Credits include: film: *The Stronger* (1980; National Film School), *The Privilege* (1982; HRP); TV: *Workhorses, Sweet Nothings, Shoot for the Sun, Down Where the Buffalo Go* – all BBC-TV; *Boon* (3 episodes; Central).

Bernard Krichefski

TV director and producer. Credits include: *Nanny* (from 1981); *Young Shoulders* (1984; *Play for Today*; producer), *Bird of Prey 2* (1984; producer), *Leaving Home* – all BBC-TV.

Stanley Kubrick

Film director. Starting as a photographer on *Look* magazine, he made his first film – a short documentary called *Day of the Fight* – in 1950. Four years later, he set up his own production company to make *The Killing* with Sterling Hayden. He followed with *Paths of Glory* (1957), *Spartacus* (1960), *Lolita* (1962), *Dr Strangelove* (1964), *2001: A Space Odyssey* (1968), *A Clockwork Orange* (1971), *Barry Lyndon* (1975), *The Shining* (1979), *Full Metal Jacket* (1987).

Barry Kyle

Theatre director. Currently associate director of the Royal Shakespeare Company. Gained a Thames TV director's bursary and went to Liverpool Playhouse where he became associate director to Antony Tuckey, and directed 21 productions including: *Saved, In Celebration, Hadrian VII, The Knack, St Joan* and *King Lear*. In 1972, he went to the Theatre Royal, York, as associate director, where *Forget-Me-Not Lane* and *The Investigation* were among his credits.

In 1973, he joined the RSC as assistant director, directing *Sylvia Plath* at The Place and co-directing *Cymbeline* and *King John* with John Barton. In 1974 he was director of The Place season in London, when he directed *Comrades* and co-directed several other productions. Work at The Other Place has included *The Churchill Play* by Howard Brenton, *The Maid's Tragedy* by Beaumont & Fletcher, *The Witch of Edmonton* (by Dekker, Ford & Rowley) and *Lear* by Edward Bond. Productions at the Warehouse have included *Sore Throats* and *Thirteenth Night* by Howard Brenton and *The Irish Play* by Ron Hutchinson. Other work for the RSC includes: *Measure for Measure; The White Guard* by Bulgakov; *The Taming of the Shrew; The Dillen* by Ron Hutchinson (adaptation of the book by Angela Hewins); Arthur Miller's *The Crucible; Golden Girls* by Louise Page; *Mary, After the Queen* (sequel to *The Dillen*); *Richard II; Two Noble Kinsmen*. In 1986, in Stratford, he directed *The Jew of Malta* and *Hyde Park*, both of which transferred to London for the 1988 season, when Kyle also directed *The Churchill Play* in the Barbican.

John Laing

Film director. Credits include: *Beyond Reasonable Doubt* (1980); *Other Halves* (1984).

Angela Langfield

Theatre director. Credits include: *Top Girls* (Leicester Haymarket); *Steaming* (Chester Gateway); *Blood Relations* (Derby Playhouse); *Season's Greetings* and *See How They Run* (Leeds Playhouse); *Billy Liar* and *Hobson's Choice* (Octagon Theatre, Bolton).

Simon Langton

TV and film director. Credits include: film: *The Whistle Blower* (with John Gielgud & Michael Caine); TV: *Smiley's People* (1982; BBC-TV), *I Remember Nelson* (1982; Central), *Thérèse Racquin; Rebecca* (1979; BBC-TV), *Anna Karenina* (CBS Ray Star), *Lost Honour of Katherine Beck* (CBS).

Sir David Lean

Film director. Credits include: *Brief Encounter* (1945); *Great Expectations* (1946); *Oliver Twist* (1948); *Bridge on the River Kwai* (1957); *Lawrence of Arabia* (1962); *Dr Zhivago* (1965); *Ryan's Daughter* (1970); *A Passage to India* (1983).

Mike Leigh

Playwright and theatre, TV and film director. Directed and designed the original production of *Little Malcolm and His Struggle Against the Eunuchs* at the Unity Theatre in 1965. Was associate director at the Midlands Arts Centre (1965–6) and assistant director at the Royal Shakespeare Company (1967–8). His first original piece for the stage was *The Box Play*, produced at the Midlands Arts Centre in 1966. All of his subsequent work, which he has scripted and directed, has evolved out of improvisation with actors. Theatre credits include: *Abigail's*

Party, Ecstasy and *Goose Pimples*, all of which began life at Hampstead Theatre. TV work includes: *Who's Who; Abigail's Party* (1977; BBC-TV); *Grown Ups* (1980); *Home Sweet Home* (1982); *Meantime* (1983); *Four Days in July*. Film credits include: *High Hopes. Smelling a Rat* recently opened at Hampstead Theatre.

David Leland

TV and film director and writer. Former actor. Wrote the screenplay for *Personal Services*, and for his directorial debut, delved further back into former madam Cynthia Payne's past with *Wish You Were Here*.

Leonard Lewis

TV, theatre and video director and producer. Credits include: *Softly Softly, When the Boat Comes In* (1975–7; producer), *The Prisoner of Zenda, Brat Farrar* and *Rockliffe's Babies* – all BBC-TV; *Flambards* and *The Good Companions* (1980; producer) (Yorkshire TV); *Tales of the Unexpected* (Anglia).

Peter Lichtenfels

Theatre director. Began his career in summer stock theatre in Canada, then trained as a director at the Traverse Theatre in Edinburgh. Currently artistic director at the Haymarket Theatre, Leicester, where he has produced commercial hits as well as creating opportunities for new young directors, designers and writers. He also wants to develop a proper youth policy, to involve and educate the future young audience at the Haymarket.

Ken Loach

Film and TV director. Credits include: *Up the Junction* (1965; BBC *Wednesday Play*); *Cathy Come Home* (1966; BBC *Wednesday Play*); *Poor Cow* (1967); *Kes* (1969); *Family Life* (1971); *Days of Hope* (1976; BBC-TV).

Richard Loncraine

Film and TV director. Credits include: film: *Brimstone and Treacle* (1982), *The Missionary* (1983); TV: *Vanishing Army* (1978; BBC *Play for Today*), *Secret Orchards* (1979; Granada), *Blade on the Feather* (1980; LWT).

Mary Longford

Theatre director, often working with experimental material. Credits include: *A Bolt Out of the Blue* and *Looking for Something* (1985; Almeida); *Hilde's Opera* (1980; The Venue); *Looking Through the Window* (1980; Drill Hall).

Vere Lorrimer

Theatre and TV director and TV producer. Directing credits include: theatre: *The Mousetrap* (1975, St Martin's); TV: *When the Boat Comes In*. As producer: *Blake's Seven* (from 1978); *Tenko* (1981–4); *Dark Side of the Sun; Maelstrom* (1985).

Robert Love

TV director and producer, currently controller of drama at Scottish TV. Credits include: *Van der Valk* (1972) and *Moody and Pegg* (1974) (Thames); *The House on the Hill* (1981; producer) and *Killer* (1983; producer) (STV); *Off-peak* (film); *The Marriage Contract* (opera); *Taggart* (STV); *Extras* (Channel 4 play).

Jonathan Lynn

Theatre and film director, actor and writer. Artistic director of the Cambridge Theatre Company (1977–81), directing 19 productions including *The Deep Blue Sea*, *Macbeth*, *The Relapse* and nine new plays and British premières. In London, has directed *The Plotters of Cabbage Patch Corner*, *The Glass Menagerie*, *The Gingerbread Man*, *The Unvarnished Truth*, *The Matchmaker*, *Arms and the Man*, *Pass the Butler*, *Loot* and *Songbook* (SWET award, 1979). For the Royal Shakespeare Company, he directed *Anna Christie*, and for the National Theatre, *A Little Hotel on the Side*. He has directed two short films – *Mick's People* and *The Case of the Shortsighted Boss* – and for Paramount, *Clue* (also wrote screenplay). In addition to many theatre and TV appearances as an actor, has written two series of *My Brother's Keeper* with George Layton and three series of *Yes Minister* (followed by *Yes Prime Minister*) with Anthony Jay. Recently, he has directed *Budgie*, the West End musical based on the early 1970s TV series.

David McGillivray

Theatre director. Specializing in wacky comedy and alternative pantomime. Credits include: *The Farndale Avenue Housing Estate Townswomen's Guild Dramatic Society Production of Macbeth*, *The Haunted Through Lounge and Recessed Dining Nook at Farndale Castle*, *The Farndale ... Murder Mystery*, *The Revenge of the Really Big Men*, *They Came from Mars ...* (all with Entertainment Machine); *Living Skills* (King's Head).

John McGrath

Theatre and TV director and writer. Founded 7:84 Theatre Company in England in 1971 and in Scotland in 1973. Has written many stage plays, including: *Events while Guarding the Bofors Gun*; *The Cheviot, the Stag and the Black, Black Oil*; *Little Red Hen*; *Yobbo Nowt*; *Baby and the Bathwater*; *There Is a Happy Land*; *Bitter Apples* (musical). Most of these were written for the 7:84 companies, and he directed many of them. He first came to prominence in TV in the 1960s, directing many of the early episodes of *Z Cars* (including the first one). At this time, he also wrote *The Diary of a Young Man* and *The Diary of a Nobody* (with Ken Russell). More recent TV productions he has written and directed include: *Come to Mecca* and *Dear Manju* (BBC-TV); *Sweetwater Memories* (1984; Channel 4); *Blood Red Roses* (1986; Channel 4); *There Is a Happy Land*. In film, he has worked with director Jack Gold on *The Bofors Gun* and *The Reckoning*, and wrote the film script for *The Virgin Soldiers*.

John Mackenzie

Film director. Credits include: *The Long Good Friday* (1980) and *The Fourth Protocol*.

Mary McMurray

TV, theatre and film director. Credits include: film: *The Assam Garden*; TV: *To Have and To Hold* (LWT), *Born in the RSA* (Channel 4), *Miss Marple* (1987; BBC-TV).

Terry Marcel

TV, film and theatre director. Credits include: theatre: *Dusa, Fish, Stas and Vi* (1985; Watermans Arts Centre); TV: *The Ferret* (1985); film: *Prisoners of the Lost Universe* (1982), *Hawk the Slayer* (1980); *There Goes the Bride* (1979); *Jane and the Lost City* (1987).

Peter Medak

Film and TV director. Film credits include: *A Day in the Death of Joe Egg* (1971), *Odd Job, Ghost in a Noonday's Sun* and *The Changeling* (1979 – all Columbia); *The Ruling Class* (1971; United Artists); *Zorro, the Gay Blade* (1981; Fox); *Negatives* (1968; Paramount). Also, over 100 hours of TV, including *Nabokov* and *The Men's Club* for US public TV (PBS).

Nicholas Meyer

Film and TV director and writer. Credits include: film: *Time after Time* (1980; also screenplay), *Star Trek II: The Wrath of Khan* (1982); *The Deceivers* (1988; Merchant Ivory Films); TV: *The Day After* (1983; ABC). He has written several novels, including the bestseller *The Seven Per Cent Solution*, and the screenplay for the film adaptation. He has also written and re-written such screenplays as *Star Trek IV* and *Fatal Attraction*.

Roger Michell

Theatre director. Won the Buzz Goodbody prize in 1977 for his production of *Bingo* at the *Sunday Times* Student Drama Festival. Worked at the Royal Court for two years, where he assisted Beckett and Osborne and directed various plays in the Theatre Upstairs, including *The Key Tag* by Mike McGrath and *The Catch* by Nick Darke. Co-wrote and directed *The White Glove* with Richard Maher, which was performed at the Lyric, Hammersmith and in the West End. He then worked at Cambridge Theatre Company, Southampton, Hampstead, Brighton, Sheffield and at the Young Vic. Joining the Royal Shakespeare Company in 1984, he worked as assistant director and then directed the première of Nick Darke's *The Dead Monkey* for The Pit in 1986. He has directed two RSC/Nat West tour productions (*The Merchant of Venice* and *Hamlet*), the British première of Vaclav Havel's *Temptation* for The Other Place and The Pit and, in 1988, *The Constant Couple*, *Restoration* and *Campesinos* for the Stratford season.

Gavin Millar

TV and film director. Credits include: film: *Dreamchild*; television: *Cream in My Coffee* (1980; LWT), *Intensive Care* (1982; BBC-TV), *The Weather in the Streets* (1984; BBC-TV), *The Russian Soldier* (1986), *Mr & Mrs Edgehill*; *Scoop*; *The Irons of Wrath*.

Jonathan Miller

Theatre and opera director and writer. Trained as a doctor of medicine, but sprang to prominence in the Cambridge Footlights in *Out of the Blue* in 1954. Co-wrote and appeared in *Beyond the Fringe* in 1960. More recent theatre credits as director include: *The Merchant of Venice* (National Theatre); *The Three Sisters*, *The Seagull* and *Long Day's Journey into Night* (London & Broadway); *The Emperor* (Royal Court); *The Taming of the Shrew* (Royal Shakespeare Company). He is currently artistic director of the Old Vic Theatre, where he has directed: *Andromache*; *One-Way Pendulum* (also Royal Alexandra Theatre, Toronto); *Bussy D'Ambois*; *The Tempest*. Opera credits include: *Arabella, Otello, Rigoletto, Don Giovanni, The Magic Flute, Tosca, The Barber of Seville* and *The Mikado* for English National Opera, and productions for Scottish Opera (including *Candide*, with John Wells), Australian Opera, Los Angeles Opera and many others. Work for TV includes *The Body in Question*, *Cosi Fan Tutte* and 12 plays for the BBC Shakespeare series. He has written a number of books: *The Body in Question*; *States of Mind*; *The Human Body*; *Facts of Life*; *Subsequent Performances*.

Robert Ellis Miller

American film and TV director. Worked in TV before moving on to films. Film credits include: *The Buttercup Chain* (1970); *Hawks* (1988).

Christopher Morahan

Theatre, TV and film director. Studied at the Old Vic Theatre School under Michel St Denis and began directing at ATV, where his credits included *Emergency Ward 10*, *Probation Officer* and *John Gabriel Borkman* (1958). From 1961 to 1971 he worked as a freelance TV director on such productions as: *The Orwell Trilogy*; *Talking to a Stranger* (1966; BBC-TV); *The Ragged Trousered Philanthropists* (1967); *A Month in the Country*; *Uncle Vanya*; *The Gorge* (1968; BBC-TV); *Hearts and Flowers* (1970; BBC-TV); *Giants and Ogres*; *The Letter*; *The Chinese Prime Minister*. From 1972 to 1976, he was head of plays for BBC-TV, and directed *The Common* (1973; *Play of the Month*) and *Old Times*. In 1982, he was co-director of *The Jewel in the Crown* for Granada, for which he received two British Academy Awards and an International Emmy.

After theatre work in the late 1960s and early '70s, which included *Little Murders*, *This Story of Yours*, *Flint* and *The Caretaker*, he joined the National Theatre and was deputy to the director (1979–80). His productions with the National have included *State of Revolution*, *Brand*, *Strife*, *The Philanderer*, *Richard III*, *Sisterly Feelings*, *Man and Superman* and, in 1984, *Wild Honey* with Ian McKellen, which won the Olivier, (London) *Evening Standard*, *Drama* and *Plays & Players* awards. Recently, he directed *In the Secret State* for the BBC, *Clockwise* for the cinema, Simon Gray's *After Pilkington* (a *Screen Two* success for the BBC) and *Troubles* (Channel 4).

Braham Murray

Theatre director and writer. Sprang to prominence while still at Oxford University when *Hang Down Your Head and Die*, which he co-wrote and directed, transferred to the West End and then to Broadway. Currently a resident artistic director of the Royal Exchange Company in Manchester, he had been artistic director of the Century Theatre and of the 69 Theatre Company in Manchester, directing, among other plays, *She Stoops to Conquer*, *Charley's Aunt*, *Mary Rose* and the musicals *'Erb* and *Catch My Soul*, all of which transferred to London. Other West End productions include *The Good Companions* (with John Mills & Judi Dench) and *The Black Mikado*. Among his many productions at the Royal Exchange are: *The Rivals*; *What the Butler Saw*; *Leaping Ginger*; *The Dybbuk*; *Measure for Measure*; *Waiting for Godot*; *Have You Anything to Declare?*; *The Nerd* (European première); *Who's a Lucky Boy?* (musical conceived with Alan Price & Gerald Scarfe); *Riddley Walker* (adaptation of the cult novel by Russell Hoban). Most recently, he has directed *Court in the Act*, *The Merchant of Venice* and the première of a new Woody Allen revue *The Bluebird of Unhappiness*.

Ronald Neame

Film director. Credits include: *The Horse's Mouth* (1958); *Tunes of Glory* (1960); *The Prime of Miss Jean Brodie* (1968); *Scrooge* (1970); *The Poseidon Adventure* (1972); *Hopscotch* (1980); *First Monday in October* (1982); *Foreign Body* (1985).

Mike Newell

TV and film director. *The Man in the Iron Mask* (1976; TV film); *The Awakening* (1980); *Dance with a Stranger* (1984); *The Good Father* (1986); *Sour Sweet* (1987).

Adrian Noble

Theatre director. Associate director of the Royal Shakespeare Company and artistic director of the 1988 Stratford season. Worked for two years in Birmingham in community and young people's theatre and was accepted on the IBA trainee director scheme. Went to Bristol Old Vic where he became an associate director; productions there included: *Ubu Rex; Man Is Man; A View from the Bridge; Love for Love; Timon of Athens; Comedians; The Recruiting Officer.* In 1979, he joined the RSC as assistant director and worked on *As You Like It, Romeo and Juliet* and *Hamlet.* After a spell with the Royal Exchange Theatre in Manchester (*The Duchess of Malfi* with Helen Mirren and *Dr Faustus* with Ben Kingsley), he returned to Stratford to direct his first RSC production, Ostrovsky's *The Forest,* which transferred to London and was named 'Best Revival' in the 1981 *Drama* awards. In 1982, he directed *King Lear* (with Michael Gambon & Anthony Sher) and *Antony and Cleopatra* (with Michael Gambon & Helen Mirren). Subsequent productions for the RSC have included: *A New Way to Pay Old Debts* by Philip Massinger; *The Comedy of Errors; Measure for Measure; Henry V; The Desert Air* by Nicholas Wright; *The Winter's Tale; As You Like It; Mephisto* by Ariane Mnouchkine; *Macbeth; The Art of Success* by Nick Dear; and for the 1988 season, *Macbeth* once again and the *Henry VI/Richard III* cycle.

Trevor Nunn

Director of theatre, opera, musicals and film. He won an ABC trainee director's scholarship to the Belgrade Theatre in Coventry and later became resident director there. In 1965, he became associate director of the Royal Shakespeare Company and, in 1968, artistic director. Work for the company in Stratford and London has included: *The Revenger's Tragedy; The Taming of the Shrew; The Relapse; King Lear; A Winter's Tale; Hamlet; Macbeth; Antony and Cleopatra; Hedda Gabler; Romeo and Juliet; The Comedy of Errors; As You Like It; The Alchemist; All's Well that Ends Well; Once in a Lifetime; Juno and the Paycock; The Life and Adventures of Nicholas Nickleby* (co-directed with John Caird) which made a successful transfer to Broadway and was shown on Channel 4. In 1982, he led the Royal Shakespeare Company into their new home in London at the Barbican, which opened with his production of *Henry IV Parts I & II.* This was followed by a Christmas production of *Peter Pan.* He has directed several highly successful musicals: *Chess, Starlight Express* and *Les Miserables* (which, with John Caird, his co-director, he also adapted from the Paris production). His Broadway production of *Cats* won a Tony award in 1983. Other recent credits include his first opera production at Glyndebourne, *Idomeneo* and the film, *Lady Jane.*

Mike Ockrent

Theatre director. From 1969 to 1973 was an ITV trainee director at the Perth Theatre, where he later became an associate director. He was artistic director of the Traverse Theatre (1973–6), where his productions included *To Damascus* and *Dream Play* by Strindberg and *Kasper* by Handke. In 1974, his production of Stanley Eveling's *Union Jack and Bonzo* played at the Hampstead Theatre, and *Schippel* (adapted by C. P. Taylor from Carl Sternheim's original) transferred to the Prince of Wales Theatre as *The Plumber's Progress* (with Harry Secombe). Other productions in the 1970s include: *The Merchant of Venice; Knickers* by Carl Sternheim; *Table Manners; The Admirable Crichton; Once a Catholic; See How They Run; A Respectable Wedding; One for the Road; A Nightingale Sang.* In 1980, he directed *Educating Rita* for the Royal Shakespeare Company, at the Warehouse, the Piccadilly Theatre and on tour. In 1982, he directed *Watch on the Rhine* by Lillian Hellman (starring Peggy Ashcroft) for the National Theatre, and Peter Nichol's *Passion Play* for the RSC and in Brussels. Other work includes: *Ducking Out* by Eduardo di Filippo at the Duke of York's Theatre; *Good* for the National Theatre of Belgium; *Short List* by Michael Rudman at the Hampstead Theatre; and *Inner Voices* by Eduardo di Filippo at the National Theatre. He has recently directed *Me and My Girl* at the Adelphi and *Follies* at the Shaftesbury.

Pat O'Connor

Film and TV director. Started with RTE in Ireland, making over 80 documentaries for them. Credits include: *Ballroom of Romance* (1982) and *One of Ourselves* (both BBC dramas), and the films *Cal* (1984), *A Month in the Country* (1987) and *Stars and Bars* (1988).

Horace Ové

Trinidadian-born film and TV director. Began his career as an independent film-maker in 1966 and, in 1986, won the BFI award for 'Independent Film and Television'. He has made the following short films: *The Art of the Needle* (1966); *Baldwin's Nigger* (1968); TV work includes: *Reggae* (1969; BBC documentary); *Coleherne Jazz and Keskidee Blues* (1972; BBC); *King Carnival* (1973; BBC *World About Us*); *Pressure* (1974); *Skateboard Kings* (1978; BBC *World About Us*); *Empire Road* (1978; BBC sit-com); *A Hole in Babylon* (1979; BBC); *The Latchkey Children* (1980; Thames); *The Professionals* (1981; LWT); *Shai Mala Khani/The Garland* (1981; BBC); *Music Fusion* (1982; Channel 4); *Good at Art* (1983; BBC); *Street Arts* (1983; Channel 4); *The Record* (1984, Channel 4); *Living Colour* (1985, Channel 4); *Moving Portraits* (1985, Channel 4); *Who Shall We Tell?* (1985; Channel 4 documentary about Bhopal); *Dabbawallahs* (1985; Channel 4); *Playing Away* (1987; *Film Four* International). Work in progress: feature film on the life of Charlie Parker and one on Phoolan Devi, the Bandit Queen of India, for Channel 4; also an adaptation of James Baldwin's novel *Giovanni's Room*.

'Here in England – all you are allowed to make is films about black people and their problems ... that's why I made *Pressure* – I was tired of reading in the papers about young blacks hanging about on street corners, mugging old ladies. Nobody tried to find out why they were doing it ... It was the same with *Hole in Babylon* (about the hold-up of the Spaghetti House restaurant by three young blacks and the resulting siege). The men in the siege were represented as a bunch of hooligans. Nobody looked at their backgrounds. They never went into the fact that they had a political motivation – that they wanted to set up a centre. One of them was a medical student, one was a poet and a writer and one of them had a background of mental illness ...' Talking about *Giovanni's Room*: 'It will be the first time a black director has made a film just about white people. It will be fascinating to see the results' (Horace Ové talking to Sylvia Paskin).

Tony Palmer

Film and TV director. Credits include: *All My Loving* (1968; BBC-TV); *There Was a Time* (1980; LWT); *Once at a Border*; *Wagner* (1983; Channel 4); *At the Haunted End of the Day* (1981; LWT); *God Rot Tunbridge Wells*; *Richard Burton*, a film biography (1988; LWT); *Shostakovich*.

Alan Parker

Film director. Credits include: *Bugsy Malone* (1976); *Midnight Express* (1978); *Fame* (1980); *Shoot the Moon* (1981); *Pink Floyd: The Wall* (1982); *Birdy*; *Angel Heart* (1987).

Julia Pascal

Theatre director. Credits include: *Men Seldom Make Passes* (1978; National Theatre); *The Caretaker* (1981; British Council tour); *James Joyce and the Israelites* (1982; Lyric Studio); *Mary's Men* (1984; Drill Hall); *Grombeen* (1985; Air Gallery); *Traitors* (Drill Hall); *The German Connection* (1986; Young Vic Studio); *Ghetto* (1987; Riverside Studios).

Raj Patel

Theatre, video and film director. Credits include: theatre: *Ahmed the Wonderful Oriental Gentleman, A Man I Never Knew, Anarkali* (all with British Asian Theatre, London); video: *Video Wicked, Caught in a Tangled Web* (also film; Star Productions).

Ron Peck

Film director. Credits include: *Nighthawks* (1979); *Empire State* (1987). *Empire State* is another film on the theme of docklands corruption, described by Mark Finch in the *Monthly Film Bulletin* as 'Not so much a side swipe at Thatcher's Britain as a last-gasp lunge at the throat.'

Harold Pinter

Playwright and theatre, film and TV director. Plays in chronological order are: *The Room, The Birthday Party, The Dumb Waiter, A Slight Ache, The Hothouse, A Night Out, The Caretaker, The Dwarfs, Night School, The Collection, The Lover, Tea Party, The Homecoming, The Basement, Landscape, Silence, Old Times, Monologue, No Man's Land, Betrayal, Family Voices, Victoria Station, A Kind of Alaska, One for the Road*. Screenplays: *The Servant* (1963); *The Pumpkin Eater* (1964); *The Quiller Memorandum* (1966); *Accident* (1967); *The Go-Between* (1970); *Langrishe Go Down; The Last Tycoon* (1976); *A la recherche du temps perdu; The French Lieutenant's Woman* (1981); *Turtle Diary*; and screenplays of his own plays: *The Caretaker* (1964); *The Birthday Party* (1968); *The Homecoming* (1973); *Betrayal* (1982). For the stage, he has directed: *The Collection* (co-directed with Peter Hall); *The Lover; The Birthday Party; The Hothouse*; Robert Shaw's *The Man in the Glass Booth*; James Joyce's *Exiles*; John Hopkin's *Next of Kin; Blithe Spirit*; William Archibald's *The Innocents* and six plays by Simon Gray (*Butley, Otherwise Engaged, The Rear Column, Close of Play, Quartermaine's Terms, The Common Pursuit*). Recent West End direction includes *Sweet Bird of Youth* by Tennessee Williams at the Theatre Royal, Haymarket (starring Lauren Bacall). For TV, he has directed *The Rear Column* and *Hothouse*, and film credits as a director include *Butley*. October 1988 saw the première at the National Theatre of *Mountain Language*, a 25-minute play which he also directed.

Stephen Poliakoff

Writer and TV and film director. Wrote his first play — *Day with My Sister* — while still at school; it was directed by David Halliwell at the Traverse Theatre, Edinburgh. Writer-in-residence at the National Theatre in 1976. As a TV scriptwriter, credits include: *Stronger than the Sun* (1977; BBC *Play for Today*); *City Sugar* (1978; STV); *Bloody Kids* (1980; ATV); *Caught on a Train* (1980; BBC); *Soft Targets* (1982; BBC). Has directed some of the later productions. Film credits: *Strawberry Fields* (1986; Marten Teagen Films/Channel 4); *Runners* (screenplay, 1983).

Angela Pope

TV director and producer. Credits include: *Lol – A Bona Queen*, *The Treble* and *Shiftwork* for BBC-TV; *A Childhood* (series for Channel 4); and recently *Sweet as You Are* with Liam Neeson and Miranda Richardson.

Tristram Powell

TV director (drama and documentary). Credits include: *The Ghost Writer* by Philip Roth (1983; WGBH (Boston)/BBC); *My Dinner with Louis* (1983; BBC-TV); *Karen Blixen*; *Out of Africa* (1985; BBC/Danish TV); *The Journey Man: Norman Lewis, Travel Writer* (1985; BBC); *Alfred Hitchcock* (2-part documentary; 1986; BBC); *East of Ipswich* by Michael Palin (1987; BBC-TV); *The Temptation of Eileen Hughes*.

Bill Pryde

Theatre director. Has worked at the Traverse Theatre, Edinburgh and was Scottish Arts Council trainee director at the Royal Lyceum, Edinburgh, associate director at the Young Lyceum and associate director of the Birmingham Repertory Theatre (main house and studio) for six years. Productions there included: *All's Well that Ends Well*; *The Merchant of Venice*; *King Lear*; *Romeo and Juliet*; *She Stoops to Conquer*; *The Elder Statesman*; *Lady from the Sea*; *The Masterbuilder*; and Rogers & Hammerstein's *Cinderella*. Also directed the premières of Stephen Bill's *The Old Order* (John Whiting Award, 1980), Vince Foxall's *Gestures* (John Whiting Award, 1979) and *Strictly Entre Nous*, as well as Michael Hasting's *Midnite at the Starlite* and the British premières of *The Wicked Cooks*, Tremblay's *Hosanna* (Half Moon, London & Birmingham) and Vampilov's *Last Summer in Chulimsk*. Productions as artistic director of the Cambridge Theatre Company include: *George and Margaret*; *The Miser*; *Hayfever*; *The Vortex*; *Canaries Sometimes Sing*. In 1986, he directed the Birmingham Repertory and Leicester Haymarket production of *Pride and Prejudice* at the Old Vic. In 1988, he resigned as director of the Cambridge Theatre Company (*see* Touring companies).

Michael Radford

Film director and writer. Credits as director include: *Another Time, Another Place* (1983); *1984* (1984); *White Mischief* (1987).

John Reardon

Television producer and director. Credits include: *Two's Company* (1976–8; LWT); *Agony* (producer; 1979–81; LWT); *Whoops Apocalypse!* (1982; LWT); *We'll Meet Again* (1982; LWT); *Drummonds* (1985; LWT); *Me and My Girl*.

Peter Richardson

Film and TV director and producer, writer and actor. Has been part of the Comic Strip team since 1979, devoting all his time to its productions. Credits include: *Five Go Mad in Dorset*, *A Fistful of Travellers Cheques*, *Gino* and, recently, *The Strike* (all seen on Channel 4); also *Supergrass* and *Eat the Rich*, which went on general release.

Bruce Robinson

Film director and writer. Has written 25 screenplays including *Withnail and I* (1986; Handmade Films) about life as a struggling actor in London at the end of the 1960s. Recently directed *How to Get Ahead in Advertising*.

Nicolas Roeg

Film director. Began as a clapper boy and worked as a cinematographer before becoming a director in the 1970s. Credits include: *Performance* (co-directed with Donald Cammell; 1970); *Walkabout* (1971); *Don't Look Now* (1973); *The Man Who Fell to Earth* (1976); *Bad Timing* (1979); *Eureka* (1983); *Insignificance* (1984); *Castaway* and *Track 20* (1987).

Michael Rudman

Theatre director. He has directed at many regional theatres, among them Sheffield Playhouse; the Belgrade, Coventry; Theatre Royal, Bath; The Palace, Watford; the Citizens, Glasgow; and for the Royal Shakespeare Company Stratford and the Dublin Festival. Assistant director at Nottingham Playhouse (1964–9), director of the Traverse Theatre, Edinburgh (1970–3), artistic director of Hampstead Theatre (1973–8) and director of the Lyttelton Theatre at the National from 1979 to 1982. West End productions have included: *Straight Up*; *Donkey's Years*; *Taking Steps*; *The Dragon's Tail*; *Camelot*. On Broadway, he has directed *The Changing Room, Death of a Salesman* and *Hamlet*. At the National Theatre (of which he is an associate director) his productions have included: *For Services Rendered*; *Death of a Salesman*; *Thee and Me*; *The Browning Version*; *Harlequinade*; *Measure for Measure*; *The Second Mrs Tanqueray*; *Brighton Beach Memoirs* by Neil Simon; *Ting Tang Mine* by Nick Darke (at the Cottesloe); *Waiting for Godot* (with Alec McCowen & John Alderton); *Six Characters in Search of an Author*; *Fathers and Sons* (a new adaptation of the Turgenev novel by Brian Friel).

Ken Russell

Film and TV director. Has worked as a ballet dancer and freelance photographer. Started working for BBC-TV as producer and director of arts programmes in the late 1950s, and gained fame by series of film biographies of leading composers. Once the *enfant terrible* of British cinema, his films are still often controversial. Credits include: *French Dressing* (1963); *Billion Dollar Brain* (1967); *Women in Love* (1969); *The Music Lovers* (1971); *The Devils* (1971); *The Boy Friend* (1972); *Savage Messiah* (1972); *Mahler* (1974); *Tommy* (1975); *Lisztomania* (1975); *Valentino* (1977); *Altered States* (1979); and, recently: *Salome's Last Dance, Gothic, The Rainbow* and *The Lair of the White Worm*.

Jan Sargent

Theatre and TV director. Credits include: theatre: *Who's Afraid of Virginia Woolf?* (1982; Bristol Old Vic); TV: *Fire at Magilligan* (1984; BBC *Play for Today*), *Flowers Tomorrow* (BBC-TV), *The Cause of Liberty* (BBC-TV), *Without Prejudice*; *Winner Stays On*; *A Long Way Away*.

Peter Sasdy

Film and TV director. Credits include: film: *The Lonely Lady* (1983); TV: Hammer House of Mystery and Suspense (3 films), *Lytton's Diary* (1985; Thames); *Secret Diary of Adrian Mole* (1985; Thames); *Blacke's Magic* (1986; NBC/MCA); *The Growing Pains of Adrian Mole*; *Imaginary Friends*.

John Schlesinger, CBE

Film director. Acted in student plays at Oxford and played character parts in the 1950s before joining the BBC as a director. In 1961, he won first prize at the Venice Film Festival for *Terminus*, a documentary about London's Waterloo Station. Credits include: *A Kind of Loving* (1962); *Billy Liar* (1963); *Darling*

(1968); *Far from the Madding Crowd* (1967); *Midnight Cowboy* (1969; Academy Awards for 'Best Picture' & 'Best Director'); *Sunday Bloody Sunday* (1971); *Marathon Man* (1976); *Yanks* (1979); *True West, Les Contes d'Hoffman; The Falcon and the Snowman; The Believers* and *Madame Sousatzka* (1988). For television: *An Englishman Abroad* (1983; BBC-TV).

Ridley Scott

Film director. A highly successful director of commercials, where he learned his craft. Film credits (mostly American) include: *The Duellists* (1977); *Alien* (1979); *Blade Runner* (1982); *Legend; Back to the Future.*

Don Sharp

Film and TV director. Credits include: TV: *Woman of Substance, Hold the Dream, Tusitala, QED; The Four Feathers* (1976; NBC); film: *Bear Island* (1979); *The 39 Steps* (1978); *Hennessy* (1975).

Bob Spiers

TV director. Long-time Comic Strip collaborator. Credits include: *Dad's Army; Fawlty Towers; Not the Nine O'Clock News;* and recently, for the Comic Strip: *Didn't You Kill My Brother?*

Max Stafford-Clark

Theatre director. Currently artistic director of the English Stage Company at the Royal Court Theatre in London. Has worked at the Traverse Theatre in Edinburgh and was a founder member of Joint Stock Theatre Group. Out of the Joint Stock adaptation of William Hinton's classic about the revolution in China, *Fanshen,* emerged the concept of a company that was run by all its constituents. Successful productions at the Royal Court have included Caryl Churchill's *Top Girls* and *Serious Money.* In 1988, after a row over the announcement, then cancellation, of Jim Allen's play *Perdition,* Stafford-Clark's contract as artistic director was not automatically renewed, but he applied for the job and, against strong opposition, won it back. He feels very much that: 'If you are involved with new work and new writing, which is where my career has been for 20 years in the theatre, then the Royal Court is the centre of the world, not just the staging post en route to the Himalayas of the South Bank' (from an interview with Jane Edwardes in *Time Out*). Recent credits include *The Recruiting Officer* and *Our Country's Good.*

Lou Stein

Theatre director. Currently artistic director at the Palace Theatre, Watford. Formerly director of the Chicago Chamber Theatre Ensemble and of the Gate Theatre Club at the Latchmere in London. Credits include: *Fear and Loathing in Las Vegas* (Gate Theatre & Fortune Theatre); *Down and Out in Paris and London* (Edinburgh Festival); *Spotted Dick; Madame Bovary; Are You Sitting Comfortably?; So Long on Lonely Street* (British première). In an interview in *Plays & Players* (May 1987), he deplores the lack of funding: 'Despite the reputation of the theatre as a leading repertory company, the Palace Theatre is funded as a small repertory company. The pressure to do 100% business is great, since it is the only way we can maintain the high standard of work.' He hopes to attract younger and more minority audiences to the theatre, and this is reflected in his choice of casting – for instance, Claire Benedict, a young black actress, in *So Long on Lonely Street.*

Simon Stokes

Theatre director. Credits include: *Lone Star, Private Wars, The Miss Firecracker Contest, Topokana Martyrs Say, When I Was a Girl I Would Scream and Shout, California Dog Fight, Kiss of the Spiderwoman* and *The Garden Girls* – all at the Bush Theatre; and *When I Was a Girl ...* at the Whitehall Theatre.

Charles Sturridge

Film and TV director. Has worked on promotional pop videos. Credits include: television: *Brideshead Revisited* (1981); film: *Runners* (1983); *A Handful of Dust* (1988).

Jeremy Summers

TV and video director, also commercials. Credits include: *Tenko* (1982 & 1984), *Strangers & Brothers* (1984) and *Big Deal* (1984–5) (all BBC-TV); *Coronation Street* (6 episodes; Granada); *Search for Tomorrow* (TV video productions; NBC). Recent credits include *Truckers* for BBC-TV.

David Thacker

Theatre director. Began work as a stage manager at York Theatre Royal, where he became assistant director in 1975. In 1976 he was awarded an Arts Council assistant director's bursary and went to the Chester Gateway Theatre. In 1978, he set up Rolling Stock Theatre Company in Crewe, which specialized in young people's and community theatre. In 1979, he became Arts Council assistant director at the Duke's Playhouse in Lancaster, in 1980 becoming director there. Appointed director of the Young Vic in 1984, and has since directed: *Othello; The Jail Diary of Albie Sachs; Stags and Hens; Macbeth; Hamlet; Measure for Measure; The Enemies Within; The Crucible; Romeo and Juliet; A Midsummer Night's Dream; Some Kind of Hero; Julius Caesar; Ghosts* (with Vanessa Redgrave); *A Touch of the Poet* (with Timothy Dalton & Vanessa Redgrave); *An Enemy of the People* (the last three all subsequently transferred to the West End).

Gerald Thomas

Film and light entertainment director. Credits include: film: *Time Lock* (1957), *Vicious Circle* (1957), *Please Turn Over* (1959), *Twice Round the Daffodils* (1962), and all *Carry On* films; TV: *Carry On* series (Thames & BBC); *Just for Laughs* (Thames).

Ralph Thomas

Film director. Credits include: *Doctor in the House* (1954); *Tale of Two Cities* (1962); *No Love for Johnnie* (1966); *The Wind Cannot Read* (1969); *The Biggest Bank Robbery* (1980); *Pop Pirates* (1984).

Wendy Toye

Theatre, opera, musicals director and producer. Credits include: *Madwoman of Chaillot* (Shaw Festival Theatre, Canada); *Kiss Me, Kate* (Copenhagen); *Once Upon a Mattress* (director & choreographer, Watermill Theatre); *Laburnham Grove* (1987; Palace Theatre, Watford); *Miranda* (1987; Chichester Festival).

Di Trevis

Theatre director. The first woman director of a company at the National Theatre. Started her career as an actor with Glasgow Citizens, Sheffield Crucible and at the National Theatre. However, a frustration with the passivity of the actor's role and a need to explore 'the whole experience' rather than one aspect of it led her into directing. Productions at the National have included: *The Taming of the Shrew; Miss Julie; Happy End; The Mother; School for Wives; Yerma.* She has also directed *The Revenger's Tragedy* for the Royal Shakespeare Company. She has directed a large proportion of classic scripts and revivals, and in an interview with Naseem Khan in *Plays & Players* (March 1987) said: '... It's a political decision. I realized quite early on that women were beginning to emerge into the fringe. And I felt there was really a place for women to work in the classical field because that history belongs to us too, even though it's being brought to us by men.'

Robert Tronson

TV and theatre director. Credits include: *Murder of a Moderate Man* (episode of *Sharing Time* series; 1984) and *Bergerac* for BBC-TV; *Boon* (Central).

Michael Tuchner

TV and film director. Credits include: TV: *Barmitzvah Boy* (1976; BBC); *The One and Only Phyllis Dixey* (1978; Thames); *Summer of My German Soldier* (1979; NBC); *The Hunchback of Notre Dame* (1982; CBS); *Adam* (1983; NBC); *Haywire* (1980); *Not My Kid* (1985); *Amos* (1985); *Trapped in Silence; At Mother's Request* (all CBS).

Colin Tucker

TV director and producer. Credits include: *The Waterfall, Fair Stood the Wind for France* (1981) and *The Gathering Seed* (producer; 1983) — all BBC-TV; *Drummonds* (producer; 1985; LWT).

David Tucker

TV and film director. Credits include: *Honeymoon* (1985; BBC *Play for Today*); *The Holy Experiment* (1985; BBC *Play of the Month*); *A Very Peculiar Practice* (1987–8; BBC-TV); *Miss Marple: Nemesis* (1986; BBC-TV); *It's in the Can* (sponsored film for Video Arts).

Jonnie Turpie

Video director. Credits include: *Out of Order* (Birmingham Film & Video Workshop, in association with British Film Institute & Channel 4). The latest in a line of remarkable collaborations between Birmingham Film & Video Workshop and Dead Honest Soul Searchers Group (DHSS) in Telford, who make videos which 'are not products of television professionals' notions of what young people are supposed to want; rather, they represent a pioneering form of direct communication between the young, using their own distinct verbal and visual language' (Julian Petley, *Monthly Film Bulletin*, August 1988).

Charles Vance

Theatre director and producing manager. Began his career as an actor at the Gaiety Theatre, Dublin, and subsequently played leading roles in numerous national tours of the UK. Directed his first production — *The Glass Menagerie* — at The Arts Theatre, Cambridge in 1960. Recent credits include: *The Mating Game; Bubbling Brown Sugar* (Germany); *Jack and the Beanstalk; Dick Whittington; Sleeping Beauty; Cinderella; A Taste of Honey; Policy for Murder* by Tony Clayton; *Verdict* by Agatha Christie.

Mike Vardy

TV, video and theatre director. Credits include: *Let's Run Away to Africa* (Yorkshire TV); *Heart Attack Hotel* (1983); *Time and the Conways, A Still Small Shout, Thunder Rock, Bon Voyage* and *Claws* (all BBC-TV).

Clare Venables

Theatre director. Artistic director of the Crucible Theatre, Sheffield. Recent credits include: *The Importance of Being Earnest, The Park* and *The Cherry Orchard* (with Steve Pimlott). 'The whirlpool of a writer meeting an audience via an actor creates energy which may, in the long term, raise us out of the depression under which we're living to remind us that it is only developed, imaginative individuals working as a group that can effect change that is worth making ... The Crucible has the perfect name for the activity — a place where high-quality ingredients are melted together to be transformed into something greater than the sum of its parts ... The reality is meetings, worries, arguments, computers, order forms, too-short rehearsals, too-small workshops ...' (from an article by Clare Venables in *Plays & Players*, August 1987).

Voytek

Theatre and TV director and designer. Credits include: TV: *Four People, Pilgrim's Progress, Frankenstein, Office Party, Callan, Joke* and *Sean* (4 episodes of adaptation of Sean O'Casey's autobiography); theatre: *Desire under the Elms*.

Glen Walford

Theatre director. Artistic director (until spring 1989) of the Everyman Theatre in Liverpool, where her credits include: *Tosca; Hamlet* and *A Winter's Tale*. Artistic director of Chung-Ying Company, Hong Kong (1979–82). Previous theatre work includes: *Return to the Forbidden Planet* (Tricycle Theatre, London); *Archangels Don't Play Pinball* (Theatre Royal, Bristol); *Much Ado about Nothing* (Rhyming Theatre Company, Tokyo); *Animal Farm* (tour of Malaysia).

Robert Walker

Theatre and TV director. Previously director of the Half Moon Theatre, London, where productions included: *Can't Pay? Won't Pay!* (also West End); *Alfredo Guarez — Twelve Shifts of Gear* by Juan Vera; *Guys and Dolls; Woyzeck; Mahagonny — The Songspiel* by Brecht & Weill; *Hamlet; Mayakovsky* by Stefan Schutz. Other credits include: theatre: *Pal Joey* (Albery Theatre & Half Moon); *Yakety Yak!* (West End); TV: *Night Kids* and *Angels in the Annexe* (BBC *Plays for Today*); *Deasey Desperate* (BBC film); *Dead Ahead* (BBC 4-part series by Howard Brenton); *Way to Go* (R. Walker Productions/Channel 4).

Deborah Warner

Theatre director. Currently resident director at the Royal Shakespeare Company. Trained as a stage manager at Central School of Speech and Drama, and worked at the Orange Tree and New End theatres and as an administrator for Steven Berkoff's London Theatre Group. In 1980, she decided to form her own theatre company to see if she could direct, and called it 'Kick' to symbolize energy. Kick quickly earned an international reputation for its highly innovative Shakespearean productions — *The Tempest, Measure for Measure, Hamlet, King Lear* and *Coriolanus* — many of which toured worldwide and three of which won Fringe Firsts at the Edinburgh Festival. Other productions with Kick were: *The Good Person of Setzuan* and *Woyzeck*. In 1986, she received the *Time Out* award for 'Director of the Year', and the next year was invited to Bangladesh to direct Bengali actors in a new version of *The Tempest*. In 1987, the Royal Shakespeare Company asked her to direct *Titus Andronicus* at the Swan Theatre in Stratford, which was a resounding critical success and transferred to The Pit. In 1988, she became a resident director at the RSC, and has directed *King John* at The Other Place and Sophocles' *Electra* at The Pit.

Keith Washington

Theatre and TV director. Credits include: theatre: *Gimme Shelter* and *An Empty Desk* (both Royal Court); TV: *Angels, Brookside, Gems, Collectors, Howard's Way*.

Les Waters

Theatre director. Credits include: *Fen* and *A Mouthful of Birds* (Joint Stock Theatre Group); *Fen* and *Rum and Coke* (Public Theatre, New York); *Abel's Sister* and *The Overgrown Path* (Royal Court); *The Seagull* (Liverpool Playhouse).

Tony Wharmby

The two police series, *Dempsey and Makespeace* and *The Gentle Touch*, were created and directed by Tony Wharmby. He also directed: episodes of *Lillie*, the biography of Lillie Langtry, actress and mistress of the Prince of Wales; *We'll Meet Again*; *Bouquet of Barbed Wire* (also adapted by him from Andrea Newman's novel); *Enemy at the Door; Love for Lydia; Helen, A Woman of Today*. As an executive producer, he has been responsible for the action adventure series *The Professionals; Eighteen Months to Balcombe Street*, a docu-drama about the IRA, nominated for the BAFTA award for Best Docu-Drama; and TV films by Dennis Potter and Alan Bennett. He has won many awards in Britain and the US.

Clifford Williams

Theatre director. Was made an associate director of the Royal Shakespeare Company in 1963 and has directed over 30 productions there, including plays by Shakespeare, Marlowe, Webster, Shaw, Durrenmatt, Rudkin, Hochhuth and Solzhenitsyn. He has also directed for the national theatres of Great Britain, Yugoslavia, Finland, Bulgaria, Mexico and Spain, as well as in Japan, France, Denmark, the US, Sweden, Canada and West Germany. West End credits include: *The Old Country* by Alan Bennett; *Born in the Gardens* by Peter Nichols; *What Every Woman Knows* by J. M. Barrie; *Too Good to Be True* by G. B. Shaw; *Wild Oats* by John O'Keefe; *Sleuth* by Anthony Shaffer; Pirandello's *Henry IV*; *Overheard* by Peter Ustinov; Lonsdale's *Aren't We All?*; Whitemore's *Stevie, Pack of Lies* and *Breaking the Code* (with Derek Jacobi) at the Theatre Royal, Haymarket and on Broadway. He has recently directed Jacobi in *Richard II* and *Richard III*.

Terence Williams

TV director and producer. Credits include: *Juliet Bravo* (producer); *The Chinese Detective* (producer, 1981); *Give Us a Break; Big Deal* (producer; 1984–5) and *Truckers* (8-part film series) — all for BBC TV.

Ronald Wilson

TV director. Credits include: *To Serve Them All My Days* (1980); *Frost in May* (1982); *Strangers and Brothers* (1984) — all BBC TV; *Sam Hughes's War* (CBC); *Drummonds* (1985; LWT); *The Black Tower* (Anglia); *The Bretts* (Central).

Michael Winner

Film director. Began making films for the BBC in the mid-1950s. Often works in Hollywood, where he has been responsible for several Charles Bronson blockbusters. Credits include: *Play It Cool* (1962); *I'll Never Forget What's 'is Name* (1967); *The Games* (1970); *Lawman* (1971); *Scorpio* (1972); *The Mechanic* (1972); *Death Wish* (1974); *Death Wish II* (1981); *The Wicked Lady* (1982); *Scream for Help* (1983); *Death Wish III* (1985); *Appointment with Death* (1987).

Peter Wood

Theatre, opera, film and TV director. In the West End, he has directed *The Bald Prima Donna/The New Tennant*; *No Laughing Matter*; *The Wit to Woo*; *The Iceman Cometh*; *The Birthday Party*; *Who's Your Father?*; *Mary Stuart*; *Five Finger Exercise*; *The Private Ear and the Public Eye*; *Loot*; *Incident at Vichy*; *The Prime of Miss Jean Brodie*; *White Liars/Black Comedy*; *Dear Love*; *Night and Day*; *Windy City*; *The Real Thing*; *Wildfire*. For the Royal Shakespeare Company, he has directed *The Devils*, *Hamlet*, *The Beggar's Opera* and *Travesties*. Wood is an associate director of the National Theatre; productions there include: *The Master Builder*; *Love for Love*; *Jumpers* (1972 & 1976); *The Guardsman*; *The Double Dealer*; *Undiscovered Country*; *The Provok'd Wife*; *On the Razzle*; *The Rivals*; *Rough Crossing*; *Dalliance*; *Threepenny Opera*; *The American Clock*. Opera credits include *Don Giovanni* at the Royal Opera House, and *Macbeth* and *Otello* at the Vienna State Opera. Recent work includes Tom Stoppard's *Hapgood* at the Aldwych Theatre.

Peter Yates

Film and theatre director. Trained at RADA, and worked as an actor and stage manager before directing his first plays — *An American Dream* by Edward Albee and *The Death of Bessie Smith* at the Royal Court. In New York, he directed Steve Tesich's *Passing Games* at the American Palace Theatre. For TV, he directed episodes for *Danger Man*, *The Saint* and other series. He has directed 16 feature films, including *Summer Holiday* (1963), *One-Way Pendulum* (1964), *Bullitt* (1968), *The Friends of Eddie Coyle* (1973), and *Breaking Away* by Steve Tesich and *The Dresser* by Ronald Harwood, for both of which he received Academy Award nominations as director and producer. Recent films include *Eleni*, starring Kate Nelligan and John Malkovich, and *The House on Carroll Street* (1988).

Robert William Young

TV director; also commercials. Credits include: *The Mad Death* (1983) and *Bergerac* (film dramas) for BBC TV; *Minder* for Euston Films; *Fairly Secret Army* (1984) for Video Arts/Channel 4; *Robin of Sherwood* for HTV/Showtime; *The Worst Witch* for HBO/Central; and *Three Wishes for Jamie* for Columbia/HTV.

18. Young actors

There is no shortage of nominations for 'promising newcomer' awards. Stage and screen are blessed with a wealth of young talent, and the following list of high achievers does not pretend to be exhaustive.

Among those who have achieved early stardom are several who give credence to the popular view that ability and persistence will overcome all obstacles. However, it has to be said that, of all the blessings a young actor might relish, being a member of a famous acting family is the best qualification for success. Instantly recognizable names figure prominently in the rollcall of the up-and-coming.

Whether they will all stay the course is, inevitably, a matter of subjective judgement. Only time and the next wave of competitors will tell.

Holly Aird   (19)

Frequently popping up on TV – *Inspector Morse*, *Echoes*, *The Muse*, *The Spider's Web* – Holly Aird is best known for her TV role as a young girl in Kenya in *The Flame Trees of Thika*. Born in Aldershot, the daughter of an army NCO and a mother who ran a bathroom design business, Holly first acted in BBC-TV's *History of Mr Polly*. A spell at the Bush Davies ballet school in East Grinstead and at an Eastbourne crammer afforded but a brief interruption to her career, which has now entered a new phase with her appearance in the Chichester production of *Ring Round the Moon*.

Frances Barber   (33)

After five years on the fringe, Frances Barber beguiled RSC audiences with her Ophelia (opposite Roger Rees's Hamlet) and a lead role in *Camille*. She made the transfer from stage to screen as a nun in Peter Greenaway's *A Zed and Two Noughts* and as Rosie in Stephen Frear's *Sammy and Rosie Get Laid*.

The daughter of a betting shop manager, Frances grew up on a council estate in Wolverhampton. From grammar school, she went to Bangor to study drama. After failing an audition for the Bristol Old Vic School, she attached herself to the Hull Truck Company where she worked with Mike Leigh and performed in what she calls 'the posh fringe'.

Latterly, she has won acclaim for her Viola in the Renaissance Company production of *Twelfth Night*.

Julia Bardsley

Recently seen as Mashenka in *Too Clever by Half* at the Old Vic, Julia Bardsley has worked extensively on the fringe as actor, director and producer.

Theatre credits include: Marie-Christine in *Ardele* (Queen's Theatre and tour); *Where the Rainbow Ends* (Kenton Theatre); *Bringing the House Down* (Nicholas Treadwell Galleries/ILEA 'Alive '85' festival); Maud, Betty and co-director, *Gaudete* (Almeida Theatre).

She is a founder member of dereck dereck productions, and has won three awards as a director: the RSC/Buzz Goodbody Award at the National Student Drama Festival, and an Edinburgh Fringe First Award for *Cupboard Man*, and another Fringe First for *Fallen* by Polly Teale. She was assistant director of *Road* at the Royal Court, and assistant producer of *A Night at the Chinese Opera* (Kent Opera), *Waiting* (monodrama for solo soprano and piano, Buxton Festival), *The Overcoat* (workshop at Royal Court) and *Bed* by Jim Cartwright at the National Theatre Studio.

Sean Bean (28)

Sean Bean's previous experience as a welder and council labourer in Sheffield, coupled with RADA training, have given him valuable background for the wide range of roles he has been called on to play — from Romeo with the Royal Shakespeare Company to Renuncio in *Caravaggio* and Brendan in the new gangster movie set in Newcastle, *Stormy Monday*.

From RADA, he went on to work at the Royal Court, the RSC, the Young Vic Studio and the Glasgow Citizen's Theatre. He also featured in *Troubles*, the notable adaptation of J. G. Farrell's novel, directed by Christopher Morahan for London Weekend Television.

Samantha Bond (26)

Daughter of Philip Bond (*The Onedin Line*) and TV producer Pat Sandys, Samantha insured herself against the hazards of an acting career by training to be a secretary. However, Bristol Old Vic Theatre School removed the need for a back-up job. She went straight to a plum role as Leo McKern's sidekick in *Rumpole of the Bailey* and, on stage, was much praised for her Beatrice in the Renaissance production of *Much Ado about Nothing*.

'I am not a small actress, either in size or manner; I am loud. We got to this scene [in *Much Ado*) which was not funny. I thought, "Jump in!" I am a great jumper-in. After that, things got better.' (*Guardian*, 20 August 1988)

Kenneth Branagh (28)

Unbowed by a surfeit of praise, Kenneth Branagh is working hard to retain his standing as the brightest hope of British acting. Having marked up two outstanding stage performances (as Tommy Judd in *Another Country* and as Shakespeare's Henry V at Stratford — where he was the youngest actor ever to play the role there — and the Barbican), a politely received film (*A Month in the Country*) and a brilliant TV debut (*Fortunes of War*), he went on to found his own Renaissance Theatre Company with fellow actor David Parfitt. Intent on escaping from the straitjacket of directors' theatre, Kenneth invited well-known performers — Judi Dench, Geraldine McEwan, Derek Jacobi — to oversee a Shakespeare trilogy that delighted both audiences and critics.

Born in Belfast, the son of a joiner, Kenneth moved with his family to Reading in 1970. He went to RADA and landed a major role in the BBC Ulster play, *Too Late to Talk to Bill*, while still a student. He won the RADA Gold Medal.

A Hollywood film, *High Season* (still to be released) in which he plays opposite Jacqueline Bisset, helped to finance Renaissance. The company started shakily with Kenneth's own 1986 production of *Romeo and Juliet* at the Lyric Hammersmith, but John Sessions' *Life of Napoleon* did better and the Shakespeare was a sell-out.

Kenneth has written two plays and is currently working on a book, but his next big project is a film of Shakespeare's *Henry V*. Having adapted the play for the cinema, he will also star in and direct the picture.

His lack of pretence shines through his favourite story of directorial inspiration: 'There were 30 of us walking around the stage "feeling the space", and [the director] said, "What would be wonderful when the king and queen come on is if you could embody the concept of honour and embody the concept of kingship and in some way absent yourself from yourself and give yourself to nationhood." And so I said, "You'd like us to bow." And he said, "Yes." '

Jason Connery

It is probably fortunate for Jason Connery that he is not the spitting image of his father, Sean Connery. Otherwise, the pressure to make him a young James Bond might have proved irresistible.

After learning the basics with Perth Rep, Jason advanced in small parts in such films as *The First Olympics* and *Dream One*, to the lead in an Australian saga of college life in the mid-1960s, *The Boy Who Had Everything*. He went on to play Robin Hood in HTV/Goldcrest series, *Robin of Sherwood*. Last year, he returned to the stage in a Nuffield Theatre production of *Journey's End*, which transferred to the West End.

Dona Croll

Dona was born in Montego Bay, Jamaica, and in 1957, her family moved to Birmingham. After training at the Birmingham School of Speech Training & Dramatic Art, she worked consistently in reps such as Leeds Playhouse and the Manchester Royal Exchange, and toured with the Cambridge Theatre Company, 7:84 and Joint Stock. At the Royal Court in London, she appeared in *God's Second in Command* and *Basin*, and at the Lyric, Hammersmith, she took the leading role in *Jelly Roll Soul* and Berintha in *The Relapse*. She also appeared as the Peruvian millionairess, Jacinta Condor, in the Royal Court's production of *Serious Money* in the West End. Television appearances have included *EastEnders*, *Boys from the Blackstuff*, *Come to Mecca*, *The Nation's Health*, *Black Silk*, *Ebony*, *The Someday Man*, *Loving Hazel* and *English*. Dona was also a presenter on the *6 O'Clock Show* (LWT) and *The Book Programme* (Channel 4).

Niamh Cusack   (29)

The third of the Cusack daughters to follow in father Cyril's footsteps, Niamh (pronounced Neeve) started working life as a musician. Having won a scholarship to the Royal College of Music, she taught the flute until she was 23. Saturday improvisation classes at the City Literary Institute, the adult education centre in Covent Garden, led to acceptance for a full-time course at the Guildhall School of Music and Drama. She left after one year 'to learn on the job' at The Gate in Dublin, a gamble which paid off with the offer to play Irina in the Manchester Royal Exchange production of *The Three Sisters*. Soon afterwards, she met Terry Hands who cast her as Desdemona opposite Ben Kingsley's Othello.

Rudi Davies

Rudi trained at the Central School of Speech & Drama and since then has appeared in three films: *Sammy and Rosie Get Laid*, *The Lonely Passion of Judith Hearne* and *Resurrected*. TV roles have included Susi in *Forever Young* (a film in the *First Love* series); many episodes of *Grange Hill* as Penny Lewis; Shirley in BBC-TV's *Inappropriate Behaviour*; and Sylvia in *Lizzie's Pictures* (BBC). Her theatre credits include Dorcas in the Royal Shakespeare Company's production of *Penny for a Song*, followed by Sally in *A Lie of the Mind* at the Royal Court. Her West End debut came about when the Young Vic production of *A Touch of the Poet*, starring Vanessa Redgrave and Timothy Dalton, transferred to the

Comedy Theatre. Following this, Rudi attracted excellent notices for her portrayal of Miranda in Jonathan Miller's production of *The Tempest* at the Old Vic.

Daniel Day-Lewis   (31)

Singled out by the movie moguls for international stardom, Daniel Day-Lewis has a chameleon-like quality that enables him to play, with equal conviction, the prissy aesthete Cecil Vyne in *Room with a View*, the gay punk in *My Beautiful Launderette* and a sex-obsessed Czech neurosurgeon in *The Unbearable Lightness of Being*.

Son of Poet Laureate Cecil Day-Lewis and actress Jill Balcon (with the legendary Ealing Studio boss, Sir Michael Balcon, as grandfather), Daniel started acting at Bedales, experience that helped to win him a place at the Bristol Old Vic Drama School. This, in turn, led to the Bristol Old Vic Theatre and to *My Brother Jonathan* on TV, a West End debut in *Another Country* (replacing Rupert Everett as Guy Bennet), bit parts in *Gandhi* and *The Bounty* and a RSC tour playing Romeo.

His latest film, *Stars and Bars*, was commissioned by David Puttnam during his brief reign at Columbia Pictures. Daniel plays Henderson Dores, an inept British art dealer encountering the lunacies of the American South. According to the *Monthly Film Bulletin*, he 'achieves an adroit blend of the burningly romantic, the normally venal and the comic schmuck'.

Penny Downie   (33)

Into her third season at the RSC, Penny is Margaret of Anjou in Adrian Noble's production of *The Plantagenets*, a role for which she attracted the sort of reviews reserved for stars in the making. Born in Australia, Penny was training to become a marine biologist in Tasmania when she decided to change course and study acting at the National Institute of Dramatic Art in Sydney. Having scored with her own TV series, she came to Britain five years ago, and since then has played Titania and Lady Capulet and was much praised for her Lady Anne opposite Antony Sher's Richard III.

Rupert Everett

Rejected by drama school but accepted by the Glasgow Citizens Theatre, Rupert Everett was the first of many young actors to win recogniton in *Another Country*, the play that made spying part of the public school ethic. Creating the role of Guy Bennet, he went on to repeat his performance on screen, and stayed with film for the well-received *Dance with a Stranger*. After a disappointing sojourn in Hollywood, when he almost came to play Orson Welles in a film biography, he decamped to Italy to play the mysterious stranger in Francesco Rosi's *Chronicle of a Death Foretold*. Continuing his association with the Glasgow Citizens — recently he was Nicky Lancaster in a revival of *The Vortex* (which transferred to the West End in early 1989) — Rupert is pursuing a tandem career as a rock singer.

Colin Firth   (29)

Claiming to have no interests outside his work, Colin Firth proved what dedication and talent can do with a towering performance as Robert Lawrence, the young Scots Guards officer in Richard Eyre's BBC Falklands film, *Tumbledown*. He went from comprehensive school to the Drama Centre and then to films, notably *Another Country* and, as the shell-shocked Birkin, in *A Month in the Country*, co-starring with Kenneth Branagh. Also *Lost Empires* for TV.

Stephen Fry   (31)

When does a comedian become an actor? With all the younger humourists, there is an overlap that makes it difficult to categorize them as one or the other. However, Stephen Fry is unique in being tipped as a future classical actor. This is the view of Simon Gray who directed him in the recent revival of his play *The Common Pursuit*. As the homosexual poet and don, Stephen was by far the best of an illustrious cast, more than fulfilling the promise of his earlier West End appearance as the junior master in the revival of *Forty Years On*.

A product of the Cambridge Footlights, who also collected a good degree, Stephen is a stalwart of the better TV comedy programmes (Cromwell and Wellington in *Blackadder*, Lord Snot in *The Young Ones*), chats endlessly but entertainingly on radio, turns out a weekly column for *The Listener* and is thinking about writing a novel. His first major television series, *This is David Lander*, a spoof of TV investigative journalism, came out at the end of 1988. It is said that Stephen Fry's agent has one of the easiest jobs in the business.

Iain Glen   (26)

Starring in the Thames TV series *The Fear*, Iain Glen more than justified the title. As the North London villain, Carl Galton, he assumed what one critic described as 'the exquisitely evil features of the devil himself'.

Iain read English at Aberdeen University for two years before making it to RADA. He hasn't stopped working since. Having made his West End debut, as Ridley in Tom Stoppard's *Hapgood*, he is awaiting reaction to two soon-to-be-released films — *Gorillas in the Mist* and *Paris by Night*.

Hugh Grant

Hugh's portrayal of Clive in the Ivory/Merchant adaptation of E. M. Forster's novel *Maurice* won him the Best Actor award at the 1987 Venice Film Festival, jointly with James Wilby.

Hugh's acting career was launched with his performance as Lord Adrian in the Oxford Film Foundation's *Privileged*, which he made while still at Oxford, studying English. After university, he worked at Nottingham Playhouse and formed a revue group, The Jockeys of Norfolk, which has played at the Edinburgh Festival and on the London fringe. They have also appeared on Tyne Tees Television, and Hugh has written and performed in radio commercials with them for Mel Smith and Griff Rhys-Jones.

Television credits include *The Last Place on Earth*, *The Demon Lover*, *Handel: Honour, Profit and Pleasure* (with Simon Callow) and, recently, *Ladies in Charge*. Recent theatre includes: *An Inspector Calls*, *Lady Windermere's Fan* and *Hamlet*. His most recent films are *White Mischief* and *Rowing in the Wind*, in which he plays Lord Byron.

Richard E. Grant   (31)

Born in Swaziland, Richard E. Grant was a virtual unknown until his collaboration with director Bruce Robinson on *Withnail and I*, playing the witty, degenerate actor Withnail.

He has worked at the King's Head Theatre Club (*Jo'burg Sis and Bremmen Coffee*); the Orange Tree (*Man of Mode*); Churchill Theatre, Bromley (*Tartuffe*); Yvonne Arnaud Theatre (*Stardust*); and Lyric Theatre, Hammersmith (*Tramway Road*). On TV, he has been seen in the spy thriller *Codename Kyril*.

His first Hollywood film is *Warlock*, and he is currently rampaging (with Bruce Robinson again) as advertising executive Dennis Dimbleby Bagley in *How to Get Ahead in Advertising*.

Rupert Graves   (25)

One of the many young actors to have been blessed by the magic touch of Merchant/Ivory, Rupert Graves is best known for his performances in two Forster adaptations for the big screen — *Room with a View* and *Maurice*.

What distinguishes him from others in the front rank is his lack of formal training. He has never had an acting lesson. After leaving school with one O-level, he was a frequent visitor to the Job Centre at Weston-super-Mare until an inspired or, possibly, a desperate employment counsellor sent him off to a circus where they were in need of a clown. 'I took being a clown very seriously and spent four whole days creating my own make-up. My main role was getting buckets of water thrown over me.'

Having found his vocation, he got himself an agent (from the back page of *The Stage*) and applied, successfully, for an Equity card. There followed a job with Peter Bowles in a children's TV series, a season at Butlin's Skegness and, the break, a lead role in *The Killing of Mr Toad* at the King's Head, Islington.

Rupert's West End debut was the Dennis Potter play *Sufficient Carbohydrate*, which was followed by *Torch Song Trilogy* with Antony Sher. But he made his strongest impact when he returned to the King's Head to play the poet Marchbanks in the Frank Hauser revival of *Candide*. It was this performance which landed him the role of Giovanni in the National production of *'Tis Pity She's a Whore*, a sad miscasting but his only serious mistake so far in a brief career embracing memorable appearances in the BBC series *Fortunes of War* and in the feature film of Evelyn Waugh's *A Handful of Dust*.

'Not being trained, I have no technique as such. I take longer in rehearsals to find my way. Some of the older actors get cross when I can't do things they learned when they were about 16. I don't have the short cuts, I have to go through the whole thing and you can waste a bit of time. But experience will teach me.'

Suzanna Hamilton   (28)

Suzanna had her first screen credit at 13, in *Swallows and Amazons*, playing Susan — 'In the best Arthur Ransome manner, I made sure everyone brushed their teeth and ate plenty of apples' — and, before leaving school, became one of the *Wildcats of St Trinians*. By the time she got to the Central School of Speech and Drama, via a London comprehensive and the Anna Scher children's theatre, she already had an Equity card and several parts, including a dairymaid in *Tess*, under her belt. Work since has included playing Julia, opposite John Hurt's Winston in *1984*, and parts in *Out of Africa* and *Wetherby*. She recently starred in *Wish Me Luck*, a TV series about women agents in occupied France.

Alex Jennings

Recently seen to good effect as the mercurial Yegor Dimitrich Gloumov in the highly successful *Too Clever by Half* at the Old Vic, Alex Jennings looks set to shine with the RSC at the Barbican.

Trained at the Bristol Old Vic Theatre School, he has worked consistently in regional theatre, at Leeds, Bath, Cambridge, Southampton, Manchester and Chichester, playing parts ranging from Weasel in *Toad of Toad Hall* to Algernon in *The Importance of Being Earnest*.

Television work has included *Smiley's People*, *The Kit Curran Radio Show* and *The Franchise Affair*. He also spent 18 months with BBC Radio Repertory. Recent work at the Barbican includes Lucentio in *The Taming of the Shrew* and Lucio in *Measure for Measure*.

Emily Lloyd

Yet to appear in *Spotlight* and short on interviews, little is known about Emily Lloyd except that she is a most compelling young actress. As the precocious teenager Lynda in the David Leland film *Wish You Were Here*, she was said to be the 'incarnation' of her role. Having previously appeared in *Everyone's a Winner* and *In Country*, her latest film is *Cookie*.

John Lynch   (28)

Educated at St Coleman's College, Northern Ireland, and the Central School of Speech and Drama, John Lynch played the title role in *Cal*, directed by Pat O'Connor. He has also played Konstantin in *The Seagull*, directed by Charles Sturridge, at the Lyric and the Queen's Theatre, London, and worked at the Contact Theatre, Manchester, the Royal Court and the Old Vic.

He has recently been seen as Stephen Dedalus in the James Joyce episode in the *Great Writers* series on LWT and in *The Strangeness of Others* at the National Theatre.

Phelim McDermott

After graduating with a BA(Hons) degree in performance arts from Middlesex Polytechnic, Phelim trained in mime with Jon Wright. He formed dereck dereck productions (with Julia Bardsley) in 1984 and produced/appeared in *Play With Me* (dance project), *Bringing the House Down*, *Cupboard Man*, *Gaudete* and *The Glass Hill*. His theatre performances include Billy in *Billy Liar* with the Manchester Royal Exchange Youth Theatre, Hamlet at the Man in the Moon and Golutvin in the highly praised Old Vic production of *Too Clever by Half*.

Kevin McNally

Born in Bristol and raised in Birmingham, Kevin trained at RADA where he won the Ronson Prize for Most Promising Actor and the Bancroft Gold Medal for Best Actor in 1975. His career began at Birmingham Repertory, followed by the National Theatre where, among other roles, he played Christ in *The Passion Plays*. Several films followed, including *The Spy Who Loved Me*, *The Long Good Friday*, *Masada*, *The Set Up* and *Bad Sister*, although most people will remember him for such TV roles as Castor in *I Claudius*, Tom Prince in *The Duchess of Duke Street* and Drake Carne in *Maria Marten*. After *Not Quite Jerusalem* at the Royal Court, which was then filmed in Israel, he played opposite Helen Mirren in *Extremities*, Greta Scacchi in *Airbase* and Diana Rigg in *Wild Fire* in the West End. Other roles included Yorkshire TV's *The Contract* and BBC-TV's *Thin Air*. More recently he appeared in two productions at the Old Vic: *Andromache* directed by Jonathan Miller, and *The Tutor* directed by Anjelika Hurwicz.

Janet McTeer   (27)

First attracting attention in stage roles in her early 20s, Janet McTeer's ability to look plain and harrowed or beautiful as required has brought her such diverse roles as a glamorous model in *Les Girls* (ITV) and a Strindberg victim in *Miss Julie* (BBC).

Daughter of a railway worker, she progressed from RADA to the Nottingham Playhouse, Manchester Royal Exchange and thence to the Royal Shakespeare Company, where comparisons were made between her and the young Judi Dench. Recently, she shone in Howard Brenton's *Greenland* at the Royal Court, and she has just made her first film, starring opposite Timothy Dalton in *Hawks*.

Imogen Millais-Scott   (20)

Descended from the Pre-Raphaelite painter Millais, Imogen trained at LAMDA and earned her Equity card by performing her own half-hour comedy show in London clubs. A succession of supporting roles on TV — The Bill, Lytton's Diary, Tenko — led to two memorable screen roles, Mrs Bee in Little Dorrit and, in sharp contrast, the wily seducer in Ken Russell's Salome's Last Dance.

Claire Moor

Born in Lancashire, the daughter of a jazz musician, Claire worked in cabaret around the North-west before joining the Royal Northern College of Music to study opera and vocal studies from 1978 to 1982. Since then, she has worked in repertory, playing Julie in Victoria Wood's Talent and appearing twice in Jesus Christ Superstar. After A Life of My Own at the Edinburgh Festival, she came to London to play Nimue in Camelot at the Apollo, Victoria, before taking over the leading role of Audrey in Little Shop of Horrors.

In 1985, Claire joined the McKellen/Petherbridge company at the National Theatre, appearing in The Duchess of Malfi, The Critic, The Real Inspector Hound and as Anya in The Cherry Orchard. While with the National, she was selected to alternate with Sarah Brightman the leading role of Christine in The Phantom of the Opera and then took over the role in March 1987.

On television, Claire has been seen in Wood & Walters, Granada's rock musical Visiting Day and Have You Met Miss Jones?, a two-handed musical in which she starred opposite Denis Lawson.

Wendy Morgan   (27)

On leaving school, Wendy toured for a year with the London Bubble Theatre Company, and while waiting to go to drama school, she landed a role in John Schlesinger's film Yanks. Television jobs followed including the title role in Bill Forsyth's Andrina and the role of Susan Layton in The Jewel in the Crown. Wendy was nominated for the Olivier 'Best Actress' award for her performance in the title role in Martine at the National Theatre, where she also appeared in Peter Shaffer's play Yonadab, directed by Sir Peter Hall.

Cyril Nri

Trained at the Bristol Old Vic Theatre School, Cyril was quickly snapped up by the Manchester Royal Exchange for Cymbeline, Great Expectations and Class K. From there, he went to the Royal Court to appear in Happy as a Sandbag, and a season for the Royal Shakespeare Company gave him the chance to appear in Julius Caesar, Volpone, Life's a Dream, Breaking the Ice and Kiss Me, Kate. Following this, he was in Manchester Contact Theatre's production of Oedipus Rex, and then Riddley Walker for the Royal Exchange. He played the roles of Nigel Ajibala, T.K. and Merrison in the Royal Court's production of Serious Money in the West End, and attracted enthusiastic reviews for his performance as Ariel in Jonathan Miller's production of The Tempest at the Old Vic. He regularly appears in the BBC Radio soap, Citizens. TV credits include Knock Knock, Umbrella and Pressures, and he has appeared in two films: Border Land and Strapless.

Gary Oldman   (31)

As the young actor with the weightiest collection of good notices, Gary Oldman is the living proof that talent can get you anywhere. Brought up in south London in what he characterizes as 'a dump' and the youngest child of a broken family, he went to a back-street school of the type that was supposed to have disappeared at the turn of the century. Not surprisingly, he was inspired to become an actor when he saw the film *If...* in which Malcolm McDowell mowed down the masters of his school with a machine-gun.

Gary won a scholarship to the Rose Bruford College, then joined Glasgow Citizens Theatre under Giles Havergal — 'surely one of the best training grounds for young actors in this country.' After a spell in provincial theatre ('I'd play in a church hall to four people, two of them the house manager and his wife, one an alcoholic, and one who would leave at the interval'), he found redemption at the Royal Court where he attracted notices as the ruthless shark in Caryl Churchill's *Serious Money*.

On screen, he extended his range of nasties with his portrayal of the heroin-addicted punk rock star Sid Vicious in *Sid and Nancy*. Then he took on the role of playwright Joe Orton in *Prick Up Your Ears*, a performance that inspired *The Times* critic to dub him a 'demonic little charmer'. After *Track 29*, the Nic Roeg–Dennis Potter collaboration in which Gary was the child–man fantasy of a bored housewife, he was snapped up by Hollywood to appear in *Criminal Law*, a psychological thriller directed by the eminently bankable Martin Campbell of *Edge of Darkness* fame.

It is all a long, long way from New Cross.

Jemma Redgrave   (23)

Daughter of Corin Redgrave, Jemma trained at LAMDA and made her stage debut as the eponymous heroine in *Lady Windermere's Fan* at the Lyric Theatre, Belfast. After touring with Pocket Theatre in the title role of *Miss Julie*, she appeared in *Easter* at the Haymarket Theatre, Leicester and in *Panorama* at the King's Head in London. Her first film role is in *Dream Demon* playing Diana, a shy English socialite whose marriage prospects to a Falklands hero are threatened by savage nightmares.

Joely Richardson   (25)

Daughter of Vanessa Redgrave and Tony Richardson, Joely was a natural to play the young Jean alongside her mother playing Jean as a middle aged woman in David Hare's film *Wetherby*. After RADA and the Liverpool Playhouse (*Miss Julie*, *Beauty and the Beast*) there was a season with the RSC when Joely played Helena in *A Midsummer Night's Dream* and the Third Witch in *Macbeth*. But her strongest role to date is Cissy III in Peter Greenaway's *Drowning By Numbers*.

Miranda Richardson   (31)

In less than a decade, Miranda Richardson has achieved more on screen than most actresses could aspire to in a lifetime. She was Ruth Ellis in *Dance with a Stranger*, the wife in William Nicholson's *Sweet as You Are* (a TV play about a married couple confronted with the news that he is carrying AIDS) and the scissor-wielding psychopath in Simon Gray's TV film *After Pilkington*. This last caused Harold Hobson to observe that, in 50 years as a drama critic, it was only the second performance he had seen that might properly be called tragic (the first was from Irene Worth in *The Cocktail Party*).

Miranda's strong line in mad or at least slightly dotty women has extended to the wayward Queenie in Rowan Atkinson's *Blackadder* series and, on stage, to Beth in Sam Shepard's *A Lie of the Mind*. Although she says she is not attracted to Hollywood, her moving portrayal of the colonial wife brought low by the Japanese invaders in *Empire of the Sun* gave notice of her ability to achieve international stardom.

The daughter of a businessman, Miranda's early years were spent in Southport where she went to grammar school. At 17, she won a place at the Bristol Old Vic

Theatre School, failed to get a grant and went to Bristol anyway to work day and evening as a barmaid, secretary and usherette. After a year, she got her grant.

Before her break in *Dance with a Stranger*, she qualified for an Equity card as an ASM at the Manchester Library Theatre, had 'a fairly bleak summer' doing TV ads, did six months in the West End in the comedy, *Moving*, and travelled the rep circuit. She reached the National last year to appear in *The Changeling*. *Plays & Players* summed up the critical response: 'This individual and intelligent actress, one of our white hopes, is completely watchable, never afraid of the almost indecent emotional thrust.'

Natasha Richardson   (26)

Daughter of Vanessa Redgrave and Tony Richardson, Natasha is said to have the 'habitually vague Redgrave smile and unfocused gaze' which is always appealing. Educated at the Lycée and at St Paul's, where she achieved the unique distinction of being asked *not* to take O-level maths, Natasha was accepted for the Central School of Speech and Drama after three auditions. Experience in alternative and provincial theatre led to her first lead, the eponymous heroine of *The Patty Hearst Story*. She was the object of Colin Firth's unspoken love in *A Month in the Country* and Mary Shelley in Ken Russell's *Gothic*. On stage, Natasha played Tracy Lord in the musical *High Society* and Nina in *The Seagull* at the Lyric and Queens Theatre in London.

Amanda Root   (25)

At 25, Amanda Root is the youngest actress ever to play Lady Macbeth for the Royal Shakespeare Company.

Since leaving the Webber Douglas Academy five years ago, she has played Juliet for the RSC touring company, and several other Shakespearean roles. She has also experienced two prolonged stretches 'out of work': 'What I really resented about those times was the feeling that other people were getting ahead. I hated wasting all that time when I could have been learning' (*Sunday Telegraph Magazine*, 1 May 1988). As Lady Macbeth, she is following in the footsteps of Helen Mirren (1974), Dame Judi Dench (1976), Sara Kestelman (1982) and Sinead Cusack (1986). But director Adrian Noble has every confidence: 'What I admire most in her is that she is completely fearless as an actress.'

Tim Roth   (29)

From comprehensive school to Camberwell Art School to television (*Made in Britain*, *King of the Ghetto*, *Driving Ambition*), Tim won praise for his role in the Stephen Frear's film *The Hit*. Other films include *Murder with Mirrors*, *To Kill a Priest*, *A World Apart* and a Mike Leigh improvisation *Meantimes*. Equally wide ranging in the theatre, Tim has worked with Steven Berkoff at the Mermaid (*Metamorphosis*), Philip Prowse at the Glasgow Citizens (*The Screens*) and Phil Young at the Royal Court (*Cries from the Mammal House*).

Greta Scacchi   (28)

It was a short step from drama school to first starring role when, at 22, Greta was selected by James Ivory for *Heat and Dust*. She followed this up with the seductive Lady Broughton in *White Mischief*, a role in which she revealed 'that mixture of blonde childishness and round adult allure which makes a supreme pin-up' (Claire Tomalin). On stage, she was in the West End run of *Uncle Vanya* playing opposite Michael Gambon.

Josette Simon   (29)

Born in Leicester, Josette joined the Royal Shakespeare Company in 1982 to play a witch in *Macbeth* along with a variety of other minor roles. According to Josette, 'I hated Shakespeare at school. They don't make him come alive. Even when I first joined the RSC I thought, "What am I doing here? I think Shakespeare's boring." I looked at the text and thought, "It's words that we don't use any more." '

Her performance as Dorcas Ableman in Louise Page's *Golden Girls* in 1984 brought great critical acclaim, and this was followed by Rosaline in *Love's Labours Lost*, which made her the first black actress to be given a major Shakespearean role by the RSC in more than 20 years. These two very different parts established Josette Simon as a name to watch. The *Financial Times* talked of her 'immense power and beauty', the *Daily Telegraph* called her one of the RSC's 'most striking discoveries in years' and added that she had 'the most extra-ordinary pair of eyes on the stage today'. Next came a role in Richard Attenborough's film, *Cry Freedom*, followed by the film, *Milk and Honey*, in which she plays a young Jamaican who goes to Toronto as a nanny. She returned to the RSC last year to take the role of Isabella in Nicholas Hynter's production of *Measure for Measure*. In a recent interview with Louise Page, Josette said – in response to 'the inevitable question about being referred to as the "black Isabella" ' – 'I suppose from the director's point of view there's always a fear that if he casts you in that kind of part, the audience will not accept you and will say "What's a black girl doing in Elizabethan England?" But audiences don't. They suspend their disbelief. I'm saddled with all kinds of prejudice. I'm a woman and I'm black, but you can't think about it all the time – you'd be a dead duck.'

Martyn Stanbridge

Martyn trained at the Drama Centre and went straight from there to the Oxford Playhouse Company in 1980. Recent theatre work has included: *Pride and Prejudice* (Cambridge Theatre Company); *Salonika* (Liverpool Playhouse); *The Three Sisters* (Greenwich Theatre); *The Vortex* (Glasgow Citizens Theatre); *Venice Preserv'd* (National Theatre); and *The Millionairess* (Greenwich Theatre).

Television credits include one of the leads in *Good and Bad at Games*; *A Pocketful of Rye*, an adaptation of one of Agatha Christie's Miss Marple novels; *Murrow*; *Paradise Postponed*; *AD 79*; and leads in *The Day After the Fair* and *Hedgehog Wedding* (both for BBC-TV).

Like much young British talent, he has been drawn to the US, where he played the lead in a pilot of a new NBC series, *Satin's Touch*.

Imelda Staunton   (31)

Encouraged to go to RADA by her elocution teacher, Imelda Staunton won the 'Most Promising Actress' award there, before making her mark at the National Theatre as Lucy Lockit in *The Beggar's Opera* and Miss Adelaide in *Guys and Dolls*. In striking contrast to these two roles, Alan Ayckbourn then cast her as the mournful Hannah in *Chorus of Disapproval*, a role that led the critics to praise her as 'extraordinarily moving' and 'giantly talented'.

Her talents range widely. In the last couple of years, she has played (as well as the underdog Hannah) a tough cookie in *The Corn Is Green*, a mean, sour staff nurse in Dennis Potter's *The Singing Detective*, the romantic pirate Captain Bess in *The Fair Maid of the West* at the RSC and Sonya in *Uncle Vanya*. All she asks is not to be typecast. Imelda is currently starring in Bill Douglas's film *Comrades*.

Juliet Stevenson (31)

One of the new generation of campaigning actresses, as made evident by her demand that the RSC should give more chances to women directors (heresy!), Juliet Stevenson is associated with original interpretations of Shakespearean roles – Isabella in *Measure for Measure*, Rosalind in *As You Like It* and Cressida in *Troilus and Cressida* – all played at Stratford and at the Barbican. But recently Juliet's screen career opened out from television (*Life Story, Stanley*) to cinema with her much praised performance as one of the trio of female conspirators in Peter Greenaway's *Drowning by Numbers*.

The daughter of an army officer, Juliet went to schools abroad before boarding at Hurst Lodge, a school noted for drawing out acting talent. At RADA, she won the Bancroft Gold Medal. Her early experience was with the RSC – she was a sea nymph in John Barton's *Tempest* – but it was seven years before she returned to play leading roles. Apart from her Shakespeare, she was Mme de Tourvel in *Les Liaisons Dangereuses*.

It is to her advantage, she argues, to have what she calls a 'weird' face, one that *Time Out* has described as a 'large, heavy-boned, mobile and, like a mountain that demands to be climbed, watchable'. Juliet's ambition is to play King Lear.

Imogen Stubbs

A dynamic combination of passion, physicality and intelligence have brought Imogen Stubbs many tributes from the critics including 'the Royal Shakespeare Company's most intriguing discovery for a decade' whose 'birthright is the big Shakespearean roles'.

After an unconventional upbringing on a wooden barge in Chiswick and much travel (her father believed it was the best education), Imogen Stubbs discovered her flair for acting at Oxford. 'I did revues and recited entire monologues in front of drunken Scots who threw things at me and didn't laugh once' (*Sunday Telegraph Magazine*).

Fresh from RADA and with a first-class degree in English from Oxford under her belt, Imogen worked at the Wolsey Theatre, Ipswich (Sally Bowles in *Cabaret* and Polly in *The Boyfriend*). She then went on to the RSC, where her performance – shinning up poles, walking on her hands and doing back flips – as the Gaoler's Daughter in *Two Noble Kinsmen* was ecstatically received. In the 1987 season, she also played Hellena in *The Rover* with Jeremy Irons, and Queen Isabel in *Richard II*. She has recently made her first film, *Nanou*, on location in France.

Suzan Sylvester

Suzan trained at the Central School of Speech & Drama and made her professional debut as Juliet in the Young Vic's production of *Romeo and Juliet*. A contract with the National Theatre followed, where she appeared in *A View from the Bridge*, attracting great acclaim for her portrayal of Catherine, and Annabella in *'Tis Pity She's a Whore*. Following this, she returned to the Young Vic to play Petra in *An Enemy of the People*. In 1987, she won the SWET Laurence Olivier award for Most Promising Newcomer.

Emma Thompson

Taught by her father, the actor and *Magic Roundabout* creator Eric Thompson, that she could do anything she wanted to, Emma Thompson has amply fulfilled his prophecy. After Cambridge Footlights and the fringe, she made the leap to stardom from the most successful British musical in years, the Leicester Haymarket production of *Me and My Girl*, which transferred to an apparently indefinite West

End run. She spent 16 months as Sally Smith singing the Lambeth Walk, before being reborn as Suzy Kettles in the BBC-TV series *Tutti Frutti* and as Kenneth Branagh's long-suffering wife in *Fortunes of War*. Her latest manifestation is as dancer, singer, comedienne and writer for her own six-part BBC comedy series.

Last year, Emma collected the Variety Club's award for the Most Promising Newcomer and the BAFTA award for Best Television Actress. It is a safe bet that there will be many more prizes to come.

Sophie Thompson

Daughter of Eric Thompson and sister of Emma, Sophie trained at the Bristol Old Vic Theatre School and from there appeared in seasons at the Bristol Old Vic Theatre. Played Laurel in the Chichester Festival Theatre production of *The Chalk Farm* and Katya in *A Month in the Country* for the Cambridge Theatre Company. In 1988 Sophie attracted rave reviews for her performance as Ophelia opposite Kenneth Branagh's Hamlet in the Renaissance Theatre Company's Shakespeare season. 'She has been a small and perfect jewel in the Renaissance crown since the first production, but here she blazes and dazzles.' (Jack Tinker, *Daily Mail*) On television she has appeared in *A Traveller in Time* (BBC), *Secret Orchards* (Granada), *The Wedding* (Tyne Tees) and *Casualty* (BBC). Her film debut was as a whore in *Missionary*.

19. Critics

Pressed to explain the secret of his success, a leading theatre critic said he was employed to give tone to his newspaper. 'You can always tell when a paper is trying to go upmarket,' he went on. 'The editor immediately gives more space to the arts.' The implication is clear. Editors are not much concerned as to what the critics say — that they exist is enough.

The question then arises, could it be the same for their readers? Perhaps that touch of class that critics bestow on a periodical is enough to justify the newsagent's bill. Actually reading their stuff is not a requirement.

There is some, admittedly highly subjective evidence for this view. Actors who masochistically devour every notice of their own and rival performances are bewildered to find that the news, which is to them so immediate, takes an awfully long time to reach the general public. Unless the triumph or failure is of such mammoth proportions as to merit a front-page story ('Actor walks off stage . . .' 'Understudy takes over . . .' 'A star is born!'), the first that most punters know of the reviews is when suitably doctored quotes appear in the advertisements. Otherwise, the news spreads by word of mouth ('I wouldn't see that, Doris. I hear the critics hated it').

Gilbert Adair, himself a distinguished critic, though of no fixed publication, said it all for film reviewers: 'People who go to the movies no longer read reviews, and people who read reviews no longer go to the movies.'

This is not to say that critics are powerless. Justified or not, a clutch of bad notices can undermine the confidence of everyone involved in a production, not least those who are taking care of the money. To shout defiance — as John Osborne once did when he plastered the stinking reviews of *The World of Paul Slickey* all over the foyer of the theatre in which it was appearing — is merely to accentuate the sense of impending doom. There is no getting away from Orson Welles's sad dictum: 'Every actor in his heart believes everything bad that is printed about him.'

The critics on the lead nationals are the ones to watch. Of the theatre, Simon Callow writes:

> There may not be any one critic in London with the *New York Times*'s make-or-break power, but the verdict of four men — those who write for *The Times*, the *Guardian*, the *Sunday Times* and the *Observer* — have been crucial to any play I've been in, except on the fringe where *Time Out* is undisputed kingmaker.

For film and television, the list is usually extended to the *Daily Telegraph* and *Sunday Telegraph*. Positive notices in these papers are enough to guarantee a viewing public either by sending a film out on circuit or by moving a television programme into primetime. Poor reviews can be taken as a sailor's farewell.

Some critics grab attention by sheer force of talent. Nancy Banks-Smith (television, *Guardian*), Christopher Dunkley (television, *Financial Times*), Jim Hiley (theatre, *The Listener*), Kenneth Hurren (theatre, *Mail on Sunday*), John

Naughton (television, *Observer*) and Charles Osborne (theatre, *Daily Telegraph*) are compulsive reading not just because they are critics but because they are also excellent writers who know how to entertain while they inform. There may well be others.

If, elsewhere, signs of world weariness are noted, it must be said that one or two of the better-known critics have been going at it for rather a long time. It would be sad if, having dedicated their careers to the pursuit of excellence, there are lead critics who are wilfully holding back talent in their own profession. Gilbert Adair, for one, is standing in the wings. Who will be the first star to move over for the understudy?

NIGEL ANDREWS	*Financial Times* (film)
NANCY BANKS-SMITH	*Guardian* (TV)
RICHARD BARKLEY	*Sunday Express* (film)
JACK BELL	*Daily Mirror* (TV/radio)
MICHAEL BILLINGTON	*Guardian* (theatre)
PETER BISHOP	*Sunday People* (film)
GORDON BLAIR	*Sunday Mirror* (radio)
DAVID BRADBURY	*Sunday Mirror* (TV)
MARY BRENNAN	*Glasgow Herald* (theatre)
CATHY BROWN	*East Anglian Daily Times* (film/theatre)
RICHARD BRUTON	(London) *Evening Standard* (radio)
EMRYS BRYSON	*Nottingham Evening Post* (theatre/film)
MICHAEL BURKE	*Star* (TV)
GARY BUSHELL	*Sun* (editor, 'Bizarre')
CHARLES CATCHPOLE	*News of the World* (TV)
DON CHAPMAN	*Oxford Mail* (theatre)
IAN CHRISTIE	*Daily Express* (film)
STEVEN CLARKE	(London) *Evening Standard* (TV)
DEREK CLEMENTS	*East Anglian Daily Times* (TV)
PAT CODD	*Star* (film)
WENDY COPE	*The Spectator* (TV)
MICHAEL COVENEY	*Financial Times* (theatre)
LIZ CURRY	*East Anglian Daily Times* (radio)
PETER DAVALLE	*The Times* (TV)
JULIE DAVIDSON	*Glasgow Herald* (TV)
PETER DAVIES	(Liverpool) *Daily Post* (TV)
CHRISTOPHER DUNKLEY	*Financial Times* (TV)
RICHARD EDMONDS	*Birmingham Post* (film/theatre)
CHRISTOPHER EDWARDS	*The Spectator* (theatre)
PAUL FERRIS	*Observer* (radio)
VAL ARNOLD FORSTER	*Guardian* (radio)
PETER FREEDMAN	*Cosmopolitan* (theatre)
PHILIP FRENCH	*Observer* (film)
JAMES GREENFIELD	*Yorkshire Evening Post* (theatre/TV)
SARA HADWIN	*Hull Daily Mail* (film/theatre)
ROBERT HANKS	*Independent* (radio)
MADELEINE HARMSWORTH	*Sunday Mirror* (film)
SUE HEAL	*Today* (film)

JIM HILEY	*The Listener* (theatre)
JOHN HOLT	*Nottingham Evening Post* (theatre/film)
KENNETH HURREN	*Mail on Sunday* (theatre)
TOM HUTCHINSON	*Mail on Sunday* (film)
SUE JAMESON	LBC (theatre)
IAIN JOHNSTONE	*Sunday Times* (film)
JULIE KAVANAGH	*Harpers & Queen* (theatre)
DOUGLAS KENNEDY	*New Statesman & Society* (theatre)
NEIL KERR	*Derby Evening Telegraph* (film/theatre)
PHILIP KEY	(Liverpool) *Daily Post* (theatre)
FRANCIS KING	*Sunday Telegraph* (theatre)
FELICITY LANDON	*East Anglian Daily Times* (film/theatre)
STEWART LANE	*Morning Star* (radio/TV)
RICHARD LAST	*Daily Telegraph* (radio/TV)
PETER LENNON	*The Listener* (TV)
KEITH MACDONALD	*Manchester Evening News* (film/radio/TV)
PETER MCGARRY	*Coventry Evening Telegraph* (film/theatre)
PAULINE MCLEOD	*Daily Mirror* (film)
JOYCE MCMILLAN	*Glasgow Herald* (radio)
W. MCMILLAN	(Exeter) *Express & Echo* (film/theatre)
DEREK MALCOLM	*Guardian & Cosmopolitan* (film)
HILARY MANTEL	*The Spectator* (film)
ADAM MARS-JONES	*Independent* (film)
VICTORIA MATHER	*Daily Telegraph* (film)
RICHARD MAYNE	*Sunday Telegraph* (film)
STEVE MILLS	(Exeter) *Express & Echo* (film/theatre)
SHERIDAN MORLEY	*Punch* (theatre)
DAVE MURDOCK	(Exeter) *Express & Echo* (radio/TV)
DAVID NATHAN	*Jewish Chronicle* (theatre)
JOHN NAUGHTON	*Observer* (TV)
BARRY NORMAN	*Film '88*, BBC-TV
CHARLES OSBORNE	*Daily Telegraph* (theatre)
KATHY O'SHAUGHNESSY	*Vogue* (film/theatre)
MAUREEN PATON	*Daily Express* (theatre)
PETER PATTERSON	*Daily Mail* (TV)
PHIL PENFOLD	(Newcastle upon Tyne) *Evening Chronicle* (theatre, film and TV)
GEORGE PERRY	*Illustrated London News* (film)
JOHN PETERS	*Sunday Times* (theatre)
EVE POLLARD	*Sunday Mirror* (theatre)
DILYS POWELL	*Punch* (film)
MICHAEL RATCLIFFE	*Observer* (theatre)
CHRIS REED	(Sheffield) *Star* (film)
HELEN REID	(Bristol) *Western Daily Press* (Film/TV/theatre)
JOE RILEY	*Liverpool Echo* (theatre)
ERIC ROBERTS	*Yorkshire Post* (TV)
DAVID ROBINSON	*The Times* (film)
JOHN RUSSELL	*Sunday Express* (TV)
WILLIAM RUSSELL	*Glasgow Herald* (film)

JEFF SAWTELL	*Morning Star* (film)
MILTON SHULMAN	(London) *Evening Standard* (theatre)
JACI STEPHEN	(London) *Evening Standard* (TV)
PATRICK STODDART	*Sunday Times* (TV)
KEITH STRONG	(Sheffield) *Star* (theatre/film)
TOM STRATHDEE	*Oxford Mail* (TV)
MIKE STUDLEY	*Liverpool Echo* (film)
ANGIE TAYLOR	*Sun* (film)
ALAN THOMPSON	*Yorkshire Evening Post* (film)
JACK TINKER	*Daily Mail* (theatre)
CHRISTOPHER TOOKEY	*Sunday Telegraph* (TV)
J. C. TREWIN	*Illustrated London News* (theatre)
CATHY TROUP	*Cosmopolitan* (TV)
KEITH TURNER	*Sunday Express* (radio)
SHAUN USHER	*Daily Mail* (film)
SALLY VINCENT	*Punch* (TV)
ALEXANDER WALKER	(London) *Evening Standard* (film)
MARGARET WALTERS	*The Listener* (film)
CHRIS WARD	*Derby Evening Telegraph* (theatre)
KEITH WARD	*Manchester Evening News* (film)
IRVING WARDLE	*The Times* (theatre)
IVAN WATERMAN	*News of the World* (film/theatre)
ROY WEST	*Liverpool Echo* (TV)
DEREK WHITFIELD	(Bristol) *Western Daily Press* (film/theatre/radio/TV)
DAVID WIGG	*Daily Express* (TV)
GEOFFREY WINTER	*Yorkshire Post* (film)
ROY WOODCOCK	*Hull Daily Mail* (radio/TV)
ALAN WRIGHT	*The Scotsman* (theatre)
ANGUS YOUNG	*Hull Daily Mail* (film/theatre)
GRAHAM YOUNG	*Birmingham Evening Mail* (TV editor)

Birmingham Evening Mail

Graham Young (TV editor) Member of international press judging panel, Golden Rose of Montreux Television Festival (1988), and committee member for Samuelson TV Award, Birmingham Film & Television Festival (1988).

Birmingham Post

Richard Edmonds (film/theatre) Director and compiler of prose and poetry recitals at various festivals; wrote and directed Alan Bates in *A Memoir of Diaghilev*. Author and director of *The English in Italy* at the Swan Theatre, Stratford-upon-Avon, and *The Venice Quartet*, a one-man play which was banned from the 1985 Edinburgh Festival. Award winner in the first BP Arts Journalist of the Year award (1987).

Cosmopolitan

Peter Freedman (theatre)
Derek Malcolm (film) See Guardian
Cathy Troup (TV)

Coventry Evening Telegraph

Peter McGarry (film/theatre)

Daily Express

Ian Christie (film)   Came to London in 1949 to play clarinet with Humphrey
Lyttleton's Band and stayed. Worked as a theatre photographer with John
Vickers, and subsequently snapped Hooray Henrys in Harrod's portrait studio.
Played clarinet with various jazz bands, including the Christie Brothers Stompers,
the Alex Welsh Band and the Mick Mulligan Band and George Melly. Wrote a
jazz column for the *Sunday Telegraph* before joining the *Daily Express* as a
feature writer, becoming their film critic in 1966.
Maureen Paton (theatre)
David Wigg (TV)

Daily Mail

Peter Patterson (TV)
Jack Tinker (theatre)   Started his career as a journalist as editor of *Brighton
Evening Argus*. Diary columnist with the *Daily Sketch*. Joined the *Daily Mail* in
1971. Author of *The TV Barons* and wrote the TV documentary *All Change for
Brighton* (BBC).
Shaun Usher (film)   Was TV critic for the *Daily Mail* before becoming its film
critic. TV reviewer for *Western Daily Press* prior to becoming broadcasting
correspondent for various national newspapers (1964–74). Contributes theatre
criticism for the *Daily Mail* and *London Weekly Diary of Events*. Writer of 200
short stories as well as plays on BBC Radio and TV. Has also been foreign
correspondent and feature writer.

Daily Mirror

Jack Bell (radio & TV)
Pauline McLeod (film)

(Liverpool) Daily Post

Peter Davies (TV)   Worked extensively in the regional media in the North-west
plus periods on national newspapers. Also editor of the *Liverpool Weekly Star*. TV
critic with the *Daily Post* since 1983; writes under the name of 'David Peters'. His
programme guide is 'the only one with subtitles for the hard of understanding'.
Philip Key (arts editor)   Writes on all aspects of the arts and reviews theatre, film,
radio, music and art (not TV). Presents annual theatre awards covering
Merseyside, Chester and N. Wales. Previously reviewed theatre for *Kentish Times*
and ran the *Daily News of Tripoli* in Libya.

Daily Telegraph

Richard Last (radio/TV)
Victoria Mather (film)   Co-author of *The English Dog at Home*. Formerly reporter
& diary editor on the *Sheffield Morning Telegraph*; presenter for BBC Radio
Sheffield. Freelances for the *Mail on Sunday, Harpers & Queen, The Times*. Art &
antiques columnist for *The Times*. Contributor to BBC Radio 4's *Loose Ends*; film
critic with the *Daily Telegraph* since 1986.
Charles Osborne (theatre)   A newcomer to the theatre critics' circle but has links
with drama going back to his young days in Australia when he acted in and
directed plays and wrote poetry and criticism. Was assistant editor of the *London
Magazine* (1958–66) and literature director of the Arts Council (1971–86).
Much of this time, he was under siege from the writers' lobby who felt that he was

unduly restrictive in his allocation of funds. Has written many books on music, ranging from *The Concert Song Companion* (1974) to *The World Theatre of Wagner* (1982). Formerly opera critic of the *Jewish Chronicle*.

Derby Evening Telegraph

Neil Kerr (film/theatre)   Has covered Nottingham's Theatre Royal for past 20+ years. Also reviews and interviews at Nottingham's Playhouse, Chesterfield and Leicester. Cut his teeth on local amateur productions many years ago, and particularly likes opera and high-quality plays.

Chris Ward (theatre)   Also reviews theatre, opera and ballet for *The Stage and Television Today*. Professional journalist since 1969.

East Anglian Daily Times

Cathy Brown (film/theatre)
Derek Clements (TV)
Liz Curry (radio)
Felicity Landon (film/theatre)

(London) Evening Standard

Richard Bruton (radio)
Steven Clarke (TV)
Milton Shulman (theatre)   Formerly a barrister and TV producer. Film critic of *Evening Standard* and book reviewer of *Sunday Express* before becoming theatre critic of the *Evening Standard* in 1953; also commentator on arts and current affairs. Film critic of *Vogue* magazine. Won IPA Award as Critic of the Year in 1966. Writer of TV play, *Kill Three*, and books including *Defeat in the West, How to Be a Celebrity, The Least Worst Television in the World*; film script: *Every Home Should Have One*.

Alexander Walker (film)   Lectured on political philosophy before turning to film, as critic on the *Birmingham Post* in the late 1950s. Joined the *Standard* in 1960. Long list of star biographies to his credit and, latterly, an autobiography, *It's Only a Film, Ingrid*. Last year was elected to the board of the British Film Institute.

(Exeter) Express & Echo

Steve Mills (film/theatre)
Dave Murdock (radio/TV)
W. McMillan (film/theatre)

Film '89 (BBC-TV)

Barry Norman   Saved from a career as a show biz writer on the popular press by a redundancy notice served in 1971, Barry Norman proceeded to carve out for himself a large chunk of peak-time radio and TV. *Film '89* is his showcase, but he has also presented many cinema specials such as *The Hollywood Greats*. Author of several novels and of film books based on his TV series.

Financial Times

Nigel Andrews (film)   Regular contributor to *Monthly Film Bulletin* and *Sight & Sound* while working for British Film Institute (1972–3). *Financial Times* film critic since 1973. Author of *Horror Films*. Regularly broadcasts on BBC Radio's *Critics' Forum* and presents *Kaleidoscope*. Critic of the Year in 1985 British Press Awards.

Michael Coveney (theatre)   Assistant editor of *Plays and Players* (1975–8). *Financial Times*: contributor since 1972; deputy arts editor and chief theatre critic since 1980.

Christopher Dunkley (TV) Started as a general reporter with the *Slough Observer* before graduating to being their cinema and theatre critic. *UK Press Gazette* feature writer and news editor, 1965–8. Moved to *The Times* as mass media correspondent and TV critic. Broadcasts on BBC Radio's *Kaleidoscope* and *Critics' Forum*; presents *Feedback*. Presenter/script writer and chairman for various TV programmes: *Real Time, Whistle Blowers*. Critic of the Year, British Press Awards, 1976 and 1986. Contributes to *The Listener, Television World, Stills, Electronic Media, Telegraph Magazine*, etc.

Glasgow Herald

Mary Brennan (theatre)
Julie Davidson (TV)
Joyce McMillan (radio)
William Russell (film)   Joined *Glasgow Herald* 1959 as reporter in Glasgow and Edinburgh. Moved to London office in 1961 to join Commons staff, reporting Scottish affairs, before becoming political correspondent. Film critic since 1985.

Guardian

Nancy Banks-Smith (TV)   TV critic of the *Sun* prior to joining the *Guardian* in 1969.
Michael Billington (theatre)   Trained as a journalist with *Liverpool Daily Post & Echo*. Was public liaison officer and subsequently director for Lincoln Theatre Company in the 1960s. Deputy drama, film and TV critic for *The Times* before becoming theatre critic of the *Guardian* in 1971. Author of *The Modern Actor* and *How Tickled I Am*. Broadcasts on BBC Radio's *Critics' Forum* and *Kaleidoscope*. Won IPC Critic of the Year award in 1975.
Val Arnold Forster (radio)   Besides being a freelance journalist, also pursued a career as an educationalist. Previously contributed to the *Daily Mirror* and the *Sunday Times*.
Derek Malcolm (film)   *Guardian* film critic since 1970 and *Cosmopolitan* film critic since 1972. Director, London Film Festival, 1984–6. Frequent broadcaster; initiated BBC-TV's *Film Club* in 1986. Past President of UK Critics' Circle. Won IPC Critic of the Year award, 1972. Author of *Robert Mitchum*.

Harpers & Queen

Julie Kavanagh (theatre)

Hull Daily Mail

Sara Hadwin (film/theatre)
Roy Woodcock (radio/TV)
Angus Young (film/theatre)

Illustrated London News

George Perry (film)
J. C. Trewin (theatre)   Drama critic for the *Western Independent*, 1928–32; deputy drama critic of the *Morning Post* in the 1930s; literary editor and second dramatic critic of the *Observer*; dramatic critic of *Punch* in the 1940s. Was with *The Sketch* and radio drama critic for *The Listener* in the 1950s. With *London Illustrated News* since 1946, *The Lady* since 1949 and the *Birmingham Post* since 1955. Has contributed to the BBC, *Times Literary Supplement, Drama* and *Plays and Players*. Author of numerous books including *The English Theatre, Edith Evans, Dramatists of Today, Verse Drama Since 1800, Peter Brook: A Biography*.

Independent

Robert Hanks (radio)
Adam Mars-Jones (film)   Has reviewed for the *Financial Times*, the *Times Literary Supplement* and *Sunday Times*. Author of *Lantern Lecture* (Somerset Maugham Award winner) and *The Darker Proof* (with Edmund White). Also editor of an anthology of lesbian and gay fiction.

Jewish Chronicle

David Nathan (theatre)

LBC

Sue Jameson (theatre)   News and current affairs presenter for LBC prior to becoming theatre critic and arts correspondent in 1981. Started in radio at Liverpool's Radio City. Contributes to *Punch, Plays and Players*.

The Listener

Jim Hiley (theatre)   After graduating from Birmingham University, worked as an actor in regional rep; actor/writer and director with Inter-Action community arts trust and at Inter-Action's Almost Free Theatre. Began to write about theatre for *Time Out* in early 1970s; contributor to the *Guardian*, the *Observer, Radio Times, Plays and Players* and *City Limits*. Broadcasting includes: *Critics' Forum, Kaleidoscope, Meridian* for BBC Radio; *Brian Hayes Show* and *The Night Is Young* for LBC; presenter of *Artbeat* for Capital Radio. TV includes *Did You See?, 01 for London* and *Thames News*. Theatre critic for *The Listener* since 1985.
Peter Lennon (TV)   Profile writer and writer on TV since 1982. Previously feature writer and TV critic for the *Sunday Times; Guardian* correspondent in Paris in 1960s. Wrote and directed *Rocky Road to Dublin* (Cannes Festival, 1968). TV critic with *The Listener* since 1987.
Margaret Walters (film)

Liverpool Echo

Joe Riley (theatre)   Arts editor with the *Liverpool Echo* since 1974. Author of *Walking in Lakeland, 50 Lakeland Poems* and *Today's Cathedrals*. Broadcasting includes contributions to *Kaleidoscope* and *Mainly for Pleasure*, and TV documentaries.
Mike Studley (film)   'Movie Scene' and 'Films on TV' columns.
Roy West (TV)

Mail on Sunday

Kenneth Hurren (theatre)   Writer on drama and the theatre since 1947. Freelance contributor to *Los Angeles Times*, the *Guardian, Radio Times, TV Times, What's On in London, Telegraph Magazine, Plays & Players*. Columnist for *Drama Quarterly*, 1970–82; theatre critic & associate editor, *The Spectator*, 1970–6; editor & theatre critic, *In London*, 1976–82. Theatre critic for the *Mail on Sunday* since 1983. Author of *Theatre Inside Out* (W. H. Allen).
Tom Hutchinson (film)   Started journalistic career with *Sheffield Telegraph*; founder, Sheffield Film Society. Worked for *Kinematograph Weekly, Picturegoer* (features editor) and *Cinema Today* before joining *Daily Express* as showbusiness reporter. Producer/scriptwriter with Tyne Tees TV. Film critic with *Nova* magazine; started (London) *Evening Standard* 'TV Preview' page; film critic of the *Sunday Telegraph* for seven years, then *Now!* and the *Sunday Standard*. Joined *Mail on Sunday* when it started up in 1982. Broadcasts review programme on Radio 2; also film critic for the *Hampstead & Highgate Gazette*.

Manchester Evening News

Keith Macdonald (film/radio/TV)
Keith Ward (film)

Morning Star

Stewart Lane (radio/TV)
Jeff Sawtell (film)

New Statesman & Society

Douglas Kennedy (theatre)   Administrator of the Abbey Theatre's second auditorium, the Peacock (1978–83). Author of three plays for Radio 4: *Shakespeare on Five Dollars a Day*; *Floating Down the Nile on the Oxford English Dictionary*; *The Don Giovanni Blues*. Stage play, *Send Lawyers, Guns and Money* produced at the Peacock, Dublin, in 1986. Has written one book – *Beyond the Pyramids: Travels in Egypt* (Unwin Hyman, 1988) – and currently working on another: *In God's Country: Travels in the Bible Belt, USA* (to be published by Unwin Hyman). Regular contributor to *The Listener*, and his journalism has also appeared in the *Sunday Times*, *New Woman*, *Time Out* and the *Irish Times*.

News of the World

Charles Catchpole (TV)
Ivan Waterman (film/theatre)   Was film critic for *East London Advertiser* before joining *News of the World* in 1975; also showbusiness editor since 1978.

Observer

Paul Ferris (radio)   Started his journalistic career on the *South Wales Evening Post* before coming to London to the *Observer* in 1953. Has written ten novels, the latest, *A Distant Country* in 1983, and five TV plays. But his widest range of work is non-fiction, including a biography of Richard Burton. His most recent book is *The Collected Letters of Dylan Thomas* (1986). Has been radio critic of the *Observer* since 1954.

Philip French (film)   Regular contributor to the *Observer* since 1963 and its film critic since 1978; senior producer in BBC Radio since 1959; producer of *Critics' Forum* since 1974. Deputy film critic of *The Times* (1973–8); chief book reviewer of *New Statesman* (1967–8); film critic, *London Magazine* (1967–8); arts columnist, *New Statesman* (1967–72). Member of the BFI Production Board (1967–74) and of BFI Publications Sub-committee since 1973. *Evening Standard* Film Award Jury since 1982; Prix Italia Documentary Jury (1981); Jury Member, Cannes Film Festival, 1986; Booker Prize judge, 1988. Contributes to numerous newspapers, magazines and anthologies in the UK and US; co-editor (with Michael Sissons), *Age of Austerity 1945–51*; editor, *The Third Dimension: Voices from Radio 3*; author of *The Movie Moguls: An Informal History of the Hollywood Tycoons*; *Westerns: Aspects of a Movie Genre*; *Three Honest Men: Edmund Wilson, F. R. Leavis and Lionel Trilling*.

John Naughton (TV)

Michael Ratcliffe (theatre)   Graduate trainee on the *Sheffield Telegraph* before becoming assistant literary editor on the *Sunday Times*. Literary editor (1967–72), chief book reviewer (1972–82) and member of TV viewing panel (1972–82), *The Times*. Theatre critic with the *Observer* since 1984. Co-author (with J. W. Lambert) of *The Novel Today*.

Punch

Sheridan Morley (theatre)   Deputy features editor for *The Times* in the 1970s. Joined *Punch* in 1975. Writes regularly for (London) *Evening Standard, Tatler, Radio Times*. Author of *A Talent to Amuse, Review Copies, Oscar Wilde, Marlene Dietrich, Sybil Thorndike, Gladys Cooper, Noel Coward and His Friends* and *The Stephen Sondheim Songbook*. Appears frequently on radio. Was an ITN newscaster and interviewer on *Late Night Line-up*. Stage appearances include walk-on in *Edward My Son* in Australia at the age of 9, followed by an appearance at the Yvonne Arnaud Theatre, Guildford, narrating *Side by Side by Sondheim*.

Dilys Powell (film)   Doyen of film critics. Was film critic of *Sunday Times*, 1939–76, and remains TV film critic of that paper. Film critic of *Punch* since 1979. Showered with honours including the CBE; was awarded BAFTA Award of Honour in 1984.

Sally Vincent (TV)

The Scotsman

Alan Wright (theatre)   Critic and arts editor with *The Scotsman* since 1965. Responsible for its comprehensive coverage of Edinburgh Festival and Fringe. Author of a new assessment of J. M. Barrie, *Glamour of Twilight*.

The Spectator

Wendy Cope (TV)   Originally a teacher. Her poems have appeared in periodicals such as the *Times Literary Supplement, Quarto* and anthologies such as *The Faber Book of Parodies* and *The Penguin Book of Limericks*. Collections of poems: *Making Cocoa for Kingsley Amis* and *Twiddling Your Thumbs*. Winner of 1987 Cholmondeley Award for poetry.

Christopher Edwards (theatre)

Hilary Mantel (film)

Star

Michael Burke (TV)   TV editor of the *Star* incorporating all TV news and feature stories. Previously crime writer for the *Birmingham Post & Mail*.

Pat Codd (film)

Sun

Gary Bushell (editor, 'Bizarre')   Formerly features editor for *Sounds* rock weekly; freelance writer for the *Sun, Daily Mirror* and (London) *Evening Standard*; joined the *Sun* in 1985.

Angie Taylor (film)   The *Sun*'s first regular critic for over ten years. 'My aim is to establish a proper film column in the paper. I see myself as the torchbearer for the younger film-going audience. Most current film critics are far too old, male and cynical and should have retired years ago! My ambition is to step into Barry Norman's shoes and become the first female TV film critic.' Before joining the *Sun*, wrote film and album reviews for magazines both here and abroad; organized and managed live shows and concerts.

Sunday Express

Richard Barkley (film)   Film critic since 1962. Also deputy theatre critic and deputy literary editor.

John Russell (TV)

Keith Turner (radio)

Sunday Mirror

Gordon Blair (radio)
David Bradbury (TV) Started as staff journalist on the *Eccles Journal*, then *Yorkshire Post, Daily Express, Sun.* Joined *Daily Mirror* in 1966. TV critic for *Sunday Mirror* since 1986.
Madeleine Harmsworth (film)
Eve Pollard (theatre)

Sunday People

Peter Bishop (film)

Sunday Telgraph

Francis King (theatre) Author of 22 novels, including *Act of Darkness, The Needle, The Custom House* and *The Woman who Was God. Sunday Telegraph* theatre critic since 1976; *Spectator* fiction reviewer since 1974. President, International PEN, 1986–9.
Richard Mayne (film) Also co-editor of *Encounter.* Regular member of BBC Radio's *Critics' Forum* panel and frequently contributes to *Kaleidoscope.* Started out as film critic of the *Cambridge Review.* Was Rome correspondent for the *New Statesman.* Author of a number of books including *Postwar: The Dawn of Today's Europe.* Edited *Western Europe: A Handbook* in 1986, and in 1978 won the Scott Moncrieff Prize for his translation of the *Memoirs* of Jean Monnet, the French 'founding father' of the European Community, whose assistant he used to be.
Christopher Tookey (TV) Film reviewer of the *Sunday Telegraph* before becoming TV critic. Contributed monthly features to *Books and Bookmen,* features for the *Observer, Review, Drama.* As a freelance TV producer and director: *After Dark, Network 7* (pilot), *Revolver, Luna, Showtime Link, The Cedar Tree, Celebrity Squares.* Was weekend editor and associate features editor for TV-AM (produced and directed *Through the Keyhole, Frankie Howerd on the Streets* and *Style by Jury*). Writer and composer of stage musicals including: *Room with a View* (Belgrade Theatre, Coventry), *An Evening with Noel & Gertie* (Phoenix, Leicester; Cadogan, London), *Him 'n' Her* (Haymarket, Leicester). Has produced/directed many stage productions since 1973 in London and the provinces.

Sunday Times

Iain Johnstone (film) Author of: *The Arnhem Report, Dustin Hoffman, The Man with No Name.* Has written and directed for American TV. Devised and produced *Film '71, Ask Aspel, Friday Night . . . Saturday Morning* for British TV. Produced current affairs programmes including *Midweek, The Watergate Hearings* and *The Frost Interviews.* Made interview–profiles of various actors including: Clint Eastwood, Marlon Brando, Woody Allen, John Wayne and Meryl Streep. Directed TV documentaries such as *Barry Norman on Broadway* and *John Cleese's First Farewell Performance.* Presented various programmes such as *Did You See . . .?* and *Film '83/'84.* Regular contributor to BBC Radio's *Kaleidoscope, Start the Week* and *Meridian.* Film critic with the *Sunday Times* since 1983.
John Peters (theatre)
Patrick Stoddart (TV) Started career as a general reporter before turning to TV criticism, first for *Broadcast,* then the (London) *Evening News.* For three years, has been TV critic for the *Sunday Times,* where he formerly edited the 'Screen' pages. Has written and presented many TV and radio programmes including *Video Age,* TV's first review programme on video, and *Read All about It* for Anglia. For eight years, he co-presented *Breakaway* on Radio 4.

The Times

Peter Davalle (TV)   As broadcasting editor for *The Times*, originated the new-style, full-page TV and radio guide. Freelance book reviewer for *The Times* and *Sunday Times*. Previously a scriptwriter and interviewer for ITV, BBC-TV and radio; programmes include: *Late Night Line-up*, *Town and Around*, *Today* and *Movie Magazine*.
David Robinson (film)
Irving Wardle (theatre)   Formerly sub-editor on the *Times Educational Supplement*, assistant theatre critic for the *Observer* in the early 1960s. Theatre critic for *The Times* since 1963. Author of play, *The Houseboy*, and book, *The Theatres of George Devine*.

Today

Sue Heal (film)

Vogue

Kathy O'Shaughnessy (theatre)
Milton Shulman (film)   See (London) *Evening Standard*

(Bristol) Western Daily Press

Helen Reid (film/TV/theatre)   Special drama interests are Shakespeare, poetic drama, 19th century and opera direction. Author of two books on cultural life in historic Bristol. Also music critic for the *Western Daily Press*.
Derek Whitfield (film/theatre/radio/TV)

Yorkshire Evening Post

James Greenfield (theatre/TV)   Prior to joining the *Yorkshire Evening Post*, worked for the Brighton Argus Group, the Press Association, Daily Mirror Publications, *Woman's Own*, *Daily Mail*, *Queen* magazine and the *TV Times*.
Alan Thompson (film)   Previously with the *Sheffield Star*, *Yorkshire Observer* and *Leicester Mercury*. Film critic with the *Yorkshire Evening Post* since 1966.

Yorkshire Post

(New theatre critic to be appointed)
Eric Roberts (TV)   Completed his education as a grave digger in Barnsley before working for newspapers in S. Yorkshire, Salford and York. Joined the *Yorkshire Post* covering subjects as diverse as rugby league and local government. 'Took up the TV critic's job at the same time as Channel 4 was born to cure my addiction to TV. It worked. Hobbies include walking and caravanning, both of which take me as far away from a TV as possible.'
Geoffrey Winter (film)   Retired as *Yorkshire Post*'s chief feature writer in 1984, but retained as freelance film critic with a weekly column.

part

4

organizations and associations

20. Associations and societies

Equity

The essential passport to an acting career is the Equity card. Without it, there is no beginning — but to get an Equity card, you must have experience as an actor. Stalemate!

Well, not quite. For the newcomer, there is a way into this most exclusive of trade unions via an allocation system set up by Equity and the theatre managers.

Until recently the deal rested on a strict quota of Equity cards to members of the Theatrical Management Association (TMA): two cards a year to each of the 125 repertory companies and the larger fringe groups, and one apiece to the smaller fringe companies. A pool of 40 cards was held in reserve for newly formed companies. The tight restrictions on entry were justified by Peter Plouviez, Equity's General Secretary, as 'one means of reducing' the number of actors on the breadline! But those who had set their hearts on joining the profession were not deterred by such petty considerations as having to earn a living. If the authorized route in was closed, they set out to jump a few fences. Stories appeared in the trade press of a lively black market in Equity cards. One actress confessed to having forged a contract for a TV commercial to make herself legitimate in the eyes of the union.

Such was the furore caused by such well-publicized abuses of the Equity charter that a campaign built up to scrap the quota system altogether. Equity leaders argued persuasively that the change would make their task of defending standards all but impossible (although why this did not apply to the Musicians' Union with their long-established policy of open entry was never adequately explained).

By way of compromise, the rules were stretched. Now students from accredited drama schools are allowed to join a register from which they automatically qualify for Equity membership immediately they are able to find work. Those who are still unemployed after two years are to be struck off the register.

The potential of the new scheme became clear when the Liverpool Playhouse announced plans for a company consisting entirely of Equity newcomers. The first nine chosen will take part in six studio productions over six months and appear in one main-house production. Equity has given a subdued welcome to the project, but warned that the new rules do not imply an increase in the overall number of engagements. However, the Liverpool Playhouse is more bullish, with Ian Kellgren, the theatre's artistic director, saying that he expects to set a precedent for other theatres across the country.

This is all well and good for young actors who adhere to conventional training, but it is not much help to those who are talented but untrained or have trained at non-recognized drama schools. For them, as always, the way in is by the back door or, perhaps more accurately, by the cellar because the work that is not restricted to Equity members but which carries an entitlement to Equity membership is often very low grade – pub entertainment, down-town night clubs, strip shows. If an actor can produce contracts for eight engagements, however bizarre, he gets his card. One of the most talented of the rising generation of young actors was accepted into Equity as a clown in a travelling circus. Rupert Graves was nominated for the role by his local Job Centre when the regular clown ran off with the tattooed lady!

However, few make the transition to the big time. There was once a young lady of visible attributes and undoubted grit who saw the chance of earning Equity recognition by touring the Gulf States as one of a trio of belly dancers. The Equity card was duly presented. Ten years on, she is still belly dancing. The money is good, but the recognition is not exactly what she had in mind when she aspired to be next in line to Vanessa Redgrave.

Equity provides the following guidelines for potential members.

EQUITY GUIDE TO MEMBERSHIP

Membership of Equity is open to anyone currently exercising professional skills in the entertainment industry.

To be eligible to apply, it is essential that you furnish proof of a current Equity contract (and details of previous engagements, if any). Upon receipt of acceptance evidence, an application form will be sent to you to complete and return, together with the specified entrance fee and annual subscription. Your completed application form will then be placed before the Equity Council who shall, in such matters, be the final arbiter.

In most areas of work, casting agreements have been made with employers which stipulate that only artists with previous professional experience, by which is normally meant membership of Equity, or an agreed quota of newcomers (who subsequently become members) are eligible to be considered for work.

In normal circumstances, it will not be possible for you to obtain your first job and Equity membership in the West End theatre, the National Theatre, television, commercials, films or radio.

Membership can be obtained through engagements in the following areas of work:

Theatre

● As a performer or assistant stage manager (ASM) in a subsidized repertory or Theatre-in-Education or young people's theatre company, under the quota of newcomer places that we have agreed with the Theatrical Management Association (TMA).*

*In the above areas, the newcomer quota does not apply to 'registered graduates' (i.e. students who have registered with us on completing acting or stage management courses accredited by the National Council for Drama Training), who are eligible for membership on obtaining an engagement.

● As a performer or ASM in a provincial commercial sessional work company (usually children's theatre) or non-subsidized repertory company, under the quota of newcomer places agreed with the TMA.
● As a performer in a provincial commercial summer season, pantomime or tour, under the quota of newcomer places agreed with the TMA.
● As an ASM with no obligation to act or understudy, in a provincial commercial theatre summer season, pantomime or tour.

- As a performer or ASM in a small-scale ('fringe') company which has a quota of newcomer places that we have agreed with the Independent Theatre Council (ITC).
- As a performer with the Royal Shakespeare Company at Stratford-upon-Avon, or with Chichester Festival Theatre, under the agreed quota of newcomers.

Opera and ballet

- As a singer engaged by an opera company on the Opera Singers' or Guest Artists' Contract.
- As a dancer with a ballet or dance company on the Ballet Contract.
- As an ASM with an opera or ballet company on the Stage Management Contract.

Directors, designers & choreographers

- As a director, designer or choreographer engaged on the appropriate theatre contract.

Variety or circus

- As a variety or circus artist, when you will need to be able to prove that you have been employed on a number of separate occasions (not less than eight) on a professional basis. The application will first be considered by the Variety Branch nearest to your permanent address.
- As a dancer with an overseas dance troupe, engaged on the approved Overseas Contract.

Other categories

- As a professional broadcaster in television or radio.
- As a concert or session singer, when you will need to be able to prove you have been employed on a number of separate occasions on a professional basis in these categories.

Work overseas

If you have worked professionally overseas and provide proof of your employment, together with the details of membership of the relevant union in that country, you may be granted exemption from the casting agreements. This will mean that, depending on the length of your previous employment, you will be entitled to seek work in the UK as though you were an existing Equity member. This arrangement, which is only available to UK or EEC citizens, or people from abroad who do not require work permits to work in this country, will not entitle you to Equity membership, but it will make it easier for you to obtain your first job in this country.

Equity's Guide to Membership issued August 1988 is available from Equity's offices.

British Actors Equity Association (incorporating Variety Artistes Federation)
8 Harley Street, London W1N 2AB
Tel (01) **636 6367/637 9311**
General Secretary Peter Plouviez

Scotland
65 Bath Street, Glasgow G2 2BX
Tel (041) **332 1669**
Scottish secretary/Secretary to Northern Ireland National Committee Jim Service

North
Conavon Court, 12 Blackfriars Street, Salford M3 5BQ
Tel (061) **832 3183**
Northern area organizer Bill Tankard

Wales & South West
34 Queen Street, Cardiff CF1 4BW
Tel (0222) **397971**
Secretary to the Welsh National Committee Christopher Ryde

Founded 1930. Membership open to actors, club and circus performers, stage management, theatre designers and directors, choreographers, dancers, singers and many others in the entertainment industry. Deputies elected in each theatre company, TV production and film unit, etc. collect subscriptions and maintain contact between members and the Equity office.

Equity's principal functions are 'to secure the best possible terms and conditions for its members through collective bargaining, and to make representations to government and other bodies on matters of policy relating to the performing arts.' Standard contracts laying down minimum terms and conditions have been negotiated in virtually every section of entertainment (*see below*). Free legal advice is available for any case of dispute in connection with professional engagements, and advice can be given on National Insurance, income tax and VAT. *Equity Journal* is issued free to members.

A number of registers are maintained for the benefit of members and are circulated or made available to employers. The list includes: Afro-Asian artists, disabled artists, foreign language speakers, ITV announcers, ITV stage managers, puppeteers, theatre choreographers, twins/triplets, walk-ons, Welsh speakers.

Subscription rates

ANNUAL GROSS EARNINGS	SUBSCRIPTION
Less than £4000	£32.00
£4001–5000	£42.00
£5001–6000	£52.00
£6001–7000	£62.00
£7001–8000	£72.00
£8001–9000	£82.00
£9001–10,000	£92.00
More than £10,000	1% of gross earnings to a

maximum of £1000 p.a.
Any member whose earnings do not exceed £3000 p.a. may pay a subscription of £20.00, subject to enclosing with the subscription a signed statement declaring those earnings.

Equity Members' *Jobgrapevine*
Room 14, Wigmore Street, London W1N 2AB

Founded 1973. A casting information service for Equity members. Run by volunteers, the *Jobgrapevine* is supported principally by funding from Equity, plus members' donations and revenue from advertising on the monthly rota. The service operates on a national basis, seven days a week, and covers all areas of work for Equity members as well as stage management, walk-ons, voice-overs, dance and some variety work (the latter to a lesser extent — volunteers with knowledge of this area of work are being sought). 'We see *Jobgrapevine*'s role as preventing time-wasting and expensive, as well as often ill-timed, letter writing, so that job applications can be more effective and accurate for all involved in the process of casting. This role as an educative service will be especially useful to those who have just entered the profession and never know where to turn to get accurate information about the do's and don'ts of the casting process.' A rota can be obtained by sending an SAE to the above address.

SELECTED EXTRACTS FROM EQUITY AGREEMENTS

TELEVISION

ITV Agreement (dated 1 January 1988)

Six transmission areas

A. London: Thames TV, LWT
B. Midlands: Central TV
C. Lancashire: Granada TV
D. Yorkshire: Yorkshire TV
E. Rest of the country: remaining independent companies
F. Channel 4: any or all of the above areas serviced by Channel 4

Payment of a negotiated programme fee entitles a company to transmit in *one area only* (except Channel 4). Each additional area transmission must be on payment of 100% of the programme fee. Payment for four areas shall include the right to transmission in the fifth area without extra payment.

Minimum rehearsal day fee: £21.00
Minimum production day fee: £31.50
Minimum programme fee: £56.00

Minimum Guaranteed rate (per week of network engagement)

When an actor is engaged in a network production, the total earnings are calculated and then the total divided by the total number of weeks of the engagement to give an average weekly earnings figure. If this average is less than the minimum weekly rate (£262.50), then the difference for the number of weeks is paid. Total earnings include production day, rehearsal day payments, programme fee, overtime, payment for location work and a gap of up to six weeks. One week consists of five out of seven consecutive days.

There must be one day of rehearsal for each six minutes of programme length.
● 90-minute programmes must have at least 15 days of rehearsal and three full days in the studio (of which one need only be an afternoon or evening run-through on the set).
● 60-minute programmes: 10 days rehearsal + 2 studio days.
● 30-minute programmes: 5 days rehearsal + 1 studio day.
The script must be sent to the actor at least three days before first rehearsal day.
Normal maximum number of production days should be:
● for programmes exceeding 60 minutes: 5 days
● for programmes exceeding 30 minutes: 4 days
● for programmes under 30 minutes: 3 days
Different guidelines exist for series and serials.

A production day in the *studio* consists of up to nine hours, during which time rehearsal and/or recording can take place and two meal breaks of one hour each. Overtime is paid for each full or part hour at £20.60; make-up and costuming at £20.60 per hour.

A production day on *location* consists of up to ten hours, including one hour break and up to one hour travelling. Overtime is paid for each full or part hour at £20.60 per hour.

Night work is work in the studio or on location scheduled to extend beyond midnight or to commence between midnight and 7 am. Payment is 1½ times the production day payment, with overtime at 1½ times the daily overtime rate.

Repeats

Programmes may not be transmitted more than twice in any one area within three years from date of first transmission in the UK without the prior consent of Equity. A repeat within two years will result in the payment of 100% of the programme fee for each area, and a repeat between two and three years from the date of first transmission in the UK will result in the payment of 150% of the programme fee for each area. Four years = 175%, with an increase of 25% for each subsequent year from date of first transmission.

BBC-TV Agreement (dated 1 January 1988)

Minimum fees
Category 1 – £260
Entitles the BBC to five rehearsal days and one performance day within seven days for programmes up to and including 30 minutes' transmission time.

Category 2 – £520
Entitles the BBC to eight rehearsal days and one performance day within 14 days for programmes between 40 and 60 minutes inclusive transmission time.

Category 2a – £390
The use of this category is restricted to serials with a guaranteed repeat within one week. Entitlement as Category 2.

Category 3 – £780
Entitles the BBC to 14 rehearsal days and one performance day with 21 days for programmes between 61 and 90 minutes' transmission time.

Category 4 – £1040
Entitles the BBC to 20 rehearsal days and one performance day within 28 days for programmes over 90 minutes' transmission time.

All these fees are negotiable by the actor or his agent, and the BBC have the right to offer 'special high' or 'special low' fees appropriate to the actor's contribution to the programme.

Knock-on fees
The amount by which a category rate is increased each year (approximately 5%).

Hours of work
Studio: an aggregate of up to 10 hours work in an overall period of 12 hours.
Location: a continuous period of nine hours, including up to eight hours' work and not less than one hour's meal break but excluding an aggregate of one hour's travelling time.
Overtime: studio: £19.25 for each 15 minutes or part thereof; location: £17.25 for each hour or part thereof.
Serials that are rehearsed and performed within seven days are subject to special rates.

Expenses
When the actor is required to travel from his own region (where he lives or normally works), the BBC pay travel and subsistence.

Repeat fees (UK)
The BBC can transmit two repeats within two years from the date of the original

transmission on both BBC1 and BBC2. 80% of the aggregate fee is paid, but if the programme is shown later than two years from the original transmission (but not more than 2½ years), the amount is 90% of the aggregate fee.*
*The aggregate fee is the sum total of the engagement fee and additional rehearsal day fees. The aggregate fee for weekly serials is calculated by dividing the total fees by the number of episodes the actor appears in that week.

* * *

Negotiation of payment takes into account the weight of the actor's contribution to the programme, an overall spread of time involved (particularly on longer individual programmes), the number of pre-rehearsal and pre-recording days involved, the actor's professional status, his earning power in other fields and his value to broadcasting.

Payment of fees entitles the BBC to transmit or permit the transmission of the artist's performance in the relevant programme once only from every transmitter of the relevant BBC-TV channel, either simultaneously or at different times in different regions.

RADIO

BBC Radio Agreement (dated 1 September 1988)

Minimum fee: £68 with a rehearsal day fee of £37.

Radio Drama Company & the Schools Rep Company: minimum weekly salary of £189 with a maximum of £265.

TELEVISION COMMERCIALS

TELEVISION COMMERCIALS AGREEMENT (dated 13 January 1988)
between Equity and the Advertising Film and Videotape Producers Association, and the Institute of Practitioners in Advertising

Auditions
1. For a first call, there is no payment, nor for videotapes and/or photographs taken.
2. For a recall, expenses are paid by the producer or advertiser for travel and out-of-pocket expenses (not less than £16.00). This also applies if the recall is on the same day as the first call.
3. For videotape at recall, the actor is paid not less than £24.00 to cover reasonable travel and out-of-pocket expenses (not in addition to No. 2 above).
4. If a script is sent to the actor prior to the first call, that call counts as a recall and the above expenses can be claimed.
5. If, for audition purposes, a voice-over artist is called in to record a script, not less than £16.00 must be paid to the artist. This is in addition to travel and out-of-pocket expenses claimed above.

Wig/wardrobe fittings
If the actor is required to attend a wig/wardrobe fitting outside the period of engagement, a payment of £27.00 is paid for a half day (up to 4½ hours) and £50.00 for a full day (up to 10 hours including an hour break).

Studio or session fees
The basic studio fee (BSF) is the fee for each working day. Minimum rate: £95.00. Repeat/use fees are based on the BSF. The life of a commercial is three years from the date of the first studio/location day.

Rehearsal call
A half-day rehearsal (up to 4½ hours) entitles the actor to 50% of his BSF. For a call of more than 4½ hours, he receives his full BSF.

Additional voice work
If the actor is required on a day other than the visual recording day(s) to do additional voice work (e.g. post synching), the actor must receive 50% of his BSF for each two-hour session.

Working hours
A working day or night is normally no more than nine hours, excluding an hour's meal break. (Time spent in make-up, hairdressing and wardrobe is included in working hours.) Day calls commence between 7.30 am and 12 noon. Dawn calls are for services rendered between 4.00 am and 7.30 am. For these calls, overtime at the rate of one-fifth of the BSF for each hour or part hour up to 7.30 am is paid in addition to the BSF. Night calls are those scheduled to extend beyond midnight or to commence between midnight and 4.00 am. A fee of 50% of the BSF is paid in addition to the BSF in respect of each session of night work. This night fee does not qualify for use fees.

Overtime
One-fifth of the BSF is paid for each hour or part hour (but a produer may use the actor for up to 15 minutes over the normal day to complete a take). Overtime (other than a night call) after midnight is paid at one-third of the BSF for each hour or part hour. No overtime payment qualifies for use fees.

Breaks between calls
Not less than 12 hours between the end of any one period of work and the time of the next call must be allowed. Additional payments are made if, for unavoidable reasons, this break is reduced.

Sundays and public holidays
Not less than 50% of the BSF (in addition to the BSF) is paid for work on these days. (This does not qualify for use fees.)

Travelling time
Where transport is not provided, time spent in travelling to and from a studio or location within a 20-mile radius of Charing Cross, London is not included in working hours. If more than 20 miles, it is included in the working hours, excluding 30 minutes each way.

Where transport is provided from a central London rendezvous, the working hours are calculated from 30 minutes after the time of call to the rendezvous until 30 minutes before the time the actor is returned to the rendezvous.

Where transport is provided from the performer's home, and when he is required to travel to and from a studio or location more than 30 miles from Charing Cross, travelling time is included in the working hours, excluding 30 minutes each way.

Meal and rest breaks
The performer is not required to work for more than five consecutive hours without a break (of not less than one hour) for rest and refreshment. If, for any reason, a main meal break is curtailed or delayed for more than 30 minutes, the actor is paid one-fifth of the BSF in compensation.

Use fees
A commercial may be shown once in each area on either ITV, Channel 4 or TV-AM without payment to the performer. Thereafter, the payments are made in a sliding scale of areas and times shown. They may be shown in blocks of ten or on a single transmission basis. There is also a different rate for a short commercial of ten seconds in length or under.

Ancillary use
The use of a commercial is limited to TV transmission in the UK. Any extension to other

media in the UK or elsewhere, such as cinema, radio or press advertising or inclusion in a film or television documentary, shall be subject to agreed terms between the performer and the producer/advertiser.

Stills
The producer/advertiser has no right to use still photographs of the actor without his consent. This consent will be subject to agreement and payment of a negotiated fee.

Overseas use
Subject to the consent of the performer.

Payment
Remuneration is due not later than the end of the same month when worksheets/invoices are received by the 15th, or not later than the 15th of the month following when worksheets/invoices have been received between the 15th and end of the month. (It seems to be common practice for the majority of advertisers not to pay before a month has elapsed.)

The advertising agency is responsible for having Performer's Work Record forms at the shoot. These should be completed and signed in duplicate at the end of the day's shoot.

WEST END THEATRES

WEST END AGREEMENT (dated 11 January 1988)
between Equity and the Society of West End Theatres (SWET)

Wages
Minimum weekly: £150.98 (once nightly) and £176.10 (twice nightly/daily).
In the case of cast replacements of actors earning less than £208.26 per week, the successor actor shall be paid not less than his immediate predecessor.

Artists under the age of 16 years: minimum salaries are one-half of the amounts stated above.

Holiday pay
Subject to at least 24 weeks (26 weeks for musicals) having elapsed since the first rehearsal of the production, and to the artist's engagement having subsisted for at least ten weeks, he is entitled to one-half day's holiday for each week (maximum annual entitlement of 18 days).

Hours of work
Not less than three weeks' rehearsal (four weeks for musicals) for every new production. In the event of 75% of more of the cast being replaced at any one time, there shall be an adequate rehearsal period of not less than two weeks. A rehearsal period shall not exceed six weeks for straight plays (eight for musicals) without Equity's consent.

Rehearsals
The working week consists of 45 hours, Monday to Saturday. Overtime is paid for any time in excess of these 45 hours.

Performance time
Defined as beginning 35 minutes (50 for full body make-up) before rise of curtain and running continuously until 15 minutes after curtain down (30 for heavy or full body make-up).

Performances
Maximum of eight performances (Monday to Saturday) per week (once nightly) or 12 per week (twice nightly/daily) and a maximum of two performances on any one day. Any performances additional to these attract an additional payment of one-eighth of the artist's salary. If, after the production has opened, the manager wishes to give

occasional additional performances, the cast shall be given not less than two weeks' prior notice, and such performances will be included in the weekly hours of work.

Photo calls

The manager shall use his best endeavours to ensure that photographs of the artist shall not be published for any purpose other than publicity for or advertisement of the play. Photographs involving any element of nudity taken by a photographer employed by the manager shall not be used for purposes other than publicizing the play.

If the manager wishes the artist to pose for photographs involving any element of nudity, the manager must obtain the artist's prior consent, and his written consent for the release of any nude photographs must also be obtained. No publication or display of these photographs shall be allowed until copies of the released photographs signed by the artist are lodged with Equity.

Understudies

Management are obliged to provide adequate and suitable understudy cover for every character in the production except for one-person shows. No walking understudy shall be required to cover more than one leading role or two non-leading roles for the minimum salary.

Minimum performance salary for each performance as an understudy is £12.49 for a leading role and £7.55 in all other cases, but half of £7.55 for understudying a role without scripted lines or crowd roles.

Responsibility payment is £10.93 per week.

Costumes, etc.

The management is responsible for supplying costumes and wig/hair-pieces, and for keeping them clean and repaired. When a performance is so strenuous that the actor needs to change his T-shirt or underwear either betwen performances or in order to go home after the performance, the management shall where appropriate provide the T-shirt(s) and underwear necessary for such change(s).

Programme notes

The artist has the right of approving all biographical material to be included in the programme. If there are any errors in the programme, it shall be slipped as soon as reasonably practical and the programme must be corrected at the next reprint.

Insurance

Where the performer is required to undertake business of a hazardous nature, including any fight sequence, management shall arrange personal accident insurance for the artist.

Medical treatment

If management refers the artist to a physician, dentist or osteopath for treatment (other than in cases where the artist's negligence has occasioned his incapacity), the management shall pay the cost of treatment and of any repeat treatment prescribed by such physician, etc.

Flying

Unless specially engaged for the purpose, the artist has the right to refuse to be lifted for flying.

Stage management

A team of not less than one stage manager (SM) or company & stage manager (CSM), one deputy stage manager (DSM) (none of whom shall act or understudy) and one assistant stage manager (ASM; who shall not act in any production or understudy in musicals with casts of more than six artists) shall be employed.

Wages

ASM: £150.98 (once nightly) & £176.10 (twice nightly)
DSM: £188.83 (once nightly) & £220.13 (twice nightly)

SM: £211.38 (once nightly) & £246.54 (twice nightly)
CSM: £226.48 (once nightly) & £264.15 (twice nightly)

PROVINCIAL THEATRES

PROVINCIAL THEATRES AGREEMENT (dated 4 April 1988)
between Equity and the Theatrical Management Association (TMA)

This agreement covers most provincial theatres not covered by the subsidized rep agreement (*see below*) — i.e. non-subsidized rep and tours.

Wages
Two tier system of payments — a higher minimum of £136.86 (once nightly) and £149.65 (twice nightly) and a lower minimum of £118.32 (once nightly) and £125.35 (twice nightly). The higher minimum weekly wage generally applies unless most of the following conditions apply:
1. None of the actors is a West End or national name.
2. The production is not advertised as pre- or post-West End.
3. The production is non-subsidized rep or uses the sessional contract.
4. The number in the cast is less than 12.
5. The theatre seating capacity is generally under 650.
6. The population within a 25-mile radius is not more than one million.

Subsistence
£35 per week for the first 12 weeks if the actor's home address is 25 miles or more from the place of employment.

Touring allowance
£15.20 per day (daily rate) and £61.45 (weekly rate). These figures are increased in line with the retail price index (RPI) every 13 weeks.

Failure to produce
If the management abandons the production, payment due to the actor is as follows:
● four or more weeks' notice given — two weeks' salary.
● less than four weeks' notice — three weeks' salary.
All monies owing until the date of notice must also be paid.

Performances per week
Eight once nightly; 12 twice nightly.

Exclusive services
Written permission is needed from the manager to perform elsewhere.

Hours of work
A week of six days (Monday to Saturday inclusive) consisting of 48 hours (including costume fittings) and not more than eight hours out of ten in any one day between 8.30 am and 11.00 pm. No actor is required to work in excess of 12 hours a day. After the first performance, rehearsals are normally limited to nine hours a week.

Holiday pay
Half a day's holiday pay per week.

Understudying
The actor may be required to cover two or three major roles. No actor can be expected to cover an 'unreasonable number of roles'.

* * *

Stage management
Minimum staff of not less than one senior stage manager (SM) — or company & stage manager (CSM) — one deputy stage manager (DSM), one assistant stage manager (ASM).

Wages
Two-tier system as for actors:
CSM: once nightly = £177.47 (lower), £205.29 (higher)
      twice nightly = £188.02 (lower), £224.47 (higher)
  SM: once nightly = £165.64 (lower), £191.60 (higher)
      twice nightly = £175.48 (lower), £209.52 (higher)
DSM: once nightly = £147.89 (lower), £171.06 (higher)
      twice nightly = £156.68 (lower), £187.06 (higher)
ASM: once nightly = £118.32 (lower), £136.86 (higher)
      twice nightly = £125.35 (lower), £149.65 (higher)

SUBSIDIZED REP

SUBSIDIZED REP AGREEMENT (dated 4 April 1988)
between Equity and the Theatrical Management Association (TMA)

Wages
Each theatre has a 'middle-range salary level' (MRSL). This is worked out by dividing the 'total basic salaries' paid by the total number of 'actor weeks' in the year. There are four levels, the minimums of which are:
1. £163.73
2. £143.26
3. £131.76
4. £122.80
Negotiation of salaries in rep is generally fairly restricted.

Subsistence
Payable for the first 12 weeks of a contract to an actor whose home address is 25 miles or more from the theatre or place of rehearsal. This currently stands at £34.22 per week.

Touring allowance
£14.60 per day (daily rate) and £72.60 (weekly rate); out-of-pocket expenses: £4.80. These figures are increased in line with the retail price index (RPI) every 13 weeks.

Hours
48 hours per week, 16 sessions of no more than four hours in a session (except dress rehearsals and performances of a production running longer than four hours, including the 'half' and 15 minutes at the end of the performance for make-up removal and/or changing).

Travel
Second-class rail fare or the equivalent is paid to and from the actor's home address at the beginning and end of the engagement.

Holiday pay
Two days' holiday pay for every four weeks worked.

Performances per week
Eight (not more than two on any one day).

* * *

Stage management
Minimum staffing: Repertory: not less than one stage manager (SM), one deputy stage manager (DSM) and one assistant stage manager (ASM) — none of whom shall act or understudy. Repertoire: not less than two teams of: 1 SM, 1 DSM, 1 ASM (none of whom shall act or understudy).

Wages
Minimum: ASM = £118.38; DSM = £135.30; SM = £149.04 (£163.73 in MRSL Grade 1 theatres).

SMALL-SCALE TOURS

SMALL-SCALE TOURING COMPANIES AGREEMENT (dated 4 April 1988) between Independent Theatre Council (ITC) & Equity

This contract generally applies to those that are not TMA, subsidized rep, West End or a No. 1 tour.

Wages
Minimum of £145 per week.

Hours
Six days — 45 hours per week.

Travelling time on performance days
Six hours maximum.

Free days
At least one in every six.

Performances
No more than twice a day. If it is a full-length play, there can be seven per week, and eight if the company is in one venue for the whole week. For a short play (one hour ten minutes), ten performances per week.

Overtime
Paid for anything over the 45 hours per week.

Subsistence
Paid for the first 16 weeks if the member is working 25 miles or more from his home address: £26 (out of London) and £29.75 (in London). This is linked to the retail price index (RPI) and changes quarterly. *NB* Subsistence is not paid if the actor is in receipt of a touring allowance that covers accommodation.

Travel
Second-class rail fare or the equivalent is paid from and to the actor's home address at the beginning and end of the contract.

Holiday pay
One-half day's pay for each week of the engagement.

Exclusive engagement
Written permission from the management must be obtained for work outside of the engagement.

Broken weeks
Count as full weeks for the purposes of wages.

Stage management
Contract terms are the same as for the actor.

The stage management team for a touring production is a minimum of two, one of whom shall not act or understudy. But if the production requires four performers or fewer (and as long as the stage manager (SM) only drives a maximum of 1½ hours in any single journey on performance day, and the set, lighting rig and sound rig are uncomplicated), the minimum team may be one SM who may not act or understudy.

The stage management team for a producing venue must be three, of whom two shall not act or understudy.

Other professional associations

Actors' Benevolent Fund
6 Adam Street, London WC2N 6AA
Tel (01) **836 6378**
President The Lord Olivier OM
General Secretary Mrs Rosemary Stevens
Minimum subscription £1.00 p.a.

> Founded 1882. The foremost representative charity of the theatrical profession in the UK. The objects of the Fund are to help, by allowances, grants and loans, elderly or distressed actors and actresses, managers, stage managers, business managers and their wives; also choristers whose efforts are entirely devoted to theatrical work. Those connected with the theatrical profession, coming within the Fund's scope, can become members on payment of the minimum subscription; they then will be entitled to participate in all matters affecting the welfare of the Fund.

The Actors Centre
4 Chenies Street, London WC1E 7EP
Tel (01) **631 3599 (membership & bookings)**
    (01) **631 3619 (administration)**
Membership £23.00 p.a.

> Founded 1980, by a group of established performers for the benefit of the acting profession. As well as enabling members to develop their professional skills and acquire fresh ones, it offers the opportunity for the exploration of new ideas and methods of work away from commercial pressures. The Centre's extensive premises provide excellent club facilities: a green room, licensed servery, changing room with showers, pay telephones, notice boards, trade journals and information on current theatrical events; three studios (two with piano) and two meeting/audition rooms for the wide range of classes and workshops programmed for Equity members. The Centre does not employ permanent staff. Classes and workshops are taken by directors and tutors, all of whom are actively working in the industry. In addition to Equity membership, there is also an Associate membership to cater for those wanting more dialogue and closer cooperation between performers and those working in production. Schedules detailing times, tutors and directors, etc. are mailed six times a year, plus a newsletter. Schedules cover: acting, audition, text, verse, writing dialect, voice, singing, TV, radio, fencing, movement, dance, tap, keep fit, musicals. All classes and workshops are at subsidized prices.

The Actors' Centre (Birmingham)

Midlands Arts Centre, Cannon Hill Park, Birmingham B12 9QH
Tel (021) **458 6838**
Administrator Ellie Darvill
Membership £3.50 per season

Founded 1988. Working under the umbrella of The Actors' Centres of London and Manchester, offers classes and workshops on TV, text, radio, auditions, etc. (plus projects with the Theatre Writers' Union sponsored by BBC-TV Pebble Mill) for Equity members living in and working from the Midlands. Spring and summer seasons for 1989 planned. Membership includes membership of the London and Manchester centres. Classes and workshops: £5.00–£20.00. Sponsored by BBC-TV, Birmingham City Council and the Actors' Centre.

The Actors' Centre (Manchester)

The Old School, Little John Street, Manchester M3 4PQ
Tel (061) **832 3430**
Administrator Simon Molloy
Membership £17.25 p.a.

Founded 1986. The second actors' centre to be set up offers a wide range of classes and workshops for Equity members. Three studios, green room with restaurant, pay telephones, information notice boards and trade journals available. A newsletter is sent out each month with the schedule of classes on offer. All classes and workshops are offered at subsidized prices.

Actors' Charitable Trust

19–20 Euston Centre, London NW1 3JH
Tel (01) **380 6212**
General Secretary Althea Stewart

Formerly the Actors' Orphanage Fund. Assists the children of actors and actresses during family crises with financial grants. The object is to help children while keeping them in their own homes with their parents. The Trust also administers Denville Hall, a residential care home for members of the theatrical professions in Northwood, Middx (the original house was donated by Alfred Denville, the actor-manager).

Actors' Church Union

St Paul's Church, Bedford Street, London WC2E 9ED
Tel (01) **836 5221**
Minimum subscription £5.00 p.a.

'The Church in action in the world of entertainment, aiming to make personal contact with all artists, technicians and other staff of any or no denomination at all wherever they may be at work. The whole purpose is to bring the Church's ministrations more easily within the reach of the theatrical profession.' Run on a voluntary basis with funding coming from members' and associates' subscriptions, and from gifts, legacies and Church collections.

The Actors' Institute

137 Goswell Road, London EC1V 7ET
Tel (01) **251 8178**
Membership £15.00 p.a.

A centre for the fostering of creativity in theatre and the arts generally. Activities include acting classes for all levels from beginners to professional, including a ten-week foundation course, with tuition by experienced professional actors, directors and writers. Also runs a series of workshops dealing with the issue of creativity in the context of performance — including 'The Mastery', 'Leadership and Creativity', 'Mastery of Excellence' — and a ten-week early-morning career course, 'Samurai'.

Association of Cinematograph, Television & Allied Technicians (ACTT)

111 Wardour Street, London W1V 4AY
Tel (01) **437 8506**
General Secretary Alan Sapper
Subscription 1% of annual income

Founded 1935. Film and television technicians' union, covering the whole of the film and broadcasting industry. Approximately 27,000 members.

Alliance of North American Artists (ANAA)

36 York Way, London N1 9AB
Tel (01) **837 7402/4**
Membership £50.00 p.a. or £35.00 covenant

The longest-running organization promoting North American arts in Great Britain. Its aims are to encourage and develop works with North American perspectives, and to create opportunities for members to meet and to develop and explore their work. It also has a funding operation with grants occasionally available to member organizations, usually for project-based schemes.

The Arts Club

40 Dover Street, London W1X 3RB
Tel (01) **499 8581**
Membership secretary Mrs Ridgway
Subscription Assessed individually: town £300 maximum, country £145 maximum

Founded 1863. Some connection with the arts necessary for membership, which is only available by application with two sponsors.

Association of Independent Producers

17 Great Pulteney Street, London W1R 3DG
Tel (01) **434 0181**
Contact Matthew Crampton
Subscription £75.00 p.a.

Founded 1976. Membership is open. Benefits include: an information service, a regular magazine, information packs on various aspects of production and a free copy of *The Independent Production Handbook*. Offers information about production, how to get in touch with producers, etc. The general aims of the association are to encourage film and TV production and to broaden the base of finance and exhibition.

BAFTA (British Academy of Film & Television Arts)

195 Piccadilly, London W1V 9LG
Tel (01) **734 0022**
Director A. J. Byrne
Ordinary subscription £80.00 p.a.

Founded 1947. Membership limited to 'those who have contributed creatively to the industry'. Provide facilities for screenings and discussions; encourage research and experimentation; lobby Parliament; make annual awards.

BETA ● *See* BROADCASTING & ENTERTAINMENT TRADES ALLIANCE.

British American Arts Association
49 Wellington Street, London WC2E 7BN
Tel (01) **379 7755**
Director Jennifer Williams

> Organization addressing the problems of transatlantic cultural exchange. Offers advice and counselling in all arts disciplines, runs a conference programme and takes on special projects. Emphasis is on the non-profit sector. BAAA is not a grant-giving organization.

British Arts Festival Association
P.O. Box 925, London N6 5XX
Coordinator Gwyn Rhydderch

> Issues a free annual brochure giving information on leading professional arts festivals that are members of the Association, including Aldeburgh, Cheltenham, Glasgow Mayfest.

The British Council
11 Portland Place, London W1N 4EJ
Tel (01) **930 8466** Fax (01) **839 6347** Telex **8952201** BRICON G
Director General R. T. L. Francis
Director of drama & dance To be announced

> Founded 1934. The British Council exists to promote a wider knowledge of Britain and the English language abroad and to develop closer cultural relations between Britain and other countries. It maintains staff in 81 countries, and from 13 offices in Britain advises and assists visitors and students from overseas. The Council organizes tours overseas by British theatre, dance and opera companies and individual recitalists and by orchestras and individual musicians, enabling them to perform in most parts of the world, including Africa, the Indian sub-continent and the Far East, where opportunities for British artists would otherwise be rare.

British Film Institute
21 Stephen Street, London W1P 1PL
Tel (01) **255 1444** Telex **27624** BFI LDNG
Membership £26.50 (includes *Monthly Film Bulletin*) or £15.75
Associateship £10.25 (plus concessions)

> Founded 1933. Committed to the development of the art and appreciation of film and TV. Runs the National Film Theatre and the National Film Archive in London and funds film theatres in the regions, as well as supporting the making of new films, video and TV programmes largely through the Regional Arts Associations, but also through direct grants. 1988 saw the opening of MOMI — the Institute's Museum of Moving Image on the South Bank: open Tuesday—Saturday (10 am to 8 pm) and Sunday (10 am to 6 pm); admission £3.25 and concessions.

British Library National Sound Archive
29 Exhibition Road, London SW7 2AS
Tel (01) **589 6603**

> An archive of over half a million discs and over 45,000 hours of tape recordings including all types of music, oral history, drama, wildlife, selected BBC broadcasts and BBC Sound Archive material. Open 9.30 am to 4.30 pm Monday to Friday; late opening Thursday to 9.00 pm. Listening service (by appointment: 9.30 am to

4.30 pm Monday to Friday; late opening Thursday to 9.00 pm).
Northern Listening Service at British Library Document Supply Centre, Boston Spa, W. Yorks. Tel: (0937) 843434. Open 9.15 am to 4.30 pm Monday to Friday.

British Music Hall Society
Honorary membership secretary Wendy Lunn, 74 Turnpike Drive, Luton, Beds. LU3 3RF

Founded 1963. An influential, worldwide group of British music hall and variety enthusiasts, including many professionals from the world of entertainment — artistes, agents and managers. The central aims of the Society are 'to preserve the history of British Music Hall and Variety, to recall the artistes who created it, and to encourage and support the entertainers of the present era — including new talent.' The Society holds regular show meetings on the first Tuesday of each month (in January 1987, they presented the first traditional variety bill at the re-opened Hackney Empire). Publish a quarterly journal, *The Call Boy*, giving news, views and information on all aspects of music hall and variety, which is issued free to members. Contributes to theatrical and hospital charities out of the proceeds of its variety shows and exhibitions. Membership application forms available from the membership secretary.

British Screen Finance
37–39 Oxford Street, London W1R 1RE
Tel (01) **434 0291** Fax (01) **434 9933** Telex **888694** BRISCR G

A private company aided by government grant, which took over from the National Film Finance Council (NFFC) in 1986; backed by consortium including Rank, Channel 4 and Cannon. Has two functions: National Film Development Fund, for script development (contact Adrian Hodges); and production investment (contact Sirnon Relph). Develop around 18 projects per year, and have invested in 26 British films in the last two years.

British Theatre Association
Regent's College, Inner Circle, Regent's Park, London NW1 4NW
Tel (01) **935 2571**
Director Sally Meades
Training director Victoria Thompson
Membership Starts at £15.00 p.a.

Founded 1919. The BTA exists to promote theatre through its research, information and training facilities. It is the only body in this country that represents all areas of theatre — professional, amateur and educational. It houses the largest and most accessible theatre library in Europe, access to which is free to all Equity members. Its training department offers the widest range of courses available outside the drama schools, including evening classes, weekend courses, full-time courses for professionals, a directors' course and summer schools. There is also a training information service that can give advice on full-time training at drama schools and universities. Discounts on many of the training courses are available to BTA members and UB40 holders. It publishes the magazine *Drama*.

British Theatre Institute (incorporating Drama & Theatre Education Council)
c/o NCA, Francis House, Francis Street, London SW1

Founded 1971. In 1976, it called a conference of educational bodies, which led to the formation of DATEC, the Drama and Theatre Education Council. The two joined forces in 1982. Because of this merger, the BTI places particular emphasis on education and training. It also acts as a resource office and consultant on all aspects of theatre and drama education. Members include both individuals and organizations.

Broadcasting & Entertainment Trades Alliance (BETA)
181–185 Wardour Street, London W1V 3AA
Tel (01) **439 7585**
Joint General Secretaries J. L. Wilson, D. A. Hearn

Founded 1984, by the amalgamation of the National Association of Theatrical Television and Kine Employees (NATTKE) and the Association of Broadcasting Staff (ABS). Covers all areas of non-performing categories in theatre, the BBC, ITV, independent local radio, IBA, cinema, film production and related areas. Negotiates minimum rates and conditions with management. All theatre staff, both full- and part-time, are eligible for membership.

Central Entertainment Agents Council
64 Port Street, Evesham, Worcs. WR11 6AP
Tel (0386) **2819/3456**
General Secretary Derek Wells

Founded 1978. 'An active trade organization open to all licensed entertainment agents, the Council has gained recognition as a consultancy for the industry, instituting branches throughout the UK. Benefits include: standard contracts for all situations, effective promotion to increase business, help for members in dispute, advice plus legal aid, regular trade showcases and a monthly news-sheet.' All applicants for enrolment are required to serve a probationary period. Further details available from the General Secretary.

Directors' Guild of Great Britain
125 Tottenham Court Road, London W1P 9HN
Tel (01) **387 7131**
Administrator Suzan Dormer

The Guild speaks for directors and their craft in all areas of the media – film, TV (where producers are included), commercials, radio, opera and dance. Covers freelance and staff directors in the UK and abroad. Campaigns for directors' copyright (in 1986, made extensive submissions to the government which should finally result in legal recognition of rights); recently published *A Directors' Guide to Copyright and Contract*. Annually publishes *The Directors' Guild Directory*, which lists all members and their principal credits, and *Direct*, the Guild magazine which is published eight times a year. Membership application forms available from the above address.

Educational Television Association
King's Manor, Exhibition Square, York YO1 2EP
Tel (0904) **629701**

An umbrella organization for individuals and organizations using TV for education and training.

Entertainment Express
P.O. Box 1, St Albans, Herts.
Tel (0727) **41175**
Membership £8.00 p.a. (Equity members only)

Offer discounts on British Rail travel and UK flights, plus full booking service for sea and coach travel; discounts on hotels in the UK and free membership of the Theatre & Concert Rail Club.

Film Artistes' Association

61 Marloes Road, London W8 6LF
Tel (01) **937 4567**

The Film Artistes' Association has over 2000 members, and provides doubles, stand-ins and background artistes for feature films that are shot in the London area and at the recognized studios; also for all filming within a 40-mile radius of London.

Independent Programme Producers Association

50–51 Berwick Street, London W1V 4RD
Tel (01) **439 7034** Fax (01) **494 2700**
Director Paul Styles
Deputy director John Woodward
Information officer Alison Selwyn
Subscription Corporate: £300 + VAT; individual: £100 + VAT

Founded 1981, to protect and advance the interests of independent TV producers supplying Channel 4; currently pressing for access to 25% of BBC and ITV output for independent producers. Membership of 550. Offers a full industrial relations service, general meetings, seminars on all aspects of production, general and production advice; close consultation with Channel 4 and BBC-TV; *IPPA Bulletin* every two months. The association is funded by subscriptions and by a 0.5% fee levied on members' production budgets for BBC and Channel 4 commissions.

Independent Theatre Council (ITC)

Old Loom House, Backchurch Lane, London E1 1LU
Tel (01) **488 1229**
Administrator Philip Bernays

The ITC is both the representative body of and the managers' association for small- to middle-scale professional theatre companies: national and regional touring companies; producing venues; Theatre-in-Education teams; community, children's and young people's theatres; mime, dance and puppet companies; cabaret, revue and street performers; also individual and associate members.

ITC campaigns for increased recognition and funding for these theatres and initiates support or opposition to any legislation or action which may affect the interests of the membership. It negotiates and administers standard contracts of employment with Equity, MSF (Manufacturing, Science, Finance — formerly ASTMS) and the writers' unions, and operates joint procedures for consultation and settling disputes. Provides an information and advice service for members on employment and other matters related to theatre management. Offers a training programme of one- and two-day courses on various aspects of running a theatre company. Regular membership mailings provide news, information and a noticeboard service. ITC produces an information pack (price £4), which contains: information sheets and application forms for ITC membership and 'approved manager status'; a reference sheet on sources of information and legal requirements for starting a theatre company; and copies of ITC's standard contracts.

International Theatre Institute

British centre: 4 St George's House, 15 Hanover Square, London W1R 9AJ
Tel (01) **486 6363** Telex **27689** SPEEDY G
Organizing secretary Maria Pattinson (01–267 5595)
Membership £20.00 p.a. (£10.00 for Equity members)

> Founded 1948 by UNESCO to 'promote international exchange of knowledge and practice of the performing arts, to stimulate creation and increase cooperation between theatre people, and to join in the defence of the ideals and aims of UNESCO.' Organizes the biennial Theatre of Nations Festival and publishes the *World Encyclopedia of Contemporary Theatre*. The Institute has over 65 centres throughout the world, which are continually in touch with each other and fed information by the international headquarters based in Paris. An award was created by the British centre in 1967 for 'Excellence in International Theatre'. Frank Dunlop won the first award for his work at the Edinburgh Festival, and in 1988, it went to Rose de Wend Fenton and Lucy Neal, directors of the London International Festival of Theatre. Membership is open to all those involved in theatre and the performing arts.

London & Provincial Theatre Councils (LTC & PTC)

Bedford Chambers, The Piazza, Covent Garden, London WC2E 8HQ
Tel (01) **836 0971**

> The Councils, which are composed of equal numbers of representatives from Equity and from management, serve as a forum for the discussion of matters in dispute between managements and artists. The Councils aim to secure the organization and cooperation of managers and artists by approving standard term contracts for use by approved managers – including all members of the Society of West End Theatre (SWET) and the Theatrical Management Association (TMA) – when employing Equity members. Managers who are not members of SWET or TMA are required to register productions with the appropriate Council and place a deposit. The Councils also provide an arbitration service for Equity members and managers in dispute, which can be convened rapidly if necessary.

Musicians' Union

National Office: 60–62 Clapham Road, London SW9 0JJ
Tel (01) **582 5566**
General Secretary John Morton
Subscription rates Weekly earnings from music up to £65: £31.72 pa + £1 entrance fee; weekly earnings over £65 but less than £120: £60.32 pa + £1 entrance fee; weekly earnings over £120 but less than £220: £68.12 + £1 entrance fee; weekly earnings over £220: £98.28 + £1 entrance fee.

> The Musicians' Union caters for all who make their living, or part of their living, from performing music; bands, groups, orchestral musicians, chamber musicians, folk and jazz. The Union negotiates basic rates of pay, recovers unpaid fees, gives advice on contracts, and provides legal assistance and aid.

New Playwrights Trust

Whitechapel Library, 77 Whitechapel High Street, London E1 7QX
Tel (01) **377 5429**
Contact Susan Croft
Subscription £9.00 waged; £4.50 unwaged; also group rates

> Organizes projects (including joint ones) such as rehearsed readings, workshops and discussions. Runs script reading service, bulletin and library service (in association with the Pub Theatre Network). There is also a 'link service' between writers and theatre companies. Monthly newsletter. Membership open to would-

be actors, playwrights and directors. Recent projects include Wordplay '88 and Bristol Express's *The Play's the Thing*.

Performing Rights Society
29–33 Berners Street, London W1P 4AA
Tel (01) **580 5544** Fax (01) **631 4138** Telex **892678 PRSLON G**

Collects and distributes royalties arising from performances and broadcasts of its members' copyright music.

Personal Managers' Association Ltd (PMA)
Rivercroft, One Summer Road, East Molesley, Surrey KT8 9LX
Liaison secretary Angela Adler

An association of artists' and dramatists' agents (membership not open to individuals). Monthly meetings for exchange of information, discussion; acts as a lobby when necessary. Applicants screened; code of conduct maintained.

Provincial Theatre Council ● *See* LONDON & PROVINCIAL THEATRE COUNCILS.

Pub Theatre Network (PTN)
178–180 Battersea Park Road, London SW11 4ND
Tel (01) **622 4553**
Contact Jessica Dromgoole, Sarah Levete (executive directors)
Membership Associate (for small theatres): £25.00 per quarter; friendship: £10.00 p.a. (individual), £15.00 p. a.(groups)

Founded 1986. PTN, now with a membership of 26, is the most active representative body for small theatre venues in and around London, the majority of which are pub theatres. It is a pioneering arts charity with a systematic programme to raise the profile of small theatre and increase public awareness of this field of work. PTN seeks to promote, protect and develop the small theatre venue and to strengthen links between community and theatre.

It is able to offer advice to actors interested in working on the small theatre circuit, with practical details on the facilities and size of venues, and availability for those wishing to mount a production. It provides a sustained publicity programme of up-to-date information on all member theatres and productions through printing tourist brochures and a fortnightly listings, and distributes all publicity material to PTN racks round London. It also maintains a clear channel of communication between theatres and companies, and provides a script service (reading/library/bulletin), organized with the New Playwrights Trust. issues the fortnightly *PTN Newsletter*. Associate membership gives access to all PTN information and involvement in and benefit from all PTN activities. Friendship of PTN includes, if desired, a subscription to the listings information or newsletter.

Royal Television Society
Tavistock House East, Tavistock Square, London WC1H 9HR
Tel (01) **387 1970/1332**
Subscription £25.00 (full UK membership)

Founded 1927. Covers all disciplines involved in the TV industry. Provides a forum for debate and conferences on technical, social and cultural aspects of the medium. Presents journalism and programme awards, and runs a wide range of training courses.

Royal Theatrical Fund

11 Garrick Street, London WC2E 9AR
Tel (01) **836 3322**
President Donald Sinden
Hon. Secretary John Berkeley

Founded 1839, by Charles Dickens and his friends to provide pensions for actors. The Fund was granted its royal charter by Queen Victoria in 1853. In 1974, it became a general charity for people in the profession, giving such help as contributions to a shortfall in nursing home fees for elderly actors or cash grants for people who are ill or convalescing. It is not a fund-raising charity — money comes from 'good house-keeping and investment'. Currently in the process of publishing a history of the Fund.

Scottish Society of Playwrights

Tron Theatre, 38 Parnie Street, Glasgow G1 5HB
Tel (041) **553 1425**
Secretary Donneil Kennedy
Membership £20.00 p.a.

Founded 1973, by a group of playwrights. The Society acts as a pressure group for playwrights and negotiates contracts with managements. Full membership is open to anyone who has had a play professionally produced on stage, TV or radio.

Society of British Fight Directors

87 Redington Road, London NW3 7RR
Tel (01) **435 2281**
Secretary Penelope Lemont
Membership £5.00 p.a. (Friend of the Society)

Founded 1969. Professional organization of fight directors, the aims of which are to raise the standard of stage fighting in this country and the status of the fight directors. It acts a a clearing house for information on fight directing in all its aspects, including historical information on weaponry and methods used. It provides names of individual fight directors. Two of its major concerns are the welfare and safety of actors who perform combat on stage, and the training of the young actor in drama school. The Society conducts a proficiency test for drama students who, if they are successful, may obtain a certificate of their safety and effectiveness as performers of stage combat. British Actors' Equity now has a Fight Directors' Committee and a Fight Directors' Register; to become a fight director and be accepted on to the Register, it is necessary to undertake a training programme run by the Society. Issue a tri-annual magazine, *The Fight Director*.

Society for Theatre Research

c/o The Theatre Museum, 1e Tavistock Street, London WC2E 7PA
Contact Hon. Secretary

Founded 1948, to 'foster research into historical and current theatre practice'. The Society provides a meeting-point for all those interested in the history and technique of British theatre — scholars, research workers, stage artists and other practitioners in theatre, as well as theatre-goers. Annual awards, ranging from £100 to £1000, are made to offset the cost of research concerned with the history and practice of the British theatre. The Society administers the William Poel Memorial Festival, an annual event at which prizes for good stage speech are awarded to two students from an accredited theatre school; candidates present a duologue from Elizabethan or Jacobean drama. Annual publications include *Theatre Notebook*, which is published three times a year and sent free to members. Lectures and events are held regularly in London. A prospectus and details of current subscription rates are available from the Hon. Secretary. All communications must be made by post.

Society of West End Theatres (SWET)
Bedford Chambers, The Piazza, Covent Garden, London WC2E 8HQ
Tel (01) **836 0971**

The Society comprises managers and proprietors of theatres and producers of shows in the West End of London, with both the commercial and the subsidized sectors represented. The Society serves to facilitate concerted action in the interest of theatre managers in cooperation with the TMA (Theatrical Management Association) and the TNC (Theatres National Committee), but concentrates its efforts on those issues of direct concern to the West End. There is a marketing division that promotes ticket sales for West End productions.

The Society also negotiates minimum rates of pay and conditions of employment with the theatrical unions: Equity (performers, stage management, directors and designers), the Broadcasting & Entertainment Trades Alliance (BETA: theatre staff) and the Musicians' Union (MU). An arbitration and conciliation service is provided for disputes between managers and artists through the Society's partnership with Equity in the London Theatre Council (LTC).

Since 1976, the Society has presented its own annual awards – now known as the Olivier Awards – to the profession to recognize talent in West End performances. The Olivier Bursary, set up in 1987 to mark Lord Olivier's 80th birthday, is awarded to a financially deprived second-year drama student to complete his/her studies. 1988 winner: Anna Healey (23) at RADA.

Stage Management Association (SMA)
Southbank House, Black Prince Road, London SE1 7SJ
Tel (01) **240 7831**

Representative organization for all professional stage management staff. Recently announced an annual award, 'For Services to the British Theatre in the field of Stage Management' – members and non-members of the SMA are eligible.

The Theatre Museum
1e Tavistock Street, London WC2E 7PA
Tel (01) **836 7891**
Open Galleries & Shop – Tuesday to Sunday 11.00 to 19.00; Cafe & Box Office – Tuesday to Saturday 11.00 to 20.00, Sunday 11.00 to 19.00

Housed in Covent Garden's old Flower Market, the Victoria & Albert's new Theatre Museum houses a rich collection of theatrical material. In addition to a semi-permanent display, there are two temporary exhibition galleries, named in honour of Sir John Gielgud and Sir Henry Irving, and a Studio Theatre where the Museum's resident repertory company, the *London Theatre Laboratory*, perform plays which have a special significance in theatre history or by authors who hold a special place in the development of theatre. Performances have included *Look Back in Anger*, and two comedies by George Bernard Shaw, *Village Wooing* and *Overruled*.

Theatres National Committee (TNC)
Bedford Chambers, The Piazza, Covent Garden, London WC2E 8HQ
Tel (01) **836 0971**

The Committee – composed of SWET, TMA and the Independent Theatre Council (ITC) – is the collective voice and representative of theatrical management on broad political, economic and social issues to the extent that they affect live theatre – e.g. safety, licensing, taxation, copyright, overseas tours. The Committee negotiates with the unions industry agreements that have national significance – for example, 'Nudity on Stage'.

The Theatres Trust

10 St Martin's Court, St Martin's Lane, London WC2N 4AJ
Tel (01) **836 8591**
Life chairman The Lord Goodman CH
Chairman Sir David Crouch
Director John Earl
Membership £7.00 p.a.; life membership: £100.00

Founded 1976. A statutory body set up 'to promote the better protection of theatres for the benefit of the nation'. The Trust must be consulted by all planning authorities before they issue a decision on any planning application affecting a theatre (used or disused). In all its work, the Trust's principal objective is not simply to see buildings preserved but to safeguard their live theatre use – or potential for such use. Membership as a 'Friend' of the Theatres Trust gives you reduced prices or other benefits at some London and provincial theatres; reduced prices at events organized by the Trust; regular reports on the work of the Trust.

The associated *Theatres Trust Charitable Fund* exists to provide small grants to theatres towards both new building and refurbishment. Its income is derived from donations and subscriptions to the Friends of the Theatres Trust.

Theatrical Management Association (TMA)

Bedford Chambers, The Piazza, Covent Garden, London WC2E 8HQ
Tel (01) **836 0971**

The Association represents those concerned with theatrical production in the provinces, both in the commercial and the subsidized sectors. Members may either be managers of theatres (or other venues) or producers of shows that are presented at such theatres. Like the Society of West End Theatre (SWET), the Association negotiates minimum terms and conditions with the theatrical unions. However, the Association also promotes the interests of its members in other areas, both in cooperation with SWET and the Theatres National Committee (TNC) and individually, and provides an arbitration service for inter-management disputes and a conciliation service through its partnership with Equity in the Provincial Theatre Council.

Writers' Guild of Great Britain

430 Edgware Road, London W2 1EH
Tel (01) **723 8074**
General Secretary Walter J. Jeffrey
Annual subscription 1% of that part of the author's income earned in the areas in which the Guild operates, with a minimum of £50 and a maximum of £480.

Founded in 1959, the Writers' Guild is the writers' trade union, affiliated to the TUC, and representing writers in film, radio, television, theatre and publishing. The Guild advises on all aspects of writers' agreements and leads the way in campaigns for minimum terms for writers working in film, radio and theatre. In 1979 the Guild, with the Theatre Writers' Union, negotiated the first ever industrial agreement for theatre writers. Along with the Society of Authors, the Guild has played a major role in advancing the Minimum Terms Agreement for authors. Membership is by a points system. One major piece of work (a full-length book, an hour-long television or radio play, a feature film, etc) entitles the author to full membership; lesser work helps to accumulate enough points for full membership, while temporary membership may be enjoyed in the meantime. Temporary members can pay a minimum subscription of £30 in their first year.

21. Arts councils and regional arts associations

Arts Councils

Arts Council of Great Britain

105 Piccadilly, London W1V 0AU
Tel (01) **629 9495**
Chairman Peter Palumbo
Secretary General Luke Rittner

The 1988/89 grant dispensed by the Arts Council stands at £150 million. From it, the Arts Council supports arts organizations, artists, performers and others; grants can also be made for particular productions, exhibitions and projects. The total amount set aside for drama in 1988/9 is £27,477,525.

Drama director Ian Brown
Deputy drama director Jean Bullwinkle

The Drama Department assesses funding of 56 professional theatre companies divided into two main categories: 23 touring and 33 theatre-based. It also looks at applications for separate new projects, often by emergent new companies. The Department also administers a number of training schemes designed to offer advanced in-service and further training to professional designers, directors, performers, technicians, stage managers and adminstrators, as well as to those working in children's theatre and puppetry. A number of bursaries are awarded to individuals to undertake short practical working attachments or specific training projects or courses. Applications are assessed on individual merit throughout the year and while funds are available. Further information available from the free Arts Council leaflet *Awards & Schemes 1988/89*.

Arts Council of Northern Ireland

181a Stranmillis Road, Belfast BT9 5DU
Tel (0232) **381591**
Drama & Dance director Denis Smith

Provides funding for the Lyric Players' Theatre, Belfast Civic Arts Theatre, Theatre Ulster, Charabanc, and Field Day Theatre Company. Supports the youth drama scheme. Individual awards are made to performers, directors and choreographers on assessment by a panel. Details and applications can be obtained from the drama & dance director.

Scottish Arts Council

12 Manor Place, Edinburgh EH3 7DD
Tel (031) **226 6051**
Drama & dance officer Anna Stapleton
Contact Charles Bell (drama officer)

The Council's bursaries scheme for theatre practitioners (actors, directors, technicians, administrators, etc.) is aimed at providing career refreshment and reinforcement by enabling candidates to extend their expertise in specific areas of work. Bursaries are generally provided to enable attendance at short-term or part-time training or to undertake a period of study or a special research project. Applicants should have a minimum of three years' professional experience in Scotland.

Welsh Arts Council

Museum Place, Cardiff CF1 3NX
Tel (0222) **394711**
Drama director Roger Tomlinson

Funding is 'tight', and as a result, most of the work of the drama department is concerned with theatres and touring companies including Theatr Clwyd, the Made-in-Wales Stage Company and Moving Being. In 1988, after much public debate, the Council approved a strategy of increased funding to Welsh-language theatre, and with additional funding from the Welsh Office and local authorities, Theatre-in-Education companies are now able to present projects in Welsh as well as English. In 1987/88, the drama department received partnership funding from Sianel Pedwar Cymru, enabling them to embark on a series of training initiatives with emphasis on assisting theatre practitioners working in Welsh, including a summer school for directors, a director's training awards scheme and the start of a series of international exchanges.

Regional Arts Associations

Council of Regional Arts Associations

Litton Lodge, 13a Clifton Road, Winchester, Hants SO22 5BP
Tel (0962) **51063**
Drama secretary Fiona Ellis (at Southern Arts Association; *see below*)

CORAA is a service organization for the corporate needs of the 13 regional arts associations of England. (Scotland, Wales and Northern Ireland have their own arts councils and are not regionally split in this way.)

The Regional Arts Associations (RAAs) are one part of a system which sustains, promotes and develops the arts. RAAs are concerned with all the arts — community arts, dance, mime, drama, literature, music, opera, the visual arts, crafts, film, video, photography and performance arts, etc. RAAs are independent and autonomous; they are neither regional branches of the Arts Council, nor are they local authority associations, but they receive funding from both. The RAAs vary in age from 14 to 30 years, with budgets varying from £1.1 million to £9.0 million. They provide financial support for professional theatre companies, dance and mime companies, music ensembles; some assistance is also given to support amateur work.

RAAs offer a number of opportunities for individual artists; many of these are aimed at helping them to reach a new and wider audience. A variety of commissions, bursaries, fellowships and residencies are available to writers, artists, craftsmen, composers, photographers, etc. Information for specific schemes offered are available on request from the RAAs.

Buckinghamshire Arts Association

55 High Street, Aylesbury, Bucks. HP20 1SA
Tel (0296) **434704**

'The Association does not offer grant-aid to actors, although its extensive programme of support for professional theatre performances is of obvious indirect benefit. Grant-aid is provided to the Limelight Theatre, Aylesbury and the Milton Keynes Theatre Consortium, both of which organize year-round pro-grammes of small-scale theatre and dance; to Theatre of Fact, the county's professional Theatre-in-Education company; and to companies from outside the county that wish to tour to schools or to areas of the county away from Aylesbury and Milton Keynes. In addition, schools, colleges, amateur companies and other groups may engage professionals for workshops, residencies or, perhaps, to direct. In these cases, the Association can contribute up to 50% of the costs.'

East Midlands Arts

Mountfields House, Forest Road, Loughborough, Leics. LE11 3HU
Tel (0509) **218292**
Drama officer Helen Flack

Covers Leicestershire, Nottinghamshire, Derbyshire (excluding the High Peak District) and Northamptonshire. 'Out of the total allocation to drama, nearly 90% is spent on resident companies and artists.' The Drama budget is split into three categories:
1. *Regional Theatre*: The bulk goes to three companies, Derby Playhouse, Northampton Repertory Players and Perspectives Theatre Cooperative. Two further allocations under this heading are grants to building-based companies to tour small communities, and grants to independent companies.
2. *Visiting companies*: Grants to promoters of visiting companies; grants to companies to tour the region; grants to promoters of residencies including workshops and performances; grants to companies that have developed a relationship with the region and offer work that cannot be provided by resident companies.
3. *Projects*: Out of this fund is supported the drama education work, notably the 'Artists at Your Service' scheme, training, new writing projects in the community, local documentaries, commissions and some workshops that do not meet the criteria of the 'Artists at Your Service' scheme.

Eastern Arts Association

Cherry Hinton Hall, Cambridge CB1 4DW
Tel (0223) **215355**
Acting drama officer Vivien Peters

Covers Bedfordshire, Cambridgeshire, Essex, Hertfordshire, Norfolk and Suffolk. Over the past year, the Association has been reconsidering the way in which support is being given to theatres, small-scale venues, regional companies and touring throughout the area. In future, the drama budget will primarily be used to support work in these areas.
One item of development is the Association's 'Theatre-in-Education and the Community' scheme, launched three years ago and designed to give groups in schools and the community the opportunity of working with professional theatre workers. Eastern Arts are inviting performers resident in the region to contact them for inclusion on their register of artists. A wide variety of experience is required – from straightforward acting, characterization and interpretation, to more specialized skills such as the use of masks, clowning and drama therapy.

Greater London Arts

9 White Lion Street, London N1 9PD
Tel (01) **837 8808**
Acting arts development officer Sue Timothy

The Drama Unit covers a wide range of both building-based and touring theatre companies, performance art, new writing and training (but not for formal, full-time courses). The Association funds a large number of drama companies with particular emphasis on black theatre, work by ethnic minority groups, disability, women's work dealing with women's issues, drama work within the community, gay and lesbian work and theatre for young people.

Lincolnshire & Humberside Arts
St Hugh's, Newport, Lincoln LN1 3DN
Tel (0522) **33555**
Principal officer (drama & dance) Alun Bond

> Lincolnshire & Humberside Arts does not operate a specific scheme related to training for the professional actor. Applications for financial support to assist qualified and experienced actors in further developing their professional skills by attendance at appropriate and recognized courses may be considered. Applications from technicians, designers and other professional theatre workers may also be considered on a similar basis. Financial support is not available to assist with full-time vocational training.

Merseyside Arts
Bluecoat Chambers, School Lane, Liverpool L1 3BX
Tel (051) **709 0671**
Acting development officer (drama/literature) Theresa Griffin

> Merseyside Arts is the regional arts association for Liverpool, Knowsley, Sefton, Wirral, St Helens, Cheshire and W. Lancashire. The Association's major recipient of funding is Merseyside Young People's Theatre Company. It is hoping to develop the small drama companies on Merseyside by the creation of a 'performing arts investment fund'. It is occasionally able to fund training for individual actors/technicians.

Northern Arts
9–10 Osborne Terrace, Jesmond, Newcastle upon Tyne NE2 1NZ
Tel (091) **281 6334**
Drama officer Sheila Harborth

> Northern Arts covers Cleveland, Cumbria, Durham, Northumberland and Tyne & Wear, and was the first regional arts association in the country to be set up by local authorities. It provides funding for small-scale touring companies able to set up a complete programme of work, such as a tour of youth clubs in the region. Priority areas for support are black and Asian communities, young people and people with disabilities.

North West Arts
4th floor, 12 Harter Street, Manchester M1 6HY
Tel (061) **228 3062**
Drama officer Ivor Davies

> Covers Cheshire, Greater Manchester, Lancashire (except W. Lancashire) and the High Peak District of Derbyshire. The Drama Panel has a strong commitment to education, both through its relationship with Theatre-in-Education (TIE) companies such as Pit Prop (Leigh), Duke's TIE (Lancaster) and M6 (Rochdale) and in a variety of other educationally based projects. Financially supports and advises emerging theatre companies.

Southern Arts
19 Southgate Street, Winchester, Hants SO23 9DQ
Tel (0962) **55099**
Drama officer Fiona Ellis

> Southern Arts is the arts development agency for central southern England, covering Berkshire, Hampshire, E. Dorset, Isle of Wight, Oxfordshire, W. Sussex and Wiltshire — a region of 4 million people and 80 arts centres, theatres and concert halls. Its support for theatre is concentrated in funding a wide range of

companies, developing audiences and supporting small- and middle-scale touring. Direct support for actors is limited, although there are some training opportunities available.

South East Arts
10 Mount Ephraim, Tunbridge Wells, Kent TN4 8AS
Tel (0892) **515210**
Drama officer Robert Henry

South East Arts covers the counties of Kent, Surrey and E. Sussex. The Drama Panel works towards the consolidation of existing theatre and drama and the nurturing of new initiatives from venues and companies. It assists innovative and experimental projects involving young people, and encourages the development of training opportunities for people active in drama. The Association revenue funds two major regional theatres and helps in the organization of regional touring. The Association is currently developing new links with northern France.

South West Arts
Bradninch Place, Gandy Street, Exeter, Devon EC4 3LS
Tel (0392) **218188**
Drama officer Moira Sutton

South West Arts covers Avon, Cornwall, Devon, much of Dorset, Gloucestershire and Somerset. 'The central theme running through the Association's constitution is development . . . increasing, improving, encouraging, advancing and coordinating.' SW Arts financially supports the Everyman Theatre in Cheltenham and gives grants to professional companies such as Theatre-in-Education (TIE), children's theatre, small-scale touring and puppetry. Support is also given for specific projects by professional companies and for the commissioning of new plays. 'We are always prepared to consider applications from any source for activities that break new ground within our overall policies.'

West Midlands Arts
82 Granville Street, Birmingham B1 2LH
Tel (021) **631 3121**
Drama officer Alan Rivett

Covers Herefordshire, Worcestershire, Shropshire, Staffordshire and Warwickshire. Open to applications for training grants only by individuals within a company existing in the West Midlands region. Priority given to developing Asian/Afro-Caribbean companies, and audience areas of special need such as people with disabilities or young people. Operate a 'Performers in the Community' scheme that focuses on community groups — play groups, old people's homes and day centres — giving them the chance to work with professional workers. Hoping in the future to set up a register of performers in the region (particularly those with special skills) who would be eligible for this scheme.

Yorkshire Arts
Glyde House, Bradford BD5 0BQ
Tel (0274) **723051**
Drama officer Shea Connolly

Yorkshire Arts offers advice, contact and support to theatre and drama projects through its performing arts department. The department includes a drama officer, dance & mime officer, music officer and two officers working across all these areas. New companies can get advice about setting up tours, making contacts, establishing good working practices, Equal Opportunities policies and financial systems. Support can be given for fees to guest practitioners or rehearsal costs, but it cannot be given towards fees for full-time study. The first point of contact is through one of the officers who can develop a plan of action with you.

22. Awards, bursaries and fellowships

Arts Council of Great Britain

Award a number of bursaries for short practical working attachments or specific training projects/courses (*see* Arts Councils & Regional Arts Associations).

Arts Council of Northern Ireland

Awards to individuals (*see* Arts Councils and Regional Arts Associations).

East Midlands Arts

Some funding for training. (*See* Arts Councils and Regional Arts Associations).

Lincolnshire & Humberside Arts

Financial support to actors, technicians and designers for courses to develop skills (*see* Arts Councils and Regional Arts Associations).

Merseyside Arts

Occasionally fund actors/technicians for training courses (*see* Arts Councils and Regional Arts Associations).

Scottish Arts Council

Bursaries for short-term or part-time training (*see* Arts Councils and Regional Arts Associations).

Society of West End Theatres (SWET)

Olivier Awards annually, and Olivier Bursary for second-year drama student at accredited drama school (*see* Associations and Societies).

Southern Arts

Limited help to actors for training (*see* Arts Councils and Regional Arts Associations).

Stage Management Association (SMA)

Annual award 'For Services to the British Theatre in the field of Stage Management' (*see* Associations and Societies).

Welsh Arts Council

Directors' training awards schemes (*see* Arts Councils and Regional Arts Associations).

Winston Churchill Travelling Fellowship

The Winston Churchill Memorial Trust, 15 Queen's Gate, London SW7 5PR.

Awarded for overseas trips in connection with specific drama-related projects. Details and application forms from the above address.

West Midlands Arts

Open to applications for training grants only by individuals within a company in the West Midland region. (*See* Arts Councils and Regional Arts Associations).

The William Poel Memorial Festival

The Society for Theatre Research, c/o The Theatre Museum, 1e Tavistock Street, London WC2E 7PA

Founded 1952. A prize for good stage speech created from the proceeds of a matinee organized at the Old Vic Theatre to celebrate the centenary of the birth of William Poel, and further donations from Dame Edith Evans. The fund has subsequently been augmented by donations from members of the Society for Theatre Research. The Festival is usually held on an afternoon in May at the National Theatre and is open to the public. Candidates from all the theatre schools in the country which offer courses accredited by the National Council for Drama Training may participate. Two students, chosen by each of the schools represented at the Festival, present a duologue from Elizabethan or Jacobean drama.

23. Publications

Amateur Stage
83 George Street, London W1H 5PL
Tel (01) **486 1732**

> Monthly. Review of amateur drama, with reviews of the latest productions and practical techniques.

Drama
British Theatre Association, Regent's College, Inner Circle, Regent's Park, London NW1 4NW
Tel (01) **935 2751**

> Quarterly. Includes reviews, articles and features on subsidized, commercial, experimental, fringe and young people's theatre in the UK and abroad.

Film Log
Subscribers: P.O. Box 100, Ramsgate, Kent and *Editorial*: P.O. Box 11, London SW15 6AY
Tel (0843) **581636** (subscribers) (01) **789 0408** (editorial)
Subscription £8.00 (3 months); £15.00 (6 months); £25.00 (12 months)

> Monthly. Listing of UK-based films in pre-production and future pre-productions, giving details of production managers and casting directors.

Films & Filming
248 High Street, Croydon, Surrey CR0 1NF
Tel (01) **681 7817** Fax (01) **688 9573**

> Monthly. Film, book and video reviews.

Jobgrapevine ● *See* 'Equity' in Associations and Societies section.

Monthly Film Bulletin
81 Dean Street, London W1
Tel (01) **437 4355**

> Monthly. Reviews of films; articles on film-makers.

Plays International
55 Hatton Garden, London EC1N 8HP
Tel (01) **720 1950**
Owner Chancery Publications
Editor Peter Roberts

> Monthly. *Plays International* is a mixture of interviews, reviews and a complete play text every month.

Plays & Players
248 High Street, Croydon, Surrey CR0 1NF
Tel (01) **681 9573** Fax (01) **688 9573**

Monthly. Focuses on the British theatre. For professionals and the general public.

Professional Casting Report (PCR)
Subscribers: P.O. Box 100, Ramsgate, Kent and *Editorial*: P.O. Box 11, London SW15 6AY
Tel (0843) **581636** (subscribers) Tel (01) **789 0408** (editorial)
Subscription £15.00 (5 weeks); £30.00 (10 weeks); £75.00 (26 weeks).

Weekly. For Equity/ACTT members only. Gives details of imminent TV, film and
theatre casting.
Who's Where, an A-to-Z of contacts within the industry (film, TV and theatre)
issued annually with addenda from time to time. Available only to subscribers of
the above at £3.00 p.a.

Repertory Report
Subscribers: P.O. Box 100, Ramsgate, Kent and *Editorial*: P.O. Box 11, London SW15 6AY
Tel (0843) **581636** (subscribers) (01) **789 0408** (editorial)
Subscription £8.00 (3 months); £15.00 (6 months); £25.00 (12 months)

Monthly. Listing of provincial theatres and their production schedules.

Screen International
6 Great Chapel Street, London W1
Tel (01) **734 9452**

Weekly. Trade news for the film industry. Good for cast lists.

Script Breakdown Service (SBS)
SBS Ltd, Suite 1, 16 Sidmouth Road, London NW2 5JX
Tel (01) **459 2781/451 2852**

Weekly. Available only to agents. A list of casting requirements for film, TV,
theatre, light entertainment, commercials, videos and documentaries.

Sight & Sound
21 Stephen Street, London W1P 1PL
Tel (01) **255 1444** Fax (01) **436 7950**

British Film Institute quarterly. Covers all aspects of the cinema for professionals in
the industry.

The Spotlight
7 Leicester Place, London WC2H 7BP
Tel (01) **437 7631**
Rates ½ page £73.50; ¼ page £40.25.

Annual. A photographic casting directory used throughout the business by agents,
casting directors and directors. Essential for all actors. *Actresses* published in
October; final date for entries 1 April. *Actors* published in April; final date for
entries 22 October. *New Actors and Actresses* published in February, through the
Conference of Drama Schools.
The Spotlight maintains computerized records for over 40,000 members of the
profession, which are continuously up-dated and are referred to at the rate of
around 500 telephone calls a day. An advisory service is available to everyone
who advertises in or subscribes to *The Spotlight*.

The Stage & Television Today
Stage House, 47 Bermondsey Street, London SE1 3XT
Tel (01) **403 1418** Fax (01) **430 1418**

Weekly. A newspaper for professionals in the entertainment industry, with new openings, jobs and reviews.

Who's Where ● *See* PROFESSIONAL CASTING REPORT (PCR).

Acknowledgements

This first edition of *The Actor's Handbook* owes everything to the help and advice generously offered by those appearing in the listings. If we ever had any doubt of the need for this book, it had long disappeared by the time we finished the compilation. Time and again it was pointed out to us that actors, particularly young actors, bemoan the lack of comprehensive, one-volume reference to essential information. Well, here it is.

We are already at work on the next edition of *The Actor's Handbook*. Suggestions for improvements and additional information will be welcome.

If thanks are due to those who have responded to our letters and telephone calls, the greater praise must go to Jill Fenner who sent out the letters and put through most of the calls. Jill's organisational talents, backed by a first hand knowledge of the job of acting, have made her contribution invaluable. At various times Jill was assisted by Thea Bennett, an assiduous researcher who also brought to her task an appreciation of the actor's life based on personal experience.

For any errors or omissions that might be spotted, the Editor alone takes responsibility.

Index